Coins & Paper Money

A Value & Identification Guide

ALLEN G. BERMAN

© 1999 by
Allen G. Berman

To Barbara, unique wife and wonderful friend

Published by

**krause
publications**

700 E. State Street • Iola, WI 54990-0001
Telephone: 715/445-2214

Please call or write for our free catalog.
Our toll-free number to place an order or obtain a free catalog is 800-258-0929
or please use our regular business telephone 715-445-2214
for editorial comment and further information.

Library of Congress Catalog Number: 99-62390
ISBN: 0-87341-7410

Printed in the United States of America

CONTENTS

INTRODUCTION

Welcome to a completely revised and updated version of *Warmans Coin & Paper Money*. For four years now it has been my privilege to be author of one of the most widely distributed introductory books on coin collecting in the United States. This book was originally conceived to be a basic guide to the hobby, written simply but intelligently for both beginning collectors and curious laymen, and it presumes no prior background in numismatics (the study of coins). I have strived to make it a unique book in that it incorporates not only pricing, but also historical backgrounds and many of my own personal observations on various aspects of coin collecting—many of which may have fallen through the cracks in more conventional coin books. It is also very distinctive in that it covers numismatics in its very broadest definition, discussing not only United States, world and ancient coins, but also tokens, medals, paper money and checks. This may be quite a bit to fit into one volume, but the point of an introduction is, among other things, to tell the curious reader what collectibles are out there. A new collector has no way of pursuing facets of numismatics which interest him if he has not been made aware of them. Moreover, beginning literature simply does not exist for many numismatic specialties. Truly, a full library is necessary to answer every question regarding this 2,700-year-old medium of exchange. And more detailed books can be searched out later as needed. But most people go through a stage where one basic book will do just fine. After three editions and lists of endorsements, I must admit, I am gratified to provide a book like this one that fills such a need.

There are a great many changes and improvements to this new third edition. Of course I have included pages of new issue commemorative listings for the United States and Canada, and updated pricing, but far more has been revised. The acquisition by Krause Publications, the world's largest numismatic publisher, of the entire Warman's Encyclopedia of Antiques and Collectibles series has put at my disposal vast reference and research facilities. Most of the illustrations are completely new. I am delighted that Krause Publications has, for the first time, entrusted me to write the chapters on ancient and medieval coins in this edition. I have long considered this early coinage a favorite specialty, having written or edited four other books on coins before our modern age.

Also for the first time, price listings for modern coins in this edition will be based primarily on the hundreds of hours of research conducted by the enormous staff of Krause Publications' numismatic division. This certainly provides a broader base of reference than any one author is likely to have at his disposal.

I have preserved in this edition a hard-boiled approach to the use of coins as investment vehicles. I give some background on the market role of the notorious "slabs," and some methods for attempting to select an honest coin dealer. (Yes, I'm pleased to say they do exist.) I try to provide the investor with enough information about market practices and safety nets that, after reading this book, that investor can comfortably say that his chances of being taken advantage of are less than before he read it. How much less depends on his willingness to do his own research and apply a good helping of common sense. I must admit, however, that I do not invest in coins, despite being a full time dealer in them. I do not believe that the best use for historical artifacts such as these is to lock them away somewhere in the hopes that they may appreciate. I would rather see them in the hands of history buffs and teachers who would be likely to share them either in a classroom, a local coin show exhibit or a coin club.

Coin collecting can be an extremely social hobby. The many joyful friendships I have made in this field have taught me this firsthand. There are hundreds of local coin clubs throughout the country, where fellow collectors get together at a restaurant or library to swap stories or show off the latest prized additions to their collections. There are also a good number of regional associations that sponsor conventions and coin shows where dealers display their wares for the collectors' perusal. On a grander scale there are national level organizations, like the American Numismatic Association, which not only sponsor shows but also have libraries and museums. I have included an entire section on clubs and museums, and I've provided information on contacting these wonderful organizations.

My beginnings in this field date back to 1970. A Civil War three cent nickel found in my grandfather's antique desk and a bag of change from a relative's trip around the world caught the imagination of an impressionable ten-year-old. I was hooked for life. Since then, my love for old coins has been my motivation for everything from travels through Europe to a graduate degree in history. I have had the rare privilege of having known no other profession, and even on the longest of days, I am still grateful. I know of few hobbies that bring together such a wide array of people from diverse states and countries as intimately and amiably as does coin collecting. It has even been shown that an interest in coins can improve students' grades.

I have never found it difficult to communicate the level of the excitement I find in coin collecting. By holding one small metal disc, the collector is capable of exploring other cultures, philosophies, artistic environments and political systems. More exciting still, a coin represents a point of contact, where an average person from another time and a modern person like myself or one of the readers of this book, come together. It is a meeting point in time and space between two individuals who could only have dreamed of the other's existence.

Any user of this or any other price guide should be warned. Coin prices can be as volatile as the stock market, and can go in either direction. Many coins go up or down with changes in the precious metals market, and some are influenced by it, but to a lesser degree. Others are unaffected. Many coins skyrocket in value based on popular fancy, and drop back down again when they become passé. Sometimes the market is stimulated by firms promoting coins to a mass market broker who, in turn, attempts to corner every available fairly priced specimen. But beware, when these firms' orders are filled, those who have accumulated in hopes of "feeding" the broker are often forced to dump the same coins at a fraction of what they may have otherwise asked. This book simply offers an idea of the normal retail value of coins at the time it was written. It is not an offer to buy or sell. In most cases, neither I nor any other dealer can make a firm offer without personally examining the coin in question.

Besides being a dealer in coins and an appraiser, I am continuously involved in writing new references and guidebooks on coins. I am always anxious to hear from any of my readers suggestions on how I can make this book more useful. I'm also open to hearing any other coin-related questions or comments they might have. I can always be reached at:

Allen G. Berman, M.A.
Professional Numismatist
P.O.Box 605
Fairfield, CT 06430
or I may be e-mailed at agberman@aol.com.

ACKNOWLEDGMENTS

This book, like the two editions that preceded it, only came to fruition with the help of a vast number of friends, experts and consultants, each of whom brought to this project contributions and advice in their own special fields of expertise. While the prices contained in this book are based on hundreds of sources, I would most like to thank the research staff at Krause Publications for the most substantive contribution. In the field of United States coin prices I would also like to extend a special thanks to Robert Walter of Sam Sloat Coins, Inc., of Westport Connecticut, who took time out of an extremely busy schedule to provide very important critical examination of the manuscript. Mr. Walter's vigilant observation of the market has provided him with some very clear insights. I would also like to extend noteworthy thanks to Alex G. Malloy, with whom I have collaborated on earlier editions of this book. It was Alex who both gave me my first "basic training" in ancient and medieval coins, as well as my first opportunity to write for publication. Without the education he provided me earlier in life, and his important consultations in the course of writing this edition, I would not have felt comfortable pursuing this project. The field of United States paper money is among the most active in all numismatics. It is because of this I am very grateful to have had the opportunity to have David Klein of RaBenco review the paper money section of the manuscript. He is both a nationally successful dealer and a friend, with great expertise in this specialized field. I would like to thank Lucien Birkler, Robert and Phyllis Cohen, Nicholas Economopoulos, Frederick Fleischer, Camden Percival, Gordon A. Singer, William B. Warden, Jr., and Joseph A. Zannella. Each contributed their own expertise or specialized advice on how to bring a project such as this to a successful conclusion. I would also like to express my gratitude to Paul Kennedy, Acquisitions Editor for Krause Publications for offering me the opportunity to write this completely revised edition, and to Randy Thern, Krause Publications' Numismatic Cataloging Supervisor, who oversaw my progress through the stages of this project. After many years of association with Randy functioning in other Krause roles, it was a joy to find myself working with him once again.

The majority of the illustrations of the coins after 1700 are from the mammoth Krause Publications' archives, and were compiled from the work of hundreds of great numismatic photographers over the years. Many selectively chosen photographs of United States coins and paper were supplied by Stack's and Spink America. A very large portion of the ancient and medieval coins have been supplied by M&M Numismatics, Italo Vecchi, and Pegasi Numismatics. Selected interesting illustrations have also been provided by Paul Bosco and Stephen Album. Some of the examples of foreign, as well as more unusual U.S. paper moneys are from the personal collections of both Frederick Fleischer and myself, as well as the inventory of RaBenco.

Lastly, and most importantly, I would like to note my dearest gratitude to my wife Barbara, who during our first months together had to put up with the worst of my craziness in order for me to get this book done on schedule. Her emotional support, material efforts, and good council were essential to the completion of this work.

ORGANIZATION

This book is organized for ease of use, but not at the expense of logic or accuracy. As a result, some changes have been made in this new third edition. Much introductory material previously at the beginning of the United States section has been moved toward the front of the book, as this information can be of equal use whether the reader is interested in collecting American tokens, African paper money, or Roman Imperial coins.

Some other changes were made to make this book quicker and handier to use. As most readers don't wish to continually refer to lists of in-depth references cited for further reading, they have all been gathered into special sections where the reader can find them conveniently listed together, often with my personal recommendations and background comments. The bibliographical sections on United States and medieval coins should now be particularly useful.

Local state coinages have been listed before the series of federally issued United States coins. This is because they were struck earlier, and sequencing them in chronological order is more logical. Most biblical coins will now be found under the ancient countries which struck them, such as Judaea and Rome, rather than in a separate section. This will make them easier to locate. All such coins, however, will now be cited in this book as having been specifically mentioned in the Bible.

Foreign coins previously listed geographically are now listed alphabetically within each continent, as this makes it quicker for the average person with only a moderate amount of geographic knowledge to locate a country's listings. Keeping the coinages of entire continents together made sense, however, as coinages of neighboring countries will frequently influence each other and reflect similar characteristics.

Each section still begins with a historical background on the origin of the series being discussed. Don't forget that these old coins we are collecting often cannot be spent, and the value we, as a society, assign to them derives significantly from the historical significance they hold for us. Included in each introduction is important background information concerning the coins' characteristics and collecting practices. It is the intent of the author to incorporate knowledge picked up from decades of experience in numismatics but not usually found in most books of this nature.

Known counterfeits are listed as a separate section for each series.

Collectors should always be aware of these. There have been counterfeits made to fool every level of consumer, from the casual and careless tourist exploring ancient ruins while on vacation, to the sophisticated collector seeking to acquire the crowning achievement of his forty-year collecting endeavor. Counterfeits have been made for thousands of years and the reader should be observant.

Two different price grades are given for United States and Canadian coins. One is high, for the collector trying to guess what that additional quality acquisition may cost him, and one is low to give the layman an idea of the replacement value of the typical "strange old coins" likely to have been handed down by an ancient relative. Prices for ancient and foreign coins are given in the grade in which they are either most commonly collected or encountered on the Western market. In all cases the exact grade that is being priced is indicated at the top of the first column to which it is being applied.

Coins in this book are chosen to be representative. Most of the coins are common examples of a particular "type," which is what a collector calls a coin design in a particular metal. Sometimes a rare date and a common date of the same type will be given for contrast. It is the intent of the author to list some rare, some average and some common type coins, and thus to give the reader an overview of what the exciting world of numismatics has to offer.

COIN DEALERS

Perhaps the most important thing a beginner can do to get started in coin collecting, besides reading, is to establish a relationship with a good coin dealer. A coin dealer is more than just someone who can sell you coins. If the dealer is a good one, and well disposed to you, he or she can be a source of immeasurable knowledge gained from years of experience. Much of the wisdom a dealer can share with regular customers they cannot readily obtain from books. Either they are fine subtleties, or are personal hints gained through the examination of hundreds of thousands of coins, or are things gleaned just the previous day via the "grape vine." You don't have to be a big spender to be treated well by a dealer. Just be serious about what you are trying to learn and be consistent. If you are not yet ready to make a purchase, say so, but when you are ready, remember the dealer who helped educate you, or you may find out when you need his advice that his fountain of wisdom has run dry for you. Realize that the dealer is trying to earn a living and that the time he is able to devote to answering your questions may be limited if it is a busy day or he trying to get an advertisement ready by a deadline. A good dealer will not begrudge you the opportunity to learn grading by examining his coins, but when he tells you to start by buying a basic grading guide or catalogue, do so. Nothing brands a free-loading customer more than the desire to be spoon fed knowledge, with no willingness to contribute to the learning process himself.

Apart from the willingness to share time and knowledge, how can a collector tell a good dealer from one he may wish to avoid? There are several factors by which to judge dealers. First of all, there is experience. Most dealers' knowledge comes from many years of experience, filtered through curiosity and common sense. A new dealer, including many very-experienced collectors, may start out with wonderful academic knowledge about coins, but may be lacking in other aspects. Understanding the subtleties of grading and the dynamics of the coin market come almost exclusively from participation, not just reading. A new dealer may be truly honest, but he may not be seasoned to the commercial aspect of numismatics. Also, most small businesses of any kind fail before their first few years. If your objective is to establish a long-term relationship, knowing that a dealer has been in business for more than his initial start-up period may indicate that he is here for the long haul.

The size of a firm should not be the sole reason for making it your regular coin firm. While larger firms may offer greater selections, smaller firms may have better prices on certain items. Also, knowledge rests in the mind of the individual numismatist, be he self-employed, or one of a dozen in a large firm. Most coin businesses are small operations with one to six full-time employees, so don't be intimidated by the lack of a corporate setting. These are the front lines of coin collecting.

There are other factors besides longevity that a new collector can use to judge dealers. There are credentials like membership in professional organizations and service awards. The largest numismatic organization in the world is the American Numismatic Association. This is open to both dealers and collectors. It has a policy of binding arbitration for any of its members involved in a numismatic business dispute. Any dealer displaying its membership logo must submit himself to such arbitration in order to maintain membership. Most dealers are members, and while that does not mean that the dealer should automatically be considered a saint, it is reasonable to presume that he would rather settle his own disputes than let them fester long enough where an ANA-member collector submits it to ANA arbitration. Other organizations with its own arbitration programs are the Professional Numismatists Guild and the International Association of Professional Numismatists. Both these organizations have worldwide membership consisting exclusively of dealers who have met certain criteria. PNG membership is primarily located in the United States and Canada, while IAPN members are mostly in Europe and Asia.

Another method of screening dealers, which is particularly useful when ordering coins by mail, is to make sure that the periodical in which the dealer's advertisement appears has a code of conduct or some other standard for enforcing dealers' proper conduct. *World Coin News* and *Numismatic News*, for example, have a set of standard mail order terms that dealers must adhere to unless specific alternative terms are stated in their ads. Both these publications, as well as other periodicals such as *The Celator*, *Coin World*, and *The Numismatist*, will generally refuse to grant advertising privileges to problem dealers. One way to identify those dealers who have long and successful track records is to ask the periodical how long the dealer in question has been an advertiser.

One distinctive program to promote proper conduct among dealers is Krause Publications' Customer Service Award. It sets a particularly high standard for mail order dealers to live up to, permitting a low number of customer complaints and no unresolved customer complaints. Those dealers achieving this standard are granted permission to display the special logo of this award in their advertising.

It is very important to point out that neither mail order dealers, nor local shop dealers, are inherently more honest than the other. There are simply different methods of selling coins, based on the convenience, collecting interests and specialties of the dealers and the collectors they serve. Local shops are probably better at establishing a personal relationship, and for main-line United States and Canadian coins, may be particularly satisfying to do business with. Those collectors interested in world, ancient, medieval, and somewhat more esoteric United States material may find that their specialized interests force them to seek the more diverse inventories of mail-order and coin show dealers.

Lastly, don't ignore the experience of your fellow collectors. Ask others what dealers they choose to order from or visit and why. Sometimes a personal introduction or a reference from an already established customer or other dealer can get you treated like a VIP the minute you walk in the door. Never forget that coin collecting is a social hobby.

BUYING COINS ON-LINE

It is entirely conceivable that, in another decade or two, one-third of all numismatic sales will be done over the Internet. At the moment, though, it is a very secondary but rapidly growing market. More and more dealers are constructing web pages with varying results. Also, there are now services that consolidate a number of dealers' offerings into a series of pages in a common location for ease of searching. At the moment, both for the dealers and for the collectors in search of dealers, the "net" is still somewhat uncharted territory. It currently lacks some of the safety mechanisms that exist with periodicals or local shops. There are no customer service awards or standard policies for advertisers, nor are there local Better Business Bureaus to which one can appeal. This does not mean there are no means by which you can discern legitimate dealers from fly-by-nights. Many of the criteria you would apply to shop, mail order and show dealers can be applied to net-dealers. Many of the more serious dealers on the "web" will also have active advertising programs in conventional media, permitting you to check with those periodicals. Also, the importance of membership in a professional organization still applies. Ask how long the dealer has been in business, and not just collecting coins as a hobby. Perhaps the most difficult part of selecting dealers on the web is discerning who is a legitimate, full-time numismatic expert and who is simply a skilled home computer buff with the dream of becoming a real coin dealer.

Whatever the medium a collector uses to seek out dealers, someone who is willing to do some research and ask the right questions is bound to end up with a few dealers in whom he can place confidence and find a certain level of comfort.

CLUBS AND ASSOCIATIONS

As mentioned earlier, coin collecting can be an extremely social hobby, with national, regional and local clubs. The largest numismatic organization in the world is the American Numismatic Association. It is an institution chartered by Congress to promote numismatic knowledge, and has over the years attracted hundreds of thousands of collectors and dealers. Not only does it provide the arbitration services mentioned above, it also holds large conventions twice each year at various locations throughout the country. The summer ANA convention is particularly important as it is one of the largest coin shows in the world and includes not only coins dealers, but also representatives of the mints of many foreign countries. Other benefits to ANA membership include a circulating numismatic library, access to its one-week summer seminar in Colorado, and an authentication service. Every member of the ANA also receives a monthly issue of the *Numismatist*, its official journal that contains many popular articles and columns, as well as ads by member dealers. Its address is:

American Numismatic Association
818 North Cascade Ave.
Colorado Springs, CO 80903

Another extremely important institution is the American Numismatic Society, which boasts the most important numismatic library in the western hemisphere. It has played a significant role in the promotion of original academic numismatic research, and there is little cutting edge scholarship in which its books or staff are not consulted. It also conducts a summer seminar for graduate students and scholarships for students who incorporate numismatic research into their theses. Its address is:

American Numismatic Society
Broadway at 155th St.
New York, NY 10032

While a great number of Canadians are active members of the ANA, there is also an important national-level organization founded specifically for Canadian numismatists. It is:

Canadian Numismatic Association
P.O.Box 226
Barrie, Ontario, Canada L4M 4T2

Many regional associations exist, and some of them sponsor very important coins shows. One of the largest such organization is F.U.N. or Florida United Numismatists, which sponsors a large show of national importance each January in Orlando. Another large regional organization is the Central States Numismatic Association, which sponsors conventions throughout the Midwest. The addresses of some of the more important regional societies are:

Florida United Numismatists
POB 951988
Lake Mary, FL 32795

Central States Numismatic Society
POB 841
Logansport, IN 46947

Great Eastern Numismatic Association
1805 Weatherstone Drive
Paoli, PA 19301

New England Numismatic Association
POB 586
Needham, MA 02192

Pacific Northwest Numismatic Association
P.O. Box 8099
Federal Way, WA 98003-0099

There are, of course, a good many state level organizations — too many to mention here.

There is also a good chance that there is a local coin club that meets regularly in your town or county. There are hundreds of such organizations throughout the United States and Canada. Rather than meeting at coin shows, most get together in a more low-key and informal manner. Many such organizations are members of the ANA themselves, and contacting the ANA may be one way of getting in touch with one. Also ask at your local library or coin shop.

MUSEUMS

For someone trying to become acquainted with numismatics, there is nothing quite like viewing the exhibits presented by a numismatic museum. It is an experience no beginner will soon forget. There are only two purely numismatic museums in the United States, but many others have respectable coin collections and numismatic exhibits. Both the American Numismatic Association in Colorado Springs and the American Numismatic Society in New York have important museums with public exhibits of coins. The exhibits at either institution provide a good overview of the evolution of coinage and money over the last couple thousand years.

The Smithsonian Institution in Washington, D.C. also has a significant numismatic collection on display, with notable pieces in the fields of United States and world gold, as well as Russian coinage, among others.

All three of the above museums will have 99 percent of their holdings stored in secure vaults, with selected representative coins on display. Museum curators, however, are notably cooperative with scholars and serious collectors, so call to the museum in advance and they can often arrange so you can view specimens not available to the general public.

Another way to see fairly interesting coins at a museum is to catch them in interdisciplinary exhibits. For example, an exhibit of medieval armor, mounted by the Metropolitan Museum of Art in New York, was accompanied by large, medieval, bracteate silver coins that depicted similar armor in a contemporary manner. Other museums have followed this method of exhibiting, too.

GRADING

The value of a coin is in part determined by its "grade," or how well-preserved it is. The most basic part of grading is determining how worn a coin is. To describe a coin as you would in written correspondence, where present for viewing,, numismatists have agreed on a series of terms to describe how much wear there is on a coin. From best (no wear at all), to worst (worn out), they are:

Uncirculated (Mint State)
Almost Uncirculated
Extremely Fine (Extra Fine)
Very Fine
Fine
Very Good
Good
Fair
Poor

For every type of United States and Canadian coin, very specific criteria have been agreed upon for each degree of wear. For United States coins, these criteria were determined under the auspices of the American Numismatic Association and have been published in the book *Official A.N.A. Grading Standards for United States Coins*, usually referred to as The Gray Book. Every coin shop carries and uses this reference. All of them, however, follow certain general principles. Below are some examples of coins that illustrate each level of wear, with some of the basic requirements for that grade.

Uncirculated (Unc.) or Mint State (MS) coins, those with no wear at all, as though they had just come from the mint, have been divided into 11 basic categories that range, from 60 to 70, the latter being best. The reason for this is that even with no circulation at all, the coins themselves do hit each other while stored at the mint in large bags, leaving minute scuffs. These scuffs are called "bag marks." While these 11 points are a continuum, the ANA has not traditionally recognized intermediate grades other than the ones listed below. Many coin dealers do. When the legendary numismatic scholar and cataloger Walter Breen was asked if he could tell an MS-61 from and MS-62, he replied "No. Neither, I think, can anyone else. It is simply ammunition for those whose motivation is dishonesty and greed."

Uncirculated or Mint State coins with absolutely no bag marks or any other problems are called MS-70 but these perfect coins do not really exist for most series. To be MS-70 a coin must be fully struck and have no unpleasant stains or discoloration. Copper must have full luster. Recent made-for-collector coins are pre-packaged at the mint have a far better chance of grading MS-70 than a coin made for circulation.

MS-67 is the nearest thing to a perfect coin that is likely to be realistically obtainable. It may have the faintest of bag marks, discernible only through a magnifying glass. Copper must have luster.

MS-65 is a grade that describes an exceptional coin. It is the highest grade that can be easily obtained when conservative grading is used. It will have no significant bag marks, particularly in open areas such as the field or the cheek. Copper may have toning. Fewer than one coin in a hundred qualifies for this grade, and it is one of the most popular coin grades for investors.

MS-63 coins are pleasant, collectible examples that exhibit a noticeable amount of bag marks, but not so many as to be considered marred, with particularly few on open areas such as the fields or a cheek.

MS-60 describes those coins that were very scuffed up at the mint before their release. They will often have nicks and discoloration. Sometimes called "commercial uncirculated," they may actually be less pleasant to behold than a higher-grade circulated coin.

About Uncirculated (AU) describes coins with such slight signs of wear that some people might need a mild magnifying glass to see them. A trace of luster should be visible. One should be careful not to confuse an attractive AU coin for Uncirculated.

Extremely Fine (EF, XF) is the highest coin grade that exhibits wear significant enough to be seen easily by the unaided eye. It is a coin that still exhibits extremely clear, minute detail. In the case of American coins featuring the word LIBERTY on a head band or shield, all letters must be sharp and clear. Many coins will exhibit luster, but it is not necessary.

Very Fine (VF) coins will show obvious signs of wear. Nevertheless, most of the detail of the design will still be clear. It is an overall pleasant coin. On American coins with LIBERTY on a headband or shield, all letters must be clear.

Fine (F) is the lowest grade most people would consider collectible. About half the design detail will show for most types. On United States coins with LIBERTY described above, the letters must be clear, if not sharp.

Very Good (VG) coins exhibit heavy wear. All outlines are clear, as is the rim in most cases. Some internal detail will also show, but most will be worn off. At least three letters of LIBERTY, described above, must be legible, and all letters on pre-1857 copper and Morgan dollars.

Good (G) coins are generally considered uncollectible, except for novelty purposes. There will usually be no internal detail to the design at all. Some of the rim may also be worn out. LIBERTY, as described above, will be worn off on most coins, and will show just trace elements on pre-1857 copper and Morgan dollars.

About Good (AG) is a grade in which only truly scarce coins are collected. Many collectors would rather do without a coin than to add it to their collections. The rim will be worn down and some outline to the design may be gone.

Poor (Pr) is the lowest possible grade. Many coins in poor will not even be identifiable. When identifiable, many will still be condemned to the melting pot. Few collectors would consider owning such a coin except in the case of the most extreme rarities.

Sometimes treated as a grade, but technically not one at all is Proof (PF). Proof quality is a special way of making coins for presentation. A proof coin is usually double struck with highly polished dies on polished blanks, which usually yields a mirror-like finish. These days proof coins are mass marketed by the mint to collectors. Earlier in the century, matte or sandblast proofs were popular, characterized by a non-reflective, but highly detailed surface. Cameo proof is a particular kind of proof that has been struck with dies polished only in the fields, but the details like the portrait are deliberately given a dull finish. For some coins these cameo proofs have a premium value above regular proofs. Proofs often grade MS-65 or higher.

Other miscellaneous factors can affect the quality of a coin. The pres-

ence of all or part of the original luster usually increases a coin's value. Be careful, however, not to be fooled by a coin that has been dipped in a brightener to simulate this luster. Toning can be either good or bad. If the toning a coin has acquired is dull, irregular or splotchy, it is likely it will be considered unpleasant, and many collectors may choose to avoid it, even if it is a high grade coin. On the other hand, if it is mild, or displays a "halo effect" around the edge of the coin, or is composed of pleasant iridescent shades, many collectors and dealers would consider paying a premium to obtain it based on its "eye appeal." Also, the mint will sometimes strike a coin on a blank that is good enough so that it's not considered an error, but is nevertheless in some minor way imperfect. The poor mixing of the metals in the alloy, or flaws left by trapped gas from this same process are examples. If trivial they may be ignored on most coins, but on more expensive or high grade pieces, the level of concern over these flaws may suddenly increase.

Even on circulated coins, few collectors wish to have coins with scratches or edge nicks. These will occur even more frequently on larger coins, like silver dollars or on coins with reeded edges. Depending on the extent, such coins may be discounted by a little or a lot.

Of course coins with damage are worth far less than coins without. Many coins have been mounted for use in jewelry, and even when the loop or bezel has been removed they still may show slight signs of this unfortunate experience. While discounted heavily, a few collectors consider these opportunities to acquire coins with high grade detail for a fraction of the cost. It should be remembered that the same heavy discount will apply when that collector goes to sell his coins.

SLABS

The word "slab" is numismatic slang for a tamper-resistant holder used to hold coins graded by third party grading services. Third party grading services came into existence to answer a market need that was particularly acute in the 1970s and early 1980s. Many investors had become aware of the impressive appreciation of certain coins. Coin values were generally on the rise, and the total population of people suddenly calling themselves coins dealers was on the rise, too. Many of these new dealers' objective was to actively promote coins as investments. With so many inexperienced customers and dealers entering the market suddenly, it became apparent that there was a dearth of knowledge. While few in the investment market were concerned if the academic numismatic knowledge was being passed along, they were very concerned that the individual either selling them their investments or buying them back may be too inexperienced or too unscrupulous to properly grade the coins. Thus a neutral arbiter was needed: The third party grading service. These firms examine coins and seal them in small, transparent, rectangular holders containing that firm's opinion of the grade. The holder does not damage the coin as embedding them in Lucite would. The coin is fully removable, but any attempt to remove it will cause the holder to exhibit evidence of tampering, thus preventing anyone from switching a low grade coin into a holder indicating a high grade.

There are obvious advantages to having someone with no vested interest in the answer determine the grade of a coin, but there are disadvantages as well. While the criteria applied to coin grading (particularly to United States and Canadian coins) are fairly clear and objective, no two coins wear in exactly the same manner, and two individuals will not necessarily evaluate a coin in precisely the same manner. It is quite common to send the same coin into different grading services and get significantly different answers. Sometimes this differs even in resubmitting the same coin to the same grading service. As a result, it has become common practice for dealers to review the coins sent into the grading services on their return. Those coins graded too conservatively are usually broken out and resubmitted in hopes of achieving a higher grade. Those that received grades the dealer believes to be higher than he would have assigned himself are left in the holders and sold as third party graded coins. It is easy to see here that simply, by means of attrition, the population of third party graded coins gradually becomes more and more skewed towards liberally graded coins. This does not mean that third party coins these days, or in the future are by definition misgraded. There are always the "middle of the road" grades coming back from the services, which often are left intact, but it does mean that no collector (or investor or dealer) should blindly accept the grade printed on a plastic holder as gospel truth. There is no substitute for study and experience, which means examining enough coins that you're to the point where you can make your own judgment.

There is nevertheless a market for "sight unseen" coins encapsulated in slabs. The values of such coins are determined by what the market perceives as the relative accuracy of the grading service that packaged the coin. *The Coin Dealer Newsletter* or "Graysheet" rates the relative merits of these grading services on a weekly basis. While most buyers do not pursue the sight unseen market, this quantifiable information is useful in determining what grading service to select for the coins you are about to either buy or sell.

As reflected in the market, some grading services are statistically more liberal at applying grading standards than others. Following is an average of the ratings of these grading services, based on information available over an extended period shortly before press time. A value of 100% would be the equivalent of the ideal, universally accurate grading service.

PCGS	96%
NGC	87%
PCI	71%
ANACS	65%
INS	42%
NCI	39%

One outgrowth of the certified grading phenomenon is "population reports." Some services maintain a record of the quantity of specimens in each grade for each coin that passes through their hands. In theory, this will indicate to the potential coin buyer how rarely a coin occurs in certain very high grades. These reports should be viewed with some caution. While it is officially expected that a dealer submitting a previously graded coin for regrading will indicate that it is the same coin, most do not. Hence one specimen can easily end up on the population reports as two different coins.

A peculiar reaction to the proliferation of slabs is "slab aversion" by pure collectors who have no interest in investment. This author has seen and heard of numerous instances where collectors have refused to buy needed coins at a grade and price which pleased them purely because the coins were in slabs. While there is no logical support for such conduct — obviously anyone who finds the holder odious can throw it away — this is a rare, but observed fact.

HANDLING AND TREATMENT OF COINS

The way in which a collector or dealer treats his coins can greatly affect how well they hold their value. Metal is softer, and more reactive, than most people would think.

The human body contains many corrosive chemicals. Simply touching a coin can in some cases contribute to its deterioration. This is especially true of coins exhibiting mint luster or iridescent toning. Touching a bright copper surface with a sweaty thumb can easily result in the materialization of a dark thumbprint several weeks or months later. All this being said, it is easy to understand why the first lesson of coin collecting should be: *Never touch a coin on its surface.* If one needs to pick a coin up with bare skin, touch only its edge. In the case of proof coins, even greater precautions must be taken. The highly reflective surfaces are so sensitive that one should avoid even breathing directly on the coin. This will cause what coin collectors call "carbon spots," which are small black dots. Also, do not leave coins out unprotected where they can be directly exposed to dust, sunlight or changes in temperature.

Coins can be stored in many ways. One of the most convenient is in two inch-square plastic "flips." These are transparent holders with two pockets — one contains the holder, one contains a cardboard ticket on which information can be recorded. It folds over on itself into a size two inches by two inches. Originally they were made only of a PVC formula plastic. This was particularly flexible and easy to work with, but eventually it broke down and deposited a green slime on the coins it contained. Today, both the PVC formula and a new, more inert, Mylar formula are available. The Mylar type is prone to cracking, but so far has not been found to damage coins. The PVC type is still popular because it is more flexible, but it is now usually used only by dealers and auction houses for temporary storage. Collectors usually repackage coins purchased in such holders before placing a coin into long-term storage.

Another common coin holder is the "two-by-two." This is a pair of cardboard squares with an adhering film of relatively inert plastic on one side. The coin is sandwiched between the two layers of plastic, and the two halves are stapled together. While this does not permit the coin to be removed and touched as easily as storage in flips, it does permit the coin to be viewed on both sides without opening the holder. It is important that when you remove coins from these holders, you must be very careful not to accidentally scratch the coin on the exposed ends with the staples that may be protruding from where the holder was pulled apart. These careless staple scratches have ruined tens of thousands of good coins.

Both flips and two-by-two's fit nicely into specially made boxes. They also fit into plastic pages designed to hold twenty of either holder. These are transparent and will fit into most loose leaf binders. It is important to remember not to place coins loose in these pages, as they are often made of PVC plastic. Moreover, some of the thumbcuts, which are made to make removing the coins easy, are large enough for some coins to fall through.

There are many specialized coin albums and folders designed to not only store and exhibit a collection, but to guide the collector through it. Each coin in the series is individually labeled, making their use extremely convenient. It is widely believed that one of the main reasons coin collecting was able to catch on with the American middle class in the 1930s is the invention of the "penny board," a one-sheet predecessor of these modern coin folders and albums. Old albums and folders were made much differently than present ones are. The cardboard in older ones contained elements that toned the coins, though they rarely corroded them. Today, this is not part of most albums' composition.

This same phenomenon occurs with the long term use of the orange-brown, two inch coin envelopes, although it is less of a problem with other colors. The toning, in this case, is caused by sulfur in the paper.

Many new collectors ask the question "How do I remove the toning?" While it can be done, it is not recommended. While there are rare exceptions, it should generally be stated that one should never clean a coin. It is highly likely that more harm than good will result. Toning is actually part of the coin. It is molecularly bonded to the metal, and the only way to remove the toning is to literally remove part of the coin. This is how most coin dips work, with a mild acid. Physical cleaning is even worse, as microscopic striations almost inevitably are scraped into the coin's surface with anything so mild as even a tissue!

A cool, dry environment is best to store a coin collection. Of course not everyone lives in such a climate. One common answer to this is to store a packet of silica gel in the same container as the coin collection. This is a desiccant and will absorb the moisture out of the air. It can sometimes be obtained at photo shops, if not through your local coin dealer.

SECURITY

For anyone who collects something of value, security is a major issue. Realize that no house is theft-proof, and take reasonable precautions. Make sure all doors are locked and that access cannot be gained through open windows. Many collectors choose to install alarm systems. If this is what you choose, do not neglect to place a sticker to that effect in the window. If your collection warrants it, you may wish to consider a home safe of suitable size. Most alarm companies provide them automatically.

Perhaps more important than locks and alarms is being discreet. Do not tell everyone you meet that you are a coin collector. Even if your collection is relatively inexpensive, some potential thieves may presume that all coin collections are valuable, and if they hear of your collection third hand, they may not realize they have stolen a $100 collection instead of a $10,000 one until it is gone.

The most intelligent choice is to keep all your more valuable coins in a safe deposit box in a bank. If your bank is conveniently located near your home or work, you are sacrificing only a small amount of convenience to the greatest amount of peace of mind. When choosing a safe deposit box it is important to consider the environment. It is better to have a box on an inside wall of the vault rather than against one along the outside of the building. This will reduce the exposure to temperature fluctuations. Also, do not forget to place a small packet of silica gel in each box. You may find it more convenient to have multiple boxes of moderate size rather than one large box if your collection is particularly heavy.

DETECTING COUNTERFEITS

There are three kinds of counterfeits the collector should be aware of. Some are more dangerous than others. The oldest type of counterfeit is often called a forgery. It is a false coin or piece of paper money struck with the intent of passing it into circulation. It is usually of adequate quality not to be obvious at a casual inspection, but is often imperfect. A successful counterfeiter who makes such a product can at most expect hope to redeem it for the face value of the item he is replicating.

A Circulating Counterfeit

He is limited by the cost of what he is willing to invest while still making a satisfactory profit for his risk. One corollary of this type of counterfeit are imitations and evasions. This type is made to circulate, but they're often not faithful to the original because they are made for use in communities that, for various reasons, have come to expect that some of their coinage will be counterfeit. Imitations vary only due to style, while evasions deliberately modify some aspect of the inscription or design to provide a meager legal defense against a charge of counterfeiting. All of these may fool a collector at first glance, but they are usually imperfect enough where they can be detected by close scrutiny. Many of them are historically significant and are frequently collected, along with, or instead of, the original series.

(Photo Enlarged)

A Collector Counterfeit

A far greater danger to the collector is the true numismatic counterfeit. These are counterfeits of higher quality, created with great care to fool numismatic experts. Many counterfeits are made by casting, even though the original coin may have been made by striking. Look for seams along the edge. They may not be centered and obvious but can be hidden to one side or the other. Also, examine the surface under magnification for a multitude of faint pimples or an unnatural porosity. The precise shapes of letters are also often neglected by counterfeiters. On modern coins an inaccurate weight, or incorrect alloy (revealed by specific gravity testing) can be a giveaway. Ancient and medieval coins can vary much more in weight. Be aware that a great many counterfeiters have sought to hide their imperfections by heavy cleaning. The idea is that a collector examining a very rare coin will attribute the problems to abuse, rather than forgery.

Souvenir marked COPY

The last type of counterfeit is of virtually no threat to collectors, but pity the poor tourist! These are counterfeits made as souvenirs. This is not to say they are never created to pass off as authentic coins, but that the forger is presuming either total credulity on the part of the buyer or an unwillingness carry out a critical inspection. Even the color of the metal is often incorrect. Tens of thousands of these replicate ancients, and have been sold at archaeological sites in Turkey and the Middle East. Other similar counterfeits are found in Italy the replicate 19th century silver dollar-sized coins. Often these types of replicas (the more accurate name) are sold clearly marked as such in museum shops, or through legitimate vendors. Often they are even marked COPY to prevent confusion with the real thing. Since the passage of the Hobby Protection Act, replicas made in the United States have been required to display this word.

VALUATIONS

The values in this book are intended to represent the average price a professional coin dealer would charge a collector who wished to purchase an item in stock for his collection. This is not to say that every dealer will charge the same price for the same coin. Local factors can influence the price of a coin, such as whether or not the dealer has more of a coin than he can use, or conversely, is running very low on it. Also a dealer must bear in mind his local clientele. Half a dozen members of a local coin club collecting the exact same field in harmony can easily deplete a dealer's stock. Other factors that can influence the retail price of a coin include a dealer's personal taste and aesthetic sensibilities. Quite simply, does the dealer like the coin? Nationally and internationally the prices of some coins can remain stable for years, whereas some coins, particularly those that are bullion related, are moving between popularity and disinterest, or are being manipulated as investments, can fluctuate weekly. Hence a book such as this, while it is able to give a general frame of reference, should not be considered an ultimate source of information. The ultimate decision makers on the legitimate retail value of a coin are the dealer selling it and the collector purchasing it.

This book makes no effort to give information on the wholesale value of coins, or what a person disposing of a collection would expect to actually get for his coins. Of course these prices fluctuate, too, both over time and throughout the country. But there are other factors involved as well. Traditionally the discount on bullion coins is fairly small. The retail values of particularly inexpensive coins include a handling charge. It costs the dealer just as much labor to sell a $1 coin as a $100 coin, so logically the percentage of the value that is to pay for the dealer's labor is much higher in the case of cheap coins. A dealer may wish to pay 50 to 60 percent of the retail value of an expensive coin that is expected to sell in a medium amount of time. In the case of a coin that sells just as quickly, but only for a dollar or so, he may be willing to pay only 20 percent of what he could get. Also, he may be willing to work much more closely on a coin thatsells quickly, than one of the same value that will take years to sell. Foreign and ancient coins will also be discounted more as they are much less popularly collected in the U.S. and Canada than the coins of North America. In short, a person attempting to sell a coin may get anywhere from 10 to 90 percent of its retail value, based primarily on the age old principles of supply and demand.

The grades that have been chosen to represent average prices for the coins are those that are considered to be ones either most commonly encountered in the market, or ones that are most likely to be sought by the average collector. In very few cases have two consecutive grades on the grading scale been chosen, as a general book such as this can stand to benefit from the inclusion of a greater diversity of grades.

ABBREVIATIONS

Numismatists often write in their own shorthand. Some commonly used numismatic abbreviations, many of which are used in this book, are listed below. Grades have been omitted, as they have already been discussed.

AB	Aluminum Bronze
AE	Copper or Bronze
Ag	Silver
AL	Aluminum
ANA	American Numismatic Association
ANS	American Numismatic Society
AR	Silver
AV or Au	Gold
B	Brass
Bil.	Billon (an alloy of copper and silver)
Ch.	Choice (i.e. nice for the grade)
CN	Copper-Nickel
Cu or C	Copper
G	Gold
IAPN	International Association of Professional Numismatists
l.	left
mm.	mintmark or mintmaster's mark
mm.	diameter in millimeters
ND	Not dated
Obv.	Obverse (Heads)
Or.	Orichalcum
PNG	Professional Numismatists Guild
r.	right
Rev. or Rx	Reverse (Tails)
S	Silver
WM	White Metal (a tin alloy)
Z or Zn	Zinc
/	separation of obverse and reverse descriptions
[ ]	not visible on coin

THE EVOLUTION OF UNITED STATES COINAGE

An average American living in the Thirteen Colonies during the 18th century would not have found many English silver or gold coins in his pocket. It was British policy to restrict the export of precious metals to the colonies. As a result, there was nothing but copper struck for the Colonies, and even that was rarely minted. Most of the silver coins circulating in colonial America were imported from the Spanish colonies in Mexico and South America. Spanish colonial reales far outnumbered English shillings. The largest Spanish colonial silver coin was a piece valued at eight reales, hence the term "piece of eight," so often associated with pirates.

The English colonists called these big coins "pillar dollars" after the Pillars of Hercules flanking the two globes on them, or "milled dollars" because of the milled design applied to the edge to prevent people from trimming away bits of silver. Because two reales were equal to one fourth of a milled dollar, the modern U.S. quarter is still sometimes referred to as "two bits." The New York stock exchange, too, still measures values in eighths of a dollar based on this tradition. Silver coins were so scarce in the Colonies that colonial Americans would use any other foreign silver or gold coin that could be pressed into service. Besides Spanish, any French, Portuguese, and occasionally German silver and gold were readily accepted when they turned up.

British copper coins were much more commonly found in the Thirteen Colonies than precious metal coins. Excavations at eighteenth century colonial sites frequently uncover halfpennies of George II (1727-1760) and George III (1760-1820), and not too rarely those of William III (1688-1702). Supplies of these, too,

were short, but the colonists were much more likely to have copper than for precious metal coins. By the mid-1700s, the counterfeiting of copper halfpennies had become a popular industry. People would knowingly accept these as a matter of convenience. Today, any counterfeit English halfpenny known to have been made at one of these private colonial "mints" is actually worth more than the real English issue in the same grade.

When neither imported nor counterfeit coins were available, the ingenious and hard-pressed colonists improvised money. They used wampum made from beads of trimmed shell. This form of currency was adopted from the local Indians. As anything of refined metal had value, nails became a standard of exchange. Another medium of exchange was the tobacco twist. Both nails and tobacco currency could also be forced back into practical uses if needed.

Some of the colonial governors also issued paper money valued in terms of discounted British currency, or in Spanish milled dollars. This will be discussed more thoroughly in the chapter on United States paper money.

After the Declaration of Independence was written, many of the same forms of currency were used. Spanish colonial silver and gold were as popular as ever. All of the new states issued their own paper money. Not only did the counterfeiting of British halfpennies continue, or perhaps even increase, but many private firms issued their own coppers and occasionally their own silver coins, too. Because the Articles of Confederation (the first United States Constitution) essentially said each state was a fully sovereign country, some of them issued their own official, state-sanctioned coinage. Usually they were cents the size of the old British halfpennies. Massachusetts, New Jersey and Vermont all authorized their issue, but by far the most common were those of Connecticut. The Continental Congress placed its own copper in circulation — the Fugio Cent. A number of other experimental coinages were struck, both by and for presentation to the Congress, but few amounted to anything.

When the Constitution took effect in 1789, it put an end to all state-issued coinage. In view of the new stronger federal union, many people began to take the idea of a single national coinage more seriously. Others argued that it was not the place of government to get involved in such things. With the personal influence of George Washington himself behind them, the proponents of the new United States mint persevered, and construction began in 1792. For both administrative and technical reasons, things got off to a slow start, but before the end of the year, silver five-cent pieces struck from the first president's tableware were in circulation in Philadelphia. The new coinage was based on a decimal system dividing a dollar into 100 cents. The idea of the dollar as the standard unit was inspired by the Spanish

piece of eight, then common in the Colonies. Suffering from a severe shortage of both bullion and labor, and annual epidemics of yellow fever, the early mint never succeeded in placing any substantial coinage in circulation on a national level. Broad circulation was also prevented by the rapid withdrawal and melting of much of the gold and silver coinage by speculators, because American coins had too high a precious metal content relative to their value. The endeavor became so futile that the striking of many denominations was frequently suspended. It wasn't until the 1830s that the weights of the coins were adjusted to prevent their export.

Two coins of same type struck by different hand-engraved dies

During the mint's first four decades, every die was engraved by hand so no two looked alike. Also, the coins were struck by hand on a screw press one at a time. Finally, in 1836 the Industrial Revolution came to the U.S. Mint. Steam-powered striking equipment was imported form England. Almost overnight, American coins became more neat and uniform. The old lettered edges were replaced by modern reeding — those hundreds of parallel lines found on coins today. Also, the quantities that could be produced in the same amount of time increased drastically. This technological improvement roughly coincided with the needed reduction in the coins' bullion content, and also with a facelift given to all silver denominations. Thus, over the mid-1830s the nation's coinage was utterly transformed.

The purity of silver coins was increased from 89.24 percent to 90 percent in 1837. Minor adjustments occurred to the weight of the silver coins in 1853 and 1873, signified by the addition of small arrows by the date. The silver three-cent piece and three, new, gold denominations, $3 (1854) and $1 and $20 (1849), were introduced, partially because of the California gold rush. But the big event of the mid-century was the coinage law of 1857. This one act eliminated the half cent, reduced the size of the one cent piece from bigger than a quarter to the diameter used today, and most importantly, caused foreign silver and gold to cease to be legal tender in the United States. The mint was finally able to produce enough to provide a true national coinage.

Civil War coin shortages not only resulted in many private tokens, but also inspired the two-cent and nickel three-cent pieces, and later possibly the five-cent nickel. It also saw the debut of the motto, "In God we trust" on the coinage. During the late 1860s and 1870s the nation was in the economic doldrums. Mintages were low for many denominations, particularly the silver dollar, hence, many of these coins are scarce today.

From the late 1870s onward, coinage was plentiful for half a century — sometimes too plentiful. A dominant political influence was the "Free Silver Movement," which didn't mean people wanted to be given free silver, but that they wanted unlimited quantities to be converted into coins. They expected to, in this way, use up the excess that was being mined, and also increase the money supply causing inflation, which, in turn, would erode debts. From 1873 to later than 1918, several laws were passed to force the government to buy silver and strike an abundance of silver dollars. Unpopular in the more developed parts of the country, they frequently sat in government or bank vaults for decades. Minor silver also became more common during this era.

Early in the present century, Theodore Roosevelt led the nation to a new level of intellectual consciousness, touching upon ideas as diverse as national parks and the artistic merits of the nation's coinage. For the latter he sought the aid of the greatest sculptors of the day, very deliberately looking outside the mint staff for talent. Most of the new coin designs reflect neoclassical artistic trends prevalent in Europe as well. These beautiful designs include the Mercury dime, the Walking Liberty half and the St. Gaudens double eagle, as well as the less classically inspired Buffalo nickel.

A commemorative coin program was also getting underway, providing an outlet for artists of various tastes. Most never saw circulation, and were sold at a premium to collectors. By 1936, however, this had gotten so far out of hand that in that year alone, 22 different half dollars were struck!

The need for strategic metals for armaments during World War II was the cause for interesting, if not pleasant, aberrations in the cent and nickel. The striking of these in steel and a silver-manganese alloy was a response to these shortages.

Idealistic images of Liberty were gradually replaced during the 1930s and 1940s with those of statesmen, while art contests replaced selecting artists.

An increase in the price of silver in 1964 prompted masses to hoard silver coins as their content's worth approached their face value. As a result, silver was all or partially removed from the coinage, in favor of clad coinage, which is readily distinguishable because of the copper core visible on the edge. Almost thirty years later the cent, too, was debased, the bronze alloy being replaced by one of zinc and simply plated with bronze.

Today the nation's coinage is characterized by a new flood of commemoratives struck for both significant and insignificant reasons, most of which are completely unknown to the American people. Traditionally sold at a high premium by the mint, 1999 will be the first time since the Bicentennial that commemoratives will be circulated at face value, this being the first year of a massive set of quarters commemorating each state.

MINTS & MINTMARKS

The first U.S. mint was constructed in Philadelphia in 1792. Over the centuries it has had several different homes in that city, and constantly grew. Officially all other mints are branch mints, but this does not mean that the largest quantities of each coin are always struck in Philadelphia.

The first branch mints were opened to strike coins from the new gold that was being mined from deposits discovered in the South. These mints, located in Charlotte, North Carolina, and Dahlonega, Georgia, were opened in 1838 and closed when the Civil War began in 1861. They never struck in any metal but gold, usually in small quantities. Open for the same duration, but of far greater importance, was New Orleans. This became the second largest mint, striking vast numbers of coins in both gold and silver.

The San Francisco mint was opened in 1854 in response to the California Gold Rush. Today it strikes most of the proof issues. In 1870 the boom in the mining of silver in Nevada caused the mint to open a branch in Carson City. It was closed in 1893 and its coins are generally scarce.

Easily rivaling Philadelphia in its present importance is the Denver mint. Opened in 1906, it sometimes strikes more coins than the primary mint itself.

Recently some coins have been struck at West Point, New York. These are not circulation strikes, but collector issues and bullion only.

One can usually tell where a coin is struck by a small letter or a mark placed on the coin. In the United States, they have usually been on the reverse, but reappeared on the obverse after they were removed from 1965 to 1967. The mintmarks used on United States coins are:

none	Philadelphia
P	Philadelphia
C	Charlotte, NC
CC	Carson City, NV
D	Dahlonega, GA
D	Denver, CO
O	New Orleans, LA
S	San Francisco, CA
W	West Point, NY

VARIETIES

In some instances, very small modifications to a certain aspect of a die are made after the year's production process has already begun. These cause subtle variations in the coins. When a new design is put into production, often its purpose is to modify trivial aspects of the design to improve striking quality. Thus, two different versions of the same type will exist for that year.

One common variety results from the use of different style or size punches to place the date in the die. This will cause some coins to have either a small or large date. In earlier times the mint wished to economize by reusing the previous year's dies re-engraved with a new date. On such dies, traces of the old date can sometimes be seen. When these dies wear out, brand new dies are prepared. Thus some years coins bear an "overdate" for part of the year's production run, but not the other.

Some varieties are caused by accident. Double die coins are not errors in manufacturing, but mistakes in the preparation of the dies themselves, visible on the coins even when they perfectly manufactured.

BOOKS ABOUT U.S. COINS

One cannot overemphasize the importance of books as a vital component to fully understanding rare coins. The difference between a person accumulating a few interesting coins and a true numismatist is not in how much a person spends, but in how much a person learns.

The following books provide a good background to United States coins in general. Other books that deal with one series are listed below, and are generally sequenced as the coins they cover are sequenced in this volume. Where it's important, I have made a few comments on these books. Do not be put off by early publication dates as a great many standard works from earlier this century have been reprinted many times and are widely available through coin dealers. This is just a sampling, and many other worthwhile books are available.

American Numismatic Association, *Official A.N.A. Grading Standards for United States Coins.*(No one has any business investing in U.S. coins, or even spending significant money on them as a hobby, if they don't have this book.)

Bowers, Q. David, *The History of United States Coinage As Illustrated by the Garrett Collection.*

Breen, Walter, *Walter Breen's Complete Encyclopedia of U.S. and Colonial Coins.* (One of the most intelligent, in-depth general catalogs of the series. Excellent!)

Breen, Walter, *Walter Breen's Encyclopedia of U.S. and Colonial Proof Coins.*

Fivaz, Bill and Stanton, J.T., *The Cherry Pickers' Guide to Rare Die Varieties.*

Yeoman, R.S., *A Guide Book of United States Coins.* (Popularly called the Red Book, it is the widely acknowledged Bible of U.S. coins.)

Yeoman, R.S., *Handbook of United States Coins.* (Popularly called the Blue Book, a companion to the Redbook above, designed for those with a desire to sell their coins.)

Counterfeit Detection

American Numismatic Association, *Counterfeit Detection,* 2 vols.

Harshe, Bert, *How to Detect Altered & Counterfeit Coins and Paper Money.*

Fivaz, Bill, *Bill Fivaz's Counterfeit Detection Guide.* (Convenient set of blow-up photos of authentic examples by a noted coin photographer.)

John, Lonesome, *Detecting Counterfeit Coins.*

John, Lonesome, *Detecting Counterfeit Gold Coins.*

Virtually every issue of *The Numismatist,* the official journal of the American Numismatic Association, has large clear photographs of newly discovered counterfeits. The listings in issues before 1988 are, in part, summarized in the above A.N.A. references.

Colonial Coins

Breen, Walter, *Walter Breen's Complete Encyclopedia of U.S. and Colonial Coins.* Despite being a general book, it is also boasts one of the best treatments of Colonials.

Crosby, S.S., *The Early Coins of America*

Kleeberg, John, *Money of Pre-Federal America.*

Maris, Edward, *A Historical Sketch of the Coins of New Jersey.*

Miller, Henry Clay, *State Coinages of Connecticut.*

Newman, Eric P., ed., *Studies on Money in Early America.*

Noe, Sydney, *The New England and Willow Tree Coinage of Massachusetts.*

Noe, Sydney, *The Oak Tree Coinage of Massachusetts.*

Noe, Sydney, *The Pine Tree Coinage of Massachusetts.*

Richardson, A.D., *The Copper Coins of Vermont.* This is an extension of the standard numbering system established in Ryder, Hillyer, *The Colonial Coins of Vermont.*

Vlack, Robert, *Early American Coins*

Half Cents

Breen, W., *Walter Breen's Encyclopedia of United States Half Cents 1793-1857.*

Cohen, Roger, *American Half Cents, The "Little Half Sisters".* Establishes a standard numbering system for die varieties.

Large Cents

Sheldon, William, *Penny Whimsy,* 1958. Covers die varieties 1793 to 1815, a standard that has lived through many reprints.

Newcomb, H., *United States Copper Cents 1816-1857.* Covers die varieties.

Small Cents

Snow, *Flying Eagle and Indian Cents.*

Taylor, *The Standard Guide to the Lincoln Cent.*

Wiles, James, The *RPM Book - Lincoln Cents.* Guide to repunched mintmark varieties.

Two Cent and Three Cent Pieces

Kilman, M., *The Two Cent Piece and Varieties,* 1977.

Flynn, Kevin, *Getting Your Two Cents Worth.*

Bowers, Q. David, U.S. *Three-Cent and Five-Cent Pieces.*

Half Dimes and Nickels

Wescott, Michael, The United States Nickel Five-Cent Piece.

Valentine, D.W., *The United States Half Dimes,* 1931. Standard reference on die varieties for the series.

Blythe, Al, *The Complete Guide to Liberty Seated Half Dimes.*

Bowers, Q. David, U.S. *Three-Cent and Five-Cent Pieces.*

Lange, David, *The Complete Guide to Buffalo Nickels.*

Dimes

Bowers, Q. *David, United States Dimes, Quarters, and Half Dollars.*

Greer, Brian, *The Complete Guide to Liberty Seated Dimes.*

Lawrence, David, *The Complete Guide to Barber Dimes.*

Lange, David W., *The Complete Guide to Mercury Dimes.*

Bowers, Q. David, *United States Dimes, Quarters, and Half Dollars.*

Rapsus, Ginger, *The United States Clad Coinage.*

Twenty Cent Pieces and Quarters

Hammer, Ted, "The Twenty Cent Piece," *The Numismatist,* vol. 60, pp. 167-69.

Browning, A. W., *The Early Quarter Dollars of the United States.* The standard reference on die varieties for the series.

Briggs, Larry, *Liberty Seated Quarters.*

Lawrence, David, *The Complete Guide to Barber Quarters.*

Cline, J.H., *Standing Liberty Quarters.*

Bowers, Q. David, *United States Dimes, Quarters, and Half Dollars.*

Rapsus, Ginger, *The United States Clad Coinage.*

Half Dollars

Overton, Al C., *Early Half Dollar Die Varieties 1794-1836.* Standard reference on die varieties for the series.

Bowers, Q. David, *United States Dimes, Quarters and Half Dollars.*

Lawrence, David, *The Complete Guide to Barber Halves.*

Fox, Bruce, *The Complete Guide to Walking Liberty Half Dollars.*

Bowers, Q. David, *United States Dimes, Quarters and Half Dollars.*

Rapsus, Ginger, *The United States Clad Coinage.*

Silver & Clad Dollars

Bolender, M.H., *The United States Early Silver Dollars from 1794 to 1803.* Standard reference on die varieties for the series.

Newman, Eric, and Bressett, Kenneth, *The Fantastic 1804 Dollar.*

Bowers, Q. David, *Silver Dollars and Trade Dollars of the United States: A Complete Encyclopedia.*

Willem, John M., *The United States Trade Dollar.*

Van Allen, Leroy, and Mallis, A. George, *Comprehensive Catalogue and Encyclopedia of U.S. Morgan and Peace Silver Dollars.*

Rapsus, Ginger, *The United States Clad Coinage.*

Gold Coinage

Bowers, Q. David, *United States Gold Coins: An Illustrated History.*

Akers, David, *Handbook of 20th-Century United States Gold Coins.*

Commemoratives

Hodder, Michael and Bowers, Q. David, *A Basic Guide to United States Commemorative Coins.*

Swiatek, Anthony and Breen, Walter, *Encyclopedia of United States Silver and Gold Commemorative Coins 1892-1989.*

Bowers, Q. David, *Commemorative Coins of the United States: A Complete Encyclopedia.*

Proofs

Breen, Walter, *Walter Breen's Encyclopedia of United States and Colonial Proof Coins.*

Patterns

Judd, J. Hewett, *United States Pattern, Experimental and Trial Pieces.*

Krause, Chester, and Mishler, Clifford, *Standard Catalog of World Coins and Standard Catalog of World Coins, 19th Century.*

Errors

Spadone, Frank, *Major Variety and Oddity.*

Margolis, Arnold, *Error Coin Encyclopedia.*

Wiles, James, and Miller, Tom, *The RPM Book*. Guide to repunched mintmark varieties.

Tokens

Rulau, Russel, *Standard Catalog of United States Tokens*.

Breen, Walter, *Pioneer and Fractional Gold*.

Kagin, Donald, *Private Gold Coins and Patterns of the United States*.

Fuld, George and Melvin, *Patriotic Civil War Tokens*.

Fuld, George and Melvin, *U. S. Civil War Store Cards*.

Schenkman, David, *Civil War Suttler Tokens and Cardboard Scrip*.

Hodder, Michael J. and Bowers, Q. David, *Standard Catalogue of Encased Postage Stamps*.

Alpert, Stephen and Smith, Kenneth E., *Video Arcade, Pinball, Slot Machine, and other Amusement Tokens of North America*.

Token and Medal Society, *TAMS Journal*. The journal of this organization is incredibly useful, with regular listings identifying "mavericks," or private tokens that don't bear specific indication of their origin.

Coffee, John, ed., *Atwood's Catalogue of United States and Canadian Transportation Tokens*, 3rd ed. and 1977 Supplement.

Sullivan, Edmund B., *American Political Badges and Medalets 1789-1892*.

Hibler, Harold and Kappen, Charles, *So-Called Dollars*. A standard work on dollar sized tokens or medals, particularly those used temporarily as a medium of exchange or to represent such satirically.

Baker, W.S., *Medallic Portraits of Washington*.

Hawaii, Alaska, U.S. Philippines

Krause & Mishler, *Standard Catalog of World Coins*.

Gould, Maurice, *Hawaiian Coins, Tokens and Paper Money*.

Yeoman, R.S., *Guidebook of United States Coins*.

Basso, Aldo, Coins, *Medals and Tokens of the Philippines*.

Confederate Coins

Reed, Fred L., III, series of articles, *Coin World*, Oct. 4, Oct. 11, Oct. 18, 1989.

PERIODICALS

Magazines have a certain immediacy not possible in books. They also put the reader in touch with the thoughts and opinions of their fellow numismatists.

CoinAge (monthly) - A popular newsstand magazine, oriented to the collector and the layman.

Coins (monthly) - Very similar to Coin-Age, but put out by Krause Publications, the world's largest numismatic publisher.

Coin World (weekly) - The largest circulation coin newspaper, covering both American and world coins.

Numismatic News (weekly) - A Krause Publications newspaper focusing primarily on United States Coins.

The Numismatist (monthly) - The monthly journal of the American Numismatic Association. All full members receive an automatic subscription.

COLONIAL AND STATE COINAGES

Coinage in colonial America was a hodge-podge of British coins, British colonial issues, local tokens and counterfeits, and imported Spanish Colonial silver and gold, usually from Mexico City, Lima, and Potosi. Sometimes small silver was made by cutting the large Spanish milled dollars or "pieces of eight" into wedge-shaped eighths. Each eighth was nicknamed a "bit." One quarter of a Spanish dollar was worth two bits. Coinage was always in short supply in colonial America, so the colonists would readily improvise for small change. The economic principles of Mercantilism prevented Britain from shipping any reasonable quantities of silver or gold to the colonies.

As for copper, even when regal coppers were brought over by the keg-full, there were never enough. Perhaps the single most common coin to circulate in the British colonies in America was the George II (1727-60) copper halfpenny. The most influential, however, may have been that of his grandson and America's last king, George III (1760-1820), shown here:

George III Halfpenny

This coin served as a pattern for numerous local colonial counterfeits. Sometimes the legends would be changed so the issuer could evade charges of out-and-out counterfeiting. Therefore, such imitations are today called "evasions." Other counterfeiters sought to make their product as accurate as possible. Legal or not, the average colonial subject was probably not too picky as to the authenticity of his coppers. After all, it was better than nothing at all, and easier than trying to barter away unneeded goods.

Several colonies were able to supplement their improvised coins with officially struck tokens. These were usually lighter than the true British issues but were sanctioned by the government to a greater or lesser extent. Some were specifically made for shipment to the American Colonies, while others were approved for shipment when they were rejected in Ireland.

After gaining independence, the colonial issues were replaced by both state copper coinages, and actual and proposed Continental Congress issues. The Continental Congress, under the Articles of Confederation, was the government of the United States before the present Constitution. That union permitted the states to keep many more of their sovereign rights, including their own coinages. Several of the state coppers were cents designed to follow very closely on the pattern of George II and especially George III halfpennies. To an illiterate public, comfort was influenced by appearance.

Private coinage did not end abruptly when the Constitution took effect in 1789. Those coins gradually transformed themselves into merchant tokens. This section lists those of the 18th century only, as most have more in common with the pre-Federal, unofficial coinages than with the later tokens. The latter is discussed separately in the section on Merchant Tokens.

Most colonial coppers, and a far larger quantity of 18th century British halfpennies, are unearthed in old colonial sites. They exhibit porous surfaces and pitting. The value of such a coin is always discounted, but if the condition is not too poor, many collectors of this early material are willing to buy it.

Also, as it had been before independence, paper money was continually issued. It also continued to merit the same bad reputation, and is perpetually subject to discount.

AMERICAN PLANTATION TOKEN

In 1688, King James II's secretary suggested that the mint be receptive to the idea of striking tin coins for the American Colonies, which he and others then referred to as the "American Plantations." Having obtained royal sanction, Richard Holt, on behalf of a consortium of tin miners, made a request that the mint prepare such coins depicting James II on a leaping horse, with four shields of arms on the reverse. This was the first official coinage for the British colonies in North America.

Their denomination was inscribed as 1/24th of a Spanish real, a common silver coin in the colonies. Conventionally they were considered to have had the value of about a British halfpenny of the time, perhaps more according to some authorities.

They met an unsuccessful end however. Minting was cut short when King James was forced to flee the advancing forces of his daughter and son-in-law, William of Orange.

Not only that, but the coins themselves soon began to crumble. It seems that tin that pure (97.5%) turns to powder in cold New England and New York winters. Most known specimens suffer from "tin pest," pitting or porosity, particularly near their edges.

Known counterfeits: In 1828, a London coin dealer struck a few hundred restrikes with original, but rusted dies. They can also be identified by a large die break to the right of the horse's face.

	G	F
James II 1/24 Real	125.00	220.00
same, 4 of 24 sideways	325.00	475.00
same, arms transposed	750.00	2,000.00
same, restrike	70.00	150.00

ROSA AMERICANA TOKENS

The next attempt at a special coinage for the American Colonies was also ill-fated. William Wood actively solicited a royal patent to strike such a coin in hopes of making a profit. It was agreed that he could strike brass pennies, half-pennies and two-pence at a standard roughly 40% the weight of British regal copper. Their weight was to be verified by none other than Sir Isaac Newton. While the document was granted by the King, it was instantly stolen by the King's mistress and held for ransom, making it impossible for Wood to have them struck in the Tower mint under controlled conditions. The 75-percent copper, 24.7-percent zinc alloy looked bright when new, but soon discolored, in large part due to the cast, rather than cut, blanks. Their arrival in New York and New England was as unwelcome as it was unexpected. Nobody could figure out their denominations!

The common obverse of these coins is the portrait of George I. The crowned, Tudor rose on the reverse is derived from a coin of Henry VIII, the uncrowned version from a coin of his son Edward VI. The reverse inscription, Rosa Americana Utile Dulci, translates variously as "American Rose, Useful [and] Sweet."

These often suffer from dark surfaces and porosity, even when not ground-finds.

Known counterfeits: 1722 second prototype halfpenny, electrotype copies of 1722 and 1733 pattern twopences. Some brass half-pennies have been silver plated to pass for the rare, 1723 silver strike.

	G	F
No Date 2 pence	60.00	190.00
1722 halfpenny	30.00	85.00

	G	F
1722 Penny	30.00	85.00
1722 2 pence	40.00	90.00
1723 1/2 penny	350.00	1,350.00
same with crown	35.00	90.00
1723 Penny	30.00	85.00
1723 2 Pence	30.00	85.00
1724 Penny pattern		Two Known
1724 2 pence pattern		Extremely Rare
1733 2 pence pattern		Four Known

HIBERNIA COINAGE

Before William Wood acquired the Rosa Americana patent, he acquired a similar one to strike coins for Ireland. It was agreed that he could strike copper halfpence and far-things at a standard roughly 1/4 lighter then British regal copper. As in the case of the previous patent, the document was granted by the King, but was instantly stolen by his mistress. It cost an additional £10,000 ransom for Wood to retrieve it. Because the Irish Parliament was not consulted before the coins were shipped, and because of the "King's Whore" scandal, these coins were widely rejected. Production ceased by the beginning of 1724. In 1736 they were demonetized. Certain merchants bought up those that remained for their scrap value, and shipped them surreptitiously to the Colonies, where they entered circulation at face value since the colonists accepted whatever coins they could get their hands on.

The common obverse of these coins is the portrait of George I. Hibernia, the allegory of Ireland, seated with a harp graces the reverse. There are a number of varieties for each date.

Porous ground finds are traded at a discount.

Known counterfeits: Any silver off metal strikes should be examined for the possibility of being silver-plated copper business strikes. Counterfeits also exist of the 1723 First Prototype farthing. Few common types have been counterfeited.

	G	F
1722 Farthing	50.00	220.00
1722 1/2 penny, rocks right (pattern)		1,800.00
1722 1/2 penny, harp left	15.00	60.00
1722 1/2 penny, harp right	15.00	60.00
1723 Farthing	20.00	65.00

	G	F
same with D:G:	40.00	90.00
1723 1/2 penny	15.00	40.00
1724 Farthing	25.00	75.00
1724 1/2 penny	15.00	60.00

HIBERNIA / VOCE POPULI COINAGE

These were originally private tokens struck by a Mr. Roche in the 1760s in Dublin. It has been suggested that the idealized head and the legend, VOCE POPULI, or "Voice of the People," could refer to Irish support for Stuart pretenders. The meaning of the "P" in the obverse field of some of these is a mystery. The common reverse is a seated figure of Hibernia with harp. When a large shipment of 1766 regal George III halfpence arrived, the Voce Populi pieces seemed to lose favor, and were bought by entrepreneurs as scrap metal and shipped to the American Colonies where they traded at face value.

Some of these appear quite crude, as many of the blanks were cast as were actual coinsl.

They're often porous, and as such are dis-counted depending on surface.

Known counterfeits: Genuine 1760 coins altered to resemble the 1700 error.

	G	F
1760 Farthing	125.00	400.00
1700 1/2 penny	500.00	1,300.00
1760 1/2 penny	30.00	90.00

	G	F
1760 1/2 penny, P	70.00	170.00
1760 1/2 penny, VOOE	35.00	110.00

PITT TOKENS

The Stamp Act of 1765 required taxes to be paid on paper — anything from forms to news-papers. It stirred major protests by the colo-nists, who were not consulted. They formed protest organizations such as the Friends of Liberty and Trade. Sir William Pitt success-fully defended the colonists' position in Parlia-ment, and the organization commissioned this medal in his honor. While commemorative in nature, it is believed to have circulated in the New York area. One tradition holds that it was engraved after a design by Paul Revere. While the larger one is usually called a halfpenny and the smaller a farthing, Breen has suggested that they both traded as halfpennies. All brass farthings were struck on cast blanks and may show natural traces of porosity.

The obverse bears a bust of Pitt, with the inscription, "The Restorer of Commerce 1766

- No Stamps." The reverse shows a ship arriving at AMERICA, with "Thanks to the Friends of Liberty and Trade."
Known counterfeits: Not extensively counterfeited.

	VG	F
1766 Farthing	2,300.00	1,250.00
1766 1/2 penny	65.00	250.00

ELEPHANT TOKENS

Most of what is known of the elephant halfpence is still conjecture. There are three different localities mentioned on their reverses: London, Carolina and New England. Some London pieces have been recovered in the New York/New Jersey area. It has been suggested that the Elephant indicates a connection to the Royal African Company, and is possibly of West African copper, but this is not known. There are die linkages between them and it is reasonable to consider them related. The date for the undated London types is not known, but they have been observed overstruck on halfpennies dated 1672. All known Carolina tokens with the correct spelling have the O repunched over an E.
Known counterfeits: Struck counterfeits of the Carolina second (commoner) type and of the New England are known.

	VG	VF
(1672-84) London	300.00	1,000.00
(1672-84) G-d		
Preserve London	80.00	150.00
1694 Carolina 1/2 penny		
PROPRIETERS		Five Known
1694 Carolina 1/2 penny		
PROPRIETORS	1,000.00	2,500.00

1694 New England 1/2 penny		Two Known

CONNECTICUT

Connecticut coppers are probably the single most commonly encountered coins from pre-federal America. The first Connecticut coppers, however, are extremely rare. Dr. Samuel Higley of Granby was a well-educated physician and metallurgist who operated a copper mine. He struck his own personal copper tokens of extremely pure metal. His first issues of 1737 bore the inscription "The Value of Three Pence," but they were the size of a mere halfpenny. Evidently encountering resistance, he changed the legend to "Value me as you please." This was not the only Higley copper that directly address the user. Others said, "I am good copper." Their obverses show a stag or a wheel, their reverses crowned hammers or an ax, with dates ranging from 1737 to 1739. They are usually found very worn or porous but are so rare they are still highly desirable — even in low grades.

It was not until after independence that another Connecticut copper was issued, this time by the state itself. In 1785, the legislature authorized the striking of coppers following the rough pattern of the British halfpenny, but with Latin legends translating "By the Authority of Connecticut," and "Independence and Liberty." The images were quite similar to the halfpenny, with a generic male bust similar to the King's, and Liberty seated looking much like Britannia. By the time the official issue of 1.4 million had been struck, these coins were suffering the fate of the British halfpenny itself: counterfeiting. Counterfeit Connecticut coppers were struck in New York, New Jersey and Massachusetts, where there was no laws against counterfeiting "foreign" coins. Some were even struck in Connecticut by the former coining contractor himself! All those dated 1788 were struck at unofficial mints. Both official and unofficial strikes were crude and struck on imperfect blanks. At least 340 varieties, including many misspellings, are known. Only broad categories are listed below.
Known counterfeit: Many modern counterfeits of diverse sorts exist of Higley coppers, some dangerous. Contemporary counterfeits of the state coppers are numerous, but are highly regarded by collectors as being simply "unofficial issues."

HIGLEY COPPERS

	G	F
1737 The Value of ThreePence / Connecticut (Three crowned hammers)	4,500.00	9,500.00
1737 The Value of Three Pence / I Am Good Copper (Three crowned hammers)		Two Known
1737 Value Me As You Please /I Am Good Copper (Three crowned hammers)	4,500.00	9,500.00

	G	F
(1737) Value Me As You Please / I Cut My Way Through (Ax)	5,000.00	9,800.00
(1737) The Wheele Goes Round (wheel) / I Cut My Way Through (Ax)		Unique
1739 Value Me As You Please / I Cut My Way Through (Ax)		Five Known

STATE COPPERS

	G	F
1785 Bust left	120.00	275.00
1785 Bust right	30.00	85.00
same, "African Head" variety with fuller features	45.00	200.00
1786 Mailed bust left	30.00	90.00
1786 Draped bust left	35.00	120.00
1786 Hercules bust left	40.00	125.00
1786 Bust right	35.00	85.00
same larger head	50.00	165.00
1787 Bust left	35.00	110.00
same, horn from bust	25.00	65.00
1787 Bust right	20.00	65.00
1788 Mailed bust left	25.00	100.00
1788 Draped bust left	20.00	55.00
1788 Bust right	25.00	85.00

MASSACHUSETTS

Confronted with continuous shortages of any kind of coinage, particularly silver, combined with British refusal to permit the latter's import, the inhabitants of Massachusetts Bay Colony were forced to barter. When the Puritan Cromwell overthrew the King, fellow Puritans in Massachusetts saw it as an opportunity. They began striking their own formerly forbidden coinage in 1652. At first these were simple silver discs stamped NE, for New England, and XII, VI, or III for the values shilling, six and three pence. Found to be easily counterfeited and clipped, the designs were made more complex, extending to the edge of the coin. The legend, "Masathvsets in New England An Dom, 1652" was ordered, surrounding a tree on one side and the value on the other. Today we call this first design a willow tree, but it is, in fact, generic. This crude willow design was struck by rough hand-hammering methods until 1560, and always carried the date 1652. This was to avoid charges of illegally striking coins in the event of the return of royal government. Thirty years of Massachusetts silver was struck with this one date. When new screw press equipment arrived, the design of the tree was modified. It is described as an oak tree. The coins struck from 1667 to 1682 have a modified tree, described as a pine tree. In 1686, a new harsh royal governor arrived in Boston with orders to restore the colony to barter. That ended silver coins from Massachusetts.

Pitted ground-finds exist and are discounted, but are still quite valuable. Some specimens were bent in the 1670s through the 1690s to use as talismans to keep away witches.

New patterns were made in 1776. Little is known about them, and whatever projects were intended were abandoned. One theory, however, is that they were proposals engraved by Paul Revere.

After independence, the new Commonwealth of Massachusetts returned to striking coins, but this time copper cents and half cents. An Indian standing with bow and arrow was depicted on them. The reverse has an eagle with an American shield in its chest; the shield is inscribed with the value. It was the first time the word "cent" appeared on an American coin. Pitted ground finds are not unusual, and are discounted.

Known counterfeits: Virtually all NE, willow, oak and pine tree coins have been counterfeited Some are dangerous collector counterfeits, made during both the 19th and 20th centuries. Others are contemporary counterfeits made to circulate, and are quite valuable. Pine tree coins are the most counterfeited of these four series. Very many crude, base metal cast replicas of all series including 1776 patterns have been made for sale by museums and as souvenirs. They can be identified by a seam around the edge.

	G	F
NE 3 pence		Two Known
NE 6 pence		Seven Known

	G	F
NE Shilling	3,500.00	11,000.00
1652 Willow 3 pence		Three known
1652 Willow 6 pence	7,500.00	15,000.00

	G	F
1652 Willow Shilling	10,000.00	18,000.00
1662 Oak 2 pence	300.00	715.00
1652 Oak 3 pence	400.00	950.00
1652 Oak 6 pence	400.00	1,000.00

	G	F
1652 Oak Shilling	300.00	725.00
1652 Pine 3 pence	320.00	550.00
1652 Pine 6 pence	300.00	650.00

	G	F
1652 Pine Shilling	350.00	850.00
1652 Pine Shilling (small diameter)	220.00	550.00
1776 Province Halfpenny Pattern		Unique
1776 Three Heads Halfpenny Pattern		Unique
1776 Penny Pattern		Unique

	VG	VF
1787 1/2 cent	70.00	285.00

1787 Cent, arrows to viewer's right	3,500.00	Rare
1787 Cent, arrows to viewer's left	60.00	240.00
1788 1/2 cent	90.00	325.00
1788 Cent	60.00	265.00

MARYLAND

One fascinating bit of colonial history is the creation of Maryland as a feudal domain in North America. Different from the other colonies, it was a territory under a Lord, similar to medieval structure. As a result of this, Cecil Calvert, Second Lord Baltimore, was able to strike a proper, European-style feudal coinage. Prior to this coinage, tobacco, along with musket balls and gunpowder, had been a primary medium of exchange, but the decline in its value caused hardships and prompted the need for coinage. They were struck at the Royal mint in 1659. Silver shillings, sixpences and groats, and copper pennies were struck. The Cromwell government challenged his right to strike these coins, but when that government fell, Calvert was vindicated. They were very European in appearance, with Calvert's bust and lordly titles on the obverse, his crowned arms on the reverse, and only a crown and flags on the penny.

In 1783, a Baltimore silversmith apparently decided to make a pattern for a proposed national coinage to show to the Continental Congress, which was meeting in Annapolis at the time. While it did not accept his proposal, he decided to continue striking coins of his own design. Thus, John Chalmers struck the first silver coins in English America in a hundred years. All his coins show clasped hands on the obverse. The reverses show interlocking rings, birds, a cross or a wreath. Another Baltimore silversmith, Standish Barry, followed him in 1790, striking a private three pence that depicted George Washington.

Known counterfeits: 19th century struck counterfeits exist of the Lord Baltimore penny, some dangerous, others with incorrect lettering style. Crude casts of other Lord Baltimore coins have been made for sale in museum shops as souvenirs. They can be identified by a seam around the edge. Counterfeits also exist of the "rings" type of Chalmers shilling.

	G	F
LORD BALTIMORE		
Penny (Denarium)		only 5 known
Groat (IV)	1,000.00	3,250.00
Sixpence (VI)	800.00	2,000.00
Shilling (XII)	900.00	2,500.00

	VG	VF
JOHN CHALMERS		
1783 3 pence	900.00	1,850.00
1783 6 pence	1,200.00	2,850.00
1783 Shilling, circle of rings on rev.		Four Known
1783 Shilling, birds on rev.	400.00	1,650.00
STANDISH BARRY		
1790 3 pence	1,200.00	2,750.00

NEW HAMPSHIRE

The New Hampshire Act of June 28, 1776, not only authorized state coinage, but permitted anyone who wanted to conform to state standards to make their own. The state issues were all cast, as they could not even get the steel for engraving dies. They all show a tree on the obverse, the reverses are either a large WM, for William Moulton, the contractor, or a harp. The authorized private imitations were sometimes hand engraved. **Known counterfeits:** Many cast and struck counterfeits are known, of various qualities. Some authorities question the authenticity of all pieces of the WM type.

VG

1776 Penny pattern, Tree / WM	Extremely Rare
1776 Halfpenny pattern, Tree / WM	Extremel Rare
1776 1/2 penny, Tree / Harp	13,000.00
1776 same, local engraved imitation	Extremely Rare

NEW JERSEY

One imported token has a special connection to New Jersey. During the English Civil War, the royalist Long Parliament struck special tokens to pay its forces, who were suppressing the 1641-42 Protestant Ulster Rebellion. The Catholics lost, and the coins, called St. Patrick coppers, were suppressed for years. After the war they reentered circulation and were still current in Ireland in the 1720s. When Mark Newbie, a Quaker, left Ireland for New Jersey in 1681, he took 14,400 of these with him. Having established the first bank in New Jersey, he was able to get the Provincial Assembly to declare his St. Patrick coppers legal tender in 1682. The obverses of these coins show Charles I as King David playing a harp. The large crown above him is struck where a drop of brass has been added to the blank, giving it a golden color on clean specimens. The reverses show St. Patrick either between a crowd and the arms of Dublin (halfpenny), or driving animals away from a church (farthing).

New Jersey coppers are perhaps the second most common of the state coinages. Three million were originally ordered struck by independent contractors. Later, unofficial pieces were also made in New York, some with official dies they had bought from the old contractors. The obverse design of a horse's head and plow is an adaptation of the crest on the New Jersey arms. The reverse is

an American shield. The obverse legend Nova Caesarea is Latin for New Jersey. Some of the latest issues are struck over other coins and tokens. Hundreds of varieties are known, and some are much rarer than others. Porous ground-finds are common and are discounted.

Known counterfeits: The silver off metal St. Patrick's farthing has been counterfeited. Counterfeits of the state cents are not abundant.

	G	F
St. Patrick Farthing	40.00	100.00
same but silver	500.00	1,450.00
same but gold		Unique

St. Patrick Halfpenny	80.00	200.00

	VG	VF
1786 Cent, date at bottom	60.00	325.00
1786 Cent, date lower right	Rare	3,300.00
1787 Cent	50.00	175.00
1788 Cent	60.00	225.00
1788 Cent, tiny fox	100.00	475.00
1788 Cent, horse head left	200.00	700.00

NEW YORK

The earliest token to be associated with New York was long considered mysterious and controversial, but recent scholarship seems to have provided it with an origin. A brass (or sometimes pewter) farthing with an eagle, surrounded by "New Yorke in America" has been attributed to Gov. William Lovelace (1663/68-1673). Its unusual reverse shows a stand of trees dividing Venus and Cupid.

After this, no official New York coins were ever struck — neither when it was a colony, nor during the pre-Federal period under the Articles of Confederation (1776-89). Many private tokens and proposals do exist.

One 1786 token struck by James Atlee shows a bust of George Washington with the legend Non Vi Virtute Vici, Not by force but by virtue. It's reverse shows Columbia seated and the legend Neo-Eboracensis, Of New York.

A pair of proposed coins were struck by Ephraim Brasher and John Bailey in 1787. One was a cent or halfpenny showing the arms of New York on the obverse, an American heraldic eagle on the reverse. The other was a bolder suggestion and has become one of the most famous American coins: the Brasher Doubloon. A gold coin worth 16 Spanish pillar dollars, it showed a sun over mountains, the central motif of the New York arms on the obverse, and an American heraldic eagle within a wreath on the reverse. When it became clear that the state legislature was not going to accept any coinage proposal, Bailey simply took a third pattern, very similar to the Connecticut cent with a generic male head and seated Liberty, but inscribed Nova Eborac for New York, and put it into production himself.

While Brasher and Bailey were making patterns to propose to the legislature, so were New Jersey engraver James Atlee and New York businessman Thomas Machin. One sample bore a portrait of New York governor George Clinton on the obverse, with the state arms on the reverse. Another showed an Indian standing with tomahawk and bow on the obverse, paired with the same reverse. A third paired the Indian obverse with an eagle standing on a globe, the crest from the state arms, on the reverses. When they made the same observation as their competitors, their answer was to go to Newburgh up the Hudson River, and set up one of the most notorious counterfeiting operations in 18th-century America. Machin's Mills not only produced counterfeit George III halfpennies by the ton, but produced imitation Connecticut, New Jersey, Vermont and Fugio cents, mixing and matching their dies with those of various tokens.

Two merchant tokens struck during the early federal period were so important to New York commerce that they are listed here. One is the Mott token of 1789, struck by a gold and silverware dealer and clock importer. The obverse showed a particular brand of grandfather clock, the reverse a heraldic eagle extremely similar to that adopted for U.S. gold coinage from 1807 to 1908. The production of these coins was so heavy that some were produced with incomplete lettering due to worn out dies.

Another producer of prolific late 18th century tokens was Talbot, Allum and Lee, importers of goods from India. Their well-made 1794 and 1795 cents were struck in Birmingham, England. The obverse legend, "Liberty and Commerce," is illustrated by a personification of Liberty standing by a bale of goods. The reverse quite naturally depicts a ship under sail. These stayed in circulation well into the next century and formed a source of blanks on which many U.S. large cents were struck.

Known counterfeits: Many copies of the Brasher Doubloon have been made with varying degrees of accuracy, and many are not dangerous at all. Wrong lettering styles and seams characterize many. One of several counterfeit George Clinton cents has an I substituted for the 1 in the date. Dangerous counterfeits also exist of the Non Vi Virtute, Excelsior, and Indian cents.

	VG	F
(1663/8-73) Farthing,		
Brass	2,750.00	4,000.00
same, pewter		Four Known
1786 Cent, Non Vi Virtute Vici (George		
Washington) / Neo-Eboracensis (seated		
Columbia)	2,800.00	3,750.00
1787 Brasher Gold Doubloon		Seven Known

	VG	F
1787 Cent, Excelsior (New York arms) /		
E Pluribus Unum (Eagle with		
shield)	925.00	1,500.00

	VG	F
1787 Cent, George Clinton / New York		
arms	4,500.00	7,500.00
1787 Cent, Standing Indian / as		
previous	3,250.00	5,000.00
1787 Cent, as previous / Eagle on		
globe	5,000.00	9,750.00
1787 Cent, as previous / Bust of		
George III		Three Known

	VG	F
1787 Cent, Male bust, Nova Eborac /		
Liberty seated right,		
Virt Et Lib	125.00	250.00
same, Liberty left	85.00	170.00

	VG	F
1789 Mott Cent	100.00	175.00
1794 Cent, Liberty standing / Ship, New York		
above	40.00	65.00
same, New York		
omitted	300.00	600.00
1795 Cent, same	25.00	50.00

VERMONT

When Reuben Harmon, Jr., was given the sole contract to supply Vermont with cents, he set out to provide quality coins. He struck the design dictated to him: a rising sun over the Green Mountains with a plow in the foreground on the obverse, and a radiant Eye of Providence within a 13-star constellation on the reverse. The Latin legend on the reverse translates as "Fourteenth star," reflecting the Republic of Vermont's dream of admission to the Union. Harmon struck his coppers even heavier than he was required to make them. This was still true of the coins of the new style; they bore Vermont legends but were similar in design to Connecticut coppers. The change was probably facilitated so they would blend together in interstate commerce. Harmon could not prepare dies quickly enough, so he entered into an arrangement with Machin's Mills in Newburgh, New York. The striking of Vermont coppers was subcontracted to the new firm. The poor Vermonter found that his once-proud cents were being struck at ever lighter weights, and were being muled with odd dies. It was out of his hands. Machin's Mills began striking Vermont coppers on their own without legal authorization. Harmon gave up and left for Ohio, abandoning his coining franchise.

The bust-type coppers were usually incompletely struck on irregular blanks. There are many other varieties. Porous ground-finds are traded at a discount.

Counterfeit alert: Contemporary counterfeits exist. Modern ones are less common.

	G	F
PLOW SERIES		
1785 Cent		
VERMONTS	125.00	400.00

	G	F
same VERMONTIS	125.00	500.00
1786 Cent	125.00	400.00

BUST & LIBERTY SERIES

1786 Cent, Bust left	75.00	275.00
1786 Cent, Bust right	125.00	500.00
1787, BRITANNIA rev.	40.00	120.00
1787 Cent, Bust left	950.00	3,500.00
1787 Cent, Bust right	45.00	175.00
1788 Cent	45.00	185.00

VIRGINIA

Virginia boasts one of the most scarce and one of the most common coins of the 18th century. The Gloucester 1714 Shilling was a private brass token struck by Dawson and Righault, local landowners in Gloucester County. The legends read "Glovcester Covrt.hovse Virginia/Righavlt Dawson Anno Dom 1714." The obverse shows the building, the reverse a star.

Virginia was the only colonial government created with the right to strike coins, and they waited more than 150 years to do so. Previously, tobacco had sufficed as small change, but the expansion of the population caused a need for coins. These halfpence were struck at the Royal mint in 1773, but by the time they could be placed in circulation, the Revolution was brewing and they were hoarded. Ironically, many entered circulation in the 1780s. Part of an original keg of these was disbursed in 1929, thus they are not unobtainable in mint state. The silver shilling struck with a larger bust of George III is a pattern.

Known counterfeits: Replicas for sale at Colonial Williamsburg are marked CWF below bust. More dangerous counterfeits also exist.

	F	VF
1714 Shilling		only 2 known
1715 Shilling		Not confirmed

	F	EF
1773 1/2 penny	50.00	170.00
1773 Shilling		Six known

WASHINGTON PIECES

One of the most common themes of private tokens of the late 1700s was George Washington. One of the earliest was the Georgius Triumpho copper, which was not only dated 1783, but actually struck then, unlike others of that date. The reverse depicts Liberty at a weaving frame, with the Latin legend for "Voice of the People." They are thought to have circulated in Georgia, Virginia and New Jersey.

Not all Washington pieces are flattering. The second oldest, the Ugly Head, was a satirical political piece. The obverse legend reads "Washington the Great D:G:" in derision of the monarchical pretensions of some Washington supporters. The reverse has the thirteen interlocking circles of the Continental Dollar.

One of several engravers who worked on proposals for a new federal coinage was Gregory Hancock, an English child prodigy. His Washington cents of 1791 were rejected by the president as being too "monarchical." In revenge for this snub, Hancock engraves a new unflattering obverse with Washington as a Roman Emperor.

The most common 1783 Washington pieces were actually struck in the early 1800s in England and shipped to the United States by merchants. The obverse is one of several military busts. Their reverse varies from ONE CENT in a wreath, to a seated Liberty, to a second bust of Washington.

This is simply a cross section of these pieces. Others exist.

	VG	VF
1783 Voci Popoli	55.00	250.00
1784 Ugly Head		Four Known
1791 Hancock's Military Bust / ONE CENT over		
Eagle	125.00	325.00
1791 same / ship	60.00	200.00

1792 same / stars over Eagle		Rare
1792 same /		
Inscription	3,250.00	7,500.00
ND (1792) same	850.00	2,750.00

	VG	VF
1792 Hancock's Roman Bust / CENT		
over Eagle		Very Rare
1783 (1820s) Roman Bust / Wreath, UNITY		
STATES	30.00	100.00
1783 (1820s) Roman Bust / Liberty seated		
left	30.00	110.00
1783 (1820s) Military Bust / Liberty seated		
left	20.00	110.00
ND (1815-20) Military Bust / Military		
Bust	30.00	100.00

PRE-FEDERAL COINAGE

There were several proposals and attempts at a national coinage under the Articles of Confederation.

In 1776 the Continental Congress anticipated a loan of silver from its French ally. It was thought that striking this silver into dollars would not only show the world a manifestation of its sovereignty but also bolster public confidence in its paper currency. Benjamin Franklin and David Rittenhouse collaborated on the design, which was engraved in secret. The obverse shows a sundial, above which is a sun and the Latin word FUGIO (I fly). Below it the phrase "Mind your business." The whole ensemble echoes Franklin's saying, "Time flies so mind your business." The reverse has a chain of thirteen links, each labeled with the name of a state. At center is "We are one," surrounded by a smaller circle inscribed "American Congress." Most of these prototypes were struck in tin. Unfortunately only three real silver ones are known, the French loan having fallen through.

In 1783 Gouverneur Morris, the Confederation's Asisstant Superintendent for Finance, proposed a decimal system that reflected the various standards of most of the states. Sample coins for 1,000, 500 and 100 in silver and 5 units in copper were struck. A radiant eye surrounded by a thirteen-star "new constellation," and the Latin Nova Constellation adorned the obverse. The value is within a wreath on the reverse. This project was soon abandoned due to lack of bullion.

One outgrowth of the project, however, was the Nova Constellatio copper. Morris made the most of his project's failure. He went to Birmingham, England, where he had quality dies engraved by George Wyon based on his failed decimal designs. Many thousands of these coppers were struck in 1785 to 86 (not 1783 as they're dated) to Morris' personal order and shipped back to America, where they became popular for a time.

Wyon quickly took the initiative and created his own 1785 patterns for a proposed American cent. The obverse has a seated figure surrounded by the Latin Immune Columbia, misspelled by his inept die letterer, Walter Mould. (Columbia was another name for America at the time.) They were not accepted but the dies were taken by the fleeing Mould, who ended up selling them to none other than the Machin's Mills counterfeiting operation in Newburgh, New York.

Besides its paper money, the single most common relic of the Continental Congress is the Fugio cent. In 1787 James Jarvis made a successful bid to strike cents for the Congress. The designs were similar to the old Continental Dollars. He acquired tons of copper from the government, bought a controlling interest in the renegade Connecticut mint in New Haven, made a limited amount of Fugios and quickly switched the majority of production (using embezzled government copper) to the more-profitable Connecticut cents. Soon he was forced to flee to Europe and his equipment, including both Connecticut and Fugio dies, was sold to, yet again, the Machin's Mills counterfeiting operation.

Known counterfeits: Both dangerous and amateurish replicas of Continental Dollars have been made in very large quantities. A counterfeit exists of Morris' decimal mark of 1,000 units. Contemporary counterfeits were made of Nova Constellatio coppers. Nineteenth century counterfeits exist of Immune Columbia coppers. "Restrikes" of the Fugio cent made with false dies were made around 1860.

	VG	VF
1776 Continental Dollar,		
Pewter	2,150.00	5,500.00
same, Brass	—	12,000.00
same, Silver		Rare
1783 Nova Constellatio "5", Copper		Unique

	VG	VF
1783 Nova Constellatio "100", Silver		Rare
1783 Nova Constellatio "500", Silver legend		Rare
1783 Nova Constellatio "500", Silver no legend		Rare

	VG	VF
1785 Immune Columbia / Nova Constellatio, Copper		Rare
1785 Immune Columbia / Eagle, Copper	450.00	1,750.00
1785 Immune Columbia / George III, Copper	1,800.00	5,000.00
1785 Immune Columbia / Vermon Auctori, Copper	1,650.00	4,750.00

	VG	VF
1783 Nova Constellatio "cent", Copper	50.00	200.00
1785 same	55.00	250.00
1786 same		Dubious
1787 Fugio Cent, Pointed rays	90.00	275.00
1787 Fugio Cent, Club rays	110.00	475.00

1792 MINT ISSUES

When the United States was created with the adoption of the Constitution in 1789 (signed 1787), it was not a given that the nation would have a mint, or even a national coinage. Many were opposed to the idea of government involvement in these matters, and those who were thought contracting out coinage contracts would be adequate. Even Washington had problems with the original coinage bill that called for his own name and portrait to appear on each coin. After much protest, the first coinage law of April 2, 1792, replaced Washington with Liberty. It is this law that determined the basic pattern of American coinage still in use today. It seems that the very first coins struck under the federal union that were the United States of America, as opposed to the Continental Congress under the Articles of Confederation, were actually struck in a saw maker's basement rather than a mint. The mint and personnel were not ready, but coins were needed, and even George Washington had pointed this out. But small silver was in particularly short supply in general commerce and no one wanted to delay production while an old distillery was converted into a mint. According to legend, the first $75 worth of half dismes included silver from Washington's own tableware. When the mint moved from the saw maker's basement to its new facilities, coinage continued with a small quantity of dismes. Many have found the early spelling "disme" to be curious. It is a synthetic word that appeared first in French in 1585, and in English in 1608, and refers to the decimal system. It continued to be the prevailing spelling for the tenth dollar until the 1830s, but its pronunciation had long since changed to that used today. The first United States cent was a matter of experimentation. Congress had called for a large copper coin, but Thomas Jefferson thought that it would be more convenient to strike a smaller coin with just a touch of silver added to compensate. They attempted both a central silver plug and a uniform alloy, but in the end, it was the original, Congressionally authorized cent that was released. All these coins share the obverse legend, "Liberty, Parent of Science and Industry." One last denomination was considered for the issues of 1792 — the quarter — but this was deferred, and only trial strikes are known.

Known counterfeits: Cent (silver center, small copper, large copper), Half Disme (copper), Quarter (copper), Be cautious of holed and plugged half dismes.

	G	F
1792 Cent, Copper		Rare
1792 same with silver center		Rare

	G	F
1792 Large Cent, Copper		Rare
1792 same, White Metal		Rare
1792 Disme, Silver	1,800.00	5,500.00
1792 same, copper		Unique?
1792 Dime, Silver		only 3 known
1792 same, Copper		Rare

1792 Quarter, Copper	only 2 known
1792 Quarter, White Metal	only 2 known

REGULAR MINT ISSUES

HALF CENTS

The half cent is far more popular today than it ever was when it actually circulated. While they permitted very precise dealings in commerce, they were considered a nuisance by those who had to spend them. Demand for them was very small, mintages were low and in some years none were struck for circulation at all. They were so low a priority that the mint sometimes allocated no blanks for them, but struck them on second hand merchant tokens instead. Even the banks didn't want them. From July 1811 until 1825, none were struck because of pressure from the banking industry. The half cent was finally abandoned in 1857.

Though not as popularly collected as the large cent, they are today considered scarce and desirable coins. Like the large cent, half cents are collected by die variety. Rare die combinations can be worth much more than common ones of the same year. Metal detector finds exhibiting porous surfaces are worth

substantially less than the prices listed. Early dates are particularly difficult to find in better than well-worn condition, the Classic Head is much easier to find well-preserved.

Known counterfeits: Cheap cast replicas of the 1793 exist, as do more dangerous counterfeits of that and the 1796 "no pole" variety. Authentic half cents exist with their dates skillfully altered to resemble the rare 1831 date. The 1840s proof restrikes were actually struck by the U.S. mint in the 1850s and 1860s.

Type Coin Price Range	aG to MS-60
1793-1797	85.00 to 15,000.00
1800-1808	18.00 to 1,050.00
1809-1836	16.00 to 250.00
1840-1857	19.00 to 195.00

LIBERTY CAP TYPE

	VG	VF
1793	2,000.00	5,000.00
1794	500.00	1,500.00
1795	325.00	1,100.00
1796 with pole	9,000.00	19,000.00
1796 no pole	30,000.00	85,000.00
1797	300.00	975.00

DRAPED BUST TYPE

1800	60.00	150.00
1802	975.00	4,750.00
1803	48.00	225.00
1804	38.00	80.00
1804 spiked chin	45.00	100.00
1805	42.00	105.00
1806	40.00	70.00
1807	45.00	110.00
1808	40.00	150.00

CLASSIC HEAD TYPE

1809	40.00	60.00
1810	45.00	140.00
1811	200.00	1,250.00
1825	35.00	75.00
1826	35.00	60.00
1828	30.00	50.00
1829	30.00	50.00
1831	2,800.00	5,600.00

	VG	VF
1831 restrikes		Unc. 6,000.00
1832	30.00	55.00
1833	30.00	45.00
1834	30.00	454.00
1835	30.00	45.00
1836		proof only 5,000.00
1836 Restrike		proof only 18,000.00

BRAIDED HAIR TYPE

	VG	VF
1840		proof only 3,800.00
1840 Restrike		proof only 3,200.00
1841		proof only 3,800.00
1841 Restrike		proof only 3,000.00
1842		proof only 3,800.00
1842 Restrike		proof only 3,200.00
1843		proof only 3,800.00
1843 Restrike		proof only 3,200.00
1844		proof only 3,800.00
1844 Restrike		proof only 3,200.00
1845		proof only 3,800.00
1845 Restrike		proof only 3,200.00
1846		proof only 3,800.00
1846 Restrike		proof only 3,200.00
1847		proof only 3,800.00
1847 Restrike		proof only 3,200.00
1848		proof only 3,800.00
1848 Restrike		proof only 3,200.00
1849		proof only 3,800.00
1849 Restrike		proof only 3,200.00
1849 Large date	40.00	60.00
1850	35.00	60.00
1851	28.00	50.00
1852		proof only 35,000.00
1852 Restrikes		proof only 3,500.00
1853	29.00	45.00
1854	32.00	45.00
1855	32.00	45.00
1856	38.00	52.00
1857	48.00	75.00

LARGE CENTS

The United States large cent was a result of the need for a decimal coin worth one one-hundredth of a dollar, and because British halfpennies and their imitations were so prevalent in the American colonies. It was slightly larger than the halfpenny, and the concept of decimal coinage was so innovative that the fraction "1/100" literally had to be written on the coin, along with the edge inscription "ONE HUNDRED FOR A DOLLAR."

The dies for striking early American coins had to be engraved by hand and no two were identical. Because of this, it has been very popular to collect them, especially the large cents, by die combination.

It is interesting to note that low mintages and mediocre acceptance by the public resulted in the very first large cents being regarded as little more than local Philadelphia coinage. Metal was in such short supply that junked copper hardware or inconsistent alloys were used for some early cents, which provided a poor-quality blank on which to strike the coin. People also resented the chain on the first design of 1793, as a symbol antithetical to liberty, and laughed at the frightened expression they per-

ceived on the face of Miss Liberty. Later they became so popular that they were considered good luck. In the early 1800s they were nailed to the rafters of new houses to bring good luck to its inhabitants. These old relics, found with characteristic square nail holes through them, have a discounted value but still hold historical interest for collectors, and have been given the nickname "rafter cents." Other large cents were stamped or hand engraved with advertising, personal initials, or risqué comments, then placed back into circulation.

During the 1850s, public irritation with the heaviness of the cent began to grow and, after eight years of research into smaller alternatives, the large cent was abandoned in 1857.

Because the hand engraved dies with which these coins were struck have been individually identified, large cents are very actively collected by die variety. Rare die combinations can be worth much more than common ones of the same year. Metal detector finds exhibiting porous surfaces are worth substantially less than the prices listed. Early dates are particularly difficult to find in better than well worn condition.

Known Counterfeits: Large cents were not frequently counterfeited in their day. A few rarer dates were later counterfeited to fool collectors. They include 1799, 1803, 1805 over 5, and 1851 over inverted 18. Some crude museum-souvenirs have been made of Chain Cents as well.

Type Coin Price Range	aG to MS-60
1793-1796	70.00 to 3,500.00
1796-1807	16.00 to 2,250.00
1808-1814	20.00 to 2,800.00
1816-1836	7.50 to 225.00
1837-1857	4.50 to 160.00

FLOWING HAIR TYPE

	VG	VF
1793 Chain Rev.	3,750.00	11,000.00
1793 Wreath Rev.	1,200.00	4,000.00

LIBERTY CAP TYPE

1793	3,950.00	20,000.00
1794	250.00	850.00
1795	240.00	630.00
1796	280.00	1,500.00

DRAPED BUST TYPE

	VG	VF
1796	175.00	1,400.00
1797	100.00	335.00
1798	85.00	385.00
1799	3,500.00	15,000.00
1800	65.00	350.00
1801	65.00	280.00
1802	55.00	225.00
1803	55.00	225.00
1804 original (open wreath)	1,100.00	2,550.00
1804 restrike (closed wreath)		Unc. 450.00
1805	55.00	300.00
1806	95.00	350.00
1807	53.00	225.00

CLASSIC HEAD TYPE

1808	75.00	425.00
1809	145.00	1,300.00
1810	75.00	600.00
1811	120.00	875.00
1812	65.00	525.00
1813	115.00	1,100.00
1814	65.00	530.00

CORONET TYPE

1816	17.00	84.00
1817 13 stars	15.00	56.00
1817 15 stars	25.00	125.00
1818	16.00	56.00
1819	14.00	63.00
1820	17.00	63.00
1821	49.00	550.00
1822	15.00	84.00
1823	110.00	625.00
1823 restrike		Unc. 600.00
1824	23.00	145.00
1825	16.00	110.00
1826	16.00	84.00
1827	15.00	75.00
1828	14.00	84.00
1829	14.00	100.00
1830	14.00	70.00
1831	14.00	63.00

	VG	VF
1832	14.00	63.00
1833	14.00	56.00
1834	14.00	56.00
1835	14.00	56.00
1836	15.00	57.00

	VG	VF
1837	14.00	51.00
1838	14.00	51.00
1839	14.00	51.00
1840	14.00	38.00
1841	14.00	38.00
1842	14.00	38.00
1843	14.00	38.00
1844	14.00	22.00
1845	12.00	19.50
1846	12.00	19.50
1847	12.00	19.50
1848	12.00	19.50
1849	12.00	28.00
1850	12.00	19.50
1851	12.00	19.50
1852	12.00	19.50
1853	12.00	19.50
1854	12.00	19.50
1855	13.00	21.00
1856	12.00	16.00
1857	49.00	65.00

FLYING EAGLE CENTS

After years of experimenting, the mint introduced its new small cent in 1857. It was less than half the weight of the large cent and was brown to beige in color due to its alloy of 88% copper and 12% nickel. It depicted an eagle flying left modeled after "Old Pete," a bird that, years earlier, had served as a mascot at the mint. Initially these were released in certain quantities at below face value to encourage their acceptance, but the old large cents were so bulky that people didn't take long to convince. It's interesting to observe, in today's health-conscious atmosphere, that the wreath on the reverse contains, among other plants, tobacco.

The 1856 is technically a pattern but was widely distributed at the time and is generally collected as part of the series.

Known counterfeits: Most of the 1856 cents encountered are counterfeit. They are usually made from authentic coins with the dates re-engraved.

Type Coin Price Range	G to MS-60
1856-58	13.00 to 200.00

	VG	VF
1856	4,250.00	5,250.00
1857	16.00	33.00
1858 Lg. Letters	17.00	38.00
1858 Small Letters	16.00	38.00

INDIAN HEAD CENTS

The origin of the Indian Head Cent is one of the most charming in the field of numismatics. According to legend, James B. Longacre, an engraver at the U.S. mint, was entertaining an Indian chief who happened to be wearing his full war bonnet. As a gesture of whimsy, the chief removed his bonnet and placed it upon the head of Longacre's little girl, Sarah. The engraver instantly perceived that this was the image destined for the next American cent. Admittedly, fewer people believe this story as time goes on, but it does add a quaint bit of sentimentality to the origin of one of America's favorite coin designs.

When the Indian Head Cent was first released, it was struck in the same copper-nickel alloy as the Flying Eagle Cent. The reverse was a simple laurel wreath encircling the words ONE CENT. The following year this was replaced by one of oak, often considered a symbol of authority, into the bottom of which was tied a bundle of arrows. Its top was open enough to fit a small American shield.

In 1864 nickel was removed from the alloy, giving the coin the bronze appearance that has since characterized the U.S. cent. It was also made thinner like our modern cent. This new bronze cent was very reminiscent in form to the private one cent "Civil War Tokens," which were circulating at the time, cost a fraction of a cent to manufacture — an obvious savings not spent on the mint.

Known Counterfeits: 1877, 1908-S and 1909-S. The latter are often made from real 1908 and 1909 Indian cents.

Type Coin Price Range	G to MS-60
1859	7.00 to 200.00
1860-64	4.00 to 70.00
1864-1909	1.30 to 24.00

(1864-1909 with original mint red are worth more.)

COPPER-NICKEL ALLOY

	F	XF
1859	15.00	70.00
1860	11.50	42.00
1861	24.00	75.00
1862	11.00	27.50
1863	10.00	25.00
1864	21.00	45.00

BRONZE

	F	XF
1864	14.00	40.00
1864 L on ribbon	80.00	175.00
1865	11.00	32.00

	F	XF
1866	45.00	125.00
1867	45.00	125.00
1868	47.00	125.00
1869	160.00	260.00
1870	140.00	260.00
1871	200.00	300.00
1872	200.00	325.00
1873	30.00	95.00
1874	27.00	80.00
1875	31.00	80.00
1876	42.00	110.00
1877	675.00	1,375.00
1878	45.00	115.00
1879	10.00	35.00
1880	5.50	20.00
1881	5.50	13.00
1882	5.50	13.00
1883	5.00	13.00
1884	6.00	23.00
1885	13.00	40.00
1886	16.00	55.00
1887	4.00	12.00
1888	4.00	15.50
1889	4.00	10.00
1890	2.50	10.00
1891	2.60	10.00
1892	3.50	10.00
1893	2.60	10.00
1894	7.50	22.50
1895	2.50	12.50
1896	2.50	11.00
1897	2.50	9.00
1898	2.50	10.00
1899	2.30	10.00
1900	2.25	7.50
1901	1.75	7.50
1902	1.75	7.50
1903	1.75	7.50
1904	1.75	7.50
1905	1.75	7.50
1906	1.70	7.50
1907	1.70	7.50
1908	1.75	8.00
1908S	49.00	75.00
1909	3.50	11.00
1909S	300.00	380.00

LINCOLN CENTS

The Lincoln cent was the first regular issue United States coin to bear the portrait of a real person. It made its debut to celebrate the one-hundredth year after Lincoln's birth. It was designed by a sculptor from outside the mint's staff, Victor David Brenner. His initials are found prominently on the very first examples to be released. Some thought they were featured too prominently, and the outcry forced their removal, causing two varieties for the first year. Later in 1918, they were added more discreetly under the truncation of the shoulder.

Lincoln cents were a bronze alloy of 95 percent copper until 1943, when they were changed to zinc-coated steel to conserve on copper for the war effort. Because some of them were confused with dimes they were replaced in 1944 and 1945 with cents made

from melted spent shell casings, resulting in a much more conventional appearance. The original alloy was restored from 1946 until 1982 when it was finally abandoned for zinc plated with copper. This was to reduce the expense of manufacturing the cent. Many people don't realize it but if you cut one of the cents struck today in half it will not be orange or brown inside. Instead, it is white, which reveals its true composition.

A new reverse was introduced in 1959 for the 150th anniversary of Lincoln's birth and the 50th anniversary of the Lincoln cent. Still in use today, it depicts the Lincoln Memorial in Washington D.C.

The Lincoln cent is one of the most popularly collected coins on earth. People collect almost all grades, and one can even find the rarities fairly easily.

Known counterfeits: The 1909S VDB, 1909S, 1914D, 1922-Plain, 1931S, and 1955 double dies have been extensively counterfeited. Most are altered cents of other dates. Counterfeits also exist of the 1972 double die. Virtually all 1943 bronze and 1944 steel cents are counterfeit. A magnet test will reveal the crudest counterfeits made by plating.

In addition to counterfeits, the collector should be aware of "reprocessed" cents. These are circulated 1943 steel cents coated in fresh zinc to make them appear uncirculated. Many hobbyists are quite willing to have them in their collections, but it is important to know the difference: Don't look for luster. Instead look for traces of flatness at the cheekbone.

Type Coin Price Range   VG to MS-63

1909-1958	.01 to .40
1943	.15 to 1.25
1959-82	.01 to .15
1982-date	.01 to .15

(Coins with original mint red are worth more than toned specimens.)

WHEAT EARS REVERSE

	VF	MS-60
1909 VDB	2.75	9.00
1909S VDB	470.00	680.00
1909	1.75	14.00
1909S	60.00	120.00
1910	.60	14.00
1910S	10.00	60.00
1911	1.95	18.00
1911D	11.00	70.00
1911S	22.00	120.00
1912	4.50	25.00
1912D	15.00	120.00

	VF	MS-60		VF	MS-60
1912S	18.50	80.00	1937D	.25	2.25
1913	3.50	23.00	1937S	.25	1.75
1913D	8.00	80.00	1938	.20	1.60
1913S	13.50	110.00	1938D	.45	2.00
1914	3.75	39.00	1938S	.60	2.25
1914D	190.00	1,000.00	1939	.20	1.00
1914S	20.00	175.00	1939D	.60	2.25
1915	12.00	80.00	1939S	.25	1.35
1915D	3.50	45.00	1940	.25	.95
1915S	11.50	100.00	1940D	.25	1.00
1916	1.25	11.00	1940S	.25	1.00
1916D	2.50	50.00	1941	.20	.85
1916S	2.50	60.00	1941D	.20	2.00
1917	.95	12.00	1941S	.20	2.25
1917D	2.50	55.00	1942	.15	.50
1917S	1.50	55.00	1942D	.15	.50
1918	.90	12.00	1942S	.15	3.50
1918D	2.00	50.00	1943 steel	.30	.85
1918S	1.50	55.00	1943D steel	.35	1.00
1919	.65	9.00	1943S steel	.35	1.75
1919D	2.00	42.00	1944	.15	.50
1919S	1.00	30.00	1944D	.15	.45
1920	.65	10.00	1944 D over S	140.00	375.00
1920D	2.50	50.00	1944S	.15	.45
1920S	1.50	75.00	1945	.15	.60
1921	1.25	35.00	1945D	.15	.70
1921S	3.50	80.00	1945S	.15	.45
1922D	11.50	65.00	1946	.15	.35
1922 plain	540.00	8,500.00	1946D	.15	.50
1923	1.65	10.00	1946S	.15	.50
1923S	5.00	170.00	1947	.15	1.00
1924	1.25	20.00	1947D	.15	.40
1924D	20.00	225.00	1947S	.15	.55
1924S	2.50	100.00	1948	.15	.50
1925	.95	8.50	1948D	.15	.45
1925D	2.00	42.00	1948S	.15	.65
1925S	1.00	55.00	1949	.15	.75
1926	.80	8.00	1949D	.15	.50
1926D	1.50	42.00	1949S	.15	1.00
1926S	4.50	92.50	1950	.15	.50
1927	.80	7.25	1950D	.15	.50
1927D	1.25	35.00	1950S	.15	.80
1927S	3.00	57.00	1951	.15	.90
1928	.80	7.00	1951D	.15	.50
1928D	.95	20.00	1951S	.15	.75
1928S	1.50	44.00	1952	.15	.50
1929	.80	6.00	1952D	.15	.50
1929D	.75	15.00	1952S	.15	1.00
1929S	1.00	8.50	1953	.15	.50
1930	.45	5.50	1953D	.15	.50
1930D	.70	12.00	1953S	.15	.45
1930S	.70	6.00	1954	.15	.75
1931	1.15	16.50	1954D	.15	.35
1931D	4.00	45.00	1954S	.15	.35
1931S	34.00	53.00	1955	.15	.30
1932	2.50	16.00	1955 double die	425.00	1,250.00
1932D	1.35	14.00	1955 minor date shift		
1933	1.90	16.00	or "poor man's		
1933D	3.00	15.00	double die"	.15	1.00
1934	.25	3.00	1955D	.15	.30
1934D	.45	15.00	1955S	.15	.60
1935	.25	1.50	1956	.15	.30
1935D	.30	4.50	1956D	.15	.30
1935S	.40	10.00	1957	.15	.30
1936	.25	1.50	1957D	.15	.30
1936D	.25	2.50	1958	.15	.30
1936S	.35	2.50	1958D	.15	.30
1937	.20	1.00			

LINCOLN MEMORIAL REVERSE

	MS-60
1959	.20
1959D	.30
1960 large date	.20
1960 small date	2.25
1960D large date	.30
1960D small date	.50
1961	.20
1961D	.20
1962	.20
1962D	.20
1963	.20
1963D	.20
1964	.20
1964D	.20
1965	.20
1966	.20
1967	.20
1968	.20
1968D	.20
1968S	.20
1969	.40
1969D	.20
1969S	.20
1970	.20
1970D	.20
1970S small date	28.00
1970S large date	.20

1970S Large Date

1970S Small Date

1971	.20
1971D	.25
1971S	.35
1972	.15
1972 double die	200.00
1972D	.15
1972S	.15
1973	.15
1973D	.15
1973S	.15

	MS-60
1974	.15
1974D	.15
1974S	.15
1975	.15
1975D	.15
1975S proof only	4.50
1976	.15
1976D	.15
1976S proof only	3.00
1977	.15
1977D	.15
1977S proof only	1.95
1978	.15
1978D	.15
1978S proof only	2.25
1979	.15
1979D	.15
1979S proof only	2.75
1980	.15
1980D	.15
1980S proof only	1.35
1981	.15
1981D	.15
1981S proof only	2.00
1982	.15
1982D	.15
1982S proof only	2.00

COPPER PLATED ZINC

1982	.30
1982D	.15
1983	.15
1983 double die rev.	200.00
1983D	.15
1983S proof only	4.00
1984	.15
1984 double die	175.00
1984D	.15
1984S proof only	3.50
1985	.15
1985D	.15
1985S proof only	3.00
1986	.15
1986D	.15
1986S proof only	7.50
1987	.15
1987D	.15
1987S proof only	2.75
1988	.15
1988D	.15
1988S proof only	2.75
1989	.15
1989D	.15
1989S proof only	2.75
1990	.15
1990D	.15
1990S proof only	5.75
1990S w/o S proof only	1,115.00
1991	.15
1991D	.15
1991S proof only	7.50
1992	.15
1992D	.15
1992S proof only	5.50
1993	.15
1993D	.15
1993S proof only	7.50
1994	.15
1994D	.15

	MS-60
1994S proof only	6.00
1995	.15
1995 double die	25.00
1995D	.15
1995S proof only	7.00
1996	.15
1996D	.15
1996S proof only	6.50
1997	.15
1997D	.15
1997S proof only	7.00
1998	.15
1998D	.15
1998S proof only	7.00

TWO CENT PIECES

Throughout the Civil War people hoarded coins, preferring to spend the less valuable private tokens and small-denomination paper money available. If the North fell, they thought that at least real coins would retain some value. A shortage in small change resulted. The two cent piece was introduced in an attempt to alleviate this shortage. It was the first coin to carry the inscription "In God We Trust."

These are usually found well worn, and fewer than one in one-hundred are in fine or better condition.

Known counterfeits: Counterfeits are not particularly common.

Type Coin Price Range	G to MS-60
1864-1873	8.00 to 70.00

	F	XF
1864 Small motto (open D in GOD)	100.00	250.00
1864 Large motto (narrow D in GOD)	20.00	32.00
1865	20.00	32.00
1866	20.00	32.00
1867	20.00	32.00
1868	20.00	65.00
1869	20.00	80.00
1870	21.00	57.00
1871	24.00	75.00
1872	174.00	400.00
1873 Closed 3	proof only	1,400.00
1873 Open 3	Restrike	1,900.00

SILVER THREE CENT PIECES

Different times have different priorities, and the reasons for striking coins in one era don't always make sense to the people living in another. This is the case of the silver three cent piece, often called the "trime." It and the three dollar gold piece were issued to make it easier to purchase single and sheets of three-cent first class postage stamps. Despite the extreme awkwardness of their small size, they were accepted enough in commerce that they were struck in significant quantities for twelve years,

Its thinness prevented it from striking up well, and the mint attempted to modify its design repeatedly. Finding a fully struck coin with no weak spots, even in higher grades, is truly difficult. Another problem that developed as a result of their thinness was frequent bending, dents and crinkling. Prices given are for flat, undamaged examples.

Known counterfeits: Counterfeits made to pass in circulation were struck in base silver and white metal for early dates, German silver (copper-nickel-zinc), dated 1860 and 1861. A struck counterfeit also exists for 1864.

Type Coin Price Range	G to MS-60
1851-1853	13.00 to 145.00
1854-1858	16.00 to 230.00
1859-1873	15.00 to 150.00

	F	XF
No Border Around Star		
1851	22.00	65.00
1851O	35.00	115.00
1852	20.00	50.00
1853	22.00	54.00
Triple Border Around Star		
1854	24.00	90.00
1855	44.00	145.00
1856	22.00	85.00
1857	22.00	85.00
1858	25.00	85.00
Double Border Around Star		
1859	22.00	70.00
1860	25.00	70.00
1861	24.00	70.00
1862	25.00	70.00
1863	280.00	350.00
1864	325.00	425.00
1865	350.00	400.00
1866	280.00	350.00
1867	350.00	400.00
1868	350.00	400.00
1869	350.00	400.00
1870	350.00	400.00
1871	350.00	400.00
1872	375.00	450.00
1873	proof only 1,100.00	

NICKEL THREE CENT PIECES

The fact that the tiny silver three cent piece survived at all dictates that there was some usefulness to this denomination, even though its size was impractical. With Civil War silver hoarding, the need for a convenient, non-silver coins of this value was even more apparent. The three cent coin was thus made bigger and changed to an alloy of 75 percent copper and 25 percent nickel — just enough nickel to give it a

white color. Despite their heavy use in commerce for decades, they are not difficult to find well preserved.

Known Counterfeits: Few if any counterfeits of this coin are known.

Type Coin Price Range	G to MS-60
1865 to 1889	7.00 to 83.00

	F	XF
1865	11.50	15.00
1866	11.50	15.00
1867	11.50	15.00
1868	11.50	15.00
1869	12.00	15.00
1870	12.00	16.00
1871	12.00	18.00
1872	12.00	17.00
1873	12.00	16.00
1874	12.00	17.00
1875	13.00	25.00
1876	17.00	38.00
1877 proof only		1,200.00
1878 proof only		700.00
1879	60.00	80.00
1880	90.00	130.00
1881	12.00	17.00
1882	84.00	110.00
1883	175.00	240.00
1884	350.00	425.00
1885	425.00	500.00
1886 proof only		700.00
1887	275.00	325.00
1888	45.00	70.00
1889	90.00	125.00

SHIELD NICKELS

The success of the 25-percent nickel, three cent piece emboldened the mint to strike a larger denomination in the same alloy the following year. Its design was an ornate shield, reminiscent of the then-popular two cent piece. One unfortunate characteristic of a coin struck in a hard alloy such as this is that its design is not always fully struck. In this case, not all of the horizontal shading lines are always clear, even on mint state coins. In its second year of issue the design was simplified — the rays between the stars on the reverse being removed.

Known counterfeits: Counterfeits intended to pass in circulation were struck bearing the dates 1870 to 1876.

Type Coin Price Range	G to MS-60
1866-1867 Rays	15.00 to 225.00
1867-1883	8.00 to 90.00

	F	XF
1866 Rays	22.00	95.00
1867 Rays	24.00	120.00
1867	14.00	34.00
1868	14.00	34.00
1869	14.00	34.00
1870	16.50	40.00
1871	50.00	120.00
1872	16.50	40.00
1873 Closed 3	25.00	270.00
1873 Open 3	16.00	40.00
1874	24.00	52.00
1875	28.00	65.00
1876	24.00	55.00
1877 proof only		1,250.00
1878 proof only		700.00
1879	345.00	440.00
1880	385.00	500.00
1881	225.00	380.00
1882	14.00	32.00
1883	14.00	32.50
1883 3 over 2	130.00	235.00

LIBERTY NICKELS

The Liberty nickel had one of the most controversial origins of all American coins. The original design had the denomination of five cents indicated simply by the Roman numeral V. The face the V was cents was simply implied. Or so the mint expected. However, some unprincipled people plated these coins in gold and passed them off as the new five dollar coin. These plated frauds became known as racketeer nickels and prompted an immediate change in the design of this coin. The word "cents" was added in bold type underneath the large V. Today, racketeer nickels have some value as collector's novelties, but not as much as a natural, unaltered coin. Interestingly, the original "no cents" nickel is quite common today in medium to high grades, perhaps because it might have been considered a novelty in its day.

The famous 1913 Liberty nickel is not an authorized mint issue, but was struck at the U.S. mint by a scheming employee with an eye for profit. Carefully marketed, the first advertisements to purchase these rare coins were placed by the original seller, knowing that no one else had any to sell, but knowing the coin's release would excite interest in the numismatic community. Today it is one of the most valuable coins in the world.

Known Counterfeits: There are counterfeits of the 1913 but they are somewhat less dangerous, as all five extant pieces are in known hands. 1912S pieces exist made from altered 1912D nickels.

Type Coin Price Range	G to MS-60
1883 No Cents	3.75 to 29.00
1883-1913	1.20 to 60.00

	F	XF
1883 No Cents	4.75	7.50
1883 With Cents	14.00	40.00
1884	16.00	42.00
1885	350.00	600.00
1886	150.00	280.00
1887	18.50	40.00
1888	22.00	60.00
1889	17.00	37.00
1890	17.00	37.50
1891	13.00	38.00
1892	13.00	36.00
1893	12.50	35.00
1894	40.00	140.00
1895	12.00	40.00
1896	14.00	42.00
1897	6.50	24.00
1898	6.00	32.50
1899	5.50	19.00
1900	5.00	17.50
1901	4.50	18.00
1902	4.25	17.00
1903	4.25	18.00
1904	4.25	19.00
1905	4.00	17.00
1906	4.00	18.00
1907	4.00	17.00
1908	4.50	18.00
1909	5.00	25.00
1910	4.00	17.00
1911	4.00	17.00
1912	4.00	17.00
1912D	6.00	42.00
1912S	85.00	475.00
1913 Proof		1,485,000.00

BUFFALO NICKELS

The Buffalo Nickel, also called the Indian Head Nickel, was one of the most artistically progressive American coins that had ever been struck when first issued. It was designed by James Earl Fraser, a noted sculptor of the era. The traditional belief was that three different Indians posed for the obverse portrait, but this theory has recently been called into question. The original reverse depicts an American bison standing on a mound. This was quickly changed the year it was issued for the practical reason the words FIVE CENTS were in such high relief that they quickly wore off. The second type of reverse has the denomination in a recess below a plane on which the bison stands. The date is also rendered in high relief on these coins, and in conditions less than very good, usually wears off. Such dateless coins are of little value.

One entertaining aside: the Buffalo nickel received a sort of tribute in the Hobo Nickel. This relic of American folk art consists of a Buffalo nickel with the portrait re-engraved by hand into a variety of different portraits. It was some individual's way of fighting the poverty of the Great Depression, by making these works of art and selling them at a modest profit. During the past few years they have come into their own and attempts to identify individual artists have met with some success.

Known counterfeits: The most famous counterfeit in the series is that of the Three-legged Buffalo variety of 1937D. It should be noted that a real 3-legged buffalo can be distinguished quite easily, not simply because it lacks a leg, but based on numerous minor details, among those, the fact that the place the design meets the field is missing. Other counterfeits are coins altered to appear to be 1913S Type II, 1918/7D, 1921S, 1924S, 1926D, and 1926S.

Type Coin Price Range — VG to MS-63

	VG to MS-63
1913 Mound	5.75 to 45.00
1913-1938	.70 to 15.00

	F	MS-60
1913 Mound	6.50	32.00
1913D Mound	12.50	50.00
1913S Mound	21.00	63.00
1913 Plain	8.50	30.00
1913D Plain	65.00	155.00
1913S Plain	165.00	345.00
1914	10.50	45.00
1914D	62.00	190.00
1914S	16.50	110.00
1915	7.00	45.00
1915D	29.00	160.00
1915S	50.00	420.00
1916	3.00	38.00
1916D	15.00	130.00
1916S	12.00	145.00
1917	4.00	48.00
1917D	27.00	275.00
1917S	30.00	290.00
1918	4.50	69.00
1918 8 over 7	1,050.00	12,500.00
1918D	30.00	320.00
1918S	29.00	300.00
1919	2.50	45.00
1919D	35.00	475.00
1919S	27.00	440.00
1920	2.25	45.00
1920D	30.00	420.00
1920S	17.50	350.00
1921	4.50	95.00
1921S	77.00	1,300.00
1923	2.75	40.00
1923S	15.00	360.00
1924	2.50	45.00
1924D	16.00	290.00
1924S	62.00	1,850.00
1925	3.00	38.00
1925D	35.00	325.00
1925S	13.50	340.00
1926	1.50	32.00
1926D	24.00	240.00
1926S	35.00	2,700.00
1927	1.50	30.00
1927D	7.00	140.00
1927S	4.60	450.00
1928	1.50	35.00
1928D	4.00	47.00
1928S	2.75	275.00

	F	MS-60
1929	1.50	30.00
1929D	3.00	45.00
1929S	1.25	39.00
1930	1.50	25.00
1930S	1.25	36.00
1931S	4.75	38.00
1934	.95	24.00
1934D	1.75	38.00
1935	.80	17.00
1935D	2.00	33.00
1935S	.80	24.00
1936	.75	14.00
1936D	.80	17.00
1936S	.75	17.00
1937	.75	13.00
1937D	.75	14.00

Detail of 1937D 3-legged Buffalo

	F	MS-60
1937D 3-Legged	240.00	1,100.00
1937S	.85	14.00
1938D	1.60	13.00
1938D D over S	10.00	39.00

JEFFERSON NICKELS

The Jefferson Nickel was the first circulating United States coin to be designed by public contest. Felix Schlag won $1,000 for his design, which featured Jefferson's portrait on one side, and his home in Monticello on the other. The initial rendition lacks the designer's initials, which were not added until 1966.

During World War II, nickel was needed for the war effort so from mid-1942 to the end of 1945 "nickels" were struck in an unusual alloy of 56 percent copper, 35 percent silver and 9 percent manganese. These War Nickels bear a large mintmark over the dome. These coins exhibit great brilliance when new, but quickly turn an ugly dull color with a moderate amount of wear.

Due to the difficulty of getting the metal to flow into every crevice of the die, many coins have steps to Monticello that are incompletely struck. Full step nickels sometimes command a premium from specialists.

Known counterfeits: 1950D. Crude casts were also made to circulate in the 1940s..

Type Coin Price Range — VG to MS-63

	VG to MS-63
1938-date	.05 to .35
1942-1945 Silver	.50 to 3.00

	VF	MS-60
1938	.80	3.50

	VF	MS-60		VF	MS-60		VF	MS-60
1938D	1.25	4.25	1961		.25	1988S proof only		4.50
1938S	1.75	3.75	1961D		.25	1989		.25
1939	.25	1.75	1962		.25	1989D		.25
1939D	4.50	30.00	1962D		.25	1989S proof only		3.00
1939S	1.50	13.00	1963		.25	1990		.25
1940	.25	1.00	1963D		.25	1990D		.25
1940D	.30	2.50	1964		.25	1990S proof only		4.50
1940S	.25	2.75	1964D		.25	1991		.25
1941	.25	.90	1965		.25	1991D		.25
1941D	.30	2.50	1966		.25	1991S proof only		5.50
1941S	.25	3.75	1967		.25	1992		.35
1942	.25	4.50	1968D		.25	1992D		.25
1942D	.60	17.00	1968S		.25	1992S proof only		4.00
Wartime Silver Alloy			1969D		.25	1993		.25
1942P	1.00	7.00	1969S		.25	1993D		.25
1942S	1.10	5.50	1970D		.25	1993S proof only		4.00
1943P	1.00	4.00	1970S		.25	1994		.25
1943P 3 over 2	60.00	250.00	1971		.50	1994D		.25
1943D	1.50	2.75	1971D		.25	1994S proof only		4.50
1943S	1.00	3.25	1971S proof only		1.50	1995		.25
1944P	1.00	4.50	1972		.25	1995D		.35
1944D	1.00	5.00	1972D		.25	1995S proof only		6.00
1944S	1.15	3.50	1972S proof only		1.50	1996		.25
1945P	1.00	3.50	1973		.25	1996D		.25
1945D	1.00	3.50	1973D		.25	1996S proof only		3.00
1945S	.80	2.00	1973S proof only		1.60	1997		.25
Regular Alloy			1974		.25	1997D		.30
1946	.25	.40	1974D		.25	1997S proof only		4.50
1946D	.25	.75	1974S proof only		1.75	1998		.25
1946S	.30	.60	1975		.25	1998D		.25
1947	.25	.40	1975D		.25	1998S proof only		3.50
1947D	.25	.90	1975S proof only		2.00			
1947S	.25	.70	1976		.25			
1948	.25	.40	1976D		.25			
1948D	.25	1.20	1976S proof only		2.00			
1948S	.25	1.00	1977		.25			
1949	.25	.80	1977D		.25			
1949D	.30	1.00	1977S proof only		2.50			
1949D D over S	40.00	170.00	1978		.25			
1949S	.45	1.50	1978D		.25			
1950	.35	1.50	1978S proof only		1.75			
1950D	5.25	6.50	1979		.25			
1951	.40	1.10	1979D		.25			
1951D	.40	1.00	1979S proof only		1.50			
1951S	.50	1.75	1980		.25			
1952	.25	.75	1980D		.25			
1952D	.30	1.25	1980S proof only		1.60			
1952S	.25	.65	1981		.25			
1953	.25	.35	1981D		.25			
1953D	.25	.35	1981S proof only		1.50			
1953S	.25	.50	1982		.75			
1954	.25	.30	1982D		1.25			
1954D	.25	.30	1982S proof only		3.00			
1954S	.25	.35	1983		1.50			
1954S S over D	7.75	22.00	1983D		1.00			
1955	.40	.75	1983S proof only		3.50			
1955D		.25	1984		1.25			
1955D D over S	8.50	33.00	1984D		.25			
1956		.25	1984S proof only		5.00			
1956D		.25	1985		.30			
1957		.25	1985D		.30			
1957D		.25	1985S proof only		3.25			
1958		.30	1986		.30			
1958D		.25	1986D		.85			
1959		.30	1986S proof only		6.50			
1959D		.25	1987		.25			
1960		.25	1987D		.25			
1960D		.25	1987S proof only		3.25			
			1988		.25			
			1988D		.25			

BUST HALF DIMES

The United States did not always have nickel five cent pieces. The original ones were very small silver coins called half dimes. Their designs almost always resembled those used on large whole dimes. Although they were one of George Washington's priorities, the production of half dimes was inconsistent in early America. Between 1805 and 1829, none were struck at all.

The bust half dime's thinness resulted in frequent bending and dents. Prices given are for flat, undamaged examples. Rare die combinations of early specimens command a premium from specialists.

Known counterfeits: 1795.

Type Coin Price Range	G to MS-60
1794-1795	540.00 to 4,500.00
1796-1797	850.00 to 5,650.00
1800-1805	625.00 to 5,050.00
1829-1837	15.00 to 270.00

FLOWING HAIR TYPE

	VG	VF
1794	875.00	1,750.00
1795	650.00	1,200.00

	VF	MS-60
DRAPED BUST / SMALL EAGLE		
1796	850.00	1,950.00
1797	925.00	2,150.00

DRAPED BUST / HERALDIC EAGLE		
1800	700.00	1,400.00
1801	750.00	1,500.00
1802	13,500.00	35,000.00
1803	700.00	1,400.00
1805	825.00	1,550.00

CAPPED BUST TYPE		
1829	25.00	50.00
1830	25.00	50.00
1831	25.00	50.00
1832	25.00	50.00
1833	25.00	50.00
1834	25.00	50.00
1835	25.00	50.00
1836	25.00	50.00
1837	25.00	50.00

SEATED LIBERTY HALF DIMES

Following the introduction of the Seated Liberty design by Christian Gobrecht on the silver dollar, the smaller coins were gradually became harmonious with this design. It is generally accepted that the seated goddess version of Liberty was directly or indirectly inspired by depictions of the Roman allegory of Britannia on British coins. The half dime and dime, because of their small size, were redesigned to have a laurel wreath encircling the denomination on the reverse, rather than an eagle.

There were several minor changes over the lifetime of this coin. After only a year the plain obverse was ornamented by thirteen stars. Two years later additional drapery was added below Liberty's elbow. The arrows by the date from 1853 to 1855 indicate a 7-1/2 percent reduction in weight. A far more obvious design change was the shift of the words UNITED STATES OF AMERICA from the obverse to the reverse in 1860.

The seated half dime's thinness resulted in frequent bending and dents. Prices given are for flat, undamaged examples.

Known counterfeits: Counterfeit half dimes are not frequently encountered.

Type Coin Price Range	G to MS-60
1837-1838 No Stars	25.00 to 600.00
1838-1859	7.50 to 130.00
1860-1873	8.00 to 145.00

	VF	MS-60
SEATED LIBERTY -		
PLAIN OBVERSE FIELD		

	VG	VF
1837	35.00	100.00
1838O	110.00	400.00

SEATED LIBERTY -
STARS ON OBVERSE

	VG	VF
1838	9.50	25.00
1839	11.00	29.00
1839O	12.00	31.00
1840	9.50	21.00
1840O	15.00	45.00
1841	9.50	22.00
1841O	15.00	40.00
1842	9.50	22.00
1842O	40.00	185.00
1843	9.50	18.00
1844	10.00	24.00
1844O	95.00	350.00
1845	9.50	22.00
1846	325.00	700.00
1847	9.50	18.00
1848	10.00	32.00
1848O	17.50	42.50
1849	9.50	18.00
1849 overdates	14.00	35.00
1849O	40.00	145.00
1850	9.25	18.00
1850O	16.00	50.00
1851	9.50	18.00
1851O	15.00	35.00
1852	9.50	18.00
1852O	35.00	110.00
1853 no arrows	38.00	85.00
1853O no arrows	190.00	550.00
1853 arrows	8.00	17.00
1853O arrows	9.50	35.00
1854	9.00	17.00
1854O	10.00	25.00
1855	10.00	20.00
1855O	20.00	55.00
1856	10.00	18.00
1856O	10.00	27.00
1857	9.00	15.00
1857O	11.50	25.00
1858	9.50	18.00
1858O	11.50	26.00
1859	12.00	33.00
1859O	10.00	30.00

	VG	VF
SEATED LIBERTY -		
LEGEND ON OBVERSE		
1860	12.00	25.00
1860O	10.00	30.00
1861	9.50	14.00
1862	9.50	16.00
1863	165.00	260.00
1863S	25.00	65.00
1864	315.00	500.00
1864S	45.00	95.00
1865	300.00	425.00
1865S	28.00	60.00
1866	250.00	415.00
1866S	24.00	50.00
1867	400.00	550.00
1867S	27.00	60.00
1868	60.00	135.00
1868S	15.00	30.00
1869	15.00	40.00
1869S	14.00	33.00
1870	10.00	17.00
1870S		Unique
1871	9.50	14.00
1871S	12.50	50.00
1872	9.00	14.00
1872S	15.00	30.00
1873	12.00	24.00
1873S	17.00	40.00

BUST DIMES

Due to limited mint capacity, dimes were not struck until 1796, even though other denominations of United States silver began to be struck two years earlier. Dime production was suspended occasionally when enough small Mexican coins were imported to satisfy demand. The initial reverse design, which showed a rather skinny eagle within a wreath, was replaced after two more years with a plumper eagle carrying a heraldic shield. In 1809 a cap was added to Liberty and her bust was turned to the left. In that same year the denomination first appeared; however it "10C" rather than "dime." Rare die combinations of early specimens command a premium from specialists

Known counterfeits: Few if any known.

Type Coin Price Range	G to MS-60
1796-1797	1,000.00 to 6,750.00
1798-1807	375.00 to 4,050.00
1809-1837	14.00 to 600.00

DRAPED BUST / SMALL EAGLE		
	VG	VF
1796	1,450.00	3,000.00
1797 13 stars	1,800.00	3,450.00
1797 16 stars	1,750.00	3,250.00

	VG	VF
DRAPED BUST / HERALDIC EAGLE		
1798 over 97,		
13 stars	3,000.00	7,500.00
1798 over 97, 16 stars	650.00	1,800.00
1798	560.00	1,125.00
1800	560.00	1,125.00
1801	556.00	1,375.00
1802	850.00	2,200.00
1803	560.00	1,125.00
1804, 13 stars	1,400.00	4,400.00
1804, 14 stars	1,700.00	4,750.00
1805	525.00	950.00
1807	525.00	975.00

CAPPED BUST TYPE	VG	VF
1809	200.00	650.00
1811 over 9	165.00	425.00
1814 Small Date	60.00	210.00
1814 Large Date	26.00	115.00
1820	24.00	105.00
1821 Small Date	25.00	125.00
1821 Large Date	23.00	105.00
1822	450.00	1,450.00
1823, 3 over 2	22.00	110.00
1824, 4 over 2	48.00	325.00
1825	25.00	145.00
1827	22.00	95.00
1828 Large Date	95.00	265.00
1828 Small Date	45.00	195.00
1829 (varieties)	17.00	60.00
1830 30 over 29	25.00	100.00
1830	17.00	60.00
1831	17.00	60.00
1832	17.00	60.00
1833	17.00	60.00
1834	17.00	60.00
1835	17.00	60.00
1836	17.00	60.00
1837	17.00	60.00

SEATED LIBERTY DIMES

Following the introduction of the Seated Liberty design by Christian Gobrecht on the silver dollar, the smaller coins gradually became harmonious with this design. It is generally accepted that the seated goddess version of Liberty was directly or indirectly inspired by depictions of the Roman allegory of Britannia on British coins. The dime and half dime, because of their small size, were redesigned to have a laurel wreath encircling the denomination on the reverse, rather than an eagle.

There were several minor changes over the lifetime of this coin. After a little more than a year the plain obverse was ornamented by thirteen stars. A year later, additional drapery was added below Liberty's elbow. The arrows by the date from 1853 to 1855 indicate a 7 percent reduction in weight, those in 1873 to 1874 a minuscule increase. A far more obvious design change was the shift of the words UNITED STATES OF AMERICA from the obverse to the reverse in 1860.

The seated dime's thinness resulted in frequent bending and dents. Prices given are for flat, undamaged examples.

Known counterfeits: Collector counterfeits of seated dimes are not frequently encountered, but circulating counterfeits were struck in copper, lead, and white metal (tin and lead alloys), particularly during the 1850s to the 1860s.

Type Coin Price Range	G to MS-60
1837-1838 No Stars	29.00 to 1,100.00
1838-1860	8.75 to 250.00
1860-1891	8.75 to 110.00

SEATED LIBERTY - **OBVERSE FIELD PLAIN**	VG	VF
1837	40.00	275.00
1838O	55.00	375.00

SEATED LIBERTY - **STARS ON OBVERSE**		
1838 (varieties)	11.00	25.00
1839	15.00	35.00
1839O	12.00	40.00
1840	15.00	30.00
1840O	22.00	70.00
1840 extra drapery		
from elbow	45.00	165.00
1841	13.00	25.00
1841O	9.00	28.00
1842	9.50	17.00
1842O	18.00	75.00
1843	9.25	17.00
1843O	65.00	250.00
1844	350.00	700.00
1845	9.25	19.00
1845O	35.00	165.00
1846	110.00	295.00
1847	25.00	60.00
1848	15.00	40.00
1849	13.00	28.00
1849O	22.00	85.00
1850	9.25	25.00
1850O	14.00	60.00
1851	9.25	19.00
1851O	15.00	75.00

	VG	VF
1852	9.25	15.00
1852O	22.00	85.00
1853 no arrows	85.00	180.00
1853 arrows	9.25	14.00
1853O arrows	13.00	45.00
1854	9.25	14.00
1854O	9.50	25.00
1855	9.25	15.00
1856	9.25	12.50
1856O	15.00	35.00
1856S	165.00	425.00
1857	9.25	13.00
1857O	10.00	25.00
1858	14.00	35.00
1858O	19.00	70.00
1858S	150.00	325.00
1859	15.00	40.00
1859O	11.00	35.00
1859S	160.00	450.00
1860S	36.00	100.00

SEATED LIBERTY - **LEGEND ON OBVERSE**		
1860	25.00	45.00
1860O	425.00	950.00
1861	10.00	18.00
1861S	80.00	225.00
1862	13.00	25.00
1862S	52.00	175.00
1863	375.00	600.00
1863S	35.00	90.00
1864	325.00	500.00
1864S	30.00	80.00
1865	350.00	550.00
1865S	45.00	100.00
1866	375.00	675.00
1866S	45.00	145.00
1867	575.00	900.00
1867S	45.00	125.00
1868	12.00	31.00
1868S	20.00	60.00
1869	16.00	55.00
1869S	17.00	38.00
1870	14.00	32.00
1870S	280.00	450.00
1871	15.00	28.00
1871CC	1,150.00	3,500.00
1871S	55.00	115.00
1872	9.50	18.00
1872CC	525.00	1,750.00
1872S	50.00	125.00
1873 Closed 3	11.00	27.00
1873 Open 3	18.00	48.00
1873CC		Unique
1873 arrows	13.00	50.00
1873CC arrows	975.00	3,750.00
1873S arrows	20.00	60.00
1874 arrows	13.00	50.00
1874CC arrows	4,500.00	9,75.00
1874S arrows	33.00	115.00
1875	9.25	12.00
1875CC	9.50	18.00

	VG	VF
1875S	14.00	25.00
1876	9.25	12.00
1876CC	9.25	18.00
1876S	13.00	20.00
1877	9.25	13.00
1877CC	9.25	18.00
1877S	15.00	27.00
1878	9.50	18.00
1878CC	75.00	165.00
1879	200.00	275.00
1880	140.00	210.00
1881	160.00	240.00
1882	9.25	12.00
1883	9.25	12.00
1884	9.25	12.00
1884S	19.00	50.00
1885	9.25	12.00
1885S	475.00	1,400.00
1886	9.25	12.00
1886S	55.00	135.00
1887	9.25	12.00
1887S	12.00	22.00
1888	9.25	12.00
1888S	13.00	25.00
1889	9.25	12.00
1889S	18.00	35.00
1890	9.25	12.00
1890S	14.00	57.50
1891	9.25	12.00
1891O	9.75	13.00
1891S	12.00	35.00

BARBER DIMES

The dime, quarter and half dollar introduced in 1892 bear a portrait head of Liberty rather than an entire figure. They were designed by Chief Engraver Charles E. Barber, after whom they have been popularly named. More practical than artistically adventurous, contemporaries thought the design rather boring, if not unpleasant. Because of its small size, the dime differed from the other two denominations in that the reverse simply has the value within a wreath, rather than an eagle — much the same as the Seated Liberty coinage.

Known counterfeits: The rare 1894S has certainly been counterfeited.

Type Coin Price Range   G to MS-60
1892-1916   1.30 to 91.00

	F	XF
1892	14.00	22.00
1892O	27.00	45.00
1892S	140.00	210.00
1893, 3 over 2	55.00	160.00
1893	17.50	32.00
1893O	90.00	135.00
1893S	25.00	49.00
1894	84.00	130.00
1894O	160.00	290.00
1894S	Very Rare Proof	451,000.00

	VG	VF
1895	200.00	450.00
1895O	690.00	1,825.00
1895S	105.00	175.00
1896	44.00	74.00
1896O	215.00	380.00
1896S	220.00	295.00
1897	5.85	23.00
1897O	225.00	345.00
1897S	72.00	140.00
1898	6.50	20.00
1898O	60.00	130.00
1898S	22.00	52.00
1899	5.85	20.00
1899O	58.00	115.00
1899S	16.50	35.00
1900	6.00	20.00
1900O	78.00	190.00
1900S	8.50	21.00
1901	5.25	20.00
1901O	12.00	42.00
1901S	280.00	380.00
1902	4.50	21.00
1902O	13.00	41.00
1902S	44.00	84.00
1903	4.50	20.00
1903O	8.75	26.00
1903S	320.00	680.00
1904	5.50	20.00
1904S	120.00	225.00
1905	4.00	19.00
1905O	30.00	58.00
1905S	7.75	30.00
1906	3.50	21.00
1906D	9.00	27.00
1906O	41.00	78.00
1906S	10.00	36.00
1907	3.50	21.00
1907D	9.00	32.00
1907O	25.00	52.00
1907S	9.75	41.00
1908	3.50	18.00
1908D	6.50	26.00
1908O	39.00	72.00
1908S	9.00	32.00
1909	3.50	18.00
1909D	58.00	105.00
1909O	8.50	27.00
1909S	78.00	145.00
1910	5.75	20.00
1910D	7.75	34.00
1910S	49.00	88.00
1911	3.00	18.00
1911D	3.75	20.00
1911S	7.75	31.00
1912	2.75	20.00
1912D	3.75	18.00
1912S	6.50	26.00
1913	2.75	20.00
1913S	67.00	175.00
1914	3.50	18.00
1914D	3.50	18.00
1914S	6.50	31.00
1915	3.90	20.00
1915S	29.00	52.00
1916	3.75	21.00
1916S	4.75	20.00

MERCURY DIMES

The name Mercury for this dime is a misnomer. Designed by Adolph Weinman, it actually depicts Liberty wearing a winged cap, to represent the freedom of thought. It was received with wide acclaim for its artistic merit when it was first released as part of a program for the beautification of United States coinage. The reverse carries the ancient Roman fasces, a symbol of authority still seen in the United States Senate. The horizontal bands tying the fasces together do not always strike up distinctly from each other, and those coins with "full split bands" often command a premium.

Known counterfeits: These include 1916D, 1916D, 1921, 1921D, 1931D, 1942/1, 1942/1D, most of which have been made by altering the mintmark on a more common date. The date 1923D is a fantasy — none were ever struck.

Type Coin Price Range   G to MS-63
1916-1945   .60 to 9.00

	VF	MS-60
1916	7.25	25.00
1916D	1,550.00	4,900.00
1916S	9.75	34.00
1917	5.50	28.00
1917D	16.00	125.00
1917S	6.00	49.00
1918	11.00	70.00
1918D	9.50	105.00
1918S	6.50	85.00
1919	5.50	35.00
1919D	15.00	140.00
1919S	13.00	175.00
1920	5.00	27.00
1920D	7.00	100.00
1920S	6.50	70.00
1921	160.00	945.00
1921D	210.00	1,000.00
1923	4.25	25.00
1923S	11.00	135.00
1924	5.00	38.00
1924D	10.00	155.00
1924S	8.00	155.00
1925	4.25	28.00
1925D	25.00	260.00
1925S	8.00	140.00
1926	4.25	28.00
1926D	7.50	70.00
1926S	34.00	770.00
1927	4.25	21.00
1927D	12.00	175.00
1927S	5.50	240.00
1928	4.25	21.00
1928D	15.00	135.00
1928S	5.00	70.00
1929	3.75	19.50
1929D	6.00	28.00
1929S	4.25	34.00
1930	4.25	22.00

	VF	MS-60
1930S	7.50	70.00
1931	5.00	35.00
1931D	18.00	77.00
1931S	7.50	63.00
1934	3.00	15.00
1934D	4.00	32.00
1935	2.15	11.00
1935D	4.75	32.00
1935S	3.00	24.00
1936	2.25	85.00
1936D	3.25	22.00
1936S	2.75	17.00
1937	2.00	10.00
1937D	3.00	21.00
1937S	3.00	18.00
1938	2.25	14.00
1938D	3.75	15.00
1938S	2.35	16.00
1939	2.00	10.00
1939D	2.25	12.50
1939S	2.50	24.00
1940	1.10	6.50
1940D	1.10	8.50
1940S	1.10	8.50
1941	1.10	5.50
1941D	1.00	8.00
1941S	1.10	10.00
1942, 2 over 1	320.00	1,450.00
1942D, 2 over 1	375.00	1,600.00
1942	1.00	5.50
1942D	1.10	8.50
1942S	1.10	10.00
1943	1.10	6.50
1943D	1.10	8.50
1943S	1.10	10.00
1944	1.10	5.50
1944D	1.10	8.50
1944S	1.10	10.00
1945	1.10	5.50
1945D	1.10	8.00
1945S	1.10	8.50
1945S micro S	3.00	17.00

ROOSEVELT DIMES

The fact that the dime was chosen to bear the image of Franklin Roosevelt is not a coincidence. It was selected to remind people of the President's involvement in the March of Dimes, as he himself was crippled by polio. The coin was designed on a tight deadline by Chief Engraver John R. Sinnock. There are no true rarities in this series.

Known counterfeits: Counterfeit Roosevelt dimes are quite rare.

Type Coin Price Range F to MS-65
1946-1964 .40 to 1.35
1965-date .10 to .50

	XF	MS-60
1946	.65	1.05
1946D	.65	1.25

	XF	MS-60
1946S	.65	2.00
1947	.65	1.00
1947D	.95	1.40
1947S	.95	1.35
1948	.95	1.75
1948D	1.20	2.00
1948S	.95	1.35
1949	1.50	6.00
1949D	1.25	3.50
1949S	2.75	9.00
1950	.95	1.35
1950D	.65	1.00
1950S	1.25	7.00
1950S, S over D	65.00	300.00
1951	.85	1.10
1951D	.65	1.00
1951S	1.05	3.25
1952	.95	1.20
1952D	.65	1.00
1952S	1.05	1.35
1953	.65	1.10
1953D	.65	1.00
1953S	.95	1.35
1954	.75	.95
1954D	.65	1.00
1954S	.65	.90
1955	.80	.95
1955D	.75	.90
1955S	.75	.90
1956	.65	.90
1956D	.65	.90
1957	.65	.90
1957D	.65	.90
1958	.65	.90
1958D	.65	.90
1959	.65	.90
1959D	.65	.90
1960	.65	.90
1960D	.65	.90
1961	.65	.90
1961D	.65	.90
1962	.65	.90
1962D	.65	.90
1963	.65	.90
1963D	.65	.90
1964	.65	.90
1964D	.65	.90

CUPRO-NICKEL CLAD COPPER

	XF	MS-60
1965		.50
1966		.50
1967		.50
1968		.50
1968D		.50
1968S proof only		.65
1969		.50
1969D		.50
1969S proof only		.65
1970		.50
1970D		.50
1970S proof only		.65
1971		.50
1971D		.50
1971S proof only		.80
1972		.50
1972D		.50
1972S proof only		.80
1973		.50
1973D		.40

	XF	MS-60
1973S proof only		.60
1974		.40
1974D		.40
1974S proof only		1.00
1975		.50
1975D		.40
1975S proof only		.60
1976		.50
1976D		.50
1976S proof only		.75
1977		.40
1977D		.40
1977S proof only		.60
1978		.40
1978D		.40
1978S proof only		.60
1979		.40
1979D		.40
1979 thick S proof only		.55
1979 thin S proof only		1.25
1980P		.40
1980D		.40
1980S proof only		.50
1981P		.40
1981D		.40
1981S proof only		4.00
1982P		1.00
1982 no mintmark error		115.00
1982D		.50
1982S proof only		.65
1983P		.60
1983D		.60
1983S proof only		1.10
1984P		.40
1984D		.50
1984S proof only		1.60
1985P		.50
1985D		.40
1985S proof only		1.10
1986P		.50
1986D		.50
1986S proof only		2.00
1987P		.35
1987D		.35
1987S proof only		1.25
1988P		.35
1988D		.35
1988S proof only		1.50
1989P		.35
1989D		.35
1989S proof only		1.45
1990P		.35
1990D		.35
1990S proof only		2.75
1991P		.35
1991D		.35
1991S proof only		3.25
1992P		.35
1992D		.35
1992S proof only		3.40
1992S Silver proof only		3.25
1993P		.35
1993D		.35
1993S proof only		2.85
1993S Silver proof only		4.00
1994P		.35
1994D		.35
1994S proof only		2.60
1994S Silver proof only		3.75

	XF	MS-60
1995		.35
1995D		.35
1995S proof only		2.60
1995S Silver proof only		3.75
1996		.35
1996D		.35
1996W		6.00
1996S proof only		2.50
1996S Silver proof only		3.50
1997P		.35
1997D		.35
1997S proof only		3.50
1997S Silver proof only		3.50
1998P		.35
1998D		.35
1998S proof only		3.50
1998S Silver proof only		3.50

TWENTY CENT PIECES

It is evident that even before its release, the mint was concerned about the public confusing this coin with a quarter. This is indicated by several of its features, which are distinct from the other silver coins of that time. The reverse design is a mirror image of the front, the word LIBERTY on the shield is in relief rather than incuse, and the edge is plain, not reeded. Nevertheless, the public was still confused, and the coin's production was halted after only two years in circulation.

Known counterfeits: 1876CC with added mintmark. Some 19th century charlatans would hand-scape reeding into the edge of pieces in hopes of passing them off as quarters.

Type Coin Price Range		G to MS-60
1875-78		45.00 to 475.00

	VG	VF
1875	70.00	120.00
1875CC	60.00	150.00
1875S	50.00	100.00
1876	125.00	200.00
1876CC Extremely Rare MS-65		148,500.00
1877		1,500.00
1878		1,300.00

BUST QUARTERS

Due to limited mint capacity, quarters were not struck until 1796, when a small quantity was produced, even though other denominations of United States silver began to be struck two years prior to that. These first rare pieces were struck on blanks with crude edges and often exhibited "adjustment marks," from filing off of excess silver before striking. The initial reverse design, which showed a rather skinny eagle within a wreath, had been in use only one year when the striking of quarters was suspended. When it was resumed a few years later, the design was replaced with a plumper eagle carrying a heraldic shield. Coinage ceased again until 1815 when a cap was added to Liberty and her bust was turned to the left. In the same year a denomination first appeared — not as "quarter dollar." Instead it was "25C." Rare die combinations of early specimens command a premium from specialists. Cleaning plagues this series, and such pieces are discounted.

Known counterfeits: Cast counterfeits exist of 1796. Other counterfeits to 1807 are possible.

Type Coin Price Range	G to MS-60
1796	4,350.00 to 28,000.00
1804-1807	210.00 to 5,850.00
1815-1838	40.00 to 900.00

DRAPED BUST / SMALL EAGLE

	VG	VF
1796	6,000.00	14,000.00

DRAPED BUST / HERALDIC EAGLE

	VG	VF
1804	1,475.00	4,750.00
1805	300.00	850.00
1806, 6 over 5	315.00	950.00
1806	285.00	800.00
1807	300.00	850.00

CAPPED BUST TYPE

	VG	VF
1815	80.00	335.00
1818 8 over 5	75.00	315.00
1818	60.00	275.00
1819	70.00	300.00
1820	65.00	275.00
1821	65.00	275.00
1822 25 over 50c	3,500.00	7,250.00
1822	90.00	400.00
1823, 3 over 2	17,500.00	27,500.00

	VG	VF
1824, 4 over 2	140.00	575.00
1825, 5 over 2	165.00	575.00
1825, 5 over 3	65.00	275.00
1825, 5 over 4	75.00	325.00
1827		39,600.00
1827 Restrike		Extremely Rare
1828	65.00	275.00
1828 25 over 50c	225.00	650.00

NO MOTTO, REDUCED SIZE

	VG	VF
1831 Small letters	50.00	90.00
1831 Large letters	50.00	90.00
1832	50.00	90.00
1833	60.00	120.00
1834	50.00	90.00
1835	50.00	90.00
1836	50.00	90.00
1837	53.00	95.00
1838	50.00	90.00

SEATED LIBERTY QUARTERS

Following the introduction of the Seated Liberty design by Christian Gobrecht on the silver dollar, the smaller coins were gradually became harmonious with this design. It is generally accepted that the seated goddess version of Liberty was directly or indirectly inspired by depictions of the Roman allegory of Britannia on British coins. The eagle on the reverse is not significantly different from that on the last capped bust coins.

There were several minor changes over the lifetime of this coin. After the first few years, additional drapery was added below Liberty's elbow. The arrows by the date from 1853 to 1855, and the rays on the reverse in 1853 indicate a 7 percent reduction in weight, while arrows in 1873 to 1874, a minuscule increase. A ribbon with the motto "In God We Trust" was added over the eagle in 1866.

Known counterfeits: Genuine 1858 quarters have been re-engraved to pass as 1853 no arrows pieces. Contemporary counterfeits struck in copper, lead and white metal (tin and lead alloys) exist.

Type Coin Price Range	G to MS-60
1838-1865	10.00 to 290.00
1853 arrows and rays	12.50 to 900.00
1854-55 arrows	12.50 to 410.00
1873-1874 arrows	12.50 to 700.00
1866-1891	12.00 to 225.00

NO MOTTO ABOVE EAGLE

	VG	VF
1838	22.00	55.00
1839	20.00	52.00
1840O	19.00	60.00
1840 extra drapery from elbow	40.00	75.00
1840O extra drapery from elbow	30.00	110.00
1841	60.00	135.00
1841O	24.00	70.00
1842	145.00	275.00
1842O Small date	500.00	1,750.00
1842O Large date	16.00	60.00
1843	16.00	45.00
1843O	33.00	175.00
1844	16.00	43.00
1844O	21.00	55.00
1845	15.00	40.00
1846	25.00	65.00
1847	15.00	45.00
1847O	40.00	110.00
1848	48.00	130.00
1849	22.00	70.00
1849O	545.00	1,675.00
1850	45.00	95.00
1850O	30.00	85.00
1851	50.00	135.00
1851O	265.00	575.00
1852	47.50	110.00
1852O	255.00	550.00
1853 no arrows	475.00	925.00

ARROWS AT DATE

	VG	VF
1853	16.00	38.00
1853, 3 over 4	47.50	165.00
1853O	26.00	75.00
1854	16.00	32.00
1854O	17.00	45.00
1854O Huge O	165.00	375.00
1855	16.00	24.00
1855O	55.00	275.00
1855S	45.00	145.00

ARROWS REMOVED

	VG	VF
1856	15.00	32.00
1856O	16.00	40.00
1856S	65.00	325.00
1856S, S over S	175.00	750.00
1857	15.00	28.00
1857O	17.00	40.00
1857S	140.00	275.00
1858	15.00	28.00
1858O	25.00	65.00
1858S	70.00	275.00
1859	15.00	30.00
1859O	25.00	50.00
1859S	125.00	275.00
1860	15.00	30.00
1860	19.00	50.00
1860S	245.00	625.00
1861	14.00	28.00
1861S	80.00	295.00

	VG	VF
1862	15.00	35.00
1862S	70.00	245.00
1863	40.00	95.00
1864	60.00	125.00
1864S	375.00	1,200.00
1865	70.00	120.00
1865S	125.00	275.00

MOTTO ABOVE EAGLE

	VG	VF
1866	310.00	475.00
1866S	290.00	650.00
1867	200.00	325.00
1867S	200.00	375.00
1868	155.00	255.00
1868S	70.00	245.00
1869	260.00	425.00
1869S	95.00	300.00
1870	48.00	135.00
1870CC	4,250.00	9,500.00
1871	40.00	115.00
1871CC	2,550.00	6,500.00
1871S	375.00	625.00
1872	40.00	100.00
1872CC	625.00	22,500.00
1872S	1,475.00	2,500.00
1873 Closed 3	265.00	525.00
1873 Open 3	37.50	95.00
1873CC		4 known

ARROWS AT DATE

	VG	VF
1873	16.00	50.00
1873CC	3,250.00	9,250.00
1873S	35.00	145.00
1874	24.00	75.00
1874S	28.00	110.00

ARROWS REMOVED

	VG	VF
1875	15.00	28.00
1875CC	80.00	295.00
1875S	30.00	80.00
1876	15.00	28.00
1876CC	16.00	35.00
1876S	15.00	28.00
1877	15.00	28.00
1877CC	16.00	35.00
1877S	15.00	28.00
1877S over horizontal S	48.00	100.00
1878	15.00	40.00
1878CC	25.00	55.00
1878S	140.00	325.00
1879	170.00	285.00
1880	170.00	285.00
1881	170.00	285.00
1882	185.00	295.00
1883	195.00	295.00
1884	245.00	375.00
1885	190.00	285.00
1886	400.00	540.00
1887	295.00	400.00
1888	205.00	295.00
1888S	15.00	30.00
1889	200.00	285.00
1890	55.00	110.00
1891	15.00	30.00
1891O	165.00	475.00
1891S	15.00	45.00

BARBER QUARTERS

The quarter, dime and half dollar introduced in 1892 bear a portrait head of Liberty instead of an entire figure. They were designed by Chief Engraver Charles E. Barber, after whom they have been popularly named. More practical than artistically adventurous, contemporaries found the design rather boring, if not unpleasant. The reverse of the quarter and the half have a fully spread heraldic eagle, a ribbon in its beak, with a field of stars above. Barber quarters are very common and well worn examples are often regarded as little better than bullion.

Known counterfeits: 1913S suspected but not confirmed. Contemporary counterfeits in a tin-lead alloy are not rare.

Type Coin Price Range — G to MS-60
1892-1916 — 3.25 to 170.00

	F	XF
1892	19.50	65.00
1892O	24.00	72.00
1892S	62.00	110.00
1893	21.00	65.00
1893O	25.00	72.00
1893S	34.00	100.00
1894	23.00	75.00
1894O	33.00	75.00
1894S	28.00	75.00
1895	22.00	65.00
1895O	35.00	82.00
1895S	40.00	75.00
1896	24.00	65.00
1896O	65.00	320.00
1896S	590.00	1,900.00
1897	22.00	65.00
1897O	75.00	310.00
1897S	150.00	325.00
1898	19.00	65.00
1898O	55.00	155.00
1898S	30.00	65.00
1899	19.00	65.00
1899O	30.00	85.00
1899S	44.00	75.00
1900	19.00	65.00
1900O	55.00	90.00
1900S	36.00	65.00
1901	20.00	65.00
1901O	85.00	275.00
1901S	4,500.00	9,500.00
1902	19.00	65.00
1902O	35.00	100.00
1902S	38.00	78.00
1903	21.00	65.00
1903O	38.00	78.00
1903S	40.00	91.00
1904	21.00	65.00
1904O	48.00	160.00
1905	24.00	65.00
1905O	36.00	130.00
1905S	36.00	83.00
1906	21.00	65.00
1906D	28.00	65.00

	F	XF
1906O	32.00	77.00
1907	19.00	65.00
1907D	25.00	75.00
1907O	21.00	65.00
1907S	40.00	100.00
1908	19.00	65.00
1908D	19.00	65.00
1908O	19.00	70.00
1908S	64.00	215.00
1909	19.00	65.00
1909D	19.00	65.00
1909O	75.00	225.00
1909S	28.00	65.00
1910	23.00	65.00
1910D	41.00	75.00
1911	21.00	72.00
1911D	65.00	260.00
1911S	45.00	115.00
1912	19.00	65.00
1912S	43.00	90.00
1913	70.00	370.00
1913D	30.00	70.00
1913S	1,900.00	3,300.00
1914	16.00	65.00
1914D	17.00	65.00
1914S	130.00	370.00
1915	17.00	65.00
1915D	17.00	65.00
1915S	28.00	72.00
1916	16.00	68.00
1916D	16.00	68.00

STANDING LIBERTY QUARTER

According to many of that time, Hermon MacNeil's Standing Liberty quarter was America's first obscene coin, while many prominent artists thought it was an excellent example of inspired neoclassical art. In either case, it was debated thoroughly at the time. Its original version, with a bare breasted Liberty stepping through a gateway while exposing a shield, was ultimately replaced by a more modest one where she is clad in chain mail. The corrective legislation, however, was careful not to criticize the coin's artistic merit or moral standing openly so as not to offend the Commission of Fine Arts, who was responsible for its approval. Physically, the coin shared with the Buffalo nickel the problem of a high relief date, susceptible to being worn off. In 1925, this was remedied by carving out the area of the date and placing it in the recess. Another technical problem with this quarter was the tendency for Liberty's head to be incompletely struck. As a result, high-grade pieces with fully struck heads command extra premiums. Specimens with worn-off dates are worth only their bullion value.

Known counterfeits: 1916 altered from 1917, 1917 Type I, 1918S 8 over 7, 1923S (altered, including all with round topped 3), 1927S (altered).

Type Coin Price Range	VG to MS-60
1916-1917 Type I	16.00 to 175.00

Type Coin Price Range	VG to MS-60
1917-1930 Type II	2.75 to 110.00

	F	XF
1916	2,150.00	2,900.00
1917	26.00	59.00
1917D	27.00	85.00
1917S	29.00	135.00

	F	XF
1917	21.00	48.00
1917D	49.00	92.00
1917S	38.00	75.00
1918	22.00	47.00
1918D	43.00	95.00
1918S	24.00	45.00
1918S, 8 over 7	1,950.00	4,500.00
1919	43.00	67.50
1919D	135.00	315.00
1919S	135.00	380.00
1920	20.00	35.00
1920D	79.00	125.00
1920S	28.00	59.00
1921	145.00	250.00
1923	25.00	40.00
1923S	250.00	450.00
1924	21.00	37.00
1924D	55.00	100.00
1924S	32.00	88.00
1925	6.30	25.00
1926	6.30	26.00
1926D	14.00	65.00
1926S	13.00	90.00
1927	6.30	25.00
1927D	19.00	95.00
1927S	48.00	1,050.00
1928	6.30	25.00
1928D	7.00	39.00
1928S	6.75	33.00
1929	6.30	30.00
1929D	11.00	35.00
1929S	6.30	30.00
1930	6.50	26.00
1930S	6.30	30.00

WASHINGTON QUARTER

The Washington quarter was intended to be a one year commemorative for the 200th anniversary of Washington's birth — not a regular issue. Its release was delayed because of the Treasury's decision have John Flanagan design it, rather than Laura Gardin Fraser, the original choice. Both designs were based the 1785 bust of Washington by Houdon. Eventually the Trea-

sury decided to replace the unpopular Standing Liberty quarter with the new commemorative, which enjoyed immense initial popularity. Several dates in the 1930s are characterized by weak rims, which makes grading difficult. 1934 and 1935 do not have this problem. 1964 pieces were aggressively hoarded in uncirculated rolls, and as such are very common.

A special reverse was used in 1975 and 1976 (both with 1976 obverse) to commemorate the American Bicentennial. It depicts the bust of a Colonial drummer, designed by Jack L. Ahr.

Known counterfeits: 1932D and 1932S exist with false mintmarks. Counterfeits of high grade 1932 and 1934 pieces also exist.

Type Coin Price Range	F to MS-65
1932-1964	1.00 to 6.50
1976	.25 to 1.20
1965-date	.25 to 1.00

	VF	MS-60
1932	4.00	21.00
1932D	60.00	490.00
1932S	45.00	290.00
1934	2.75	20.00
1934D	7.50	195.00
1935	2.75	21.00
1935D	7.00	180.00
1935S	5.00	59.00
1936	2.75	20.00
1936D	10.00	325.00
1936S	7.00	56.00
1937	5.75	20.00
1937D	7.00	37.00
1937S	12.00	100.00
1938	7.50	59.00
1938S	8.00	59.00
1939	2.75	16.00
1939D	4.50	29.00
1939S	8.00	55.00
1940	3.25	12.00
1940D	9.00	63.00
1940S	4.25	16.00
1941	2.00	7.50
1941D	2.00	18.00
1941S	2.00	15.00
1942	2.00	6.50
1942D	2.00	10.00
1942S	2.00	50.00
1943	2.00	5.00
1943D	2.00	14.00
1943S	2.00	29.00
1944	2.00	4.50
1944D	2.00	9.00
1944S	2.00	9.00
1945	2.00	5.00
1945D	2.00	7.50
1945S	2.00	6.00
1946	2.00	4.75
1946D	2.00	4.00

	VF	MS-60
1946S	2.50	4.00
1947	2.00	6.50
1947D	2.00	5.50
1947S	2.00	5.00
1948	2.00	4.00
1948D	2.00	5.00
1948S	2.00	5.00
1949	2.00	19.00
1949D	2.00	8.75
1950	2.00	5.00
1950D	2.00	4.50
1950D, D over S	60.00	275.00
1950S	2.50	7.25
1950S, S over D	90.00	425.00
1951	1.75	4.75
1951D	1.75	3.25
1951S	1.75	12.00
1952	1.75	3.00
1952D	1.75	3.25
1952S	2.00	8.50
1953	1.75	3.25
1953D	1.25	2.25
1953S	1.75	4.00
1954	1.25	2.00
1954D	1.50	2.00
1954S	1.50	2.00
1955	1.50	2.00
1955D	1.75	2.50
1956	1.50	2.00
1956D	1.75	2.75
1957		2.75
1957D		2.00
1958		2.50
1958D		2.00
1959		2.00
1959D		2.00
1960		2.75
1960D		2.00
1961		1.75
1961D		1.75
1962		1.75
1962D		1.75
1963		1.75
1963D		1.75
1964		1.75
1964D		1.75

CUPRO-NICKEL CLAD COPPER

		MS-60
1965		.75
1966		.75
1967		1.00
1968		.75
1968D		1.00
1968S proof only		1.00
1969		1.00
1969D		1.00
1969S proof only		1.00
1970		.75
1970D		.75
1970S proof only		.95
1971		.75
1971D		.70
1971S proof only		.95
1972		.75
1972D		.75
1972S proof only		.95
1973		.75
1973D		.75
1973S proof only		.95

	VF	MS-60
1974		.75
1974D		.75
1974S proof only		1.25

		MS-60
1976 Bicentennial		.75
1976D Bicentennial		.75
1976S Bicentennial proof only		.90
1976S Bicentennial Silver Clad		1.50
1977		.75
1977D		.75
1977S proof only		.95
1978		.75
1978D		.75
1978S proof only		.95
1979		.75
1979D		.75
1979 thick S proof only		.95
1979 thin S proof only		1.45
1980P		.75
1980D		.75
1980S proof only		.95
1981P		.75
1981D		.75
1981S proof only		.95
1982P		1.00
1982D		1.00
1982S proof only		2.25
1983P		2.00
1983D		1.75
1983S proof only		1.75
1984P		1.00
1984D		1.00
1984S proof only		1.60
1985P		1.25
1985D		1.75
1985S proof only		1.25
1986P		2.00
1986D		1.50
1986S proof only		2.00
1987P		.75
1987D		.75
1987S proof only		1.10
1988P		.75
1988D		.75
1988S proof only		1.25
1989P		.75
1989D		.75
1989S proof only		1.35
1990P		.75
1990D		.75
1990S proof only		3.60
1991P		.75
1991D		.75
1991S proof only		5.00
1992P		.75
1992D		.75
1992S proof only		4.00
1992S Silver proof only		4.00
1993P		.75
1993D		.75
1993S proof only		4.75

	VF	MS-60
1993S Silver proof only		5.00
1994P		.75
1994D		.75
1994S proof only		3.25
1994S Silver proof only		4.50
1995P		.75
1995D		.75
1995S proof only		3.00
1995S Silver proof only		4.75
1996P		.75
1996D		.75
1996S proof only		3.00
1996S Silver proof only		4.75
1997P		.75
1997D		.75
1997S proof only		3.00
1997S Silver proof only		4.75
1998P		.75
1998D		.75
1998S proof only		3.00
1998S Silver proof only		4.75

FIFTY STATE QUARTERS

In 1992, to commemorate its 125th anniversary, Canada released a set of circulating commermorative quarters honoring each province and territory. These quarters were greeted with immense popularity by the general public. Partially inspired by this Canadian series, the United States has begun issuing a similar set of quarters honoring the fifty states. It was the intent of Congress to "promote the diffusion of knowledge among the youth of the United States about the individual states, their history and geography, and the rich diversity of the national heritage."

Five each year will be released from 1999 to 2000. Their release dates will be in the order which each state ratified the constitution, with a new quarter appearing roughly every ten weeks. These will be the only quarters issued during these years, with one of the old eagle reverse quarters being produced at all.

The designs must meet certain federal criteria, but well be designed and submitted at a state level. Many will be provided by public competitions held in individual states. At this writing it is not too late for citizens of most states to submit design proposals.

The quarters will be released into circulation in the years listed below. The earlier date is the date each state ratified the Constitution or was admitted into the Union. In addition to clad circulation strikes, special silver and clad proof coins will be produced for collectors, much as they have in previous years.

1999

Delaware	1787
Pennsylvania	1787
New Jersey	1787
Georgia	1788
Connecticut	1788

2000

Massachusetts	1788
Maryland	1788
South Carolina	1788
New Hampshire	1788
Virginia	1788

2001

New York	1788
North Carolina	1789
Rhode Island	1790
Vermont	1791
Kentucky	1792

2002

Tennessee	1796
Ohio	1803
Louisiana	1812
Indiana	1816
Mississippi	1817

2003

Illinois	1818
Alabama	1819
Maine	1820
Missouri	1821
Arkansas	1836

2004

Michigan	1837
Florida	1845
Texas	1845
Iowa	1846
Wisconsin	1848

2005

California	1850
Minnesota	1858
Oregon	1859
Kansas	1861
West Virginia	1863

2006

Nevada	1864
Nebraska	1867
Colorado	1876
North Dakota	1889
South Dakota	1889

2007

Montana	1889
Washington	1889
Idaho	1890
Wyoming	1890
Utah	1896

2008

Oklahoma	1907
New Mexico	1912
Arizona	1912
Alaska	1959
Hawaii	1959

EARLY HALF DOLLARS

The half dollar, along with the half dime and dollar, was one of the first silver denominations released by the new United States mint. As a result, it first appeared with the briefly used flowing hair design. These first rare pieces were struck on blanks with crude edges and often exhibited "adjustment marks," made by filing off of excess silver before striking. The initial reverse design showed a rather skinny eagle within a wreath, which was used even after the flowing hair obverse was replaced by the rather voluptuous, draped bust design. After a brief gap in the issue of halves, this eagle was replaced with a plumper eagle carrying a heraldic shield. In 1807 a cap was added to Liberty's head and her bust was turned to the left. In that same year the coin's denomination first appeared, but it wasn't written "quarter dollar." Instead, it read "50C." The eagle was also made slightly more realistic, though he still bore a heraldic shield. With the introduction of this type, production began to increase. By the teens and twenties, halves became so common that banks began to use them as cash reserves to back up their own privately issued paper money. As a result many half dollars between 1807 and 1839 can be found very good condition. Unfortunately their high relief caused many of them to be incompletely struck, particularly at the motto over the eagle, and the broach. In 1836 new machinery was introduced and the edges were reeded instead of lettered. Rare die combinations of early specimens command a premium from specialists. This series' specimens were often cleaned too much, and such pieces are discounted.

Known counterfeits: Cast counterfeits exist of 1796 coins. Other counterfeits of 1794 to 1802 are possible. Contemporary counterfeits of capped-bust halves exist in German silver. Hold coins are sometimes deceptively plugged.

Type Coin Price Range	G to MS-60
1794-1795	450.00 to 15,000.00
1796-1797	9,500.00 to 100,000.00
1801-1807	115.00 to 5,000.00
1807-1836 lettered	27.50 to 500.00
1836-1839 reeded	32.00 to 750.00

FLOWING HAIR TYPE

	VG	VF
1794	1,750.00	3,700.00
1795 two leaves	625.00	1,550.00
1795 three leaves	1,450.00	3,750.00

DRAPED BUST / SMALL EAGLE

1796, 15 stars	11,500.00	25,500.00
1796, 16 stars	12,000.00	27,000.00
1797	11,500.00	24,000.00

DRAPED BUST / HERALDIC EAGLE

1801	300.00	825.00
1802	240.00	775.00
1803 Small 3	170.00	450.00
1803 Large 3	150.00	350.00
1805, 5 over 4	200.00	500.00
1805	150.00	350.00
1806, 6 over 5	160.00	350.00
1806	130.00	290.00

Note: many varieties of 1806 exist.

1807	135.00	300.00

CAPPED BUST / LETTERED EDGE

	VG	VF
1807 Small stars	90.00	325.00
1807 Large stars	80.00	300.00
1807, 50 over 20	60.00	175.00
1808, 8 over 7	50.00	125.00
1808	42.50	90.00
1809	42.50	85.00
1810	38.00	90.00
1811, 11 over 10	40.00	125.00
1811	37.50	60.00
1812, 2 over 1, small 8,	50.00	110.00
1812, 2 over 1, large 8,	1,875.00	3,750.00
1812	37.50	60.00
1813	37.50	70.00
1813, 50 C over inverted UNI	70.00	195.00
1814, 4 over 3	60.00	145.00
1814	38.00	60.00
1815, 5 over 2	850.00	1,500.00
1817, 7 over 3	105.00	275.00
1817, 7 over 4	60,000.00	145,000.00
1817	33.00	60.00
1818, 8 over 7	40.00	85.00
1818	33.00	60.00
1819, 9 over 8	33.00	70.00
1819	33.00	60.00
1820, 20 over 19	53.00	130.00
1820	50.00	120.00
1821	35.00	70.00
1822, 2 over 1	49.00	125.00
1822	34.00	55.00
1823	33.00	50.00
1824, 4 over 1	40.00	65.00
1824, 4 over 4	40.00	65.00
1824	33.00	47.00
1825	33.00	50.00
1826	33.00	50.00
1827, 7 over 6	40.00	60.00
1827	33.00	45.00
1828	33.00	43.00

Note: date varieties of 1828 exist.

	VG	VF
1829, 9 over 7	40.00	85.00
1829	33.00	43.00
1830	33.00	43.00
1831	33.00	43.00
1832	33.00	43.00
1833	33.00	43.00
1834	33.00	43.00
1835	33.00	43.00
1836	33.00	43.00
1836, 50 over 00	80.00	185.00

CAPPED BUST / REEDED EDGE

	VG	VF
1836	675.00	1,150.00
1837	38.00	60.00
1838	38.00	60.00
1838O proof only		90,000.00
1839	38.00	60.00
1839O	145.00	280.00

SEATED LIBERTY HALF DOLLARS

Following the introduction of the Seated Liberty design by Christian Gobrecht on the silver dollar, the smaller coins were gradually brought into harmony with this design. The half dollar was the last to make the change. It is generally accepted that the seated goddess version of Liberty was directly or indirectly inspired by depictions of the Roman allegory of Britannia on British coins. The eagle on the reverse is not significantly different from that on the last capped-bust coins.

There were several minor changes over the lifetime of this coin. During its first year additional drapery was added below Liberty's elbow. In those made from 1853 to 1855, the arrows by the date and the rays on the reverse in 1853, accompany a 7 percent reduction in weight. Arrows in 1873 to 1874 coins signify a minuscule increase. Most of the 1861O pieces were struck after Louisiana seceded from the Union. A ribbon with the motto "In God We Trust" was added over the eagle in 1866. Seated halves are often found cleaned, and watch for retoned specimens.

Known counterfeits: Genuine 1858O halves have been re-engraved to pass as 1853O no-arrows pieces. Some pieces with arrows have had the arrows removed for the same reason. Contemporary counterfeits struck in tin and lead alloys are often found.

Type Coin Price Range	G to MS-60
1839-1866	16.00 to 410.00
1853 arrows and rays	16.50 to 1,700.00
1854-55 arrows	16.00 to 500.00
1873-1874 arrows	16.50 to 950.00
1866-1891	15.00 to 340.00

NO MOTTO ABOVE EAGLE

	VG	VF
1839 No drapery below elbow	65.00	250.00
1839 With drapery	28.00	75.00
1840 Sm. rev. letters	20.00	60.00
1840 Med. rev. letters (struck at New Orleans with 1838 reverse die)	165.00	325.00
1840O	27.50	80.00
1841	45.00	140.00
1841O	25.00	85.00
1842 Small date	37.50	95.00
1842 Large date	21.00	50.00
1842O Small date	800.00	2,250.00
1842O Large date	23.00	115.00
1843	21.00	50.00

	VG	VF
1843O	21.00	55.00
1844	21.00	50.00
1844O	21.00	55.00
1844O Double date	650.00	1,375.00
1845	40.00	90.00
1845O	21.00	45.00
1845O No Drapery	35.00	115.00
1846	20.00	40.00
1846, 6 over horizontal 6	215.00	375.00
1846O, Med. date	18.00	45.00
1846O, Tall date	245.00	575.00
1847, 7 over 6	2,750.00	4,250.00
1847	30.00	60.00
1847O	25.00	50.00
1848	55.00	135.00
1848O	25.00	50.00
1849	35.00	85.00
1849O	25.00	60.00
1850	275.00	400.00
1850O	25.00	55.00
1851	300.00	465.00
1851O	45.00	105.00
1852	350.00	600.00
1852O	90.00	325.00
1853O no arrows Rare		154,000.00

ARROWS AT DATE / RAYS ON REVERSE

	VG	VF
1853	27.00	90.00
1853O	31.00	100.00

ARROWS AT DATE / NO RAYS

	VG	VF
1854	22.00	50.00
1854O	22.00	50.00
1855 over 1854	60.00	125.00
1855	30.00	60.00
1855O	22.00	50.00
1855S	425.00	1,300.00

ARROWS REMOVED

	VG	VF
1856	25.00	47.50
1856O	21.00	45.00
1856S	65.00	225.00
1857	18.00	45.00
1857O	21.00	55.00
1857S	95.00	285.00
1858	18.00	60.00
1858O	17.00	45.00
1858S	30.00	90.00
1859	27.50	55.00
1859O	25.00	50.00
1859S	38.00	85.00
1860	25.00	75.00
1860O	20.00	45.00
1860S	30.00	75.00
1861	16.00	45.00
1861O	25.00	50.00
1861S	28.00	60.00
1862	32.00	95.00
1862S	27.00	60.00
1863	28.00	70.00

	VG	VF
1863S	25.00	50.00
1864	32.00	85.00
1864S	20.00	60.00
1865	27.50	70.00
1865S	21.00	50.00
1866		Unique
1866S	110.00	325.00

MOTTO ABOVE EAGLE

	VG	VF
1866	24.00	50.00
1866S	24.00	58.00
1867	35.00	85.00
1867S	24.00	50.00
1868	45.00	120.00
1868S	24.00	50.00
1869	24.00	45.00
1869S	27.00	50.00
1870	27.00	60.00
1870CC	800.00	2,650.00
1870S	24.00	60.00
1871	24.00	50.00
1871CC	180.00	485.00
1871S	24.00	50.00
1872	24.00	55.00
1872CC	85.00	300.00
1872S	28.00	85.00
1873 Closed 3	24.00	90.00
1873 Open 3	2,700.00	5,500.00
1873CC	185.00	575.00
1873S	No Known Specimens	

ARROWS AT DATE

	VG	VF
1873	25.00	85.00
1873CC	160.00	550.00
1873S	75.00	225.00
1874	25.00	85.00
1874CC	350.00	975.00
1874S	35.00	135.00

ARROWS REMOVED

	VG	VF
1875	24.00	40.00
1875CC	34.00	95.00
1875S	24.00	42.00
1876	24.00	40.00
1876CC	30.00	85.00
1876S	24.00	40.00
1877	24.00	40.00
1877CC	33.00	75.00
1877S	24.00	40.00
1878	28.00	50.00
1878CC	365.00	850.00
1878S	11,000.00	17,500.00
1879	220.00	350.00
1880	210.00	310.00
1881	195.00	300.00
1882	240.00	390.00
1883	210.00	390.00
1884	300.00	425.00
1885	235.00	360.00
1886	345.00	450.00
1887	385.00	550.00
1888	210.00	310.00
1889	200.00	300.00
1890	200.00	300.00
1891	50.00	90.00

BARBER HALF DOLLARS

The half dollar, quarter, and dime introduced in 1892 bear a portrait of Liberty's head instead of an entire figure. They were designed by Chef Engraver Charles E. Barber, after whom they have been popularly named. More practical than artistically adventurous, contemporaries thought the design rather boring if not unpleasant. The reverse of the half and the quarter have a fully spread heraldic eagle with a ribbon in its beak, with a field of stars above. This new design for the half dollar came only a year after it was resurrected to an actively minted denomination. Barbers are very common, and well-worn examples are often regarded as little better than bullion. Strong middle grades, on the other hand, are surprisingly difficult to obtain.

Known counterfeits: Contemporary counterfeits in a tin-lead alloy are not rare. Altered 1913, 1914, and 1915 coins exist with their mintmarks removed.

Type Coin Price Range	G to MS-60
1892-1916	5.50 to 390.00

	VG	VF
1892	283.00	90.00
1892O	190.00	285.00
1892S	195.00	295.00
1893	20.00	80.00
1893O	34.00	125.00
1893S	95.00	285.00
1894	33.00	100.00
1894O	19.00	95.00
1894S	18.00	80.00
1895	15.00	85.00
1895O	22.00	100.00
1895S	26.00	125.00
1896	23.00	90.00
1896O	35.00	145.00
1896S	80.00	200.00
1897	10.00	75.00
1897O	85.00	650.00
1897S	125.00	400.00
1898	8.00	71.00
1898O	35.00	160.00
1898S	17.00	86.00
1899	8.00	71.00
1899O	13.00	90.00
1899S	22.00	88.00
1900	7.75	71.00
1900O	10.00	90.00
1900S	12.00	95.00
1901	7.75	71.00
1901O	13.00	115.00
1901S	28.00	225.00
1902	7.75	71.00
1902O	11.00	77.00
1902S	12.00	87.00
1903	10.00	78.00
1903O	12.00	75.00
1903S	12.00	75.00
1904	8.00	71.00
1904O	17.00	110.00
1904S	27.00	325.00
1905	19.00	78.00
1905O	29.00	130.00

	VG	VF
1905S	11.00	79.00
1906	7.50	71.00
1906D	7.50	71.00
1906O	7.50	74.00
1906S	12.00	80.00
1907	6.75	75.00
1907D	8.25	75.00
1907O	8.25	71.00
1907S	12.00	125.00
1908	7.50	74.00
1908D	9.00	71.00
1908O	7.50	71.00
1908S	13.00	78.00
1909	7.50	60.00
1909O	12.00	84.00
1909S	8.50	71.00
1910	20.00	115.00
1910S	8.25	71.00
1911	6.75	60.00
1911D	11.00	82.00
1911S	8.25	74.00
1912	7.50	60.00
1912D	8.25	71.00
1912S	8.25	71.00
1913	25.00	175.00
1913D	10.00	73.00
1913S	11.00	80.00
1914	43.00	295.00
1914S	9.00	71.00
1915	29.00	190.00
1915D	7.00	71.00
1915S	7.00	71.00

WALKING LIBERTY HALF DOLLAR

This artistic new half dollar was designed by Adolph Weinman, the designer of the Mercury dime that was released that same year. It features Liberty, the American flag draped about her and flowing in the breeze, progressing towards the dawn of a new day. It was received with wide acclaim for its artistic merit when it was first released, and was part of a program for the beautification of United States coinage. The reverse carries an eagle perched on a rocky crag. The obverse design proved so popular that it was resurrected in 1986 for use on the new silver one-ounce bullion coins. Originally the mintmarks on this coin appeared on the reverse, but after mere months, they were moved to the reverse. Due to the arrangement of the design Liberty's head does not always strike perfectly. High grade examples with fully struck heads are worth more.

Known counterfeits: 1916S, 1938D coins with added mintmark exist. 1928D halves are all counterfeit.

Type Coin Price Range	VG to MS-63
1916-1947	2.40 to 35.00

	F	XF
1916	57.00	160.00
1916D	30.00	145.00
1916S	125.00	525.00
1917	10.50	35.00
1917D Obv.	39.00	165.00
1917D Rev.	21.00	230.00
1917S Obv.	55.00	665.00
1917S Rev.	13.50	55.00
1918	17.00	145.00
1918D	22.00	155.00
1918S	14.00	56.00
1919	30.00	400.00
1919D	48.00	540.00
1919S	30.00	650.00
1920	11.00	56.00
1920D	25.00	350.00
1920S	14.00	160.00
1921	175.00	1,350.00
1921D	230.00	2,350.00
1921S	57.00	5,000.00
1923S	24.00	210.00
1927S	11.00	90.00
1928S	12.50	90.00
1929D	13.00	80.00
1929S	10.00	68.00
1933S	10.00	45.00
1934	2.95	11.00
1934D	5.50	25.00
1934S	4.50	25.00
1935	2.95	9.00
1935D	5.50	25.00
1935S	4.50	25.00
1936	3.50	9.00
1936D	4.50	17.00
1936S	4.50	17.00
1937	3.50	9.00
1937D	7.00	28.00
1937S	6.00	18.00
1938	4.50	11.00
1938D	28.00	90.00
1939	3.50	10.00
1939D	4.50	10.50
1939S	6.00	12.50
1940	3.00	9.00
1940S	3.00	10.00
1941	3.00	7.00
1941D	3.00	6.00
1941S	3.00	7.00
1942	3.00	5.50
1942D	3.00	6.00
1942D, D over S	42.00	78.00
1942S	3.00	7.00
1943	3.00	5.50
1943D	3.00	6.00
1943S	3.00	6.00
1944	3.00	5.50
1944D	3.00	6.00
1944S	3.00	6.25
1945	3.00	5.50
1945D	3.00	6.00
1945S	3.00	6.00
1946	3.00	5.50
1946D	6.00	9.50
1946S	3.50	5.50
1947	3.50	7.00
1947D	3.50	7.00

FRANKLIN HALF DOLLAR

Like the design for the Washington quarter, the design for the Franklin half dollar was used in spite of the Commission of Fine Arts' recommendation. The reverse depicts the Liberty Bell as its primary motif, despite a law that required all coins larger than a dime to bear an eagle. This is why a small eagle was added at the side of the bell as an afterthought. While the coin was designed by Chief Engraver John R. Sinnock, the minute eagle was actually engraved by a young Frank Gasparro.

The biggest striking problem of the Franklin half dollar is the horizontal lines on the Liberty Bell. Those mint state examples with fully struck bell lines often sell for significantly more.

Known counterfeits: It is possible that none exist.

Type Coin Price Range	VF to MS-65
1948-1963	1.90 to 50.00

	XF	MS-60
1948	3.50	13.75
1948D	4.75	9.50
1949	7.00	28.00
1949D	7.50	29.00
1949S	8.00	48.00
1950	6.00	20.00
1950D	6.50	16.00
1951	4.00	8.75
1951D	5.00	19.00
1951S	3.50	18.00
1952	3.00	7.00
1952D	3.00	6.25
1952S	3.75	33.00
1953	5.00	12.00
1953D	4.00	6.00
1953S	4.75	11.00
1954	3.75	5.50
1954D	3.50	4.75
1954S	4.00	6.50
1955	5.50	6.50
1955 Bugs Bunny Teeth		15.50
1956	3.50	5.00
1957	3.00	4.00
1957D	2.25	3.50
1958	2.50	3.75
1958D	2.00	3.25
1959	2.00	3.75
1959D	2.00	3.75
1960	2.00	2.80
1960D	2.00	3.50
1961	2.00	3.25
1961D	2.00	3.25
1962	2.00	2.80
1962D	2.00	2.80
1963	2.00	2.50
1963D	2.00	2.50

KENNEDY HALF DOLLAR

Only three days elapsed between the assassination of President John F. Kennedy on Nov. 22, 1963, and the first notice from the director of the mint to the chief engraver to prepare for the issue of a coin bearing his portrait. Gilroy Roberts fashioned its obverse portrait based on the Kennedy inaugural medal to save time. The reverse is Frank Gasparro's rendition of the presidential seal. Remarkably, working dies were ready by January 2. Kennedy halves have been struck in three different compositions. The 1964 issue was struck in the traditional 90 percent silver alloy. The following year when dimes and quarters were changed to cupro-nickel clad copper, the half dollar was preserved as a silver alloy coin by striking it in a silver clad version that contained 80 percent silver in its outer layers, and 21 percent silver in its middle layer. The remaining alloy was copper. Finally, silver was abandoned in 1971, and only sporadic collectors' issues were struck in that metal since. Circulation issues are now struck in the same clad composition as dimes and quarters. Coins dated 1970D, 1987P and 1987D were not issued for circulation, but are widely available from broken up mint sets.

A special reverse was used in 1975 and 1976 (both with 1976 obverse) to commemorate the American Bicentennial. It depicts Independence Hall in Philadelphia, and was designed by Seth G. Huntington.

Known counterfeits: It is possible that none exist.

Type Coin Price Range	XF to MS-65
1964	1.90 to 3.50
1965-70	1.00 to 2.00
1971-date	1.25
1976	1.50

	MS-60
1964	2.50
1964D	2.50
SILVER CLAD	
1965	1.25
1966	1.25
1967	1.00
1968D	1.00
1968S proof only	3.50
1969D	1.00
1969S proof only	3.50
1970D	9.00
1970S proof only	7.50
CUPRO-NICKEL-CLAD COPPER	
1971	1.50
1971D	1.00

	MS-60		**MS-60**		**MS-60**
1971S proof only	2.75	1979 Filled S proof only	2.00	1990D	1.00
1972	2.00	1979 Clear S proof only	14.00	1990S proof only	9.75
1972D	2.00	1980P	1.00	1991P	1.00
1972S proof only	2.50	1980D	1.25	1991D	1.00
1973	1.35	1980S proof only	1.25	1991S proof only	15.00
1973D	1.35	1981P	1.25	1992P	1.00
1973S proof only	1.75	1981D	1.25	1992D	1.00
1974	1.00	1981S proof only	1.75	1992S proof only	16.00
1974D	1.20	1982P	1.00	1992S Silver proof only	13.50
1974S proof only	3.00	1982D	1.25	1993P	1.00

BICENTENNIAL REVERSE

	MS-60		**MS-60**		**MS-60**
		1982S proof only	3.50	1993D	1.00
		1983P	1.00	1993S proof only	14.00
		1983D	1.00	1993S Silver proof only	14.75
		1983S proof only	3.00	1994P	1.00
		1984P	1.00	1994D	1.00
		1984D	1.00	1994S proof only	9.75
1976 Bicentennial	1.00	1984S proof only	6.50	1994S Silver proof only	13.00
1976D Bicentennial	1.00	1985P	1.00	1995P	1.00
1976S Bicentennial proof only	1.25	1985D	1.00	1995D	1.00
1976S Bicentennial Silver Clad	2.50	1985S proof only	4.50	1995S proof only	13.00

REGULAR ISSUE CONTINUED

	MS-60		**MS-60**		**MS-60**
		1986P	1.25	1995S Silver proof only	13.00
1977	2.60	1986D	1.00	1996P	1.00
1977D	2.60	1986S proof only	15.00	1996D	1.00
1977S proof only	1.75	1987P	2.00	1996S proof only	13.00
1978	1.25	1987D	2.00	1996S Silver proof only	13.00
1978D	1.00	1987S proof only	3.50	1997P	1.00
1978S proof only	1.75	1988P	1.25	1997D	1.00
1979	1.50	1988D	1.25	1997S proof only	13.00
1979D	1.25	1988S proof only	7.50	1997S Silver proof only	13.00
		1989P	1.25	1998P	1.00
		1989D	1.25	1998D	1.00
		1989S proof only	3.50	1998S proof only	5.00
		1990P	1.00	1998S Silver proof only	13.00

EARLY SILVER DOLLARS

The intent of the first American silver dollar was to fill the same role in commerce as the old Spanish colonial milled dollar. The dollar, along with the half dollar and half dime, was one of the first silver denominations to be released by the new United States Mint. As a result, it first appeared with the briefly used flowing hair design. These first rare pieces were struck in 1794 and 1795 on crude blanks, often exhibiting "adjustment marks" from the filing off of excess silver before striking. While considered part of the manufacturing process, these marks nevertheless reduce the value of a specimen. The initial reverse design, showing a rather skinny eagle within a wreath, continued to be used after the flowing hair obverse was replaced by the rather voluptuous draped bust design. After four years of use this eagle was replaced with a plumper eagle carrying a heraldic shield.

As with the smaller denominations, the government's lack of bullion and skilled labor made it impossible to strike enough pieces to have a significant role in the economy. Another complication soon ended the life of the silver dollar altogether The average silver content of these coins slightly exceeded that of the Spanish dollar, though it was exchangeable for them at par. Most of them were thus exported and melted, worn Spanish dollars being shipped back in their place. Not willing to change the dollar's specifications, the government simply ceased to strike it for thirty years! During the last year they were struck for circulation in 1804 only old dies — probably dated 1803 — were used. In the 1830s when a few dollars were needed as gifts for foreign heads of state, the mint struck bust dollars that looked like what the 1804 dollars would have looked like if they had borne that date. These exceedingly rare "1804" dollars have become among the most famous United States coins A small number were also restruck somewhat later for collectors.

Rare die combinations of early coins can command a premium from specialists.

Known counterfeits: It is likely that all dates of early dollars have been counterfeited. Some of the cruder counterfeits can be easily distinguished by the plain or reeded edges they have, as opposed to the lettered edges of the authentic pieces. Other counterfeits are more dangerous. A great many counterfeit 1804s exist. Holed coins are sometimes deceptively plugged. Cleaning is a frequent problem, both on real and counterfeit pieces. On the latter it can sometimes make authentication more difficult.

Type Coin Price Range   G to MS-60

1794-95 Flowing Hair

800.00 to 40,000.00

1795-98 Small Eagle

585.00 to 16,000.00

1798-1804 Heraldic Eagle

350.00 to 7,500.00

FLOWING HAIR TYPE

	VG	VF
1794	13,500.00	27,500.00
1795	9,000.00	2,200.00

DRAPED BUST / SMALL EAGLE

		VG	VF
1795		800.00	1,825.00
1796		765.00	1,400.00
1797 9 & 7 stars, Small letters		2,000.00	4,500.00
1797 9 & 7 stars, Large letters		775.00	1,400.00
1797 10 stars l. & 6 stars r.		775.00	1,400.00
1798 15 stars		1,600.00	3,150.00
1798 13 stars		1,150.00	2,400.00

		VG	VF
DRAPED BUST /HERALDIC EAGLE			
1798		440.00	700.00
1799, 9 over 8, 15 stars		500.00	1,150.00
1799, 9 over 8, 13 stars		440.00	700.00
1799		425.00	700.00
1799 8 stars l. & 5 stars r.		500.00	1,100.00
1800		440.00	700.00
1801		475.00	850.00
1802, 2 over 1		450.00	850.00
1802		450.00	875.00
1802	Proof Restrike		70,000.00
1803		440.00	850.00
1803	Proof Restrike		70,000.00
1804 (struck 1834-35)	Proof		700,000.00
1804 (struck 1859)	Proof		200,000.00

GOBRECHT DOLLARS

It is ironic that the coin for which the Seated Liberty design was first prepared was the last to have it appear on pieces actively struck for circulation. It was the intent that when the striking of silver dollars was resumed, that a design of exceptional artistic merit be used. For this reason Christian Gobrecht was asked to prepare dies based on a drawing of Liberty seated by artist Thomas Sully. It is generally accepted that his seated goddess concept of Liberty derives from depictions of the Roman allegory of Britannia on British coins. The reverse design was also a radical departure from the staid old heraldic eagle. The new eagle was seen in the realistic attitude of flight. It was prepared by Gobrecht based on a drawing of Old Pete by the famous Titian Peale. Old Pete was an eagle who lived at the mint ca.1830-36 and who met an unfortunate end, getting caught in the machinery. While Gobrecht dollars are not all patterns, very few were ever struck for circulation, never more than a thousand or so of any one variety. Only circulating issues are listed here. Pattern pieces with the engraver's name in the field as opposed to on the base, as well as 1838 issues, are listed in that section. Later some were restruck for collectors. These can usually be distinguished by the misaligned dies that make the eagle appear to be flying horizontally when the coin is turned around. Originals have the eagle flying slightly upward. Known counterfeits: Gobrecht experimental dollars are less often counterfeited than other early dollars. Cleaning and polishing are problems, however.

STARS ON REVERSE

	VF	EF
1836 (coin alignment)	3,500.00	4,400.00
1836 (struck 1837, medal alignment)	3,500.00	4,600.00

STARS ON OBVERSE

1839	3,800.00	5,000.00

SEATED LIBERTY DOLLARS

The active production of silver dollars finally resumed in 1840. However, the reverse design especially created for it was replaced by a more mundane heraldic eagle similar to that in use on the minor coinage. While production of these coins continued for most years, those struck from 1853 to about 1867 were primarily intended as bullion pieces for export, each containing more than a dollar's worth of silver. A ribbon with the motto "In God We Trust" was added over the eagle in 1866. These dollars are often found cleaned. Be careful of retoned specimens as well.

Known counterfeits: Counterfeits of this type are not common.

Type Coin Price Range   G to MS-60

1840-1865	100.00 to 900.00
1866-1873	100.00 to 1,250.00

NO MOTTO ABOVE EAGLE

	F	EF
1840	225.00	575.00
1841	180.00	375.00
1842	175.00	300.00
1843	175.00	300.00
1844	300.00	575.00
1845	250.00	500.00
1846	175.00	275.00
1846O	190.00	475.00
1847	175.00	300.00
1848	400.00	700.00
1849	190.00	350.00
1850	750.00	1,100.00
1850O	350.00	1,400.00
1851 Original	8,000.00	13,500.00
1851 Restrike	Proof	20,000.00
1852 Original	6,500.00	11,500.00
1852 Restrike	Proof	16,000.00
1853	270.00	575.00
1854	1,500.00	3,500.00
1855	1,300.00	2,650.00
1856	375.00	975.00
1857	550.00	1,500.00
1858	2,750.00	5,500.00
1859	350.00	700.00
1859O	175.00	265.00
1859S	400.00	1,350.00
1860	230.00	475.00
1860O	175.00	265.00
1861	600.00	1,250.00
1862	625.00	1,250.00
1863	400.00	800.00
1864	315.00	675.00
1865	290.00	625.00
1866		2 Known

	F	EF
MOTTO ABOVE EAGLE		
1866	250.00	550.00
1867	300.00	600.00
1868	225.00	525.00
1869	200.00	500.00
1870	175.00	325.00
1870CC	325.00	1,050.00
1870S	50,000.00	200,000.00
1871	175.00	315.00
1871CC	3,750.00	8,500.00
1872	165.00	315.00
1872CC	1,600.00	4,250.00
1872S	400.00	1,100.00
1873	200.00	350.00
1873CC	6,500.00	17,500.00
1873S	None known to exist	

TRADE DOLLARS

Trade dollars were coins struck deliberately for export as bullion, usually for the Far East. Their chief intent was to compete against the Mexican peso which had slightly more silver than a standard dollar. They were distinguished by a Liberty and eagle facing in the direction opposite that of standard dollars. From the very beginning their legal tender status was limited in the United States, but in 1876 when the price of silver dropped, they ceased to have legal tender altogether, not having it restored until 1965. Eight million were redeemed by the government in 1887, however. Any struck between

1879 and 1885 are Proof Only collectors' issues. Those prices are for circulated examples.

It was typical for Oriental merchants to impress a character into these and other silver coins to confirm that they accepted them as good quality. These "chop marks" are commonly found on trade dollars, sometimes in quantity. They reduce the value of the coin as a form of mutilation, but have recently been the subject of serious research. Chop marked dollars may not be as valuable, but are still collectible.

Known counterfeits: Counterfeits are not abundant and are more likely to be contemporary counterfeits. Be cautious of cleaned coins.

Type Coin Price Range

Chopped to MS-60

1873-1885	50.00 to 475.00

	F	EF
1873	125.00	250.00
1873CC	225.00	475.00
1873S	160.00	260.00
1874	125.00	225.00
1874CC	105.00	240.00
1874S	95.00	165.00
1875	425.00	675.00
1875CC	105.00	200.00
1875S	85.00	120.00
1875S, S over CC	400.00	825.00
1876	100.00	160.00
1876CC	150.00	325.00
1876S	85.00	120.00
1877	85.00	130.00
1877CC	175.00	350.00
1877S	85.00	120.00
1878	Proof only	1,250.00
1878CC	675.00	1,750.00
1878S	85.00	120.00
1879	Proof only	950.00
1880	Proof only	950.00
1881	Proof only	1,000.00
1882	Proof only	1,000.00
1883	Proof only	1,100.00
1884	Proof only	10 known
1885	Proof only	5 known

MORGAN DOLLARS

The Morgan dollar was introduced as a result of pressure from the silver mining lobby. For decades silver dollars had been scarce in circulation. With the boom in silver mining the price of the metal dropped as more became available. Something needed to be done to remove the excess silver from the market. The new design coincided with the reintroduction of the silver dollar. Because they were inconvenient, however, many, perhaps hundreds of thousands, of these dollars sat for decades in bags, held as private, bank, and government reserves. The U.S. Treasury was stuck with such an excess that thousands remained on hand for almost a century, prompting the famous GSA auction of silver dollars in the 1970s. Those coin, in distinctive GSA cases, often command a slight premium.

Artistically, many consider the Morgan dollar, named after it's designer George T. Morgan, an aesthetically pleasing but unoriginal design. Morgan's competence (and perhaps his interesting use of Gothic script) may be able to be attributed to his training at the Royal Mint in London. A long gap exists between 1904 and the last Morgan issue in 1921. During this time the master dies were lost and new ones had to be prepared. As a result there are subtle differences of relief in the 1921 issue. It is less pleasing, and dealer "bids" are often less for that year than for other bulk Morgan dollars. Another subtle variation in the appearance of Morgan dollars is the variation in quality of strike from mint to mint. San Francisco-made examples are usually fully struck, Philadelphia are medium, and New Orleans dollars are usually the most weakly struck. The eagle's breast on high grade pieces is usually the spot where these differences are most obvious.

Morgans have been among the most popular coins to invest in. This is partially due to their availability in great quantities in uncirculated condition, the typical grade favored by investment promoters and the mass of investors. It is ironic that their sheer commonness has contributed to their desirability.

Known counterfeits: Genuine coins have been known to be altered to pass for 1879CC, 1889CC, 1892S, 1893S, 1894, 1895, 1895S, 1896S, 1901, 1903S and 1904S dates. Cast counterfeits are known of 1878, 1878S, 1879S, 1880O, 1881, 1883, 1883S, 1885, 1888O, 1889, 1889O, 1892O, 1899O, 1901, 1902, 1903, 1904S, 1921D and 1921S. Struck counterfeits of certain rare dates are also possible. Cleaned coins are common and are heavily discounted, as are scuffed and heavily edge knocked pieces. Be careful to avoid coins with false toning.

Type Coin Price Range   G to MS-65

1878-1904	7.00 to 110.00
1921	6.50 to 110.00

	VF	MS-60
1878, 8 tail feathers	17.50	70.00
1878, 7 over 8 tail feathers	19.00	85.00
1878, 7 feathers	15.00	32.00
1878, same, rev. of 1879	16.50	38.00
1878CC	40.00	95.00
1878S	13.00	28.00
1879	12.50	25.00
1879CC	112.00	1,400.00
1879O	13.00	50.00
1879S	12.50	21.00
1880	12.50	21.00
1880CC	69.00	205.00
1880O	11.00	43.00
1880S	11.00	21.00
1881	11.00	20.00
1881CC	120.00	190.00
1881O	11.00	21.00
1881S	11.00	21.00
1882	11.00	21.00
1882CC	40.00	84.00
1882O	11.00	21.00
1882O, O over S	20.00	135.00
1882S	11.00	21.00
1883	11.00	21.50
1883CC	40.00	84.00
1883O	11.00	21.00
1883S	12.50	365.00
1884	11.00	21.00
1884CC	45.00	84.00
1884O	11.00	20.00
1884S	14.00	3,400.00
1885	11.00	20.00
1885CC	175.00	240.00
1885O	11.00	20.00
1885S	15.00	95.00
1886	11.00	20.00
1886O	11.00	275.00
1886S	19.00	140.00
1887, 7 over 6	22.00	150.00
1887	11.00	20.00
1887O, 7 over 6	22.00	270.00
1887O	11.00	39.00
1887S	11.50	57.00
1888	11.00	21.00
1888O	11.00	21.00
1888S	31.00	140.00
1889	11.00	20.00
1889CC	400.00	6,550.00
1889O	11.00	85.00
1889S	22.00	125.00
1890	11.00	20.00
1890CC	37.50	240.00
1890O	11.00	31.00
1890S	11.00	39.00
1891	11.00	38.00
1891CC	37.50	175.00
1891O	11.00	73.00
1891S	11.00	39.00
1892	12.00	120.00
1892CC	69.00	390.00
1892O	11.50	95.00
1892S	39.00	14,000.00
1893	82.00	330.00
1893CC	175.00	1,170.00
1893O	110.00	1,300.00
1893S	1,550.00	29,000.00
1894	295.00	900.00

	VF	MS-60
1894O	31.00	480.00
1894S	45.00	390.00
1895	Proof only	19,000.00
1895O	145.00	8,200.00
1895S	190.00	1,250.00
1896	11.00	20.00
1896O	11.00	630.00
1896S	41.00	680.00
1897	11.00	21.00
1897O	12.00	470.00
1897S	11.00	39.00
1898	11.00	21.00
1898O	13.00	22.00
1898S	13.75	155.00
1899	33.00	76.00
1899O	11.00	22.00
1899S	16.00	155.00
1900	11.00	21.00
1900O	11.00	24.00
1900O, O over CC	27.50	170.00
1900S	16.50	115.00
1901	27.00	1,500.00
1901O	11.00	21.00
1901S	24.00	250.00
1902	11.00	32.00
1902O	11.00	21.00
1902S	56.00	175.00
1903	15.00	32.00
1903O	125.00	180.00
1903S	62.00	2,400.00
1904	11.50	57.00
1904O	11.00	21.00
1904S	37.00	950.00
1921	8.50	13.00
1921D	8.50	25.00
1921S	8.50	21.00

PEACE DOLLARS

Like the Morgan dollar before it, the Peace dollar was the result of Congressional authorization for a new large coinage of silver dollars. When the famous numismatist Farran Zerbe learned that this new issue of dollars was to bear the old Morgan design he agitated for a new, more artistically progressive replacement. A new, radiant Liberty head by sculptor Anthony de Francisci. It was not only in harmony with the new designs for the other denominations (especially those by Weinman and St. Gaudens), but also commemorated the end of World War I. The word PEACE can be seen upon the rocky perch on which the eagle stands. The old silver dollar was last made for circulation in 1935. The very first Peace Dollars — those struck in 1921 only — were struck in a much higher relief. Later issues have a lower relief more suitable to mass production. The Peace dollar outlived this death sentence for thirty years in the form of the mysterious issue of 1964. While none have been officially verified there have long been rumors, generally accepted by the numismatic community, that several escaped the mint's melting pot.

Like the Morgan dollar, this coin is available in mint state in abundant quantities. The broad, smooth surfaces, however, permit many mint state pieces to reveal unsightly bruises and bag marks.

Known Counterfeits: 1928 altered from 1923 or 1928S, as well as other counterfeits of this date.

Type Coin Price Range	G to MS-65
1921	16.00 to 2,200.00
1922-35.	6.50 to 145.00

	VF	MS-60
1921	38.00	135.00
1922	8.25	13.00
1922D	8.25	18.00
1922S	8.25	18.00
1923	8.25	13.00
1923D	8.25	32.00
1923S	8.25	18.00
1924	8.25	13.00
1924S	11.50	160.00
1925	8.25	13.00
1925S	10.00	57.00
1926	10.00	21.00
1926D	9.50	50.00
1926S	9.00	32.00
1927	16.50	46.00
1927D	14.00	120.00
1927S	16.00	100.00
1928	125.00	175.00
1928S	12.50	100.00
1934	15.00	70.00
1934D	14.00	70.00
1934S	42.00	1,000.00
1935	11.50	49.00
1935S	13.00	120.00
1964D	No confirmed examples known	

EISENHOWER DOLLARS

The "Ike" dollar was struck as much to commemorate the first manned moon landing in 1969, as it was to honor President Dwight D. Eisenhower. The reverse of this coin was an adaptation of the Apollo XI insignia, depicting an eagle clutching and olive branch and landing on the moon. The obverse shows a left-facing portrait of Eisenhower. Circulation strikes were of the same cupro-nickel clad composition as the dime and quarter. Special collectors' issues were also struck in a silver clad version similar to the alloy used for the half dollars of 1965-1970. These special silver coins bearing the "S" mint mark were released in special blue envelopes for the uncirculated issues, and brown boxes for the proofs. Most dealers and collectors require that they be in the original packaging.

A special reverse was used to commemorate the bicentennial. It featured the Liberty Bell superimposed on the moon, as arranged by design contest winner Dennis R. Williams. While all bicentennial dollars are dated "1776 1976" they were struck in both 1975 and 1976, the reverse of the former year uses heavy block lettering, the latter mostly used slightly finer letters.

Known counterfeits: None likely.

Type Coin Price Range

	MS-60 to PF-65
1971-78	1.25 to 4.75
1976	1.25 to 4.60

	MS-63	PF
1971	2.50	
1971D	2.50	
1971S Silver	4.25	4.75
1972	2.25	
1972D	2.25	
1972S Silver	4.25	4.75
1973	3.40	
1973D	3.40	
1973S Proof only		5.00
1973S Silver	4.75	17.00
1974	2.25	
1974D	2.25	
1974S Proof only		5.00
1974S Silver	4.50	5.00

BICENTENNIAL REVERSE

	MS-63	PF
1976 Block letters	2.25	
1976 Finer letters	2.00	
1976D Block letters	2.25	
1976D Finer letters	2.00	
1976S Block letters	Proof only	5.60
1976S Finer letters	Proof only	4.60
1976S Silver, Block letters	10.00	10.00

REGULAR ISSUE CONTINUED

	MS-63	PF
1977	2.25	
1977D	2.25	
1977S Proof only		4.75
1978	2.25	
1978D	2.50	
1978S Proof only		4.75

SUSAN B. ANTHONY DOLLARS

The Anthony "mini-dollar" was struck to achieve two specific ends. It was intended to save the government money, by replacing the quickly worn out one dollar bill with a coin designed to last in circulation for decades. It was also a coin greatly supported and pushed for by he vending machine lobby. The large Ike dollars were inconvenient for vending machines, but a coin of its value was necessary to facilitate the sale of more expensive items in such machines.

Its obverse depicts Frank Gasparro's portrait of Susan B. Anthony who was instrumental in gaining women the right to vote. The reverse design is the same Apollo XI motif as on the Eisenhower dollar.

Certainly one of the least popular coins in the history of the United States, it was far too close in diameter to the quarter, with which it as frequently confused. The last year of issue was not even placed into circulation and was obtainable only in mint sets. **Known counterfeits:** None likely.

	MS-63	PF
1979P Narrow rim, far date	1.30	
1979P Wide rim, near date	4.00	
1979D	1.30	
1979S	1.60	
1979S Filled S		4.50
1979S Clear S		69.00
1980	1.40	
1980D	1.40	
1980S	1.80	4.50
1981	3.60	
1981D	3.50	
1981S	3.50	
1981S Filled S		5.50
1981S Clear S		100.00

GOLD DOLLARS

Although the gold dollar was originally planned as early as 1791, and patterns were prepared in 1836, it was not until 1849 that they were finally approved. Earlier demand was being filled by privately struck Georgia and Carolina gold of standard United States coinage weight, and the mint director personally opposed their issue. When Congressional intervention was coupled with the new flow of gold from California the mint had to give in. The first gold dollars, designed as one of James Longacre's early projects, were a mere 12.7 mm. in diameter and were easily lost. The diameter was increased to 14.3 mm. and the coin made thinner in 1854 to make them easier to handle, but the new narrow head design was of too high relief and parts of the date on the reverse did not always strike up. The gold dollar's final modification came in 1856, when the wide flan was retained but a lower relief portrait of Liberty similar to that on the Three Dollar piece was used.

Many gold dollars were used at the time in jewelry and bear solder marks, especially the first type. These coins are worth a fraction of the value of unmutilated coins. Mutilated examples are far more common than worn ones, with few examples grading lower than VF.

Known counterfeits: Type I: Altered 1849C Open Wreath and 1854C, 1850-54 cast and struck counterfeits. Type II: Most dates have been counterfeited. Type III: most dates 1868-1878, including 1873 and 1874, as well as 1883 and 1887.

Type Coin Price Range   F to MS-60

1849-1854, Type I	100.00 to 275.00
1854-1856, Type II	210.00 to 3,000.00

1856 to 1889, Type III	110.00 to 280.00

CORONET HEAD - TYPE I

	VF	EF
1849 Open wreath	120.00	165.00
1849 Closed wreath	120.00	165.00
1849C Open wreath		Extremely Rare
1849C Closed wreath	425.00	750.00
1849D	410.00	800.00
1849O	165.00	210.00
1850	135.00	150.00
1850C	585.00	950.00
1850D	550.00	1,150.00
1850O	260.00	370.00
1851	135.00	165.00
1851C	410.00	650.00
1851D	400.00	750.00
1851O	175.00	195.00
1852	120.00	150.00
1852C	450.00	750.00
1852D	600.00	1,150.00
1852O	150.00	210.00
1853	130.00	150.00
1853C	475.00	1,200.00
1853D	675.00	950.00
1853O	160.00	195.00
1854	150.00	160.00
1854D	860.00	1,850.00
1854S	300.00	440.00

NARROW INDIAN PRINCESS HEAD - TYPE II

1854	265.00	370.00
1855	265.00	370.00
1855C	950.00	2,650.00
1855D	2,300.00	4,500.00
1855O	550.00	800.00
1856S	650.00	1,100.00

LARGE INDIAN PRINCESS HEAD - TYPE III

1856 upright 5	160.00	180.00
1856 slanted 5	140.00	170.00
1856D	3,500.00	5,500.00
1857	130.00	170.00
1857C	500.00	1,000.00
1857D	825.00	1,650.00
1857S	500.00	600.00
1858	140.00	170.00
1858D	775.00	1,300.00
1858S	375.00	500.00
1859	140.00	160.00
1859C	500.00	1,250.00
1859D	780.00	1,150.00
1859S	250.00	480.00

	VF	EF
1860	140.00	170.00
1860D	2,500.00	3,800.00
1860S	325.00	475.00
1861	140.00	170.00
1861D (Struck by the Confederacy)	6,000.00	8,500.00
1862	120.00	155.00
1863	450.00	875.00
1864	370.00	475.00
1865	370.00	585.00
1866	380.00	450.00
1867	440.00	550.00
1868	295.00	400.00
1869	360.00	520.00
1870	285.00	500.00
1870S	475.00	800.00
1871	285.00	440.00
1872	315.00	480.00
1873 Closed 3	425.00	700.00
1873 Open 3	120.00	155.00
1874	120.00	155.00
1875	2,500.00	3,600.00
1876	250.00	360.00
1877	175.00	350.00
1878	215.00	365.00
1879	190.00	300.00
1880	160.00	200.00
1881	160.00	200.00
1882	175.00	210.00
1883	165.00	200.00
1884	160.00	190.00
1885	160.00	200.00
1886	165.00	200.00
1887	165.00	200.00
1888	165.00	200.00
1889	165.00	200.00

GOLD 2-1/2 DOLLARS

The first strikes of the quarter eagle (2-1/2 dollar gold) came the year following the first introduction of American gold coinage, the half eagle and eagle preceding it in 1795. However, it preceded the other denominations as the first coin to depict the heraldic eagle with a shield on its chest, which later was featured on all denominations besides copper. Its first obverse features a bust of Liberty wearing a tall conical cap, traditionally but inaccurately referred to by numismatists as a turban. This first bust by Robert Scott was replaced by one designed by John Reich, and wearing a smaller cap. A reverse eagle similar, but more realistic, was paired with the new obverse. A large gap in the striking of quarter eagles followed immediately upon the release of this new design, which was finally restored on the same standard but at a slightly smaller diameter in 1821.

Through most of its history, until the 1830s, the quarter eagle was plagued by mass meltings, because it was undervalued relative to its gold content, particularly by European standards. In 1834 this was remedied by reducing the coin's gold content. This was indicated to the public by the removal of the motto over the eagle on the reverse, and by a new capless Liberty head,

the "Classic Head" by William Kneass. The final Coronet type Liberty head design was a rendition by Christian Gobrecht, which continued in use from 1840 to 1907 without change. Those 1848 pieces countermarked CAL. were struck with gold shipped east by the military governor of California.

In 1908, as part of the same coin design beautification program which later introduced the Walking Liberty half dollar and St. Gaudens double eagle, sculptor Bela Lyon Pratt was asked to prepare new designs for the quarter and half eagle in secret under the authority of President Theodore Roosevelt. His work showed the bust of an Indian chief on the obverse and an eagle with closed wings on the reverse. It was both controversial and innovative in that it bore its design in relief, but recessed below the surface of the coin. While some criticized it both for aesthetic reasons and for fear of it spreading germs in dirt trapped in the recesses, it proved to be a very successful method of shielding the design from wear.

Known Counterfeits: 1841, 1848 CAL (altered 1848), 1858, 1873, 1875 (altered from 1875S), 1878, 1883 and 1883 Proof, 1884, 1885 and 1885 Proof, 1895 Proof, 1899, 1903, 1904, 1905, 1905S (no real ones exist), 1907, 1908, 1911, 1911D (added mint mark, 1914, 1915, 1928. Be cautious of false C mintmarks altered by cutting down an authentic O mintmark. Beware of traces of solder on earlier coins that may have been used as jewelry. Look for interruption in the pattern of edge reeding. Be cautious of cleaned coins. This is harder to detect on gold which usually does not tone naturally.

Type Coin Price Range   VG to MS-63

1796-1807	2,000.00 to 36,000.00
1808-1834	2,200.00 to 15,000.00
1834-1839	200.00 to 5,250.00
1840-1907	75.00 to 790.00
1908-1929	75.00 to 775.00

TURBAN BUST RIGHT

	F	XF
1796 No stars on obverse	9,500.00	31,000.00
1796 Stars	8,500.00	20,000.00
1797	8,500.00	12,500.00
1798	3,500.00	7,750.00
1802, 2 over 1	3,000.00	5,000.00
1804, 13 stars	16,000.00	55,000.00
1804, 14 stars	3,250.00	5,750.00
1805	3,000.00	5,400.00
1806, 6 over 4	3,000.00	5,000.00
1806, 6 over 5	6,500.00	22,000.00
1807	2,800.00	5,000.00

CAPPED BUST TYPE

	F	XF
1808	9,000.00	22,000.00
1821	3,250.00	4,500.00
1824, 4 over 1	3,000.00	4,250.00
1825	3,000.00	4,250.00
1826, 6 over 5	3,500.00	5,500.00
1827	3,600.00	5,000.00
1829	3,000.00	4,000.00
1830	3,000.00	4,250.00
1831	3,000.00	4,250.00
1832	3,000.00	4,250.00
1833	3,000.00	4,250.00
1834	6,750.00	19,500.00

CLASSIC HEAD (NO MOTTO)

1834	250.00	550.00
1835	250.00	400.00
1836	250.00	400.00
1837	250.00	425.00
1838	250.00	425.00
1838C	550.00	2,500.00
1839	250.00	600.00
1839C	400.00	1,800.00
1839D	475.00	2,250.00
1839O	340.00	1,100.00

CORONET TYPE (NO MOTTO)

	F	EF
1840	180.00	700.00
1840C	325.00	1,250.00
1840D	500.00	4,100.00
1840O	225.00	900.00
1841	—	27,500.00
1841C	275.00	1,250.00
1841D	600.00	2,600.00
1842	350.00	3,000.00
1842C	525.00	2,600.00
1842D	700.00	2,900.00
1842O	375.00	1,500.00
1843	200.00	250.00
1843C, Crosslet 4, small date	1,000.00	5,500.00
1843C, Plain 4, large date	500.00	900.00
1843D	400.00	1,100.00
1843O, Crosslet 4, small date	200.00	325.00

	F	EF
1843O, Plain 4, large date	250.00	450.00
1844	200.00	850.00
1844C	325.00	1,550.00
1844D	325.00	1,200.00
1845	200.00	290.00
1845D	325.00	1,125.00
1845O	750.00	1,900.00
1846	300.00	725.00
1846C	550.00	2,000.00
1846D	450.00	1,200.00
1846O	200.00	525.00
1847	200.00	400.00
1847C	300.00	1,000.00
1847D	300.00	1,000.00
1847O	200.00	425.00
1848	350.00	1,000.00
1848 CAL.	7,000.00	15,000.00

Quarter eagles with CAL over the eagle were struck with gold shipped to the Dept. of War by the governor of California.

	F	EF
1848C	400.00	1,200.00
1848D	400.00	1,200.00
1849	175.00	500.00
1849C	400.00	1,750.00
1849D	400.00	1,200.00
1850	175.00	225.00
1850C	275.00	1,400.00
1850D	350.00	1,200.00
1850O	200.00	575.00
1851	115.00	170.00
1851C	375.00	1,500.00
1851D	275.00	1,300.00
1851O	200.00	350.00
1852	115.00	170.00
1852C	350.00	1,550.00
1852D	450.00	2,750.00
1852O	200.00	300.00
1853	115.00	180.00
1853D	500.00	2,650.00
1854	175.00	210.00
1854C	250.00	1,650.00
1854D	1,800.00	6,000.00
1854O	200.00	300.00
1854S	15,000.00	37,500.00
1855	175.00	185.00
1855C	500.00	2,850.00
1855D	2,000.00	8,000.00
1856	125.00	180.00
1856C	500.00	2,000.00
1856D	4,000.00	13,000.00
1856O	200.00	715.00
1856S	200.00	435.00
1857	175.00	210.00
1857D	565.00	2,000.00
1857O	160.00	350.00
1857S	150.00	400.00
1858	135.00	225.00
1858C	350.00	1,300.00
1859	150.00	300.00
1859D	600.00	3,000.00
1859S	200.00	1,200.00
1860	200.00	300.00
1860C	350.00	1,400.00
1860S	200.00	700.00
1861	115.00	170.00
1861S	200.00	950.00
1862, 2 over 1	650.00	2,150.00
1862	200.00	300.00
1862S	650.00	2,500.00
1863	Proof only	25,000.00
1863S	400.00	1,500.00
1864	2,500.00	13,500.00
1865	2,000.00	8,500.00
1865S	200.00	630.00
1866	550.00	5,000.00
1866S	200.00	975.00
1867	225.00	840.00
1867S	200.00	875.00
1868	200.00	500.00
1868S	200.00	500.00
1869	200.00	500.00
1869S	200.00	600.00
1870	210.00	550.00
1870S	200.00	350.00
1871	210.00	350.00
1871S	225.00	350.00
1872	225.00	825.00
1872S	225.00	500.00
1873 Closed 3	125.00	200.00
1873 Open 3	125.00	225.00
1873S	200.00	575.00
1874	200.00	500.00
1875	1,500.00	5,250.00
1875S	200.00	400.00
1876	175.00	625.00
1876S	210.00	600.00
1877	325.00	600.00
1877S	125.00	210.00
1878	125.00	165.00
1878S	125.00	165.00
1879	125.00	165.00
1879S	125.00	165.00
1880	215.00	350.00
1881	700.00	2,750.00
1882	125.00	300.00
1883	125.00	400.00
1884	125.00	400.00
1885	500.00	1,500.00
1886	125.00	300.00
1887	125.00	225.00
1888	125.00	225.00
1889	125.00	250.00
1890	125.00	200.00
1891	125.00	250.00
1892	135.00	200.00
1893	125.00	200.00
1894	125.00	200.00
1895	125.00	200.00
1896	125.00	165.00
1897	125.00	165.00
1898	125.00	165.00
1899	125.00	165.00
1900	125.00	165.00
1901	125.00	165.00
1902	125.00	165.00
1903	125.00	165.00
1904	125.00	165.00
1905	125.00	165.00
1906	125.00	165.00
1907	125.00	165.00

INDIAN HEAD TYPE

	VF	AU
1908	130.00	200.00
1909	130.00	200.00
1910	130.00	200.00
1911	130.00	200.00
1911D	700.00	1,600.00
1912	130.00	200.00
1913	130.00	200.00
1914	140.00	210.00
1914D	130.00	200.00
1915	130.00	200.00
1925D	130.00	200.00
1926	130.00	200.00
1927	130.00	200.00
1928	130.00	200.00
1929	130.00	200.00

THREE DOLLAR GOLD PIECES

The 1851 law which lowered the rate for first class mail from 5¢ to 3¢ also authorized a 3¢ coin that could be used to purchase the new stamps. The prevailing thought at the time continued, and in 1853 another law authorized a $3 gold piece that could be used to conveniently purchase entire sheets of stamps, as well as be exchanged for 100 of the small silver trimes. Popularly called a portrait of an Indian princess, the design is more specifically that of Liberty wearing a feathered headdress, and was also used on the type III gold dollars of 1856. It was never particularly popular, with most years outside the 1850s being struck in insignificant quantities. Mintages became almost ceremonial until striking was finally suspended in 1889.

In its day it was popularly used as jewelry so collectors must be very careful to inspect coins for traces of solder. Look for irregularities in the reading or discoloration near the edge. Cleaning is both a problem and a hint to other flaws like mount marks.

Known counterfeits: 1857, 1877 (both altered and struck), 1882/82, as well as most other dates.

Type Coin Price Range   **F to MS-60**

1854-1889	400.00 to 730.00

	VF	EF
1854	575.00	625.00
1854D	7,250.00	13,500.00
1854O	425.00	750.00
1855	575.00	625.00
1855S	1,000.00	1,750.00
1856	600.00	690.00
1856S	760.00	900.00
1857	600.00	690.00
1857S	1,000.00	1,800.00
1858	800.00	1,050.00

	VF	EF
1859	600.00	675.00
1860	700.00	850.00
1860S	760.00	1,800.00
1861	760.00	1,000.00
1862	760.00	900.00
1863	700.00	850.00
1864	760.00	1,150.00
1865	800.00	1,600.00
1866	700.00	950.00
1867	700.00	950.00
1868	700.00	900.00
1869	700.00	1,000.00
1870	700.00	1,000.00
1870S		1,500,000.00
1871	750.00	1,200.00
1872	700.00	1,200.00
1873 Closed 3	4,000.00	6,500.00
1873 Open 3	Proof only	25,000.00
1874	550.00	600.00
1875	Proof only	55,000.00
1876		10,000.00
1877	1,100.00	2,750.00
1878	550.00	625.00
1879	550.00	850.00
1880	750.00	1,200.00
1881	1,000.00	2,100.00
1882	700.00	1,250.00
1883	700.00	1,250.00
1884	900.00	1,500.00
1885	900.00	1,500.00
1886	825.00	1,400.00
1887	625.00	800.00
1888	625.00	800.00
1889	625.00	800.00

FIVE DOLLAR GOLD PIECES

The first American gold coin to be struck was the half eagle, or $5 gold piece, in 1795. Its first obverse features a bust of Liberty wearing a tall conical cap, traditionally but inaccurately referred to by numismatists as a turban. Originally this was paired with a reverse design featuring a skinny eagle similar to that on the first dollars, but instead of standing within a wreath it is seen holding one above its head. As with the other denominations this was replaced by a plumper heraldic eagle bearing a shield on its chest, which later was featured on all denominations besides copper. The original bust by Robert Scott was replaced in 1807 by one designed by John Reich, and wore a smaller cap. A reverse eagle similar, but more realistic, was paired with the new obverse. While the design and net gold content did not change for almost thirty years the coin's diameter was at first increased and then reduced.

Through most of its history until the 1830s the half eagle was plagued by mass meltings, being undervalued relative to its gold content, particularly by European standards. In 1834 this was remedied by reducing the coin's gold content. This was indicated to the public by the removal of the motto over the eagle on the reverse, and by a new capless Liberty head, the "Classic Head" by William Kneass. The final Coronet type Liberty head design was a rendition by Christian Gobrecht, which continued to be used from 1839 to 1908, the motto being replaced over the eagle in 1866.

In 1908, as part of the same coin design beautification program which later introduced the Walking Liberty half dollar and St. Gaudens double eagle, sculptor Bela Lyon Pratt was asked to prepare new designs for the quarter and half eagle in secret under the authority of President Theodore Roosevelt. His work showed the bust of an Indian chief on the obverse and an eagle with closed wings on the reverse. It was both controversial and innovative in that it bore its design in relief, but recessed below the surface of the coin. While some criticized it both for aesthetic reasons and for fear of it spreading germs in dirt trapped in the recesses, it proved to be a very successful method of shielding the design from wear.

Known counterfeits: 1811, 1815 (altered), 1841O (probable), 1852C, 1854S (altered), 1858, 1870CC (altered), 1875, 1877 (altered), 1885, 1885S, 1887 Proof (altered), 1892, 1892O (altered), 1906S, 1907D, 1908 (Liberty), 1908D, 1909 Matte Proof, 1909D, 1909O, 1914D, 1914S, and 1915D (all counterfeit), among others. Be cautious of false C mintmarks altered by cutting down an authentic O mintmark. Beware of traces of solder on earlier coins from use as jewelry. Look for interruption in the pattern of edge reeding. Be cautious of cleaned coins. This is harder to detect on gold which usually does not tone naturally.

Type Coin Price Range VG to MS-63

1795-1798	4,000.00 to 82,000.00
1795-1807	900.00 to 11,750.00
1807-1834	1,000.00 to 12,000.00
1834-1838	150.00 to 5,750.00
1839-1866	95.00 to 5,750.00
1866-1908	95.00 to 500.00

TURBAN BUST / SMALL EAGLE

	F	VF
1795	5,250.00	7,250.00
1796, 6 over 5	6,000.00	9,100.00
1797, 15 stars	7,500.00	10,000.00
1797, 16 stars	7,000.00	9,000.00
1798		23,000.00

TURBAN BUST / HERALDIC EAGLE

	F	VF
1795	6,500.00	7,500.00
1797, 7 over 5	5,000.00	7,000.00
1797, 16 star obv.		Unique
1798 Small 8	1,500.00	1,850.00
1798 Large 8, 13 star rev.	1,200.00	1,850.00
1798 Large 8, 14 star rev.	1,600.00	2,300.00
1799	1,300.00	1,600.00
1800	1,150.00	1,550.00
1802, 2 over 1	1,150.00	1,550.00
1803, 3 over 2	1,150.00	1,550.00
1804, Small 8	1,150.00	1,550.00
1804, Small 8 over Large 8	1,150.00	1,550.00
1805	1,150.00	1,550.00
1806, Pointed 6	1,150.00	1,550.00
1806, Round 6	1,150.00	1,550.00
1807	1,150.00	1,550.00

CAPPED BUST TYPE

	F	VF
1807	1,250.00	1,650.00
1808, 8 over 7	1,400.00	1,550.00
1808	1,250.00	1,650.00
1809, 9 over 8	1,250.00	1,500.00
1810 Small date, small 5	10,000.00	20,000.00
1810 Small date, tall 5	1,300.00	1,650.00
1810 Large date, small 5	14,000.00	25,000.00
1810 Large date, large 5	1,250.00	1,400.00
1811 Small 5		1,250.00
	1,400.00	
1811 Tall 5	1,150.00	1,350.00
1812	1,000.00	1,350.00
1813	1,300.00	1,500.00
1814, 4 over 3	1,600.00	2,000.00
1815	EF	35,000.00
1818	1,500.00	1,900.00
1818 STATESOF	1,600.00	2,100.00
1818, 5D over 50	2,100.00	4,000.00
1819	6,250.00	12,500.00
1819, 5D over 50	17,000.00	
1820, Curved-base 2	1,500.00	1,900.00
1820, Square-base 2	1,500.00	1,900.00
1821	2,200.00	8,000.00
1822		1,000,000.00
1823	1,600.00	2,000.00
1824	4,500.00	8,750.00
1825, 5 over 1	4,500.00	6,750.00
1825, 5 over 4		Only 2 known
1826	2,750.00	6,000.00
1827	6,000.00	9,000.00
1828, 8 over 7	7,000.00	10,000.00
1828	4,250.00	6,500.00

	F	VF
1829		Extremely Rare

CAPPED BUST / REDUCED DIAMETER

	F	VF
1829	20,000.00	35,000.00
1830	3,500.00	5,000.00
1831	3,500.00	5,100.00
1832, 12 stars		Only 6 known
1832, 13 stars	2,000.00	3,000.00
1833	3,500.00	5,000.00
1834 Plain 4	3,500.00	5,000.00
1834 Crosslet 4	4,000.00	6,000.00

CLASSIC HEAD (NO MOTTO)

	VF	EF
1834 Plain 4	300.00	500.00
1834 Crosslet 4	1,150.00	2,375.00
1835	300.00	500.00
1836	300.00	500.00
1837	325.00	525.00
1838	300.00	500.00
1838C	1,550.00	4,250.00
1838D	1,450.00	3,500.00

CORONET TYPE (NO MOTTO)

	VF	EF
1839	250.00	435.00
1839C	950.00	1,300.00
1839D	800.00	1,700.00
1840	225.00	350.00
1840C	700.00	1,650.00
1840D	700.00	1,500.00
1840O	325.00	700.00
1841	375.00	850.00
1841C	675.00	1,450.00
1841D	600.00	1,250.00
1841O		2 Known
1842 Small letters	300.00	1,300.00
1842 Large letters	700.00	2,000.00
1842C Small date	6,500.00	25,000.00
1842C Large date	750.00	1,500.00
1842D Small letters	650.00	1,250.00
1842D Large letters	2,250.00	6,000.00
1842O	1,000.00	5,000.00
1843	165.00	195.00
1843C	600.00	1,400.00
1843D	550.00	1,000.00
1843O Small letters	550.00	1,400.00
1843O Large letters	325.00	900.00
1844	180.00	250.00
1844C	725.00	2,700.00
1844D	550.00	1,050.00
1844O	225.00	600.00
1845	165.00	195.00
1845D	850.00	1,850.00

	F	VF
1845O	350.00	1,100.00
1846 Small date	200.00	325.00
1846	180.00	210.00
1846C	900.00	2,500.00
1846D	550.00	1,350.00
1846O	350.00	1,450.00
1847	165.00	195.00
1847C	575.00	1,450.00
1847D	500.00	1,100.00
1847O	2,300.00	10,500.00
1848	180.00	250.00
1848C	650.00	1,600.00
1848D	500.00	1,500.00
1849	180.00	300.00
1849C	500.00	1,100.00
1849D	700.00	1,350.00
1850	350.00	550.00
1850C	550.00	1,100.00
1850D	500.00	1,500.00
1851	165.00	200.00
1851C	600.00	1,100.00
1851D	525.00	1,375.00
1851O	650.00	1,500.00
1852	165.00	195.00
1852C	550.00	1,100.00
1852D	500.00	1,000.00
1853	180.00	210.00
1853C	525.00	1,000.00
1853D	500.00	900.00
1854	200.00	500.00
1854C	600.00	1,600.00
1854D	500.00	1,000.00
1854O	300.00	500.00
1854S		Extremely Rare
1855	200.00	250.00
1855C	625.00	1,750.00
1855D	600.00	1,500.00
1855O	700.00	2,900.00
1855S	425.00	1,100.00
1856	310.00	340.00
1856C	600.00	1,300.00
1856D	600.00	1,300.00
1856O	800.00	2,800.00
1856S	300.00	800.00
1857	200.00	250.00
1857C	600.00	1,300.00
1857D	600.00	1,250.00
1857O	700.00	2,000.00
1857S	300.00	700.00
1858	275.00	800.00
1858C	800.00	1,250.00
1858D	600.00	1,200.00
1858S	650.00	2,600.00
1859	275.00	600.00
1859C	525.00	1,400.00
1859D	725.00	2,000.00
1859S	1,250.00	4,750.00
1860	300.00	600.00
1860C	800.00	2,000.00
1860D	800.00	1,800.00
1860S	1,200.00	2,800.00
1861	165.00	195.00
1861C	1,500.00	3,400.00
1861D	4,000.00	7,000.00
1861S	1,100.00	4,500.00
1862	750.00	2,500.00
1862S	4,500.00	10,500.00
1863	1,150.00	3,450.00
1863S	1,200.00	4,750.00

	F	VF
1864	600.00	2,100.00
1864S	6,750.00	15,000.00
1865	1,200.00	3,150.00
1865S	1,200.00	3,600.00
1866S	1,600.00	6,000.00

CORONET TYPE (WITH MOTTO)

	F	VF
1866	725.00	1,800.00
1866S	1,350.00	4,500.00
1867	550.00	2,500.00
1867S	1,600.00	5,000.00
1868	650.00	1,800.00
1868S	500.00	2,400.00
1869	875.00	2,300.00
1869S	375.00	2,400.00
1870	700.00	2,800.00
1870CC	4,400.00	9,500.00
1870S	1,200.00	4,000.00
1871	875.00	2,150.00
1871CC	975.00	3,000.00
1871S	550.00	2,000.00
1872	750.00	2,000.00
1872CC	850.00	3,500.00
1872S	525.00	1,850.00
1873 Closed 3	225.00	250.00
1873 Open 3	225.00	250.00
1873CC	2,200.00	6,500.00
1873S	875.00	2,700.00
1874	625.00	2,200.00
1874CC	675.00	1,750.00
1874S	725.00	3,750.00
1875	45,000.00	55,000.00
1875CC	1,500.00	5,400.00
1875S	950.00	3,300.00
1876	1,000.00	2,600.00
1876CC	1,500.00	5,750.00
1876S	1,700.00	5,000.00
1877	800.00	2,400.00
1877CC	1,000.00	3,300.00
1877S	325.00	900.00
1878	165.00	225.00
1878CC	3,500.00	9,000.00
1878S	165.00	190.00
1879	165.00	175.00
1879CC	350.00	1,300.00
1879S	200.00	275.00
1880	165.00	175.00
1880CC	350.00	875.00
1880S	165.00	175.00
1881, 1 over 0	350.00	600.00
1881	165.00	175.00
1881CC	500.00	1,500.00
1881S	165.00	175.00
1882	165.00	175.00
1882CC	375.00	650.00
1882S	165.00	175.00
1883	165.00	175.00
1883CC	375.00	800.00
1883S	195.00	225.00
1884	150.00	175.00
1884CC	450.00	825.00
1884S	165.00	175.00

	F	VF
1885	165.00	175.00
1885S	165.00	175.00
1886	175.00	185.00
1886S	165.00	175.00
1887	Proof only	25,000.00
1887S	165.00	175.00
1888	175.00	250.00
1888S	190.00	275.00
1889	260.00	440.00
1890	250.00	400.00
1890CC	300.00	400.00
1891	165.00	235.00
1891CC	250.00	375.00
1892	165.00	175.00
1892CC	300.00	600.00
1892O	600.00	1,250.00
1892S	175.00	225.00
1893	165.00	185.00
1893CC	300.00	400.00
1893O	200.00	300.00
1893S	170.00	180.00
1894	165.00	185.00
1894O	195.00	350.00
1894S	275.00	350.00
1895	165.00	175.00
1895S	190.00	275.00
1896	175.00	185.00
1896S	225.00	275.00
1897	165.00	175.00
1897S	175.00	190.00
1898	165.00	175.00
1898S	165.00	175.00
1899	165.00	175.00
1899S	165.00	175.00
1900	165.00	175.00
1900S	175.00	200.00
1901	165.00	175.00
1901S, 1 over 0	170.00	200.00
1901S	165.00	175.00
1902	165.00	175.00
1902S	165.00	175.00
1903	165.00	175.00
1903S	165.00	175.00
1904	165.00	175.00
1904S	180.00	225.00
1905	165.00	175.00
1905S	165.00	175.00
1906	165.00	175.00
1906D	165.00	175.00
1906S	165.00	175.00
1907	165.00	175.00
1907D	165.00	175.00
1908	165.00	175.00

INDIAN HEAD TYPE

	VF	EF
1908	190.00	225.00
1908D	190.00	225.00
1908S	225.00	450.00
1909	190.00	225.00
1909D	190.00	225.00
1909O	600.00	900.00
1909S	215.00	235.00
1910	190.00	225.00
1910D	190.00	225.00
1910S	190.00	240.00
1911	190.00	225.00
1911D	350.00	475.00
1911S	190.00	240.00
1912	190.00	225.00
1912S	215.00	240.00
1913	190.00	225.00
1913S	250.00	270.00
1914	190.00	225.00
1914D	190.00	225.00
1914S	215.00	235.00
1915	190.00	225.00
1915S	300.00	325.00
1916S	190.00	250.00
1929	2,000.00	3,500.00

TEN DOLLAR GOLD PIECES

Among the first two American gold coins to be struck was the eagle or $10 gold piece in 1795. It was George Washington himself who received the first example. Its first obverse features a bust of Liberty by Robert Scot, wearing a tall conical cap, traditionally but inaccurately referred to by numismatists as a turban. Originally this was paired with a reverse design featuring a skinny eagle similar to that on the first silver dollars, but instead of standing within a wreath, it is seen holding one above its head. As with the other denominations this was replaced by a plumper heraldic eagle bearing a shield on its chest, which later was featured on all denominations other than copper. All these early eagles were struck on a primitive screw press with hand engraved dies, no two of which were identical. Many will show evidence of adjustment marks, a scraping of metal from the blank before striking to prevent the coin from being overweight. While not desirable, they are not considered damage, as they are part of the manufacturing process.

The initial issue of 1795-1804 was plagued by mass meltings and wholesale export, and were undervalued relative to its gold content, particularly by European standards. As a result, its coinage was completely suspended for more than thirty years. It was reintroduced in 1838 on the reduced gold standard adopted in 1834 to prevent these abuses. The new gold eagle featured a Liberty head wearing a coronet, being Christian Gobrecht's interpretation of a painting of Venus by Benjamin West. A new, more realistic reverse eagle still wore a heraldic shield. This design was used until 1907, with the motto taking the place of the eagle in 1866.

In 1908, as part of the same coin design beautification trend which introduced later the Walking Liberty half dollar and Mercury dime, noted sculptor Augustus St. Gaudens was asked to prepare new designs for the eagle and double eagle by President Theodore Roosevelt. His work showed the head of Lib-

erty wearing an Indian war bonnet. The headdress was added to St. Gauden's head, which was originally designed as Victory at the President's instruction. The reverse featured a very proud eagle with closed wings.

Because Roosevelt believed that using the motto "In God We Trust" on coinage debased the divine name, it was omitted from the initial issues. This upset Congress so much that a law was enacted that replaced it in 1908.

Known counterfeits: 1799, 1858 (altered), 1889 (altered from Ps), 1901S, 1906D, 1907, 1908 with Motto Proof, 1908S, 1909 Matte Proof, 1909S, 1910 Proof, 1910S, 1911 Proof, 1911D, 1911S, 1912S, 1913, 1913S, 1914S, 1915S, 1916S, 1926, 1932, 1933, among others especially 1870 to 1933. Be cautious of false C mintmarks altered by cutting down an authentic O mintmark. Beware of traces of solder on earlier coins from being used as jewelry. Look for interruption in the pattern of edge reeding. Be cautious of cleaned coins. This is harder to detect on gold, which usually does not tone naturally.

Type Coin Price Range   VG to MS-63

1795-1797	4,500.00 to 79,000.00
1797-1804	2,000.00 to 22,500.00
1838-1866	200.00 to 11,500.00
1866-1908	190.00 to 700.00
1907-1908	200.00 to 1,750.00
1908-1933	180.00 to 750.00

TURBAN BUST / SMALL EAGLE

	F	VF
1795, 9 leaves below eagle	17,000.00	35,000.00
1795, 13 leaves	6,000.00	8,500.00
1796	6,000.00	9,500.00
1797	7,500.00	12,500.00

TURBAN BUST / HERALDIC EAGLE

	F	VF
1797	2,500.00	3,500.00
1798/97, 9 stars l., 4 r.	4,500.00	7,500.00
1798/97, 7 stars l., 6 r.	10,000.00	22,000.00
1799	2,400.00	3,000.00
1800	2,400.00	3,250.00
1803	2,400.00	3,000.00
1804	3,750.00	4,200.00

CORONET TYPE (NO MOTTO)

	VF	EF
1838	1,175.00	2,900.00
1839 Large letters	1,175.00	1,950.00
1839 Small letters	1,600.00	5,500.00
1840	425.00	750.00
1841	415.00	650.00
1841O	2,450.00	5,400.00
1842 Small date	425.00	1,200.00
1842 Large date	415.00	750.00
1842O	395.00	700.00
1843	415.00	700.00
1843O	415.00	600.00
1844	1,300.00	2,900.00
1844O	425.00	600.00
1845	750.00	950.00
1845O	490.00	625.00
1846	900.00	1,275.00
1846O	490.00	975.00
1847	295.00	325.00
1847O	300.00	400.00
1848	350.00	400.00
1848O	600.00	1,400.00
1849	295.00	360.00
1849O	800.00	3,000.00
1850 Large date	295.00	325.00
1850 Small date	575.00	1,500.00
1850O	400.00	600.00
1851	325.00	525.00
1851O	300.00	550.00
1852	425.00	525.00
1852O	700.00	1,200.00
1853, 3 over 2	475.00	950.00
1853	295.00	800.00
1853O	400.00	575.00
1854	400.00	700.00
1854O Small date	400.00	1,000.00

	VF	EF
1854O Large date	600.00	2,250.00
1854S	300.00	575.00
1855	295.00	325.00
1855O	600.00	2,000.00
1855S	1,900.00	4,250.00
1856	330.00	360.00
1856O	600.00	2,000.00
1856S	380.00	625.00
1857	380.00	1,000.00
1857O	1,000.00	2,000.00
1857S	525.00	800.00
1858	5,000.00	8,000.00
1858O	380.00	850.00
1858S	2,150.00	3,250.00
1859	380.00	825.00
1859O	3,500.00	9,000.00
1859S	2,000.00	4,500.00
1860	380.00	800.00
1860O	575.00	1,000.00
1860S	2,700.00	6,000.00
1861	295.00	325.00
1861S	1,900.00	2,750.00
1862	475.00	1,000.00
1862S	1,950.00	3,000.00
1863	3,650.00	9,000.00
1863S	1,700.00	3,500.00
1864	1,900.00	3,000.00
1864S	5,800.00	11,500.00
1865	2,150.00	3,500.00
1865S	5,000.00	14,500.00
1865S, 865 over inverted 186	2,500.00	6,000.00
1866S	3,000.00	3,600.00

CORONET TYPE (WITH MOTTO)

	VF	EF
1866	750.00	3,000.00
1866S	1,750.00	3,900.00
1867	1,750.00	4,500.00
1867S	2,600.00	8,500.00
1868	600.00	1,800.00
1868S	1,250.00	2,000.00
1869	1,750.00	3,000.00
1869S	1,800.00	3,200.00
1870	750.00	1,450.00
1870CC	7,000.00	19,000.00
1870S	2,000.00	3,250.00
1871	1,600.00	2,875.00
1871CC	2,250.00	6,000.00
1871S	1,750.00	4,700.00
1872	2,500.00	3,900.00
1872CC	2,500.00	10,000.00
1872S	530.00	1,000.00
1873	4,200.00	14,000.00
1873CC	2,700.00	12,000.00
1873S	1,600.00	5,000.00
1874	300.00	350.00
1874CC	875.00	2,900.00
1874S	1,700.00	3,375.00

	VF	EF
1875	36,000.00	47,000.00
1875CC	3,500.00	9,000.00
1876	3,000.00	6,750.00
1876CC	3,000.00	10,000.00
1876S	2,100.00	4,000.00
1877	3,500.00	9,000.00
1877CC	2,400.00	4,550.00
1877S	500.00	6,750.00
1878	280.00	350.00
1878CC	3,500.00	8,000.00
1878S	450.00	715.00
1879	280.00	290.00
1879CC	5,000.00	12,500.00
1879O	2,200.00	3,800.00
1879S	310.00	360.00
1880	280.00	290.00
1880CC	425.00	675.00
1880O	400.00	600.00
1880S	280.00	290.00
1881	280.00	290.00
1881CC	400.00	550.00
1881O	400.00	875.00
1881S	280.00	290.00
1882	280.00	290.00
1882CC	475.00	1,800.00
1882O	400.00	850.00
1882S	280.00	290.00
1883	280.00	290.00
1883CC	400.00	850.00
1883O	3,200.00	8,500.00
1883S	295.00	375.00
1884	280.00	290.00
1884CC	525.00	1,300.00
1884S	280.00	290.00
1885	280.00	290.00
1885S	280.00	290.00
1886	280.00	290.00
1886S	280.00	290.00
1887	300.00	310.00
1887S	280.00	290.00
1888	300.00	325.00
1888O	280.00	290.00
1888S	280.00	290.00
1889	400.00	500.00
1889S	280.00	290.00
1890	300.00	315.00
1890CC	375.00	450.00
1891	280.00	290.00
1891CC	300.00	350.00
1892	280.00	290.00
1892CC	300.00	310.00
1892O	280.00	290.00
1892S	300.00	310.00
1893	280.00	290.00
1893CC	380.00	600.00
1893O	280.00	290.00
1893S	300.00	310.00
1894	280.00	290.00
1894O	280.00	290.00
1894S	300.00	475.00
1895	280.00	300.00
1895O	280.00	290.00
1895S	280.00	400.00
1896	280.00	290.00
1896S	280.00	350.00
1897	280.00	290.00
1897O	280.00	290.00
1897S	280.00	325.00
1898	280.00	290.00

	VF	EF
1898S	280.00	290.00
1899	280.00	290.00
1899O	300.00	315.00
1899S	280.00	290.00
1900	280.00	290.00
1900S	300.00	330.00
1901	280.00	290.00
1901O	300.00	325.00
1901S	280.00	290.00
1902	280.00	290.00
1902S	280.00	290.00
1903	280.00	310.00
1903O	280.00	290.00
1903S	280.00	290.00
1904	280.00	290.00
1904O	280.00	290.00
1905	280.00	290.00
1905S	280.00	350.00
1906	280.00	290.00
1906D	280.00	290.00
1906O	280.00	310.00
1906S	280.00	290.00
1907	280.00	290.00
1907D	280.00	290.00
1907S	280.00	310.00

INDIAN HEAD / NO MOTTO

	VF	EF
1907 Wire rim, periods		4,500.00
1907 Rounded rim, periods		12,500.00
1907 No periods	330.00	450.00
1908	480.00	525.00
1908D	430.00	440.00

INDIAN HEAD / WITH MOTTO

	VF	EF
1908	290.00	300.00
1908D	290.00	300.00
1908S	290.00	300.00
1909	290.00	300.00
1909D	290.00	300.00
1909S	290.00	300.00
1910	290.00	300.00
1910D	290.00	300.00
1910S	290.00	300.00
1911	290.00	300.00
1911D	290.00	550.00
1911S	290.00	460.00
1912	290.00	300.00
1912S	290.00	300.00
1913	290.00	300.00
1913S	290.00	650.00

1914	290.00	300.00
1914D	290.00	300.00
1914S	290.00	300.00
1915	290.00	300.00
1915S	290.00	300.00
1916S	290.00	385.00
1920S	6,500.00	7,500.00
1926	290.00	300.00
1930S	3,500.00	5,000.00
1932	290.00	300.00
1933	MS-63	264,000.00

TWENTY DOLLAR GOLD PIECES

The California Gold Rush of the 1840s resulted in large quantities of bullion being received at the mint for coinage. Partly to make this massive coinage more expedient and partly because of the obvious convenience of using fewer coins for large international payments, the bill proposing the introduction of gold dollars was amended to include a large $20 gold piece called a "double eagle." James B. Longacre engraved a bust of Liberty wearing a coronet similar to, but of much more refined style than, the one in use on smaller gold since 1838. A facing heraldic eagle with a circlet of stars and a radiant arc above graced the reverse, the two motto ribbons at its sides suggesting the denomination of two eagles. This design continued to be used beginning in 1907, and the motto was replaced with the circlet over the eagle in 1866. Two other minor modifications were attempted. The first (1861), called the Paquet reverse, is a subtle rearrangement of details, and for technical reasons was abandoned almost immediately. The other was the replacement in 1877 of the abbreviation D. with the word dollars.

In 1908, as part of the same coin design beautification trend which introduced later the Walking Liberty half dollar and Mercury dime, noted sculptor Augustus St. Gaudens was asked by President Theodore Roosevelt to prepare new designs for the double eagle and eagle. His work showed a full figure of Liberty, holding a torch and olive branch, striding toward the viewer. It is very much inspired by Hellenistic sculpture, as correspondence between the two men clearly confirms. The reverse featured an eagle in mid-flight with a rising sun and rays in the background.

As Roosevelt didn't believe in using the motto "In God We Trust" on coinage, it was omitted from the initial issues. This upset Congress so much that a law was enacted to replace it in 1908. To avoid public confusion, the date was changed from Roman numerals to Arabic ones, and because the initial design was of such high relief that it took three strikes by the dies, its relief was lowered as well.

Both the Liberty type and the Saint Gaudens type are often found with heavy bag marks due to their soft metal and heavy weight. Examples virtually free from bagging command a substantial premium.

Known counterfeits: 1879, 1879O, 1881 (altered), 1882 (altered), 1887 (altered), 1891, 1894, 1897S, 1899S, 1900, 1900S, 1901S, 1903, 1903S, 1904, 1904S, 1906, 1906S, MCMVII, 1907 (Saint-Gaudens), 1908, 1911D, 1919, 1920, 1921, 1924, 1925, 1926, 1927, 1927D (altered), 1928, among others especially 1870 to 1932. This series generally has been extensively counterfeited so be cautious. Beware of traces of solder on earlier coins from use as jewelry. Look for interruption in the pattern of edge reeding. Be cautious of cleaned coins. This is harder to detect on gold which usually does not tone naturally.

Type Coin Price Range	F to MS-63
1849-1866	475.00 to 7,800.00
1866-1876	400.00 to 7,800.00
1877-1907	400.00 to 650.00
1907-1908	400.00 to 635.00
1908-1933	400.00 to 575.00

LIBERTY HEAD - TYPE I

	VF	EF
1849		Unique
1850	600.00	625.00
1850O	780.00	1,250.00
1851	600.00	625.00
1851O	715.00	810.00
1852	600.00	625.00
1852O	685.00	815.00
1853, 3 over 2	650.00	1,500.00
1853	600.00	625.00
1853O	700.00	1,000.00
1854	600.00	625.00
1854O	17,500.00	52,000.00
1854S	700.00	880.00
1855	600.00	625.00
1855O	3,000.00	6,000.00
1855S	600.00	625.00
1856	600.00	715.00
1856O	19,000.00	30,000.00
1856S	600.00	625.00
1857	600.00	625.00
1857O	1,075.00	1,850.00
1857S	600.00	625.00
1858	835.00	1,075.00
1858O	1,175.00	1,950.00
1858S	600.00	625.00

	VF	EF
1859	975.00	2,600.00
1859O	3,150.00	6,800.00
1859S	600.00	625.00
1860	600.00	625.00
1860O	3,450.00	6,250.00
1860S	600.00	625.00
1861	600.00	625.00
1861O	1,500.00	3,550.00

Most of these were struck by Louisiana and the Confederacy after withdrawal from the Union.

	VF	EF
1861S	600.00	625.00
1861 Paquet rev.	Proof-67	660,000.00
1861S Paquet rev.	5,850.00	11,000.00
1862	910.00	1,600.00
1862S	600.00	625.00
1863	600.00	750.00
1863S	600.00	625.00
1864	600.00	950.00
1864S	600.00	625.00
1865	600.00	700.00
1865S	600.00	700.00
1866S	1,850.00	3,750.00

LIBERTY HEAD (WITH MOTTO) - TYPE II

	VF	EF
1866	685.00	780.00
1866S	665.00	850.00
1867	625.00	650.00
1867S	615.00	650.00
1868	850.00	1,125.00
1868S	625.00	675.00
1869	725.00	810.00
1869S	625.00	665.00
1870	775.00	885.00
1870CC	35,000.00	65,000.00
1870S	625.00	640.00
1871	750.00	910.00
1871CC	3,000.00	4,700.00
1871S	625.00	665.00
1872	625.00	650.00
1872CC	1,150.00	1,500.00
1872S	560.00	575.00
1873 Closed 3	625.00	750.00
1873 Open 3	560.00	575.00
1873CC	850.00	1,700.00
1873S	625.00	650.00
1874	625.00	650.00
1874CC	685.00	780.00
1874S	560.00	575.00

	VF	EF
1875	560.00	575.00
1875CC	665.00	780.00
1875S	560.00	575.00
1876	560.00	575.00
1876CC	690.00	775.00
1876S	560.00	575.00

LIBERTY HEAD - TYPE III

	VF	EF
1877	595.00	600.00
1877CC	730.00	975.00
1877S	485.00	595.00
1878	585.00	600.00
1878CC	975.00	1,300.00
1878S	485.00	585.00
1879	650.00	665.00
1879CC	1,050.00	1,650.00
1879O	3,250.00	4,700.00
1879S	485.00	585.00
1880	485.00	600.00
1880S	485.00	625.00
1881	4,050.00	6,800.00
1881S	485.00	585.00
1882	7,800.00	15,000.00
1882CC	730.00	780.00
1882S	485.00	580.00
1883	Proof only	40,000.00
1883CC	715.00	775.00
1883S	485.00	580.00
1884	Proof only	71,000.00
1884CC	650.00	775.00
1884S	485.00	580.00
1885	7,400.00	9,100.00
1885CC	1,025.00	1,600.00
1885S	485.00	585.00
1886	8,800.00	11,000.00
1887	Proof only	30,000.00
1887S	485.00	585.00
1888	485.00	575.00
1888S	485.00	490.00
1889	575.00	600.00
1889CC	795.00	875.00
1889S	485.00	490.00
1890	540.00	550.00
1890CC	675.00	775.00
1890S	485.00	490.00
1891	3,600.00	5,500.00
1891CC	1,900.00	2,900.00
1891S	485.00	490.00
1892	1,200.00	1,600.00

	VF	EF
1892CC	745.00	810.00
1892S	485.00	490.00
1893	485.00	490.00
1893CC	815.00	875.00
1893S	485.00	490.00
1894	485.00	490.00
1894S	485.00	490.00
1895	485.00	490.00
1895S	485.00	490.00
1896	485.00	490.00
1896S	485.00	490.00
1897	485.00	490.00
1897S	485.00	490.00
1898	485.00	490.00
1898S	485.00	490.00
1899	485.00	490.00
1899S	485.00	490.00
1900	485.00	490.00
1900S	485.00	490.00
1901	485.00	490.00
1901S	485.00	625.00
1902	485.00	485.00
1902S	485.00	490.00
1903	485.00	490.00
1903S	485.00	490.00
1904	485.00	490.00
1904S	485.00	490.00
1905	485.00	620.00
1905S	520.00	575.00
1906	585.00	600.00
1906D	485.00	490.00
1906S	485.00	490.00
1907	485.00	490.00
1907D	485.00	490.00
1907S	485.00	490.00

SAINT-GAUDENS / NO MOTTO

	VF	EF
1907 High relief, wire rim	2,500.00	4,000.00
1907 High relief, flat rim	3,000.00	4,200.00
1907 Arabic numerals	500.00	615.00
1908	495.00	525.00
1908D	500.00	595.00

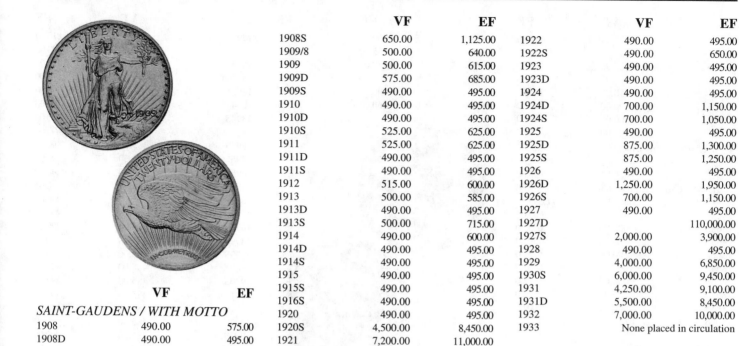

SAINT-GAUDENS / WITH MOTTO

	VF	EF
1908	490.00	575.00
1908D	490.00	495.00

	VF	EF		VF	EF
1908S	650.00	1,125.00	1922	490.00	495.00
1909/8	500.00	640.00	1922S	490.00	650.00
1909	500.00	615.00	1923	490.00	495.00
1909D	575.00	685.00	1923D	490.00	495.00
1909S	490.00	495.00	1924	490.00	495.00
1910	490.00	495.00	1924D	700.00	1,150.00
1910D	490.00	495.00	1924S	700.00	1,050.00
1910S	525.00	625.00	1925	490.00	495.00
1911	525.00	625.00	1925D	875.00	1,300.00
1911D	490.00	495.00	1925S	875.00	1,250.00
1911S	490.00	495.00	1926	490.00	495.00
1912	515.00	600.00	1926D	1,250.00	1,950.00
1913	500.00	585.00	1926S	700.00	1,150.00
1913D	490.00	495.00	1927	490.00	495.00
1913S	500.00	715.00	1927D		110,000.00
1914	490.00	600.00	1927S	2,000.00	3,900.00
1914D	490.00	495.00	1928	490.00	495.00
1914S	490.00	495.00	1929	4,000.00	6,850.00
1915	490.00	495.00	1930S	6,000.00	9,450.00
1915S	490.00	495.00	1931	4,250.00	9,100.00
1916S	490.00	495.00	1931D	5,500.00	8,450.00
1920	490.00	495.00	1932	7,000.00	10,000.00
1920S	4,500.00	8,450.00	1933	None placed in circulation	
1921	7,200.00	11,000.00			

COMMEMORATIVE COINAGE

From the beginning of Federal coinage in 1792 until a century later in 1892, there was no such thing as commemorative coins. Then came a celebration of world class proportions. The World's Colombian Exposition, or what we would today call the 1892-93 World's Fair, gave America its first chance to show the entire world that it could put on an exposition equal to its European counterparts. It was a matter of national pride, and for the first time, a specific event was noted on United States coinage. The exposition's success was considered so important in the eyes of the government that two special coins were struck and sold at over their face value in order to subsidize the construction and operation of the exposition site. America's otherwise mundane coinage had taken a new and innovative turn, and it provided a proud manifestation for the nation's medallic artists. It also served the collectors, whose numbers had grown steadily with the development of America's middle class. (It is no coincidence that these were the days of the A.N.A.'s birth as well.) During the next forty years, commemorative half dollars — usually sold at a premium as fund raisers for civic causes — became a normal part of the nation's coinage. Commemoratives were struck in gold as well, and between the two metals the mint produced commemorative coins at a rate of slightly less than one per year. By 1934, these issues had become little more than pork for congressmen and special interests. In the short span of five years—from 1934 to 1938, forty-three different commemorative half dollars were issued. Many collectors considered it a national scandal, and a debasement of the dignity of the coinage. Clearly they were not alone, as the flow of commemoratives trickled off to one or two per year, and after 1954, the series ended. It took the Bicentennial of American Independence to embolden anyone to approve commemoratives again.

Commemorative coins of this early period are often more available in uncirculated than circulated grades. This is primarily due to the surcharges the original purchasers were required to pay. Sometimes they are even available in their original packaging. These boxes or envelopes can add anywhere from a dollar to a hundred dollars to the value of the coin.

Because many of these coins were held by laymen who prized them but had little numismatic knowledge, many have been cleaned. One telltale sign is very fine striations. Cleaned specimens are worth less than the prices quoted. The lowest grade in which these are usually collected is XF. Lower grades are often not considered collectible at all.

The following silver commemorative coins are all half dollars, except for the Isabella quarter and the Lafayette dollar. Despite the historical logic of chronological listing, it has long been traditional to sequence the earlier series U.S. commemorative coins alphabetically. This provides for quick reference, and is the way they are listed here:

ISABELLA QUARTER

	AU	MS-60
1893	215.00	225.00

Struck to raise funds for the Board of Lady Managers of the World's Colombian Exposition, it depicts Queen Isabella and a kneeling woman holding distaff and spindle, emblematic of woman's industry. Its issue was instigated by Susan B.. Anthony.

ALABAMA CENTENIAL

	AU	MS-60
1921, with 2x2	145.00	275.00
1921, no 2x2	80.00	195.00

This was the first U.S. coin to bear the portrait of a living person. Depicted are Alabama's first governor, William W. Bibb, and then governor, Thomas E. Kilby. Struck to raise money for the Alabama Centennial Commission two years after the centennial.

ALBANY, NEW YORK

1936	175.00	190.00

Struck to celebrate the 250th anniversary of Albany's city charter. The obverse depicts a beaver, the basis for the city's 17th century economy. The reverse shows the colonial governor of New York and the city's two founders.

Known counterfeits: Some counterfeits have been sold as proofs.

ANTIETAM

1937	390.00	400.00

Struck for sale at the commemoration of the 75th anniversary of the Civil War Battle of Antietam. They depict Union General George McClellan and Confederate General Robert E. Lee. Offered at $1.65 each, most went unsold and were melted.

Known counterfeits: Some are known in high grade.

ARKANSAS CENTENNIAL

	AU	MS-60
1935	54.00	57.00
1935D	60.00	75.00
1935S	60.00	75.00
1936	50.00	60.00
1936D	60.00	75.00
1936S	60.00	75.00
1937	60.00	70.00
1937D	60.00	75.00
1937S	60.00	75.00
1938	75.00	105.00
1938D	75.00	105.00

	AU	MS-60
1938S	75.00	105.00
1939	115.00	190.00
1939D	115.00	195.00
1939S	115.00	195.00

These were struck for the Arkansas Centennial Commission, which originally sold the 1935 Philadelphia for $1 each. Other issues were sold in their entirety to dealers at such high prices that the public outcry stimulated Congress to end the entire commemorative program. Another coin for the same purpose was the Robinson-Arkansas half.

BAY BRIDGE

	AU	MS-60
1936S	80.00	90.00

Not only were these coins struck to commemorate the opening of a world-class bridge from San Francisco to Oakland, they could actually be purchased by motorists at that bridge without even getting out of their cars. The Grizzly bear on the obverse was actually a San Francisco resident. The reverse view of the bridge is from the San Francisco side.

DANIEL BOONE

	AU	MS-60
1934	57.00	65.00
1935	60.00	70.00
1935D	65.00	75.00
1935S	65.00	75.00
1935 w/"1934"	100.00	120.00
1935D w/"1934"	150.00	230.00
1935S w/"1934"	150.00	230.00

	AU	MS-60
1936	60.00	70.00
1936D	65.00	75.00
1936S	65.00	75.00
1937	90.00	120.00
1937D	95.00	230.00
1937S	95.00	230.00
1938	210.00	250.00
1938D	210.00	250.00
1938S	210.00	250.00

Originally made to raise money to restore historic sites, this issue was characterized by high handed marketing tactics. The distribution price increased consistently and the Commissioner responsible for their issue falsely announced the 1937 issue as the final year to promote sales.

BRIDGEPORT, CONNECTICUT

	AU	MS-60
1936	85.00	90.00

The world's most famous circus promoter and former Bridgeport mayor, P.T. Barnum, was featured on a half commemorating the 100th anniversary of Bridgeport, Connecticut's incorporation as a city. Sold at $2 each, they were distributed rather equitably, and were available locally through official channels for forty years! Many have said that the eagle on the reverse, when inverted, resembles a shark. Original boxes are common.

CALIFORNIA DIAMOND JUBILEE

	AU	MS-60
1925S	85.00	100.00

This attractive half depicts a "Forty-Niner" panning for gold, with a ferocious grizzly bear on the reverse. It celebrates the 75th anniversary of California statehood.

CARVER - WASHINGTON

	AU	MS-60
1951	9.00	11.00
1951D	12.00	30.00
1951S	12.00	30.00
1952	10.00	12.00
1952D	12.00	30.00
1952S	12.00	30.00
1953	12.00	30.00
1953D	12.00	30.00
1953S	10.00	12.00
1954	12.00	30.00
1954D	12.00	30.00
1954S	10.00	10.00

The original legislation pushed this coin "to oppose the spread of communism among Negroes in the interest of National Defense," but this was just to hook the McCarthy-ites into passing the bill. In reality it was to help pay off the debts of S.J.Phillips, marketer of the Booker T. Washington half. The reverse design is a replacement for one rejected by the State Department. Many actually saw circulation.

CINCINNATI MUSIC CENTER

	AU	MS-60
1936	195.00	210.00
1936D	195.00	210.00
1936S	195.00	210.00

This coin was made for the 50th anniversary of nothing! It was struck almost exclusively for coin dealer Thomas Melish, who worked with promoters to drive up the price per set from $7.75 to $75 within months. The 1886 date noted on the coin has not been found to have any historical relevance. However, Stephen Foster, composer of "Oh! Susannah," whose bust appears, did live in Cincinnati.
Known counterfeits: Dangerous casts exist.

CLEVELAND - GREAT LAKES

1936	54.00	57.00

While this coin was legitimately struck for the Great Lakes Exposition at which some were sold, most of them, like the Cincinnati half, fell to the control of coin dealer Thomas Melish who contrived their issue. The Exposition coincided with Cleveland's 100th anniversary, and its founder, Gen. Moses Cleveland is portrayed.

COLUMBIA, SOUTH CAROLINA

1936	140.00	150.00
1936D	140.00	150.00
1936S	140.00	150.00

These were struck for the March 1936 festivities in celebration of Columbia's 150th anniversary as capital of South Carolina. Unfortunately they arrived in October. The figure depicted is that of Justice. The tree on the reverse is a palmetto.

COLUMBIAN EXPOSITION

	AU	MS-60
1892	12.00	24.00
1893	12.00	24.00

This is the first United States commemorative coin. It was struck to help raise funds for the 1892-93 World's Colombian Exposition held in celebration of the 400th anniversary of Columbus's voyage of discovery. The obverse portrait is a conjectural one of Christopher Columbus, and the reverse shows his ship the Santa Maria. While initially sold to fair-goers at a premium, too many were ordered and a great many of them later entered circulation at face value.

CONNECTICUT TERCENTENARY

1935	155.00	170.00

Struck to subsidize the statewide celebrations of Connecticut's 300th anniversary,

this coin depicts the Charter Oak, where the colonists hid their royal charter from a governor who sought to revoke it The distribution of this coin was notably fair, and many went to non-collectors.
Known counterfeits: Multiple examples reported.

DELAWARE TERCENTENARY

1936	175.00	195.00

Struck to commemorate the landing of Swedish settlers in Delaware in 1638, this coin features Old Swedes Church (1699), as well as the ship that brought the first settlers.

ELGIN, ILLINOIS

	AU	MS-60.
1936	150.00	155.00

This coin was struck to help pay for construction of the statue *Pioneer Memorial* by Trygve Rovelstad, the same sculptor who designed the coin, The statue itself, never completed, is seen on the reverse. The obverse is the head of a typical pioneer of the 1830s. The date 1673 is incorrect.

BATTLE OF GETTYSBURG

| 1936 | 230.00 | 245.00 |

Struck to commemorate the 75th anniversary of the Battle of Gettysburg, as well as the coinciding Blue and Gray Reunion, this coin displays a gathering of Civil War veterans on the field of battle.

GRANT MEMORIAL

| 1922 star in r. Field | 620.00 | 910.00 |
| 1922 no star | 63.00 | 80.00 |

This coin was struck in celebration of the 100th anniversary of Grant's birth. A Mathew Brady photograph formed the basis for Laura Gardin Fraser's bust of Grant used on both the half dollar and the gold dollar. The proceeds from this coin were supposed to fund the construction of four museum buildings and a highway. None were ever built. A minority of these have an incuse star in the obverse field.

Known counterfeits: Some plain-field Grant halves have been altered by punching a false star in the field. On these a corresponding flat spot may show on the reverse.

HAWAII SESQUICENTENNIAL

	AU	MS-60
1928	1,000.00	1,200.00

Struck for the 150th anniversary of Capt. Cook's discovery of Hawaii, his bust is featured on the obverse. While the warrior chief on the reverse is not technically King Kamehameha I, it is based on a statue of him. This is one of the scarcest commemorative-type coins. It was distributed almost exclusively in Hawaii at $2 each.

Known counterfeits: Counterfeits are a serious problem for this issue.

HUDSON, NEW YORK

| 1935 | 400.00 | 450.00 |

The 150th Anniversary of Hundson, New York, was not an event of national importance, but in 1935 it was reason enough to create a commemorative half dollar. Even worse, after one coin dealer was given permission to purchase 75 percent of them before they were released, only 2,500 remained for the general public to buy at $1 each. The designs are Hudson's ship and the city's seal.

Known counterfeits: Both regular strikes and matte proofs have been counterfeited.

HUGUENOT-WALLOON TERCENTENARY

| 1924 | 68.00 | 80.00 |

This coin was struck to commemorate the 300th anniversary of Protestant settlement in America and the founding of New Netherlands—or today's new York. The ship Nieuw Nederlandt is on the reverse, while the obverse shows Adm. Coligny and William the Silent, two 16th century Protestant martyrs. More than one-third are reported to have entered general circulation.

ILLINOIS STATEHOOD

| 1918 | 61.00 | 80.00 |

Struck to finance the celebration of Illinois's 100th anniversary of statehood, a statue of a beardless Lincoln depicted on the coin was unveiled at the celebrations. Many were spent.

IOWA STATEHOOD

| 1946 | 55.00 | 61.00 |

Struck to celebrate Iowa's 100th anniversary as a state, Iowa residents were allowed to purchase them at $2.50, others at $3. The design is the state seal and the Old Stone Capitol in Iowa City. Specimens are often riddled with bag marks.

LEXINGTON-CONCORD

	AU	MS-60
1925	49.00	61.00

This coin commemorates the beginning of the Revolutionary War in 1775. The obverse depicts an 1875 statue of a Minuteman, the reverse the Old Belfry, which called them to arms. The original wooden box of this coin is among the most common original holders.

LONG ISLAND TERCENTENARY

| 1936 | 58.00 | 65.00 |

Struck to commemorate the 300th anniversary of Dutch settlement on Long Island, this coin shoes a Dutch settler and Algonquin Indian, with a 17th century ship on the reverse. Unlike some 1930s commemoratives, this coin was very fairly distributed to the public through Long Island's local banks. Bag marks are a particular problem.

LYNCHBURG, VIRGINIA

	AU	MS-60
1936	135.00	150.00

This coin was struck in recognition of the "150th Birthday" of Lynchburg, Virginia. Sen. Carter Glass, who was alive at the time, is depicted. Liberty is on the reverse. Glass was the founder of the FDIC.

MAINE CENTENNIAL

| 1920 | 68.00 | 80.00 |

This half showing the Maine arms honored the centennial of its admission as a state. It was, unlike most halves, distributed by the state treasurer, and was very popular with the public.
Known counterfeits: Those of proof have been seen.

MARYLAND TERCENTENARY

| 1934 | 95.00 | 110.00 |

Subsidizing the 300th anniversary celebration of Maryland's settlement, this half portrays Cecil Calvert, Lord Baltimore, showing his full arms on the reverse. It was well distributed and fairly popular at the time.
Known counterfeits: There are many false matte proofs that were modified from authentic regular issues.

MISSOURI CENTENNIAL

| 1921, 2★4 in field | 340.00 | 460.00 |
| 1921, no 2★4 | 210.00 | 400.00 |

This coin was struck a year too late to finance the Missouri Centennial Exposition, and also a year after the statehood centennial. The portrait is that of Daniel Boone, who helped settle Missouri. The 2´4 in the field of some of them indicates that it is the 24th state. On early strikes it is incuse, not in relief.
Known counterfeits: Type with plain field.

MONROE DOCTRINE

	AU	MS-60
1923S	27.00	36.00

This coin, allegedly to commemorate the Monroe Doctrine, was instigated by promoters of a film industry exposition; hence, "Los Angeles" is on the reverse. The continents shown are formed of two allegorical figures. John Quincy Adams is shown with Monroe because Adams actually wrote this policy against European intervention in the Americas. Most of these ended up in circulation.
Known counterfeits: Actual counterfeits are not common, but cleaned or AU coins often pass for MS-60.

NEW ROCHELLE, NEW YORK

	AU	MS-60
1938	230.00	245.00

This coin was made for the 250th anniversary of the settlement of New Rochelle, New York, by Huguenots from La Rochelle, France. They owed John Pell, from whom they obtained their land "one fat calf" every June 24th. Pell received it is depicted.
Known counterfeits: Matte proofs.

NORFOLK, VIRGINIA

	AU	MS-60
1936	310.00	330.00

Despite the 1936 date of the celebration of Norfolk's anniversary, the legislation allowing for this coin was not even passed by Congress until 1937. The Royal Mace depicted was presented to the city in 1753.

OREGON TRAIL MEMORIAL

1926	80.00	90.00
1926S	80.00	95.00
1928	140.00	155.00
1933D	215.00	230.00
1934D	120.00	140.00
1936	95.00	110.00
1936S	110.00	120.00
1937D	115.00	130.00
1938	110.00	130.00
1938D	110.00	130.00
1938S	110.00	130.00
1939	300.00	350.00
1939D	300.00	350.00
1939S	300.00	350.00

This was struck to finance the Oregon Trail Memorial Association's placement of landmarks along the historic route west. The reason this issue was divided between various mints and dates, instead of one large production run, was the OTMA's realization that it would force collectors to buy many coins instead of one or two coins to have a complete set.

PANAMA PACIFIC EXPOSITION

	AU	MS-60
1915S	180.00	300.00

Struck for San Francisco's celebration of the opening of the Panama Canal, this coin sold individually at $1 each, and as part of five-piece sets with four gold commemoratives (or in ten-piece double sets). The original copper frames are valuable.
Known counterfeits: Some exist with less distinct details.

PILGRIM TERCENTENARY

1920	46.00	61.00
1921	85.00	105.00

Struck to honor the 300th anniversary of the Pilgrims' landing at Plymouth Rock. The bust is a hypothetical one of Gov. William Bradford. The reverse ship represents the Mayflower. The 1921 issue is scarcer as many were melted.
Known counterfeits: Reported, not verified.

RHODE ISLAND TERCENTENARY

	AU	MS-60
1936	55.00	63.00
1936D	60.00	68.00
1936S	60.00	68.00

For the 300th anniversary of the founding of Rhode Island by Roger Williams, the obverse and reverse are adaptations of the Providence and Rhode Island arms respectively. Most went to Rhode Island Hospital National Bank and to Grant's Hobby Shop, with far fewer distributed nationally.

ROANOKE ISLAND, NORTH CAROLINA

1937	140.00	155.00

This coin was struck to honor the 1587 settlement founded by Sir Walter Raleigh, and the birth of the first European child in the New World.

ROBINSON - ARKANSAS

1936	68.00	73.00

The Arkansas Centennial Commission decided that if there were more varieties of its coins it would sell more, so it got approval to replace the allegorical portraits on its half with one of the still-living Sen. Joseph Robinson of Arkansas, who was then the Senate Majority Leader! The entire publicly available mintage was handled by the numismatic firm of Stack's who offered them at $1.85 each.

SAN DIEGO CALIFORNIA PACIFIC EXPOSITION

	AU	MS-60
1935S	49.00	55.00
1936D	54.00	58.00

Struck to promote the World's Fair in San Diego, the original 1935 quantities did not sell well to attendees, so they were shipped back to the mint, melted and restruck with a 1936 date, forcing collectors to buy them to maintain a complete set.

SESQUICENTENNIAL OF INDEPENDENCE

1926	46.00	61.00

Intended for distribution at the exposition celebrating the 150th anniversary of American independence, most did not sell. This may have been due to their low relief, and they were melted. President Calvin Coolidge, who was in office at the time, is depicted with George Washington. A $2-1/2 gold piece was also struck for this celebration.

Known counterfeits: Beware of false proofs made from treating regular issues.

OLD SPANISH TRAIL

	AU	MS-60
1935	730.00	750.00

This coin was designed by, struck for, and entirely purchased by L.W.Hoffecker, who later became ANA president. Some proceeds went to El Paso Museum. Shown is Alvar Cabeza de Vaca's route west.

Known counterfeits: Matte proofs are a possibility. Those of regular strikes sometimes lack normal die polish marks.

STONE MOUNTAIN MEMORIAL

	AU	MS-60
1925	30.00	36.00

Struck to raise funds for the construction of the mammoth sculpture (completed 1970) honoring Confederate heroes at Stone Mountain, near Atlanta. Depicted is a section showing "Stonewall" Jackson and Robert E. Lee. About half were put into circulation.

TEXAS CENTENNIAL

	AU	MS-60
1934	76.00	80.00
1935	82.00	92.00
1935D	82.00	92.00
1935S	82.00	92.00
1936	82.00	92.00
1936D	82.00	92.00
1936S	82.00	92.00
1937	85.00	95.00
1937D	85.00	95.00
1937S	85.00	95.00
1938	145.00	181.00
1938D	145.00	181.00
1938S	145.00	181.00

Struck to commemorate the centennial of Texas' independence from Mexico. The obverse shows an eagle against a Lone Star background. The complex reverse shows Victory holding the Alamo, busts of Sam Houston and Stephen Austin at her sides. The reason this issue was divided between various mints and dates, instead of one large production run, was the realization that it would force collectors to buy many coins instead of one coin to maintain a complete set.

FORT VANCOUVER

1925	215.00	270.00

Struck to pay for the celebration of the centennial of the founding of Ft. Vancouver, Washington, the bust is that of Dr. John McLoughlin, the chief Hudson's Bay Company representative in the area.

Known counterfeits: Exist both for proofs and regular strikes. They lack sharpness.

VERMONT SESQUICENTENNIAL

	AU	MS-60
1927	130.00	150.00

Made to commemorate the 150th anniversary of the Battle of Bennington and to raise money for local museums. Depicted is Ira Allen, a leader of the Green Mountain Boys, and an inaccurately rendered Vermont catamount. The relief on this coin is notably high.

BOOKER T. WASHINGTON

1946	9.00	11.00
1946D	9.00	12.00
1946S	9.00	12.00
1947	11.00	14.00
1947D	11.00	14.00
1947S	11.00	14.00
1948	18.00	30.00
1948D	18.00	30.00
1948S	18.00	30.00
1949	35.00	57.00
1949D	35.00	57.00
1949S	35.00	57.00
1950	30.00	38.00
1950D	30.00	38.00
1950S	9.00	10.00

	AU	MS-60
1951	9.00	11.00
1951D	35.00	52.00
1951S	35.00	52.00

This coin was ostensibly struck to fund construction memorials to the great educator, and "to perpetuate [his] ideals and teachings." Many, however, considered them a profit making scheme of S.J.Phillips, their promoter. Some dates are scarce, while other more common ones ended up in circulation.

WISCONSIN CENTENNIAL

1936	140.00	155.00

This coin wasn't struck for the centennial of Wisconsin's statehood, but rather for its establishment as a territory. One side displays a badger, the other side shows an arm with pickax.

YORK COUNTY, MAINE

1936	130.00	135.00

This coin was struck in honor of the 300th anniversary of the founding of Brown's Garrison in York County, Maine. One-third of the production was reserved for Maine residents, who were able to buy them for twenty years.

LAFAYETTE DOLLAR

	AU	MS-60
1900	270.00	500.00

This was the only silver dollar in the original commemorative series. Profits were to pay for an equestrian statue (depicted on reverse) of Lafayette at the 1900 Paris Exposition. The portraits are those of Washington and Lafayette.

Known counterfeits: Several counterfeits have been reported.

GRANT MEMORIAL GOLD DOLLARS

	AU	MS-60
1922 with star	1,100.00	1,250.00
1922 no star	1,000.00	1,050.00

This was struck for the 100th anniversary of Grant's birth. A Mathew Brady photograph was the subject for Laura Gardin Fraser's bust of Grant on both the half dollar and the gold dollar. The proceeds were supposed to fund four museum buildings and a highway, none of which were constructed. Some of these have a star above the word GRANT on the obverse.

Known counterfeits: Casts are known.

LEWIS AND CLARK EXPE-DITION GOLD DOLLARS

1904	470.00	700.00
1905	470.00	800.00

These were struck to commemorate Lewis and Clark's 1804-05 expedition to discover the newly acquired Louisiana Territory. They were sold to finance an exposition honoring their explorations in Portland, Oregon, and to construct a memorial to Sacagawea. A bust of one explorer is on each side.

Known counterfeits: Both pieces have been counterfeited.

LOUISIANA PURCHASE EXPOSITION GOLD DOLLARS

	AU	MS-60
1903 Jefferson	300.00	395.00
1903 McKinley	280.00	350.00

Struck to raise money for the 1904 Louisiana Purchase Exposition in St. Louis, Missouri, and ultimately to commemorate Jefferson's 1803 Louisiana Purchase from France. The McKinley obverse also serves as a memorial, as he was assassinated in 1901.

Known counterfeits: Both have been counterfeited.

WILLIAM McKINLEY MEMORIAL GOLD DOLLARS

1916	245.00	325.00
1917	300.00	470.00

These were struck to pay for the construction of a memorial to the assassinated president in Niles, Ohio. They sold poorly and 10,000 of the remainders were bought by coin dealer B. Max Mehl.

Known counterfeits: Those of the 1917 date are known.

PANAMA-PACIFIC EXPOSI-TION GOLD SERIES

1915S $1	295.00	330.00

1915S $2-1/2	1,110.00	1,250.00

	AU	MS-60
1915S $50 round	22,000.00	24,000.00
1915S $50 octagonal	20,000.00	22,000.00

This coin was struck for San Francisco's celebration of the opening of the Panama Canal. At the Exposition, the gold dollar that depicted a canal worker was available for $2, the $2-1/2 with Columbia astride a sea horse for $4, while the giant $50 depicted Minerva and an owl was often bought as part of five-piece sets with one silver and four gold commemoratives (or in ten-piece double sets). This was the first time the United States issued a $50 coin, and the last until 1986. The original copper frames are valuable.

Known counterfeits: Certainly the $1 and $2-1/2, possibly the $50 as well.

INDEPENDENCE SESQUI-CENTENNIAL $2-1/2 GOLD

	AU	MS-60
1926	240.00	265.00

The intent for this coin was that it be distributed at the exposition celebrating the 150th anniversary of American independence. Most did not sell, perhaps due to their low relief or expense, and were melted. The design is Liberty standing with torch and the Declaration of Independence, Independence Hall in Philadelphia on the reverse. A half dollar was also struck for this celebration.

Known Counterfeits: Beware of false proofs made by treating regular issues. Regular issues have also been counterfeited.

RECENT COMMEMORA-TIVE COINAGE

After the Bicentennial, with the War of Independence still on the populace's consciousness, it seemed only right and fitting to strike a commemorative half dollar to honor the 250th anniversary of the birth of the Father of our country. Unlike the Bicentennial coins, however, no circulation strikes were ever made. Washington halves were sold at a high premium and most Americans never knew of their existence. Congress and the mint had entered the world of modern mass marketing and there was no turning back. Within very few years the mint was selling so many different specialized numismatic products that former president Gans of the ANA, then on the mint's committee on commemorative coins, announced that the full annual coin budget of the average American collector could not even afford to purchase one of each item, let alone do so and have money left over for older coins.

Conversely, the fact that certain coins have been oversold via mass marketing to soon-disinterested non-collectors, has placed a great many on the secondary market. Some of these can now be bought at below what the government originally charged for them.

Unlike the earlier commemoratives, which are considered special if in the original holders, these are considered undesirable without them. Original holders are the norm. Also, unlike the previous series, these are listed in chronological order, rather than alphabetically, as many of them are collected in sets of issue.

Known counterfeits: Perhaps none.

WASHINGTON HALF DOLLAR

	MS-65	PF
1982D	4.50	
1982S		4.50

These were issued to honor the 250th anniversary of George Washington's birth in 1732.

LOS ANGELES OLYMPICS

	MS-65	PF
1983P $1 Silver	8.25	
1983D $1 Silver	8.75	
1983S $1 Silver	8.50	8.50

	MS-65	PF
1984P $1 Silver	14.00	
1984D $1 Silver	21.00	
1984S $1 Silver	23.00	10.00

	MS-65	PF
1984P $10 Gold		245.00
1984D $10 Gold		240.00
1984S $10 Gold		220.00
1984W $10 Gold	220.00	220.00

Struck to raise funds for the U.S. Olympic committee, the 1983 dollar shows three stylized discus throwers, and most collectors didn't like it. The 1984 depiction of the headless statues before the Los Angeles Coliseum was rejected by the national Fine Arts Commission. The first gold eagle since 1933 depicts runners carrying the Olympic Torch.

STATUE OF LIBERTY

	MS-65	PF
1986D $1/2 Clad	4.50	
1986S $1/2 Clad		4.65

	MS-65	PF
1986P $1 Silver	9.00	
1986S $1 Silver		10.00

	MS-65	PF
1986W $5 Gold	114.00	115.00

The 100th anniversary of the Statue of Liberty was an occasion for three coins to benefit it, and Ellis Island reconstruction. The half dollar depicts an immigrant family of the turn of the century. The dollar features the Statue of Liberty with Ellis Island in the background, and the $5 gold, the head of the Statue of Liberty as seen from slightly below.

CONSTITUTION BICENTENNIAL

	MS-65	PF
1987P $1 Silver	8.25	
1987S $1 Silver		8.25

	MS-65	PF
1987W $5 Gold	114.00	114.00

These two coins, celebrating the drafting of the Constitution, were deigned by invitational competition. It is interesting to observe the quill pen in the eagle's talons rather than arrows, alluding to the power of words.

SEOUL OLYMPICS

	MS-65	PF
1988D $1 Silver	8.50	
1988S $1 Silver		8.25

	MS-65	PF
1988W $5 Gold	114.00	114.00

These two coins were struck to benefit the U.S. Olympic committee, and to finance U.S. participation in the Olympics held in Seoul, South Korea, that year.

CONGRESS BICENTENNIAL

	MS-65	PF
1989D $1/2 Clad	11.00	
1989S $1/2 Clad		5.00

	MS-65	PF
1989D $1 Silver	12.50	
1989S $1 Silver		11.25

	MS-65	PF
1989W $5 Gold	114.00	114.00

Because the Constitution did not go into effect in 1789, the Congress celebrated its bicentennial two years after the Constitution itself, hence another series of coins. Part of the profits from this issue went to repair the Capitol building and to pay on the national debt.

EISENHOWER CENTENNIAL

	MS-65	PF
1990W $1 Silver	11.00	
1990P $1 Silver		11.00

In addition to the "Ike" dollar of 1971-78, it was decided that a coin was needed to honor the 100th anniversary of the birth of Eisenhower. He is depicted both as general and as president.

MOUNT RUSHMORE

	MS-65	PF
1991D $1/2 Clad	9.00	
1991S $1/2 Clad		8.50

	MS-65	PF
1991P $1 Silver	28.00	
1991S $1 Silver		28.00

	MS-65	PF
1991W $5 Gold	114.00	114.00

Despite the depiction of his sculpture on the 1925 Stone Mountain half, Gutzon Borglum's most famous work, Mt. Rushmore, was not honored on a coin until its 50th anniversary. The eagle on the $5 is shown wielding the sculptor's tools, a hammer and chisel.

KOREAN WAR MEMORIAL

	MS-65	PF
1991D $1 Silver	16.00	
1991P $1 Silver		16.50

Struck to honor veterans of the Korean War and to finance construction of the Korean War Memorial.

USO ANNIVERSARY

	MS-65	PF
1991D $1 Silver	15.00	
1991S $1 Silver		14.00

This coin was issued to commemorate the 50th anniversary of the USO, the United Service Organization, famous for providing services for American troops worldwide.

BARCELONA OLYMPICS

	MS-65	PF
1992P $1/2 Clad	5.00	
1992S $1/2 Clad		8.00

	MS-65	PF
992D $1 Silver	21.00	
1992S $1 Silver		28.00

	MS-65	PF
1992W $5 Gold	125.00	114.00

These three coins were struck to benefit the U.S. Olympic committee, and to finance U.S. participation in the Olympics held in Barcelona, Spain, that year.

WHITE HOUSE BICENTENNIAL

	MS-65	PF
1992D $1 Silver	23.00	
1992W $1 Silver		19.00

This coin was issued to mark the bicentennial of the laying of the cornerstone of the White House. The building was designed by architect James Hoban, who is depicted on this dollar's reverse.

COLUMBUS QUINCENTENARY

	MS-65	PF
1992D $1/2 Clad	13.00	
1992S $1/2 Clad		12.50

1992D $1 Silver	29.00	
1992P $1 Silver		29.00

	MS-60	PF
1992W $5 Gold	135.00	125.00

Among the better executed designs in recent years, this set of three coins commemorates the 500th anniversary of Columbus' voyage of discovery. It was this historical event that prompted the very first U.S. commemorative in 1892.

BILL OF RIGHTS

	MS-65	PF
1993W $1/2 Silver	12.50	
1993S $1/2 Silver		12.50

1993D $1 Silver	16.50	
1993S $1 Silver		16.50

1993W $5 Gold	135.00	110.00

These three coins honor the 1789 approval of the first ten amendments to the Constitution, which guaranteed American liberties and are collectively called the Bill of Rights.

WORLD WAR II

	MS-65	PF
1993P $1/2 Clad	10.00	
1993P $1/2 Silver		11.00

1993D $1 Silver	21.00	
1993W $1 Silver		23.00

1993W $5 Gold	150.00	130.00

This three piece set was struck to commemorate the 50th anniversary of World War II. The dollar also commemorates D-Day, the decisive allied landing in Normandy that led to the end of the war.

WORLD CUP

	MS-65	PF
1994 $1/2 Clad	9.00	
1994 $1/2 Silver		10.00

1994D $1 Silver	26.50	
1994S $1 Silver		29.00

1994W $5 Gold	135.00	125.00

Struck to note the World Cup, the biggest international soccer competition, which was held in the United States that year for the first time.

JEFFERSON MEMORIAL

	MS-65	PF
1993P (1994)	25.00	
1993S (1994)		20.00

This coin was struck to commemorate the 250th anniversary of the birth of Thomas Jefferson, third president and author of the Declaration of Independence.

VIETNAM WAR MEMORIAL

1994P $1 Silver	28.00	
1994S $1 Silver		30.00

This was issued to mark the tenth anniversary of the Vietnam Veteran's War Memorial in Washington, D.C. The obverse depicts the memorial's primary element, its famous wall of names.

PRISONERS OF WAR

	MS-65	PF
1994P $1 Silver	25.00	
1994S $1 Silver		25.00

Struck to remember American prisoners of war, proceeds were used to support the National Prisoner of War Museum.

WOMEN VETERANS

1994P $1 Silver	20.00	
1994S $1 Silver		23.00

This coin was struck to honor women who have served in the nation's five different branches of the military.

U.S. CAPITOL

	MS-65	PF
1994P $1 Silver	18.00	
1994S $1 Silver		15.00

Struck to commemorate the beginning of the construction of the Capitol building in 1793, it was finally completed in 1830.

SPECIAL OLYMPICS

	MS-65	PF
1995W $1 Silver	24.00	
1995P $1 Silver		15.00

This coin honors the Special Olympic World Games held in the United States, and the movement's founder, Eunice Kennedy Shriver. Considered scandalous by many, this is one of the rare instances where a living person is depicted on a United States coin.

CIVIL WAR BATTLEFIELDS

	MS-65	PF
1995S $1/2 Clad	9.00	
1995S $1/2 Clad		10.00

	MS-65	PF
1995P $1 Silver	23.00	
1995S $1 Silver		18.50

	MS-65	PF
1995W $5 Gold	280.00	150.00

These mark the 100th anniversary of the establishment of Gettysburg as a national park. Like two commemoratives of the 1930s, these coins were made, in part, to raise money to help preserve Civil War sites.

ATLANTA OLYMPICS

	MS-65	PF
1995D $1/2 Clad Basketball	10.00	
1995S $1/2 Clad Basketball		10.00
1995D $1/2 Clad Baseball	9.00	
1995S $1/2 Clad Baseball		9.50
1995D $1/2 Clad Swimming	11.50	
1995S $1/2 Clad Swimming		10.00
1995D $1/2 Clad Soccer	11.50	
1995S $1/2 Clad Soccer		10.00

	MS-65	PF
1995D $1 Silver Gymnast	33.00	
1995P $1 Silver same		33.00
1995D $1 Silver Paralympics	33.00	
1995P $1 Silver same		33.00
1995D $1 Silver Track & Field	32.00	
1995P $1 Silver same		33.00
1995D $1 Silver Cycling	32.00	
1995P $1 Silver same		35.00

	MS-65	PF
1996D $1 Silver		
Tennis	37.00	
1996P $1 Silver same		33.00
1996D $1 Silver		
Wheelchair Athlete	37.00	
1996P $1 Silver same		33.00
1996D $1 Silver		
Rowing	37.00	
1996P $1 Silver same		35.00
1996D $1 Silver		
High Jump	38.00	
1996P $1 Silver same		35.00

	MS-65	PF
1995W $5 Gold Torch		
Runner	190.00	150.00
1995W $5 Gold		
Stadium	190.00	175.00
1995W $5 Gold		
Flag Bearer	245.00	220.00
1995W $5 Gold		
Cauldron	245.00	220.00

In 1996 the Olympics were held in Atlanta. This extensive set of commemoratives honors the many facets of these games.

COMMUNITY SERVICE

1996P $1	35.00	
1996S $1		36.00

Struck to commemorate those who volunteer for community service, part of the money raised from their sale was donated to an organization dedicated to helping encourage such activities.

SMITHSONIAN

	MS-65	PF
1996D $1 Silver	33.00	
1996P $1 Silver		30.00

1996W $5 Gold	255.00	190.00

This two piece set was struck to commemorate the 150th anniversary of the founding of the Smithsonian Institution.

BOTANIC GARDEN

1997P $1	33.00	32.00

Struck two years after the fact to honor the 175th anniversary of the founding of the United States Botanic Garden.

JACKIE ROBINSON

	MS-65	PF
1997S $1 Silver	34.00	37.00

1997W $5 Gold	240.00	265.00

This two piece set was struck to honor the nation's first African American baseball player to play in the major leagues, on the 50th anniversary of that important event.

LAW ENFORCEMENT

1997P $1	40.00	47.00

This coin was struck to honor those who serve in law enforcement, and the memorial to those who died in the line of duty.

ROBERT F. KENNEDY

	MS-65	PF
1998S $1 Silver	40.00	46.00

Struck to memorialize Robert F. Kennedy, former Senator and Attorney General, who was assassinated in 1968.

BLACK PATRIOTS

1998S $1	38.00	40.00

Struck to honor the Black patriots, Crispus Attucks, in particular, who was the first American killed during the Revolutionary War.

ROOSEVELT

1997W $5 Gold	240.00	240.00

Struck to honor Franklin Delano Roosevelt, the only president to be elected to four terms (1933-1945).

U.S. PROOF SETS

Proof coins originated centuries ago when special, carefully produced strikings were prepared as examples of the "ideal" coin, very often as a reference used to seek royal approval. American proof coins are known at least from the early 1800s, but those proofs were not widely available, They were struck for VIPs and for those special collectors and coin dealers with personal connections at the mint.

As the proof coin developed through the late 19th and early 20th centuries, certain criteria began to characterize their manufacture. Generally, these days, they are struck twice with highly polished dies on carefully prepared polished blanks. Early this century the dies were given a matte or sandblast finish, but this soon fell out of favor. Recently some proofs have been struck with a combination of finishes: a dull matte finish on some motifs, such as those of portraits, with a highly reflective, mirror-like surface in the fields. These are called cameo proofs and are more desirable than conventional proofs.

Beginning in 1936, the mint began the active sale of proof sets to the general public. Each set usually contains one coin of each circulating denomination. They have been released every year since with the exceptions of 1943-1949 and 1965-1967. Proof sets of the 1950s were originally sold in cardboard boxes, and later in flat cellophane sheets inside a special envelopes. Today, they come in hard plastic cases. Proof sets that aren't in their original holders are usually traded at a discount. Such removal can damage their fragile surfaces by exposure to air and humidity. Such maltreatment can cause "carbon spots" to form. This is what collectors call tiny black spots that form as a result of this exposure.

Since then the mint has begun active marketing of recent commemoratives. Plus, they have offered special proof sets containing a commemorative dollar as well as the minor coins. These are called Prestige sets. Another option the government offered to proof-set buyers since 1992 is the traditional alloy of 90 percent silver, despite the fact that no coins for circulation are struck in that composition.

Known counterfeits: Proof sets are not generally counterfeited, but regular coins can occasionally be treated by pickling and are made to look like matte proofs.

1936	3,700.00
1937	1,950.00
1938	760.00
1939	910.00
1940	680.00
1941	560.00
1942 5 coins	600.00
1942 6 coins	640.00

1950	400.00
1951	285.00
1952	145.00
1953	110.00
1954	62.00
1955 box	63.00
1955 flat pack	63.00
1956	32.00
1957	13.50
1958	28.00
1959	15.50
1960	12.50
1960 small date cent	24.00
1961	8.40
1962	8.40
1963	8.40
1964	7.75
1968S	4.90
1968S no mint mark dime	7,500.00
1969S	4.90
1970S large date cent	10.00
1970S small date cent	57.00
1970S no mintmark dime	365.00
1971S	5.40
1971S no mintmark nickel	630.00
1972S	6.20
1973S	9.90
1974S	9.75
1975S	10.00
1975S no mintmark dime	Rare
1976S	9.50
1976S 3-pc. silver	15.00
1977S	9.00
1978S	9.75
1979S Filled S	8.20
1979S Clear S	90.50
1980S	6.20
1981S	8.50
1982S	4.80
1983S	6.00
1983S no mintmark dime	340.00

1983S Prestige	88.00
1984S	8.00
1984S Prestige	26.00
1985S	6.00
1986S	12.50
1986S Prestige	24.00
1987S	5.40
1987S Prestig.	21.00
1988S	6.50
1988S Prestige	31.00
1989S	6.00
1989S Prestige	35.00
1990S	8.50
1990S no mintmark cent	1,150.00
1990S Prestige	22.00

1990S Prestige, no mintmark cent	1,150.00
1991S	17.00
1991S Prestige	50.00
1992S	11.00
1992S Prestige	46.00
1992S Silver	14.00
1992S Silver Premier	15.50
1993S	27.00
1993S Prestige	43.00
1993S Silver	28.00
1993S Silver Premier	28.00
1994S	14.00
1994S Prestige	60.00
1994S Silver	41.00
1994S Silver Premier	60.00
1995S	46.50
1995S Prestige	110.00
1995S Silver	45.00
1995S Silver Premier	41.00
1996S	10.00
1996S Prestige	125.00
1996S Silver	30.00
1996S Silver Premier	36.00
1997S	27.50
1995S Prestige	225.00
1995S Silver	30.00
1995S Silver Premier	39.00
1998S	27.50
1998S Silver	35.00
1998 Silver Premier	41.00

U.S. MINT SETS

Mint sets do not necessarily contain coins superior to those in circulation. They are sold as a convenience to collectors who wish to obtain one example of each coin struck for circulation from each mint used to strike that denomination.

Mint sets from 1947 to 1958 contain two of each coin. No conventional mint sets were packaged from 1965 to 1967. The Special Mint Sets of these years were of a superior quality (despite initial government claims to the contrary) perhaps to compensate the public for the lack of proof sets available in those years. While Philadelphia, Denver and San Francisco were all striking coins for circulation, no mintmarks were used, so their products cannot be told apart. The 1966 and 1967 sets came in rigid cases in a tight fitting cardboard box. When the use of mintmarks resumed in 1968 the coins of the different mints were separated by placing them in blue or red plastic sleeves. Some recent mint sets also contain commemoratives. In 1982 and 1983, mints began to sell souvenir sets, which replaced mint sets.

Even more than with proof sets, mint sets must be in their original packaging to command a premium above loose, uncirculated coins. Removing them from the protective packaging can damage mint-state coins by exposure to air and humidity. Such maltreatment can cause "carbon spots" to form, much as they do on proof coins.

Known counterfeits: When mint sets are presented in unofficial holders, be careful that a slightly circulated coin has not been inserted in hopes of passing it off as new. Coins that originally constituted a mint set and have simply been changed to another holder will usually have matching toning, typical of early sets. The plastic holders of 1966 and 1967 can easily be opened and other coins substituted.

1947	595.00
1948	225.00
1949	400.00
1950	—
1951	370.00
1952	265.00
1953	225.00
1954	105.00
1955	73.00
1956	63.00
1957	95.00
1958	81.00
1959	18.00
1960	19.00
1961	28.00
1962	11.00
1963	11.00
1964	9.00
1965 Special Mint Set	3.50
1966 Special Mint Set	3.65
1967 Special Mint Set	6.00
1968	2.50
1969	5.00
1970	10.50
1970 small date cent	37.00
1971	3.50
1972	3.25
1973	9.50

1974	7.40
1975	9.50
1976	9.00
1976S 3-pc. silver	13.50
1977	8.25
1978	8.25
1979	5.50

Above set was incomplete in that it lacks the Susan B. Anthony dollar.

1980	6.75
1981	12.50
1982	Souvenir Sets Only
1983	Souvenir Sets Only
1984	5.25
1985	5.00
1986	9.50
1987	6.00
1988	4.90
1989	5.50
1990	3.80
1991	8.00
1992	9.00
1993	5.50
1994	11.00
1995	24.00

1996	11.00
1997	10.00
1998	8.00

BULLION ISSUES

A bullion coin is a coin with a value in precious metal intended to be higher than its face value. They are sold by the issuing authority at or near the value of the metal. People buy these as a means of investing in precious metal, much as they might otherwise buy ingots. The difference is that a bullion coin is not only guaranteed by the government that issued it, but also can be spent in the unlikely event that the value of its metal should evaporate. On Jan. 1, 1975, for the first time since the Depression, it again became legal for Americans to own gold bullion. From then until 1980, the United States market in bullion was dominated by imported coins.

An attempt was made to capitalize on this domestic market with a product the U.S. government could easily produce. The first endeavor was the American Arts Medallion series of gold pieces. Struck in one and half ounce sizes, they depicted important Americans in the arts on the obverse, and a reverse emblematic of their works. Despite some limited success at direct distribution and sales through post offices, this series was not deemed successful, perhaps due to their lack of a denomination and legal tender status.

In an effort to capture a greater share of that market, and specifically, to compete with the South African Krugerrand, which had fallen out of favor because of the anti-Apartheid movement, the United States started issuing its own gold bullion coin. The new gold Eagle, with a face value of $50 rather than $10 like the eagle of 1795-1933, is virtually identical to the Krugerrand. It contains one ounce of pure gold, but weighs a bit more because of an added alloy to harden it. Its purity is 97.67 percent. Despite the denominations, it is generally customary in the bullion market to refer to these pieces by their net gold contents instead.

The obverses of both these coins hark back to the Hellenistic designs of the early 20th century. The gold ounce and its fractions have Liberty striding toward the viewer as on St. Gaudens' $20 gold piece of 1907-1933. The silver revives Weinman's Walking Liberty, used on half dollars of 1916-1947. The new reverses depict a family of eagles on the gold, and a dignified heraldic eagle on the silver.

In 1997 this series was rounded out by the addition of a $100 one-ounce platinum eagle. The proof versions of this coin depict a bust of the Statue of Liberty and a soaring eagle is unusual in its rendering. Rather than having its fields brilliant and its details matte, it is reversed. The major part of the surface has a matte texture, with only elected details reflective. Not only does this make for a striking appearance, it is one more tool to help discern a genuine coin from a counterfeit.

In an effort to maintain a very low premium over the bullion content, U.S. bullion coins are only available in bulk quantities. This is not true of proof strikes, which are available individually by mail order. When buying these coins retail, remember that the larger the size the smaller the premium. Smaller fractions are usually better as gifts than investments.

Known counterfeits: Despite the fact that the U.S. bullion coins are not counterfeited as much as many others, it is important to be cautious. Check for detail and for any trace of an edge seam. When the coin is placed on the tip of a finger and the edge is struck with a pencil, an extended ring should be heard. Many privately made silver bullion pieces resemble the U.S. silver Eagle but differ in their inscriptions. All those larger than one ounce are privately made.

NOTICE: The values of most of these issues, including many proofs, vary at least daily with the value of their metal content. The prices listed here are based on a platinum value of $360, gold $285, and silver $4.90. Updated prices on commodities such as precious metals, though not on single coins, can be found both in most newspapers and on the Internet. However, for any firm quote on bullion it is best to call your local coin or bullion dealer.

AMERICAN ARTS GOLD MEDALLIONS

1/2 oz.	BU
1980 Marian Anderson	165
1981 Willa Cather	165
1982 Frank Lloyd Wright	165
1983 Alexander Calder	165
1984 John Steinbeck	165

1 oz.	BU
1980 Grant Wood	325
1981 Mark Twain	325
1982 Louis Armstrong	325
1983 Robert Frost	325
1984 Helen Hayes	330

AMERICAN EAGLE SILVER COINS

1 oz. / $1	Unc.	PF
1986	10.00	
1986S		22.00
1987	7.65	
1987S		22.00
1988	7.65	
1988S		34.00
1989	7.65	
1989S		22.00
1990	7.60	
1990S		22.00
1991	7.60	
1991S		23.00
1992	7.60	
1992S		23.00
1993	7.60	
1993P		49.00
1994	7.60	
1994P		45.00
1995	7.60	
1995P		43.00
1995W		682.00
1996	7.60	
1996P		34.00
1997	7.60	
1997P		30.00
1998	7.60	
1998P		25.00

AMERICAN EAGLE GOLD COINS

1/10 oz. / $5	Unc.	PF
1986	45.00	
1987	45.00	
1988	48.00	
1988P		58.00
1989	48.00	
1989P		60.00
1990	48.00	
1990P		58.00
1991	48.00	
1991P		60.00
1992	48.00	
1992P		71.00
1993	48.00	
1993P		66.00
1994	41.00	
1994W		60.00
1995	38.00	
1995W		68.00
1996	38.00	
1996W		38.00
1997	38.00	
1997		95.00
1998	38.00	
1998W		60.00

1/4 oz. / $10	Unc.	PF
1986	100.00	
1987	105.00	
1988	110.00	
1988P		90.00
1989	110.00	
1989P		150.00
1990	110.00	
1990P		150.00
1991	135.00	
1991P		150.00
1992	110.00	
1992P		150.00
1993	110.00	
1993P		
1994	105.00	150.00
1994W		
1995	100.00	150.00
1995W		
1996		
1996W		
1997		
1997		
1998		

1/2 oz. / $25	Unc.	PF
1986	179.00	
1987	194.00	
1987P		283.00
1988	284.00	
1988P		283.00
1989	344.00	
1989P		283.00
1990	344.00	
1990P		283.00
1991	374.00	
1991P		283.00
1992	224.00	
1992P		283.00
1993	194.00	
1993P		283.00
1994	179.00	
1994W		283.00
1995	179.00	
1995W		283.00
1996	264.00	
1996W		283.00
1997	179.00	
1997W		283.00
1998	179.00	
1998W		283.00

1 oz.		
1986		
1986W		
1987		
1987W		
1988		
1988W		
	PF	
	311.00	
	76.00	

1 oz. / $50	Unc.	PF
1989	311.00	
1989W		576.00
1990	313.00	
1990W		576.00
1991	313.00	
1991W		576.00
1992	311.00	
1992W		576.00
1993	311.00	
1993W		576.00
1994	313.00	
1994W		576.00
1995	311.00	
1995W		576.00
1996	316.00	
1996W		576.00
1997	311.00	
1997W		576.00
1998	325.00	
1998W		576.00

AMERICAN EAGLE PLATINUM COINS

1/10 oz. / $10	BU	PF
1997	45.00	
1997W		125.00
1998	45.00	
1998W		115.00

1/4 oz. / $25	BU	PF
1997	175.00	
1997W		210.00
1998	105.00	
1998W		225.00

1/2 oz. / $50	BU	PF
1997	425.00	
1997W		370.00
1998	200.00	
1998W		410.00

1 oz. / $100	BU	PF
1997	390.00	
1997W		725.00
1998	385.00	
1998W		715.00

PATTERNS

Patterns are trial or experimental coins. They are projects that have surpassed being just sketches and plaster sculpture, and are now at the point where engraving dies and striking examples have been made. These show what the coin might look like if it went into production. Such patterns are useful to government officials trying to determine if a particular design is suitable, or if a size, shape or denomination is practical. Also they are useful to mint employees in determining how to adjust the dies or mix the alloy for the best strike. Patterns of successful designs sometimes exist dated before the year they were first put into circulation, from the period when they were being developed.

During the 19th and very early 20th centuries, those patterns the mint was no longer using were given or sold to the employees, politicians, or simply well-connected coin collectors or dealers. Since 1916 it is forbidden to release them. At some points mint employees even struck extra patterns or used pattern dies to strike examples in off metals so they could sell them.

Distinguishing tiny differences among composition varieties may require specific gravity testing.

All patterns are scarce and all pricing is conjectural, as the arrival or departure of as few as thirty serious collectors in the pattern market can alter the pricing structure.

Known counterfeits: Restrikes are known of the 1836 2¢. They are of incorrect weight and show signs of die failure. Electrotype copies have been made of some patterns. One should also not confuse private proposals or fantasies for actual U.S. mint pattern coins. However, this overt counterfeiting is not extensive. Serious research is recommended.

EF-Unc.

1794 Half Dollar, as regular issue but no stars on obv., struck in copper .... Unique

1808 $5, obv. as regular issue, reverse heraldic eagle as type of 1795-1807, struck in silver, Restrikes only .... Scarce

1814 Half Dollar, as regular issue but struck in platinum, obv. counterstamped with 33 P's, reverse engraved *Platina* over eagle.......... Three Known

1836 2¢, Eagle standing with wings open on cloud, rev. TWO CENTS in wreath, 90% copper, 10% silver. 60 grs. 3,000.00

1836 Dollar, Seated Liberty, rev. flying eagle, copper, reeded edge..................................... Rare
    same, plain edge, Restrike 14,500.00

In an effort to maintain a very low premium over the bullion content, U.S. bullion coins are only available in bulk quantities. This is not true of proof strikes, which are available individually by mail order. When buying these coins retail, remember that the larger the size the smaller the premium. Smaller fractions are usually better as gifts than investments.

Known counterfeits: Despite the fact that the U.S. bullion coins are not counterfeited as much as many others, it is important to be cautious. Check for detail and for any trace of an edge seam. When the coin is placed on the tip of a finger and the edge is struck with a pencil, an extended ring should be heard. Many privately made silver bullion pieces resemble the U.S. silver Eagle but differ in their inscriptions. All those larger than one ounce are privately made.

NOTICE: The values of most of these issues, including many proofs, vary at least daily with the value of their metal content. The prices listed here are based on a platinum value of $360, gold $285, and silver $4.90. Updated prices on commodities such as precious metals, though not on single coins, can be found both in most newspapers and on the Internet. However, for any firm quote on bullion it is best to call your local coin or bullion dealer.

AMERICAN ARTS GOLD MEDALLIONS

1/2 oz.	BU
1980 Marian Anderson	165
1981 Willa Cather	165
1982 Frank Lloyd Wright	165
1983 Alexander Calder	165
1984 John Steinbeck	165

1 oz.	BU
1980 Grant Wood	325
1981 Mark Twain	325
1982 Louis Armstrong	325
1983 Robert Frost	325
1984 Helen Hayes	330

AMERICAN EAGLE SILVER COINS

1 oz. / $1	Unc.	PF
1986	10.00	
1986S		22.00
1987	7.65	
1987S		22.00
1988	7.65	
1988S		34.00
1989	7.65	
1989S		22.00
1990	7.60	
1990S		22.00
1991	7.60	
1991S		23.00
1992	7.60	
1992S		23.00
1993	7.60	
1993P		49.00
1994	7.60	
1994P		45.00
1995	7.60	
1995P		43.00
1995W		682.00
1996	7.60	
1996P		34.00
1997	7.60	
1997P		30.00
1998	7.60	
1998P		25.00

AMERICAN EAGLE GOLD COINS

1/10 oz. / $5	Unc.	PF
1986	45.00	
1987	45.00	
1988	48.00	
1988P		58.00
1989	48.00	
1989P		60.00
1990	48.00	
1990P		58.00
1991	48.00	
1991P		60.00
1992	48.00	
1992P		71.00
1993	48.00	
1993P		66.00
1994	41.00	
1994W		60.00
1995	38.00	
1995W		68.00
1996	38.00	
1996W		38.00
1997	38.00	
1997		95.00
1998	38.00	
1998W		60.00

1/4 oz. / $10	Unc.	PF
1986	100.00	
1987	105.00	
1988	110.00	
1988P		90.00
1989	110.00	
1989P		150.00
1990	110.00	
1990P		150.00
1991	135.00	
1991P		150.00
1992	110.00	
1992P		150.00
1993	110.00	
1993P		150.00
1994	105.00	
1994W		150.00
1995	100.00	
1995W		150.00
1996	100.00	
1996W		150.00
1997	100.00	
1997		150.00
1998	85.00	
1998W		150.00

1/2 oz. / $25	Unc.	PF
1986	179.00	
1987	194.00	
1987P		283.00
1988	284.00	
1988P		283.00
1989	344.00	
1989P		283.00
1990	344.00	
1990P		283.00
1991	374.00	
1991P		283.00
1992	224.00	
1992P		283.00
1993	194.00	
1993P		283.00
1994	179.00	
1994W		283.00
1995	179.00	
1995W		283.00
1996	264.00	
1996W		283.00
1997	179.00	
1997W		283.00
1998	179.00	
1998W		283.00

1 oz. / $50	Unc.	PF
1986	311.00	
1986W		
1987	311.00	
1987W		576.00
1988	311.00	
1988W		576.00

1 oz. / $50	Unc.	PF
1989	311.00	
1989W		576.00
1990	313.00	
1990W		576.00
1991	313.00	
1991W		576.00
1992	311.00	
1992W		576.00
1993	311.00	
1993W		576.00
1994	313.00	
1994W		576.00
1995	311.00	
1995W		576.00
1996	316.00	
1996W		576.00
1997	311.00	
1997W		576.00
1998	325.00	
1998W		576.00

AMERICAN EAGLE PLATINUM COINS

1/10 oz. / $10	BU	PF
1997	45.00	
1997W		125.00
1998	45.00	
1998W		115.00

1/4 oz. / $25	BU	PF
1997	175.00	
1997W		210.00
1998	105.00	
1998W		225.00

1/2 oz. / $50	BU	PF
1997	425.00	
1997W		370.00
1998	200.00	
1998W		410.00

1 oz. / $100	BU	PF
1997	390.00	
1997W		725.00
1998	385.00	
1998W		715.00

PATTERNS

Patterns are trial or experimental coins. They are projects that have surpassed being just sketches and plaster sculpture, and are now at the point where engraving dies and striking examples have been made. These show what the coin might look like if it went into production. Such patterns are useful to government officials trying to determine if a particular design is suitable, or if a size, shape or denomination is practical. Also they are useful to mint employees in determining how to adjust the dies or mix the alloy for the best strike. Patterns of successful designs sometimes exist dated before the year they were first put into circulation, from the period when they were being developed.

During the 19th and very early 20th centuries, those patterns the mint was no longer using were given or sold to the employees, politicians, or simply well-connected coin collectors or dealers. Since 1916 it is forbidden to release them. At some points mint employees even struck extra patterns or used pattern dies to strike examples in off metals so they could sell them.

Distinguishing tiny differences among composition varieties may require specific gravity testing.

All patterns are scarce and all pricing is conjectural, as the arrival or departure of as few as thirty serious collectors in the pattern market can alter the pricing structure.

Known counterfeits: Restrikes are known of the 1836 2¢. They are of incorrect weight and show signs of die failure. Electrotype copies have been made of some patterns. One should also not confuse private proposals or fantasies for actual U.S. mint pattern coins. However, this overt counterfeiting is not extensive. Serious research is recommended.

EF-Unc.

1794 Half Dollar, as regular issue but no stars on obv., struck in copper .... Unique

1808 $5, obv. as regular issue, reverse heraldic eagle as type of 1795-1807, struck in silver, Restrikes only .... Scarce

1814 Half Dollar, as regular issue but struck in platinum, obv. counterstamped with 33 P's, reverse engraved *Platina* over eagle .... Three Known

1836 2¢, Eagle standing with wings open on cloud, rev. TWO CENTS in wreath, 90% copper, 10% silver. 60 grs. 3,000.00

1836 Dollar, Seated Liberty, rev. flying eagle, copper, reeded edge.................................... Rare

same, plain edge, Restrike 14,500.00

EF-Unc.

1855 Large Cent, Flying eagle, rev. Value in wreath,
copper 1,750.00
1858 Small Cent, Indian head and wreath as regular
1859 issue, Copper Nickel, plain edge. 1,250.00
1866 5¢, Washington, rev. Value in wreath,
Nickel 1,800.00

1870 Trade Dollar, Liberty Seated on Globe, rev. 1
Dollar, silver, reeded edge 3,500.00
1880 $4 "Stella," Liberty Head with flowing hair,
rev. Star, gold 60,000.00
1891 Dime, as Barber type of 1892-1916,
Silver ....Rare

1896 1¢ Shield, rev. Value within circular branch,
Aluminum 2,750.00
1916 Half Dollar, Walking Liberty with LIBERTY
to right, Walking Eagle, Value above,
silver 35,200.00
1942 1¢, Plasticised Fiber .... None Released
1974 1¢, Lincoln Memorial type,
Aluminum .... None Released

ERRORS

An error is a coin which is manufactured incorrectly, or one manufactured correctly with dies on which a mistake has been made or the die damaged. There are a great many types of errors, from the wrong metal being used to the coin being struck off center. The mint usually tries to prevent such coins from getting

out. They are usually caught and melted. Because the modern automated manufacturing process creates far fewer errors and greater uniformity than in ancient times, collectors of modern coins actually prize such mistakes. Errors in larger coins, proofs and commemoratives tend to be scarcer because more attention is paid to the inspection process. Over the last fifty years there have been more getting out than in the past, and as a result recent errors are not as valuable as early ones.

How each basic type of error occurs is explained below, along with what a typical example of such an error would retail for. Prices are for coins struck within the past 30 years. Values for most popular double die cents appear in the regular listings.

Known counterfeits: Most major double die cents have been counterfeited. Virtually every example of a 1943 copper and 1944 steel cent is counterfeit. A magnet test will reveal plating, but not cleverly altered dates. Also, it is very easy to cause apparent errors by striking a coin with a coin or hammering foreign matter into it. Apparent off metal strikes can simply be a coin plated after it was released from the mint. Some very thin coins have been bathed in acid. (Is the surface abraded?) Clipped coins are easily confused for clip errors. All two-headed American coins are concoctions. Do not presume a coin is a mint error until you determine how it was made. There are thousands of such "hoax coins" out there.

Some illustrations here are of foreign coins in order to best show the effects of these errors.

EF-MS-60

BIE Cent - A special kind of die chip in which a small chip out of the die between B and E in "liberty" looks like an extra letter I. Fairly common in the 1950s 25

Blank - A blank, or planchet, is the piece of metal on which a coin is struck. Sometimes they escape the mint with no processing whatsoever. Other times they escape unstruck, but do make it through the machine which upsets the edge slightly. These are called type I and type II blanks respectively.
Cent .... .50
Nickel 2.50
Dime 2.00
Quarter.. 4.00
Half 10.00
Anthony Dollar 30.00

Broadstruck - Coin struck without the collar that keeps it round, thus the metal spreads out.
Cent 1.00
Nickel 7.50
Dime 5.00
Quarter... 10.00
Half 36.00
Anthony Dollar 35.00

Brockage - A coin struck with a coin and a die instead of two dies. Caused by the previous coin adhering to one die. If it covers the whole die it causes a "full brockage."
Cent 12.00

Nickel 35.00
Dime 45.00
Quarter.. 45.00
Half 250.00
Anthony Dollar... 250.00

Clashed Dies - Coin struck with a die that has been previously struck by another die leaving some of its impression behind. On the coin the image of the primary die will be bold, the image of the residual impression will be very faint.
Cent.. .50
Nickel 1.00
Dime 1.50
Quarter.. 5.00
Half 15.00
Anthony Dollar.. 15.00

Clip (2 types) - A coin struck on a blank which has part of its edge missing. There are two causes. A regular clip is caused by the punching device attempting to cut out the form of another coin before a previously punched blank is out of the way. A straight clip is caused when a blank is punched out from too near to the end of the sheet of metal.
Cent.. .50
Nickel 2.50
Dime 2.00
Quarter.. 2.50
Half 10.00
Anthony Dollar   22.00

Cud - A cud is a raised area of the coin near its edge. It is caused by a piece of the die chipping away. There is no striking surface in that spot to force the coin's metal down.
Cent... 1.00
Nickel 3.00
Dime 3.00
Quarter.. 6.00
Half 20.00
Anthony Dollar.. 30.00

Die chip - A die chip is similar to a cud but it can be very small and occur anywhere in the die, not just the edge.
Cent..25 to 1.00
Nickel ....25 to 3.00
Dime ....50 to 3.00
Quarter...2.00 to 6.00
Half ....5.00 to 20.00
Anthony Dollar....................................5.00 to 30.00

Die crack - A crack in the die will cause a very fine raised line across the surface of the coin it strikes. Larger cracks are worth more than values listed.
Cent.. .25
Nickel .... .50

Dime...50
Quarter..1.00
Half...2.00
Anthony Dollar......................................5.00

Double Die - Caused by several factors, all occurring in the die-manufacturing process. They will appear blurred at first glance but upon inspection the details will appear doubled

Prices vary widely, often $10 to $500

Double Struck - When the coin that has been struck fails to eject from between the pair of dies it will receive a second impression, which isn't usually centered.

Cent.. 10.00
Nickel.. 10.00
Dime... 12.00
Quarter.. 40.00
Half... 135.00
Anthony Dollar.................................... 350.00

Lamination - Occasionally called an Occluded Gas Lamination, it is caused by improper mixture of the metal when the alloy is being made. It will appear as flaking on the surface.

Cent...25
Nickel.. 3.00
Dime.. 4.00
Quarter.. 7.00
Half... 12.00
Anthony Dollar...................................... 25.00

Off Center - When the blank is not lined up with the dies, only part of the impression is made. The other part of the blank remains just that — blank!

Cent...75
Nickel.. 2.00
Dime.. 2.00
Quarter.. 4.00
Half... 12.00
Anthony Dollar...................................... 35.00

Struck through - A coin that had foreign matter on the blank. This matter was impressed into the surface by the force of the die.

Cent.. 1.00
Nickel.. 1.00
Dime.. 1.00

Quarter.. 3.00
Half.. 8.00
Anthony Dollar...................................... 10.00

Wrong Metal - When a blank intended for one coin is accidentally mixed into blanks designed for another and gets struck with those dies.

Cent.. 65.00
Nickel.. 30.00
Dime.. 30.00
Quarter.. 30.00
Half... 75.00
Anthony Dollar.................................... 350.00

CALIFORNIA AND OTHER PRIVATE GOLD COINAGES

In the 1830s there was a gold boom in Georgia. People were using flakes of freshly mined gold as means of payment. This was, of course, awkward, but it was too great a risk and a nuisance to ship their gold all the way to the Philadelphia mint to be coined into money. The trip was long and the journey was unsafe. Jewelers such as Templeton Reid and Christopher Bechtler saw an opportunity. For a nominal fee they offered to melt down gold flakes and strike the gold into coins of their own. They made plain looking coins conforming to U.S. government specifications. Some federal assays found that Bechtler may have been even a bit better than the U.S. mint. When he passed on, his heirs continued the coining business. Eventually, with the opening of U.S. mints in Georgia and North Carolina, the need for these tokens faded.

Following the discovery of gold in California, the state underwent a massive and sudden increase in population. It increased more quickly than the quantity of small change needed for petty commerce. Fortunately, there was lots of gold, and gold at that time was relatively cheap. It didn't take long before people realized that if the government could make a tiny gold dollar, then they could make private tokens of even smaller sizes. The assay companies were refining gold and producing ingots anyway. It was not difficult to add the production of these tiny gold pieces to their array of services. Larger gold tokens were made as well, both in California and other mining territories such as Oregon and Colorado. Some of the these pieces were, in a sense, government sanctioned, since they were struck by U.S. government assay offices.

The designs on these pieces, both in Georgia and out West, were simply inscriptions. As the Western tokens evolved, they became more coin-like by using the same motifs (such as Liberty heads), as the then-circulating coin. Many of these gold tokens were octagonal, and some were shaped like the ingots that preceded them, but bore values in dollars, not just ounces.

Known counterfeits: The preponderance of examples of California fractional gold that coin shops are offered by the layman are counterfeit. Most of them are not particularly dangerous. They began to be struck as souvenirs as early as the turn of the century. One key to weeding out the worst of these pieces is the absence of a denomination, which is present on all authentic pieces. Many of these counterfeits have the word Eureka or a bear, both emblems of California. Also, examine near the edge where on some poorly made counterfeits the base metal may be exposed. Much of the larger territorial gold has also been counterfeited. They fall into two categories. Some are very poorly cast replicas sold in souvenir shops. These make no attempt to hide their casting seam and are easy to discern. Others are very dangerous, faithful copies made to fool collectors. Because this series is relatively expensive, it is worth the counterfeiter's while to make a quality product.

Specific counterfeits of the 1857 $1/4 octagonal, 1855 $1/4 round, 1868 $1/2 octagonal; $1/2 round 1854, 1863; $1 octagonal 1858K, and 1863 for fractional issues have been reported, although some are quite old. Larger denomination counterfeits include Baldwin $20 1851, and Blake $20 1855, among others.

CALIFORNIA

Fractional Gold	VF	XF
25¢/$1/4 Round, Liberty Head	55.00	65.00
25¢/$1/4 Round, Indian Head	55.00	65.00
25¢ Round, Eagle	—	23,000.00
$1/4 Round, Washington Head	185.00	285.00
25¢/$1/4 Octagonal, Liberty Head	55.00	65.00
25¢/$1/4 Octagonal, Indian Head	55.00	65.00
$1/4 Octagonal, Washington Head	175.00	275.00
50¢/$1/2 Round, Liberty Head	75.00	85.00
50¢/$1/2 Round, Indian Head	85.00	100.00
$1/2 Round, California Arms	—	1,250.00
50¢/$1/2 Octagonal, Liberty Head	55.00	60.00
50¢/$1/2 Octagonal, Indian Head	65.00	90.00
$1 Round, Liberty Head	400.00	550.00
$1 Round, Indian Head	500.00	650.00
$1 Octagonal, Liberty Head	90.00	150.00
$1 Octagonal, Indian Head	250.00	350.00

	VF	XF
Augustus Humbert, U.S. Assayer		
1852 $10	2,500.00	4,750.00
1852 $20	6,000.00	9,500.00
1851 $50 Lettered edge	12,000.00	22,000.00

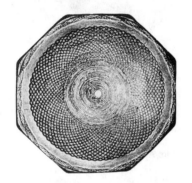

	VF	XF
same reeded edge	8,000.00	18,500.00
Baldwin & Co.		
1850 $5	6,500.00	10,000.00

	VF	XF
1850 $10	27,500.00	45,000.00
1851 $10	15,500.00	30,000.00
1851 $20	—	52,800.00
Cincinnati Mining & Trading Co.		
1849 $5		Rare
1849 $10		104,500.00
Dubosq & Co.		
1850 $5	42,500.00	Rare
1850 $10	45,000.00	Rare
Dunbar & Co.		
1851 $5	32,500.00	52,500.00
Kellogg & Co.		
1854 $20	2,250.00	4,350.00
1855 $20	2,500.00	4,650.00
1855 $50		Rare
F.D. Kohler, State Assayer		
1850 $50, rectangular		200,000.00
Massachusetts & California Co.		
1849 $5	55,000.00	Rare
Miners Bank		
ND $10	12,000.00	24,500.00
Moffat & Co.		
ND $16 Rectangular		Rare

	VF	XF
1849 $5	1,350.00	4,000.00
1850 $5	1,550.00	5,000.00
1849 $10	3,500.00	6,000.00

	VF	XF
1852 $10	4,000.00	8,500.00
1853 $20	3,750.00	6,000.00
Norris, Gregg & Norris		
1849 Half Eagle	3,000.00	6,000.00
J.S. Ormsby		
ND $5	137,500.00	Two Known
ND $10		Rare
Pacific Company		

	VF	XF
1849 $5	180,000.00	—
1849 $10	60,000.00	100,000.00
Schultz & Co.		
1851 $5	25,000.00	45,000.00
United States Assay Office of Gold		
1852 $10	2,500.00	3,850.00
1853 $10	4,200.00	6,500.00
1853 $20	2,750.00	4,250.00
1852 $50	6,500.00	14,500.00
Wass, Molitor & Co.		
1852 $5	4,000.00	6,750.00
1852 $10	2,750.00	5,000.00
1855 $10	8,000.00	12,000.00
1855 $20	11,500.00	20,000.00
1855 $50	14,500.00	28,000.00

COLORADO

Clark, Gruber, & Co.	VF	XF
1860 $2-1/2	1,300.00	2,500.00
1861 $2-1/2	1,500.00	2,750.00
1860 $5	1,950.00	3,350.00
1861 $5	2,500.00	4,500.00
1860 $10	3,950.00	9,000.00
1861 $10	2,500.00	4,500.00

	VF	XF
1860 $20	60,000.00	80,000.00
1861 $20	10,000.00	20,000.00
J.J. Conway & Co.		
ND $21/2	45,000.00	70,000.00
ND $5	30,000.00	44,000.00
ND $10	60,000.00	Rare
John Parsons & Co.		
ND $21/2	85,000.00	Rare
ND $5	100,000.00	Rare

GEORGIA

Templeton Reid	VF	XF
1830 $2.50	39,500.00	55,000.00
1830 $5	75,000.00	200,000.00
1830 $10		Rare
Not dated $10		Rare

NORTH CAROLINA

Christopher Bechtler	VF	XF
$1 Carolina	1,200.00	1,700.00
$1 N. Carolina	1,100.00	2,000.00

	VF	XF
$2.50 Carolina	2,150.00	5,500.00
$2.50 North Carolina	5,000.00	7,000.00
$2.50 Georgia*	2,650.00	5,000.00
$5 Carolina	3,250.00	6,000.00
$5 North Carolina	4,500.00	8,500.00
$5 Georgia*	3,500.00	5,500.00

Georgia on coins refers to the source of the gold, not the location of the mint, which is actually in Rutherford County, N.C.

August Bechtler

	VF	XF
$1 Carolina	650.00	1,150.00

	VF	XF
$5 Carolina	4,000.00	6,500.00

OREGON

Oregon Exchange Co.	VF	XF
1849 $5	17,500.00	28,600.00
1849 $10	35,000.00	55,000.00

UTAH

Mormon Issues / State of Deseret

	VF	XF
1849 $2-1/2	5,000.00	7,750.00

	VF	XF
1849 $5	4,250.00	6,500.00
1850 $5	5,500.00	8,500.00
1860 $5	9,000.00	14,500.00
1849 $10		Rare

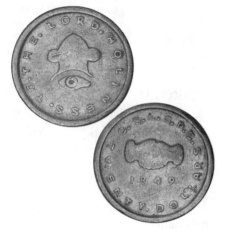

1849 $20	42,500.00	65,000.00

HARD TIMES TOKENS

The "Hard Times" was a period of depression beginning in 1837. For some time before this, the national banks, and land speculation, which were based on unbacked, bank-issued paper money, had been a point of public anxiety. Andrew Jackson attempted to put the nation's financial house in order by withdrawing the government's money from the national bank and by requiring that purchases of public land be made with gold and silver only. There was a flow of precious metal to the West where most public land was being bought. The East, depleted of money, went into a financial panic. Banks suspended payments of gold and silver and businesses began collapsing.

Many of the large cent-sized tokens of the 1830s and 1840s have themes that relate to these issues. Others are advertising pieces, promoting certain products while they circulated as a cent. They provide an interesting glimpse into the political arguments of a distant era.

POLITICAL TOKENS VF

Head of Andrew Jackson r. / The Bank Must Perish, around Wreath 5,750.00
Bust of Andrew Jackson as Roman Emperor / Inscription 150.00
Perish Credit Perish Commerce, Boar running l. / My Substitute For The U.S. Bank, Small Bust over Inscription...12.00

POLITICAL TOKENS VF

Webster Credit Currency 1841, Ship sailing / Van Buren Metallic Currency 1837, Ship foundering on Rocks 12.00
Gulian C. Verplanck Our Next Govnr, Bust l. / A Faithful Friend to Our Country, Eagle 125.00
Executive Experiment, Turtle carrying chest / Illustrious Predecessor, Mule leaping l............. 12.00
1838, Liberty Head wearing LOCO FOCO on coronet / MINT DROP within Wreath 12.00
Substitute For Shinplasters, Phoenix rising from flames / Specie Payments Suspended, around Wreath.. 12.00

I Take The Responsibility, Andrew Jackson popping out of box / The Constitution as I Understand It, Mule with LLD on side 12.00
Henry Clay and the American System, Bust r. / United We Stand, in Wreath................. 30.00

Am I Not a Woman and a Sister 1838, Female Slave Kneeling / United States of America 1838, Wreath.. 40.00

LOCAL TOKENS VF

Alabama: Stickney & Wilson Montgomery, ALABAMA / Dry Goods, etc..., Leaf ornament. 2,500.00
Connecticut: Davenport Chapel St. New Haven Combs, Comb / Davenport Hemmings Genuine Needles.. 25.00
Georgia: J. & D. Morrison Grocers, AUGUSTA GEO. / Wholesale & Retail 8,000.00
Louisiana: Gasquet Parish & Co. New Orleans, 47 CHARTRES STREET / Heraldic Eagle. 750.00
Maryland: Sailing Ship / James Cole Baltimore, Fells Point, flower 300.00

LOCAL TOKENS VF

Massachusetts: American Institute New York, Liberty Seated with Eagle and Shield / R & W Robinson, etc. 12.00
Missouri: Burrows & Jennings, Dealers in Groceries. / Boat Stores and Ship, etc. 8,500.00
New Hampshire: E.F.Sise & Co....Portsmouth, N.H. / Importers of Crockery, etc. ...12.00
New Jersey: Agriculture & Commerce Bas Canada, Bouquet / T. Duseaman Butcher Belleville, Eagle and Shield 32.50
New York: Eagle l. on rock / Feuchtwanger's Composition, THREE CENTS in Wreath (German silver)...1,200.00

Time is Money, Face of Clock / Smiths Clock Establishment, etc. 60.00
Ohio: A. Loomis...Cleveland, Ohio, Eagle / Keg 200.00
Pennsylvania: Dickson White & Co. Philadelphia, Pocket Watch / Importers of Watches, etc. 125.00
Rhode Island: Washington Row Providence, Heraldic Eagle / W.A. Handy, Merchant Taylor.. 15.00
South Carolina: Soda Water 1837, Soda Urn / R.L. Baker Charleston S.C., Good For 1 Glass...2,000.00
Tennessee: Kohn Daron & Co., ornament / Good for One Load, Wreath 325.00
Vermont: Gustin & Blake, Tin Copper Sheet Iron Workers Chelsea, Vt/ Stoves & Tin Ware 1,000.00
Virginia: Time is Money, Face of Clock / S.N. Botsford Clock & Watch...Norfolk, etc. 125.00

CIVIL WAR TOKENS

Throughout the Civil War coinage was scarce. Much of what the mint produced was simply hoarded. Even base metal coins were hoarded. People thought that if the their side fell, at least real coins would retain some value. The government's answer was tons of small size paper money valued at 3¢ to 50¢, but the merchants had a better idea. They began using small, cent size copper tokens as business cards and spending them. They cost the merchant less than a cent to have made, they were of more intrinsic value than potentially worthless paper money, and they even advertised his product and location. Of course signing one's name to a token does imply that you will honor or redeem it. Soon anonymous tokens began to appear. No issuing merchant was indicated — only patriotic sayings and images. No one benefited from the advertising but the person who spent them first, since those people could never again be found to redeem them. Collectors call these two kinds of Civil War Tokens "Store Cards" and "Patriotics."

Similar situations existed in both the North and the South, but Southern Civil War Tokens are far scarcer, with paper money being more dominant there.

It is enjoyable to use these tokens to trace local history because their issue was far more widespread than tokens were at any time before. Some people also collect them by topic, such as those issued by restaurants or book sellers. Those issued by military provisioners, called suttler, are particularly scarce and valuable.

Most Civil War Tokens are struck in copper or brass. Fewer were struck in lead. Some of these tokens even caught on with 19th century collectors. Special presentation pieces in silver were occasionally made for them. Many of these were actually struck over American coins. The tokens listed here are copper or brass unless noted.

Known counterfeits: While virtually no Civil War Tokens were counterfeited to fool collectors, some were imitated by competing manufacters, causing a vast array of similar, but distinct varieties. Decades later some token dies were found by individuals who restruck them, often in more desirable metals, or in unknown obverse/reverse combinations.

VF

Alabama: Huntsville, White & Swan, Indian
Head... 800.00

Connecticut: Bridgeport, E.W. Atwood Dealer in
Books / Liberty Head 6.00
__. Willimantic, Arch Saloon / Crude Lincoln
Head..Rare
Illinois: Cairo, D. Ford Watchmaker / Mercury
Head...10.00
__: Chicago, Baierle's Saloon / Beer Mug.
(14mm)...Rare
__: Chicago, C. & S. Stein Dry Goods / Child's
Manfr Chicago, Female Head 8.00
__: Elgin, M.MCNeil Dealer in Dry Goods / Heraldic
Eagle.. 85.00
__: Paris, Collins Bro's Druggist / Indian Head 40.00
Indiana: Brazil, Connely's New York Store /
Indian Head 20.00
__: Brazil, same but Carl Haas, Rabbit instead of
Indian Head ....Rare
__: Indianapolis, A.D. Wood Hardware Merchant,
Compass and Square / Indian Head 35.00
Iowa: Cedar Rapids, Reynolds & Co. New York
Store, Head l. / You Can Buy Goods Cheap at
the New York Store 150.00

__: Lyons, Gage, Lyall & Keeler Grocers / "Business
Card" in Wreath.............................. 135.00
Kansas: Leavenworth, A. Cohen, Clothing and
Gents Furnishing Goods, / Liberty
Head... 1250.00

Kentucky: Covington, Cov. & Cin. Ferry Company
/ Indian Head...Rare
__: Louisville, H. Preissler / Soda Water, Two
Crossed Arrows ....Scarce
Maine: Bangor, R.S. Torrey, Inventor of the Maine
State Bee Hive / Eagle over Shield............ 40.00
Maryland: Baltimore, Mount Vernon Club, 5 / Liberty
Head.. 250.00

Massachusetts: Boston, G. F. Tuttle's Restaurant,
Steer's Head / Good For 5 Cents 70.00
__: Worcester, Charles Lang, Bearded Head l. /
Die Sinker & Gen'l Engraver 35.00
Michigan: Addison, Smith Brothers, Sheaf of
Wheat / Dealers in Dry Goods Groceries &
Hardware...25.00
__: Detroit, American Coffee Mills / Indian
Head 25.00

__: Pontiac, A. Parker Dealer in Drugs.../ French's
Hair Restorative, Bottle 50.00
Minnesota: St. Paul, Wheeler & Wilsons Sewing
Machines / Sewing Machine 175.00
__: Winona, Coe & Hayden Dry Goods Crockery
Boots.../ The Regulator, No.2, Simpson
Block 175.00
Missouri: St. Joseph, John Kenmuir Man'fg Jeweler
/ John Kenmuir Watch Maker ....Rare
New Hampshire: Concord, A.W. Gale, Restorator
at Depot / Good for One Cent in Goods.... 25.00
New Jersey: Jersey City, Terhune Brothers Hardware
/ Eagle on Globe 12.00

__: Trenton, E.W.Titus / Dry Goods Oil Clothes
Carpets 6.00
New York: J.J.Benson, Good for 25 Cents, Suttler
1st Mtd. Riffles 75.00
__: Albany, Benjamin & Herrick Fruit Dealers /
Redeemed at 427 Broadway....................... 6.00

__: Binghamton, Evans & Allen Watches & Jewelry
/ "Business Card" in Wreath..................... 12.00
__: Brooklyn, T.Ivory Billiard Saloon / -I-O-U-
1 Cent 8.00
__: Buffalo, Alberger's Meat Store / Indian
Head..8.00
__: New York, Felix ___ (i.e. Kosher) Dining
Saloon / Indian Head............................... 35.00

__:__ Feuchtwanger's Composition, "3 Three Cents"
within Wreath / Eagle grasping snake
1864 ....Rare
__:_, Fr. Freise, Leichenbesorger, Indian Head / Fr.
Freise, Undertaker, Coffin within Wreath ...6.00
__: Oswego, M.L.Marshall, Fish / Toys, Fancy
Goods, Fishing Tackle and Rare Coin.........8.00
Ohio: Berea, D.E.Stearns, Grindstone in mounting /
Grindstones Mounted with Patent Adjustable
Rest...,...8.00
__: Cambridge, A.C. COCHRAN, Lock / Eagle15.00
__: Cincinnati, A. Bruggemann Grocer / Compass
and Square within Stars 15.00
__:_, Carl Haas 493 Vine St. / Carl Haas, Rabbit
(See Brazil, Indiana). 10.00

__:__, One Hair Cut Hill / Blank 40.00
__: Kenton, J.M. Brunson, Dealer in Dry Goods /
Fancy & Staple Dry Goods &c., Flag......... 15.00
__: Warren, Robbin's Card / Photographic Albums
15 Market St... 15.00
Pennsylvania: Lancaster, S.H. Zahm, Dealer in
Coins, Tokens, Medals &c / Benjamin
Franklin.. 50.00
__: Philadelphia, M.C.Campbell's Dancing Academy
/ Skating Acadamy, Washington
Hall 12.00
__: Pittsburgh, Pittock News Dealer / Indian
Head 6.00
Rhode Island: Providence, H.Y. LeFavre, Pro
Empire Saloon, UNION in wreath / Beer
Mug.. 20.00
__:_, Pohle 1863, Grapes / Elmwood Vineyard,
Anchor...Rare
Tennessee: Clarksville, Andrew King Merch't / See
Best Stock in City at King's....................... Rare

__: Nashville, Walker & Napier / Indian Head Rare
Virginia: Norfolk, F.Pfeiffer & Co., VA in wreath /
Good for a Scent 1863, Dog Head 125.00
West Virginia: Wheeling, Bassett's Cheap Dry
Goods 55 Main St. / Mercury Head 20.00

VF

Wisconsin: Columbus, William's Bros. Chemists & Druggists, Mortar and Pestle / Liberty Head 15.00

__: Milwaukee, D.J. Doornink, Beehive / Groceries & Dry Goods Cor. of 10th & Cherry St. 15.00
__: Oshkosh, Allen Vosburg & Co. Music Store / Steinway's Pianos, Smith's Melodeons & Tremolo Harmoniums 60.00
Anonymous Patriotic Tokens: Liberty, Liberty Head r. / Shield surrounded by Stars 6.00
__: Indian Princess Head l. / Union For Ever, Shield 6.00
__: Benjamin Franklin, Franklin's Bust r. / 'Penny Saved is a Penny Earned, wreath 6.00

__: 'The Union Must and Shall be Preserved, Bust of Andrew Jackson / Beware, Coiled Snake 6.00
__: The Flag of Our Union 1863, Flag, Liberty Cap on pole / If Anybody Attempts to Tear It Down, Shoot Him on the Spot, DIX in center 6.00
__: As previous but Spoot for Spot in error 7.00

__: Anchor / HOPE, ornaments above and below Rare
__: Our Little Monitor, Ironclad Ship / Anchor and 1863 in Wreath 6.00
__: Pro Bono Publico, Shield on Star / NEW YORK in wreath 6.00
__: Money Makes the Mare Go, Go it Buttons, Person Walking / United States Copper, Eagle on Globe 6.00
__: First in War, First in Peace, Equestrian Statue of Washington / Union for Ever over Shield, all in Wreath 6.00

ENCASED POSTAGE STAMPS

As mentioned above, throughout the Civil War coinage was scarce. Much of what the mint produced was hoarded — even base metal coins. People thought that if the their side fell at least real coins would retain some value. The government's answer was small size paper money, while merchants began using cent size copper tokens. A third interesting answer to the Civil War coin shortage was the encased postage stamp patented in August 1862. These consisted of unused U.S. postage stamps placed in a round brass holder and covered with a disc of mica, a transparent mineral. Thus the stamp was protected and its value could be read. Both in spirit and evolution, they were halfway between loose postage stamps and Civil War Tokens. Stamps actually did see some use as money during this emergency, but they were found to be inconvenient, not durable and ultimately messy. The brass side of encased postage stamps often carried advertisements. One of the advertisers on these was their inventor, John Gault of Boston. Encased postage was much less popular than Civil War Tokens. This is because they cost more to make than their face value as opposed to tokens, which were the opposite. Consequently, they are far scarcer today. One advantage of the encased postage stamp was its flexibility, which permitted values anywhere from one cent to 90 cents. Few people would take the Civil War Tokens at more than a cent.

Among the problems encountered with collecting these is there is often broken or missing mica. The prices given here are for examples with intact mica. Because of their thinness, bends are also a problem.

Known counterfeits: Specimens are known with modern mica replacing original but damaged mica. One should also be cautions to look for signs that they might have been bent, then straightened.

Aerated Bread Company, New York
  1¢ 750.00
Take Ayer's Pills
  1¢ 180.00
  5¢ 200.00
The Currency To Pass, Ayer's Cathartic Pills
  1¢ 180.00
  12¢ 510.00
Ayer's Sarsaparilla To Purify the Blood
  3¢ 175.00
Joseph L. Bates Fancy Goods, Boston
  1¢ 180.00
Brown's Bronchial Troches for Coughs and Colds
  5¢ 200.00
F. Buhl & Co., Detroit
  12¢ 750.00
Burnett's Cocoaine Kalliston Toilet Sets
  90¢ 2,000.00
Burnett's Standard Cooking Extracts
  3¢ 180.00
Dougan, (picture of top hat), New York
  3¢ 1,000.00

Drake's Plantation Bitters
  1¢ 275.00
J. Gault (mostly blank)
  2¢ 2,000.00
  3¢ 300.00
  10¢ 325.00
  24¢ 1,250.00
Kirkpatrick & Gault, Applications for Advertising, New York
  5¢ 225.00
Lord & Taylor, Dry Goods, New York 3¢ 750.00
  30¢ 1,900.00
No. American Life Insurance Co., N.Y.
  1¢ 250.00
Pearce, Tolle & Holton, Cincinnati
  5¢ 1,250.00
Sands Ale
  30¢ 3,000.00
Schapker & Bussing, Dry Goods, Evansville, Ind.
  10¢ 700.00

CONFEDERATE COINAGE

While the Confederacy struck hundreds of thousands of coins, those readily distinguishable as Confederate are virtually unobtainable. This is because most coins struck by the Confederacy were struck with old dies when Union mints were taken over. Most notable examples of this include the 1861-O half dollar, and the 1861-C and 1861-D half eagles.

Still, some patterns of half dollars and cents using distinctive Confederate dies were struck. A New Orleans die cutter prepared the half dollar reverse die, and four proof patterns were struck at the New Orleans mint, which combined the Confederate reverse with the regular Union Seated Liberty obverse. In 1879 when the Confederate half die was discovered by numismatists, it was used to strike 500 pieces in tin alloy, the other side bearing an historical inscription. After this press run, 500 strikes were made on 1861 half dollars, obliterating the union eagle reverse. Thus the appearance of these restrikes is roughly that of the four pieces struck by the Confederacy, except for flattened highpoints on Liberty caused by striking pressure on an already struck coin. Most are also lighter than an original Confederate half because most coins were prepared by the eagle side being planed off before striking. Coins with the Confederate reverse and a horseman obverse were made from completely new dies prepared in the early 1960s for the centennial of the Civil War.

Confederate cents were actually struck in the North. Before hostilities broke out, representatives of the Confederacy offered Philadelphia token manufacturer Robert Lovett, Jr., a contract to strike copper nickel cents. Lovett completed the dies, and struck a dozen trial pieces. After hostilities bagan he though it wise to hide the evidence of this project, and they were not revealed until 1873. The following year numismatist John Haseltine used the dies to strike very few in gold, silver and copper. Some time between 1874 and 1961 they were partially defaced but not destroyed. For the hundredth anniversary of the Confederate cent the original damaged dies were used to prepare virtually identical transfer dies. These transfer dies were used by coin dealer Robert Bashlow to coin second restrikes, mostly in silver, bronze and brass, but also small quantities each in several other metals.

Counterfeit alert: Modern replicas are quite common.

Unc.

Original

1861 1¢ Copper-nickel	12 Struck

1874 Haseltine Restrikes

1861 1¢ Copper	4,000.00
1861 1¢ Silver	only 12 struck
1861 1¢ Gold	only 7 struck

1961-1962 Bashlow Restrikes

1861 1¢ Platinum	3 Struck
1861 1¢ Gold	3 Struck
1861 1¢ Silver	12.00
1861 1¢ Nickel Silver	50 Struck
1861 1¢ Bronze	10.00
1861 1¢ Brass	10.00
1861 1¢ Lead	50 Struck
1861 1¢ Aluminum	50 Struck
1861 1¢ Tin	50 Struck
1861 1¢ Zinc	50 Struck
1861 1¢ Red Fiber	50 Struck
1861 Half Dollar	4 struck
same, 1879 restrike	3,000.00
1861 Scott Token with Confederate reverse	900.00

1862 The Confederate States of America : 22 February 1862 ★ Deo Vindice ★, Horseman in Wreath / Confederate half dollar reverse from new die (struck ca.1962)..10.00

MERCHANTS' TOKENS AND "GOOD FORS"

Merchants have long seen the value of having their names on tokens and medals. This practice goes back hundreds of years, and by the 1600s in England it was quite common. There are several different reasons for doing this. In times of financial crisis when real coins are in short supply, people are willing to take coin substitutes. An innovative merchant can alleviate his own shortage of small change and at the same time, advertise his business. Not only will the customer read his advertisement on it, but hundreds of people who come in contact with it in circulation might also. Another benefit to making such tokens is to increase the purchases of customers the merchant has already. If, for example, during the Great Depression, a merchant gave a new customer a token good for 5c at his store that customer was more likely to return to spend that token, rather than simply abandon its purchasing power. Many numismatists call this type of token a "good for" after its typical inscription. Similarly, merchant tokens are used to force a minimum purchase or a loan. Many video arcades sell game tokens in multiple piece lots. If a customer buys ten and only uses five, the arcade makes additional profit. If the customer uses the final five six months later, the merchant has enjoyed a loan of that amount of money for six months. Some merchant tokens simply proved payment of a fee, such as parking or locker tokens. Merchant tokens with no exchangeability were also useful as business cards, permitting the customer to keep a durable record of the merchant's address. Some of these tokens are uses as premiums for purchases, and are, in a sense, a gift to the customer. During the 1960s and 1970s, many gas stations distributed tokens displaying antique automobiles as gifts with a purchase.

Many people collect merchant tokens as a way of studying the history of their local area. The bear evidence of long lost business and community founders. In the Northeast, and to an extent the Midwest, this record is abundant and early tokens are cheap. In the Southwest, century old tokens are often nonexistent and even early twentieth century tokens can be desirable and pricey.

The biggest challenge to token collectors are the so-called mavericks. These are tokens that bear no indication of a home state and often no city. Because no one book fully catalogues all tokens, these mavericks often defy identification.

Prices on merchant tokens sometimes vary regionally. Those listed here are averages. In the area of issue, scarcer tokens can sell for double these prices or more. Conversely, outside of that area, they may be virtually impossible to sell at above more than a nominal price.

Known counterfeits: Late nineteenth and twentieth century merchant tokens are virtually never counterfeited. The largest exception to this is the series of brass bordello tokens inspired by ones used in the wild West. Virtually all of those encountered are recent falsities.

VF

Alabama: Birmingham. The Dude Saloon, Gentleman in top hat, standing / I O U ONE DRINK (nickel silver, 1866-89) 350.00

Alaska: ARRC (=Alaska Rural Rehabilitation Corp.) 25¢ Issued by the federal government (AL, 1935)..................................18.00

same, $5 (brass, 1935).........................65.00

_: Juneau. NUGGETT / Billiard 12 1/2¢ Parlor (brass, late 1890s) 3.50

Arizona: Tucson. Good for One Drink at Depot Beer Garden / George Sicocan Dealer in Wines Liquors and Cigars (Brass, 1966-89) 650.00

Arkansas: Little Rock. Herman Kahn Co. Wholesale Agents / This Check Will be Redeemed by Any Dealer, Good for One Fontella Cigar (Copper, 1866-89) 10.00

California: San Francisco. Cornell Watch Co., across Face of Clock / Tenth Industrial Fair of the Mechanics Institute (WM, 1875).........30.00

_: Good for a 10¢ cup of coffee at Sambo's anywhere, tiger and Sambo / What this country needs is a good 10¢ cup of coffee, Sambo's has it, hand with coffee (wood, c.1960s) 50

Colorado: Durango. Good for One Drink at Windsor Bar (Brass, 1880s)............................65.00

Connecticut: Hartford. Value Me as You Please, Stag standing l. / Alfred S. Robinson Banker Numismatist & Notary Public Dealer in... (Copper, 1861) The obverse of this token is copied from that of a Higley Copper of 1737. ....3.00

_: Trumbull. Amusement Technology Trumbull Shopping Park, Carosel with one horse / Token Not Refundable for Money, ´ 1 ´ (brass, ca.1982)..25

Delaware: Leipsic. S.H.L.'s Sons 3C / 3 within rays (brass, 1880-99) 25.00

Georgia: Savannah. Eldorado Saloon, 10 / blank (Nickel Silver, 1870s) 150.00

Idaho: Burke. Hunt & Moore Proprietors, Star / Good for 1 Drink (Brass, 1866-89) 15.00

Hawaii: Kona. Kona Dollar, Coat of Arms / Aloha, Kona Chamber of Commerce, Beach scene (brass, 1975)..................................2.00

Illinois: Chicago. Lyceum Theatre Finest Vaudeville House on Earth / Laughing Headquarters Burlesque Novelty Minstrels Spectacular Comedy (Nickel Silver, 1870-90)......................5.00

VF

Iowa: Harlan. One Only Good for $1.00 in Payment for Land, Lot, Farm Loan or Abstract from O.P.Wyland / A Residence in Shelby Co. Iowa - $1.00 - Since 1856(AL, c.1920s)...................... 5.00

Kansas: Athol. Freely Merchantile Co., Genl. Mdse. / Good for 5¢ in Trade (brass, ND).. 1.00

Kentucky: Louisville. Progress, Locomotive / Jewell & Beddo Jewelers, Masonic Temple (Brass, 1870s) 50.00

Louisiana: New Orleans. 1884 February / Mardi Gras Souvenir (Brass, 1884) 17.50

Maine: Houlton. Smiler Blake, Houlton, Maine / Good for Nickel in Trade (ND).................. 6.00

Maryland: Baltimore. For Benefit of Bohemian Cemetery / 5 within rays (brass, 1884-1900)................................Scarce

Massachusetts: Springfield. Massachusetts, Eagle r. / Springfield Antiquarieans...(names) (copper, 1866) 15.00

Michigan: Caro. 5 in circle of stars / Good For 5¢ Jake Hobson in Trade (brass, 1889)........... 8.50

Minnesota: St. Paul. Western Land Securities Co., view of farm / Upper Peninsula of Mich. Lands 712,000 Acres - Good for Refund of Railroad Fare... (bronze, ND).................................. 10.00

Mississippi: Canton. Take Me Back to Vic Trolio / Canton, Miss. Solid Silver (silver, ca.1880s)... 60.00

Missouri: St. Louis. Realtors, Saint Louis to the Front, Equestrian statuue of St. Louis / St. Louis Million Dollar Bond Issue, Large ** (brass, 1923)....................................... 5.00

Montana: Poplar Creek. P.W. Lewis Trader Poplar Creek M.T. / Good For $1.00 in Merchandise (brass, 1870-85)........................ 500.00

Nebraska: West Point. Drahos Bros., ornament / IOU 5¢ Drink (ND).................................. 10.00

Nevada: Goldfield. Red Top Bar Ajax & Martin / Good for 61/4¢ in Trade....................... 15.00

New Hampshire: Manchester. Compliments of W.P.Farmer Fine Footware 823 Elm. St. / 1846 Semi-Centennial Sept. 7.8.9 1896... (brass 1896)..20.00

New Jersey: Perth Amboy. Mrs. Schverlichovsky P.A.N.J., Anchor / Good for 5¢ in Trade (brass, 1866-89)......................... 15.00

New Mexico: Albuquerque. The J.M. Brunswick & Blake Cos. Check, Pool Table / Chas. E. Bonsall 121/2¢ (CN, 1886)................................. 150.00

New York: New York. Matthew's Soda Water Apparatus, Female Head l. / Cupid weilding wrench to ward off bear from soda water apparatus (copper, 1876)............................. 10.00

__:__. Cafe Lindinger, 56 & 58 Liberty St. New York / Fritz Lindinger 21/2 56 & 58 Liberty St. (CN, 1900)... 10.00

VF

__:__. Woman holding book and lamp before youth examining coin, Rare Coins below / Guttag Bros, Cartouche inscribed: Bonds Bank Stocks Foreign Money (bronze, 1920s-1930s)....... 4.00

North Carolina: Greensboro. Barrell inscribed Wines Liquors / In Newcomb We Trust, V cents (nickel, 1891)............................. 35.00

North Dakota: Mayville. Traill County Farms, Cream of the Red River Valley Luther Nelson / Good for $25 if You Buy Land of Luther Nelson...(AL, ND)............................... 5.00

Ohio: Cincinnati. Billigheimer's Billiard Hall Nos. 210 & 212 Vine St. / Four Leaf Clover (copper, 1880-88)......................... 12.50

Oklahoma: Tulsa. Peter Adamson Coal & Mdse. / Good for 5¢ in Merchandise (AL, ND).......Rare

Oregon: Astoria. Finnish Socialist Club / Good for 5¢ in Trade (brass, c.1890s)..................... 20.00

Pennsylvania: Greensburg. Star Brewing Co. / Good for 5¢ Hotel Merchants. (brass, octagonal, 1866-1889)......................... 8.00

__: Philadelphia. Benjamin Franklin 1706-1790, Head of Franklin / Souvenir Benjamin Franklin Memorial, Building, (AL, c.1970s)............... .25

Rhode Island: Pawtucket. Our Country's Pride Admiral Dewey, Bust of Dewey / We Will Redeem this from Any Dealer at 5c, Houston's Hand Made 5c Cigar F.J.Houston, 5c (AL, 1899) 15.00

South Carolina: Ridgeland. At Pickney Oyster Co. Store / Good for 50¢ in Merchandise (brass, c.1890s)...................................... 15.00

South Dakota: Blunt. Otis Land Co. Right Land Right Prices / Good For Railroad Fare in Payment of Land - Bought of Otis Land Co. (AL, ND) 15.00

Tennessee: Briceville. Cambria Coal Company This Order Payable in Merchandise Only / Payable Only to Employees Not Transferable, 1, ... (brass, ND)...............................1.00

Texas: El Paso. N.F. Newland, in oval / Good for 1 Acme Drink (CN, 1881)........................... 12.50

Utah: Salt Lake City. Hogle Zoo, Animal / My Country Good Luck, Flag and map (c.1960s)... .25

Vermont: St. Albans. Dowlings' Seegar Store / Good For 71/2¢ in Trade (c.1900-30s)...... 35.00

Virginia: Rosann. Panther Coal Co. 5 Not Transf., Panther / MMISC Des. Pat. In Trade (brass, ND) 2.00

Washington: Seattle. Bussell Land Co. Yakima Fruit Lands, Apple (in background) / Membership Emblem of the Don't Worry Club Good Luck, Swastika (brass, c.1920s)................. 5.00

West Virginia: Hinton. Wickham House Bar / 5 in circle surrounded by stars (brass, 1883-84).75.00

Wisconsin: Iola. Good for 5¢ Olson Bros. Iola Wis. in Trade / 5¢, small Indian riding above, ornament below (brass, 1880s)........................... 8.50

VF

Non-Local: Green Duck Corporation. No Cash Value, GDC monogram / Four interlocking circles.. .25

__: Chevrolet Superior 1924, Antique car / Antique Coin Series, Sunoco and DX logos (AL, 1968)...25

__: At Shopwell Food Stamp Credit Token 5¢ / Food Stamp Credit Token Redeemable only in Eligible Foods 5¢ (octagonal, AL, 1970s) 25

TRANSPORTATION TOKENS

Transportation tokens have been present for at least two centuries, possibly longer. In the United States they have been quite common for about a century. They are a specialized form of token usually used to indicate payment of a fare. There are several reasons to use tokens instead of money. Perhaps the most practical reason is that it prevents the driver from having to make change, and therefore to continue on their route without delay. Another reason is for security. If drivers and conductors collect only company tokens instead of cash, there is far less risk of robbery. It also reduces chances of embezzlement. There are many other reasons that are similar to the reasons for using merchant tokens: the forced loan that is implicit in purchasing tokens in advance and the additional profit made on non-redeemed tokens. Often, multiple fares can be sold in one transaction, reducing labor. The use of transportation tokens also permits a special class of people, like students, to ride for free. Many municipalities also permit senior citizens to purchase tokens at a discount. Sometimes quantity purchasers are also given this opportunity.

One distinctive feature of transportation tokens is that they frequently use cut out designs. These cut outs are often the initial of the issuing firm or its symbol. Most are of moderate size, generally between the size of a United States dime and quarter.

One of the most exciting aspects of collecting transportation tokens is that the majority of counties in the United States can claim one piece or another, thus most people can collect their own local history.

Dates listed below are often the first release date. Many tokens stayed in production or distribution for years.

Known counterfeits: There are very few counterfeits in this series. Some restrikes of scarcer tokens are known.

XF

Alabama: Birmingham Transit Company, Statue of Vulcan. Cut-out: 2 slots. (bronze)............... 1.00

Alaska: Juneau Transit System (bronze, 1949) ...25

Arizona: Tucson Rapid Transit Co., T (WM, 1947-55 .... .25

Arkansas: Uptown is Downtown, logo / Little Rock Unlimited Progress, Inc..... (brass, 1975)... .35

XF

California: Pasadena City Lines, Inc., Rose / Good For One Fare, Rose (CN, 1948) 25

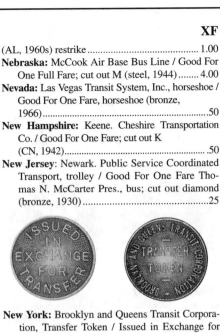

Connecticut: State Shield of Arms / Connecticut Turnpike Good for 1 Fare, Map (brass, c.1980) 25

__: Bridgeport Auto Transit Co., B / Good for One Fare, B (WM, 1948) 25

Delaware: Wilmington. Delaware Coach Company / Good For One Fare; Cut out W (steel, 1943) 25

Florida: Miami Transit Company, Monogram / Miami Transit Company, Monogram; cut out ball (CN, 1940-74) 35

Georgia: Rome Street Railway, 5 / J.D. Williamson President, 5 (celluloid, early 20th century) 125.00

Hawaii: Honolulu Rapid Transit Co. 1924 Ltd. / , Good For One Fare; Cut out H (zinc, 1943)......................................25

Idaho: Moscow. Neely's Taxi / Good For 25¢ Taxi Service (AL, ND) 20.00

Illinois: The Chicago & South Side Rapid Transit R.R. Co. Good for One Continuous Ride, large 31 / Deposit this in Gateman's Box, large 31 (AL, pre-1924)................................. 6.00

Indiana: Elwood Transit / Good For One City Fare; cut out E (bronze, 1946)..............................25

Iowa: Des Moines City Railway Co. One Fare, Diamond / Des Moines City Railway Co. One Fare, Diamond, (AL, 1893-1909) 5.50

Kansas: Manhattan Transit, Inc. / Good For One Fare (bronze, 1949) 1.00

Kentucky: Louisville. Bridge Transit Company / Good For One Fare (zinc, ND) 50

Louisiana: New Orleans. N.O. & Carrollton R.R. Co. Employee Pass / numbers (AL, ND) 75.00

Maine: The Bill Johnson Insurance Agency Inc., BJ / Ride the Bus Free Expires 5-17-81 (wood, 1981) 50

Maryland: The Roland Park Homeland Company / One Fare Hemeland-Guilford; cut out H (CN, 1927)..50

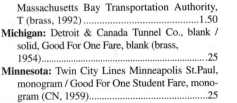

Massachusetts: Sail Boston 1 9 9 2, waves / Massachusetts Bay Transportation Authority, T (brass, 1992) 1.50

Michigan: Detroit & Canada Tunnel Co., blank / solid, Good For One Fare, blank (brass, 1954)..25

Minnesota: Twin City Lines Minneapolis St.Paul, monogram / Good For One Student Fare, monogram (CN, 1959)...25

Missouri: Full Fare, K.C.RYS.Co / Full Fare, K.C.RYS.Co., cut out bar (CN, 1917) 50

Montana: Baker Street Ferry M.L.Lynch, 25 / Fort Benton 1860, Two Indians in canoe (brass, late 1800s) 100.00

XF

(AL, 1960s) restrike 1.00

Nebraska: McCook Air Base Bus Line / Good For One Full Fare; cut out M (steel, 1944) 4.00

Nevada: Las Vegas Transit System, Inc., horseshoe / Good For One Fare, horseshoe (bronze, 1966)...50

New Hampshire: Keene. Cheshire Transportation Co. / Good For One Fare; cut out K (CN, 1942)..50

New Jersey: Newark. Public Service Coordinated Transport, trolley / Good For One Fare Thomas N. McCarter Pres., bus; cut out diamond (bronze, 1930) 25

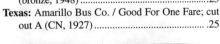

New York: Brooklyn and Queens Transit Corporation, Transfer Token / Issued in Exchange for Transfer (CN, 1929).................................... 1.00

New York City Transit Authority, NYC / Good For One Fare, NYC; cut out Y (brass, 1953).......25

___: Diamond Jubilee Seventy Fifth Anniversary NYC Subway 1904-1979, subway car / NYC Subway 1904-1979 People Moving People, subway station entrance; cut out diamond (brass).. 1.00

Ohio: Cleveland. Municipal Traction Co. / 3 Cent Ticket 1908 (AL) large central hole 3.00

Oklahoma: Oklahoma City. Oklahoma Railway Co., O / Good For One City Fare, O (iron, 1943).......................................25

Pennsylvania: Beaver Falls. H.T.B. Line / Good For One Fare, 15¢ (brass, 1937)................... 1.00

___: Pittsburgh. 43rd St. Bridge, large 2 / C.Siebert-Treas. (brass, 1870-1912) 7.00

Rhode Island: Providence. R.I.P.T.A., roadrunner / R.I.P.T.A., roadrunner; cut out star (AL, 1972)..25

South Carolina: Columbia. S.C. Electric & Gas Co., bus / Good For One Fare, bus; cut out ball (brass, 1950)...................................... 25

South Dakota: Rapid City. Rapid Transit Line / Fare Token; cut out R (steel, 1944) 50

Tennessee: Southern Coach Lines Inc. Nashville / Good For One Fare; cut out N (bronze, 1948)...25

Texas: Amarillo Bus Co. / Good For One Fare; cut out A (CN, 1927) 25

Utah: U L A T C O Salt Lake City, bee hive / Good For Child's Fare Ages 5 to 12 R.H.Jones Treas. (square, brass, 1942)......................................50

XF

Vermont: Burlington. Chittenwood C.T.A., bus / Good For One Fare, bus; cut out slots (brass, 1973) 25

Virginia: Virginia Electric & Pwr. Co. / One Fare Norfolk Div.; cut out N (CN, 1941)...............25

Washington: Seattle Municipal Railway / Full Fare D.W.Henderson Supt.; cut out triangle (copper, c.1920)..25

POLITICAL TOKENS

Political tokens are a natural outgrowth of buttons, pins and other ornaments, which people wore to show their political affiliations or promote the candidates they endorsed. The earliest campaign tokens were almost exclusively designed with holes so that they could be sewn onto a garment, such as on a lapel. As political trinkets evolved, the pin and the tokens went in different directions, to the point where today they are very distinct items. Lapel pins are outside the realm of numismatics and this book.

There were no campaign pins for our first president, but some ornaments were worn to celebrate his inauguration. Tokens first played a role in Andrew Jackson's 1824 presidential campaign. They were struck only intermittently until the 1840s, and in relatively small quantities. It was with the presidential campaign of William Henry Harrison in 1840 that they finally came into their own, being distributed in unprecedented quantities. They continued to be popular for wearing and increasingly as pocket pieces through the 1930s. In the last sixty years they have again taken a new turn. The late twentieth century political token is often larger and more artistic than the smaller pocket piece, which continues to be struck, but in smaller numbers and more sporadically. Large size pieces were also struck in the 1800s but they were not as common as the smaller ones. As they have grown larger in the post-war era their compositions have changed. The small pocket pieces were traditionally brass, the earlier large medals often "white metal," a tin alloy. The new incarnation of the large political medal is more likely bronze, copper-nickel or silver.

The study of these tokens is particularly interesting because of their images and inscriptions. Not only are the candidates from both (or several) sides usually depicted, but the hotly debated issues of the day are often discussed, sometimes with biting satire. Also, styles of popular iconography scan be traced.

Known counterfeits: Restrikes are more dangerous than counterfeits in this series. Many dies were dug out of storage years after the campaigns for which they were created, and used to strike new issues for collectors. These restrikes can sometimes be distinguished by differences in edge or in alloy. Specialized references are of great use here.

Note: All examples listed here are brass and smaller than an Anthony dollar unless indicated.

VF

1789 George Washington
Long Live the President, GW in oval (large silvered copper button)..Rare

1824 Andrew Jackson
Bust facing / Hero of New Orleans, in wreath 40.00

1828 Andrew Jackson
Bust facing, 1829 below / Eagle with arrows and olive branch, stars around (large, white metal) 400.00

1832 Andrew Jackson
Bust facing / The Gallant & Successful Defender of N.Orleans, eagle in wreath This is also a Hard Times Token 350.00

1836 Martin van Buren
Bust right / Democracy and Our Country, Temple surmounted by eagle................................. 100.00

1840 William Henry Harrison
Bust left / The People's Choice The Hero of Tippecanoe, Log Cabin 25.00

1844 James K. Polk
Bust of Polk / Bust of George M. Dallas (large, white metal) 150.00

1848 Zachary Taylor
Major General Zachary Taylor, Hero of Palo Alto Resaca de la Palma Monterey and Buena Vista 1847, Bust facing / United States of America 1847, eagle... 40.00

1852 Franklin Pierce
Gen. Franklin Pierce The Statesmen & Soldier, three-quarters bust / Pierce & King the People's Choice, eagle 35.00

1856 James Buchanan
No Sectionalism, Bust right / United States of America, eagle... 15.00

1860 Abraham Lincoln
Hon. Abraham Lincoln, Bust right / The Rail Splitter of the West, Lincoln splitting wood while formally dressed gentleman hods wedge in place 25.00

1864 Abraham Lincoln
For President Abraham Lincoln, Head right / For Vice President Andrew Johnson, Head right (copper) This is also a Civil War Token. 45.00

1868 Ulysses S. Grant
General U.S.Grant 1868, Facing Bust / I Propose to Fight It Out on This Line If It Takes All Summer, wreath 20.00

VF

1872 Ulysses S. Grant
President U.S.Grant 1872, Bust left / Patient of Toil, Serene Amidst Alarms, Inflexible in Faith, Invincible in Arms (copper) 20.00

1876 Rutherford B. Hayes
Rutherford B. Hayes for President of the United States, Centennial America 1876, Bust half-left / Wm. A. Wheeler for Vice President of the United States, Centennial 1876 America, Bust half-right 20.00

1880 James Garfield
Conjoined busts of Garfield and Arthur left / J.A.Garfield C.A. Arthur, UNION on ribbon across shield... 15.00

1884 Grover Cleveland
Conjoined busts of Cleveland and Hendricks / Cleveland and Hendricks on a Broad Platform of Good Planks Will Lead All to Victory, 1884 Fasces... 15.00

1888 Benjamin Harrison
Harrison & Morton, Conjoined busts right / Protection to American Industry 1888, arm and hammer 15.00

1892 Grover Cleveland
Public Office a Public Trust Grover Cleveland, Conjoined busts of Mr. & Mrs. Cleveland left / Democracy's Trump Card an Honest Administration..15.00

XF

1896 "Bryan Money"
A Government Dollar Contains 4121/2 Grains Coin Silver 900/1000 Fine, This Piece

VF

Contains 823 Grains Coin Silver in Value the Equivalent of One Gold Dollar.../ Size of Government Dollar Containing 4121/2 Grains of Silver 900/1000 Fine, inscribed on edge of spoked wheel which is smaller than medal and off center (large, silver)..........................150.00

1900 William McKinley
William McKinley, bust left / Republican Candidate 1900, eagle 15.00

1904 Theodore Roosevelt
Facing Bust surrounded by stars / St. Louis 1904 World's Fair..., domed building (silvered brass)...20.00

1928 or 1932 Herbert Hoover
Hoover Lucky Pocket Piece, elephant / Good for 4 Years of Prosperity.......................................5.00

1932 Franklin D. Roosevelt
Keep This Coin for Good Luck, Conjoined busts of Roosevelt and Garner, swastika and anchor at sides / Elect the Democratic Party, Happy Days are Here Again (large, brassed copper)...7.00

1936 Franklin D. Roosevelt
Onward America A New Deal Franklin D. Roosevelt, bust left / Member NRA We Do Our Part, eagle holding gear and lightning (red fiber).............5.00

1960 John F. Kennedy   **BU**
Kennedy and Johnson...The Best Men for the Job, facing busts of Johnson and Kennedy / Put a Democrat Back in the White House Vote in November Vote Democratic, cartoon donkey head (large, CN) 5.00

1972 Richard M. Nixon
Richard M. Nixon, head right / Re-elect the President, stylized elephant (large, bronze).........5.00

1976 Gerald Ford
Ford & Dole in 1976 for President and Vice-President, Conjoined busts left / With a Job a Person Has a Chance, workers (large, nickel silver) 7.00

1984 Ronald Reagan
Medal of Merit Ronald Reagan Founder, facade of White House / Republican Presidential Task Force, heraldic eagle (very large, bronze)...5.00

U.S. MINT MEDALS

Medals are coin-like items struck for artistic and commemorative purposes, but that lack any face value, and aren't considered legal tender. They are often of higher relief and larger than most coins.

The United States has been striking medals even longer than it has had a mint, and for most of its history the mint has done more than just make coins. On March 25, 1776, the Continental Congress began a tradition that has survived to this day. It voted to award General George Washington a gold medal of a special design to honor his liberation of Boston from the British. Over the course of the Revolutionary War, several heroic leaders were honored with similar medals. However, years later, not one had yet been awarded! Because the United States did not have a mint of its own, it had to rely on French engravers and the Paris mint to produce its medals. It was several years before Thomas Jefferson could prod the artists into completing their tasks. In addition to the gold medals actually being awarded, some examples of these first medals were also struck in silver for presentation to officials and for reference. During the bicentennial celebrations a large quantity were also restruck in pewter with new dies for public distribution. The tradition of awarding special gold medals to national heroes, both military and civilian has continued. These include people as diverse as Robert Frost and Gen. Colin Powell. Quite frequently the public is given an opportunity to purchase bronze strikes of these gold medals both at the mint and by mail order.

The special series of medals struck to honor each president at his inauguration has an interesting origin. Originally, special large medals were prepared bearing a depiction of the president and, on the reverse, symbols of peace like clasped hands. These were for presentation to Native American chiefs. For this reason these are today known as Indian Peace Medals. The very first ones, presented before the U.S. mint was in operation, were hand engraved. Later they were struck. Over the span of time the designs became more elaborate and by the end of the nineteenth century this series naturally evolved into modern presidential inauguration medals.

After the mint became established, and particularly after the mid-1800s, many other medals were struck for sale to the public. A large number were sold as souvenirs of the 1876 and 1892. Others were authorized by Congress to commemorate special events, officials or buildings. Many have been restruck, but even some century old originals are today very inexpensive.

In addition to government issued medals, such as the ones listed here, many private firms have struck tens of thousands of other medals, both here and abroad. This is a specialized field of collecting, and many dealers may choose not to purchase medals offered to them.

Known counterfeits: One should not confuse official restrikes and reissues for original medals. Often, special expertise is needed, with differences in alloy and finish being the best clues.

NOTE: Date listed first is date on medal, not necessarily the date struck. Values are for average grade. This means VF to XF for early medals, Mint State for those manufactured (not dated) during the past hundred years.

Average

1776 Georgio Washington Svupremo Dvci Exercitvvm Adsertori Libertatis Comitia Americana, Bust of Washington r. / Hostibus Premo Fugatis, Washington and officers, mounted, on highlands, overlooking the evacuation of British from Boston (gold) ....Extremely Rare
same, restruck in 1974 (pewter) 3.00

1781 Libertas Americana 4 Juil. I776, Liberty head l., Liberty Cap on Pole behind / Non Sine Diis Animosus Infans, Allegory of France saving the infant America from a British Lioness (copper, 48mm.).. 1,200.00
1793 Indian Peace Medal. Indian and George Washington sharing a peace pipe, farmer plowing in background / Heraldic eagel (silver, large oval)... Rare
1849 Indian Peace Medal. Bust of Zachary Taylor / Peace and Friendship, Two hands clasped. (silver, 51mm) ....Rare
1863, Lieut. General T.J. Jackson, Stonewall..., Head l. / Kernstown, Front Royal, Middletown..., surrounded by wreath inscribed with Bull Run, Chantilly, ..., armaments below. (white metal, 2") This was an issue of the Confederate government. 120.00

Average

1871 Bust of Ulysses S. Grant, "Let us have peace." above, Liberty Justice and Equality below / On Earth Peace Good Will Towards Men, Globe, Bible, and farm implements (copper, 64mm)..300.00

1876, In Commemoration of the Hundredth Anniversary of American Independence..., Liberty standing crowning Industry and Art who kneel at her side / These United Colonies Are, and of Right Ought to be, Free and Independent States 1776, America kneeling with sword (bronze, 21/4")... 75.00

Average

1893 U.S. GovT Building, Domed Building with flags / Treasury Department United States Mint Exhibit, World's Columbian Exposition Chicago 1893 (bronze, Dollar size) 7.00

1926 Sesquicentennial - International - Exposition Philadelphia, Head of Washington r. / Liberty Riding Pegasus r. (brass, dollar size) 15.00

Unc.

1961 John F. Kennedy Innaugural medal R: Presidential seal (gold, 70mm).......................Unique

same (bronze, 1 5/6") 2.00

1969 Opening of the New Philadelphia Mint. Main Entrance / Eagle holding balance scales, map superimposed (silver, 76mm).................... 85.00

same (bronze, 1 5/16") 2.00

(reduced)

1976 Half figure of Statue of Liberty, 1776 1976 at sides / Heraldic eagle, American Revolution Bicentennial We the People, ARBA logos (gold, 3") 4,500.00

1972-76 American Revolution Bicentennial Medal. Many varieties authorized by A.R.B.A. usually depicting one of the Founding Fathers on obverse. (bronze, dollar size) 1.50

same canceled in first day cover.................. 2.25

similar but struck in pewter and in a case ... 2.50

1992 Battle scene / Persian Gulf Veterans National Medal, Dedicated to..., Eagle, (bronze, 11/2") 12.50

General Colin Powell Chairman Joint Chiefs..., Facing bust (gold, 3")...................................Unique

same (bronze, 11/2") 2.00

TAX & RATION TOKENS

During the Great Depression many states imposed new sales taxes. It was quickly found that collecting sales tax on a purchase of 10 cents or less was a complicated matter. Either the tax had to be waived or, in terms of percentages, significantly more than the actual amount due had to be collected. In this era of poverty, people seriously objected to paying almost a whole cent extra, but the states would not forgo their revenue. The answer was a token valued at a fraction of a cent — usually between 1/10¢ and 5/10¢. Thirteen states and numerous localities issued these tokens not only in metal, but in plastic and fiber as well.

The Federal government also used fiber tokens, although for a different reason. During World War II, the Office of Price Administration issued tokens to indicate that the purchaser was authorized to buy certain quantities of rationed goods. Their color indicated what sort of commodity was authorized.

It is interesting to note that Missouri plastic tokens were issued because the O.P.A. refused to permit the use of zinc because of war time rationing.

Known counterfeits: Possibly none.

Unc.

Alabama. Luxury Tax 1 mill. Inscriptions (AL, holed, 1937-38).. .25

Arizona. Sales Tax 1 mill. State Seal (zinc, 1942)... 1.00

__. same (copper, 1937-40) .... .25

Colorado. Retail Sales Tax 2 mills. Inscriptions (AL, cruciform hole, 1937-42) .... .25

Illinois. Retailers' Occupation 11/2 mills. Inscriptions (AL, square, 1935-36) .... .25

Kansas. Sales Tax 2 mills. Large K (zinc, 1937-39)... .25

Louisiana. Public Welfare Tax 1 mill. Octagon (AL, triangular hole, 1938-40) .... .25

Mississippi. Sales Tax 1 mill. Inscriptions. (plastic, 1943-52)... .25

Missouri. Sales Tax Receipt 1 mill. Map. (zinc, 1937-42)... .25

__. Sales Tax 1 mill. 1 in Target. (plastic, 1943-61)...25

New Mexico. Emergency School Tax. 1 mill. Eagle / Sun. (AL, 1935-42)...................................... .25

__. School Tax. 5 mills. Inscriptions (fiber, 1942-49) 10.00

Oklahoma. Consumer's Tax Check. 1 mill. Target (AL, holed, 1936-37)................................... .25

Unc.

Utah. Emergency Relief Fund. 1 mill. Circle of stars. (AL, 1937-38)...................................... .25

Washington. Tax on Purchase 10 Cents of Less. Horizontal line. (AL, holed, 1935-41)........... .25

Federal WWII Ration Token

★OPA★RED★POINT, 1 / same (red fiber)........ .25

same (blue fiber)... .25

HAWAII

Before becoming a part of the United States, Hawaii was an independent kingdom with its own coinage. Because of close economic ties with the United States, Hawaiian coinage was deliberately struck to American coinage standards. All of it was engraved and struck under contract in the United States.

The first Hawaiian coin was a large cent depicting King Kamehameha III (1825-54). These were prepared in Attleboro, Massachusetts. A year before this coin was demonetized in 1884, a new set of coins was struck in silver. These were designed by Charles Barber and struck at the San Francisco mint.

When Hawaii became an American territory, many of the silver coins were withdrawn and melted. Others were made into jewelry, such as cuff links, pins and bracelets. Solder marks from such uses are often seen on dimes and quarters. These mutilated coins sell at a heavy discount. Another problem with surviving Hawaiian coins is they've been cleaned.

During this period many Hawaiians also spent copper or brass plantation tokens. These were tokens struck by the owner of the plantation on which they worked, and good at the company store. Sometimes it was the only medium in which workers were paid.

Known counterfeits: Beginning 1947 brass replicas of the 1847 cent have been struck as souvenirs.

	F	XF
1847 Cent	225.00	425.00
1883 Dime	45.00	250.00
1883 Quarter	45.00	90.00
1883/1383 Quarter	50.00	100.00

	F	XF
1883 Half Dollar	65.00	250.00
1883 Dollar	250.00	600.00

PLANTATION TOKENS

Grove Ranch Plantation
G.R.P. over date / Value

1886 12 1/2¢	275.00	650.00
1887 12 1/2¢	350.00	800.00

Haiku Plantation
Trees around border / Star with rays

1882 1 Real	150.00	400.00

Thomas Hobron Railroad
R.R. over date / T.H.H. over value

1879 12 1/2¢	125.00	325.00
1879 25¢		Rare

Kahului Railroad
Obv. & Rev. Inscriptions only

1891 10¢	250.00	600.00
1891 15¢	250.00	600.00
1891 20¢	250.00	600.00
1891 35¢	250.00	600.00
1891 75¢		Rare

Wailuku Plantation
HI and star / W.P. and value

ND 6¢	175.00	500.00
1871 12 1/2¢	200.00	650.00

W.P. 1880 in wreath / Value

1880 Half Real	250.00	700.00

W.P. 1880 within stars / Value

1880 1 Real	175.00	600.00

John Thomas Waterhouse
Bust of Kamehameha IV / Beehive

(1862)	400.00	1,250.00

U.S. PHILIPPINES

After centuries as a Spanish colony the Philippine Islands were taken by the United States as a conquest of the Spanish-American War in 1898. In 1935 it was made a United States Commonwealth with more autonomy. During World War II the Islands endured a harsh Japanese occupation during which many local guerrillas fought for the American cause. The Philippines were granted independence in 1947 following the war.

From 1903 to 1906 the standards of Philippine silver coinage approximated that of domestic United States coins. In 1907 it was reduced by about a third. From 1925 onwards some coins bear the M mintmark for Manila. Beginning in 1936 the coat of arms of the Commonwealth of the Philippines replaces that of the United States, although "United States of America" continued to surround the arms.

Commemoratives were issued in 1936 for the change to commonwealth status. Many of these were dumped into Manila Bay at the Japanese invasion. After the war they were recovered, but show obvious corrosion. While some are willing to collect them, their values are substantially discounted depending on extent of corrosion.

Known counterfeits: 1906S Peso. Casts of the 1936 Commonwealth issues have been made.

HALF CENTAVO (bronze) — VF

1903	1.00
1904	1.00
1905	Proof only 100.00
1906	Proof only 80.00
1908	Proof only 80.00

ONE CENTAVO (bronze) — VF

1903	1.00
1904	1.00
1905	1.00
1906	Proof only 80.00
1908	Proof only 80.00
1908S	2.00
1909S	10.00
1910S	2.00
1911S	2.00
1912S	2.00
1913S	2.00
1914S	2.00
1915S	25.00
1916S	10.00
1917S, 7 over 6	5.00
1917S	2.00
1918S	2.00
1918S, Large S	50.00
1919S	2.00
1920	2.00
1920S	12.00
1921	1.00
1922	1.00
1925M	1.00
1926M	1.00
1927M	1.00
1928M	1.00
1929M	1.50
1930M	1.50
1931M	1.50
1932M	2.75
1933M	.75
1934M	2.00
1936M	1.00

1937M	1.00
1938M	.75
1939M	1.00

ONE CENTAVO (bronze) — VF

1940M	.75
1941M	1.00
1944S	.15

FIVE CENTAVOS (cupronickel) — VF

1903	1.00
1904	1.50
1905	Proof only 135.00
1906	Proof only 120.00
1908	Proof only 120.00
1916S	20.00
1917S	2.00
1918S	2.00
1918S mule with 20c rev.	200.00
1919S	3.00
1920	4.00
1921	4.00
1925M	4.00
1926M	4.50
1927M	4.00
1928M	4.50
1930M	2.00
1931M	2.00
1932M	2.00
1934M	3.00
1935M	2.00

1937M	1.50
1938M	1.25
1941M	1.50
1944 (copper-nickel-zinc)	.15
1944S (copper-nickel-zinc)	.15
1945S (copper-nickel-zinc)	.15

TEN CENTAVOS (silver) — VF

1903	2.00
1903S	10.00
1904	12.50
1904S	2.00
1905	Proof only 135.00
1906	Proof only 125.00

Reduced Size

1907	3.00
1907S	2.50
1908	Proof only 160.00
1908S	1.75
1909S	20.00
1910S	Not confirmed
1911S	3.50

TEN CENTAVOS (silver)

	VF
1912S	4.00
1913S	4.50
1914S	5.00
1915S	15.00
1917S	1.75
1918S	1.75
1919S	1.75
1920	5.00
1921	1.50
1929M	1.50
1935M	1.50

	VF
1937M	1.00
1938M	.75
1941M	1.00
1944D	.50
1945D	.50

TWENTY CENTAVOS (silver)

	VF
1903	3.00
1903S	20.00
1904	20.00
1904S	3.00
1905	Proof only 185.00
1905S	8.00
1906	Proof only 190.00

Reduced Size

	VF
1907	4.00
1907S	3.00
1908	Proof only 145.00
1908S	3.00
1909S	8.00
1910S	8.00
1911S	8.00
1912S	5.00
1913S	5.00
1913S, S over S	15.00
1914S	3.00
1915S	3.00
1916S	3.00
1917S	2.00
1918S	2.00
1919S	2.00
1920	3.00
1921	2.00
1928M, 8 over 7	12.00
1929M	2.00

	VF
1937M	1.50
1938M	1.00
1941M	1.00
1944D	.75
1944D, D over S	20.00
1945D	.75

FIFTY CENTAVOS (silver)

	VF
1903	6.00
1903S	3,500.00
1904	25.00
1904S	6.50
1905	Proof only 350.00
1905S	8.00
1906	Proof only 300.00

Reduced Size

	VF
1907	5.00
1907S	4.00
1908	Proof only 275.00
1908S	4.00
1909S	6.00
1917S	6.00
1918S	4.00
1919S	4.50
1920	4.00
1921	4.00

	XF
1936M Commemorative	35.00

1944S	2.50
1945S	2.50

ONE PESO (silver)

	VF
1903	15.00
1903S	12.00
1904	65.00
1904S	14.00
1905	Proof only 850.00
1905S	18.00
1906	Proof only 500.00
1906S	1,200.00

Reduced Size

1907	2 known
1907S	4.50
1908	Proof only 500.00
1908S	4.50
1909S	4.50
1910S	5.50
1911S	15.00
1912S	15.00

	XF
1936M Roosevelt and Quezon	55.00
1936M Murphy and Quezon	55.00

UNITED STATES PAPER MONEY

INTRODUCTION

Before the Civil War there was no such thing as United States government paper money. During the Revolutionary War the states and the Continental Congress printed so much paper money to finance their expenses that its value evaporated and it became nearly worthless. As a result, when the Constitution was written it contained the words "No state shall ... make anything but gold and silver coin a tender in payment of debts (1§10)." Because of this the government avoided issuing paper money until the Civil War, and even then it was issued under limited circumstances. The first type of paper money, Demand Notes, even bore interest.

Most of the paper money issued by the United States over the following century was in fact redeemable for gold or silver. There are many different kinds of American paper money, as the following sections will show. Their names, usually found at the top of the note as a heading, and often the colors of their seals, indicate the law that authorized their issue and the nature of their backing.

Almost all United States paper currency bears a date, but this is not necessarily the year it was actually printed. It was the year of the act authorizing the series or the year the series went into production. The signature combinations on banknotes can often be used to date them.

Originally paper money was larger than today. Until 1928 they were about 7-1/2" by 3-1/8". Beginning with the series of 1928 (released 1929) they have been 6-1/8" x 2-5/8". The fractional notes of the Civil War were smaller than current notes, but varied in size.

GRADING PAPER MONEY

State of preservation is as important for paper money as it is for coins. Paper money is primarily graded to describe the amount of wear. Other factors can influence value, though. Many of the terms used to describe the grades of paper money are the same as for coins. Of course the physical nature of paper requires a whole different set of definitions. They are briefly described here.

Crisp Uncirculated (CU) - This is a note that is pristine as issued. It is literally crisp, with sharply pointed corners. It must have absolutely no folds, tears, or edge rounding. It can have no stains or staple holes either.

Extremely Fine (XF) - This is a particularly nice note with only the slightest sign of wear. It will still be crisp to the touch. Slight rounding of the corner points is possible but no significant folds or creases. No tears, stains or staple holes at all.

A convenient method of detecting creases in a note is to hold the note pointed at a narrow light source and look at it from an acute angle, though not directly in the direction of the light.

Very Fine (VF) - This is a nice clean note with obvious but moderate signs of wear. Creases that break the ink will be visible, but generally only one in each direction, and not too deep. Its corner points will be dull. While not limp, it will have only some of the crispness of better grade notes. No significant stains are visible.

Fine (F) - This is a worn but not worn out note. It has no crispness left. It will have heavy creases, but none that threaten the structural integrity of the note. Its edges may not be perfectly smooth, but are not irregularly worn. Trivial ink marks and smudges are acceptable.

Very Good (VG) - This note is worn and limp. It has serious deep creases. The edges are worn and uneven. Some ink marks or smudges are visible. Tiny tears may be present but no parts missing. Small staple or pin holes are acceptable.

Good (G) - This condition is not considered collectible for most purposes. Only the rarest of notes in this grade could find a home with most collectors. It is usually limp, heavily creased, stained, ripped. and pinned or stapled. Some of the creases will permit spots of light to shine through the note at their intersections.

HANDLING AND TREATMENT OF PAPER CURRENCY

The most important thing to know about handling currency is to NEVER FOLD PAPER MONEY. This instantaneously reduces its value. When in doubt as to whether a note has value or not, place it flat in a book until you can consult a numismatist or coin dealer. Do not carry an interesting note around in your wallet. Remember when handling a note remember that its most fragile parts are its corners. Never touch them. Also never repair a tear in a note with tape. The tape usually is of greater detriment to the note's value than the tear.

Attempts to clean a note are also likely to cause damage.

DETECTING COUNTERFEITS

Detecting counterfeit notes is not as difficult or as mysterious a business as many presume. Also many of the methods used by merchants are so inefficiently used as to be of no value.

First it must be realized that almost since its beginning, United States paper money has been printed not on paper, but on cloth. It is part cotton and part linen with some silk. The silk is in the form of minute red and blue threads that dive in and out of the surface of the note. A color copier may be able to reproduce the colors of these tiny threads, but it cannot reproduce the texture of them entering and leaving the surface of the note. Use a magnifying glass. Another key to detecting counterfeits is crispness of the ink in the design. Images and lines should appear sharp and distinct.

In recent years Federal Reserve Notes have incorporated many new counterfeit detection devices. These are fully described in that section.

Certain practices are designed to take an authentic note and make it appear to be a better grade than it is. These include ironing a note to make it look less worn, and expertly gluing tears. Hold your note up to a light. light will pass through the glue differently than through normal currency.

BOOKS ABOUT UNITED STATES PAPER MONEY

Bressett, Kenneth, *Guide Book of United States Currency.*
Donlon, William, et al., *United States Large Size Paper Money 1861 to 1923.*
Friedberg, Robert, *Paper Money of the United States.* An important basic reference.
Gengerke, Martin, *United States Paper Money Records.* A compilation of price history for rare notes.
Lloyd, H. Robert, *National Bank Notes,* Federal Reserve Bank Notes, Federal Reserve Notes 1928-50.
Schwan, C.F. and Boling, J.E., *World War II Military Currency.*
Schwartz and Oakes, *U.S. Small Size Currency.*
Continental and State Issues
Newman, Eric, *The Early Paper Money of America.*
Obsoletes
Haxby, James, *Obsolete Bank Notes.*
Fractionals
Rothert, Matt, *A Guide Book of United States Fractional Currency.*
Nationals
Hickman and Oakes, *National Bank Notes.*
Confederate
Slabaugh, Arlie, *Confederate States Paper Money.*
Scrip
Mitchell, Ralph & Schafer, Neil, *Standard Catalog of Depression*
Schingoethe, H. and M., *College Currency.*
Personal Checks
Scott Publishing Co., *Specialized Catalogue of United States Stamps.*

Periodicals
Bank Note Reporter
Society of Paper Money Collectors' Paper Money.

CONTINENTAL AND STATE CURRENCY

The very first paper money to circulate in the United States was issued in the Colonial era. The colonial assemblies of all of the original Thirteen Colonies issued small squarish notes valued in either English Pounds or in Spanish milled dollars. Due to British mercantilist policies there was always a shortage of precious metal coinage in the colonies and these notes helped fill the void.

During the Revolutionary War, the governors and legislatures of the newly independent states continued to print paper money, as did the Continental Congress. There was at the time the additional motivation of raising money to help finance the American Revolution. Unfortunately, printing unbacked paper currency in order to raise money for arms is inflationary. This situation worsened when the public realized that redeeming their money for real silver or gold varied from difficult to impossible. Rapid inflation soon caused these notes to be devalued, and they popularly traded at a sharp discount. Continental Currency issued by the Congress has such a poor reputation that the saying "Not worth a Continental" sprang up. The slang term "shinplasters" for these notes also implies their worthlessness, recalling how 1700s Americans would stick them in their boots to keep warm.

Designs on state notes varied, but the majority featured inscriptions in elaborate borders. Coats of arms and, initially, crowns were also common. During the mid-1770s designs got more elaborate and farm panoramas and buildings came into vogue. This coincided with the appearance of Continental Currency, almost all of which bore intricate circular seals of an allegorical nature.

There are many interesting aspects to American paper currency of the eighteenth century. The most fascinating was a unique form of printing whereby an actual leaf was used in the printing process, producing very fine detail difficult to artificially duplicate. This was intended to deter counterfeiting, as was the saying "To counterfeit is death" featured on so many notes. Another was the fact that each note bore a hand signature. This is of particular interest to the historian as many of these signers were either then or soon to be very important people. Some became signers of the Declaration of Independence or the Constitution. Signatures of these more important historical figures add to the value of a note. There is also the quaint eighteenth century habit of sewing together, instead of gluing, torn notes.

Known counterfeits: The most common counterfeits are those made during the mid-twentieth century as souvenirs and novelty items. They can be identified by their crinkled brownish-yellow paper. Real notes are printed on thick, soft white paper with a coarse grain. Contemporary counterfeits made to spend at the time are known and are collectible. Serious counterfeits meant to fool collectors are less common.

Note: There are a great many types and varieties. The prices given here are for representative common types.

	VG	VF
Connecticut		
Colony 1709-64	800.00	Rare
Colony 1770-76	20.00	55.00
State 1777-80	20.00	55.00
Delaware		
Colony 1723-60	80.00	200.00
Colony 1776	22.00	75.00
State 1777	20.00	70.00
Georgia		
Colony 1735-75	400.00	Scarce
State 1775-86	100.00	250.00

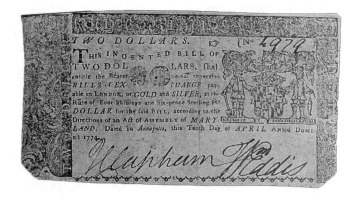

	VG	VF
Maryland		
Colony 1733	40.00	100.00
Colony 1740-56		Rare
Colony 1767-74	22.00	75.00
State 1775-81	20.00	60.00
Massachusetts		
Colony 1690-174		Rare
Colony 1750-76	525.00	Rare
State 1776-80	20.00	60.00
New Hampshire		
Colony 1709-63		Rare
Colony 1775-76 (hole canceled)	100.00	400.00
State 1777-80	40.00	175.00
New Jersey		
Colony 1709-Jan. 1756		Rare
Colony June 1756-76	20.00	60.00
State 1780-86	20.00	80.00
New York		
Colony 1709	1,700.00	Rare
Colony 1711-55		Rare
Colony 1756-76	25.00	90.00
State 1776-88	30.00	100.00
North Carolina		
Colony 1712-35		Rare
Colony 1748-61	80.00	250.00
Colony & Province 1768-76	40.00	150.00
State 1778-85	30.00	90.00
Pennsylvania		
Colony 1723-49		Rare
Colony 1755-56	40.00	100.00
Colony 1757-76	20.00	60.00
Commonwealth 1777-85	20.00	50.00
Rhode Island		
Colony 1710-67	500.00	Rare
Colony 1775-76	50.00	150.00
State 1776-86	20.00	60.00
South Carolina		
Colony 1703-70		Rare
Colony 1774-75		Scarce
State 1776-87	65.00	235.00

	VG	VF
Vermont		
State 1781	2,000.00	Rare
Virginia		
Colony 1755-70		Rare
Colony 1771-76	30.00	160.00
State 1776-81	30.00	160.00

Continental Currency

1775	20.00	75.00
1776	20.00	75.00
1777	30.00	120.00
1778	20.00	70.00
1779	22.00	95.00

OBSOLETES

Before the Civil War the United States government did not issue paper money. It was generally held that it would violate the Constitution. Instead paper money was issued privately by banks and other firms throughout the country. No one had to accept it. People were at liberty to refuse any note if they thought the issuing bank unsound or unfamiliar or simply too far away. Usually these notes would simply pass from one consumer to another as modern government issue notes do. Sound banks keep coin reserves on hand to back the notes and this is why bust half dollars are commonly available in high grades today. Some fraudulent banks released notes without any backing at all. They were produced in especially large numbers in the 1830s and 1850s. These notes ceased to be issued in the 1860s when many of the banks went bankrupt and others simply redeemed these notes and stopped issuing them. This is why today they are called obsolete notes, or more informally, broken bank notes. They are a wonderful way to trace local history. Many of the vignettes are very artistic and represent local industries such as shipping or cotton. Others have generic patriotic vignettes provided by the printer. Some even show their value in coins: a $1.25 note would show pictures of two half dollars and a quarter. Most notes are one sided.

Known counterfeits: Many notes were counterfeited at the time. These counterfeits are of some value today, but usually less than the real ones. Also some authentic notes were stamped "counterfeit" by rival banks so they would not have to honor them. Most Bank of the United States notes of this period are modern replicas, particularly those of high denomination. They can be identified by their crinkled brownish-yellow paper. Real notes are printed on thin, limp paper.

	VG	VF
Connecticut: Bridgeport, The Connecticut Bank,		
$3, 1856 (Locomotive)	22.00	55.00
__: Fairfield, Fairfield Loan & Trust Company, $1 ,		
1839 (Coins, cows and pigs)	150.00	300.00
Delaware: Wilmington, Bank of Wilmington		
and Brandywine, $5, 1839	150.00	300.00

	VG	VF
District of Columbia: Washington, Columbia Bank,		
Washington, 1852, $1	8.00	20.00
Florida: State of Florida, $50, 1861	25.00	110.00
Georgia: Savannah, Farmers and Mechanics Bank, $5,		
1860 (Statue of Columbia)	3.00	7.00
Illinois: Lockport, State Bank, $10, 1839	5.00	15.00
Indiana: Bloomfield, Indiana State Bank, $2, 1856	30.00	90.00
Maine: Calais, Washington County Bank, $5, 1835		
(Blacksmith, Mercury, Agriculture)	15.00	40.00

	VG	VF
Massachusetts: Boston, Cochituate Bank, $5, 1853		
(Early steam ship and sailor)	15.00	40.00
Mississippi: State of Mississippi, $1, 1864	8.00	35.00
Nebraska: Omaha, Western Exchange Fire & Marine		
Insurance, $2, 1856 (Indian, horse & train)	10.00	35.00
New York: Roundout, Bank of Roundout, $10	20.00	95.00
__: Ithica, Village of Ithica, 3¢, 1863	25.00	100.00
North Carolina: Lexington, Bank of Lexington, $5,		
1860 (Cotton picker at left)	4.00	8.00
Ohio: Wilmington, Goshen, Wilmington & Columbus		
Turnpike Co., $10, 1840	30.00	125.00
Virginia: Fincastle, Farmers Bank of Fincastle, $10, 1857	100.00	250.00

FRACTIONAL AND POSTAL CURRENCY

As a result of the Civil War, people began to hoard coins, not only precious metal but copper too. Much of the silver coinage was also being shipped to Canada. One improvised answer to the shortage created was to spend postage stamps as small change. The Treasury even sanctioned this practice, much to the chagrin of the Post Office, which was running out of stamps. It was a useful concept, but impractical. Small envelopes printed with a value were devised to convey the stamps as they were spent, but the stamps soon became a sticky mess, and the envelopes quickly deteriorated. Merchants discovered an alternative: give customers their own miniature paper currency for small change. This required the customers to return with more business in order to spend them. These were made illegal. The problem was solved in 1862 by a hybrid between postage stamps and paper money. Small rectangles of paper depicting stamps and labeled "Postage Currency" were issued. They could, of course, be redeemed for postage at any post office, but generally they circulated at the value of the stamps depicted. The sheets initially had stamp-like perforations around the edges, but they were soon removed. These miniature notes were a more convenient size and lacked the adhesive that had made stamps a mess. These special stamps were replaced in March of the following year by small notes of a similar size, but that were designed more in the form of paper money, with no reference to stamps. They were now labeled "Fractional Currency." These continued through several issues, surviving throughout the Civil War well into the period of Reconstruction. More than 99 percent of these notes were redeemed and destroyed. Despite this recall, fractionals are today quite common, and are a very inexpensive type of nineteenth century currency, far more so than contemporary larger denominations. They are a popular and easy series to collect. They are available in virtually every state of preservation form crisp to pulverized. The latter have only novelty value.

Fractional currency can be conveniently divided into four different series. The first is the Postage Currency already mentioned. It contains several varieties of ink and paper color, as well as notes with and without "ABNCo." This is the initials of the American Bank Note Co., the printing contractor.

When these were replaced by the new "Fractional Currency" notes of the second series an interesting counterfeit prevention device was incorporated. A metallic bronze ink was used to frame Washington's bust and to overprint the value on the reverse. Like bronze coins they can both tone down and corrode green. Collectors, of course, prefer those notes with the bright original color. These new notes were printed by the government itself instead of by a private contractor.

Attempts to prevent counterfeiting continued with new hard-to-imitate details incorporated into a set of all-new designs. (The notes of the second series were all identical.) Actual hand signatures were also tried. This series has the interesting distinction of having two government officials place their portraits on different notes. Both United States Treasurer Spinner and Superintendent of the National Currency Bureau, Spencer M. Clark deemed themselves worthy of depiction. Evidently Congress did not agree with them. It quickly passed a law to prevent the likeness of a living person from being depicted on these notes again. It has been suggested that Clark accidentally placed himself on the 5¢ note in a case of mistaken identity with the explorer of the Northwest William Clark! Nevertheless, these notes were printed for two more years.

A new anti-counterfeiting measure was also introduced for the fourth series. Perhaps even more important, these notes incorporated new almost inimitable paper containing silk threads. It was an over-sized treasury seal, superimposed over the entire height of the face of the note. Some also have a bright pink background over the entire face, and are worth more than prices listed.

The final series of notes lasted only two years. It was decided that the country had recovered from the Civil War enough to redeem its fractional paper. New silver coins were struck and virtually all fractional paper was turned in. Like series four, some have a bright pink background over the face, and are worth a premium.

Known counterfeits: Contemporary counterfeits of fractional currency were a problem from the very first series of postal currency. It continued to an extent for years into the following series. Still, most of these counterfeits were destroyed in the 1860s and 1870s, and they are not abundant today. The bronze metallic ink overprints can be removed in order to create what appears to be a rare variety.

Postal Currency

FIRST ISSUE - POSTAGE CURRENCY

	VG	VF
5¢ Washington, perforated edges	15.00	32.00
5¢ Washington, straight edges	5.00	13.00
10¢ Washington, perforated edges	20.00	32.00

	VG	VF
10¢ Washington, straight edges	5.00	13.00
25¢ Five Stamps, perforated edges	20.00	42.00
25¢ Five Stamps, straight edges	6.00	16.00
50¢ Five Stamps, perforated edges	20.00	42.00
50¢ Five Stamps, straight edges	12.00	23.00

SECOND ISSUE - 1863-64

	VG	VF
5¢ Washington in bronze oval	5.00	12.00
10¢ same	5.00	12.00
25¢ same	8.00	19.00
50¢ same	12.00	32.00

Fractional Currency - Third Issue

THIRD ISSUE - 1864-69

Note: All read "Act of March 3, 1863"

	VG	VF
3¢ Washington	10.00	19.00
5¢ Clark	6.00	13.50
10¢ Washington	6.00	13.50
15¢ Specimen only		CU55.00
25¢ Fessenden	8.00	19.00
50¢ Justice seated	32.00	85.00
50¢ Spinner	25.00	67.00

FOURTH ISSUE - 1869-75

Note: All read "Act of March 3, 1863" and have large treasury seal on face.

	VG	VF
10¢ Liberty bust	4.00	10.00
15¢ Columbia bust	11.00	27.00
25¢ Washington	6.00	13.50
50¢ Lincoln	16.00	47.00
50¢ Stanton	10.00	21.00
50¢ Samuel Dexter	8.00	19.00

Fractional Currency

	VG	VF
FIFTH ISSUE - 1874-76		
10¢ Wm. Meredith	3.00	10.00
25¢ Robert. Walker	3.50	11.00
50¢ Wm. Crawford	8.00	16.00

DEMAND NOTES

The demand notes of 1861 were the very first regular paper money issued by the United States. They were put into circulation under the emergency circumstances of the Civil War. The bad result of the over-production of paper money during the Revolutionary War was still fresh in people's minds, so limits were set on the uses for these notes. They differed from modern currency, mostly in that they were not actually legal tender, but rather were described as "receivable in payment for all public dues." That is to say they were not good for "all debts public and private," and not by initial obligation for any private debts at all. One could use them to pay taxes, but did not have to accept them otherwise. Later a law was passed that required their acceptance. Their name, Demand Note, is derived from another phrase on their face, "The United States promises to pay to the bearer on demand."

On the other hand, there were limits as to how they could be redeemed. These notes were issued at five cities and could only be redeemed by the Assistant Treasurers in the city that issed that partic-ular note. Designs were uniform from city to city. The $5 notes show at left the statue of Columbia from the Capitol building, and a portrait of Alexander Hamilton on the right. The $10 shows Lincoln, then in office, left, an eagle centered, and an allegorical figure of art right. The $20 depicts Liberty holding a sword and shield.

The nickname "green back" for paper money began with these notes, which have a distinctive green back. The privately issued paper money circulating until then had blank backs.

There are two major varieties of these, which resulted from the government's poor preparation for the practical reality of hand signing millions of notes. The original intent was that clerks would be able to sign them "N. for the" Register of the Treasury and "N. for the" Trea-surer of the United States. The time it took to sign the words "for the" millions of times quickly became excessive, so the notes were modi-fied so the words were printed instead. The earlier varieties are worth more than the prices listed here.

High grade notes in this series are very rare.

Known counterfeits: Examine detail, check to make sure notes are hand signed, and use reasonable caution.

Demand Notes

	G	VG
$5 Boston	400.00	950.00
$5 Cincinnati		Rare
$5 New York	400.00	950.00
$5 Philadelphia	400.00	950.00
$5 St. Louis	2,500.00	5,000.00
$10 Boston	500.00	1,500.00
$10 Cincinnati		Rare
$10 New York	500.00	1,500.00
$10 Philadelphia	500.00	1,500.00
$10 St. Louis	2,500.00	6,000.00
$20 Boston	5,500.00	12,000.00
$20 Cincinnati		Rare
$20 New York	5,500.00	12,000.00
$20 Philadelphia	5,500.00	12,000.00

TREASURY NOTES

These notes, designated "Treasury Notes" by the titles on their face inscriptions, are also called "Coin Notes." This was because according to law, the Secretary of the Treasury was instructed to redeem these notes in coin, either gold or silver, at his choosing. Inter-estingly, they were not actually backed by coin at all, but rather by sil-ver bullion.

This series was of very short duration, issued only in 1890 and 1891. Both years have the same face designs, generally of military heroes. The original reverse designs featured the values spelled out in large letters. For 1891 they were redesigned to allow more blank space. The ornamentation of the two 0s in 100 on the reverse of the $100 note is reminiscent of the pattern on the skin of a watermelon, hence it is known by the collecting community as "watermelon notes."

Known counterfeits: Examine detail, silk threads in paper and use reasonable caution.

Treasury Note

	F	XF
$1 1890 Edwin M. Stanton	440.00	900.00
$1 1891 same	85.00	250.00
$2 1890 Gen. James D. McPherson	650.00	2,400.00
$2 1891 same	225.00	500.00
$5 1890 Gen. George H Thomas	425.00	1,600.00
$5 1891 same	290.00	625.00
$10 1890 Gen. Philip H. Sheridan	690.00	1,850.00
$10 1891 same	440.00	900.00
$20 1890 John Marshall	2,500.00	5,750.00
$20 1891 same	2,750.00	6,900.00
$50 1891 William H. Seward	10,500.00	22,500.00
$100 1890 Adm. David G. Farragut	12,000.00	22,500.00
$100 1891 same	22,500.00	35,000.00
$1000 1890 Gen. George Meade		Rare
$1000 1891 same		Rare

NATIONAL BANK NOTES

National bank notes are a hybrid of government issued and private paper money. The notes, titled "National Currency" on their face, were issued by individual private banks, but printed by the U.S. government. Not every bank could issue them, only "national banks." To qualify, each bank had to meet certain criteria, which included keeping a predetermined value of U.S. government bonds on deposit with the United States Treasurer. In exchange for this commitment, the notes issued by any bank were considered legal tender of the United States and were good anywhere United States currency was good. The Treasury would stand behind these notes.

Designs didn't vary from bank to bank, but they used those types designated by the Treasury. The face of each note indicated the issuing bank's name (usually including the word "national") and its charter number. Many earlier notes also showed the coat of arms of its native state.

Each of over 1,300 issuing bank was assigned a charter number. There were three periods under which banks could apply a for a twenty-year charter. The first period was 1863-1882. Those banks securing their charters during this period could issue notes of the first charter reverse design as late as 1902. Those banks receiving their charters from 1882 to 1902, the second period, issued notes of a new type back designed for second charter banks. These were actually printed 1882 to 1922. Those banks receiving their charters during the third period of authorization (1902 to 1922) issued yet a third series of different designs from 1902 to 1929. It is apparent that this system determines the design (and often apparent "date") on a note not by when it was issued but by when the issuing bank first received its charter. Hence, different designs of National Bank Note could be issued at the same time with different dates! A very confusing situation.

Just like all other currency, Nationals were reduced in size in 1929. Type 1 notes (1929-33) have the charter number one the face twice. Type 2 notes (1933-35) have it four times. When, in May 1935, the Treasury recalled many of the bonds the national banks were using as security, National Bank Notes ceased to be issued

Nationals have been among the most sought after notes in a generally active U.S. paper money market. Not all nationals of a given type are worth the same since certain states and cities are more popularly collected than others. Also some banks ordered very small quantities of notes. The values below are for the most common and least expensive banks issuing that type of note. Large size Nationals from Alaska, Arizona, Hawaii, Idaho, Indian Territory, Mississippi, Nevada, New Mexico, Puerto Rico, and South Dakota are automatically worth more. The same is true for small size nationals from Alaska, Arizona, Hawaii, Idaho, Montana, Nevada and Wyoming.
Known counterfeits: Examine detail, silk threads in paper and use reasonable caution.

	VG	VF
FIRST CHARTER (1863-1875)		
$1 Allegory of Concord / Pilgrims Landing,		
ND (Original series)	125.00	280.00
same, 1875	125.00	280.00

	VG	VF
$2 Lazy 2 / Sir Walter Raleigh, ND		
(Original series)	500.00	1,300.00
same, 1875	500.00	1,300.00

$5 Columbus Sighting Land / Landing of		
Columbus, ND (Original series)	150.00	475.00
same, 1875	150.00	475.00

	VG	VF
$10 Franklin experimenting with lightning /		
DeSoto, ND (original series)	200.00	600.00
same, 1875	200.00	600.00
$20 Battle of Lexington / Baptism of Pocahontas,		
ND (original series)	750.00	1,250.00
same, 1875	750.00	1,250.00

	VG	VF
$50 Washington Crossing Delaware and at prayer /		
Pilgrims, ND (original series)	2,500.00	6,000.00
$100 Battle of Lake Erie / Signing of the		
Declaration of Independence, ND (original series)	3,000.00	7,500.00
$500		Unique
$1000		Unique

SECOND CHARTER / Series of 1882
"Brown Backs" with charter number

	VG	VF
$5 James Garfield	110.00	265.00
$10 as 1st charter	130.00	310.00
$20 as 1st charter	185.00	425.00
$50 as 1st charter	800.00	1,700.00
$100 as 1st charter	975.00	2,200.00

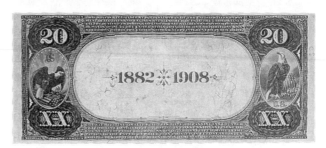

SECOND CHARTER / Series of 1882
"Date Backs" with large "1882*1908"

	VG	VF
$5 James Garfield	100.00	225.00
$10 as 1st charter	110.00	275.00
$20 as 1st charter	120.00	375.00
$50 as 1st charter	760.00	1,200.00
$100 as 1st charter	850.00	1,600.00

	VG	VF

SECOND CHARTER / Series of 1882
"Value Backs" large spelled-out value

	VG	VF
$5 James Garfield	130.00	325.00
$10 as 1st charter	155.00	430.00
$20 as 1st charter	185.00	475.00
$50 as 1st charter		Extremely Rare
$100 as 2nd series		Extremely Rare

THIRD CHARTER / Series of 1902
Red Treasury Seal on face

	VG	VF
$5 Benjamin Harrison / Pilgrims Landing	115.00	200.00
$10 William McKinley / Columbia between ships	145.00	250.00
$20 Hugh McCulloch / Columbia and Capitol	215.00	315.00
$50 John Sherman / Train	775.00	1,450.00
$100 John Knox / Eagle on Shield	875.00	1,800.00

THIRD CHARTER / Series of 1902
Blue Treasury Seal, "1902 1908" on back

	VG	VF
$5 as Red Seals	35.00	65.00
$10 as Red Seals	40.00	70.00
$20 as Red Seals	49.00	80.00
$50 as Red Seals	300.00	575.00
$100 as Red Seals	375.00	625.00

	VG	VF

THIRD CHARTER / Series of 1902
Blue Treasury Seal, "Plain Backs" without dates

	VG	VF
$5 as Red Seals	38.00	55.00
$10 as Red Seals	39.00	65.00
$20 as Red Seals	50.00	75.00
$50 as Red Seals	250.00	500.00
$100 as Red Seals	300.00	550.00

THIRD CHARTER / Series of 1929
Brown Treasury Seal, Small Size Notes

	VG	VF
$5 Type 1	10.00	15.00
$5 Type 2	12.00	20.00
$10 Type 1	12.00	20.00
$10 Type 2	13.00	20.00
$20 Type 1	24.00	35.00
$20 Type 2	25.00	38.00
$50 Type 1	55.00	85.00
$50 Type 2	75.00	165.00
$100 Type 1	110.00	140.00
$100 Type 2	130.00	200.00

NATIONAL GOLD BANK NOTES

These notes were like National Bank Notes, but they were specifically redeemable in gold coin. They were a cooperative issue of the individual National Gold Bank which held the obligation, and the U.S. Treasury. Every bank had to be a regular national bank as well, and meet all the reserve requirements. But these national banks were authorized by the Treasury to issue notes redeemable in gold.

The reason for their issue from 1870-75 was to relieve the banks in California of the daily handling of massive quantities of gold coin. All but one of the banks authorized to issue these was located in California. The very design of these notes reflect their basis on gold. Their paper is a golden yellow, and the reverse bears an array of United States gold coins of every denomination. Their remarkably fine engraving gives the coins a very realistic appearance. Because other types of notes were not very popular in California, these notes got some very hard use and today are rare in all but worn out condition.

Known counterfeits: Examine detail, and look for correct yellow paper, which occasionally may tone down. Use reasonable caution.

National Gold Bank Note

	G	F
$5 Columbus Sighting Land	700.00	1,500.00
$10 Franklin experimenting with lightning	850.00	2,900.00
$20 Battle of Lexington	1,200.00	5,400.00
$50 Washington crossing Delaware and at prayer	4,000.00	Rare
$100 Battle of Lake Erie	11,250.00	Rare

UNITED STATES / LEGAL TENDER NOTES

While most of these notes will carry the title "United States Note" at the top or bottom of their face, some earlier ones actually say "Treasury Note" instead. The very first notes omit both. They are, however, the same according to the legislation that authorized them. They are the longest lasting kind of American paper money, and were issued for over a century, from 1862 until 1966. There are a great many different designs, of which the "Bison Ten" is the most famous and most popular. Just like all other currency, United States Notes were reduced in size with the "series of 1928" in 1929. Small size notes are occasionally found in circulation today and are characterized by a red Treasury seal. The latter, when worn, are not generally considered collectible.

This series includes popular "star" notes. These are notes with part of the serial number replaced by a star. They were printed to replace notes that were accidentally destroyed. These were introduced first on $20 notes in 1880 and eventually descended to $1 notes by 1917. They usually are worth more.

Known counterfeits: Examine detail, silk threads in paper and use reasonable caution. In addition to counterfeits made to fool collectors, early circulation counterfeits of the 1863 $50, 1869 $50, and 1863 $100 exist

	F	XF
$1 1862 Salmon P. Chase, red seal	275.00	640.00
$1 1869 Washington, Columbus scene /		
US intertwined	310.00	625.00

	F	XF
$1 1874-1917 same / Large X	35.00	60.00
$1 1923 Washington bust	50.00	100.00
$2 1862 Alexander Hamilton / Double circle	400.00	950.00

	F	XF
$2 1869 Jefferson and Capitol / II 2TWO	370.00	1,350.00
$2 1874-1917 same / II TWO omitted	40.00	75.00
$5 1862 Statue of Columbia l., Alexander Hamilton r.	325.00	725.00
$5 1863 same, different obligation on back	325.00	725.00

	F	XF
$5 1869 Jackson l., Pioneer family center /		
Circle with 5	335.00	775.00
$5 1875-1907 same, red seal / Circle with		
concentricpattern	80.00	140.00
$5 1880 same, brown seal	150.00	450.00
$10 1862 Lincoln and allegory of Art	650.00	1,200.00
$10 1862-63 same, different obligation on back	650.00	1,200.00

	F	XF
$10 1869 Daniel Webster and Pocahontas / Inscription centered	560.00	1,100.00
$10 1875-80 same / Inscription at right	325.00	590.00
$10 1880 same, brown seal	325.00	650.00

United States Note - 1901 "Bison Ten"

	F	XF
$10 1901 Bison / Columbia standing between pillars	625.00	1,150.00
$10 1923 Andrew Jackson / Value	580.00	1,225.00
$20 1862 Liberty with sword and shield 2,650.00		1,550.00
$20 1862-63 same, different obligation on back	1,550.00	2,650.00

	F	XF
$20 1869 Alexander Hamilton l., Victory standing r.	1,600.00	3,400.00
$20 1875-80 same / No inscription at center	275.00	750.00
$20 1880 same, brown seal	575.00	1,150.00
$50 1862 Alexander Hamilton	7,000.00	14,500.00
$50 1862-63 same, different obligation on back	6,750.00	14,000.00
$50 1869 Peace and Henry Clay	12,750.00	30,000.00
$50 1874-80 Franklin and Columbia	2,600.00	5,200.00
$50 same, brown seal	2,800.00	6,000.00
$100 1862 Eagle	10,000.00	20,000.00
$100 1862-63 same, different obligation on back	10,000.00	20,000.00
$100 1869 Lincoln and allegory of Architecture / Inscription centered	10,000.00	18,000.00

	F	XF
$100 1875-80 same, Inscription at left	4,000.00	9,000.00
$100 1880, same, brown seal	5,500.00	17,000.00
$500 1862 Albert Gallatin		Rare
$500 1862-63 same, different obligation on back		Rare
$500 1869 John Quincy Adams		Rare
$500 1874-80 Gen. Joseph Mansfield		Rare
$500 1880 same, brown seal		Rare
$1000 1862 Robert Morris		Rare
$1000 1862-63 same, different obligation on back		Rare
$1000 1869 Columbus and DeWitt Clinton / Inscription centered		Rare
$1000 1878-80 same, Inscription at left		28,000.00
$1000 1880 same, brown seal		Rare

SMALL SIZE NOTES - RED SEAL

$1 1928	Washington / ONE
$2 1928-63A	Jefferson / Monticello
$5 1928-63	Lincoln / Lincoln Memorial
$100 1966-66A	Franklin / Indep.Hall

	F	XF
$1 1928	20.00	50.00
$2 1928	12.50	18.00
$2 1928A	35.00	65.00
$2 1928B	45.00	150.00
$2 1928C	15.00	30.00
$2 1928D	10.00	18.00
$2 1928E	15.00	25.00
$2 1928F	4.50	10.00
$2 1928G	5.00	8.00

	CU
$2 1953	7.50
$2 1953A	5.00
$2 1953B	5.50
$2 1953C	6.50
$2 1963	5.00
$2 1963A	7.50

	F	XF
$5 1928	8.00	15.00
$5 1928A	12.00	30.00
$5 1928B	8.00	12.00
$5 1928C	10.00	15.00
$5 1928D	16.00	40.00
$5 1928E	9.50	16.00
$5 1928F	9.50	16.00
$5 1953	8.50	15.00
$5 1953A	7.00	12.00
$5 1953B	7.00	8.50
$5 1953C	7.50	12.00
$5 1963	7.00	9.00

	XF	CU
$100 1966	175.00	300.00
$100 1966A	300.00	750.00

GOLD CERTIFICATES

As the title on these notes implies, these were notes both backed by reserves in gold coin and payable to the bearer in that coin. The first Gold Certificates were issued in 1865-75 but were used for transactions between banks. Notes of this period not listed below are not known to have survived. The issue of 1882 was the first for general circulation. Again the issues of 1888-89 were only of $5,000 and $10,000 and not widely circulated. Regular issues were again placed in circulation in 1905-07. This series includes a $20 note so beautifully colored with black, red and gold ink on white gold-tinted paper that it has come to have the nickname of "technicolor." Those of the series of 1913-28 are the most common Gold Certificates.

Like all other notes of the 1928 series, these gold certificates were printed on the reduced size paper still used today. These are distinguished from other kinds of small size notes by a gold Treasury seal. The final issues, those of 1934, were again just for bank transactions. The government recalled these notes from general circulation in 1933 when it withdrew gold coinage. Today they are perfectly legal to own but far scarcer due to this earlier destruction.

Known counterfeits: Examine detail, on 1882 and later silk threads in paper, and use reasonable caution.

	F	XF

FIRST ISSUE - 1863
$20 Eagle on Shield		Extremely Rare
$100 Eagle on Shield		Extremely Rare

SECOND ISSUE - 1870-71
None notes known to have survived.

THIRD ISSUE - 1870s
$100 Thomas H. Benton	Extremely Rare	

FOURTH ISSUE - Series of 1882

$20 James Garfield	530.00	1,700.00
$50 Silas Wright	725.00	2,100.00
$100 Thomas Benton	700.00	1,350.00
$500 Abraham Lincoln		Rare
$1000 Alexander Hamilton		Rare
$5000 James Madison		Rare
$10,000 Andrew Jackson		Rare

FIFTH ISSUE - Series of 1888
$5000 James Madison		Rare
$10,000 Andrew Jackson		Rare

SIXTH ISSUE - Series of 1900
$10,000 Jackson		Rare

SEVENTH ISSUE - Series of 1905-07
$10 Michael Hillegas	65.00	160.00
$20 Washington 1905 "technicolor note"	900.00	3,200.00
$20 Washington 1906	110.00	335.00

EIGHTH ISSUE - Series of 1907
$1000 Alexander Hamilton		Rare

NINTH ISSUE - Series of 1913
$50 Ulysses S. Grant	500.00	975.00

	F	XF

TENTH ISSUE - Series of 1922

$10 Michael Hillegas	80.00	225.00
$20 Washington	145.00	290.00
$50 Ulysses S. Grant	450.00	850.00

Gold Certificate

$100 Thomas Benton	500.00	975.00
$500 Abraham Lincoln		Rare
$1000 Alexander Hamilton		Rare

SMALL SIZE - Series of 1928

$10 Alex. Hamilton	35.00	75.00
$20 Andrew Jackson	55.00	110.00
$50 Ulysses S. Grant	125.00	350.00
$100 Ben.Franklin	275.00	450.00
$500 W. McKinley	1,850.00	4,000.00
$1000 G. Cleveland	2,300.00	4,500.00
$5000 James Madison		Rare

SILVER CERTIFICATES

On the same day, February 28, 1878, as the authorization by Congress of the striking of millions of silver dollars, it also passed legislation authorizing Silver Certificate. This is not pure coincidence. Silver Certificates were not simply backed up by silver bullion, but represented actual silver dollars held by the Treasury. The issue of this series of notes was what in part made it necessary to strike millions of Morgan dollars, which was due mainly to heavy lobbying by the silver mining industry.

Some of the most famous or beautiful banknotes issued by the U.S. are Silver Certificates. These include the "Educational" $1, $2, and $5 of 1896, the "Onepapa Five," and the "Porthole Five." The name "Onepapa Five" is a misnomer. It depicts Chief Running Antelope of the Uncpapa Sioux, but because the name sounded so unfamiliar to early collectors it was quickly mispronounced "Chief One Papa."

Just like all other currency, Silver Certificates were reduced in size with the "series of 1928" in 1929.

During World War II there was fear that supplies of U.S. currency would fall into enemy hands if certain territories were overrun. The response to this was to make sure that notes distributed in these territories had distinguishing features which would permit their identification and repudiation if captured. Those Silver Certificates issued to troops in North Africa were printed with a yellow Treasury seal instead of a blue one. Notes distributed in Hawaii feature the word HAWAII overprinted very large on the back.

The motto "In God We Trust." was added to the one dollar note for the 1935 G and H and all 1957 series. They continued to be issued until the 1957B series in 1963. Small size silver certificates are occasionally found in circulation today and are easily recognized by a blue Treasury seal. These notes, when worn, are not generally considered collectible, but do have some novelty value. They have not been redeemable for silver since 1968.

This series includes popular "star" notes. These are notes with part of the serial number replaced by a star. They are printed to replace accidentally destroyed notes. These were introduced first in 1899. They often but not always are worth somewhat more.

Known counterfeits: Examine detail, silk threads in paper and use reasonable caution. Circulating counterfeits exist for this series and are slightly less dangerous.

	F	XF
$1 1886 Martha Washington / Inscription in oval	230.00	540.00
$1 1891 same / Inscription in rosette	190.00	425.00
$1 1896 History Instructing Youth / George and Martha Washington	160.00	450.00
$1 1899 Eagle	45.00	85.00
$1 1923 Washington	22.00	30.00
$2 1886 Gen. Winfield Scott Hancock	400.00	900.00
$2 1891 Sen. William Windom	330.00	1,100.00
$2 1896 Science Presenting Steam and Electricity to Commerce and Industry / Fulton and Morse	400.00	1,250.00
$2 1899 Washington, Mechanics and Agriculture	100.00	250.00
$5 1886 Ulysses S. Grant / Morgan Silver Dollars	560.00	1,900.00
$5 1891 same / Inscription	450.00	1,200.00
$5 1896 Winged Electricity lighting the World	850.00	2,250.00
$5 1899 Chief "Onepapa"	380.00	750.00

	F	XF
$5 1923 Lincoln in porthole-like frame / Great Seal	375.00	1,000.00
$10 1878-80 Robert Morris / S I L V E R	1,075.00	2,700.00

	F	XF
$10 1886 Thomas Hendricks in tombstone-like frame	750.00	2,200.00
$10 1891-1908 same / UNITED STATES in oval	350.00	950.00

	F	XF
$20 1878-80 Capt. Stephen Decatur / S I L V E R	2,500.00	5,200.00
$20 1886 Daniel Manning / Double Diamond	2,900.00	7,000.00
$20 1891 same / Double Circle	900.00	2,000.00
$50 1878-80 Edward Everett / S I L V E R	5,200.00	13,000.00

	F	XF
$50 1891 same / Inscription in center	1,550.00	3,450.00
$100 1878-80 James Monroe / S I L V E R	10,500.00	22,000.00
$100 1891 same / Inscription in center	5,900.00	11,000.00
$500 1878-80 Sen. Charles Sumner / S I L V E R		Rare
$1000 1878-80 William Marcy		Rare
$1000 1891 Columbia and Marcy		Rare

SMALL SIZE NOTES - BLUE SEAL

$1 1928-28E	Washington / ONE	
$1 1934-57B	Washington / Great Seal	
$5 1934-53C	Lincoln / Lincoln Memorial	
$10 1933-53B	Hamilton / Treasury	

	F	XF
$1 1928	8.00	12.00
$1 1928A	6.00	10.00
$1 1928B	6.00	10.00
$1 1928C	50.00	150.00
$1 1928D	35.00	90.00
$1 1928E	300.00	500.00
$1 1934	8.00	15.00
$1 1935	5.00	7.50
$1 1935A	3.00	4.00
$1 1935A HAWAII	13.50	16.00

	F	XF
$1 1935A Yellow seal	16.00	20.00
$1 1935A Red R	20.00	43.00
$1 1935A Red S	20.00	36.00
$1 1935B	2.00	3.00
$1 1935C	2.50	3.50
$1 1935D	2.00	3.00

	XF	CU
$1 1935E		5.00
$1 1935F		5.00
$1 1935G		6.00
same with motto	4.00	15.00
$1 1935H		6.50
$1 1957		4.50
$1 1957A		5.00
$1 1957B		4.50
$5 1934	10.00	20.00
$5 1934A	10.00	15.00
$5 1934A Yellow seal	40.00	100.00
$5 1934B	18.00	35.00
$5 1934C	18.00	20.00
$5 1934D	15.00	20.00
$5 1953		17.50
$5 1953A		12.00
$5 1953B		15.00
$10 1933	3,500.00	6,500.00
$10 1933A		Unique
$10 1934	35.00	50.00
$10 1934A	35.00	80.00
$10 1934 Yellow seal	3,500.00	6,000.00
$10 1934A Yellow seal	45.00	125.00
$10 1934B	150.00	1,250.00
$10 1934C	45.00	80.00
$10 1934D	40.00	90.00
$10 1953	45.00	100.00
$10 1953A	50.00	125.00
$10 1953B	40.00	75.00

FEDERAL RESERVE NOTES

The Federal Reserve System was created in 1913. Under this system there are twelve Federal Reserve Banks. They are governed in part by the U.S. government through the Federal Reserve Board, appointed by the President and confirmed by the Senate. Each of the Federal Reserve Banks is composed of various member banks. Today in the United States the paper currency is not directly issued by the Treasury but by the Federal Reserve Banks. Originally Federal Reserve Notes bore an obligation of the government to redeem them in gold. This was changed in 1934. Today Federal Reserve Notes are the only type of paper money issued in the United States.

Just like all other currency, Federal Reserve Notes were reduced in size with the "series of 1928" in 1929.

Since 1993 major new innovations have been gradually incorporated into these notes to prevent counterfeiting. At first micro printing was incorporated into the design and around the frame of the portrait. Also a transparent strip bearing the value and USA was embedded inside the paper. It can only be seen when the note is held up to the light and cannot be photocopied.

These improvements were only a precursor to the first major overhaul of the designs of the currency since the 1920s. It incorporated these two, as well as other safeguards. Beginning in 1996 with the $100 note the portraits were enlarged to show more detail. The reverse was modified to incorporate more white space, making it possible to successfully use a watermark incorporated into the paper. This is an image not printed on nor embedded inside the paper, but one created by the pressure of a pattern pressed against the paper during its drying stage. Like the transparent printed strip, it can only be seen when the note is held up to the light. Among the most ingenious high-tech safeguards on the new notes is the use of color shifting ink, which alters its shade depending on the angle of the light hitting it. The green Treasury seal has been retained but the old letter seal indicating the Federal Reserve Bank of distribution is now replaced by the seal of the Federal Reserve system. These innovations have also been incorporated into the $50 and $20 notes, with the $10 note planned for the near future.

A recent experiment with the use of a Web Press in the manufacture of $1 notes has resulted in less than total success. Interestingly enough for collectors however is the fact that this has resulted in some paper money being printed outside the Bureau of Engraving and Printing for the first time since the nineteenth century, and the appearance of an actual mintmark, FW being used to designate Fort Worth, Texas.

Most Federal Reserve Notes since the 1930s are only collected in high grade. Dealers may be unwilling to buy even scarce pieces if not crisp uncirculated. Star replacement notes are quite popularly collected in this series, but again, must usually be crisp to be desirable. Very recent ones command no premium at all, and are sold at face value plus a handling fee to cover the dealer's labor.

Known counterfeits: Examine detail, silk threads in paper and use reasonable caution. Circulating counterfeits exist, particularly $20 and $10 denominations, but most are imperfect, and can be easily detected on close examination.

	F	XF

RED SEAL - SERIES OF 1914
	F	XF
$5 Abraham Lincoln / Columbus and Pilgrims	60.00	175.00

	F	XF
$10 Andrew Jackson / Reaper and Factory	70.00	185.00
$20 Grover Cleveland / Train and Ship	115.00	500.00
$50 Ulysses S. Grant / Allegory of Panama	475.00	1,000.00
$100 Franklin / Five allegories including commerce and agriculture	585.00	1,100.00

BLUE SEAL - SERIES OF 1914

	F	XF
$5 Abraham Lincoln / Columbus and Pilgrims	35.00	50.00
$10 Andrew Jackson / Reaper and Factory	35.00	50.00
$20 Grover Cleveland / Train and Ship	45.00	60.00
$50 Ulysses S. Grant / Allegory of Panama	130.00	300.00

	F	XF
$100 Franklin / Five allegories including commerce and agriculture	300.00	450.00

BLUE SEAL - SERIES OF 1918

	F	XF
$500 John Marshall / DeSoto discovering Mississippi	1,500.00	3,500.00
$1,000 Alexander Hamilton / Eagle	2,200.00	4,000.00
$5,000 Madison		Extremely Rare
$10,000 Chase		Extremely Rare

SMALL SIZE NOTES - GREEN SEAL

$1 1963—	Washington / Great Seal
$2 1976—	Jefferson / Signing Declaration
$5 1928—	Lincoln / Lincoln Memorial
$10 1928—	Hamilton / Treasury Building
$20 1928—	Jackson / White House
$50 1928—	Grant / Capitol
$100 1928—	Franklin / Independence Hall

	F	XF
$500 1928-34A	McKinley / 500	
$1000 1928-34A	Cleveland / Inscription	
$5000 1928-34B	Madison / 5000	
$10,000 1928-34B	Chase / 10,000	

One Dollar

	CU
$1 1963	3.00
$1 1963A	3.00
$1 1963B	3.50
$1 1969	2.50
$1 1969A	2.50
$1 1969B	2.50
$1 1969C	2.50
$1 1969D	2.50
$1 1974	2.00
$1 1977	2.00
$1 1977A	2.00
$1 1981	2.00
$1 1981A	2.00
$1 1985	2.00
$1 1988	2.50
$1 1988A	2.00
$1 1988A Web Press	18.00
$1 1993	2.00
$1 1993 Web Press	8.00
$1 1995	2.00
$1 1995 Web Press	6.00

Two Dollars

	CU
$2 1976	3.00
$2 1995	3.00

Five Dollars

	XF	CU
$5 1928	25.00	60.00
$5 1928A	25.00	40.00
$5 1928B	20.00	40.00
$5 1928C	200.00	575.00
$5 1928D	350.00	1,000.00
$5 1934	6.50	20.00
$5 1934A	6.50	20.00

	XF	CU
$5 1934 HAWAII	65.00	200.00
$5 1934A HAWAII	65.00	185.00
$5 1934B	6.50	30.00
$5 1934C	6.50	30.00
$5 1934D	6.50	30.00
$5 1950		30.00
$5 1950A		16.00
$5 1950B		15.00
$5 1950C		15.00

	XF	CU
$5 1950D		15.00
$5 1950E		20.00

Five Dollars

	XF	CU
$5 1963		14.00
$5 1963A		12.00
$5 1969		10.00
$5 1969A		12.00
$5 1969B		14.00
$5 1969C		10.00
$5 1974		10.00
$5 1977		10.00
$5 1977A		10.00
$5 1981		10.00
$5 1981A		10.00
$5 1985		10.00
$5 1988		10.00
$5 1988A		10.00
$5 1993		10.00
$5 1995		10.00

Ten Dollars

	XF	CU
$10 1928	60.00	100.00
$10 1928A	60.00	190.00
$10 1928B	25.00	55.00
$10 1928C	60.00	120.00
$10 1934	18.00	25.00
$10 1934A	15.00	25.00
$10 1934A HAWAII	75.00	210.00
$10 1934B	15.00	25.00
$10 1934C	15.00	20.00
$10 1934D	15.00	25.00
$10 1950	25.00	50.00
$10 1950A	20.00	35.00
$10 1950B		30.00
$10 1950C		35.00
$10 1950D		35.00
$10 1950E		30.00
$10 1963		20.00
$10 1963A		20.00
$10 1969		20.00
$10 1969A		20.00
$10 1969B		25.00
$10 1969C		18.00
$10 1974		17.00
$10 1977		17.00
$10 1977A		16.00
$10 1981		15.00
$10 1981A		15.00
$10 1985		15.00
$10 1988		15.00
$10 1988A		15.00
$10 1993		15.00
$10 1995		15.00

Twenty Dollars

	XF	CU
$20 1928	35.00	75.00
$20 1928A	55.00	75.00
$20 1928B	40.00	65.00
$20 1928C	200.00	500.00
$20 1934	30.00	40.00
$20 1934A	30.00	40.00
$20 1934 HAWAII	110.00	800.00
$20 1934A HAWAII	55.00	500.00
$20 1934B	32.00	40.00
$20 1934C	30.00	35.00
$20 1934D		35.00
$20 1950		50.00
$20 1950A		40.00
$20 1950B		40.00
$20 1950C		40.00

Twenty Dollars

	XF	CU
$20 1950D		40.00
$20 1950E		60.00

Twenty Dollars

	XF	CU
$20 1963		35.00
$20 1963A		30.00
$20 1969		30.00
$20 1969A		30.00
$20 1969B		40.00
$20 1969C		30.00
$20 1974		30.00
$20 1977		30.00
$20 1981		30.00
$20 1981A		30.00
$20 1985		30.00
$20 1988A		30.00
$20 1990		30.00
$20 1993		30.00
$20 1995		30.00
$20 1996 Large Portrait		30.00

Fifty Dollars

	XF	CU
$50 1928	100.00	200.00
$50 1928A	90.00	150.00
$50 1934	80.00	160.00
$50 1934A	80.00	160.00
$50 1934B	75.00	125.00
$50 1934C	60.00	85.00
$50 1934D	75.00	250.00
$50 1950	60.00	120.00
$50 1950A	60.00	120.00
$50 1950B	60.00	120.00
$50 1950C	60.00	110.00
$50 1950D	60.00	150.00
$50 1950E	60.00	150.00
$50 1963A		100.00
$50 1969		100.00
$50 1969A		90.00
$50 1969B		90.00
$50 1969C		70.00
$50 1974		100.00
$50 1977		85.00
$50 1981		75.00
$50 1981A		80.00
$50 1985		75.00
$50 1988		65.00
$50 1990		65.00
$50 1993		65.00
$50 1996 Large Portrait		60.00

One Hundred Dollars

	XF	CU
$100 1928	150.00	200.00
$100 1928A	175.00	200.00
$100 1934	175.00	225.00
$100 1934A	150.00	200.00
$100 1934B	175.00	250.00
$100 1934C	175.00	200.00
$100 1934D	150.00	225.00
$100 1950		250.00
$100 1950A		130.00
$100 1950B		250.00
$100 1950C		225.00
$100 1950D		250.00
$100 1950E		250.00
$100 1963A		200.00
$100 1969		175.00
$100 1969A		175.00
$100 1969C		150.00
$100 1974		150.00

One Hundred Dollars	XF	CU
$100 1977		150.00
$100 1981		200.00
$100 1981A		200.00
$100 1985		175.00

One Hundred Dollars	XF	CU
$100 1988		150.00
$100 1990		125.00
$100 1993		120.00

$100 1996 Large Portrait		115.00

Five Hundred Dollars

	XF	CU
$500 1928	750.00	1,000.00
$500 1934	550.00	750.00

$500 1934A	550.00	700.00
$500 1934B	550.00	650.00
$500 1934C	550.00	650.00

One Thousand Dollars

$1000 1928	1,200.00	1,400.00
$1000 1934	1,200.00	2,750.00
$1000 1934A	1,200.00	2,300.00
$1000 1934C	1,200.00	1,500.00

Five Thousand Dollars

$5000 1928		32,000.00
$5000 1934		32,000.00
$5000 1934A		32,000.00
$5000 1934B		32,000.00

Ten Thousand Dollars

$10,000 1928		126,500.00
$10,000 1934		45,000.00
$10,000 1934A		30,000.00
$10,000 1934B		30,000.00

FEDERAL RESERVE BANK NOTES

Federal Reserve Bank Notes are a type of National Currency issued not by individual National Banks but directly by the twelve Federal Reserve Banks. These are regional banks under the partial control of the Board of Governors of the Federal Reserve, appointed by the President. Unlike Federal Reserve Notes, these were legal tender but not a government obligation. The obligation to redeem Federal Reserve Bank Notes fell with the individual Federal Reserve Banks and not directly with the Treasury. They were issued for a fairly short duration.

Small size Federal Reserve Bank Notes are actually emergency currency printed on notes originally intended to become regular 1929 series National Currency. The identity of the Federal Reserve Bank is printed where the name of the National Bank would have been, and small details of text are either blocked out or added. They were issued in 1933 and have a brown Treasury seal, unlike the large size notes which feature a blue one.

Star replacement notes are scarce and command a significant premium. **Known counterfeits:** Examine detail, silk threads in paper and use reasonable caution.

	F	XF
$1 1918 George Washington / Eagle on Flag	45.00	80.00
$2 1918 Thomas Jefferson / Battle Ship	145.00	290.00
$5 1915 Abraham Lincoln / Columbus, Pilgrims landing	75.00	175.00
$5 1918 same	60.00	165.00
$10 1915 Andrew Jackson / Horse-drawn Reaper and Factory	300.00	750.00
$10 1918 same	275.00	725.00

$20 1915 Grover Cleveland / Train and Ship	540.00	1,100.00
$20 1918 same	575.00	1,100.00
$50 1918 Ulysses S. Grant / Allegory of Panama	3,000.00	5,000.00

	F	XF
SMALL SIZE NOTES - BROWN SEAL		
$5 Boston	15.00	35.00
$5 New York	15.00	25.00
$5 Philadelphia	15.00	25.00
$5 Cleveland	15.00	25.00
$5 Atlanta	15.00	35.00

$5 Chicago	12.00	25.00
$5 St. Louis	90.00	250.00
$5 Minneapolis	25.00	95.00
$5 Kansas City	12.50	35.00
$5 Dallas	20.00	50.00
$5 San Francisco	350.00	750.00
$10 Boston	15.00	35.00
$10 New York	15.00	25.00
$10 Philadelphia	15.00	30.00
$10 Cleveland	15.00	30.00
$10 Richmond	15.00	35.00
$10 Atlanta	15.00	30.00
$10 Chicago	15.00	25.00
$10 St. Louis	15.00	25.00
$10 Minneapolis	15.00	30.00
$10 Kansas City	15.00	25.00
$10 Dallas	100.00	250.00
$10 San Francisco	15.00	35.00
$20 Boston	25.00	75.00
$20 New York	25.00	35.00
$20 Philadelphia	25.00	35.00
$20 Cleveland	25.00	45.00
$20 Richmond	25.00	45.00
$20 Atlanta	25.00	45.00
$20 Chicago	25.00	45.00
$20 St. Louis	25.00	45.00
$20 Minneapolis	25.00	45.00
$20 Kansas City	25.00	45.00
$20 Dallas	35.00	125.00
$20 San Francisco	30.00	100.00
$50 New York	65.00	110.00
$50 Cleveland	65.00	110.00
$50 Chicago	65.00	100.00
$50 Minneapolis	75.00	110.00
$50 Kansas City	75.00	100.00
$50 Dallas	400.00	600.00
$50 San Francisco	85.00	150.00
$100 New York	125.00	175.00
$100 Cleveland	135.00	160.00
$100 Richmond	125.00	175.00
$100 Chicago	125.00	175.00
$100 Minneapolis	125.00	175.00
$100 Kansas City	125.00	150.00
$100 Dallas	150.00	325.00

INTEREST BEARING NOTES

In an effort to raise money during the Civil War, Congress authorized a form of paper money that was a cross between a bank note and a bond. This was called an Interest Bearing Note. Issued in 1861 and 1863, they were legal tender for their face value but they also bore inter-

est. Those issued with one and two year maturity could be redeemed at that time for more than their face value. Those that matured in three years actually had coupons attached that allowed them to be redeemed at six month intervals for interest payments. They were issued in $10, $20, $50, $100, $1,000, and $5,000 denominations.

These notes are incredibly rare because most were redeemed. They are far too specialized to include a complete listing here but an example of an 1863 $10 one-year note is illustrated below.

Known counterfeits: All such notes should be examined by an expert for authenticity and value.

	VF
$10+5% 1863 Salmon Chase, eagle and Peace	6,000.00

COMPOUND INTEREST TREASURY NOTES

Continuing with the precedent set by the Interest Bearing Notes of 1861-63, and because the Civil War had vastly depleted the Treasury, Congress authorized another form of paper money that incorporated the features of a zero-coupon bond.

This was called a Compound Interest Treasury Note, a name displayed conspicuously in gold letters. On some notes this overprint has been known to dissolve through the note or to turn green. Issued in 1863 and 1864, they were legal tender for their face value but they also bore compounded interest payable at maturity in three years. An interest calculation table was displayed on the back. They were issued in $10, $20, $50, $100, $500, and $1,000 denominations.

Most of these notes were turned in at maturity, hence they too are incredibly rare and are too specialized to include a complete listing here. The face design of a $10 note is very similar to the Interest Bearing Note depicted above, but with its gold overprint.

Known counterfeits: All such notes should be examined by an expert for authenticity and value.

CONFEDERATE STATES ISSUES

The story of Confederate paper money is in some ways reminiscent of that of Continental Currency. Under desperate war time circumstances and with the best intentions, the government attempted to finance the war effort by printing unbacked paper currency. The initial series, backed by cotton, held its value at first, and restraint was used in the quantities issued, but as the war continued more and more was printed, causing inflation. According to the legends on the later notes, they could not be redeemed until "two years after the ratification of a treaty of peace between the Confederate States and United States." Ultimately, the seventh and final issue was authorized in unlimited quantity. After two billion dollars were issued, the currency's value eroded almost completely. Measured in gold dollars, its decline can be seen as follows, along with rough quantities issued or authorized:

1861 March	$150,000,000	95¢
1862	$265,000,000	
1863	$515,000,000	33¢
1864	$1,000,000,000	
1865 April	none	1-2/3¢
1865 May	none	1/12¢

For many years Confederate currency was synonymous with worthlessness, and some people even burned it. From the 1960s onward, however, it has taken on value as a collectible. The late 1990s have been a particularly good time for this series. Prices have increased drastically.

The first issue of confederate currency of March 1861 was initially issued in Montgomery, Alabama, but the wording was changed to Richmond, Virginia. This is because the capital of the Confederacy was moved to Richmond in May, shortly after Virginia withdrew from the Union. Throughout the war the production of confederate notes was plagued with difficulties. The Northern printers, who had originally been hired to print notes prior to the hostilities, were no longer available. Paper was in short supply. It was also not always practical to import notes, paper or even plates due to the Union blockade of Southern ports. Some paper was brought in from the North by smugglers, and from Great Britain by blockade runners. As a result, some of the designs use improvised images not initially prepared for Confederate currency. More suitable images used include portraits of President Jefferson Davis and members of his cabinet, as well as of Southern agriculture.

Known counterfeits: It has been suggested that contemporary counterfeits were made of virtually every type of Confederate currency. True or false, it stands that a vast array of contemporary counterfeits of confederate notes have survived. Most are printed from very crudely engraved plates. Like real examples they are often printed on thin, limp paper. Not all the counterfeits made during the Civil War were actually meant to circulate. Samuel Upham of Philadelphia made 1-1/2 million confederate and Southern state notes as a spoof, all with the notice "Facsimile Confederate Note - Sold wholesale and retail, by S.C. Upham, 403 Chestnut Street, Philadelphia" in the margin. Many had this notice cut off and intact examples are worth at least a few dollars each. In 1954, Cheerios cereal distributed reproductions as a promotion. Other similar notes printed on brittle brownish-yellow paper were printed in the 1960s. Many, but not all, have the word FACSIMILE near the margin.

Some "fantasy" notes were also made to circulate during the Civil War period. These were notes claiming to be Confederate, but with designs the Confederate. government had never used. The most famous of these notes is the "female riding a deer" note, which was actually Artemis riding a stag. It is illustrated here. Most of the coun-

terfeits — both contemporary and modern — have printed signatures, all authentic notes are hand signed except for the 50¢ denomination.

	VG	VF
FIRST ISSUE, MONTGOMERY 1861		
$50 Three slaves hoeing cotton	700.00	3,200.00
$100 Train	800.00	3,300.00
$500 Train on bridge, Cattle below	1,300.00	7,700.00
$1000 John Calhoun and Andrew Jackson	1,500.00	6,900.00
FIRST ISSUE, RICHMOND 1861		
$50 Industry and Agriculture seated on cotton	100.00	575.00
$100 Train	125.00	650.00
SECOND ISSUE, July 25, 1861		
$5 Inscription	225.00	1,400.00
$5 Liberty and Eagle, Sailor left	200.00	1,100.00
$10 Liberty and Eagle, Commerce left	34.00	350.00
$20 Sailing Ship	17.00	68.00

	VG	VF
$20 Artemis riding Stag, Indian seated left Contemporary Fantasy	17.00	60.00
$50 Washington	20.00	88.00
$100 Ceres and Proserpina	100.00	560.00
THIRD ISSUE, September 2, 1861		
$2 Confederacy striking down Union, Judah Benjamin l	80.00	38.00
$5 Cotton being loaded onto Steamboat left, Indian Princess right	1,200.00	6,750.00
$5 Commerce seated on bale of cotton	15.00	38.00
$5 Allegories of Commerce, Agriculture, Liberty, Industry and Justice, Minerva left	75.00	385.00
$5 Sailor with cotton bales, C.G. Memminger left	30.00	65.00
$5 Boy's bust left, Blacksmith seated right	120.00	575.00
$5 C.G. Memminger, V at lower right	25.00	75.00
$5 same, but FIVE at lower right	25.00	75.00
$10 Liberty with Eagle left	625.00	3,250.00
$10 Ceres and Commerce left	15.00	65.00
$10 Indian Family	75.00	335.00
$10 Cotton Picker	30.00	160.00
$10 Revolutionary War Generals with sweet potatoes, Minerva standing r.	15.00	65.00
$10 Wagon with cotton, John Ward left	175.00	850.00
$10 Robert Hunter left, Child right	25.00	115.00
$10 Hope with Anchor, Robert Hunter left, C.G. Memminger rt.	20.00	120.00
$10 same, with X X overprint	25.00	95.00
$20 Ceres between Commerce and Navigation	75.00	385.00

	VG	VF
$20 Sailing Ship	15.00	45.00
$20 Navigation seated with globe	335.00	1,300.00
$20 Industry seated behind large 20	10.00	38.00
$20 Alexander Stephens	35.00	155.00
$50 Moneta & chest	18.00	65.00
$50 Train	435.00	2,900.00
$50 Jefferson Davis	25.00	135.00
$100 Loading cotton onto wagon, Sailor left	25.00	75.00

FOURTH ISSUE, April 17, 1862

	VG	VF
$1 Steamship	20.00	65.00
$1 same with ONE overprint	24.00	95.00
$2 Confederacy striking down Union, Judah Benjamin l.	20.00	65.00
$2 same with "2 TWO" overprint	25.00	95.00
$10 Commerce reclining		Rare
$10 Ceres seated		Rare
$20 Liberty with shield	600.00	2,900.00
$100 Train	25.00	65.00
$100 Hoeing Cotton	25.00	65.00

FIFTH ISSUE, December 2, 1862

	VG	VF
$1 Clement Clay	24.00	75.00
$2 Judah Benjamin	20.00	65.00
$5 Confederate Capitol at Richmond, Memminger right	8.00	32.00
$10 South Carolina Capitol, Robert Hunter right	8.00	32.00
$20 Tennessee Capitol, Alexander Stephens right	20.00	80.00
$50 Jefferson Davis	25.00	95.00
$100 Lucy Pickens	30.00	95.00

SIXTH ISSUE, April 6, 1863

	VG	VF
50¢ Jefferson Davis	8.00	25.00
$1 Clement Clay	20.00	65.00
$2 Judah Benjamin	20.00	85.00
$5 Confederate Capitol at Richmond, Memminger right	8.00	25.00

	VG	VF
$10 South Carolina Capitol, Robert Hunter right	8.00	25.00
$20 Tennessee Capitol, Alexander Stephens right	8.00	30.00

	VG	VF
$50 Jefferson Davis	20.00	65.00
$100 Lucy Pickens center, Soldiers left, George Randolph right	25.00	75.00

SEVENTH ISSUE, February 17, 1864

	VG	VF
50¢ Jefferson Davis	7.00	25.00
$1 Clement Clay	30.00	80.00

	VG	VF
$2 Judah Benjamin	25.00	75.00
$5 Confederate Capitol at Richmond, Memminger right	7.00	25.00
$10 Field Artillery, Robert Hunter right	6.00	20.00
$20 Tennessee Capitol, Alexander Stephens right	7.00	20.00
$50 Jefferson Davis	20.00	50.00

$100 Lucy Pickens, Soldiers left, George Randolph right	25.00	60.00

$500 Flag and seal left, Stonewall Jackson right	120.00	350.00

ADVERTISING AND OTHER SCRIP

During the Great Depression there was very little money in circulation. In order to facilitate local commerce, many chambers of commerce, city governments and various firms printed their own paper money. Through various methods, which varied by issuer, it could be placed into circulation at a more rapid rate than normal money could. To force it into the stream of currency, rather than being sidetracked into savings, it usually carried an expiration date.

Even in times when there is no shortage of coin or currency it is often useful for businesses to print their own paper money-like certificates, which can be redeemed for products or services. Sometimes this is issued as a reward for patronage. Other times, it facilitates purchases of goods in a closed economic environment, such as a camp or convention. Very often these notes serve no practical purpose at all besides being reminders to the customer of the merchant's business in an entertaining way. One less common, and to an extent outmoded form of scrip is college currency. This is essentially "play money" used by business schools for practicing use of money in commercial situations. "Real" play money of course has a very long history too, and some early issues can actually have numismatic value.

There is no thorough reference for this type of material, so it is a wide open area for those interested in doing original research in local history. Prices for these types of notes are often minimal.

Known counterfeits: Negligible risk.

		XF-CU
1860-85 National School Bank, 2 left, girl right $2		30.00
1860-85 Salt Lake City, Utah, Latter Day Saints College Currency	$1000	350.00
1912 (actually 1998) United States of DiCaprio, Bust of Leonardo DiCaprio,	$20,000,000	.25

		XF-CU
ND. Astor and Colonial Theatre Auction Scrip-Lincoln Silhouette		20.00
1930 R-K-O Proctor's 58th St. Theatre, R.C.A. Victor Radio Auction, 100 Shekels		5.00
1933 San Diego (Calif.) Clearing House Certificate, Inscription	$20	40.00
1933 St. Petersburg (Florida) Citizens Emergency Committee, 10¢		35.00
1935 State of Washington Tax Token Scrip, 10¢		1.00
1935 Parker Brothers, Monopoly $5, house l., locomotive r. (salmon paper)		1.00
(1940) "Buck Benny Rides Again," Portrait of Jack Benny, 1 Benny Buck		10.00
1970s (Parker Brothers, Monopoly) $5, house l., locomotive r. (pink paper)		.10
1970s Fairfield County (Conn.) Council, Boy Scouts of America, Eagle, Cub Bucks		$1.50
1988 American Numismatic Association, ANA logo right, ANA Collector	Currency $1	1.00

		XF-CU
1990 Krause Publications Currency Collector Series, Five Cherubs with oversized Seated Liberty Dollars / Krause building $5		5.00
1994 Chicago International Coin Fair, Three women and Cupid frolicking in Water, Revolutionary War Soldier left, $1		.50
1997 Stack's, New York, Stack's logo (inscription and borders as colonial note of the 1700s) £5		.25

MILITARY PAYMENT CERTIFICATES

Military Payment Certificates are special currency paid to U.S. military personnel overseas. It is good only at military installations. The reason for its issue is to prevent the speculation in U.S. currency by merchants in surrounding communities. To prevent local entrepreneurs from speculating in the certificates themselves, they are frequently recalled and demonetized with little notice, at which time the military base is sealed off. Even the GI's off base run the risk of being stuck with worthless paper if they ignore the notice. The use of MPC also affords some of the advantages of the old World War II North Africa and Hawaii notes in that if captured by the enemy they can be easily identified and easily repudiated without reflecting poorly on the integrity of the U.S. dollar.

Most MPC is smaller than regular currency. While very humble in their appearance, earlier examples can be quite valuable in high grade. Dates do not appear on MPC but they can be dated by their series number.

Known counterfeits: Few known.

	VF	CU
Series 461 (1946) $1	7.00	100.00
Series 471 (1947) $5	600.00	5,000.00
Series 472 (1948) 5¢ Great Seal / Great Seal	.75	4.00

1988 International Association of Millionaires, Statue of Liberty, $1,000,000 (engraved printing)		2.00
1988 Attorney Lester E. Blank (Bridgeport, Conn.), Bust of Blank,	$1,000,000	.25

	VF	CU
Series 481 (1951) 5¢ Seated female with compass and sphere	2.50	20.00
Series 521 (1954) $10 Female wearing wreath	200.00	1,250.00
Series 541 (1958) 25¢ Female wearing wreath / same	6.00	35.00
Series 591 (1961) 50¢ Bust of statue of Liberty	35.00	235.00
Series 641 (1968) 50¢ Female head l.	2.00	12.00

	VF	CU
Series 661 (1968) $5 Female holding flowers	2.00	10.00
Series 681 (1969) 25¢ Submarine	1.00	12.00

	VF	CU
Series 692 (1970) $20 Indian Chief Ouray	120.00	400.00

PERSONAL CHECKS

The use of personal checks has its origins in the letters of credit of the Renaissance. They represent the transfer of a certain sum of money stored in a bank from one specific individual to a second individual's account at another bank. It permits a great amount of convenience and security in not having to transfer actual precious metal or currency from one distant location to another. Because it is usually not a document issued to a bearer but rather to a specific individual, if it is lost or stolen the funds are usually recoverable.

Checks have been used in the United States for most of its exist-

ence. From 1862 to 1882 all checks written were required to have a revenue stamp either affixed to its face or pre-printed on its paper. For a brief time during the Spanish American War these tax stamps were again required. Most checks have traditionally been boring and utilitarian in appearance. Earlier this century, certain firms began to display their logos on them. New styles of artistic checks have become more popular in recent years, and depice background images ranging from Star Trek themes to prairie scenes.

Checks are usually collected as an adjunct to other collections. Traditionally depictions of actual local buildings are of interest to local history collectors. They will also peruse checks written by important community founders. National Bank Note collectors find interest in checks drawn from banks that also issued paper money. Autograph collectors also can find checks of interest as even famous historical figures are known to have signed checks. Finally. stamp collectors have long found great interest in the varieties of revenue stamps found on checks, some of which can be valuable.

While economists have long considered personal checks a form of money, it is only recently that collectors have begun to give them reasonable attention in their own right.

Known counterfeits: The alterations and other frauds which are occasionally a concern when checks are used in commerce are irrelevant to the collector of canceled checks.

Bank (Personal) Check - B. Max Mehl, Ft. Worth, Texas

XF Canceled

1870 Connecticut National Bank of Bridgeport (Connecticut), pre-printed 2¢ stamp depicting eagle	1.50
1874 First National Bank of Rushville, Ill., $112.30, Semi-nude woman and eagle	2.25
1879 Shawmut National Bank, Boston, Mass., $600.00, Steam Locomotive	20.00
1882 City National Bank of Bridgeport, Connecticut, $17.15, blue 2¢ stamp affixed, cut canceled	.75
1895 Centennial National Bank of Phila-delphia, $15.00, Bank Building	30.00
1899 Dime Savings Bank / Western Savings and Deposit Bank, $21.20, three revenue stamps affixed.	5.00
1899 Bank of Clinch Valley, Tazewell, Va., $100.00, 2¢ stamp depicting battle ship affixed	.75
1906 Central National Bank, Philadelphia, Penn., $27.00	.75
1912 All Night and Day Bank, Los Angeles, CA, $420.00	2.00
1916 The First-Bridgeport National Bank, Connecticut, $7.50	.50
1930 Fort Worth National Bank, Ft. Worth, Texas, issued on account offamous coin dealer B. Max Mehl, $30.00, Mehl Building and Fugio Cent	3.00
1998 First National Bank of Chicago, $69.00, View of Chicago shore	.10

CANADA

Like the situation south of the border in the United States and formerly in the Thirteen Colonies, Canadian coinage before the 1870s was a hodgepodge of various coins and tokens struck by a number of authorities, firms countries and individuals. Throughout the 1700s and early 1800s the British policies of Mercantilism prevented the royal government from shipping reasonable quantities of sterling to British North America. By the time the idea was seriously considered, there was already chaos. When official coinage was finally struck by the various pre-Confederation colonial provinces, they had already recognized slightly different standards, sometimes as much as 20 percent different from each other in value. The first coins to be struck in the name of "Canada" were not struck by the Canadian Confederation, but rather by the Province of Canada. This was the collective name for Upper Canada (Ontario) and Lower Canada (Quebec). Bronze cents and silver five, ten and twenty cents were struck in 1858-59. In the intervening years before these two provinces combined with New Brunswick and Nova Scotia to form the independent Canadian Confederation in 1867, all of them had already struck their own unique coins. Despite all this complexity of coinage, there still persisted a shortage of small change in circulation. Neither bank tokens nor poorly made "black smith" counterfeits could be suppressed. During the American Civil War, when U.S. silver coins were being discounted in terms of gold, some firms bought it up in quantity and imported it. Unfortunately it soon became the tool of scams, whereby it was paid out at par but only taken for deposit at a discount. Finally in 1869-70, a three step program was used to cure this dilemma. The United States silver was bought up and four million dollars worth re-exported south. An order was placed with the Royal Mint for an issue of millions of new sterling silver Canadian 5¢, 10¢, 25¢ and 50¢ pieces. Lastly, a temporary issue of fractional paper money redeemable in gold was released immediately to make due until the new coins arrived. (This small paper money proved so popular that was continued to be issued until the 1930s.)

The new Canadian silver coins, nominally valued at one United States dollar worth of gold per Canada Dollar, were struck in quantity, except for the depression of the late 1870s, supplemented by a large initial issue of cents in 1876. These were slightly heavier than the Province's old cents, and continued from 1881 onward. The standards for cents and silver remained unchanged until World War I. During the 1800s, Canadian coins were struck at the Royal Mint in London, and sometimes by contract by the Heaton Mint, Birmingham, England. In 1908, after years of agitation a branch of the Royal mint was opened in Ottawa. With it came the ability to mint the gold then being mined in Canada into internationally recognized British design sovereigns, and soon after that a domestic gold coinage was initiated.

While the basic designs for most Canadian coins remained fairly stable from the beginning until 1937, many smaller changes occurred as needed. Of course with the passing of each monarch, a new royal portrait was designed, one for Edward VII in 1902, another for George V in 1911. The gold sovereigns only, instead of using the crowned busts, used bare headed ones to match British gold sovereigns. There was a bit of a ruckus in 1911 when the new obverse of George V was found to be lacking the Latin Dei Gratia for "by the grace of God." The mint responded to the public outcry, and beginning in 1912, these titles were added. World War I and its aftermath resulted in more modifications. The large cent was replaced in 1920 by a small cent, and the 5¢ silver in 1922 was replaced by one of pure nickel, both similar in size to their American counterparts. Also as a result of a war time increase in the price of silver the alloy of coins in that metal was reduced from 92.5 percent pure (sterling) to 80 percent beginning in 1920.

The entire visual style of Canadian coins began to change in 1935, when a new artistic, commemorative silver dollar for the jubilee of George V was released. It depicted the now famous design of a fur trapper and an Indian paddling a canoe. When the obverses were changed to portray the new King George VI in 1937, the opportunity was taken to revise all the reverses of the smaller denominations with creative, and distinctly Canadian designs. The cent was given a more naturalistic sprig of maple leaves, the five cents a beaver on its dam, while a schooner graced the ten cent pieces and the bust of a caribou the 25 cent. The fifty cent coins displayed a more conservative coat of arms. Because of the time taken to design the new coinage, some 1936 dated coins were struck in 1937 bearing a minute dot to distinguish them. These are quite rare. The reverses introduced in 1937 have, with some alteration, are still used today.

Like World War I, the second World War had its effects on the coinage. Shortages of nickel caused the five cent piece to be struck in a brass alloy called tombac, and later in chromium plated steel. It was not restored to its original composition of old nickel alloy until 1955. A special reverse design was used to boost war time morale — that of a torch superimposed on a V for victory. Because of the time taken to modify the royal titles to reflect the independence of India, some 1947 coins were struck in 1948 with a tiny maple leaf after the date. While not at all rare, these are quite popular.

No monarch has had as many different portraits on Canadian coins as Elizabeth II. The first portrait, designed by Mary Gillick, had some minor difficulties in striking and as a result was subtly modified after being placed in production. In 1965 a new bust, wearing a tiara, was introduced — years before Britain itself began using it. When a mature head of the Queen was desired, the Canadian choice for the first time differed from that of Britain. A design by Canadian artist Dora de Pédery-Hunt was used beginning in 1990.

The centennial of Canadian independence was cause for issue of some of Canada's most beautiful and dignified wildlife coins. Animals emblematic of Canada shown against stark open backgrounds were portrayed on the reverses of the 1967 issues, along with a $20 gold piece with the national arms. Unfortunately, the rising price of silver forced these animal coins out of circulation, In mid-year the 10¢ and 25¢ pieces were reduced to 50 percent pure, and beginning in 1968 pure nickel replaced all circulating silver.

Throughout the 1970s through 1990s, various modifications were made to reduce the expenses of producing coins, which no longer had any tie to their intrinsic value. The cent went through several modifications in weight and shape before they were switched to copper plated steel in 1996. In 1982, the five cent piece was changed from nickel to cupronickel., then to nickel plated steel in 1996, along with the 10¢, 25¢ and 50¢ pieces. Radical new dollar and two dollar coins were introduced to save the expense of producing perishable paper money. A small golden-bronze plated nickel dollar was introduced in 1987 depicting a swimming loon. In 1996 a two dollar coin depicting a polar bear and composed of a nickel ring surrounding an aluminum bronze center followed. Today these two coins are popularly know as the "loonie" and "twonie" respectively.

Since the 1970s Canada has had an aggressive collector coin program, with several different designs in various precious metals being offered in quality strikings each year. Some of these are quite scarce and are made in limited quantities, while others, particularly those of the 1970s are so common as to be frequently meted for scrap. Some of the more unusual pieces are the silver Canadian Aviation series, which actually boasts a small portrait inlay of gold. This decade also saw the old cellophane packaged proof-like sets supplemented with the more market-oriented cased proof sets.

Circulating commemoratives were struck for the 125th anniversary of the Canadian Confederation in 1992. While most coins just bore the 1867-1992 legend, an extremely popular series of 25¢ coins bore reverses emblematic of each province and territory. A dollar depicting children before parliament was issued as well.

As one of the world's richest nations in terms of precious metals, it is not surprising that Canada has for years produced some of the world's most popular bullion coins. Silver one ounce, gold 1/20 to one ounce, and platinum 1/20 to one ounce pieces are struck bearing an intricate and difficult-to-counterfeit maple leaf reverse.

CANADIAN MINT MARKS

C	Ottawa, Ontario
H	Heaton, Birmingham, England
none (1858-1907)	Royal Mint, London
none (1908—	Ottawa, Ontario
none (1968)	Philadelphia, USA
none (1973-)	Hull, Quebec,
none (1975—)	Winnipeg, Manitoba
W (1998)	Winnipeg, Manitoba

GRADING CANADIAN COINS

There are certain convenient key reference points which greatly facilitate the grading of Canadian coins. In the case of the portraits of Queen Victoria it is the hair over or braid below the ear. In the case of both Edward VII and George V it is the band of the crown.

Two special bit of wisdom should be imparted to those who grade Canadian coins. Firstly, even though the typical reverse of a pre-1937 Canadian coin is usually in better grade than the obverse, the value of a coin in the real marketplace is primarily determined by the grade of its obverse. Secondly, pure nickel George V five cent pieces are very difficult to grade. Because of nickel's hardness the dies did not always leave a sharp impression. Thus the understanding of the texture and surface of the metal is always useful in grading this series.

Uncirculated coins with particularly unpleasant bagging, color or toning may trade at a heavy discount.

MS-65 or Gem Uncirculated - This is the highest grade one is likely to encounter. It has utterly no wear. It has no significant bag marks, particularly in open areas such as the field or cheek. Copper must have luster.

MS-63 or Choice Uncirculated - This is a pleasant coin with absolutely no wear but enough bag marks to be noticed. Still, there are few enough bag marks not to be considered marred, particularly few in open areas such as the field or cheek.

MS-60 or Uncirculated - While there is technically no wear at all on an MS-60 coin, it is not necessarily attractive. It will bear scuffs and bagmarks acquired from handling at the mint before release. Copper will usually be toned and some coins of either metal may be discolored.

AU or Almost Uncirculated - This describes a coin with such slight signs of wear that some people may in fact need a mild magnifying glass to see them. One should be careful not to confuse an attractive AU coin for uncirculated. Look for the texture of the metal.

XF or Extremely Fine - This is the highest grade of coin that exhibits wear significant enough to be seen easily by the unaided eye. It still exhibits extremely clear, minute detail. In

the case of Victorian coins the hair over ear and jewels of diadem, or segments of braid, are sharp. In the case of Edward VII and George V, the jewels in the band of the crown are sharp. George VI coins will have only the slightest wear in the hair over the ear.

VF or Very Fine - These coins will show obvious signs of wear. Nevertheless, most of the detail of the design is still clear. In the case of Victorian coins, the hair over ear and jewels of diadem, or segments of braid, are visible but not sharp. The same is true of the jewels in the diadem. In the case of Edward VII and George V, the jewels in the band of the crown are visible but not sharp. George VI coins will have about 80 percent of hair detail visible.

F or Fine - This is the lowest grade most people would consider collectible. About half the design detail will show for most types. In the case of Victorian coins, the strands of the hair over ear or segments of braid begin to run into each other. Some of the details in the diadem will be obscured. In the case of Edward VII and George V, the jewels in the band of the crown will be unclear, but the band will be distinct from the head. George VI coins will have only about half the hair detail visible.

VG or Very Good - These coins exhibit heavy wear. All outlines are clear, as is generally the rim. Some internal detail will also show, but most will be worn off. In the case of Victorian coins, the details in the strands of the hair over ear or segments of braid will be obscured. Most of the details in the diadem will be obscured. In the case of Edward VII and George V, the band of the crown will be worn through at its center. George VI coins will have only about one third the hair detail visible.

G or Good - These coins are generally considered uncollectible except for novelty purposes. There will usually be little or no internal detail to the design. Some of the rim may also be barely visible on silver. In the case of Victorian coins, the hair over ear or the braid will be very much obscured, as will the majority of the diadem. In the case of Edward VII and George V, the band of the crown will be worn through along most of its width. George VI coins will have no hair detail at all.

BOOKS ON CANADIAN COINS

Charlton, J.E., *The Standard Catalogue of Canadian Coins*

Charlton, J.E., *The Charlton Standard Catalogue of Canadian Colonial Tokens*

Harper, David C., ed., *North American Coins & Prices*

Haxby, James, *The Royal Canadian Mint and Canadian Coinage: Striking Impressions*

Haxby, James, and Willey, R.C., *Coins of Canada*.

Periodical

Canadian Coin News.

CENTS

One-inch wide large cents were among the first coins to be struck by the Province of Canada in 1858-59 before the formation of the Confederation. These coins with a young head of Queen Victoria were struck in such quantities that they were still in bank coffers until 1875. The following year another large order for cents was placed, this time with a heavier weight and a mature head of the queen. This order lasted for five years. Since 1881 Canadian cents have been struck almost continuously.

With the passing of Queen Victoria a new portrait was designed for Edward VII in 1902, another for George V in 1911. There was a bit of a ruckus in 1911 when the new obverse of George V was found to be lacking the Latin Dei Gratia for "by the grace of God." The mint responded to the public outcry and beginning 1912 these titles were added. More public complaint was heard about the traditional size of the cent. The large cent was replaced in 1920 by a small cent much like America's.

When the obverse was changed to portray the new King George VI in 1937, the opportunity was taken to revise the reverse of the cent. It was given a more naturalistic sprig of maple leaves, designed by G.E. Kruger-Gray. Because of the time taken to design the new cents, some 1936 dated coins were struck in 1937 bearing a minute dot to distinguish them. These are quite rare. The reverse introduced in 1937 is, with some alteration, still in use today.

Because of the time taken to modify the royal titles to reflect the independence of India, some 1947 cents were struck in 1948 with a tiny maple leaf after the date. While not at all rare, these are quite popular.

No monarch has had as many different portraits on Canadian coins as Elizabeth II. The first portrait, designed by Mary Gillick, had some minor difficulties in striking and as a result was subtly modified after being placed in production. In 1965, a new bust of her, wearing a tiara, was introduced — years before Britain itself began using it. When a mature head of the Queen was desired, the Canadian choice, for the first time, differed from that of Britain. A design by Canadian artist Dora de Pédery-Hunt was used beginning in 1990.

As part of a set of wildlife coins struck for the centennial of Canadian independence the 1967 cent depicted a rock dove. For its 125th anniversary the double date 1867-1992 was displayed.

In an economy measure the weight of the cent was reduced in 1978, 1980 and 1982. Finally it was switched to copper plated steel in 1996. From 1982 to 1995 Canadian cents were twelve-sided.

Known counterfeits: The 1936 dot variety is a prime target.

VICTORIA	VG	VF
1858	35.00	60.00
1859, 9 over 8	22.00	40.00
1859, Narrow 9	1.50	3.00
1859, Double punched 9 (2 vars.)	32.00	60.00
1876H	1.50	4.00
1881H	2.50	5.00
1882H	1.50	3.00
1884	2.00	4.00
1886	3.25	7.00
1887	2.50	5.00
1888	1.50	3.00
1890H	4.00	11.50
1891 Large date	4.50	11.00
1891 Small date, Large Leaves	40.00	85.00
1891 Small date, Small Leaves	30.00	60.00
1892	3.00	6.00
1893	2.00	4.00
1894	5.50	13.00
1895	3.00	7.00
1896	1.75	3.50
1897	2.00	5.00
1898H	4.00	8.00
1899	1.50	3.00
1900	5.00	12.00
1900H	1.50	3.50
1901	1.50	3.00

EDWARD VII	VG	VF
1902	1.25	2.00
1903	1.25	2.00
1904	1.50	3.25
1905	2.50	6.00
1906	1.25	2.00
1907	1.50	3.50
1907H	6.00	16.00
1908	2.25	4.50
1909	1.25	2.00
1910	1.25	1.75

GEORGE V - LARGE	F	XF
1911	1.25	3.50
1912	1.00	2.50
1913	1.00	2.50
1914	1.40	3.50
1915	1.10	2.75
1916	.65	2.00
1917	.50	1.50
1918	.50	1.50
1919	.50	1.50
1920	.75	2.00

GEORGE V - SMALL	F	XF
1920	.50	2.00
1921	.75	4.00
1922	10.00	22.00
1923	16.25	34.00
1924	4.75	11.50
1925	14.25	28.00
1926	3.00	8.75
1927	1.25	4.00
1928	.25	1.50
1929	.25	1.50
1930	1.80	5.00
1931	1.00	3.50
1932	.25	1.50
1933	.25	1.50
1934	.30	1.50
1935	.30	1.50
1936	.25	1.50
1936 Dot below date		Rare

GEORGE VI	XF	MS-63
1937	1.60	6.00
1938	1.00	6.50
1939	1.00	5.00
1940	1.00	6.00
1941	1.00	35.00
1942	.75	25.00
1943	.75	12.00
1944	1.00	32.00
1945	.50	5.00
1946	.60	5.00
1947	.50	6.00
1947 Maple Leaf	.50	5.00
1948	.80	8.00
1949	.50	4.00
1950	.40	4.00
1951	.40	4.00
1952	.40	4.00

Gillick bust   Machin bust

ELIZABETH II	MS-63
1953 without fold	2.00
1953 with fold	35.00
1954 without fold	Proof like only 250.00
1954 with fold	4.00
1955 without fold	950.00
1955 with fold	1.00
1956	.90
1957	.70
1958	.70
1959	.50
1960	.50
1961	.40
1962	.25
1963	.25
1964	.25

de Pedery-Hunt bust   125th Anniv. rev.

1965	.25
1966	.20
1967 Centennial	.20
1968	.20
1969	.20
1970	.20
1971	.20
1972	.20
1973	.20
1974	.20
1975	.20
1976	.20
1977	.20
1978	.20
1979	.20
1980	.15
1981	.15
1982	.15
1983	.15
1984	.15
1985	.15
1986	.15
1987	.15
1988	.15
1989	.15
1990	.15
1991	.15
1992 "1867-1992"	.15
1993	.15
1994	.15
1995	.15
1996	.15
1997	.15
1998	.15
1998	.15
1998W	.20
1998 Large Cent as 1908	17.50

FIVE CENTS

Tiny sterling silver five cent pieces were among the first coins to be struck by the Province of Canada in 1858 before the formation of the Confederation. These coins bore a young head of Queen Victoria. Twelve years later the new Confederation started issuing five cent silver coins, making no significant changes from the earlier provincial piece.

With the passing of Queen Victoria a new portrait was designed for Edward VII in 1902, followed the next year by a change of the reverse crown from St. Edward's to the Imperial crown. There was a bit of a ruckus in 1911 when the new obverse with George V's portrait was found to be lacking the Latin Dei Gratia, for "by the grace of God." The mint responded to the public outcry and beginning 1912 these titles were added.

As a result of World War I, silver prices increased and the lloy was reduced from 92.5 percent pure (sterling) to 80 percent beginning with 1920. Public complaint persisted about the small size of this coin, since they were easy to lose or drop, and their thinness resulted in the dents, edge dings, and bends collectors object to today. It was replaced in 1922 by a larger coin much like America's but of pure nickel.

When the obverse was changed to portray the new King George VI in 1937, the opportunity was taken to revise the reverse of the five cent piece. A naturalistic beaver on its dam was portrayed, designed by G.E. Kruger-Gray. This new reverse is, with some alteration, still used today.

Like World War I, the second World War had its effects on the coinage. Shortages of nickel caused the five cent piece to be struck in a brass alloy called tombac from 1942-44, and later in 1944-45 and 1951-54 in chromium plated steel. A special reverse design was used to boost war time morale, that of a torch superimposed on a V for victory.

Because of the time taken to modify the royal titles to reflect the independence of India, some 1947 coins were struck in 1948 with a tiny dot or maple leaf after the date. The dot is scarce, the leaf common, but both are quite popular.

No monarch has had as many different portraits on Canadian coins as Elizabeth II. The first portrait, designed by Mary Gillick, had some minor difficulties in striking and as a result was subtly modified after being placed in production. In 1965 a new bust wearing a tiara was introduced, years before Britain itself began using it. When a mature head of the Queen was desired, the Canadian choice for the first time differed from that of Britain. A design by Canadian artist Dora de Pédery-Hunt was used beginning 1990.

As part of a set of wildlife coins struck for the centennial of Canadian independence, the 1967 five cent piece depicted a running rabbit. For its 125th anniversary the double date 1867-1992 was displayed.

In an economy measure, the alloy of the five cent coin was changed to 75 percent copper and 25 percent nickel in 1982. It was switched to nickel-plated steel in 1996, with proofs being struck in sterling.

Modern counting machines occasionally leave an X-shaped scratch on these coins, and such damaged coins are virtually worthless unless scarcer dates.

Known counterfeits: For the small size pieces, only the 1921 is problematic, and most were remelted. For the large size, crude contemporary counterfeits are occasionally encountered.

VICTORIA	VG	VF
1858	10.00	25.00
1858, Large date over small date	100.00	250.00
1870 Flat rim	9.00	25.00
1870 Wire rim	9.00	25.00
1871	9.00	25.00
1872H	6.00	25.00
1874H Plain 4	12.50	55.00
1874H Crosslet 4	10.00	40.00
1875H Large date	125.00	325.00
1875H Small date	80.00	250.00
1880H	4.00	16.00
1881H	4.25	17.50
1882H	5.00	18.00
1883H	11.50	60.00
1884	75.00	225.00
1885	7.50	35.00
1886	4.50	17.50
1887	12.50	45.00
1888	3.50	14.00
1889	13.50	60.00
1890H	4.50	18.00
1891	3.00	10.00
1892	4.50	16.00
1893	3.00	10.00
1894	9.50	40.00
1896	3.50	12.00
1897	3.75	12.00
1898	8.00	30.00
1899	2.75	7.50
1900 Oval 0's	3.00	8.00
1900 Round 0's	13.00	45.00
1901	2.75	8.00

EDWARD VII	VG	VF
1902	1.50	3.25
1902H Broad H	2.00	4.50
1902H Narrow H	5.00	20.00
1903	4.00	14.00
1903H	1.75	7.00

EDWARD VII	VG	VF
1904	1.75	7.00
1905	1.75	6.00
1906	1.50	4.00
1907	1.50	4.00
1908	4.00	12.00
1909	2.00	7.00
1910	1.50	3.25

GEORGE V - SILVER	VG	XF
1911	1.75	11.00
1912	1.50	6.00
1913	1.25	5.00
1914	1.50	7.00
1915	6.50	40.00
1916	2.75	12.50
1917	1.25	4.00
1918	1.25	4.00
1919	1.25	4.00
1920	1.25	4.00
1921	1,700.00	5,000.00

GEORGE V - NICKEL	VG	XF
1922	.25	7.00
1923	.40	12.00
1924	.30	7.00
1925	25.00	150.00
1926 near 6	3.00	45.00
1926 far 6	65.00	300.00
1927	.15	6.50
1928	.15	6.50
1929	.15	6.50
1930	.15	6.50
1931	.15	6.50
1932	.15	7.00
1933	.40	10.00
1934	.15	6.50
1935	.15	6.50
1936	.15	6.50

GEORGE VI	XF	MS-60
1937	2.50	9.00
1938	7.00	65.00
1939	4.50	40.00
1940	1.50	14.00
1941	1.50	17.00
1942 Nickel	1.75	14.00
1942 Brass	1.75	3.00

GEORGE VI

	XF	MS-60
1943 Brass	1.00	2.00
1944 Brass		Rare
1944 Steel	1.00	2.25
1945 Steel	1.00	2.25
1946	2.00	10.00
1947	1.25	10.00
1947 Dot	50.00	220.00
1947 Maple Leaf	1.25	8.00
1948	2.00	15.00
1949	.75	4.00
1950	.75	4.00
1951 Steel	1.00	2.50
1951 Nickel	.75	2.00
1952 Steel	1.00	3.00

ELIZABETH II

	MS-60
1953 Steel, without strap	3.00
1953 Steel, with strap	3.50
1954 Steel	4.50
1955	3.00
1956	1.75
1957	1.50
1958	1.50
1959	.65
1960	.25
1961	.20
1962	.20
1963	.20
1964	.20

1965	.20
1966	.20
1967 Centennial	.20
1968	.20
1969	.20
1970	.55
1971	.20
1972	.20
1973	.20
1974	.20
1975	.20
1976	.20
1977	.20
1978	.20
1979	.20
1980	.20
1981	.20

ELIZABETH II MS-60

Cupro-Nickel

1982		.20
1983		.20
1984		.20
1985		.20
1986		.20
1987		.10
1988		.10
1989		.10
1990		.10
1991		.20
1992 "1867-1992"		.10
1993		.10
1994		.10
1995		.10
1996		.10
1996 Silver	Proof only	4.00
1997		.10
1997 Silver	Proof only	4.00
1998		.10
1998W		.15
1998 "1908-1998" Silver		3.00

TEN CENTS

Sterling silver ten cent pieces were among the first coins to be struck by the Province of Canada in 1858 before the formation of the Confederation. These coins bore a young head of Queen Victoria. Twelve years later the new Confederation started issuing five cent silver coins, making no significant changes from the earlier provincial piece.

With the passing of Queen Victoria a new portrait was designed for Edward VII in 1902. There was a bit of a ruckus in 1911 when the new obverse with George V's portrait was found to be lacking the Latin Dei Gratia, for "by the grace of God." The mint responded to the public outcry and beginning in 1912 these titles were added.

As a result of a World War I increase in the price of silver, the alloy was reduced from 92.5 percent pure (sterling) to 80 percent beginning in 1920.

When the obverse was changed to portray the new King George VI in 1937, the opportunity was taken to revise the reverse of the ten cent piece. A fishing schooner under sail is depicted, designed by Emmanuel Hahn. Because of the time taken to design the new reverse some 1936 dated coins were struck in 1937, and bore a minute dot to distinguish them. These are quite rare. This new reverse is, with some alteration, still in use today.

Because of the time taken to modify the royal titles on the dies to reflect the independence of India, some 1947 coins were struck in 1948 with a maple leaf after the date. These are common, but quite popular.

No monarch has had as many different portraits on Canadian coins as Elizabeth II. The first portrait, designed by Mary Gillick, had some minor difficulties in striking and as a result was subtly modified after being placed in production. In 1965 a new bust, wearing a tiara, was introduced — years

before Britain itself began using it. When a mature head of the Queen was desired, the Canadian choice for the first time differed from that of Britain. A design by Canadian artist Dora de Pédery-Hunt was used, beginning in 1990.

As part of a set of wildlife coins struck for the centennial of Canadian independence, the 1967 ten cent piece depicted a mackerel. Unfortunately the rising price of silver forced the centennial coins out of circulation. In mid-year the ten cent piece was reduced to 50 percent pure, and beginning in 1968 to pure nickel. It was switched to nickel plated steel in 1996, with proofs being struck in sterling.

For the Confederation's 125th anniversary the double date 1867-1992 was displayed on the regular type. The 1997 issue commemorates the voyages of John Cabot.

Modern counting machines occasionally leave a circular scratch on these coins, and such damaged coins are virtually worthless unless scarcer dates.

Known counterfeits: The 1936 dot should be examined by an expert.

VICTORIA

	VG	VF
1858, 8 over 5	325.00	875.00
1858	13.50	45.00
1870 Narrow 0	12.00	50.00
1870 Wide 0	17.00	60.00
1871	15.00	70.00
1871H	18.00	70.00
1872H	70.00	225.00
1874H	8.00	30.00
1875H	175.00	575.00
1880H	7.00	25.00
1881H	8.50	40.00
1882H	8.50	35.00
1883H	25.00	125.00
1884	140.00	575.00
1885	22.00	125.00
1886 Small 6	12.00	50.00
1886 Large 6	15.00	60.00
1887	23.00	125.00
1888	6.75	30.00
1889	400.00	1,450.00
1890H	11.50	45.00
1891, 21 leaves	12.00	50.00
1891, 22 leaves	12.00	50.00
1892/1	115.00	325.00
1892	9.50	37.50
1893 Flat top 3	14.00	70.00
1893 Round 3	425.00	1,700.00
1894	13.00	55.00
1896	7.00	25.00
1898	7.00	30.00
1899 Small 9's	6.75	25.00
1899 Large 9's	10.00	35.00
1900	6.75	25.00
1901	6.75	25.00

EDWARD VII	VG	VF
1902	3.50	18.00
1902H	2.75	12.50
1903	8.00	60.00
1903H	3.00	15.00
1904	4.50	20.00
1905	4.00	25.00
1906	2.75	14.00
1907	2.75	12.50
1908	5.00	27.00
1909 Victorian Leaves	3.50	20.00
1909 Broad Leaves	5.50	25.00
1910	2.75	12.50

GEORGE V	VG	XF
1911	4.00	40.00
1912	1.75	22.00
1913 Large Leaves	75.00	650.00
1913 Small Leaves	1.50	17.50
1914	1.50	18.50
1915	4.00	80.00
1916	1.00	11.00
1917	.75	8.75
1918	.75	8.75
1919	.75	8.75
1920	.75	9.00
1921	1.25	12.50
1928	1.00	10.00
1929	1.00	9.50
1930	1.25	14.00
1931	1.00	10.00
1932	1.50	20.00
1933	2.00	25.00
1934	3.00	55.00
1935	3.00	55.00
1936	.60	8.75
1936 Dot		4 Known

GEORGE VI	XF	MS-60
1937	4.50	10.00
1938	7.00	40.00
1939	6.00	35.00
1940	3.00	14.00
1941	6.00	35.00
1942	4.00	25.00
1943	4.00	12.00
1944	4.50	20.00
1945	4.00	12.00
1946	4.50	20.00

GEORGE VI	XF	MS-60
1947	6.00	32.00
1947 Maple Leaf	3.00	10.00
1948	17.00	40.00
1949	2.00	7.00
1950	1.50	6.00
1951	1.50	5.00
1952	1.50	5.00

ELIZABETH II	XF	MS-60
1953 without straps	1.25	3.00
1953 with fold	1.25	3.50
1954	1.50	6.00
1955	.75	3.00
1956	.75	2.25
1956 Dot below date	5.00	12.50
1957		1.25
1958		1.25
1959		1.00
1960		.75
1961		.75
1962		.75
1963		.75
1964		.75

1965		.75
1966		.75
1967 Centennial		.75
1968		.60
Nickel		
1968		.25
1969		.25
1970		.65
1971		.25
1972		.25
1973		.25
1974		.25
1975		.25
1976		.25
1977		.25
1978		.25
1979		.25
1980		.25
1981		.25
1982		.25
1983		.25
1984		.25
1985		.25
1986		.25
1987		.25
1988		.25
1989		.25
1990		.25
1991		.25
1992 "1867-1992"		.35
1993		.25
1994		.25
1995		.25

ELIZABETH II	XF	MS-60
Nickel-Plated Steel		
1996		.25
1996 Silver		Proof Only 4.00
1997		.25
1997 Silver		Proof Only 4.00
1997 John Cabot, Silver		Proof Only 12.50
1998		.25
1998W		.30
1998 "1908-1998" Silver		6.00

TWENTY CENTS

Sterling silver twenty cent pieces were the largest of the first coins to be struck by the Province of Canada in 1858 before the formation of the Confederation. These coins bore a young head of Queen Victoria. Twelve years later the new Confederation started issuing five cent silver coins, making no significant changes from the earlier provincial piece. During the American Civil War, when U.S. silver coins were being discounted in terms of gold, some firms bought it up in quantity and imported it. With so many United states quarters circulating at the same time it became easy to confuse the twenty cent piece with them. Because of this, it was decided to withdraw the denomination in 1870.

It has since become one of the most desirable and salable Canadian coins
Known counterfeits: Few.

	VG	VF
1858	40.00	90.00

TWENTY-FIVE CENTS

Sterling silver twenty-five cent pieces were first struck in 1870 after the decision to abandon the old twenty cent denomination. The new coin was more in harmony with the flood of United States quarters that had been imported into Canada during the American Civil War. These coins bore an older head of Queen Victoria. These coins saw hard service, not being actively replaced by the government as they wore out, hence they are more difficult than one would expect in middle to upper grades.

With the passing of Queen Victoria, a new portrait was designed for Edward VII in 1902. There was a bit of a ruckus in 1911 when the new obverse with George V's portrait was found to be lacking the Latin Dei Gratia, for "by the grace of God." The mint responded to the public outcry and beginning in 1912 these titles were added.

As a result of a World War I increase in the price of silver the alloy was reduced from 92.5 percent pure (sterling) to 80 percent in 1920.

When the obverse was changed to portray the new King George VI in 1937, the opportunity was taken to revise the reverse of the twenty-five cent piece. A Caribou's bust is depicted, designed by Emanuel Hahn. Because of the time taken to design the new reverse, some 1936 dated coins were struck in 1937, and bore a minute dot to distinguish them. These are quite rare. This new reverse is, with some alteration, still in use today.

Because of the time taken to modify the royal titles on the dies to reflect the independence of India, some 1947 coins were struck in 1948 with a tiny dot or maple leaf after the date. The dot is scarce, while the leaf is not, but both are quite popular.

No monarch has had as many different portraits on Canadian coins as Elizabeth II. The first portrait, designed by Mary Gillick, had some minor difficulties in striking and as a result was subtly modified after being placed in production. In 1965 a new bust, wearing a tiara, was introduced — years before Britain itself began using it. When a mature head of the Queen was desired, the Canadian choice for the first time differed from that of Britain. A design by Canadian artist Dora de Pédery-Hunt was used beginning 1990.

As part of a set of wildlife coins struck for the centennial of Canadian independence the 1967 twenty-five cent piece depicted a bobcat. Unfortunately the rising price of silver forced the centennial coins out of circulation. In mid-year this coin was reduced to 50 percent pure, and beginning in 1968, to totally pure nickel. It was switched to nickel plated steel in 1996, with proofs being struck in sterling.

A special reverse was used in 1973 to commemorate the centenary of the Royal Canadian Mounted Police. A whole set of circulating commemorative twenty-five cent pieces was struck for the 125th anniversary of the Canadian Confederation in 1992. While one of the coins simply bore a "1867-1992" legend, a dozen others of the extremely popular series bore reverses emblematic of each province and territory. Most common 1912-1968 pieces in Very Good or lower are worth only their scrap value. Modern counting machines occasionally leave a circular scratch on these coins, and such damaged coins are virtually worthless unless scarcer dates.
Known counterfeits: The 1936 dot should be examined by an expert.

VICTORIA	VG	VF
1870	11.00	45.00
1871	14.00	65.00

VICTORIA	VG	VF
1871H	16.00	80.00
1872H	6.00	25.00
1874H	7.00	27.00
1875H	225.00	1,200.00
1880H Narrow 0	30.00	165.00
1880H Wide 0	95.00	350.00
1880H Wide over narrow 0	90.00	350.00
1881H	12.00	55.00
1882H	13.00	65.00
1883H	10.00	45.00
1885	75.00	325.00
1886, 6 over 3	12.00	65.00
1886	10.00	60.00
1887	75.00	325.00
1888	10.00	50.00
1889	95.00	350.00
1890H	15.00	70.00
1891	45.00	190.00
1892	9.00	45.00
1893	75.00	275.00
1894	15.00	70.00
1899	6.00	27.00
1900	6.00	27.00
1901	6.00	27.00

EDWARD VII	VG	VF
1902	7.00	40.00
1902H	4.00	32.00
1903	5.00	30.00
1904	9.75	95.00
1905	5.50	65.00
1906 Small crown		Rare
1906 Large crown	5.00	27.00
1907	4.00	27.00
1908	6.00	45.00
1909	5.00	40.00
1910	3.00	26.00

GEORGE V	F	XF
1911	14.00	75.00
1912	3.50	40.00
1913	3.50	40.00
1914	4.00	50.00
1915	22.00	350.00
1916	3.00	30.00
1917	3.00	20.00
1918	3.00	18.00
1919	3.00	18.00
1920	3.00	22.00
1921	16.00	180.00
1927	30.00	200.00
1928	3.00	22.00

GEORGE V	F	XF
1929	2.75	22.00
1930	3.50	25.00
1931	3.50	27.50
1932	4.00	30.00
1933	4.50	40.00
1934	6.00	55.00
1935	5.00	42.00
1936	3.00	20.00
1936 Dot	60.00	275.00

GEORGE VI	XF	MS-60
1937	5.00	10.00
1938	6.50	55.00
1939	6.50	50.00
1940	4.50	10.00
1941	4.50	12.00
1942	4.50	12.00
1943	4.00	15.50
1944	4.50	17.00
1945	4.00	10.00
1946	5.00	35.00
1947	6.00	40.00
1947 Dot after date	115.00	200.00
1947 Maple Leaf	4.00	12.00
1948	5.00	40.00
1949	2.00	9.00
1950	2.25	9.00
1951	2.25	6.00
1952	2.25	6.00

With Strap   Without Strap

ELIZABETH II	XF	MS-60
1953 without strap	2.00	4.00
1953 with strap	2.00	6.00
1954	6.00	20.00
1955		3.50
1956		3.00
1957		2.00
1958		2.00
1959		1.50
1960		1.50
1961		1.50
1962		1.50
1963		1.25
1964		1.25

ELIZABETH II	XF	MS-60
1965		1.25
1966		1.25
1967 Centennial		1.25
1968		1.00
Nickel		
1968		.50
1969		.50
1970		1.00
1971		.50
1972		.50
1973 R.C.M.P.		.50
1974		.50
1975		.50
1976		.50
1977		.50
1978		.50
1979		.50
1980		.50
1981		.50
1982		.50
1983		.75
1984		.50
1985		.50
1986		.50
1987		.75
1988		.75
1989		.50
1990		.50
1991		8.00
1992 "1867-1992"		7.00

1992 Alberta		.50
1992 Alberta Silver Proof		7.50
1992 British Columbia		.50
1992 Br. Columbia Silver Proof		7.50
1992 Manitoba		.50
1992 Manitoba Silver Proof		7.50

1992 New Brunswick		.50
1992 New Brunswick Silver Proof		7.50
1992 Newfoundland		.50
1992 Newfoundland Silver Proof		7.50
1992 North West Terr.		.50
1992 North West Terr. Silver Proof		7.50

1992 Nova Scotia		.50
1992 Nova Scotia Silver Proof		7.50

ELIZABETH II	XF	MS-60
1992 Ontario		.50
1992 Ontario Silver Proof		7.50
1992 Prince Edward Island		.50
1992 Prince Edward Island Silver Proof		7.50

1992 Quebec		.50
1992 Quebec Silver Proof		7.50
1992 Saskatchewan		.50
1992 Saskatchewan Silver Proof		7.50
1992 Yukon		.50
1992 Yukon Silver Proof		7.50
1993		.75
1994		.75
1995		.75
Nickel Plated Steel		
1996		.75
1996 Silver	Proof Only	5.00
1997		.75
1997 Silver	Proof Only	5.00
1998		.75
1998W		.85
1998 "1908-1998" Silver		17.50

FIFTY CENTS

Sterling silver fifty cent pieces were the largest coin struck for domestic circulation from the beginning of Confederation coinage in 1870 until 1912. These coins bore an older head of Queen Victoria. Initial mintages were moderate and for some time it was not the government's policy to replace worn out coins, so these coins saw hard service. They are more difficult than one would expect in middle to upper grades.

With the passing of Queen Victoria, a new portrait was designed for Edward VII in 1902. The very first coin struck at the new Canadian mint in 1908 was one of these pieces. There was a bit of a ruckus in 1911 when the new obverse with George V's portrait was found to be lacking the Latin Dei Gratia, for "by the grace of God." The mint responded to the public outcry and beginning in 1912 these titles were added.

As a result of World War I, silver prices increased and the alloy was reduced from 92.5 percent pure (sterling) to 80 percent beginning in 1920. Most 1921 pieces were melted before they could be released, and no more fifty cent pieces were struck until 1929. The former year is today one of the greatest of Canadian rarities.

When the obverse was changed to portray the new King George VI in 1937, the opportunity was taken to revise the reverse of the fifty cent piece. The crowned coat of arms of Canada was selected, as designed by George Kruger-Gray. This new reverse motif is, with many alterations, still used today.

Because of the time taken to modify the royal titles on the dies to reflect the indepen-

dence of India, some 1947 coins were struck in 1948 with a tiny maple leaf after the date. This is not quite popular.

No monarch has had as many different portraits on Canadian coins as Elizabeth II. The first portrait, designed by Mary Gillick, had some minor difficulties in striking, and as a result, was subtly modified after being placed in production. In 1965, a new bust wearing a tiara, was introduced — years before Britain itself began using it. When a mature head of the Queen was desired, the Canadian choice for the first time differed from that of Britain. A design by Canadian artist Dora de Pédery-Hunt was used, beginning in 1990.

During this reign, the coat of arms on the reverse went through its own evolution. A version with a motto and more elaborate crest was introduced in 1959, only to be modified the next year. The 1959 version was heraldically inaccurate, using the symbol for blue instead of white in the lowest section. In 1997 a additional collar was added around the shield.

As part of a set of wildlife coins struck for the centennial of Canadian independence, the 1967 fifty cent piece depicted a howling wolf. Unfortunately, the rising price of silver forced the centennial coins out of circulation. Production of the silver fifty cent piece was suspended, and beginning in 1968 it was reduced in size and produced in pure nickel. It was switched to nickel plated steel in 1996, with proofs being struck in sterling.

For the Confederation's 125th anniversary the double date "1867-1992" was displayed on the regular type.

Most common 1937-1968 pieces in Fine or lower are worth only their scrap value.

Known counterfeits: Any 1921 should be examined by an expert.

VICTORIA	VG	VF
1870	550.00	1,800.00
1870 LCW	40.00	160.00
1871	45.00	220.00
1871H	90.00	425.00
1872H	40.00	170.00
1872H inverted		
A over V	95.00	425.00
1881H	40.00	175.00
1888	110.00	490.00
1890H	700.00	2,000.00
1892	45.00	225.00
1894	245.00	920.00

VICTORIA	VG	VF
1898	45.00	225.00
1899	95.00	435.00
1900	40.00	160.00
1901	42.00	165.00

EDWARD VII	VG	VF
1902	11.00	75.00
1903H	18.00	110.00
1904	80.00	300.00
1905	100.00	435.00
1906	10.00	70.00
1907	10.00	70.00
1908	20.00	120.00
1909	13.00	120.00
1910 Victorian Leaves	9.00	65.00
1910 Edwardian Leaves	9.00	65.00

GEORGE V	F	XF
1911	70.00	475.00
1912	16.00	200.00
1913	16.00	210.00
1914	45.00	400.00
1916	14.00	125.00
1917	12.00	90.00
1918	8.00	70.00
1919	8.00	70.00
1920	8.50	110.00
1921	13,500.00	25,000.00
1929	8.00	100.00
1931	22.00	200.00
1932	100.00	500.00
1934	25.00	200.00
1936	20.00	150.00

GEORGE VI	XF	MS-60
1937	10.00	25.00
1938	28.00	100.00
1939	16.50	70.00
1940	5.00	22.00
1941	5.00	22.00
1942	5.00	22.00
1943	5.00	22.00
1944	5.00	22.00
1945	5.00	22.00
1946	9.00	60.00
1946 Hoof in 6	110.00	975.00
1947 Straight 7	12.00	80.00
1947 Curved 7	12.00	80.00
1947 Straight 7, Maple Leaf	60.00	160.00
1947 Curved 7, Maple Leaf	2,000.00	3,000.00
1948	90.00	145.00
1949	10.00	35.00
1949 Hoof over 9	60.00	350.00
1950	20.00	175.00
1950 Lines in 0	4.00	11.00
1951	3.50	8.00
1952	3.50	8.00

ELIZABETH II	XF	MS-60
1953 Small date, without strap	2.50	5.50
1953 Large date, without strap	12.00	70.00
1953 Large date, with fold	5.00	20.00
1954	7.00	20.00
1955	5.00	12.00
1956	3.00	4.50
1957	2.00	3.50
1958	2.00	3.00
1959	2.00	2.50
1960		2.25
1961		2.00
1962		2.00
1963		2.00
1964		2.00

ELIZABETH II		XF	MS-60
1965			2.00
1966			2.00
1967 Centennial			4.00
Nickel			
1968			.65
1969			.65
1970			.65
1971			.65
1972			.65
1973			.65
1974			.65
1975			.65
1976			.65
1977			1.50
1978			.75
1979			.65
1980			.65
1981			.65
1982			.65
1983			.65
1984			.65
1985			.65
1986			.85
1987			.85
1988			1.50
1989			.85
1990			2.00
1991			.85
1992 "1867-1992"			1.75
1993			.85
1994			.75
1995			.75
Nickel Plated Steel			
1996			.65
1996 Silver	Proof Only		7.50
1997			.75
1997 Silver	Proof Only		7.00
1998			.75
1998W			1.00
1998 "1908-1998" Silver			35.00
1998 Speed Skaters	Proof Only		15.00
1998 Ski Jumper	Proof Only		15.00
1998 Soccer Players	Proof Only		15.00
1998 Race Car	Proof Only		15.00
1998 Killer Whales	Proof Only		15.00
1998 Humpback Whales	Proof Only		15.00
1998 Beluga Whales	Proof Only		15.00
1998 Blue Whale	Proof Only		15.00

DOLLARS

Despite patterns having been produced as early as 1911, Canada did not issue a silver dollar until 1935. The entire visual style of Canadian coins began to change then, when a new artistic, commemorative dollar for the jubilee of George V was released. It depicted the now famous Voyageur design of a fur company agent and an Indian paddling a canoe past an islet. This design was retained when the reverses of all the other denominations were modernized with appearance of the new George VI portrait in 1937.

Because of the time taken to modify the royal titles to reflect the independence of India, some 1947 coins were struck in 1948 with a tiny maple leaf after the date. While not at all rare, these are quite popular. The 1950-52 Arnprior varieties have only 1-1/2 water lines to the right of the canoe, due to over-polishing of the die.

No monarch has had as many different portraits on Canadian coins as Elizabeth II. The first portrait, designed by Mary Gillick, had some minor difficulties in striking and as a result was subtly modified after being placed in production. In 1965 a new bust wearing a tiara was introduced, years before Britain itself began using it. When a mature head of the Queen was desired, the Canadian choice for the first time differed from that of Britain. A design by Canadian artist Dora de Pédery-Hunt was used beginning 1990.

The 1967 centennial of Canadian independence was cause for issue of some of Canada's most beautiful and dignified wildlife coins. On the dollar, a majestic Canada goose is shown against stark open background. Unfortunately the rising price of silver forced this coin out of circulation. Beginning in 1968 the 80 percent silver dollar was replaced by a smaller one of pure nickel.

In 1987, a radical new dollar coin was introduced to save the expense of producing perishable paper money. A small golden-bronze plated nickel dollar was introduced that depicted a swimming loon. It was originally intended to use the standard Voyageur reverse but the master dies were temporarily lost in transit! Today this coin is popularly know as the "loonie."

With a long history of being used as a commemorative, with one or more being struck every decade since its creation, it is natural that one dollar commemoratives would spearhead the modern aggressive collector coin program initiated during the 1970s. Most years, a special cased silver alloy dollar is produced for the numismatic market. In many years a base metal commemorative is also issued, available in both circulation and collector's versions. Cased versions in either silver or base metal should always be kept in their cases of issue. Otherwise they are considered less salable.

Known counterfeits: Any 1948 dollar should be examined by an expert.

GEORGE V	XF	MS-60
1935 Jubilee	30.00	39.00
1936	18.50	36.00

GEORGE VI	XF	MS-60
1937	13.50	26.00
1938	55.00	75.00

GEORGE VI	XF	MS-60
1939 Royal Visit	8.00	14.00
1945	145.00	200.00
1946	42.00	75.00
1947 Pointed 7	120.00	285.00
1947 Blunt 7	100.00	140.00
1947 Maple Leaf	165.00	270.00
1948	700.00	850.00
1949 Newfoundland	22.00	25.00
1950, 4 water lines	11.00	15.00
1950, Arnprior	15.50	38.00
1951, 4 water lines	8.00	12.50
1951, Arnprior	47.00	105.00
1952, 4 water lines	8.00	12.00
1952, Arnprior	70.00	175.00
1952, No water lines	9.00	16.50

ELIZABETH II	XF	MS-60
1953 Wire rim, without shoulder strap	4.50	8.00
1953 Flat rim, with shoulder strap	4.50	8.00
1954	10.50	16.50
1955, 4 water line	10.50	16.50
1955, Arnprior	75.00	110.00
1956	14.50	19.00
1957, 4 water lines	4.75	8.00
1957, Arnprior	7.50	14.00

	XF	MS-60
1958 British Columbia	5.50	7.00
1959		5.00
1960		5.00
1961		5.00
1962		5.00

	XF	MS-60
1963		5.00
1964 Charlottetown		4.50

	XF	MS-60
1965		5.00
1966		4.50
1967 Centennial		9.00

Nickel, Voyageur unless noted MS-63

	XF	MS-60
1968		1.50
1969		1.50

	XF	MS-60
1970 Manitoba		2.00
1971 British Columbia		2.00
1971 British Columbia, silver	PL	10.00
1972		2.00

	XF	MS-60
1973 Pr. Edward Is.		2.00
1973 R.C.M.P., silver	PL	11.00

	XF	MS-60
1974 Winnipeg		2.00
1974 Winnipeg, silver	PL	7.00
1975		2.00
1975 Calgary, silver	PL	6.00
1976		2.50

	XF	MS-60
1976 Library of Parliament, silver	PL	9.00
1977		2.50
1977 Queen's Jubilee, silver	PL	7.00
1978		2.00

	XF	MS-60
1978 Edmonton Games, silver	PL	7.00
1979		2.00
1979 Sailing Ship, silver	PL	15.00
1980		2.00

	XF	MS-60
1980 Arctic Territories, silver	PL	28.00
1981		2.00
1981 Railroad, silver	PF	22.00

	XF	MS-60
1982		2.00
1982 Constitution		3.00
1982 Regina, silver	PF	7.00
1983		2.00

	XF	MS-60
1983 Edmonton Games, silver	PF	8.00
1984		2.00

	XF	MS-60
1984 Cartier		2.25

1984 Toronto, silver	PF	7.00
1985		2.00
1985 National Parks, silver	PF	8.00
1986		2.00

1986 Vancouver, silver		10.00
1987		2.00
1987 Davis Strait, silver	PF	13.50

Aureate-bronze Plated
Nickel, Loon unless noted   MS-63
1987		3.75
1988		3.75
1988 Ironworks, silver	PF	28.00
1989		3.75

Aureate-bronze Plated
Nickel, Loon unless noted   MS-63
1989 MacKenzie River, silver	PF	30.00
1990		3.00
1990 Kelsey, silver	PF	20.00
1991 Loon		3.50

1991 S.S. Frontenac, silver	PF	22.00
1992 "1867-1992" Loon		2.50

1992 "1867-1992" Parliament		2.50
1992 Stagecoach, silver	PF	20.00
1993		2.50

Aureate-bronze Plated
Nickel, Loon unless noted   MS-63
1993 Stanley Cup, silver	PF	18.50
1994		2.00
1994 War Memorial		2.50

1994 R.C.M.P. Dog Sled, silver	PF	20.00
1995		2.00
1995 Peacekeeping Monument		2.50

1995 Hudson's Bay Co., silver	PF	20.00
1996		2.00
1996 McIntosh Apple, silver	PF	24.00
1997		2.50

1997 Loon Flying		9.50
1997 Loon Flying, silver	PF	65.00
1997 Hockey, silver	PF	22.50
1998		2.50
1998W		2.75
1998 R.C.M.P. - G.R.C	PF	22.50

TWO DOLLARS

In 1996 a radical new two dollar coin was introduced to save the expense of producing perishable paper money. It is composed of a central disc of aluminum-bronze, surrounded by a washer-like ring of nickel. The reverse design is that of a polar bear.

The is not unique, and such bimetallic coins have been appearing in more and more countries since 1982.

Known counterfeits: Beware of false "errors" created outside the mint by separating the inner and outer sections of the coin. These are of no numismatic value.

	MS-63
1996	3.50
1996 gold, silver ring	PF365.00
1996 silver, center gold plated	PF80.00
1997	3.50
1997 gold, silver ring	PF ——
1997 silver, center gold plated	PF23.50
1998	3.50
1998W	4.00

GOLD FIVE DOLLARS

Part of the motivation for establishing a Canadian mint in 1908 was it would enable them to convert domestically mined gold into coin. Four years after the mint's opening this dream was realized. The crowned portrait of George V is the same as on the minor coins. The coat of arms on the reverse is the original one granted in 1868, reflecting the four original provinces: Ontario, Quebec, New Brunswick, and Nova Scotia. Bag marks and edge knock can be a problem on these, and cleaning, although to a lesser extent.

Known counterfeits: It is believed counterfeits exist for this type.

	VF	XF
1912	160.00	190.00
1913	160.00	190.00
1914	300.00	375.00

SILVER FIVE DOLLARS

Among the most over-sold coins marketed to the general public were the silver

commemoratives struck to raise money for the 1976 Olympics in Montreal. Produced over four years, the majority were sold to laymen, leaving no secondary market for those who no longer wanted to own them. Literally tons were melted during the great silver boom of 1979-80. Ambiguous redemption procedures and limits to their legal tender status also contributed to the collapse of the market for this series.

This denomination was revived for commemorative use in 1998.

Known counterfeits: None.

	MS-63	PF
1973 Sailboats	5.25	6.50
1973 Map	5.25	6.50
1974 Olympic Symbol	5.25	6.50
1974 Ancient Athlete	5.25	6.50
1974 Rowing	5.25	6.50
1974 Canoeing	5.25	6.50
1975 Running	5.25	6.50
1975 Javelin Thrower	5.25	6.50
1975 Swimmer	5.25	6.50
1975 Diver	5.25	6.50
1976 Fencing	5.25	7.00
1976 Boxing	5.25	7.00
1976 Olympic Village	5.25	7.00
1976 Olympic Flame	5.25	7.00
1998 Norman Bethune		38.00

GOLD TEN DOLLARS

Part of the motivation for establishing a Canadian mint in 1908 was it enable them to convert domestically mined gold into coin. Four years after the mint's opening this dream was realized. The crowned portrait of George V is the same as on the minor coins. The coat of arms on the reverse is the original one granted in 1868, reflecting the four original provinces: Ontario, Quebec, New Brunswick, and Nova Scotia. Bag marks and edge knock can be a problem on these, and cleaning, although to a lesser extent.

Known counterfeits: It is believed counterfeits exist for this type.

	VF	XF
1912	350.00	400.00
1913	350.00	400.00
1914	375.00	425.00

SILVER TEN DOLLARS

Among the most over-sold coins marketed to the general public were the silver commemoratives struck to raise money for the 1976 Olympics in Montreal. Produced over four years, the majority were sold to laymen, which left no secondary market for those who no longer wanted to own them. Literally tons were melted during the great silver boom of 1979-80. Ambiguous redemption procedures and limits to their legal tender status also contributed to the collapse of the market for this series.

Known counterfeits: None.

	MS-63	PF
1973 Montreal Skyline	10.25	13.00
1973 World Map	10.25	13.00
1974 World Map		235.00
1974 Head of Zeus	10.25	13.00
1974 Temple of Zeus	10.25	13.00
1974 Bicycling	10.25	13.00
1974 Lacrosse	10.25	13.00
1975 Indian Head	10.25	13.00
1975 Ladies' Shot Put	10.25	13.00

	MS-63	PF
1975 Sailing	10.25	13.50
1975 Canoeing	10.25	13.50
1976 Soccer	10.25	14.00
1976 Field Hockey	10.25	14.00
1976 Round Stadium	10.25	14.00
1976 Velodrome	10.25	14.00

SILVER FIFTEEN DOLLARS

This pair of odd denomination coins was struck as part of an international series commissioned by the International Olympic Commission. It commemorates the Centennial of the founding of the modern Olympic Games. The Gold $175 piece is also part of this series.
Known counterfeits: None.

	PF
1992 Track	28.00
1992 Gymnast, Skater, Jumper	28.00

GOLD TWENTY DOLLARS

In addition to the wildlife cent through the dollar, the 1967 Confederation centennial was commemorated by Canada's first gold coin since 1919. The reverse of this coin, all of which were originally released in proof-like sets, bears a coat of arms very similar to the half dollar of 1960-96. Its proof-like surface makes it particularly susceptible to fingerprinting and other mishandling.
Known counterfeits: Dangerous counterfeits of this coin are known but are not common.

	PL
1967	225.00

SILVER TWENTY DOLLARS

To help raise money for the 1988 Winter Olympic Games in Calgary, a set of coins was sold. Its issue extended over four years and all pieces were proof $20 pieces. The normal edge is lettered, and all plain edge coins were struck in error.
Known counterfeits: None.

	PF
1985 Downhill Skier	22.50
1985 same, plain edge	180.00
1985 Speed Skater	22.50
1985 same, plain edge	180.00
1986 Biathlon	22.50
1986 same, plain edge	180.00
1986 Hockey	22.50
1986 same, plain edge	180.00
1986 Cross-country Skier	22.50
1986 Free-style Skier	22.50
1986 same, plain edge	180.00
1987 Figure Skaters	22.50
1987 Curler	22.50
1987 Ski Jumper	22.50
1987 Bobsledders	22.50

GOLD ON SILVER TWENTY DOLLARS

This ongoing series honors Canadian pioneers in the field of powered aviation. It is distinctive in having the portrait of each hero set on a small, oval gold inlay.
Known counterfeits: None.

	PF
1990 Lancaster Bomber	190.00
1990 Two 1940s Airplanes	60.00
1991 1909 Biplane	45.00
1991 1947 Pontoon Airplane	45.00
1992 Curtis Canuck left	45.00
1992 de Haviland Gypsy Mother.	45.00
1993 Pontoon Airplane	45.00
1993 Lockheed 14 Super Electra	45.00
1994 Curtiss HS-2L and Trees	45.00
1994 Canadian Vickers Vedette	45.00
1995 Fleet Canuck flying l.	50.00
1995 "Chipmunk" flying upward	50.00
1996 Two Jets right	50.00
1996 Two Jets left	50.00
1997 Sabre Jet left	45.00
1997 Tutor Jet right	45.00
1998 Anti-submarine Bomber	45.00
1998 Waterbomber Aircraft	45.00

PLATINUM THIRTY DOLLARS

Another ongoing set of collectors' coins are the platinum wildlife proof sets of four. These coins are not sold individually. Despite reports to the contrary, these are not bullion coins and are all scarce due to the small quantities struck.
Known counterfeits: None.

	PF
1990 Polar Bear Bust	90.00
1991 Snowy Owl Bust	90.00
1992 Cougar Bust	100.00
1993 Arctic Fox Bust	90.00
1994 Sea Otter Bust	95.00

	PF
1995 Canadian Lynx Bust	100.00
1996 Falcon Bust	130.00
1997 Bison	130.00
1998 Gray Wolf Bust	135.00

PLATINUM 75 DOLLARS

See Remarks on the Platinum $30 above.
Known counterfeits: None.

	PF
1990 Polar Bear	200.00
1991 Snowy Owls	220.00
1992 Cougar	220.00
1993 Arctic Foxes	230.00
1994 Sea Otter	235.00
1995 Canadian Lynx kittens	250.00
1996 Falcons	210.00
1997 Bisons	215.00
1998 Gray Wolf	215.00

GOLD 100 DOLLARS

Similar to the collectors' issue silver dollars, each year a different topic of Canadian history or culture is selected to be honored. Except for the first year, only proof versions are struck. They are all released in special mint packaging and are priced below for examples in that packaging. Those without may occasionally be discounted. From 1976-86 all proofs have contained one-half ounce pure gold, and one-quarter ounce from 1987 onward.
Known counterfeits: None likely.

	MS-63	PF
1976 Olympics	105.00	185.00
1977 Queen's Jubilee		225.00

	PF
1978 Geese flying	190.00
1979 Year of the Child	190.00

MS-63	PF
1980 Arctic Territories	190.00
1981 National Anthem	190.00

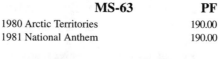

	PF
1982 New Constitution	185.00
1983 St. John's, Newfoundland	185.00

	PF
1984 Jacques Cartier	200.00
1985 National Parks	200.00

	PF
1986 Peace - Paix	185.00
1987 Calgary Olympics	110.00

	PF
1988 Whales	125.00
1989 Sainte-Marie, Ontario	120.00

	PF
1990 Literacy Year	120.00
1991 Ship Empress of India	140.00

	PF
1992 Montreal founding	150.00

MS-63	PF
1993 Antique 1893 Car	165.00

	PF
1994 WWII: Home Front	170.00
1995 Louisbourg	170.00

	PF
1996 Klondike Gold Rush	190.00
1997 Alexander Graham Bell	190.00
1998 Discovery of Insulin	195.00

PLATINUM 150 DOLLARS

See Remarks on the Platinum $30 above.
Known counterfeits: None.

	PF
1990 Polar Bear	360.00
1991 Snowy Owl Flying	375.00
1992 Cougars	375.00
1993 Arctic Fox	400.00
1994 Two Sea Otters	435.00
1995 Canadian Lynx	450.00
1996 Falcon on Branch	445.00
1997 Bisons	430.00
1998 Two Gray Wolf cubs	445.00

GOLD OLYMPIC 175 DOLLARS

See remarks on the Silver $15 above. Each coin contains one half ounce of gold.
Known counterfeits: None.

PF

1992   325.00

GOLD 200 DOLLARS

Similar to the collectors' issue dollars and $100 coins, each year a different topic of Canadian history or culture is selected to be honored. Only proof versions are struck. They are released in special mint packaging and are priced below for examples in that packaging. Those without may occasionally be discounted. Each contains slightly over half an ounce pure gold.
Known counterfeits: None likely.

PF

1990 Canadian Flag Jubilee   210.00
1991 Hockey   250.00

1992 Niagara Falls   265.00
1993 Mounted Police   255.00

1994 Anne of Green Gables   255.00
1995 Maple Syrup Harvesting   270.00

PF

1996 Transcontinental Railway   290.00
1997 Haida Mask   300.00
1998 White Buffalo   300.00

PLATINUM 300 DOLLARS

See remarks on the Platinum $30 above.
Known counterfeits: None.

PF

1990 Polar Bears   700.00
1991 Snowy Owl with chicks   650.00
1992 Cougar in Tree   650.00
1993 Arctic Fox with kits   800.00
1994 Sea Otters   850.00
1995 Lynx with kittens   875.00
1996 Falcon with chicks   840.00
1997 Bisons   825.00
1998 Gray Wolf and two cubs   840.00

GOLD 350 DOLLARS

This largest denomination of all Canadian coins depicts Canada's heraldic flowers: the English rose, Scottish thistle, Irish shamrock, and French fleur-de-lis.
Known counterfeits: None.
1998   PF   750.00

BULLION COINS

GOLD SOVEREIGNS

It was the production of gold sovereigns that was part of the motivation for the opening of a Canadian mint in 1908. It is also the reason, that until 1931 it had the status of "British Royal Mint, Ottawa Branch." These coins are identical in every aspect to those made for Great Britain. The reverse design of St. George slaying the dragon was originally designed in 1816 by Benedetto Pistrucci. The mintmark C for Canada is found on the ground below the horse's hoof. Their production permitted the convenient coinage of locally mined gold into an internationally standard coin (.2354 Troy oz. net) During World War I they also permitted the transfer of gold from Britain to the United States without the risk of being sunk during a transatlantic crossing.
Known counterfeits: A great many sovereign counterfeits are known. Some are more dangerous than others. Look for an even border pattern, and crispness where the field meets the design. Avoid any with a pebbly texture in field.

	VF	XF
EDWARD VII		
1908C	1,750.00	2,350.00
1909C	220.00	285.00
1910C	175.00	250.00
GEORGE V		
1911C	115.00	125.00
1913C	550.00	750.00
1914C	250.00	325.00
1916C	12,500.00	14,000.00
1917C	120.00	130.00
1918C	120.00	130.00
1919C	120.00	130.00

MAPLE LEAF BULLION COINS

A bullion coin is a coin intended to be a storage vessel for precious metal, and they are not necessarily for circulation. While they have face values on them, their values in precious metal are usually much higher; therefore, no one would reasonably spend them. Bullion coins are not collectors' coins, but are sold by the mint at a modest premium above the value of the metal they contain.

The Maple Leaf series is one of the most popular and difficult-to-counterfeit bullion series in the world. It began in 1979 with the .999 pure, one Troy ounce gold piece. At the time it was considered unusual to manufacture a bullion gold piece with no alloy at all. Most other countries' pieces weighed over an ounce to compensate for the addition of a alloy. The metal was further refined to .9999 pure in 1982, and the first fractional gold pieces, the tenth oz. and quarter oz. were released, followed by a half ounce four years later. Having established a high degree of recognition in the bullion market, the mint decided to expand into silver and platinum in 1988, releasing a one ounce coin in the former metal, and three different sizes in the latter. Very small gold and platinum pieces, mostly suitable for gift giving were added to the array in 1993 and 1994.
Known counterfeits: None, but the one ounce gold is always a potential target due to its liquidity.
Notice: The values of most of these issues vary at least daily with the value of their metal content. The prices listed here are based on a platinum value of $360, gold $285 and silver $4.90. Updated prices on commodities such as precious metals, though not on single coins, can be found both in most newspapers and on the Internet. For any firm quote on bullion, however, it is best to call your local coin or bullion

dealer. Values given here for gold and platinum are in terms of percent premium typically charged above the actual bullion content. Some dealers will add a handling charge to very small orders.

SILVER MAPLE LEAF

1 ounce / $5	MS-63	PF
1988 to date	7.00	
1989		42.50
10 ounce / $50		
1998		148.00

GOLD MAPLE LEAF

	MS-63	PF
1/20 oz. ($1) 1993-	22%	
1/15 oz. ($2) 1994-	80%	
1/10 oz. ($5) 1982—	15%	
1/10 oz. ($5) 1989		75.00
1/4 oz. ($10) 1982—	11%	
1/4 oz. ($10) 1989		175.00
1/2 oz. ($20) 1986—	7%	
1/2 oz. ($20) 1989		275.00
1 oz. ($50) 1979—	5%	
1 oz. ($50) 1989		450.00

PLATINUM MAPLE LEAF

	MS-63	PF
1/20 oz. ($1) 1993-	25%	
1/15 oz. ($2) 1994-	80%	
1/10 oz. ($5) 1988—	17%	
1/10 oz. ($5) 1989		90.00
1/4 oz. ($10) 1988—	12%	
1/4 oz. ($10) 1989		175.00
1/2 oz. ($20) 1988—	8%	
1/2 oz. ($20) 1989		350.00
1 oz. ($50) 1988—	6%	
1 oz. ($50) 1989		700.00

PROVINCIAL COINS & TOKENS

Like the situation in the United States and formerly in the Thirteen Colonies, Canadian coinage before the 1870s was a hodgepodge of various coins and tokens struck by a number of authorities, firms countries and individuals. Throughout the 1700s and early 1800s the British policies of Mercantilism prevented the royal government from shipping reasonable quantities of sterling to British North America. Chaos ensued. Numerous merchants throughout the country struck or imported hundreds of local copper tokens. Some were well made, like most bank issues, others were wretched.

When official coinage was finally struck by the various pre-Confederation colonial provinces, they had already recognized slightly different standards, sometimes as much as 20 percent different from one another other in value. Generally provincial coins start out on the British sterling system, but change over to a decimal system in the 1860s.

The union of Upper Canada (Ontario), Lower Canada (Quebec), New Brunswick and Nova Scotia formed the independent Canadian Confederation in 1867, though it was not enough to bring order from discord — at least not immediately. There still persisted a shortage of small change in circulation. Neither bank tokens nor poorly made "black smith" counterfeits could be suppressed. In 1870, the government announced that certain specified bank tokens would be officially recognized as one cent and two cent pieces.

The provincial coinage of Newfoundland continued for decades and is far more extensive than the others. This is because Newfoundland did not join Canada until 1949. Mintages of these coins are often remarkably low, but the prices have remained very moderate despite that fact. Contrary to this, Newfoundland fifty cent pieces are often more common than contemporary Canadian ones.

Known counterfeits: Contemporary counterfeits of George III Irish halfpennies circulated in Canada and are worth more than real ones. Those of George IV Nova Scotia halfpennies are common and worth about the same as real ones.

LOWER CANADA BANK TOKENS

UN SOU - HALF PENNY
(after 1870 1¢)

Boquet / Wreath	VG	VF
Montreal	2.00	6.00
Bank of Montreal	2.00	6.00
Banque du Peuple	3.00	13.00

Standing figure / Oval shield		
1837 City Bank	2.00	5.00
1837 Bank of Montreal	2.00	6.00
1837 Banque du Peuple	3.00	7.00
1837 Quebec Bank	2.00	5.00
Side View Building / Oval shield		
1838 Bank of Montreal	70.00	275.00
1839 Bank of Montreal	70.00	275.00
Front View Building / Oval Shield		
1842 Bank of Montreal	2.00	4.00
1844 Bank of Montreal	2.00	4.00
1845 Bank of Montreal		Rare
Standing figure / Allegorical scene		
1852 Quebec Bank	2.00	5.00

DEUX SOU - ONE PENNY

(after 1870 2¢)	VG	VF
Standing figure / Oval shield		
1837 City Bank	2.00	7.00
1837 Bank of Montreal	2.00	6.00
1837 Banque du Peuple	2.50	8.00
1837 Quebec Bank	2.00	7.00
Side View Building / Oval shield		
1838 Bank of Montreal	150.00	525.00
1839 Bank of Montreal	150.00	525.00
Front View Building / Oval Shield		
1839 Banque du Peuple		Rare
1842 Bank of Montreal	2.00	6.00
Standing figure / Allegorical scene		
1852 Quebec Bank	2.50	9.00

NEW BRUNSWICK

HALFPENNY	VG	VF
1843	3.00	11.50
1854	3.00	11.50

PENNY		
1843	3.75	15.00
1854	3.75	15.00

HALF CENT

1861	65.00	150.00

ONE CENT	VG	VF
1861	2.00	6.00
1864	2.00	6.00

FIVE CENTS

1862	35.00	125.00
1864	35.00	125.00

TEN CENTS

1862	35.00	125.00
1864	35.00	125.00

TWENTY CENTS

1862	16.00	65.00
1864	16.00	65.00

NEWFOUNDLAND

LARGE CENT

Victoria	VG	VF
1865	2.00	6.00
1872H	2.00	6.00
1873	2.50	10.00
1876H	2.00	6.00
1880 Round 0	2.00	6.00
1880 Oval 0	85.00	180.00
1885	16.50	55.00
1888	15.00	45.00
1890	2.00	5.50
1894	2.00	5.50
1896	2.00	5.50

Edward VII	VG	VF
1904H	4.50	20.00
1907	1.50	4.00
1909	1.50	4.00

George V		
1913	.75	2.00
1917C	.75	2.00
1919C	.75	2.25
1920C	.75	3.50
1929	.75	2.00
1936	.75	1.75

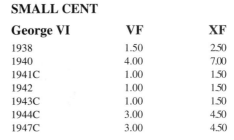

SMALL CENT

George VI	VF	XF
1938	1.50	2.50
1940	4.00	7.00
1941C	1.00	1.50
1942	1.00	1.50
1943C	1.00	1.50
1944C	3.00	4.50
1947C	3.00	4.50

SILVER FIVE CENTS

Victoria	VG	VF
1865	20.00	60.00
1870	35.00	90.00
1872H	22.00	60.00
1873	45.00	145.00
1873H	710.00	1,875.00
1876H	75.00	200.00
1880	22.00	80.00
1881	15.00	45.00
1882H	15.00	40.00
1885	90.00	250.00
1888	20.00	50.00
1890	6.00	30.00
1894	6.50	30.00
1896	4.00	20.00

Edward VII	VG	VF
1903	3.00	18.00
1904H	2.00	14.00
1908	1.75	11.50

George V		
1912	1.00	5.00
1917C	1.00	4.00
1919C	2.00	10.00
1929	1.00	3.25

George VI	VF	XF
1938	2.00	4.00
1940C	2.00	4.00
1941C	2.00	3.00
1942C	2.50	3.00
1943C	2.00	3.00
1944C	2.50	3.00
1945C	2.00	3.00
1946C	355.00	435.00
1947C	9.00	15.00

SILVER TEN CENTS

Victoria	VG	VF
1865	13.50	55.00
1870	120.00	335.00
1872H	13.50	50.00
1873	15.00	90.00
1876H	20.00	75.00
1880, 80 over 70	22.00	100.00
1882H	12.50	70.00
1885	50.00	210.00
1888	11.50	70.00
1890	5.50	20.00
1894	5.50	20.00
1896	5.00	20.00

Edward VII		
1903	5.00	35.00
1904H	2.50	20.00

George V	VG	VF
1912	1.50	9.00
1917C	1.25	6.50
1919C	1.50	9.00

George VI	VF	XF
1938	2.50	7.00
1940	2.50	5.00
1941C	2.00	3.25
1942C	2.00	3.25
1943C	2.50	5.00
1944C	2.00	5.00
1945C	2.00	3.25
1946C	10.00	20.00
1947C	7.00	12.00

SILVER TWENTY CENTS

Victoria	VG	VF
1865	11.00	45.00
1870	12.00	60.00
1872H	7.00	30.00
1873	9.00	60.00
1876H	10.00	50.00
1880, 80 over 70	15.00	65.00
1881	5.00	35.00
1882H	5.00	27.50
1885	8.00	40.00
1888	5.00	32.00
1890	4.00	22.00
1894	4.00	22.00
1896	3.00	20.00
1899	3.25	18.00
1900	3.00	15.00

Edward VII		
1904H	9.00	50.00

George V		
1912	2.00	10.00

SILVER TWENTY-FIVE CENTS

George V	VG	VF
1917C	1.50	4.00
1919C	1.50	4.25

SILVER FIFTY CENTS

Victoria	VG	VF
1870	12.00	45.00
1872H	10.00	40.00
1873	28.00	150.00
1874	20.00	80.00
1876H	18.00	80.00
1880	18.00	80.00
1881	10.00	70.00
1882H	8.00	40.00
1885	12.00	70.00
1888	15.00	80.00
1894	5.00	50.00
1896	4.00	26.00
1898	5.00	35.00
1899	5.00	28.00
1900	5.00	28.00

Edward VII	VG	VF
1904H	3.25	15.00
1907	4.00	20.00

Edward VII	VG	VF
1908	3.25	12.50
1909	3.25	12.50

George V		
1911	2.75	8.00
1917C	2.75	6.00
1918C	2.75	6.00
1919C	2.75	6.00

GOLD TWO DOLLARS

Victoria	F	XF
1865	150.00	275.00
1870	175.00	325.00
1872	200.00	385.00
1880	1,000.00	1,600.00
1881	120.00	225.00
1882H	110.00	210.00
1885	120.00	235.00
1888	110.00	210.00

NOVA SCOTIA

HALFPENNY

Bust / Thistle	VG	VF
1823	3.00	8.00
1824	3.00	12.50
1832	3.00	7.50
1382 error	150.00	1,650.00
1840	2.50	7.50
1843	3.00	9.00

Bust / Mayflowers

1856	2.00	7.50

ONE PENNY

Bust / Thistle	VG	VF
1824	3.00	10.00
1832	3.00	10.00
1840	2.50	7.50
1843, 3 over 0	12.00	40.00
1843	3.00	10.00

Bust / Mayflowers

1856 No LCW	2.50	8.50
1856 with LCW	2.50	7.00

HALF CENT	VG	VF
1861	3.00	8.00
1864	3.00	8.00

ONE CENT		
1861	2.00	5.00
1862	15.00	40.00
1864	2.00	5.00

PRINCE EDWARD ISLAND

MERCHANTS' TOKENS

	VG	VF
Ships, Colonies & Commerce / Sailing Ship	2.50	9.00
1855 Self Government and Free Trade	2.50	9.00

ONE CENT		
1871	1.75	4.50

UPPER CANADA

HALFPENNY BANK TOKENS

St. George slaying dragon / Bank emblem

	VG	VF
1850	1.50	4.00
1852	1.50	4.00
1854	1.50	4.00
1854 Crosslet 4	12.00	35.00
1857	1.50	4.00

ONE PENNY BANK TOKEN

St. George slaying dragon / Bank emblem

	VG	VF
1850	1.75	5.00
1850 Dot between cornucopias	3.00	12.00
1852	1.75	5.00
1854	1.75	5.00
1854 Crosslet 4	4.00	15.00
1857	1.75	5.00

ANCIENT COINS

Ancient coins are among the most universally popular coins to collect. While most Americans consider them strange and exotic, perhaps even museum pieces, few can grow up in countries like England, Italy or Israel without seeing common a Roman or Greek coin that some friend or relative found while on a hike or plowing a field. While most dealers in North America have junk boxes filled with coins left over from tourists' trips across the globe, dealers in most European capitals have junk boxes filled with coins left over from mankind's trip across the centuries. Much to the surprise of visiting Americans, these Roman coins, while not very well preserved, sell for as little as a dollar or two each. Many other ancient coins, the great rarities of art or grade, can sell at European auctions for tens of thousands of dollars. Clearly, collectors around the world have created an active market in these small relics.

Not only hobbyists find them interesting. Many teachers and professors have found that providing genuine ancient coins for their students to examine has stirred a vital and unexpected interest in the cultures which created them. Coins are among the earliest things humanity has mass-produced. Because Greek and Roman coins have survived in the millions, they are today the only genuine ancient artifact an average person can, if he or she desires to, own.

THE EVOLUTION OF COINAGE

The ancient Egyptians in the days of the pyramids, or the Babylonians in the days of Hammurabi had no coins. They traded precious metal, often in convenient shapes such as rings, but the purity and weight of these items varied, and at each transaction they had to be weighed out and sometimes even tested. In Asia Minor, in present-day Turkey, irregular clumps of electrum, a natural alloy of gold and silver, were popularly traded for their bullion value. As time went by it became apparent that making these clumps of a known alloy with a regular weight made commercial transactions much easier. By the seventh century B.C. the Kings of Lydia, in western Asia Minor, started impressing their symbols on one side of these clumps to guarantee weight and purity to their subjects. At first these symbols were engraved at the end of an iron punch. Soon after, the symbols were engraved on the surface of an anvil and a chisel was used to force the metal down into the design. It wasn't long until people realized that if the end of the chisel point could leave its impression on the reverse of the coin, so could a second design engraved into the end of the chisel point. At first this secondary design was little more than a simple geometric pattern, but it quickly took on the complexity of the primary design. In this way the modern concept of a two-sided, struck coin was invented.

GRADE VS. QUALITY

When collecting, it is important to remember that ancient coins were not made by the same methods as modern coins. You should not expect to find perfectly round ancient coins, though there are many exceptions. This is because they were not struck within collars like modern coins, so when the dies pressed down on the metal it would spread out in unpredictable directions. Also, because the blanks were placed between the dies by hand, they may not have been perfectly centered. Modern automation has caused off center coins to be scarce collectors' items, but slightly off center coins were far more common in ancient times. Except for the most radically off-center specimens, modern collectors of Greek and Roman coins consider off-center specimens less desirable, and they often command lower prices. This is especially true if the portrait is affected. Would you want a portrait of a Greek god or Roman emperor with the nose missing?

Another thing that many collectors consider more important than whether or not an ancient coin is worn is the strength of the strike. A coin's design is made by metal being forced into the recessed parts of a die engraved with a negative image of the design. Today this metal is forced to flow by powerful machines striking the dies against the blank with thousands of pounds of pressure. In ancient times it was only the strength of the minters arm that determined how much pressure the dies would exert — and maybe whether or not he was paying attention while he was striking. If the craftsman struck the dies with too little pressure the metal would not flow into every crevice of the die, and even when brand new, the resulting coin would not have a fully detailed image.

Most ancient coins survive today because they were buried in the ground. Most ancient civilizations did not have banks in the modern sense. To protect their wealth from thieves or invading armies, many ancient people would place their wealth in a pottery jar or a cloth or leather bag, and bury it in a secret place until they could safely retrieve it. Unfortunately for them, many did not live long enough to recover their fortunes, and their secrets died with them. Coins buried in sealed pottery usually survive to modern times very well preserved. Those buried in cloth are usually recovered with porous or pitted surfaces. Such porous coins, even if high grade pieces with little circulation wear and much detail, are considered by many collectors undesirable, and are usually sold at a discount.

All these factors together — centering, strike, and surface texture — probably affect the value of an ancient coin far more than its technical grade in point of wear. It is not unusual for a dealer to pay more for a coin in Very Fine than for the same type of coin in Extremely Fine if the strike and centering are superior on the lower grade coin.

GREEK COINS

As the concept of uniform, predictable coinage took root, electrum was generally replaced by separate coinages of gold and silver. During this early stage of development there were no copper coins. If small values were needed, extremely small coins of gold or silver were struck. Some of these minute coins were less than one-tenth the size of a United States dime. In the early sixth century B.C., coinage was still too new a concept for people to accept copper coins of a convenient size just because the government would promise to redeem them for silver. During this early first stage of coinage, it was confined to Asia Minor and Greece. Gradually, coinage spread westward to Italy and Gaul (France) as Greeks established colonies of settlers on their coasts. Coinage expanded eastward to Phoenicia (Lebanon), Syria and Judaea (Israel) as people of these lands came into contact with Greek coinage and found it convenient. The Phoenicians spread the use of coinage to North Africa and Spain through their settlement of Carthage.

Ancient Greek coinage has long been divided by numismatists into specific stages based on artistic and political developments. The first stage, beginning with the invention of coinage, is called "archaic." The style of archaic art is very stiff, formal and unrealistic. Like ancient Egyptian art, from which it derives, eyes are usually shown in full facing view, even when the head looks towards the side. Faces also have what is called an "archaic smile," and body movements are seen with unnatural exaggeration. Some coin designs continued to use archaic design forms, particularly the simple geometric reverse designs, long after Greek painting and sculpture moved beyond this stage. This was to convince people of the coin's stable weight and value. The idea was that if there was no change in the coin's appearance, there was, theoretically, no change in its content. (Similar logic to that of the United States one dollar bill, the design of which has not changed since 1923.)

Much of the authority for issuing archaic coinage came from the many Greek city-states. The designs of these coins usually consisted of the patron deities of these cities, symbols of those gods, or sometimes plants or animals important to the local economy. One example is Athens, named after the goddess Athena. Most ancient Athenian coins bear her portrait on one side, and an owl on the other. The owl was considered a symbol of Athena, who was goddess of wisdom. Coins of ancient

Sicily sometimes bore an octopus or a crab, important food animals in Sicily both then and now. Some designs even had puns! Coins of the island of Rhodes in the Aegean Sea usually bore a rose because the Greek word rhodos meant both Rhodes and rose.

The next stage in the evolution of Greek coinage is called the Classical period. Roughly mid-fifth to mid-fourth century B.C., was the period of the finest artistic achievement. The same imagery persisted, but was rendered in a more realistic style and with greater ornateness. As designs became more complex, the quality of die engraving became so important that some of the dies were actually signed by the engraver as though they were works of art. Many believe that this was the all-time high point of numismatic art, and that it has, to this day, never been equaled. By this time virtually all coins were struck with two fully engraved dies. Also, the acceptance of the role of coinage was such that token copper coins replaced minute silver pieces for local use. Copper coins were usually not accepted outside their region of origin, but larger silver and gold coins were available for international commerce. In order to enforce some responsibility for the purity of the metal, at this time some of the magistrates responsible for the coinage were required to sign their name clearly on the dies.

Alexander the Great (r.336-323 B.C.) changed the political structure of the Western World forever. Before Alexander, the typical government was the city-state. Alexander's world conquests introduced the concept of a large multiethnic state. Even after he died and his empire was divided by his generals, the "Successors," the Western World continued to be divided mostly into large kingdoms and federations rather than city-states. This new third period of Greek history and coinage is called "Hellenistic." The most notable innovation to be found at this stage is the introduction of real human portraits. Many accept the idea that Alexander, depicted as though he were Hercules wearing a lion's skin, was the first living human being to appear on a coin. Even if this were not true, the generation of the coins which followed his death certainly saw dozens of Hellenistic kings placing their somewhat idealized portraits on their coins. Coins during this period were extremely common and many actually bear the year of issue indicated in many different local calendars, often based on the founding date of a city or dynasty, or a king's accession.

The eclipse of the Hellenistic kingdoms and the Greek federations by the Roman Empire did not completely eliminate Greek coinage. Some of the most important internationally accepted Greek silver coins, such as the shekel of Tyre and the tetradrachm of Philip Philadelphos, continued to be struck under Roman domination. Often, especially in Asia Minor and the Mideast, the new Roman overlords would permit large municipalities to

continue striking Greek style coinage for local use, with no apparent change. Also many lands, rather than being conquered by the Romans, would submit to them as client states, preserving much of their autonomy and usually keeping their traditional style coinage.

Greek gold coins were usually called staters. Most staters weighed eight to ten grams and were the size of a cent or nickel.

Greek silver coins were usually called drachms, obols and staters. While the size of a drachm could vary from city to city, many shared standards. An average drachm weighed about 4-1/2 grams and resembled a thick dime. One sixth of a drachm was called an obol. The term, stater as used at Corinth, referred to its principle coin, worth three drachms.

For both gold and silver, the prefix hemi- always meant half. Deka-, octa-, tetra-, and di- meant ten times, eight times, four times, and double, respectively.

In most cases we do not know the names of ancient Greek bronze coins. Generally numismatists call them by diameter in millimeters. A coin 15mm. in diameter is called an AE15, one 20mm. an AE20.

The images on most Greek coins are either of ancient deities or their symbols. Natural products of an area, such as a horse or a plant are also common.

Some of the most common ancient gods and goddesses depicted on coins can be recognized by their attire, or their symbols as follows:

Ammon - Bearded older male, rams horns on sides of head. Mostly Egyptian.

Aphrodite (Venus) - Female, usually nude or semi-nude. Symbols: Apple, poppy, dove, swan.

Apollo - Beardless male with slightly feminine face, often seen seated on a thimble shaped object called an omphalos. Symbol: lyre, arrow, tripod (three-legged altar).

Artemis (Diana) - Female with bow and arrow. Symbol: stag.

Ares (Mars) - Helmeted male.

Athena (Minerva) - Woman wearing crested helmet. Symbol: owl.

Baal - Semitic equivalent of Zeus.

Dionysus (Bacchus) - Young man, bearded or not, wearing ivy wreath. Symbols: panther, ivy, grapes.

Dioscuri - The twins Castor and Pollux, usually riding horses together. Symbol: two conical caps, two stars

Eros (Cupid) - Winged boy. Symbol: bow and arrow.

Heracles (Hercules) - Male , usually bearded, wearing lion's skin. Symbol: club.

Hermes (Mercury) - Beardless male wearing winged broad felt hat. Symbol: caduceus.

Janus - Bearded male with two faces.

Poseidon (Neptune) - Bearded older male, often naked, wearing wreath or diadem. Symbol: trident, dolphin.

Serapis - Bearded older male, wearing modius on head. A modius is an ancient conical

grain measure, with extended feet.

Nike (Victory) - Winged female. Symbol: trophy of arms.

Tyche (Fortuna) of the city - Female wearing turreted city wall as crown.

Zeus (Jupiter, Jove) - Bearded older male, usually with wreath, often enthroned.

Symbols: Thunderbolt, eagle.

This list will also prove useful for identifying the reverses of Roman and Greek Imperial coins. The Roman counterparts are named above in parentheses.

BOOKS ABOUT GREEK COINS

Hundreds of pages can be written on books about ancient Greek coins. The list here will be confined to only the most basic or the most important references.

British Museum, Catalogue of Greek Coins in the, 29 vols. (various authors).

Danish National Museum. *Sylloge Numorum Graecorum* (SNG).

Head, Barclay. *Historia Numorum.*

Klawans, Zander. *Handbook of Ancient Greek and Roman Coins.* Certainly the easiest introduction.

Kraay, Colin. *Archaic and Classical Greek Coins.*

Melville Jones, John. *A Dictionary of Ancient Greek Coins.*

Sayles, Wayne. *Ancient Coin Collecting: Numismatic Art of the Greek World.*

Sear, David. *Greek Coins and their Values*, Vol. 1 & 2. The most commonly used catalogue of representative coins.

The Celator. Popular monthly magazine devoted to ancient coins.

Certain specialized works not mentioned here will be noted in each subsection.

> Values for Greek coins are for Very Fine examples for gold (**AV**) and silver (**AR**), Fine for bronze and copper (**AE**).

SPAIN & GAUL

The chief cities in ancient Spain were the Phoenician colonies of Carthage. By the first century B.C., most had fallen under Roman control. The coins of ancient Spain show a blend of Carthaginian, Roman, Greek and local Iberian influences. The alphabet used is unique to the area.

Greek influence in Gaul was primarily focused at the colony of Massalia on the southern coast. The interior was inhabited by Celts.

Additional Specialized Books: Heiss, *Description Generales Des Monnaies Antiques de L'Espagne.*

Osca. 150-100 BC. AR Denarius. Bearded head r. / Horseman r. 125.00
Rhoda. before 250 BC. AR Drachm. Head of Persephone l. / Rose viewed from beneath (leaves appear as four spokes) 500.00
Gaul: Massalia (Marseilles). 375-200 BC. AR Drachm. Head of Artemis r. / Lion r. 125.00

THE CELTS

The Celts were an ancient people that inhabited an area stretching from Bulgaria and the Danube to Spain and Ireland. As the eastern areas became inhabited by other peoples, the Celts remained more dominant in the British Isles and Gaul throughout the Roman era. Most Celtic coins, beginning in the third century B.C. and ending in the first A.D., derive their types from Hellenistic and Roman Republican types. These usually show a distinctive artistic interpretation, often showing the person or animal as disjointed and conveying more of a sense of motion than a realistic depiction.

Distinctive features also include the use of tin and the casting rather than striking of some base metal issues in the West.

Additional Specialized Books: Allen, Derek. *Catalogue of the Celtic Coins in the British Museum*, 3 vols.

Nash, Daphne. *Coinage in the Celtic World.*
VanArsdell, R.D. *Celtic Coinage of Britain.*

England. 45-20 BC. AV Stater. Abstract design devolved from head of Apollo / Horse leaping r. 300.00
__: Thames and South, 1st century BC. Tin 18mm. Linear abstract head / Linear abstract bull 60.00
__: **The Iceni.** 10 BC - AD 60. AR Unit (14mm.). Geometric pattern / Horse r., ECEN below... 150.00
Channel Islands. Armorican. 75-50 BC. Billon Stater. Stylized head r. / Abstract horse r...125.00

Gaul: Aedui or Lingones. 1st century BC. AR Quinarius. Helmeted head l. / Horse l., wheel below... 85.00
Allobroges. 1st century BC. AR Quinarius. Helmeted head of Roma r. / Horseman r., BR COMA below. Crude imitation of coin of Roman Republic. 80.00
Volcae Tectosages. 3-2nd cent. BC. AR Drachm. Degenerate head of Persephone l. / Cross dividing field, crescent in each angle. *Crude imitation of the coin of Rhoda above*................ 75.00

Eastern Celts. 200s BC. AR Tetradrachm. Stylized head of Zeus / Stylized horseman l. This coin is based on one of Philip II of Macedon. 250.00
__: 3-2nd century BC. AR Drachm. Crude head of Alexander the Great in extremely high relief / Disjointed figure of Zeus std. l. 90.00

GREEK ITALY

Before the expansion of Rome, the majority of settlements of southern Italy and eastern Sicily were Greek, not Italian. They were usually settlements of larger Greek cities, such as Corinth, and their coinage was very much in line with Greek traditions. Greek Syracuse in particular was notable for the quality of its numismatic art, to the point where some engravers actually signed their works.

Known counterfeits: High quality Greek silver has been the target of counterfeiters for more than a century. Many counterfeits are quite deceptive.

Agrigentum, Sicily. 500-450 BC. AE Trias (tooth-shaped). Eagles' heads / crab / Three pellets...125.00
Brettian League, Bruttium. 215-205 BC. AE22. Head of Zeus r. / Naked warrior r. with spear and shield 35.00

Neapolis (Naples), Campania. 300-276 BC AR Didrachm. Head of Nymph r. / Man-headed bull r., Victory above...................................... 300.00
__: 270-240 BC. AE20. Head of Apollo l. / Man-headed bull r., Victory above 30.00

Caulonia, Bruttium. c.525 BC. AR Stater. Apollo, stg. naked, stag stg. r. looking back, KAVL / same incuse and reversed 3,500.00
Posedonia, Lucania. c.400 BC. AE14. Poseidon walking r. / Bull r. 25.00

Rhegium, Bruttium. 415-387 BC. AR Tetradrachm. Lion's face / Hd. of Apollo r. 2,500.00

Syracuse, Sicily. 405-344 BC. AE18 Hd. of Arethusa l. / Dolphin r. over shell.................................35.00
__: Agathokles, 317-289 BC. AV Tetraobol. Head of Apollo l. / Chariot r........................... 1,200.00

.. __. Hieron II, 274-216 BC. AE18. Head of Poseidon l. / Trident..35.00
Tarentum, Calabria. 4-3rd century BC. AR Didrachm. Naked young horseman / Taras riding dolphin 200.00
Velia, Lucania. 350-300 BC. AE16. Zeus / Owl with wings spread.. 35.00

GREECE & ASIA MINOR

As mentioned above, coinage was invented in Lydia, Asia Minor (Turkey). It soon spread throughout the Greek cities of western Asia Minor, the Aegean, and the Greek mainland.

Because Alexander the Great of the Kingdom of Macedon, in northern Greece, conquered most of the Greek world and vast regions to its east, he made Greek standards for coinage almost ubiquitous in the ancient world. His coins continued to be struck by dozens of mints throughout his vast former empire for more than a century after his death.

Known counterfeits: High quality Greek silver has been the target of counterfeiters for more than a century. Many counterfeits are quite deceptive. The works of famous nineteenth century counterfeiters such as Becker command values as collectibles themselves. Counterfeit diobols of Apollonia Pontica and Mesembria were widely distributed in 1988.

Achaean League. 200-146 BC. AR Hemidrachm. Head of Zeus r. / AX monogram in wreath 65.00
Apollonia Pontica, Thrace. 400-350 BC. AR Diobol. Facing head of Apollo / Anchor................... 75.00
Amisus, Pontus. 121-63 BC. AE21. Shield with Medusa head / Victory walking r. 20.00
Aspendos, Pamphylia. 370-333BC. AR Stater. Two wrestlers / Slinger r. 225.00

Athens, 478-419 BC. AR Tetradrachm. Helmeted head of Athena with archaic eye r. / Owl., leaves and crescent moon l., AΘE r., all in incuse square 400.00
__. similar, clumpy and irregular.................. 200.00

Corinth, 370-320 BC AR Stater, Pegasus l., Q below / Helmeted head. of Athena l.250.00

Cyzicus, Mysia. 480-450 BC. AR Obol. Forepart of running boar / Forepart of lion 75.00

Ephesus, Ionia. 280-258 BC. AE18. Bee, E Φ at sides / Stag stg. r., quiver above 30.00

Lydia, Kingdom, Croesus, 561-546 BC. AR 1/2 Stater. Busts of lion and bull facing each other / Two incuse squares 500.00

See Persia for Lydia under that empire.

Macedon, Kingdom. Amyntas III, 389-383 BC. AE15. Head of Hercules r. / Eagle r., wings closed, AMYNTA 30.00

__: Philip II, 359-336 BC. AR Tetradrachm. Head of Zeus r. / King riding l. 450.00

__: Alexander III the Great, 336-323 BC. AV Stater. Helmeted head of Athena r. / Victory stg. 1,350.00

__:__. AR Tetradrachm. Head of Alexander as Hercules r. / Zeus std. l., legs parallel. *Usually struck before his death, unlike the following.* 300.00

__:__. same, legs crossed. *Almost always struck after his death.* 250.00

__:__. similar, but AR Drachm 110.00

__:__. AE20. Head of Alexander as Hercules / club and bow in case... 40.00

Maroneia, Thrace. 400-350 BC. AE15. Horse galloping r. / Vine in square 20.00

Mesembria, Thrace. Crested helmet facing / Four-spoked wheel, META 75.00

Mytilene, Lesbos. 450-330 BC. Electrum 1/6 Stater. Head of Apollo r. / Female head in square..275.00

Pergamum, Mysia. 190-50BC. AR Tetradrachm. Serpent emerging from container, all in wreath / Bow case between two coiled serpents ... 225.00

Rhodes, Caria. 3rd century BC. AE10. Rose / Rose, P O at sides 20.00

Tenedus, Troas, 160-140 BC. AR Tetradrachm. Jani-form head with male and female faces / Double axe in wreath 2,000.00

Tarsus, Cilicia. 300s BC. AR Stater. Baal std. l. / Lion attacking bull 375.00

__,__. 2nd-1st century BC. AE17. Zeus std. l. / Club in wreath... 20.00

Thasos, Thrace. 411-350 BC. AR Trihemiobol. Satyr kneeling l. / Amphora 125.00

ANCIENT NEAR EAST

At first dominated by the municipal issues of the Phoenician cities in the 500s B.C., as well as of the Persian Empire, this region was incorporated by Alexander the Great (336-323 B.C.) into his vast empire. From his death until the Roman conquest of the area the municipal issues combined with those of the larger Hellenistic kingdoms, particularly the Seleucids, descended from one of Alexander the Great's generals.

Additional Specialized Books:

Houghton, Arthur. *Coins of the Seleucid Empire from the Collection of Arthur Houghton.*

Known counterfeits: High quality Greek silver has been the target of counterfeiters for more than a century. Many counterfeits are quite deceptive.

Seleucid Empire

Seleucus I, 312-280. AR Tetradrachm. Head of Alexander as Hercules / Zeus std. l., ΣΕΛΕΥΚoΥ r. 300.00

Antiochus I, 280-261 BC. AE18. Head of Apollo / Tripod 20.00

Antiochus II, 261-246. AE17. Head r. / Apollo stg. l...22.00

Seleucus II, 246-226 BC. AE17. Head of Hercules / Apollo std. l.. 20.00

Antiochus III, 223-187 BC. AR Tetradrachm. Diad head r. / Apollo std. l................................ 300.00

Molon, 222-220 BC. AE18. Head of Apollo / Victory stg. l..45.00

Seleucus IV, 187-175 BC. AE17. Bust of Artemis, quiver at shoulder / Artemis stg. with deer 20.00

Antiochus IV, 175-164BC. AE16. His radiate head r., AX l. / Tyche std. l. holding small Victory 20.00

Alexander I, 150-145BC. AR Tetradrachm. Alexander's bust r. / Eagle l. on prow, club l...285.00

Antiochus VII, 138-129 BC. AR Tetradrachm. Diademed bust r. / Athena stg. l.....................200.00

__. AE18. Bust of Eros r. / Headdress of Isis ..25.00

Alexander II, 128-123 BC. AE21. Radiate bust r. / Cornucopia...25.00

Tigranes II of Armenia, 95-56 BC. AR Tetradrachm. Bust in Armenian tiara / Tyche std. r......... 600.00

__. AE22. similar 38.00

Philip Philadelphos, 93-83 BC. AR Tetradrachm. Philip's bust r. / Zeus std. l holding victory and scepter, four line inscription, all in wreath 175.00

Syria

Antioch. 1st century BC. AE20 Head of Zeus r. / Zeus std. l. 20.00

Phoenicia

Arados. 2nd century BC. AE17. Head of Zeus r. / Ram of galley 16.00

Sidon. AD 44. AE15. Turreted head of Tyche r. / War galley l., ΣΙΔΩΝΟΣ... above 20.00

Tripolis. 2nd century B.C. Veiled bust of Tyche / Prow of galley, two caps above.................. 20.00

Tyre. 2nd-1st century BC. AR Shekel (tetradrachm). Head of Melkarth r. / Eagle l., club *l. There is great demand for this coin for its Biblical connection. It is believed the most likely coin to have been used to pay Judas the thirty pieces of silver.* 475.00

JUDAEA

There were no coins in the time of the Patriarchs. The first ones to be made in Judaea were tiny silver pieces struck during the Persian occupation and marked "Yehud." Independent Jewish coinage began under John Hyrcanus I, nephew of Judah Maccabee who led the fight against the Seleucid King Antiochus IV. Ancient Jewish coins are virtually all crudely made small bronzes. Except for two periods of revolt against the Romans, there are no proven silver coins of the Judaean kingdom. During the end period when Judaean kings were clients of the Romans some of their coins actually depict the Roman emperor on one side, while referring to the king on the other.

The revolt coins are often struck over Roman coins, which sometimes had their designs partially filed off first. Occasionally a fragment of the old coin actually shows through the new design.

Despite their crudeness, Judaean coins are extremely popular because of their Biblical connection.

Additional Specialized Books: Hendin, David. *Guide to Biblical Coins, 3rd ed.*

Known counterfeits: Many poor replicas have been made over the last century, often recognizable by their extreme uniformity or blatant edge seams. High quality counterfeits exist of many of the revolt silver pieces.

Persian Period, before 333 BC. AR Hemiobol. Head of Persian king / Falcon, *Yhd* r. 650.00

__,__. AR Drachm. Helmeted , bearded head r. / Male deity std. on winged wheel. ....Unique

John Hyrcanus I, 134-104 BC. AE Prutah. *Yehohanan the High Priest and the Council of the Jews,* in wreath / Two cornucopias, pomegranate between 30.00

Anonymous. 1st century BC. AR Shekel (tetradrachm). Head of Melkarth r. / Eagle l., club l., KP r. *Some scholars believe that Tyre shekels with KP were struck in Jerusalem to use as donations at the Temple.*.......................... 475.00

Alexander Jannaeus, 103-76 BC. AE Prutah. Anchor / Star within diadem. *This is the coin most often considered the widow's mite mentioned in the New Testament. Because of this it is always popular despite its usual crudeness and poor grade.* 15.00

same, low grade 6.00

Herod I the Great, 40 BC - AD 4. AE27. Cap on couch between branches / Tripod............ 250.00

__. AE Prutah. Anchor, HPωΔ BACI / Two cornucopiae, caduceus between...................... 30.00

Herod Archelaus, 4 BC - AD 6. AE Prutah. Bunch of Grape / Helmet with plumes 30.00

Herod Antipas, 4 BC - 40 AD. AE19. HPωΔ TETPAP, Reed / TIBEPIAC in wreath 350.00

Agrippa I, 37-44. AE Prutah. Umbrella / Three ears of barley............................... 20.00

Pontius Pilate, 26-36, for Tiberius. AE Lepton. Astrologer's staff / LIZ in wreath............. 75.00

Nero, 54-68. AE Lepton. Palm branch / NEPωNOC in wreath................................. 20.00

Agripa II, 56-95. AE 18. Bust of Roman Emperor Domitian / Victory writing on shield, ETO KΔ BA AΓPIΠΠ around 150.00

First Revolt, 66-70. AE Prutah. Amphora / Vine leaf..25.00

Second Revolt, 132-135. AR Tetradrachm. Facade of Temple / Lulav and etrog, "For the freedom of Jerusalem" around 1,200.00

__. AR Denarius. Bunch of grapes / Lyre 285.00

ANCIENT PERSIA

Ancient Persian coins are among the most common coins of the 6th century B.C. Gold darics and silver sigloi were struck in quantity, both in the homeland of their large empire, and in their possessions in Asia Minor. Many of these coins have test punches applied by ancient bankers. They reduce the value, but if they're only on the reverse the value is not significantly reduced.

After a century of being part of Greek empires, Persia again asserted its independence (238 B.C.) as Parthia. It is interesting to see the evolution of the artistic style of the Parthian drachm, from Hellenistic Greek realism to a stylized and linear oriental rendering.

Three vassal kingdoms of Parthia also struck coins: Characene, Elymais, and Persis.

The Sassanian dynasty of Persis overthrew the Parthians, their former overlords (A.D.224), but continued their empire, calling it Ayran. They also continued the trend toward oriental portraiture. Their drachms are notable for their broad, thin fabric and the elaborate crowns worn by their emperors.

Additional Specialized Books: Gobl, Robert. *Sassanian Numismatics.*

Sellwood, David. *An Introduction to the Coinage of Parthia.*

Sellwood, Whitting, and Williams. *An Introduction to Sassanian Coins.*

Shore, F. Parthian Coins and History.

Known counterfeits: While not as aggressively counterfeited as Greek coins, collector counterfeits of varying quality have been made of these series for almost a century.

Note: All Parthian and Sassanian coins below are silver drachms unless otherwise noted.

PERSIAN EMPIRE

500-330 B.C. AV Daric. King kneeling r. holding spear and bow / Crude incuse square 800.00

500-330 BC. AR Siglos. similar 90.00

Also struck by Persians in Lydia.

PARTHIA

Arsaces I, 238-211 BC. Beardless bust l. wearing leather cap / Archer std. l. 2,250.00

Arsaces II, 211-191 BC. AR Drachm. Beardless bust l. wearing leather cap / Archer std. r.......... 375.00

Mithradates I, 171-138 BC. similar, but archer seated on omphalos 140.00

Phraates II, 138-127 BC. Bearded bust l. wearing diadem / similar.................................... 200.00

Artabanos I, 127-124 BC. similar to above ...250.00

Mithradates II, 123-88 BC. similar but archer on chair.. 90.00

__. AE17. similar / Horse head 30.00

Gotarzes I, 95-87 BC. Bearded bust in tiara l. / Archer std. r. on chair 70.00

Orodes I, 90-77 BC. similar. 70.00

Sinatruces, 77-70 BC. similar but anchor behind head 250.00

Phraates III, 70-57 BC. Bust l. wearing short beard and diadem / similar to above 200.00

Mithradates III, 57-54 BC. similar.................... 90.00

Orodes II, 57-38 BC. similar............................60.00

Pakoros I, 50 BC. Beardless bust l. / as above .... Rare

Phraates IV, 38-2 BC. Bust l. with short beard and diadem / as above 60.00

Phraataces, 2BC - AD4. similar but Nike behind head 60.00

Vonones I, 8-12 AD. Bearded bust l. / Victory flying r. 150.00

Artabanos II, 10-38. Bearded bust l. / Archer std. r. 45.00

Vardanes I, 40-45. similar 90.00

Gotarzes II, 40-51. similar 75.00

Vonones II, 51. Facing bust / Archer std. r. ...125.00

Vologases I, 51-78. Bust l. with beard and diadem / as above 80.00

Vardanes II, 55-58. similar.............................. 90.00

Vologases II, 77-80. Bust l. with beard and tiara / above 300.00

Pakoros II, 78-105. Beardless bust l. / as above 175.00

Artabanos III, 80-90. Bust l. with beard and diadem. / as above 90.00
Vologases III, 105-147. similar........................ 45.00
Osroes I, 109-129. similar but hair is gathered in puffy balls 750.00

___. AR Tetradrachm. Beaded bust l. in diadem...1,250.00
Parthamaspates, 116. Bearded bust l. in tiara / similar 200.00
Mithradatess IV, 140. Bust l. with beard and diadem / similar 70.00
Vologases IV, 147-191. Bust l. with beard and tiara / similar 55.00
___. similar / Tyche giving diadem to seated king 150.00
Osroes II, 190. similar 55.00
Vologases V, 191-208. Facing bearded bust with hair gathered in puffy balls / Crude archer std. r...750.00
Vologases VI, 208-228. Bust l. with beard and tiara, I r. / as above 55.00
Artabanos IV, 216-224. similar, >_ to r. 350.00
Characene. Attambelos III, 53-72. AE Tetradrachm. Beardless head r. / Hercules std. l. 60.00
Elymais. Orodes II, c.150-200. AE Drachm. Facing bust with tiara, anchor r. / dashes 10.00
Persis. 1-2nd cent. AR Hemidrachm. Bust in tiara l. / double diadem 75.00

Sassanian. Ardashir I, 224-241. Bust in high crown / Fire altar aflame..................................... 150.00
Shapur I, 241-272. Crowned bust / Fire altar between attendants 85.00
Hormazd I, 272-273. similar 2,000.00

Varhran I, 273-276. Bust in spiked crown / as above 300.00
Varhran II, 276-293. Bust in winged crown / as above... 225.00

Narseh, 293-303. Bust in floral crown / as above 175.00
Hormazd II, 303-309. Bust in eagle crown / as above 140.00
Shapur II, 309-379. Crowned bust / as above . 60.00
Ardashir II, 379-383. Bust in cap-crown / as above 225.00
Shapur III, 383-388. Bust in low crown / as above 100.00
Varhran IV, 388-399. Bust in winged crown / as above 55.00
Yazdgard I, 399-420. Bust in cap-crown / as above 65.00
Varhran V, 420-438. Crowned bust / as above, face within flames................................. 55.00
Yazdgard II, 438-457. Crowned bust / Fire altar between attendants..................................... 40.00
Firuz, 457-484. similar................................... 30.00

Valkash, 484-488. similar 135.00
Zamasp, 497-499. Crowned bust, small bust before / as above.. 120.00
Kavad I, 484-531. Crowned bust / as above.... 27.00
Khusru I, 531-579. Similar 27.00
Hormazd IV, 579-590. similar 27.00
Varhran VI, 590-591. similar 300.00
Vistahm, 591-597. similar............................. 210.00
Khusru II, 590-628. Bust in winged crown / as above 25.00
Kavad II, 628. Crowned bust / as above 300.00
Ardashir III, 628-630. similar 115.00
Buran, 630-631. Beardless bust / as above.... 700.00
Azarmidukht, 631-632. Bust in winged crown / as above 5,000.00
Hormazd V, 631-632. similar 225.00
Khusru V, 631-33. Beardless bust / as above 300.00
Yazdgard III, 632-651. similar....................... 135.00
Sassanian Kushanshahs. Peroz II, 325-28. Peroz in tiara / Altar 13.00

FURTHER ASIA

Despite the brevity of Alexander the Great's occupation of further Asia, areas as far as modern Afghanistan, Pakistan and even India, his cultural and monetary influence was lasting. The Hellenistic kingdom of Bactria continued for hundreds of years until wiped out by invaders from the North. On many of their coins, a Greek obverse inscription is combined with a reverse legend in local Karoshti characters. The later reverse types also show a synthesis of Greek and Indian cultures. Other unusual features of their coinage were the use of a natural nickel alloy, thousands of years before the isolation of the element nickel,

and the use of square coins, again centuries before they were widely used.

Additional Specialized Books: Mitchiner, Michael. *Oriental Coins and their Values: Ancient and Classical World.*

Known counterfeits: The heroic bust coins of Bactria are a magnet for counterfeiters. All must be examined by an expert.

Bactria. Euthydemus I, 230-190 BC. AE22. Bearded head r. / Horse running r. 90.00
___. Demetrius I, 190-171 BC. Head of Elephant / Caduceus 150.00

___. Antimachus I, 185-170 BC. AR Tetradrachm. Bust in broad hat / Poseidon stg. 2,200.00
___. Diomedes, 110-80 BC. AE17x22 rectangular. Dioscuri stg. / Humped bull 75.00
Indo-Greeks. Menander I, 155-130 BC. AR Tetradrachm. Heroic bust l. throwing spear / Athena stg. l... 500.00
___.___. AR Drachm. similar 90.00
___. Strato I, 130-110 BC. AE20 square. Bust of Hercules r. / Victory walking r. 30.00
Indo-Scythians. Azes I, 57-35 BC. AR Tetradrachm. Zeus stg. l. / Victory walking r. 300.00

EGYPT & AFRICA

The Egyptians found little use for coinage before Alexander the Great. With the founding of the Greek Ptolemaic dynasty, descended from one of his generals and the increase in Greek influence, its coinage became prolific. Silver was similar to that of the other Hellenistic kingdoms, but its copper coins were unique for the immense size of their larger denominations. Their "centration holes," actually dimples, are a distinct feature of their manufacturing process.

Carthage was a Phoenician city in North Africa, near modern Tunis. A bitter rival of the Roman Republic during the Punic Wars, it colonized Spain, western Sicily, and Sardinia.

Egypt. Nektanebo II, 361-350BC. AV Stater. Horse galloping r. / Ornamented collar over heart and wind-pipe (hieroglyphic for fine gold) 3,500.00
Ptolemy II, 285-246BC. AE16. Head of Zeus-Ammon / Eagle stg. l. on thunderbolt, wings open, D between legs 20.00

Ptolemy IV, 221-204 BC. AE34. Head of Zeus-Ammon r. / Eagle l. on thunderbolt. cornucopia l. 250.00
Ptolemy VIII, 145-116BC. AR Tetradrachm. Idealized head of Ptolemy I / Eagle l. on thunderbolt l., PA r. 150.00
Cleopatra VII, 51-30BC. AE26. Her bust r. / Eagle stg. on thunderbolt. 500.00

Carthage. 320-280 BC Electrum Stater. Head of Tanit l. / Horse stg. r. 600.00
__. 250-200 BC. AE18. Horse head r. / Palm-tree 20.00

ROMAN COINS

Roman coins are among the most universally collected. In fact, the origin of coin collecting in the West and the rediscovery of realistic portraiture evolves from the finding of Roman coins by Italians at the dawn of the Renaissance. Roman coins are divided into three different stages, although the middle one actually overlaps the first. They are the Roman Republic, Imperatorial, and Roman Empire. The evolution of coinage from the first to the last is a development from primitive to nearly modern.

ROMAN REPUBLIC

The Roman word for money, *pecunia*, derives from their very earliest measure of wealth: sheep (*pecus*). But sheep were often inconvenient. Less sophisticated than the Greeks at the time, the Romans' next step was to trade in large cast bars of copper (*aes*). Alas, the Greek invention of coinage was still more convenient, and as the Romans expanded their territories and traded over greater distances, their cast bronze ingots gradually became round and took on the form of coins. When Rome began producing its first silver coins, they didn't cast in the Roman tradition, but

were struck in the Greek manner. Their weights and values were Greek as well. The coast of southern Italy and Sicily then were covered with Greek colonies. In the late third century B.C. the Romans were powerful enough to decide to strike a silver coin on their own standard, and replaced the *drachm* with the new, dime-sized *denarius*. In the meantime, the old cast copper aes had evolved into a struck copper coin of large size, the *As*. It was originally called the liberal *As*, because it weighed one pound or *libra*. The new denarius was valued at 10 of these, and later at 16. Most Romans were illiterate, so a system was devised for reading the value of coins by counting dots or simple symbols. It survived for many years as follows:

Roman Republic Bronze

(none)	= Semuncia	1/2 Uncia
•	= Uncia	(ounce)
••	= Sextans	1/6 As
•••	= Quadrans	1/4 As
••••	= Triens	1/3 As
S	= Semis	1/2 As
I	= As	12 Unciae

Roman Republic Silver

IIS	= Sestertius	2-1/2 Asses
V	= Quinarius	5 Asses
X	= Denarius	10 Asses
X—	= Denarius, late	16 Asses

Most bronzes of the republic depicted a god or goddess on the obverse, and the prow of a ship on the reverse. Silver, particularly the denarius, usually had a portrait of the personification of Roma on the obverse, and a chariot on the reverse. Living people were not depicted, but late in the Republic the magistrates responsible for managing the mint would sometimes depict their famous ancestors or deities from which they claimed descent.

> Values for Greek coins are for Very Fine examples for gold (**AV**) and silver (**AR**), Fine for bronze and copper (**AE**).

BOOKS ABOUT ROMAN REPUBLIC & IMPERATORIAL COINS

Because the imperatorial period is technically the end of the Republic, many of the same books can be useful for both series. Hundreds of pages can be written on books about ancient Roman coins. The list here will be confined to only the most basic or the most important references.

Klawans, Zander. *Handbook of Ancient Greek and Roman Coins.* The most simple introduction.

Sayles, Wayne. *Ancient Coin Collecting: The Roman World - Politics and Propaganda.*

Melville Jones, John. *A Dictionary of Ancient Roman Coins.*

Sear, David. *Roman Coins and their Values.* The most used catalogue of representative coin.

Sear, David. *Roman Silver Coins,* v. I.

AV 60 Asses, after 211 BC. Head of Mars / Eagle stg. r. 2,500.00

AR Quadrigatus, 225-217 BC. Beardless janiform head / Jupiter and Victory in chariot r., ROMA below 200.00

AR Denarius, c.154 BC. Helmeted head of Roma r., X behind / Dioscuri galloping r., CSCR, ROMA below 85.00
AR Denarius, 90 BC. Head of Apollo / Horseman r., L.PISO.FRVGI. 75.00
AR Denarius, 90 BC. Bearded head r. / Pegasus r...85.00

AR Denarius, 79 BC. Head of Juno / Griffin leaping r., L.PAPI. This coin has a serrate edge, which looks like a series of cuts 85.00
AR Victoriatus, 206-195 BC. Head of Jupiter / Victory crowning trophy.................................75.00
AR Quinarius, 98 BC. similar but Q at bottom of reverse 70.00
AR Sestertius, 211-207 BC. Head of Roma, IIS behind / Dioscuri galloping r. 225.00

AR Denarius, c.54 BC. Head of Juno in goatskin r. / Girl stg. with coiled serpent, FABATI below..110.00

AE Semuncia, c.215 BC. Head of Mercury / Prow r., no mark of value 65.00

AE Uncia 217-215 B.C. Helmeted head. of Roma l., • r. / Prow r., ROMA above, • below. 125.00
AE Uncia, 211-207 B.C. same but smaller 90.00
AE Sextans, 211-207 B.C. Head of Mercury, •• above / Prow r., •• below 90.00
AE Quadrans, 2nd cent. B.C. Head of Hercules, ••• behind / Prow r. 60.00

AE Semis, 211-209 B.C. Head of Saturn r., S behind / Prow, S above 125.00

AE As, 206-195 BC. Head of Janus, I above / Prow r., bird and rudder above, I r., ROMA below.. 150.00

AE As, c.190-150 BC. Head of Janus, I above / Prow r., monogram above......................... 125.00

ROMAN IMPERATORIAL

Toward the end of the Roman Republic many important generals took control from each other, eclipsing the power of the senate. During this time their power and audacity caused them to do what had been previously unthinkable: place their own names and even images on the coinage. These generals include the famous Julius Caesar, who died before his nephew Octavian became the first Roman Emperor under the name of Augustus. Numismatists call this coinage, named for the rulers whose civil wars caused the demise of the Republic, Imperatorial, after the Latin word for general, *Imperator*.

Pompey the Great, d. 48 BC. AE As, 45 BC. Janiform head of Pompey / Prow 300.00

Sextus Pompey, d. 35 BC. AR Denarius, 44-43 BC. Head of Pompey the Great / Galley 2,000.00

Julius Caesar, d. 44 BC. AR Denarius, 44 BC. Bust of Julius Caesar / Venus stg. holding Victory..1,600.00

___. AR Denarius. Elephant r. trampling serpent, CAESAR below / Priestly implements..... 250.00

Marc Antony, d. 30 BC. AR Legionary Denarius, 32-31BC. Galley / Legionary eagle between two standards 165.00

Marc Antony and Octavian. AR Denarius. 41 BC. Head of Marc Antony / Head of Octavian.. 350.00

Lepidus and Octavian. AR Denarius. c. 42 BC. Head of Lepidus / Head of Octavian...... 1,500.00

ROMAN EMPIRE

As Rome grew from a city to a Republic and then to an Empire, larger denominations were needed to facilitate even greater financial transactions. The monetary system as it looked during most of the Empire (27 B.C. to A.D. 286) follows, but not all coins were struck during all periods.

Roman Copper and Brass to 295 A.D.

coin	value	size
Quadrans	1/4 As	16 to 15
Semis	1/2 As	21 to 18
As	1/16 Denarius	28 to 23
Dupondius	2 Asses	28 to 23
Sestertius	4 Asses	34 to 30

Roman Silver to 286 A.D.

Quinarius	8 Asses	15 to 14
Denarius	16 Asses	18 to 15
Antoninianus	2 Denarii	24 to 18

(Late silver alloy coins appear copper)

Roman Gold to 286 A.D.

Quinarius	12-1/2 Denarii	16 to 15
Aureus	25 Denarii	20 to 19

At the end of this 300-year span there was great inflation. The amount of silver in the *antoninianus* (double denarius) was not a whole lot more than that in the original denarius. The denarius itself declined from a dime size coin of good silver to one of less than half silver by the 250s, and by 270s it was a small copper containing only a trace of silver. When silver is less than 50 percent pure it is called billon.

Diocletian (284-305) attempted to put the degenerate Roman coinage in order. He based his reforms on a heavier gold *aureus* weighing 1/60th instead of 1/70th Roman pound, a small coin of good silver, the *argenteus*, and a large bronze coin, the *follis*, almost the size of an American half dollar.

The *argenteus* was particularly innovative as it had been decades since a good quality silver coin had been minted.

Unfortunately, with Diocletian's passing, his currency began to erode. Constantine the Great (307-337) replaced the *aureus* with the slightly lighter *solidus* (1/72 Roman pound), but from then on the purity and weight of the gold coinage was maintained for centuries into the Byzantine period. He renamed the *argenteus* the *siliqua* and added a 1-1/3 *siliqua*, called a *miliarense*, and maintained the purity of both. However, he let the *follis* continue to deteriorate. By His death in 337 it had declined to a size smaller than a dime.

During the late Roman period the sizes of bronze coins declined so rapidly and surviving records are so scarce that numismatists have taken to categorizing them by diameter instead of name.

name	size	similar to U.S.
AE1	over 24 mm.	mini-dollar
AE2	21-24 mm.	quarter
AE3	17-20 mm.	cent
AE4	below 17 mm	half dime

IMPERIAL COIN DESIGNS

The obverses of most coins of the Roman Empire show the portrait of the emperor or a member of his family. AVG for *augustus* or *augusta* on the obverse meant the person was emperor, or empress. *Caesar*, after the first dynasty, meant junior emperor. The portrait could also tell the average Roman the face value of the coin. If the emperor wore a radiate (spiked) crown, the value was doubled. Dupondii and Antoniniani (the double denarius) both had radiate crowns. For an empress, a crescent below the shoulder substituted for a crown.

First and second century Roman coins have very realistic portraits. This realism begins to fade somewhat by the 250s. The Tetrarchy period replaces realistic portraiture altogether with well executed, angular images of an emperor, still conveying a strong sense of authority. The addition or deletion of a beard aside, these stereotyped images persist through the end of the Empire, although usually lacking the original inspiration.

Most base metal coins until well into the third century have the letters SC in the reverse field. This indicates that they were issued with the consent of the Senate.

The reverses often depicted gods and goddesses just as the Greeks had. The descriptions of deities given in the Greek section above will help for Roman coins too. The Romans depicted virtues in allegorical form perhaps more than they showed deities. Often their names were clearly written. Their Latin names and English translations are given here, with an attribute or two given afterward. The V was used both for V and U on Roman coins. Allegories are female unless noted.

ABVNDANTIA - Abundance. Cornucopia and ears of grain.

AEQVUITAS - Equity. Balance scales.

AETERNITAS - Eternity. Globe, torch, scepter, phoenix.

ANNONA - Harvest. Ears of grain, grain measure (*modius*), cornucopia.

CLEMENTIA - Clemency. Branch, scepter.

CONCORDIA - Concord. Dish (*patera*), cornucopia.

CONCORDIA MILITVM - Military Concord. Two military standards.

CONSTANTIA - Firmness. Right hand to face, spear.

FECVNDITAS - Fertility. Child or children, scepter.

FELICITAS - Felicity. Caduceus, cornucopia, scepter.

FIDES - Faith. *Patera*, cornucopia, grain-ears, fruit basket.

FORTVNA - Fortune. Rudder, cornucopia, wheel.

GENIVS - Spirit. Male holding *patera* and cornucopia.

HILARITAS - Cheerfulness. Palm branch, cornucopia, scepter, patera.

INDVLGENTIA - Mercy. Patera, scepter.

IVSTITIA - Justice. Olive branch, *patera*, scepter.

LAETITIA - Joy. Wreath, scepter.

LIBERALITAS - Liberality. Tablet, cornucopia.

LIBERTAS - Liberty. Pointed cap in hand, scepter.

MONETA - Money. Scale, cornucopia.

PAX - Peace. Olive branch, scepter, cornucopia, caduceus.

PIETAS - Piety. Veil, *patera*, scepter, altar by feet.

PROVIDENTIA - Providence. Baton, globe, scepter.

PVDICITIA - Modesty. Veil, scepter.

SALVS - Health. Scepter, serpent.

SECVRITAS - Security. *Patera*, scepter, column.

SPES - Hope. Raises dress slightly.

VBERITAS - Fertility. Cornucopia, purse, bunch of grapes.

VICTORIA - Victory. Depicted as a winged female. Wreath, palm branch.

VIRTVS - Military Virtue, Courage. Armored male, holding Victory, sword, spear, shield.

Roman Mints

There were many mints throughout the Roman Empire, some as distant from each other as England and Egypt. Most of those operating during the 280s and later placed mintmarks very clearly on the reverse.

A Roman mintmark most often consisted of three parts. One was an indication of money, and were generally denoted by P, M, and SM to mean *Pecunia*, *Moneta*, or *Sacra Moneta*. Next, the city was abbreviated. Also a letter indicating the workshop within the mint, called an *officina*, often fol-

lowed or preceded the city abbreviation. Some of the more common city abbreviations used in mintmarks are:

AL .... Alexandria, Egypt
AN or ANT .... Antioch, Syria
AQ .... Aquileia, Italy
AR .... Arles, France
CON or CONS .... Constantinople, Turkey
CON or CONST .... Arles, France
H or HERAC .... Heraclea, Turkey
K or CVZ .... Cyzicus, Turkey
K or KART .... Carthage, Tunisia
L or LON........................... London, England
LG or LVG .... Lyons, France
N, NIC or NIK .... Nicomedia, Turkey
R or ROM................................. Rome, Italy
S or SIR..................... Sirmium, Yugoslavia
SIS or SISC .... Siscia, Croatia
TS or TES .... Thessalonica, Greece
T .... Ticinum, Italy
TR .... Trier, Germany

Coins from more popularly collected and smaller mints, such as London, command a premium above others.

BOOKS ABOUT ROMAN IMPERIAL COINS

Hundreds of pages can be written on books about Roman Imperial coins. The list here will be confined to only the most basic or the most important references.

Carson, Hill, & Kent. *Late Roman Bronze Coinage.*

Cohen, Henri. Description *Historique des Monneis Frappees sous L'Empire Romain.*

Klawans, Zander. *Handbook of Ancient Greek and Roman Coins.*

Mattingly, H. and Sydenham, E.A. *The Roman Imperial Coinage*, 10 vols.

Melville Jones, John. *A Dictionary of Ancient Roman Coins.*

Sear, David. *Roman Coins and their Values.*

Sear, David. *Roman Silver Coins*, vols. II-V.

Julio-Claudian Dynasty

Augustus, 27 BC - AD 14. AR Denarius. Caius and Lucius Caesars stg. with shields and spears...175.00

Tiberius, 14-37. AR Denarius. Livia as Peace std. r. This coins is mentioned in the Bible and is often called the "Tribute Penny"......................250.00

Caligula, 37-41. AE As. Vesta veiled, std. l. .. 175.00

Caligula was a nickname. His real name Caius, or C., appears on his coins.

Claudius, 41-54. AE Quadrans. Modius / SC 30.00

Nero, 54-68. AE As. Victory flying l. with shield inscribed SPQR 90.00

Galba, 68-69. AE As. Liberty stg. holding pileus and scepter..350.00

Otho, 69. AR Denarius. Security stg. l. 975.00

Vitellius, 69. AR Denarius. Tripod altar, dolphin above, raven on base 650.00

Flavian Dynasty 69-96

Vespasian, 69-79. AR Denarius. Female Jew std. r., trophy of arms behind, IVDAEA below 500.00

__: AR Denarius. Peace std. l. 125.00

Titus, 79-81. AR Denarius. Chair 150.00

Domitian, 81-96. AR Denarius. Minerva stg. l. with spear 110.00

The Good Emperors 96-180

Nerva, 96-98. AE As. Clasped hands. 75.00

Trajan, 98-117. AE Sestertius. Hope stg. l. raising skirt 75.00

Hadrian, 117-138. AV Aureus. Hadrian riding horse r... 1,500.00
Antoninus Pius, 138-161. AR Denarius. Emperor sacrificing at tripod altar 75.00
Marcus Aurelius, 161-180. AR Denarius. Fortune std. 80.00

__. AE Sestertius. Minerva stg. with spear and shield.. 60.00
Lucius Verus, 161-169. AR Denarius. Roma walking l. Holding trophy 135.00
Commodus, 177-192. AE Dupondius.
Minerva...40.00

Pertinax, 193. AR Denarius. Laetitia stg. with wreath and scepter 800.00
Pescennius Niger, 193-194. AR Denarius. Basket of fruit 1,500.00
Clodius Albinus, as Caesar 193-195. AE As. Felicity stg. 200.00

The Severan Era 193-235

Septimius Severus, 193-211. AR Denarius. Victory walking with shield............................ 60.00

Caracalla, 198-217. AE Sestertius. Providence stg. holding rod over globe and long scepter ... 85.00
Caracalla was a nickname. His real name, Antoninus, appears on his coins.
Geta, as Caesar, 198-209. AR Denarius. Genius stg. l. holding dish and grain ears..................... 60.00
__, as Emperor, 209-212. AR Denarius. Genius stg. l. holding dish and grain ears..................... 90.00

Macrinus, 217-218. AR Denarius. Jupiter stg. holding thunderbolt and scepter 115.00
Elagabalus, 218-222. AR Denarius. Health feeding serpent 60.00

Elagabalus was a nickname. His real name, Antoninus, appears on his coins.

Severus Alexander, 222-235. AR Denarius. Aequitas stg. with scales and cornucopia............ 40.00

Maximinus, 235-238. AR Denarius. Emperor stg. between two military standards.................. 85.00
Maximus, Caesar 235-238. AR Denarius. Maximus stg., two standards to r. 220.00
Gordian I, 238. AR Denarius. Roma std. l. . 950.00
Gordian II, 238. AE Sestertius. Victory walking l.. 700.00

Balbinus, 238. AE Sestertius. Emperor stg. holding sword and branch. 300.00
Pupienus, 238. AR Antoninianus. Clasped hands 350.00
Gordian III, 238-244. AE Sestertius. Emperor sacrificing at altar. 40.00

Philip I, 244-49. AR Antoninianus. Peace running l...40.00
Philip II, 247-249. AR Antoninianus. Sol walking l. holding whip 45.00
Pacatian, 248. AR Antoninianus. Fortune std. holding rudder and cornucopia. .... Rare
Jotapian, 248. AR Antoninianus. Victory walking l... Rare
Trajan Decius, 249-251. AR Antoninianus. Allegory of the province of Pannonia stg.........40.00

__. AE Double Sestertius. Felicity stg. holding caduceus and cornucopia. 350.00
Herennius Etruscus, as Caesar 250-251. AR Antoninianus. Priestly implements...................85.00
Hostillian, as Caesar 251. AR Antoninianus. Apollo std. with lyre 110.00
Trebonianus Gallus, 251-253. AR Antoninianus. Liberty. 40.00

Volusian, 251-253. AR Antoninianus. Virtue...45.00
Aemilian, 253. AR Antoninianus. Mars leaning on shield...150.00
Valerian, 253-260. AR Antoninianus. Faith stg. with two military standards 35.00
Gallienus, 253-268. Billon Antoninianus. Virtue stg. l. 15.00
Saloninus, as Caesar 255-59. Billon Antoninianus. Priestly implements...................................50.00

Macrianus, 260-261. Billon Antoninianus. Jupiter std. l. 150.00

Quietus, 260-261. Billon Antoninianus. Equity stg. l. 150.00

Postumus, 259-268 in Gaul. AE Antoninianus. Health stg. r. feeding serpent. 10.00

Laelianus, 268 in Gaul. AE Antoninianus. Victory walking r. 365.00

Marius, 268 in Gaul. AE Antoninianus. Felicity stg. l. 150.00

Victorinus, 268-270 in Gaul. AE Antoninianus. Piety stg. l., altar at feet 12.00

Tetricus I, 270-273 in Gaul. AE Antoninianus. Joy stg. with wreath and anchor 10.00

Claudius II Gothicus, 268-270. AE Antoninianus. Felicity stg. l. 8.00

Aurelian, 270-275. AE Antoninianus. Security leaning on column 12.00

__. AE Denarius. Victory walking l. 35.00

Vabalathus, with Aurelian, 270-271. AE Antoninianus. 40.00

Tacitus, 275-276. AE Antoninianus. Providence stg. l. globe at feet.............................. 20.00

Probus, 276-282. AE Antoninianus. Jupiter giving globe to Probus 12.00

Carus, 282-283. AE Antoninianus. Female giving wreath to Carus.................................... 25.00

Numerian, 283-284. AE Antoninianus. Roma std. l.. 20.00

Carinus, 283-285. AE Antoninianus. Virtue holding spear and sword.................................. 20.00

Julian I, 284-285. AE Antoninianus. Felicity..1,800.00

The Tetrarchy 284-324

Diocletian, 284-305. AE Follis. Genius (spirit) of the Romans stg. l. 20.00

Carausius, 287-293 in Britain. AE Antoninianus. Peace stg. 65.00

Allectus, 293-296 in Britain. AE Quinarius. Galley. 70.00

Domitius Domitianus, 296-297 in Egypt. AE Follis. Genius of the Romans stg. l............... 500.00

Maximianus, 286-305. AE Antoninianus. Jupiter stg., eagle at feet 10.00

Constantius I, 305-306. AE Follis. Genius of the Romans stg... 35.00

Galerius, as Caesar 293-305. AR Argentius. Four emperors, city gate in background. 325.00

__. AE Follis. Genius of the Romans stg. 20.00

On his coins as Caesar, Galerius is often called *Maximianvs Nob Caes*, not Galerius

__, as Emperor 305-311. AE Follis. Genius of Imperator stg... 30.00

Severus II, 306-307. AE Antoninianus. Severus and Jupiter stg.. 45.00

Maximinus II, 309-313. AE Follis. Jupiter stg., eagle at feet 18.00

Maxentius, 306-312. AE Follis. Roma std. in temple.. 35.00

__. Bust l. with spear and shield / same rev. ....Scarce

Alexander, 308-311 in Carthage. AE Follis. Carthage stg. 1,500.00

Licinius I, 308-324. AE3. Jupiter stg., eagle at feet... 10.00

Martinian, 324. AE3. Jupiter with eagle and captive at feet. 1,500.00

House of Constantine 307-363

Constantine I the Great, 307-337. AE3. Victory running r. over captive, *Sarmatia Devicta* around 20.00

__. AE3 Two soldiers standing........................ 10.00

Fausta, wife of Constantine I. AE3. Salus holding two children in arms, Salus Reipublicae around 18.00

Constantine II, as Caesar 317-337. AE3. Wreath..10.00

Constans, 337-350. AE4. Two Victories 10.00

Constantius II, 337-361. AE Centenionalis. Roman soldier dragging barbarian child from hut ...20.00

Magnentius, 350-353. AE Double Centenionalis. Christogram..75.00

Vetranio, 350. AE Centenionalis. Vetranio stg...150.00

Nepotian, 350. AE Centenionalis. Roma std. l...1,200.00

Julian II the Apostate, 360-363. AE 3. Wreath. 35.00

Jovian, 363-364. AE3. Wreath........................50.00

Valentinian I, 364-375. AE3. Emperor dragging captive 18.00

Valens, 364-378. AE3. Victory........................ 18.00

Procopius, 365-366. AE3. Emperor stg........ 150.00

Gratian, 367-383. AE3. Victory walking l..... 18.00

Valentinian II, 375-392. AR Siliqua. Roma std. l. 125.00

__. AE4. Victory with trophy and captive 20.00

Theodosius I, 379-395. AE 2. Theodosius stg. raising kneeling female.....................................30.00

Magnus Maximus, 383-388. AE4. Camp gate 50.00

Flavius Victor, 387-388. AR Siliqua. Roma std...500.00

Eugenius, 392-394. AR Siliqua. Roma std..... 600.00

Arcadius, 383-408. AE4. Victory with trophy and captive 15.00

Honorius, 393-423. AE3. Honorius crowned by Victory. 18.00

Theodosius II, 402-450. AV Solidus. Victory stg. holding large cross 300.00

Constantine III, 407-411. AR Siliqua. Roma std...600.00

Constans (II), 408-411. AR Siliqua. Roma std..4,000.00

Maximus, 409-411. AR Siliqua. Roma std. 4,000.00

Priscus Attalus, 409-415. AE3. Victory....... 400.00

Jovinus, 411-413. AR Siliqua. Roma std......950.00

Sebastianus, 412-413. AR Siliqua. Roma std...6,000.00

Constantius III, 421. AV Tremissis. Victory with wreath and globe..................................5,000.00

Johannes, 423-425. AE4. Victory with trophy and captive. 200.00

Valentinian III, 425-455. AV Solidus. Emperor stg. holding cross and Victory........................ 450.00
__. AE4. Camp gate...................................... 60.00
Marcian, 450-457. AE4. Monogram............. 50.00
Petronius Maximus, 455. AV Solidus. Emperor stg. holding cross and Victory.....................Rare
Avitus, 455-456. AV Tremissis. Cross in wreath...4,000.00
Leo I, 457-474. AE4. Monogram. 50.00
Leo II, 473-474. AV Tremissis. Victory. 800.00

Majorian, 457-461. AV Solidus. Emperor stg. with cross and Victory 3,500.00
__. AE4. Victory 300.00
Severus III, 461-465. AE4. Victory 250.00
Anthemius, 467-472. AE4. Monogram 300.00
Olybrius, 472. AV Tremissis. Cross in wreath..7,000.00
Glycerius, 473-434. AR Siliqua. Victory walking l. 4,000.00
Julius Nepos, 474-480. AE4. Monogram. ... 400.00
Romulus Augustus, 475-476. AV Tremissis. Cross in wreath 4,000.00
Zeno, 474-491. AE4. Monogram. 50.00

GREEK IMPERIALS

In most of the Mediterranean, Greek coinage was replaced with a unique type of coinage, blending Greek, local non-Greek, and Roman traditions. Numismatists usually call these coins "Greek Imperial." Greek was the international language of business in the Eastern Mediterranean, even in Roman times. These Greek Imperial coins usually bore the portrait of the Roman Emperor or a member of his family, but instead of Latin, their titles were usually translated into Greek. Also, the denominations of these coins didn't match the values of regular Roman coins, but were intended to match the values of old Greek style coins, which had been in use for centuries. Lastly the images on the reverses were not always the favorite Roman deities, but often local ones such as river gods. Also local industries were reflected on the coins, such as grapes in wine producing areas like Thrace and Moesia (Bulgaria), or horses in Asia Minor. Some of the most desirable Greek Imperials depict local temples and shrines, thus preserving a tangible record of numerous buildings which have since fallen into ruin.

Greek Imperial coins provide an exciting avenue for collectors who wish to follow uncharted paths. While the literature on them is extensive, so much work needs to be done that new types of coins are able to be discovered by the average hobbyist. On the other hand, those who are particularly concerned about surface

quality may find the series disappointing. The majority of Greek Imperial coins are found with slightly to very porous surfaces.

BOOKS ABOUT GREEK IMPERIAL COINS

Burnett, Amandry, and Ripoles, *Roman Provincial Coinage, vol. I, 44 BC - AD 69.*

Butcher, Kevin. *Roman Provincial Coins: An Introduction to the Greek Imperials.* A coherent introduction.

Curtis, James. *The Tetradrachms of Roman Egypt.*

Sayles, Wayne. *Ancient Coin Collecting: Roman Provincial Coins.*

Sear, *Greek Imperial Coins and their Values.*

Note: All coins have a bust of an emperor on obverse unless noted otherwise.

Province of Syria, 61-35BC. AR Tetradrachm. Bust of Philip Philadelphos r. / Zeus std. l holding victory and scepter, four line inscription, Greek numbers 3 to 29 below throne, all in wreath.. 200.00

Augustus, 27 BC - AD 14. Antioch, Syria. AR Tetradrachm. Tyche std. r., river-god swimming at feet... 225.00
Caligula, 37-41. Caesaraugusta, Spain. AE As. Priest plowing r. with yoke of oxen......... 175.00
Nero, 54-68. Caesarea, Cappadocia. AR Didrachm. Bust of Agrippina, Jr. r............................. 500.00
Domitian, 81-96. Ascalon, Judaea. AE19. War-god Phenebal... 65.00

Trajan, 98-117. Caesarea, Cappadocia. AE17. Winged caduceus. 25.00
Hadrian, 117-138. Side, Pamphylia. AE20. CIΔHTωN, Athena l. 35.00

__. Alexandria, Egypt. Billon Tetradrachm. Serapis std. with Cerberus before........................... 75.00
Marcus Aurelius, 161-180. Alexandria, Egypt. Billon Tetradrachm. Tyche std. 40.00

Septimius Severus, 193-211. Nicopolis, Moesia Inferior. AE26. Dionysus stg. naked holding pitcher and staff... 25.00
Elagabalus, 218-222. Nicaea, Bithynia, Asia Minor. AE20. Three military standards..... 20.00
Severus Alexander, 222-235. Alexandria Troas, Asia Minor. AE22. Horse feeding r. 22.00

Gordian III, 238-44. Odessus, Thrace. AE27. Confronted heads of Gordian and Sarapis / Sarapis stg. with modius on head 75.00
Philip I, 244-49. Viminacium, Moesia Inferior. Female between bull and lion. 25.00

Gallienus, 253-268. Side, Pamphylia. AE30. Bust over eagle / Apollo stg. 60.00

BYZANTINE

Byzantine is the name historians have given to the Eastern Roman Empire, which did not fall in the fifth century like the Western part, but continued on for another thousand years. As far as the gold coinage is concerned, there is little difference between early Byzantine and late Roman coinage. What little silver was struck was also initially on the late Roman standard.

The copper coinage underwent a fundamental change under Anastasius in 498, and it is for this reason that numismatists usually call him the first Byzantine emperor. (Other historians often do not.) Before Anastasius there was only one copper coin, the *nummus* (an AE4), and if a moderate purchase was made a bag of them had to be traded. This awkwardness was ended when the emperor introduced a whole range of copper denominations, up to forty nummi. This coin, called a *follis*, formed the basis of Byzantine minor coinage until 1092, almost six hundred years. Initially it was very easy to tell the denominations of Byzantine copper, because they were written in very large Greek numbers on the reverse. They were valued in nummi as:

Follis	M	40
	ΛΓ	33
3/4 Follis	Λ	30
Half Follis	K	20
	IS	16
	IB	12
Decanummium	I	10
	S	6
Pentanummium	E	5
	Γ	3
Two Nummi	B	2
Nummus	A	1

Those denominations in *italics* were not used throughout the empire, but were struck to meet special local needs, mostly in Egypt.

One satisfying aspect of Byzantine coin collecting is that they can often be dated to an exact year. The dates are usually not by any calendar, but indicate the reigning year of the emperor.

There were many mints as well and most of them placed mintmarks very clearly on the reverse. A letter, indicating the workshop within the mint, called an *officina* often followed the mintmark. Some of the most common mint marks are:

Some Byzantine Mint Marks

ΑΛεΖ............................... Alexandria, Egypt
ANTIX .... Antioch, Syria
CAT ....Catania, Sicily
CON ....Constantinople, Turkey
KART ....Carthage, Tunisia
KYZ .... Cyzicus, Turkey
NIKO............................Nicomedia, Turkey
RAV.. Ravenna, Italy
ROM...Rome, Italy
SCL ....Syracuse, Sicily
TES, ΘεC .... Thessalonica, Greece
THEUP.............Theoupolis (Antioch), Syria

Byzantine coins usually depict the emperor, alone or with his family. Notable in Byzantine coin design is a vast array of religious iconography. Among the most popular, then and now, was the bust of Christ. The Virgin Mary was also very common, as well as a host of other patron saints. Emperors often depicted a saint with whom they shared a name. A cross on steps was used particularly frequently on silver, sometimes with a medallion at the center containing either the emperor or Christ. Most Byzantine emperors have a distinctive monogram and very often only knowing what these monograms look like can distinguish a coin of one from that of another.

Some designs consisted of nothing but an inscription. It was inevitably a title, either of

the reigning emperor or of Christ. The latter usually translates either "Christ Conquers," or "Jesus Christ King of Kings."

The most unusual Byzantine coins are cup shaped. Called scyphate, they exist of bullion, silver, electrum and gold. They should not be mistaken for damaged as they were made like this deliberately.

Known counterfeits: Byzantine gold is remarkably common. Nevertheless, so are quality counterfeits. The letter forms and shade of color are often hints. Counterfeits of other metals are far less common.

BOOKS ABOUT BYZANTINE COINS

Grierson, Philip. *Byzantine Coins.*
Sear, David. *Byzantine Coins and their Values.*

> Values for Greek coins are for Very Fine examples for gold (**AV**) and silver (**AR**), Fine for bronze and copper (**AE**).

Note: Byzantine copper is frequently found in lower grades than Fine condition, which is priced here.

Anastasius I, 491-518. AE Half Follis. Bust r. / Large K, stars at sides, cross above, CON at bottom 20.00

Justin I, 518-527 AE Follis. Bust r. / Large M, stars at sides, cross above, CON at bottom........ 30.00
Justin I and Justinian, 527. AE Follis. Facing busts of two emperors / Large M, stars at sides, cross above, ANTIX at bottom................ 300.00

Justinian I, 527-565. AE Follis. Facing, helmeted bust of Justinian / Large M, cross above, ANNO l., XXXI r., THUP below 35.00
Justin II, 565-578. AE Pentanummium. Monogram / ε... 15.00
Tiberius II Constantine, 578-582. AE Decanummium. Crowned bust facing / Large X, small cross above. 30.00
Maurice Tiberius, 582-602. AV Solidus. Helmeted facing bust / Angel standing facing 275.00
__. AE Follis. Crowned facing bust / Large M, ANNO l., III r., cross above, THEUP below. 20.00

Phocas, 602-610. AE Follis. Crowned bust facing / large XXXX, ANNO above, CONR below 25.00
Heraclius, 610-641. AR Hexagram. Two emperors enthroned / Cross on globe on steps 200.00
Constans II, 641-668. AE Follis. Constans stg. facing / Large M, ANA l., NεOS r., * above 12.00

Constantine IV, 668-685. AE Follis. Constantine stg. with spear / Large M, monogram above, emperors at sides..40.00
Justinian II, 685-695 & 705-711. AE Follis. Emperor stg. facing / Large M, monogram above, SCL below 45.00
Leontius, 695-698. AE Follis. Facing bust of emperor / Large M, monogram above, SCL below 200.00
Tiberius III, 698-705. AE Follis. Facing bust of emperor / Large M, monogram above, palm branch on each side 110.00

Philippicus, 711-713. AV Solidus. Facing bust with globus and eagle scepter / Cross on steps 950.00

Anastasius II, 713-715. AE Follis. Facing bust of emperor / Large M, monogram above, palm branch on each side 250.00

Theodosius III, 715-717. AE Half Follis. Facing bust of emperor / Large K, ANNO l., II r., cross above 250.00

Leo III, 717-741. AE Follis. Leo stg. ΛεON l., ΔεCΠ r. / Emperor stg., KωNS l., ΔεCΠ r. 30.00

Constantine V, 741-775. AE Follis. Busts of two emperors / Facing bust of emperor holding cross potent 30.00

Leo IV, 775-780. AE Follis. Busts of two emperors / Bust of two emperors B A at sides, Large M between X N below 40.00

Constantine VI, 780-797. AE Follis. Facing bust of Empress Irene / Facing bust of emperor over large M 150.00

Irene, 797-802. AV Solidus. Bust of Irene / Bust of Irene 2,400.00

Nicephorus I, 802-811. AE Follis. Facing bust of Nicephorus holding cross potent, N IKH around / Bust of Stauracius, C TAV around 35.00

Michael I, 811-813. AE Follis. Busts of two emperors / Large M, XXX l., NNN r. 35.00

Leo V, 813-820. AE Follis. Busts of two emperors / Large ΛK 30.00

Michael II, 820-829. AE Follis. Busts of two emperors, MIXAHL S ΘεOΛ / Large M, Θ below........................ 30.00

Theophilus, 829-42. AE Follis. Facing bust of emperor, ΘεOFILOS bAS / Large M, XXX l., NNN r., Θ below 30.00

Michael III, 842-867. AE Follis. Facing bust of emperor, MIXAHL b / Large M, Θ below 40.00

Basil I, 867-886. AV Solidus. Christ enthroned facing / Basil and Constantine holding patriarchal cross between them 300.00

Leo VI, 886-912. AE Follis. Facing bust of emperor / +LεOn εn ΘεO bASILεVS ROMεOn 30.00

Alexander, 912-913. AV Solidus. Christ enthroned facing / Alexander stg. crowned by St. Alexander.................. 35,000.00

Constantine VII, 913-959. AV Solidus. Facing bust of Christ / Facing busts of Constantine VII and Romanus II........................ 400.00

Romanus I, 920-944. AE Follis. Facing bust of emperor / +RωmAn εn Θεw bASILεVS RωMAIωn 30.00

Romanus II, 959-963. AE17mm. Monogram / cross on steps, pellet each side 50.00

Nicephorus II, 963-969. AR Miliaresion. Cross on steps, bust of emperor at center / +NICHF εN Xω AVTOCRAT εVSεb bASILεVS RωMAIω...150.00

John I, 969-976. AR Miliaresion. Cross on steps, bust of emperor at center / +IωANN εN Xω AVTOCRAT εVSεB BASILεVS RωMAIω 150.00

Basil II, 976-1025. AV Histamenon Nomisma. Bust of Christ facing / Facing busts of Basil II and Constantine VIII holding patriarchal cross between them. 350.00

Anonymous, c.969-1028. AE Follis. Bust of Christ facing / +IhSUS XRISTUS BASILEU BASILE.................................25.00

Constantine VIII, 1025-1028. AV Histamenon Nomisma. Bust of Christ facing / Bust of emperor 300.00

Romanus III, 1028-1034. AV Histamenon Nomisma. Christ enthroned / Emperor stg. crowned by the Virgin 300.00

Michael IV, 1034-1041. AV Histamenon Nomisma. Bust of Christ facing / Bust of emperor. scyphate. 500.00

Constantine IX, 1042-55. AV Histamenon Nomisma. Bust of Christ facing / Bust of emperor. scyphate. 300.00

__. similar but stars in rev. field 950.00

Theodora, 1055-56. AV Histamenon Nomisma. Christ stg. / Theodora and the Virgin stg. holding standard between them. scyphate. 1,000.00

Michael VI, 1056-57. AV Tetarteron Nomisma. Facing bust of the Virgin / Michael stg. with long cross. 950.00

Isaac I, 1057-59. AV Histamenon Nomisma. Christ enthroned / Emperor stg. holding sword. scyphate 375.00

Constantine X, 1059-1067. AV Histamenon Nomisma. Christ enthroned / Emperor stg. holding standard and globus. scyphate ... 250.00

Romanus IV, 1068-71. AE Follis. Bust of Christ facing / C R P Δ in angles of cross 28.00

Michael VII, 1071-1078. AE Follis. Bust of Christ facing / Bust of Michael holding standard 28.00

Nicephorus III, 1078-1081. AE Follis. Figure of Christ / C Φ N Δ in angles of cross 25.00

Alexius I, 1081-1118. Electrum AV Histamenon Nomisma. Christ enthroned / Facing bust of emperor holding cross and globus. scyphate........................ 200.00

John II, 1118-1143. AE Tetarteron. Christ stg. / John stg........................ 15.00

Manuel I, 1143-80. AE Half Tetarteron. Bust of Manuel / Monogram 15.00

Andronicus I, 1183-1185. Billon Aspron Trachy. Virgin stg. facing / Emperor stg. crowned by Christ. Scyphate 25.00

Isaac II, 1185-95. Billon Aspron Trachy. Virgin enthroned / Emperor stg. scyphate 15.00

Alexius III, 1195-1203. Billon Aspron Trachy. Bust of Christ / Emperor and St. Constantine stg. scyphate 12.00

From 1204 to 1261 the Byzantine Empire was submerged by the Crusader states.

Michael VIII, 1261-1282. AE Trachy. Archangel Michael stg. / Emperor stg. scyphate.........20.00

Andronicus II, 1282-1328. AV Hyperpyron. The Virgin within city walls / Christ crowning Andronicus and Michael. scyphate 200.00

Andronicus III, 1328-1341. AE Assarion. Bust of St. George / Bust of Emperor 75.00

John V, 1341-1391. AR 1/16 Hyperpyron. Bust of Christ / Bust of John. 200.00

Manuel II, 1391-1423. AE Follaro. Christ stg. in ellipse / Manuel II stg. 60.00

John VIII, 1423-1448. AR Stavraton. Bust of Christ / Bust of emperor 100.00

Constantine XI, 1448-1453. AR Quarter Hyperpyron. Bust of Christ / Bust of emperor 8,000.00

__. Similar but Sixteenth Hyperpyron 2,000.00

MEDIEVAL & RENAISSANCE COINS

Among the best opportunities for the collector to buy historically interesting European coins at a minimal price are the coins of the Middle Ages. The Middle Ages were the centuries between the fall of the Roman Empire and the resurgence of Western Civilization with the Renaissance. Except for the earliest period, called the Dark Ages, the typical medieval coin is very thin, and made of silver (sometimes debased) or gold. They are poorly hand struck with crude hand engraved dies. Usually the metal does not flow evenly into the dies. Because of this, many coins appear to have spots worn out even if they are mint state. Because of this, many collectors prefer exceptionally well struck middle grade coins over exceptionally high grade pieces with normal strikes.

Medieval civilization existed during a period initiated by a significant governmental and technological decline. This can readily be seen in the coinage. The practice of realistic portraiture had been abandoned by the beginning of the Middle Ages, and completely lost soon after. Medieval coin portraits vary from simplified, generic portraits — which remained unchanged from decade to decade — down to a crude assemblage of dots and dashes, purporting to be a human. The inscription on medieval coins are often illiterate, reflecting the wrote copying of poor grammar, or at worst complete gibberish. In virtually every case, the actual or attempted language was Latin, the language of the collapsed Roman Empire. The medieval Europeans pined for its stable government and extended civilization, and it was the standard by which many later institutions were judged.

THE EVOLUTION OF MEDIEVAL COINAGE

Medieval coins evolved in stages, although some countries evolved more slowly than others. The Carolingian penny (also called denier, pfennig, denaro) and its descendants continued as the primary coin in Western Europe until at least the 1200s, though it was debased in many countries. From its introduction onward, one iconographic innovation spread like wildfire: an equally armed cross dominated one side. This continued as the dominant design in many lands almost until modern times. It not only had religious connotations, but was a convenient guide by which to cut a coin into halves or quarters to make small change.

As the European economy expanded in the late Middle Ages, the need for larger valued coins arose. During the 1200s, many multiples of the denier were introduced, some worth 4, 12 or even 24 deniers. Called by various names, meaning "of great size" such as groat, gros, groschen or grosso, most were of similar sizes, with a 24 denier grosso simply meaning that the issuing state had suffered more inflation than the state striking the 4 denier grosso. In the following century gold was re-introduced into the expanding economy in a big way. Some of the larger gold coins of the 1300s and 1400s, engraved in the Gothic style of art, are among the most exquisite examples of medieval engraving available. The complexity of their designs not only helped discourage counterfeiting, but today provides an important primary source for the study of medieval iconography and history.

The word renaissance means rebirth. Much of this economic rebirth can already been seen in European coinage before the actual Renaissance in the 1400s, but there were other changes not purely economic. This period included the reintroduction of realistic portraiture. The newly developed heavy silver coins, the Testone (1471-73, Venice; 1474, Milan) and the silver dollar sized taler (1486, Tyrol) permitted the artists great opportunity to exercise their talents in depicting their princes and lords. Indicating specific dates became common on coins in the 1500s. Before this, only the name of the king and the design served to identify the age of a coin.

Perhaps more than any other period, the value of a medieval coin can vary by quality of strike. Depending on the series, one grade difference in preservation can change the value anywhere from 30 to 200 percent. When these combine one realizes that the values of such coins are very subjective and vary based on aesthetic tastes. It should be remembered that coins of either exceptionally poor strike or those that are poorly preserved can be worth a fraction of the prices listed.

BOOKS ABOUT MEDIEVAL COINS

Erslev, Kristian. *Medieval Coins in the Christian J. Thomsen Collection.* The only general catalogue of Western European medieval coins in print.

Grierson, Philip. *Coins of Medieval Europe.* Well illustrated text by a venerable authority. Indispensable.

Walker, Ralph. *Reading Medieval European Coins.* Inexpensive and an excellent first step.

> Medieval coins listed are silver (**AR**) and silver colored silver alloys, of 15 to 25 mm. diameter unless noted. Gold is indicated **AV**, copper **AE**, and copper colored base silver is **Billon**

THE DARK AGES

When the barbarian tribes overran the Roman Empire, they not only adopted the remaining fragments of Roman civilization, but attempted to continue the already declining Roman coinage in their own rough way.

During the final stage of Western Roman coinage, silver and large bronze had become scarce. The only small coin actually circulating was the tiny copper nummus, often no broader than a pea! Roman society had become militarized and gold was necessary to pay the troops, so coinage in that metal survived intact. The solidus, a nickel-sized coin equal to 1/72 of a Roman pound of gold was struck, along with its half, the semis, and third, the tremissis. These coins were the pattern the barbarians tried to imitate. Because skilled engravers and mint administrators were not available to the barbarians, the coins soon degenerated in both appearance and purity. Ultimately, the images on these coins became scarcely recognizable as human. Surprisingly, the invaders acknowledged the primacy of the eastern Roman (Byzantine) Emperor on most of their gold coins. It was over a century before barbarian kings would strike coins exclusively in their own names.

The most Romanized of the barbaric tribes was the Ostrogoths. They conquered Italy in 493 and went to great efforts to preserve the Roman structures of government, even while they were fighting against the Eastern Roman armies. Their coins were faithful to Roman artistic form and quality, and of relatively good purity. They even permitted municipal copper coins under the Roman Senate and Ravenna.

The Vandals migrated through Italy, Gaul and Spain, eventually conquering Roman North Africa. Their first improvised coins were made by simply scraping new values onto worn Roman coins. After settling in around Carthage, their coins took on more conventional forms, sometimes calling attention to the former glories of their captive city. Still, the allegories sometimes did not mature beyond complex stick figures, which only somewhat improved before they were subdued and North Africa was reincorporated into the eastern Roman Empire.

The Visigoths conquered Roman Spain in the 470s. Visigothic coins in any metal but gold are very rare. Their first coins were close imitations of Roman solidi but they progressively degenerated. Eventually the portraiture became so crude that it became a mere abstraction of lines and curves. The reverse image of a winged victory became progressively more insect-like!

As barbarian invaders go, the Lombards were latecomers. They arrived in Italy as the Byzantines were taking the peninsula back from the Ostrogoths. They established a kingdom in the north, based at Pavia. They also founded a smaller duchy in the south at Beneventum. Their stylized and simple coins were distinctive in their wide flans and broad annular borders.

The barbarians who finally dominated Gaul were the Merovingian Franks. Most of their coins were derived from the small gold tremissis introduced in late Roman times. Their tremisses were small, base and among the crudest of all. By the eighth century, this popular coin had become so corrupted it was mostly silver alloy. The patron saint of numismatists, St. Eligius, was a blacksmith pressed into service as a minter for one of the Merovingian kings.

Additional Specialized Books: Grierson and Blackburn, *Medieval European Coinage I: The Early Middle Ages.*

Roberts, James. *The Silver Coins of Medieval France.* Updated Merovingian coverage.

Known counterfeits: There are a few nineteenth century counterfeits of these coins, mostly of Visigothic gold.

ARMENIA

Ancient Armenia reasserted itself from Byzantine and Moslem domination as a result of the Crusades. It was raised from a barony to a kingdom in 1198. While there is some Western influence, the overall appearance of these coins is quite distinctive, including a unique alphabet. One must be able to read the inscriptions to identify some of these coins. They are usually weakly struck. Coins are valued here in F as an average, but silver is usually found in higher grades, copper, Very Good or worse.

Additional Specialized Books: Nercessian, Y.T., *Armenian Coins and their Values.*

Known counterfeits: While there is an array of counterfeits for this series, they are not frequently encountered.

BARONY   F

Roupen I, 1080-95. AE20 Cross / Cross 200.00
Toros I, 1100-1123. AE18 Similar 650.00
Toros II, 1144-68. AE18. Cross / Castle 700.00
Roupen II, 1175-87. AE21. Castle / Cross.... 800.00
Levon II, 1187-98. AE24. Knight riding l. /
    Cross 250.00

KINGDOM   VF

Levon I, 1198-1218. Tram. King enthroned / Two
    lions rampant, cross between 22.00
Hetoum, 1226-1270. Tram. Hetoum and Queen
    Zabel stg. / Lion r. 22.00
Levon II, 1270-89. Tram. King riding r. /
    Lion l. 25.00

Hetoum II, 1289-1305. AE Kardez. King std. facing
    on pillow / Cross (22mm).......................... 20.00
Smpad, 1296-98. AE Pough. King riding r. /
    Cross 22.00
Gosdantin I, 1298-99. AE Kardez. King standing /
    Cross 125.00

KINGDOM   VF

Levon III, 1301-07. AE Kardez. King std. facing /
    Cross 25.00
Oshin, 1308-20. AE Pough. Similar but
    smaller......................... 25.00
Levon IV, 1320-42. Takvorin. King riding r. / Lion
    walking r. 25.00
Guy, 1342-44. Takvorin. Similar 60.00
Gosdantin III, 1344-63. Takvorin. Similar 25.00
Gosdantin IV, 1365-73. Takvorin. Similar....... 30.00
Levon V, 1374-75. AE Pough. Lion r. /
    Cross 40.00

AUSTRIA

The first Austrian coins were struck to capitalize on local silver mines around the 1150s. It was in the 1190s, however, when the Vienna mint got its big boost: It had the opportunity to strike some of the many tons of silver paid to the Austrian duke by England as ransom for the freedom of Richard the Lionheart. Most Austrian coins of the 1200s through 1400s were small silver pfennigs. They were square-shaped, very crude, and usually the design of the reverse was effaced in the manufacturing process. One almost never encounters a completely struck example. Values given below are for average crude strikes.

Improvement came in the last half of the fifteenth century with better striking methods, larger denominations and the introduction of real portraits. The artistic quality of the coinage continued to develop through the Renaissance and Baroque periods, co-inciding with the dynastic expansion of the Austrian empire. Many of the Austrian mints striking coins in the 1600s are today far outside the borders on modern Austria. Some coins from this era are truly impressive. During this era coins were usually struck on "roller dies" causing the coins to have a slightly curved appearance. This is not damage and does not detract from the value of a coin.

Various nobles, both of the House of Hapsburg and of lesser houses were authorized to strike coins. This practice did not end until Napoleonic times.

Additional Specialized Books: Metcalf, D.M. *Coinage of South Germany.*

Miller zu Aichholz, *Oesterreichische Munzpragungen, 1519-1938.*

Szego, Alfred. *Coinage of Medieval Austria, 1156-1521.*

Known counterfeits: Counterfeiting is generally not widespread in this series.

                                     F

Heinrich II, 1156-77. Pfennig. Tree / Lion r............
Leopold VI, 1198-1230. Pfennig. Panther r. under
    tree / Eagle, hd. r. 35.00

Ottokar II, 1261-76. Pfennig. Dog running l., tree in
    background / Head between eagles 15.00

                                       F

Albrecht I, 1282-1308. Pfennig. Unicorn / Towers
    over arch......................... 15.00
Frederick the Handsome, 1308-30. Pfennig. Squirrel / Eagle in arched border...................... 15.00
Albrecht III, 1358-97. Pfennig. Ram's head /
    blank 15.00

Frederich V (III), 1436-93. Pfennig. F R I around
    shield 15.00
Ferdinand I, 1521-64. Sechser. Crowned bust r. /
    Cross, shield in each angle........................ 75.00
Rudolf II, 1576-1612. Taler. Bust r. / Crowned
    shield 150.00

Ferdinand II, 1619-37. 3 Kreuzer. Bust r. / Three
    shields......................... 30.00

SALZBURG   F

Eberhard II, 1200-46. Pfennig. εBεRHARDS εPS,
    Bishop facing between fleur-scepters / Bust
    between steeples, tower behind   30.00
Mathäus Lang, 1519-40. Zweier. Two shields, Cardinal's hat above, 40 below, all in three-arched
    border 12.00

TYROL   F

Sigismund, 1439-96. Sechser. Crowned bust r. /
    Long cross, shields in angles 75.00
__. Kreuzer. Double cross / Eagle................... 15.00

BALKANS

The medieval Balkan states consisted primarily of Serbia and Zeta (in modern Yugoslavia), Slavonia and Ragusa (in modern Croatia), Moldavia, Transylvania and Wallachia (in modern Romania), Bosnia, and Bulgaria. Most of their coinages first developed in the later Middle Ages. These evolved in the shadow of the declining Byzantine Empire, while it was under heavy commercial domination by the West, Balkan coinages reflect these two influences. Generally, the denominations, metals and form of the coins reflect Venetian and Hungarian influence. This is partly due to the wide availability of silver in this mining region. The art, however, can be pure Byzantine. Medieval Balkan coinages were prevented from reaching their fullest development by the Ottoman invasions, which also put an end to the Byzantine Empire.

Transylvania, though today part of Romania, was very closely tied to Hungary. Its coinage, first beginning during the Renaissance, usually follows Hungarian and occasionally Polish standards.

Many coins previously considered rare in the west are now available due to the opening of trade with Eastern Europe. Prices have dropped precipitously on a few of the most common types, but only slightly on most others.

The names for some denominations vary from authority to authority.

Additional Specialized Books: Buzdugan, et al. *Monede si Bancinote Romanesti.*

Dochev, Konstantin. *МОНЕТИ И ПАРИЧНО ОБРЪЩЕНИЕ В ТЪРНОВО XII-XIV в*

Jovanovic, *Srpski Srednjevekovni Novac.*
Metcalf, *Coinage of South Eastern Europe.*
Rengjeo, *Corpus der Mittelalterlichen Munzen von Kroatien, Slavenien, Dalmatien und Bosnien.*
Resch, A. *Siebenbürgische Münzen und Medaillen.*

Known counterfeits: Until recently there have been few, but several types have been produced in quantity at workshops in Eastern Europe since the mid-1990s. These include coins of Mircea the Old of Wallachia, Alexander the Good of Moldavia, and Ivan Alexander of Bulgaria.

BOSNIA VF

Tvrtko II, 1420-43. Grosch. Elaborate crest on angled shield / St. Gregory stg. 175.00
Thomas Ostojic, 1443-61. Grosch. Similar... 175.00
Nikola Ilocki, 1471-77. Denar. Shield / Madonna and Child.................... 300.00

BULGARIA VF

Ivan Asen I, 1218-41. Grosch. Saint giving banner to Ivan / Christ enthroned........................ 300.00
Constantine Tikh, 1255-77. AE Trachy. Bust of Christ / Tsar riding r. scyphate. 100.00
George I, 1280-92. Grosch. St. George giving banner to George / Christ enthroned............. 500.00
Teodor Svetoslav, 1300-30. Grosch. Christ enthroned / Tsar stg. 250.00
Michael III, 1323-30. AE Trachy. Monogram / Michael and Ivan, cross between. scyphate.................... 125.00

Ivan Alexander, 1331-71. Grosch. Two tsars stg. / Christ enthroned. Very linear style art 40.00
Ivan Stratzimir, 1370-1396. Grosch. King std. / Bust of Christ........................ 30.00

BULGARIA VF

Ivan Shishman, 1371-93. Gros, reduced standard. Bust of Madonna and child, barbarically engraved / Tsar stg. 25.00

CATTARO F

Venetian period. Folar, 1492-1565. St. Trifon stg. / Bust of winged lion, small shield below. .. 50.00

MOLDAVIA F

Alexander the Good, 1400-23. Billon Half Grosch. Bull's head / Shield.................... 35.00

RAGUSA VF

Anonymous, 1300-1500. Grosso. St. Blasius stg. / Christ stg. in ellipse. 75.00
—, 1600-1700s. Grosetto. Similar but smaller...................... 40.00

SERBIA VF

Anonymous, 1270s-1320s. Grosch. St. Mark giving banner to Doge / Christ enthroned. This is a slightly smaller imitation of a Venetian grosso of 1268-75..................... 65.00
Stefan V Dragutin, 1276-1282. Dinar. St. Stephen giving banner to Dragutin / Christ enthroned....................... 90.00

Stefan VI Milutin, 1282-1321. Dinar. Similar. 90.00
Stefan VII Decanski, 1321-31. Dinar. Christ enthroned / Decanski std. with sword on lap..................... 135.00
Stefan VIII Dusan, 1331-55. Dinar. Helm with elaborate crest / Christ enthroned.................... 90.00
Stefan IX, 1355-71. Dinar. Two rulers, patriarchal cross between / Helm with elaborate crest 90.00
Vukashin, 1366-71. Dinar. Christ enthroned / Five line legend.................... 125.00

St. Lazar, 1371-89. Dinar. Lazar stg. / Christ stg. in ellipse 85.00
Vuk Brankovic, 1389-97. Dinar. Vuk stg. / Christ enthroned 125.00
George Brankovic, 1427-56. Dinar. Monogram / Lion 85.00

SLAVONIA F

Various Governors, 1200s. Denar. Martin running l., stars above and below / Patriarchal cross between two crowned heads..................... 35.00

TRANSYLVANIA VF

John Zapolya, 1527-40. Denar. Arms / Madonnna and Child..................... 40.00
Stephan Bocskai, 1604-06. 3 Groschen. Bust r. / Inscription 85.00

TRANSYLVANIA VF

Gabriel Bathori, 1608-13. Groschen. Ducal crown / Eagle..................... 75.00
Gabriel Bethlen, 1613-29. Breit- groschen. Shield / Madonna and Child within rays 60.00

WALLACHIA VF

Radu I, 1377-83. Ducat. Shield / Eagle on helm..................... 85.00
Dan I, 1383-86. Ducat. Similar....................... 75.00

Mircea the Old, 1386-1418. Ducat. Mircea stg. / Elaborate crest on angled shield. Mircea was Dracula's grandfather. 95.00

ZETA VF

Balscha III, 1405-21. Grosch. Elaborate crest on angled shield / BALSE D GORGI, St. Lawrence stg. 500.00

BALTIC

The coinage of the medieval Baltic follows three paths. The greatest strand of this cord is coinage of the Grand Dukes of Lithuania. Lithuania was a very large state during this period, reaching far inland. In 1386, as a result of its grand duke's marriage to Poland's queen, its crown was united with that of Poland, but it still retained its own identity and coinage. Not only was its coinage abundant through most of the fifteenth through the seventeenth centuries, it has become a very inexpensive way of obtaining interesting Renaissance portraiture.

Another important contributor to the development of Baltic coinage are the issues of the knights of the Teutonic and Livonian orders, who conquered these territories in order to convert the mostly Slavic pagans.

There was also city coinage, mostly from Riga (today in Latvia). During the Baroque period Sweden conquered much of the Baltic, and continued to produce some of the city coinage, along with some other related issues. These coins were usually struck with roller dies and are usually either slightly curved or off center.

At present Baltic coinage is abundant in the marketplace.

Additional Specialized Books: Davenport, John. *East Baltic Regional Coinage.*

Gumowski, M. *Handbuch des Polnischen Numismatik.* Convenient for the issues of Lithuania after 1386.

Known counterfeits: Counterfeits of the Swedish issues were struck in Romania in the 1600s. They have some collector value.

DORPAT F

Dietrich II, 1379-1400. Schilling. TIRICVS €PV, Facing head of bishop / Crossed key and sword..................... 65.00

LITHUANIA VF

Anonymous, 1370s-1430s. Denar. Spear head, cross at side / Stylized castle.................... 275.00

LITHUANIA
VF

Alexander, 1501-06. Half Groschen. Knight riding
l. / Eagle 35.00
Sigismund I, 1506-48. Half Groschen. Knight
riding l. Eagle 35.00

Sigismund II, 1547-72. Half Groschen. Eagle /
Knight riding l..35.00

F

John Casimir, 1649-68. AE Schilling (Solidus)
Head r. / Horseman riding l. 12.00

LIVONIAN ORDER
VF

Anonymous, 1400s. Schilling. Shield / Cross, three
pellets in each angle. 75.00
Bernd of the Borg, 1471-83. Schilling. Three birds
on shield / Long cross.............................. 75.00

RIGA
VF

City, 1566-79. Billon Schilling. City gate / Crossed
keys. 35.00

Sigismund III, 1587-1632. 3 Groschen. Crowned
bust r. / City gate amid inscription. ....
Christina of Sweden, 1632-54. Billon Schilling
(Solidus). Sheaf in crowned C / Crossed keys on
shield... 20.00

TEUTONIC ORDER
VF

Anonymous, c.1250. Hohlpfennig. Cross on shield.
bracteate... 65.00

Paul of Russdorf, 1422-41. Schilling. MAGS PAV-
LVS PRIM, Shield on cross / Cross on
shield.. 65.00
Friedrich of Saxony, 1498-1510. Groschen. MAGI
STER FRID ICVS, as above................... 100.00

BOHEMIA

Bohemia, now roughly the Czech Repub-
lic, was one of the earliest civilized and Chris-
tianized of the north Slavic states. Its original
coins, struck by Boleslav I c.955, were silver
denars, similar to the deniers introduced by
Charlemagne. In the 1040s the coins began to
shrink somewhat. The quality and diversity of
the engraving on these small coins became
notable during the following century.

After the discovery of major silver
reserves in 1298, Bohemia became a major
coinage exporter. The large coin made from
this silver, the Prager Groschen, became an
internationally traded coin in Central Europe
during the Middle Ages. Bohemia was inherited by the Hapsburg empire in 1526, but
retained a separate coinage for centuries.

Cach, F. *Nejstar i _eské mince* 3 vols.

Fiala, E. *Sammlung böhmischer Münzen
& Medaillen Max Donebauer.*

VF

Bretislaw I, 1037-55. Denar. King stg. holding flag /
St. Wenceslaus std. with cross, cross r. ... 125.00
Wratislas II, 1086-92. Denar. Crowned bust r. /
Hand l. holding banner., small
building r. 90.00
Premysl I, 1192-1230. Denar. Angel spearing
demon / Bust in building 95.00
Wladislaus I, 1109-25. Denar. Duke std. between
two knights / Bust of St. Wenceslaus 90.00

F

John the Blind, 1310-46. Prager groschen. Crown
within double legend / Double tailed
lion... 40.00
Charles IV, 1346-78. AV Florin. Crowned bust fac-
ing / Double tailed lion l. 1,200.00
Anonymous, 1440-71. Pfennig. Double tailed lion l.
/ blank 15.00
Wladislaus II, 1471-1516. Prager groschen. Crown
within double legend / Double tailed
lion. 25.00
Louis I, 1516-26. Pfennig. Double tailed lion l. /
blank... 15.00
Ferdinand I, 1526-64. Prager groschen. Crown
within double legend / Double tailed
lion. 25.00
Rudolf, 1576-1612. Maly Groschen. Double tailed
lion l. / Crowned R, MALY GROSS 25.00

CRUSADER

The Crusaders carved out new states in
the territories they conquered, beginning in
1098. These mostly clustered in two areas:
the coast of the eastern Mediterranean (modern Israel, Lebanon and Syria) and the
former Byzantine lands (modern Greece,
Cyprus, and western Turkey).

The first coins used by the Crusaders were
mostly common deniers carried over from
France and elsewhere in western Europe, combined with local Byzantine copper and Islamic
silver and gold. When they started striking their
own coinage it reflected these influences.

Byzantine style coinage was soon abandoned. Some of the coins with Arabic inscriptions are easily identified by a cross or Roman
letters, but the more faithful imitations require
an expert to discern from true Arabic coins. The
Western European style coins, while somewhat
crude, are both common and popular.

After the Muslim conquered the Crusader
Middle East again, some Crusader states survived in Cyprus, Rhodes and the Greek Islands.
Additional Specialized Books: Malloy, Pre-
ston and Seltman. *Coins of the Crusader
States.* A convenient price guide keyed to the
reference numbers used in this book is also
available.

Known counterfeits: While few counterfeits of
these coins have been made to fool collectors,
some contemporary counterfeits are known.

ACHAEA
F

William, 1245-78. Denier tournois. G: PRINCE
ΛCh, Cross / CLΛRENTIΛ, Stylized
castle 25.00
Philip of Taranto, 1306-13. Denier tournois. PhS P
ACh TAR DR, Cross / D CLAReNCIA, Styl-
ized castle 25.00
Maud, 1316-18. Denier tournois. MΛhΛVTΛ P ΛCh,
Cross / De CLAReNCIΛ, Stylized castle ... 25.00

ANTIOCH
F

Bohemond I, 1098-1204. AE Follis. Θ ΠETPOC,
Bust of St. Peter / Cross, B H M T in
angles 300.00
Roger, 1112-19. AE Follis. Christ stg. / Cross, DNE
SAL FT RO in angles 60.00
Raymond, 1136-49. Denier. RAMVDVS, Head r. /
ANTIOCHIE, Cross 100.00
Bohemond III, minority 1149-1163. Denier. BOAM-
VNDVS, Crude head r. with swept back hair /
ANTIOCHIA, Cross................................... 65.00

__, majority 1163-1201. Denier. BOAMVNDVS,
Helmeted head wearing chain-mail l. / ANTIO-
CHIA., Cross, crescent in one angle.......... 35.00
Raymond Roupen, 1216-19. Denier. RVPINVS,
Helmeted head wearing chain-mail l. / AMTIO-
CHIA., Cross, crescent in one angle........ 125.00
Anonymous, 1200s. AE Pougeoise. Fleur /
Cross..40.00

ATHENS
F

William, 1280-87. Denier. G DVX ATENES, Cross
/ THEBE CIVIS..25.00

CYPRUS VF

Hugh IV, 1324-59. Gros grand. hVGVε RεI Dε, King enthroned facing / Cross, * in each angle 125.00

BEIRUT F

Raymond, 1148-86. AE Pougeoise. TVRRIS, Tower of David / DAVIT, Star.................. 90.00

EDESSA F

Baldwin II, 1108-18. AE Follis. ΒΑΛΔΟΙΝ, Count stg. / Cross ending in floral scroll at base 150.00

EPIRUS F

Philip of Taranto, 1294-1313. Denier tournois. PhS P ACh TAR DR, Cross / NEPANTI CIVIS, Stylized castle.. 30.00

JERUSALEM F

Baldwin III, 1143-63. Denier. BALdVINVS REX, Cross / Tower of David.............................. 45.00

Amaury, 1163-74. Denier. AMALRICVS REX, Cross / Church of the Holy Sepulchre 50.00
Anonymous, 1100s. AV Cut fragment. Hexagram / Gate. No intact example of these coins exist. 75.00
__, 1200s. Dirham. Arabic inscription in hexagram, after type of Aleppo.................................. 25.00

LATIN CONSTANTINOPLE F

Anonymous, 1204-19. AE Trachy. MP ΘV, Virgin enthroned facing / ΜΛΝΟVΗΛ ΔΕΠΟΤΗC, Byzantine style emperor stg. 13.00

RHODES VF

Robert de Juilly, 1374-1377. Gigliato. Grandmaster kneeling l. before cross / Floral cross 225.00

SIDON F

Balian Grenier, 1204-40. Billon Denier. DENIER, Cross / DESEETE, Cathedral.................. 200.00

TRIPOLI VF

Raymond II-III, 1136-1187. AV Dinar. pseudo-Arabic inscriptions in four lines and around.....300.00
Bohemond VII, 1275-87. Gros. Cross in arched border / Three towered gateway in arched border 125.00

TYRE F

Philip, 1243-70. AE Pougeoise. PhELIPε, Cross / DE SVR, Temple 200.00

FRANCE

By the eighth century the most popular medieval coin in the West, the gold tremissis, had become so corrupted it was mostly silver alloy. The Caroligian King of the Franks refined this coinage. He introduced a large, relatively pure silver denarius or denier of dependable weight. When the powerful Frankish King, Charlemagne, became the first Holy Roman Emperor, he was able to get most of Europe to accept his improved, heavier denarius as an international standard.

As the power of Charlemagne's dynasty weakened, local nobles and bishops became more powerful and usurped the right to strike coins. During most of the middle ages there were two kinds of French coins, royal coins struck by the kings, and feudal coins struck by the nobility. Until the 1200s however, both types of coins consisted primarily of deniers derived (and degenerated) from the Carolingian denier, or its half, the obol. Many coins were struck for hundreds of years without outward change at all to increase the perception of stability. As a result, many coins appear to have been struck by Charlemagne or Charles the Bald even though they actually struck years after their deaths. A posthumous "Charles" coin is worth a fraction of a real Charlemagne. Feudal coinage eventually faded away as the French kings gradually reasserted their sovereign rights throughout the land. Those few feudal powers still producing coins after the 1300s struck a more diverse array of denominations than earlier, from gold to copper, as did the kings themselves.

One actively collected type of feudal coinage is called Anglo-Gallic. These were struck by English kings in hereditary lands in France. These lands were held as feudal vassals of the King of France. The tensions of this arrangement was a frequent cause of war.

Another small territory in France held by a foreign ruler was Avignon in the south. It was under the rule of the Pope from 1274 through the modern era.

France had more inflation than England, so even though its first large silver coin, the Gros tournois was struck earlier, in 1266, it took 12 deniers to equal one, not 4 as across the Channel. Gold coins were reintroduced in 1290, inspired by the gold florins flowing in from Florence. Many French gold coins

of the following century are true works of Gothic art.

By the 1300s there was so much inflation that most of the small silver had been debased enough to look copper colored. The list of denominations continued to expand. Faithful portraiture was introduced during the Renaissance on the new large silver testone of Francis I.

Additional Specialized Books (Royal):
Duplessy, *Les Monnaies Francaises Royales*, 2 vols. The best catalogue.
Mayhew, Nicholas. *Coinage in France From the Dark Ages to Napoleon.*
Roberts, James. *Silver Coins of Medieval France.*

Additional Specialized Books (Feudal):
Boudeau, E. *Monnaies Francaises Provinciales.*
Elias, E.R. Duncan. *The Anglo-Gallic Coins.*
Mayhew, Nicholas. *Coinage in France From the Dark Ages to Napoleon.*
Roberts, James. *Silver Coins of Medieval France.* Makes identification much easier.

Known counterfeits: There are a number of counterfeits of Charlemagne, made both recently and in the last century. Similar counterfeits of other Carolingian dynasty coins also exist. After this period, counterfeits are less common. Counterfeits made to circulate during the 1200s through 1500s are somewhat common and have collector value.

CAROLINGIAN VF

Peppin, 751-768. Denier. R:P: / Δ/T TRΔ- NO in three lines 1,500.00
Charlemagne, 768-814. Denier. CARO LVS / METVLO (barbarous) around star 1,350.00
Louis the Pious, 814-840. Denier. HLVDOV-VICVS REX, Cross / XRISTIANA RELIGIO, Temple..225.00

Charles II the Bald, 840-877. Denier. Carolus monogram, GRATIA D-I REX / Cross, AVRE-LIANIS CIVITAS..................................180.00

Odo, 887-898. Denier. Odo Rex monogram / Cross, BLESIANIS CASTRO. 225.00
Charles the Simple, 897-922. Denier. Karolus monogram, GRATIA D-I REX / PARISI CIVITΛ 175.00
Raoul, 923-36. Denier. Raoul monogram, GRATIA D-I REX / Cross, CARNOTIS CIVITAS...225.00

ROYAL F

Hugh Capet, 987-996. Denier. HERVEVS HVGO REX, Cross / CROLS monogram............200.00

ROYAL   F

Robert II, 996-1031. Denier. ROB FRAN REX,
Facing crowned bust / ADALBERO LAD, Fac-
ing bust.. 250.00

Henry I, 1031-1060. Denier. AW suspended under
vertical lines, HAINRICVS REX /
Cross 500.00

Philip I, 1060-1108. Denier. Stylized city gate,
PHIL¹PVS X REX D-I / Cross, AVREL¹ANVS
CIVITA 90.00

Louis VI, 1108-1137. Denier. ⊞ | ⊞, LVDOV-
ICVS REX / Cross, LANDONIS
CASTA 90.00

Louis VII, 1137-1180. Denier. Crowned facing
head, LVDOVICVS REX / Cross, fleur at three
upper ends, VRBS BITVRICA................. 80.00

Philip II Auguste, 1180-1223. Denier tournois.
Cross, PHILIPVS REX / Stylized castle, SCS
MARTINVS 35.00

Louis VIII, 1223-1226 and St. Louis to 1245.
Denier tournois. Cross, LVDOVICVS REX /
Stylized castle, TVRONVS CIVI 30.00

St. Louis IX, 1226-1270. Denier tournois. Cross,
LVDOVICVS REX / Stylized castle,
TVRONVS CIVIS.................................... 35.00

Philip III, 1270-1285. Denier tournois. Cross, PhIL-
IPVS' REX / Stylized castle, TVRONVS
CIVIS 30.00

Philip IV, 1285-1314. Gros tournois. Cross within
double border of legends / TVRONVS CIVIS,
Stylized castle within, border of fleurs
(26mm)..125.00

Philip V, 1316-1322. Gros tournois. As Philip IV
except for addition of mintmarks. 500.00

Charles IV, 1322-1328. Double parisis. Large
crown, KAROLVS REX / Cross with fleur ends,
DVPLEX MOnETA................................... 30.00

Philip VI, 1328-1350. Double parisis. Crowned
FRA NCO / Floral cross........................... 20.00

John II the Good, 1350-1364. Billon Denier parisis.
FRA, IOhANNES REX / Cross, PARISIVS
CIVIS.. 40.00

ROYAL   F

Charles V, 1364-80. AV Franc a Pied. King standing
under Gothic arch / Cross in arch
border 700.00

Charles VI, 1380-1422. Blanc dit Guenar. Shield /
Short Cross, Fleurs and crowns in alternate
angles (26mm) 40.00

Charles VII, 1422-1461. Billon Denier tournois.
Two fleurs in three-arch border / Cross in four-
arch border. Legends begin with ⊞ 30.00

Louis XI, 1461-1483. Billon Liard. Fish-like dolphin l. / Cross, fleurs and crowns in alternate
angles 30.00

Charles VIII, 1483-98. Billon Denier tournois. Two
fleurs in three-arch border / Cross in four-arch
border. Legends begin with crown 30.00

Louis XII, 1498-1515. Billon Double tournois.
Three fleurs in three-arch border / Cross in four-
arch border... 30.00

Francis I, 1515-47. Douzain. Crowned shield in
arched border / Cross in arched border 35.00

ROYAL   F

Henry II, 1547-1559. Teston. Crowned bust r. /
Crowned shield, Crowned H each side....250.00

__. Douzain. Crowned shield, crowned crescents at
sides / Cross formed of crescents and
fleurs.. 30.00

Francis II, 1559-60, in name of Henry II. Douzain.
Crowned shield, crowned crescents at sides /
Cross formed of crescents and fleurs 45.00

Charles IX, 1560-1574. Douzain. Crowned shield,
C at each side / Cross, fleurs and crowns in
alternate angles......................................35.00

Henry III, 1574-1589. Douzain. Crowned shield, H
at each side / Cross, crowns in each
angle 35.00

Charles X, 1589-90. Douzain. Crowned shield, C at
each side / Cross, fleurs and crowns in alternate
angles..45.00

Henry IV, 1589-1610. Douzain. Crowned shield, H
at each side / Cross, fleurs and crowns in alternate angles..35.00

Louis XIII, 1610-1643. AE Double tournois. Bust r.
/ Three fleurs 20.00

FEUDAL   F

Angouleme, 1100s. Denier. Cross, LODOICVS /
Four annulets around open cross, ECOLIS-
SIME 30.00

Anjou. Charles, 1246-85. Denier. Cross, CAR-
OLVS COMES / ANDEGAVENSIS, Fulk
monogram 30.00

Aquitaine, 1050-1137. Denier. Four crosses, GVIL-
ILMO / Cross, BVRDECTVLA...............30.00

Avignon. Urban VIII, 1623-44. AE Patard. Crossed
keys / Cross 35.00

Béarn, 1200s. Denier. Cross, CENTVLLO COMES
/ P A X, ONOR FORCAS 30.00

__. 1200s. Obol. similar 65.00

Blois. 1000-1200, Denier. Picasso-esque head r. /
Cross, BEISIS CASTRO 50.00

Châteaudun, 1100s. Denier. Degenerate head r. /
Cross, DVNIOSTIH................................40.00

Dombes. Gaston, 1627-50. AE Double tournois.
Bust r. / Three fleurs...............................25.00

Brittany. John the Red, 1237-86. Denier. Cross,
IOhANNES DVX / Shield, BRITAIN 35.00

La Marche, Hugh X, 1208-49. Denier. Cross, VGO
COHES / Cross, annulets and crescents at alternate ends, MARCHIE..............................30.00

Le Puy, 1200s. Denier. Six armed cross /
Cross 25.00

FEUDAL   F

Lorraine. René II, 1473-1508. Demi-plaque. Arm with sword / Crowned shield...................... 65.00

Maine, 1030-1246. Denier. Herbert monogram, COMES CNEONINIS / Cross, SIGNVM DEI VIVI.. 35.00

Meaux. Gautier I, 1045-82. Denier. Hand in benediction, GALTERIVS PESV / Cross, MELDIS CIVITA 45.00

Melgueil, 1130-1316. Cross of bar and two miters / Four annulets 30.00

Metz. Etienne, 1120-63. Denier. Cross, STEPHANI / Temple, SPINA.. 40.00

__. Thierry V, 1365-84. Gros. Bishop stg. with crozier / Cross, double legend 125.00

Normandy, 1050-1150. Denier. Degenerate temple in form of cross / Cross in circle, ROTO-MAGVS.. 90.00

Penthiévre, 1100s. Denier. Degenerate head r., GVINGAMP / Cross, STEPhAN COM 35.00

Poitou. Alfonse, 1241-71. Denier tournois. Cross, ALFVNS COMES / Stylized castle, PICTAVI-ENSIS 30.00

Souvigny. Denier. Bust of saint, SCS MAIOLVS / Cross, SILVINIACO 30.00

Valence, 1100-1300. Denier. Cross, S APOLLI-NARS / Angel (eagle according to some), VRBS VALENTIAI................................ 25.00

Vienne. 1100s Denier. Stylized head of Saint Maurice l. / Cross, pellets in angles.................. 25.00

ANGLO-GALLIC   F

Aquitaine. Edward II, 1307-1327. Maille Blanche. Short cross, double legend around / Stylized castle, DnS hIBERnIE, Leaf border 125.00

Poitou. Richard the Loinheart, 1189-1199. Denier. Cross, RICARDVS REX / PIC TAVIE NSIS in three lines 85.00

GERMANY

Few series of coins are as complex as that of medieval and Renaissance Germany. Initially German coins of the 900s were struck only by the Holy Roman Emperor and a few very powerful nobles.

The Holy Roman Emperor was a line that began with Charlemagne in 800, who was to be the ruler of the Christian world. By the late 800s he was, in effect, the emperor of Germany and most of the lands surrounding it. Theoretically, he was subject to election by the few most powerful nobles and bishops. The Empire itself struck virtually no coins after the 900s. Most coins struck in the name of the Emperor were struck by him in lands which he would have held by heredity anyway, or by cities and nobles striking coins themselves and paying homage to the Emperor on one side of the coin.

As time went on, the Emperor gave the right to strike coins to more and more nobles. Ultimately there were several hundred authorities in the Empire with such a "mint right."

From the 800s through the 1100s German coins were silver denars, also called pfennigs, derived from the denier of Charlemagne. As authority became more and more diffuse, it began to erode, its size shrinking. By the 1200s the pfennig had declined from nickel size to the size of a half dime. One way to prevent the coinage from shrinking in diameter was to make it thinner. Eventually coins became so thin that the designs on both sides would show through in negative impressions, making either difficult to see. An innovative solution to this was to strike the coin only on one side, and make it a very high relief. The resulting coins were often quite fragile, but very beautiful. They were called bracteates, although particularly small ones came to be called hohlpfennigs. With the increase in the availability in silver in the later Middle Ages, thicker large coins replaced these thin ones, with the exception of the very smallest denominations.

The earliest multiple-pfennig coins of the 1300s were called groschen, meaning big. Gold ducats, florins and gulden became common in the 1300s, following the lead of Italy and fueled by an increase in trade and mining. By the end of the 1480s, talers (large silver dollar type coins) were gaining popularity. This provided a great opportunity to reflect the new realistic portraiture of the Renaissance. On the opposite end of the scale, copper and very base silver (billon) became common, filling the need for small change in an increasingly money driven economy.

Additional Specialized Books: Craig, W.D. *Germanic Coinages.*

Davenport, John. *German Talers, 1500-1600; German Church and City Talers 1600-*

1700; German Secular Talers, 1600-1700; Silver Gulden, 1559-1763.

Metcalf, D.M. *Coinage of South Germany in the Thirteenth Century.*

Reichmann, A., & Co. *Die Mittelalterlichen Münzen...*

Saurma, H. *Die Saurmasche Münzsammlung deutscher, schweitzerischer und polnischer.*

These are just a few of the most basic books. Hundreds of catalogues, often specializing on a narrow period or locale, exist.

Known counterfeits: Contemporary counterfeits exist of some medieval gold coins.

VF

Aachen. HRE Freidrich I, 1152-90. Denar. Emperor std. facing / ROMA CAPVT MVNDI, City walls 100.00

Augsburg. Udalschalk, 1184-1202. Denar. Facing bust of bishop. semi-bracteate. 200.00

Bardowik. Heinrich, 1142-80. Denar. Cross, ring in each angle / very degenerate church..........75.00

Bavaria. Ludwig II, 1253-94. Pfennig. Bust of monk r...30.00

__. Otto III, 1290-1312. Pfennig. Facing bust, H O at sides / Busts of bishop and duke facing..35.00

__. Heinrich IV, 1393-1450. Pfennig. Dog l. under flowers / oho 30.00

__. Maximilian I, 1597-1651. 2 Kreuzer. M C P V B D S R I A E E, Shield / SOLI DEO GLORIA, 2 on orb 30.00

Brandenburg. Joachim II, 1535-71. Dreier. Scepter shield / Eagle shield 30.00

Bremen. Christopher, 1511-58. 2 Groten. St. Peter std. facing, shield under feet / Key 250.00

Brunswick. 1300s. Hohlpfennig. Lion l. bracteate...25.00

Cologne. Dietrich II, 1414-63. Groschen. Half figure of St. Peter under Gothic canopy / Shields in arched border..225.00

Goslar. HRE Otto III, 983-1002. Denar. Cross, ODDO in angles / Temple 65.00

__. HRE Heinrich III, 1046-56. Denar. Crowned facing head / Crowned head l., scepter l. 200.00

Hall. 1300s. Heller. Open hand / Cross........... 25.00
Hamburg. HRE Freidrich III, 1440-93. Goldgulden.
   St. Peter / Orb 750.00

__. 1400s. Schilling. City gate / Cross 150.00
Hannau-Lichtenberg. Philip V, 1590-99. 3 Kreuzer.
   Shield, date at sides / Double headed eagle,
   titles of HRE Rudolf around 40.00
Hesse-Cassel. Ludwig II, 1413-58. Groschen. Lion
   l. supporting small shield / Elaborate cross in
   four-arched border 125.00
__. Wilhelm IV, 1567-92. Dreier. Lion shield /
   Helm with crest.. 25.00

Hildesheim. Heinrich I, 1247-57. Pfennig. Bust
   under arch with three towers.
   bracteate... 225.00
Leuchtenberg-Hals, 1443-1517. Pfennig. Austrian
   shield, h above, I l., v^ r. / blank 20.00
Meissen. Dietrich, 1197-1221. Pfennig.. Dietrich
   std. facing. bracteate. 150.00

Nürnburg. 1200s. Pfennig. Bust l. with cross and
   sword / Figure std. 50.00
Passau. Leonard, 1423-51. Pfennig. Wolf l., crozier
   r. / blank 20.00
Prussia. Albert, 1525-68. Groschen. Bearded bust /
   Eagle 40.00
__. Georg Wilhelm, 1619-40. 1/24th Taler.
   Crowned shield / Royal orb...................... 25.00
Saxony. Denar, 1040s. Cross, pellet in each angle /
   Triple knot 150.00

Saxony. Johann Friedrich, 1547-52. Groschen.
   Angel holding shield / Shield 125.00
Speier. Marquard, 1560-81. Pfennig. Four-part
   shield, M above... 25.00
Württemberg. Christof, 1550-68. Pfennig. Postal
   horn, C H above 30.00

GREAT BRITAIN & IRELAND

Before the tenth century, England was divided into several Anglo-Saxon kingdoms. The Anglo-Saxons were Germanic invaders who displaced much of the Romano-Celtic population in the sixth century. Their first coins, introduced in the 630s, were gold thrymsas, patterned after the already corrupted tremissis of the nearby Merovingian Franks. By the 670s they were debased into small silver pieces with stylized or crude portraits and few inscriptions. Crosses, animals and geometric designs — some of vaguely Roman inspiration — were used on the reverses. In turn, these small silver sceats became so base as to be virtually pure copper, and legends replaced the designs.

After the popularization of the silver penny (denier) by Charlemagne, the various Anglo-Saxon kingdoms adopted that standard. It continued to be the basis of English coinage for a thousand years, and suffered far less inflation than on the Continent. When England was conquered by William, Duke of Normandy, in 1066, he changed nothing about the coin quality and mint organization of England as he recognized their great success. Few smaller denominations and virtually no larger ones were struck until 1344. When a need for half pennies or farthings would arise, pennies were simply cut into halves or quarters. Larger purchases were made with bags of individual pennies. During the reign of Edward III both gold and large silver were successfully introduced. Many of these new larger coins continued to be used up until 1970. Their initial values in pennies and the years they were first coined follow:

Half Groat	1351	2
Groat	1279, 1351	4
Sixpence	1551	6
Testoon	1502	12
Shilling	1549	12
Crown	1526	54; 60
Noble	1344	80
Angel	1464	80
Rose Noble, Ryal	1464	120
Sovereign	1489	240

After 973 virtually all silver bore the portrait of a king on the obverse, and a cross on the reverse. While the portraits varied from clear to barbaric, none of them before Henry VII was a wholehearted attempt to portray the face of any individual, but rather they represented the concept of a king. Even more complicated for collectors, some kings kept the name of their predecessors on their coins as a sign of stability. Generally those coins can only be distinguished by careful examination

of minute details. Henry VII also introduced the royal arms and a seated figure into the repertoire of silver coin designs. Gold, however, from its very beginning, was far more creative in its imagery, and most often depicted images alluding to England's naval power.

No matter how well or poorly the dies were engraved, most English coins of the twelfth and thirteenth centuries are very poorly struck. Sometimes only half of the die's image was impressed on the coin. When very weakly struck, collectors either avoid these coins or expect to pay a significantly reduced price.

The English penny's reputation for purity was so strong that on the continent many princes tried to make their coins look like it. Usually they changed the legends to include their own names, on the presumption that in illiterate society few could tell the difference. Occasionally they would counterfeit it outright. A similar copying occurred with the English gold noble. Originating mostly in the Low Countries and the German Rhineland, these medieval counterfeits are actively collected but sometimes require an expert to identify them.

The English Civil War between Charles I and Parliament created a complicated array of varieties and denominations. Many of these coins are excellently engraved creative designs; however, they are struck so poorly that their beauty is destroyed. Other coins of cities under siege or the victorious Commonwealth were extremely simple in design.

Additional Specialized Books: North, J.J. *English Hammered Coinage.*, 2 vols. Good for discerning varieties.

Seaby, et al. *Coins of England and the United Kingdom.* The basic reference.

West, R., ed. *British Coins Market Values.* Current updated values but minimal numismatic information.

Known counterfeits: There are a number of quality older counterfeits of Anglo-Saxon pennies. Alfred the Great portrait pennies with the reverse legend WEMBLEY are all modern fantasies. Quality recent counterfeits include the unique penny of Howell Dda of Wales. Coins counterstamped WRL were produced after 1972.

ANGLO-SAXON KINGDOMS

East Anglia, 690-725. Sceat. Crude bust r., runes
   before / TT o / \ in square 250.00

Kent, 690-725. Sceat. Diademed head r. / Cross
   between annulets, bird above................... 250.00
Mercia. Burgred, 852-874. Penny. Bust r. / MON
   CENRED ETA in three lines 250.00
Northumbria. Aethelred II, 854-62. AE Sceat.
   +EDILRED, Cross / +MONNE, : :........... 95.00

Wessex. Alfred the Great, 871-899. Penny. +AEL-FRE, Cross in circle / DVDIE + +MON in two lines 575.00

VIKING INVADERS

VF

Danish East Anglia, 885-915. Penny. Large A, SCFDNI / Cross, AOARFRI 225.00

KINGS OF ENGLAND

Aethelred II the Unready, 978-1016. Penny. Bust l. with radiate helmet and shield, AEDELRED REX AN / Long cross, ornament in each angle 240.00

Cnut, 1016-1035. Penny. Bust l. with scepter, +CNVT REC / Short cross 225.00

Edward the Confessor, 1042-1066. Penny. Helmeted bust r. with scepter, +EDPERD R / Short cross, three crescents at each end 250.00

Harold II, 1066. Penny. Crowned bust l. with scepter, +HAROLD REX ANGLO / PAX across field 1,200.00

William I the Conqueror, 1066-1087. Penny. Facing crowned bust, PILLEM REX / Short cross, P A X S, each in circle in angles 275.00

William II, 1087-1100. Penny. Facing crowned bust, PILLEM REI / Short voided cross, _ in each angle 1,250.00

Henry I, 1100-1135. Penny. Crowned facing bust with scepter, HENRICVS / Quadrilateral on floral cross 350.00

Stephen, 1135-1154. Penny. Crowned bust r. with scepter, STIEFNERE / Cross moline 325.00

F

Henry II, 1154-89. Penny. Crowned facing head and hand with scepter, hENRICVS REX / Short voided cross, x in each angle 40.00

Richard I, 1189-1199. Penny. Similar 100.00

John, 1199-1216. Penny. Similar..................... 95.00

Henry III, 1216-1272. Penny. Crowned facing head and hand with scepter, hENRICVS REX III / Long voided cross, three pellets in each angle 35.00

F

Edward I, 1272-1307. Penny. Crowned facing bust, ЄDW R ANGL' DNS hVB / Long cross, three pellets in each angle 33.00

Edward II, 1307-27. Penny. Similar but ЄDWA R ANG DNS hVB 35.00

Edward III, 1327-77. Penny. Similar but ЄDW R' AnGL DnS hVB 40.00

Richard II, 1377-99. Halfpenny. Similar but RICARDVS REX ANGL 50.00

Henry IV, 1399-1413. Penny. Similar but +hЄNRIC REX AnGLIЄ 300.00

Henry V, 1413-22. Penny. Similar but +hЄnRICVS REX AnGLIЄ 55.00

Henry VI, 1422-61 and 1470-71. Groat. Crowned bust with annulets at nick, facing in arched border / Long cross, three pellets in each angle, two lines of legend around 80.00

Edward IV, 1461-70 and 1471-83. Penny. Crowned facing bust, G and key at neck, ЄDWARD DI GRA REX AnG / Long cross, three pellets in each angle 50.00

Edward V, 1483. It is likely that no dies were prepared exclusively to strike Edward V's coins.

Richard III, 1483-85. Groat. Crowned bust facing in arched border, boar's head at beginning of legends / Long cross, three pellets in each angle, two lines of legend around 750.00

VF

Henry VII, 1485-1509. AV Angel. Angel spearing demon / Shield on ship 850.00

Henry VIII, 1509-47. Groat. Crowned clean-shaven bust r. / Shield on cross 275.00

VF

Edward VI, 1547-53. AV Half Sovereign. Crowned bust r. / Crowned shield 1,250.00

F

Mary, 1553-54. Groat. Crowned bust l. / Shield on cross (24mm) 110.00

Philip and Mary, 1554-58. Sixpence. Confronted busts of Philip and Mary, crown above / Crowned oval shield (27mm) 250.00

Elizabeth I, 1558-1603. Sixpence. Crowned bust l., rose r. / Shield on cross (27mm) 90.00

James I, 1603-1625. Halfgroat. Crowned Rose / Crowned Thistle 50.00

Charles I, 1625-1649. AE Farthing. Crown and crossed scepters / Crowned Harp.............. 25.00

F

__. Sixpence. Crown, C R VI around / OBS.
NEWARK 1646. Royalist under siege at
Newark 300.00
Commonwealth, 1649-60. Halfgroat. Shield within
wreath / Two shields, II above..................50.00

SCOTLAND

Scottish coins did not exist before 1136.
Originally they were struck to the same fine
standard as the English penny. They often
echoed English artistic style, although with a
distinctive interpretation. While the English
kings soon settled down to a facing portrait,
those of Scotland often preferred a side view.
Large silver was introduced at about the
same time as in England, but gold was not
introduced successfully until 1390. Inflation
affected Scottish coinage more than the
English, and during the fifteenth and sixteenth centuries it became more debased. By
the 1600s the Scottish penny, originally the
same value as the English, was worth twelve
to the English penny.

While the thrones of Scotland and
England were united in 1603, when the Scottish king inherited England, the countries
were not united until 1707. It was then that
separate Scottish coinage ended.

Additional Specialized Books: Seaby, P.
and P. Frank Purvey, *Coins of Scotland, Ireland and the Islands.* Best basic catalogue
but values outdated.

West, R., ed. *British Coins Market Values.* Updated values but minimal numismatic
information.

Known counterfeits: The most common
Scottish counterfeits are contemporary ones
of 1-1/2 penny "hardheads" of 1558.

F

David I, 1124-1153. Penny. Crowned bust r. with
fleur-scepter, DAVIT REX / Cross
moline..700.00
Malcolm IV, 1153-65. Penny. Crowned bust l. with
fleur-scepter, MALCOLM REX / Cross with
fleur ends...4,000.00
William I the Lion, 1165-1214. Penny. Leonine head
l., Lɛ RɛI WILAM / Short voided cross, star in
each angle (mostly struck 1205-30)...........110.00
Alexander II, 1214-1249. Penny. Head r., scepter r. /
same 975.00

Alexander III, 1249-1286. Penny. Crowned head l.,
scepter l. / Long cross, star in each angle . 50.00
John Baliol, 1292-1296. Penny. As above but
IOhANNES DɛI GRA.............................165.00
Robert the Bruce, 1306-1329. Penny. As above but
ROBERTVS DɛI GRA.............................450.00
David II, 1329-1371. Penny. As above but DAVID
DɛI GRA REX..60.00

F

Robert II, 1371-1390. Groat. Crowned bust l., scepter l. within arched border / Long cross, star in
each angle, double legend (28mm) 115.00
Robert III, 1390-1406. Groat. Same, but three pellets in each angle (27mm).......................115.00

James I, 1406-37. AV Demy. Lion in diamond
shaped shield / X-cross in ornate
border 600.00
James II, 1437-1460. Groat. Crowned facing bust
within arched border / Long cross, crowns in two
angles, three pellets in each other.
(26mm) 275.00
James III, 1460-1488. Plank (4 pence). Crowned
shield between crosses, in arched border / Long
cross, opening at center. (26mm) 60.00
James IV, 1488-1531. Billon Plank. Similar but
shield between crowns...............................55.00
James V, 1531-1542. Billon Bawbee (6 pence).
Crowned thistle, I 5 at sides / Large X, crown at
center..55.00
Mary, 1542-1567. Billon Bawbee (6 pence).
Crowned thistle, M R at sides / Large X, crown
at center..50.00
__. Lion or Heardhead (1-1/2 pence). Crowned FM
Monogram / Crowned Lion..........................35.00
James VI, 1567-1625. AE Turner (2 pence). Triple
thistle / Crowned lion l., : r. 35.00
Charles I, 1625-1649. AE Turner. Crowned C R /
Crowned thistle...32.00

IRELAND

The first Irish coins were struck by
Viking settlers in Dublin. They imitated the
English pennies of Aethelred II the
Unready, often with a change of name or a
corruption of style. It was struck in quantity
throughout the entire eleventh century.

Irish coins were struck under the English
from 1190. One distinctively Irish feature
of the early English series is a portrait
within a triangular frame. From the 15th
century on, most Irish coins were virtually
identical to contemporary English ones, the
exceptions being those with crown motifs.
Most are scarce. Henry VIII struck special
coins in good silver, on which he mentioned
three of his wives. Like on their English
coins, Elizabeth and James I's portraits are
very low relief and were prone to rapid
wear. Unlike their English coins, they were
of a distinctly baser alloy.

Many crude pieces were struck by both
sides during the Irish phase of the English
Civil War.

Additional Specialized Books:

Seaby, P. and P. Frank Purvey, *Coins of
Scotland, Ireland and the Islands.* Best basic
catalogue but values outdated.

West, R., ed. *British Coins Market Values.* Updated values but minimal numismatic
information.

Known counterfeits: Quality recent counterfeits include Hiberno-Norse pennies of Sihtric.

VF

Anonymous, 1035-60. Penny. Corrupt bust of
Aethered II l. / Voided long cross, stylized hand
in two angles 300.00
John, 1199-1214. Penny. Crowned and sceptered
bust facing in triangle pointing up / Sun, moon
and three stars in triangle pointing up 125.00
Henry III, 1216-72. Penny. Crowned and sceptered
bust facing in triangle pointing up / Voided long
cross, three pellets in each angle..............125.00

VF

Edward I, 1272-1307. Penny. Crowned bust facing
in triangle pointing down / Solid long cross,
three pellets in each angle 90.00
Edward IV, 1461-83. Double Groat. Crowned facing bust / Rose at center of sun's rays
(27mm)..5,000.00
Henry VIII, 1509-47. Groat. Crowned shield /
Crowned harp, h I at sides. For Henry and Jane
Seymour. (26mm) 175.00

F

Elizabeth I, 1558-1603. AE Penny. Shield /
Crowned harp..35.00
James I, 1603-25. Sixpence. Crowned bust r. /
Crowned harp..70.00

Lords Justices, "Ormonde Sixpence" of 1643-44.
Crowned CR / VI, d above......................135.00
Confederate Catholics, "Blacksmith Halfcrown" of
1642-43. Line engraving of King riding l. / Oval
arms 500.00

HUNGARY

The very first Hungarian coin was struck
by the nation's patron saint, who both organized the state and introduced Christianity to
the county. He struck a slightly small version
of the standard European silver denier introduced by Charlemagne. By the early 1100s it
had greatly shrunk to a minuscule size. During the following century, Hebrew letters can
be found on many coins, indicating their
manufacture by Jewish moneyers. After the
reign of Sigismund the denar's diameter
recovered, although the alloy was somewhat
less pure.

This is among the most prolific of coinages of medieval and Renaissance Europe,
although most denominations besides the
denar, goldgulden, and later taler, are scarce.
It is popularly collected because it is possible
to assemble long runs of inexpensive dated
coins beginning as early as 1503.

Additional Specialized Books: Huszar, L.
Münzkatalog Ungarn.

Known counterfeits: Contemporary counterfeits of the Madonna and Child type denars are
common. Modern counterfeits were unknown
until the late 1990s. Thousands are known to
have been made in eastern Europe but few have

entered the North American market so far. Dates include but may not be confined to 1585, 1586 and 1587.

VF

St. Stephen, 997-1038. Denar. STEPNANVS REX, Cross / Cross.. 225.00

VF

Peter, 1038-41, 1044-46. Denar. PETRVS RE+, Cross / PANONIA, Cross........................ 200.00
Samuel Aba, 1041-44. Denar. REX SAMVHEL, Cross / Cross.. 275.00
Ladislaus I, 1077-95. Denar. LADISLΛS RE+, Three long crosses / Cross........................ 100.00

Coloman, 1095-1116. Denar. CΛLMΛN RE, Cross / Cross. 35.00
Anonymous, 1100s. Denar. Cross, crosslet in each angle / Cross in two circles 15.00
Geza II, 1141-62. Denar. GEICΛ RE, Cross / Cross in two circles..Scarce

Bela III, 1172-96. AE Follis. Two kings enthroned / Madonna and child 75.00
Stephen V, 1270-72. Denar. MONETΛ VNGΛRIЄ, Crowned head l. / Hebrew letter À between birds 75.00
Louis I, 1342-82. Denar. Saracen head / Patriarchal cross 30.00
Mary, 1385-95. Denar. Crown / Patriarchal cross. 25.00
Sigismund I, 1387-1437. Patriarchal cross / Shield 15.00
__. Goldgulden. Shield / St. Ladislaus stg. ... 275.00
Matthias I, 1458-90. Denar. Shield with raven at center / Madonna and Child 17.00
Wladislaus II, 1490-1516. Denar. Shield / Madonna and Child... 15.00
Louis II, 1516-26. Denar. Similar 17.00
Ferdinand I, 1516-64. Denar. Similar.............. 15.00
Maximilian II, 1564-76. Denar. Similar......... 15.00
Rudolf II, 1576-1608. Denar. Similar.............. 15.00
Matthias II, 1608-19. Denar. Similar 17.00
Ferdinand II, 1619-37. Denar. Similar 17.00
Ferdinand III, 1637-57. Denar. Similar........... 30.00
__. Taler. Bust r., Hungarian shield and Madonna and Child amid legend / Double headed eagle...250.00

ITALY

The coinage of Italy was perhaps the most diverse and most important of the Middle Ages. Italy was always a focus of commerce, banking and religion. It developed such things as the large silver coins, it reintroduced gold and realistic portraiture, and replaced very base silver (billon) with thicker copper coins, which were accepted based on trust in the state. The central location of the Italian peninsula, at the crossroads of the Byzantine, Islamic, Germanic, and Slavic cultures, fostered the spread of Italian trade (and the Renaissance) as well as the Italian assimilation of many diverse monetary, artistic and commercial practices.

Numismatically, Italy is easily divided into three regions. The South, later becoming the of the Kingdom of Naples and Sicily, was until the 1200s subject to domination by, or at least the influence of, the Byzantine Empire and of Islamic dynasties. As a result, distinctive coinages that were truly more Byzantine and Islamic than Western European developed. These regional characteristics included the continued use of copper and gold coins, as well as the cup-shaped scyphate shape used in the Byzantine Empire. Inscriptions in the Arabic language were also quite common. Under the royal houses of Anjou and Aragon, its coinage fell more in line with northern patterns.

The North consisted of many small feudal and ecclesiastical territories and independent cities. Its coinage after the 700s consisted primarily of the carolingian penny or denaro, just as that of France and Germany. Like in France and Germany the denaro began to erode, becoming smaller and baser as the Emperor's authority was delegated more widely, or usurped. But it was in Italy that the artistic and commercial flowering of the Renaissance began. Because the need came first, the Italians were the first to introduce (1190s) a grosso, a silver coin worth multiples of a denaro. They were also the first to reintroduce gold. A few Northern cities such as Florence and Venice created gold coins for international trade in the late 1200s. The earlier small gold pieces in Sicily and the South fell more into the system of Islamic coinage and had less international influence. Large, half dollar size silver coins bearing portraits also began in Northern Italy, being particularly favored in Milan. Such a coin was called a testone, meaning "big head," because of immediate use of Renaissance portrait heads as a motif.

In many aspects the commercial destiny of central Italy followed that of the north. Politically, however, it was dominated by the papacy. Originally the Pope struck proper Byzantine and Carolinian style coins, one side citing the authority of the emperor, the other the Pope. When the political power of the Pope weakened in the 1000s, his coinage was replaced by that of the Roman Senate, and by the coinage of a number of powerful cities. It was not until the 1300s that the Pope was able to regain his full power as a secular ruler. From that time onward, papal coinage was an artistic leader. Papal coins of the Baroque era were themselves works of art. Papal coins inscribed Sede Vacante were struck between popes.

Additional Specialized Books: Berman, Allen. *Papal Coins*.

Berman, Allen. *Papal Numismatic History: The Emancipation of the Papal State*.

Biaggi, Elio. *Monete e Zecche Medievali Italiane*.

Spahr, R. *Le Monete Siciliane*. 2 vols.

Varesi, Alberto. *Monete Italiane Regionali: Emilia; Lombardia, zecche minori; Piemonte, Sardegna, Liguria...Corsica*. These are the first three volumes of a planned series.

Many other specialized references are considered standard, some are difficult to obtain.

Known counterfeits: There are a number of seventeenth and eighteenth century counterfeits of papal coins, some of coins which were never struck! The Venetian gold ducat was counterfeited from the Middle Ages to the eighteenth century. They vary widely in accuracy and alloy. Papal coins are frequently encountered with mount marks from use as jewelry, and as such are traded at a discount.

NOTE: Italian coins in this section are valued in Fine for copper (AE) and dark billon, in Very fine for gold (AV), silver and silver colored billon.

VF

Amalfi, 1050-1100. AV Tari. Pseudo-Arabic legend around small cross....................................600.00
Ancona. 1300s. Billon Denaro. PP S QVIRIA, C V S / DE ANCONA, Cross 15.00
Bologna, 1191-1337. Bolognino. BONONI, Large A / I P R T cruciform.............................75.00.

Florence. 1300s-1500. Fiorino. St. John the Baptist stg. / Fleur de lis......................................300.00

Genoa. 1139-1339. Denaro. CVNRADI REX, Cross / IANVA, Gateway...........................30.00
Lucca. 1039-1125. Denaro. TT / V < C Λ (=LVCA). Very barbaric 25.00

Milan. 1039-1125. Denaro. HE RIC H in three lines / MEDIOLANV, Cross. scyphate. 50.00

VF

Milan. Henry VII, 1310-13. Grosso of 2 Soldi. Two
saints stg. / St. Ambrose enthroned........ 700.00
__. Gian Galeazzo Visconti, 1395-1402. Grosso. G
3, Serpent devouring child / St. Ambrose
enthroned. 90.00
__. Republic, 1447-50. Billon Denaro. Head of St.
Ambrose / Cross 20.00

__. Galeazzo Maria Sforza, 1468-76. Testone. Bust
r. / G3 M, Shield with elaborate crest. 600.00

Naples. Charles II, 1285-1309. Saluto d'argento.
Angel and Mary / Shield 150.00
__. Ferdinand I, 1458-94. Carlino. King enthroned /
Circular arms 150.00
__. __. AE Cavallo. Crowned bust r. /
Horse r. 30.00
__. Charles V and Joanna, 1516-19. AE Cavallo.
Large I C / Jerusalem cross. 40.00

Naples. Philip II, 1556-98. Half Ducato. Bust r. /
Crowned shield.. 225.00
__.__. AE Tornese. Crowned head r. /
Cornucopia 35.00
Papal States. St. Gregory III, 731-741. Eighth Sili-
qua. Bust of Byzantine Emperor / Gregory
monogram...Rare

VF

__. St. Leo IV, 847-55. Denaro. SCS PETRVS,
LEO PA monogram / HLOTHARIVS. IMP
monogram 750.00
__. Urban V, 1362-70. Bolognino. VRBANVS PP
QNTS, Mitred facing bust / S PET E PAL,
U R B I cruciform..................................... 95.00
__. Pius II, 1458-1464. Bolognino. Similar but
PIVS PP SECV. 135.00
__. Alexander VI, 1492-1503. Grosso. Borgia arms
with papal tiara / Saints Peter and Paul
stg. 185.00

__. Paul III, 1534-49. AV Scudo d'oro. Farnese arms
with papal tiara / St. Paul stg. with sword. 550.00
__. Pius IV, 1559-65. Giulio. Medici arms with
papal tiara / St. Peter stg. 185.00
__. Pius V, 1566-72. Bianco of Bologna. Bust r. /
Lion with pennant l................................ 275.00
__. Gregory XIII, 1572-85. Billon Quattrino. Papal
arms / St. Peter stg. 25.00
__. Clement VIII, 1592-1605. Testone. Papal arms /
Holy door 200.00
__. Paul V, 1605-21. Testone of Ferrara. Borghese
arms / St. George riding r. searing dragon 225.00
__. Urban VIII, 1623-44. AE Quattrino. Barberini
arms with papal tiara / Archangel expelling
Lucifer... 35.00

Clement X, 1670-76. AV Quadrupla. Arms / King
David std. r. playing harp............................Rare
__.__. Testone. Similar. 350.00
Pavia. Galeazzo II Visconti, 1354-78. Pegione
(grosso) Elaborate crest over small shield / St.
Sirus enthroned 90.00

VF

Perugia. after 1471. Billon Quattrino. *P* / Cross, *
in angle..25.00

Piacenza. Alexander Farnese, posthumous 1599.
AV Quadrupla. Bust l. / She-wold stg. before
crowned lilies. 1,500.00
Ravenna. 1232-1300s. Billon Denaro.
ARCIEPISCO, P V S / DE RAVENA, Cross,
scepter and pellets in alternate angles 25.00
Roman Senate. Charles of Anjou, 1263-66. Grosso.
Lion walking l. / Roma std. facing 450.00
__. Denaro Provisino. Comb, S above / Cross 30.00
Savoy. Denaro. Amedeo III, 1103-48. Cross /
SECVSIL, Three pellets 75.00
__. Carlo Emanuele, 1580-1630.. Billon Quarto di
Soldo. Crowned CE / Savoy cross............. 15.00
Sicily. William I, 1154-66. AE Fractional Follaro.
Bust of Madonna and child / REX W, Arabic
around. scyphate..30.00

__. William II, 1166-89. Trifollaro. Lion face / Palm
tree..40.00
__. Manfred, 1258-66. AV Multiple Tari. Eagle /
Cross, I C NI KA in angles.....................225.00
__.__. Billon Denaro. Cross / Large S.............20.00
__. James, 1285-96. Billon Denaro. Crowned head
l. / Cross 20.00

__. Frederick the Simple, 1355-77. Pierreale. Eagle
in border / shield in border........................75.00
__. Philip IV, 1621-65. 4 Tari. Bust r. / Eagle
(27mm)..150.00
Siena. 1279-1350. Billon Piccolo. SENA VETVS,
Large S / Simple cross 30.00
Venice. Lorenzo Tiepolo, 1268-75. Grosso. LA
TEVLP..., St. Mark handing banner to Doge /
Christ enthroned..65.00
__. Pietro Gradenigo, 1289-1311. Grosso. Similar
but PE GRADONICO... ....65.00

VF

__. Francesco Dandolo, 1328-39. Soldo. Doge kneeling l. with banner / Lion l. with banner........45.00
__. Antonio Venier, 1382-1400. Billon Tornesello. ANTO VENERIO DVX, Cross / Bust of winged lion 20.00
__. Francesco Erizzo, 1631-46. Soldo. FRANC ERIZ, Doge kneeling before winged lion / Christ stg... 20.00

LOW COUNTRIES

The Low Countries are Belgium, Netherlands and Luxembourg. During most of the Middle Ages they were composed of many semi-independent feudal states, most of them paying homage to some greater lord.

During the Dark Ages, silver sceats similar to English ones were struck on the Freisian coast. The Dutch city of Dorestad was a major mint of silver deniers for the Carolinginn Emperors. As elsewhere, while that dynasty grew weak, the power of local nobles grew strong. Through marriage and alliance, the Dukes of Burgundy transformed most of the Low Countries into a powerful state between France and the Holy Roman Empire. Much of the coinage reflects a strong influence of French feudal and royal coins. As in neighboring areas of France, the deterioration of the denier revealed itself not in a more base coin but in a smaller one of good purity called a petit denier. These lands passed to Spain in 1506 with the inheritance of Charles V. The territories that eventually became Belgium and the Netherlands began their different turns as a result of the Reformation, when the latter became Protestant. It broke away from Spanish rule and established itself as the United Netherlands. Each province continued to strike its own coins, but usually on a shared standard.

Many of the coins of the Burgundian dependencies bore A.D. dates in the 1400s. This is far ahead of the practice in the rest of Europe, which rarely did this before the 1500s. Such coins are actively sought by collectors.

Additional Specialized Books: de Mey, J. *Les Monnaies des Comtes de Flandre 1244-1384; Les Monnaies des Comtes de Flandre 1384-1556; Les Monnaies des Comtes de Louvain et Ducs de Brabant 1015-1467; Les Monnaies des Ducs de Brabant 1467-1598; Les Monnaies des Souverains Luxembourgeois.*

de Mey, and Van Keymeulen. *Les Monnaies de Brabant 1598-1790.*

Haeck, A. *De Munten van de Graven van Vlaanderen.* 2 vols.

As in the case of German coinage, many specialized books exist for individual locales.

Known counterfeits: During the Renaissance many counterfeits were made of gold ducats. These were often gilt silver.

F

Alost. 1220-53. Petit Denier. Bust of knight l. in chainmail / Long cross over circle 65.00
Brabant. John I, 1268-94. Denier. Shield / Long voided cross 75.00
__. John III, 1312-55. Gros. MOnЄTA BRΛBΛn, Lion l., leaf border / Cross, double legend 80.00
__. Philip the Handsome, 1482-1506. Briquet. Lion std. holding shield / Floral cross, dated 1492...225.00
__. Fifth Ecu. Bust of Philip II of Spain (1556-98)/ Shield (28mm) 75.00

Flanders. Robert, 1305-22. Sterling. R COMES FLANDRIE, Bust like Edward I of England / Long cross, three pellets in each angle...... 95.00
__. Louis II, 1346-84. Double Gros Botdraeger. Lion wearing helmet std. l. / Short floral cross, double legend (32mm)............................. 150.00
__. John the Fearless, 1404-19. Double Gros. Two shields, helm above / Cross, lions and fleurs in angles (35mm) 150.00
__. Philip the Good, 1419-67. Billon Mite. Shield / Long cross, fleur in one angle, lion in another...30.00

VF

Frisia. 700-750. Sceatta. Crude head appearing as porcupine / Square design 125.00
Hainault. William IV, 1404-17. Gros. Lion and shield within fence / Long cross (30mm) 250.00

Holland. Floris III, 1157-1190. Petit Denier. Head r. / Voided cross 85.00
__. AV Ducat, 1586-1668. Knight stg. / Tablet with inscription 150.00
Luxembourg. Josse, 1388-1402. Gans. Shield in three arch border / Long cross, double legend (27mm)... 175.00
Utrecht. 1500s. Lion Daalder. Knight holding shield / Lion 125.00

POLAND

The first common Polish coins were struck by anonymous 11th century bishops who imitated the temple denar of Goslar, which itself was an imitation of the Carolinginn temple denier. Most other contemporary or earlier coins are rare and were not made in significant quantity.

As with German, many Polish coins of the 1100s and 1200s are bracteats, struck only on one side. During these centuries Hebrew letters can be found on many coins, indicating their manufacture by Jewish moneyers.

While some coins became one-sided because of their thinness, many thin Polish coins kept being struck with two dies. This made both sides very difficult to interpret due to ghosting of one side onto the other.

By the 1300s, Polish coinage took on a more conventional appearance and by the end of the following century they were again quite common. As elsewhere the Renaissance saw the dawn of modern realistic portraiture on coins, Sigismund I being the first Polish king so depicted. This fine portraiture was wasted on the coins of the 1600s, since most were very unevenly struck.

While the majority of coins are for Poland proper or Lithuania (see Balkans) there were many special issues for individual cities such as Gdansk.

Additional Specialized Books: Gumowski, M. *Handbuch der Polnischen Numismatik.*

Kopicki, E. *Katalog podstawowych typów monet i banknotów Polski.*

Known counterfeits: 1600 (and possibly 1602) six groschen. They are distinguished by a broken S in Sigismun, and by their sharp edges.

VF

Anonymous, 1000s. Denar. Temple / Church 125.00
Similar but smaller 75.00
Wladislaw II, 1138-46. Denar. Helmeted bust of Wladislaw facing with shield and sword / Bust of Bishop facing with crozier and book ..125.00
Casimir II, 1177-81. Denar. Bust of bishop, seems ברכה קזי (=Blessing on Casimir) bracteate. 500.00
Boleslaw V, 1243-79. Denar. Two stg. figures / D- O L I in arms of cross 125.00

F

Casimir IV, 1447-92. Half Groschen. MOnЄTA KA3IMIRI, Eagle / Crown 30.00
John Alexander, 1492-1501. Half Groschen. Similar but I ALBERTI 25.00
Alexander, 1501-06. Half Groschen. Similar but ALЄXAnDЄR....................................25.00
Sigismund I, 1506-48. Half Groschen. Similar but SIGISMVNDI..25.00
Stephan Bathory, 1576-86. Three Groschen. Crowned bust r. / Inscription.....................45.00

Sigismund III, 1587-1632. Six Groschen. Crowned bust r. / Crown and three shields...............40.00
__. Three Polker (1-1/2 Groschen) Crowned Shield / Orb..12.00

F

Wladislaw IV, 1633-48. Taler. Crowned bust r. / Shield. .... VF 500.00
John Casimir, 1649-68. AE Schilling (Solidus). Head r. / Eagle 20.00

John Sobieski, 1676-96. Six Groschen. Bust laureate r. / Crown and three shields 35.00

PORTUGAL

Portugal was created relatively late, a byproduct of the final conquest of the Iberian peninsula. By the time its founder, Count Afonso, declared its independence from Castile in 1143, the standard medieval denier or dinheiro had already collapsed into a small coin of a base silver alloy.

Multiples of the dinheiro were struck but were usually scarce. Medieval and Renaissance Portuguese coins are distinctive in their failure to develop realistic portraiture, adhering to other design motifs such as heraldry, monograms and crosses.

From 1580 to 1640 the Kings of Spain also ruled Portugal. They were very careful not to alter the coinage, and there is nothing distinctly Spanish about their issues.

There were a number of times when the government restamped the silver with marks indicating new values, sometimes in preparation for export.

Additional Specialized Books: Gomes, *Moedas Portuguesas.*

Vaz, J. *Book of the Coins of Portugal.*

Known counterfeits: Counterfeits of this series are not particularly common.

F

Afonso I, 1128-85. Billon Dinheiro. HLFONSIS, Pentacle / RεX POR, Latin cross, T V at sides..300.00
Sancho II, 1223-48. Billon Dinheiro. SANCIVS REX, Four shields cruciform / Long cross......................40.00
Dinis I, 1279-1325. Billon Dinheiro. D RεX PORTVGL, Cross / Five shields cruciform........................30.00
Ferdinand I, 1367-83. Billon Barbuda, Crowned bust in helmet / Five shields cruciform, Castles in angles 90.00
John I, 1385-1433. Billon Real. Crowned IhNS in arched border / Five shields cruciform, Castles in angles 38.00
Edward I, 1433-38. AE Ceitil. Crowned ΣD in arched border / Five shields cruciform, Ca stles in angles 50.00
Afonso V, 1438-81. AE Ceitil. Castle / Shield........................30.00
John II, 1481-95. Vintem. Crowned Y / Crowned shield 50.00
Manuel I, 1495-1521. AE Ceitil. Castle / Shield 30.00

F

John III, 1521-57. AV Cruzado Calvario. Crowned shield / Cross on mound 400.00
Sebastian I, 1557-78. Half Tostao. Shield / Simple cross 65.00
Philip II, 1598-1621. Tostao. Crowned shield / Simple cross, five pellets in each angle 95.00

RUSSIA

The first Russian state was Kievian Rus founded by the Viking Rurik in 862. His descendants divided Russia into over sixty small and moderate sized principalities. About thirty struck coins. Many were suppressed during the Mongol invasion and occupation. After this, the Grand Dukes of Moscow emerged the most powerful, declaring independence from the Mongols in the 1400s. They eventually conquered all those remaining states. In 1547 Ivan IV the Terrible, the reigning Grand Duke of Moscow, became the first "Tsar of All the Russias."

The coins of Kienian Rus are too rare to be considered obtainable. From the 1300s to the 1600s most Russian coins consisted of very small copper puls and silver dengas, and later kopeks. These coins are usually nicknamed "wire money" by collectors because most of them were literally hand struck on rods of silver wire. Four different mints struck wire money under the czars. While mint identification is outside the scope of this book, it is not necessarily difficult.

The dies were engraved to be much larger than the blanks they were striking. As a result no one coin will have a complete design. Also the strikes were frequently incomplete. There are few series where brockage errors (see US coins, Errors) are more common than in this.

As a result of the conservative adherence to this method of manufacture, medieval coinage did not end in Russia until the reign of the great reformer Peter I the Great (1689-1725).

There has never been a better time to collect Russian coins. Vast quantities of material have been flooding out of post-Soviet Russia, greatly diminishing prices. The rate at which this material can be replenished through excavations or the liquidation of estates will be much slower than the rate of export, so this depressed market may be only a short term opportunity. Even rare coins, while still rare, are at least somewhat obtainable at moderate prices.

Additional Specialized Books: Kleshchinov, V. & Grishin, I. *Catalogue of Medieval Coins of Russia from Reign of Tzar Ivan IV Vasilievich till Swedish Occupation of Novgorod (1533-1617).* Bilingual.

Lapa, F. *Russian Wire Money.* Incomplete but convenient.

Spassky, I.G. *Russian Monetary System.* An excellent history.

Known counterfeits: There are fewer recent ones than would be expected. In the 1960s, however, one unscrupulous American dealer produced some wire money. Novodels are government issue "restrikes" of coins which may have never existed. They are rare and collectible.

All inscriptions below are approximate. The actual inscriptions will vary from die to die, both in spelling and letter forms. The personal name of the ruler, or in the case of feudal coins the state, has been underlined below for ease of recognition.

FEUDAL COINAGE

VF

Moscow, 1400s. AE Pul. Siren / ПОVΛО МОСК-OBЬCKOE 75.00
__. Vasiliy the Blind, 1425-46. Denga. Horseman holding falcon / Samson fighting lion 90.00
Ivan III, 1462-1505. Horseman r. / ωСП ОΔАРЬ ВСНА РYCН.................45.00
Ivan IV the Terrible, 1533-47. Denga. Horseman with sword / KHSb BEΛИКИ IBAHЪ BC P 20.00
Novgorod, 1420-56. Denga. Suppliant before Grand Duke holding sword / Inscription 120.00
__, 1400s. AE Pul. Crowned facing head in silhouette / ПVΛО НОВАГОРОΔА 50.00
__,__. AE Pul. Double headed eagle / Same... 50.00
Pskov, 1400s. Denga. Crowned facing head / Panther.....................................125.00

Ryazan, 1380s. Countermark resembling two eyes and a big nose, usually on Tartar silver coin.....................................100.00
Tver, 1450-1500. AE Pul. Bird l. or right / ПОVΛО ТВЄРЬСКОЕ................................45.00
__,__. AE Pul. Bird with flower in mouth / Similar.....................................45.00

CZARS OF RUSSIA

VF

Ivan IV the Terrible, 1547-84. Kopek. Horseman with spear / ЦРЬИ КHSb BEΛИКI ИBAHЪ BCEГA РЧСИ...20.00
Feodor Ivanovich, 1584-98. Kopek. Similar but ЦРЬИ BEΛИКI КHS ФЄΔОР BCEA РYСI...25.00
Boris Godunov, 1598-1605. Kopek. Similar but ЦРЬИ BEΛИКI КHS БОРIС ФЄΔОРОВIЧ ВCEA РYСI...20.00
Dmitry Ivanovich, 1604/5-06 Kopek. Similar but ЦРЬI BEΛИКI КHSb ΔМIТРE IBAHOBIЧЬ B...35.00
Vasilii Shuiskii, 1606-10. Kopek. Similar but ЦРЬI BEΛИКI КHSb BACIΛEИ IBAHOBIЧb ВCEA РVСI...25.00

VF

Vladislav IV Prince of Poland, 1610-12. Kopek. Similar but ЦРЬІ ВЕΛІКІ КНАЗ ВΛАΔІСΛАВ ЖІΓІСМонΔовичь ВОСЕ.. 175.00
Michael Feodovich, 1613-45. Kopek. Horseman with spear r. / ЦР ЬІΛІКНІ КS МНХАІΛО ΘΔРОВИЧ ВІСЕ РVСІ 15.00

Alexei Mikhailovich, 1645-76 Kopek. Similar but ЦРЬ І ВЕΛІКНІ КНАS АΛЕКСІВІ МИХАІΛОВІЧь ВСЕ 15.00
same in copper 15.00
Feodor Alexievich, 1676-82. Kopek. Similar but ЦРЬ І ВЕΛІКНІ КНАS ФЕОΔωР АΛЕКСІЕВІ Чь ВСЕА РVСІИ 35.00
Ivan Alexievich, 1682-89. Kopek. Similar but ЦРЬ І ВЕΛИКИ КНАS ІОЯНН АΛЕЗІЕВІЧь ВСЕА РVСІ 60.00
Peter I, 1689-1725. Kopek. Similar but ЦРЬ І ВЕΛИИКИ КНА ПЕТРЬ АΛЕЗИЕВИЧ ВСЕА Р 10.00

SCANDANAVIA

Scandinavian coinage originated in the late 900s and early 1000s. It was greatly influenced by the dependable English penny of the day, to which the first penigs bear a great resemblance. They are a good metal and weight. As Vikings raided down the Volga they brought back Byzantine coins which also contributed to the array of tenth century designs. Only in Denmark was coinage truly successful, however.

Later medieval Scandinavian coinage was an outgrowth of medieval German coinage, and it follows much the same pattern of development in terms of standards. It did manage to avoid the pitfalls of a prolonged period of feudal coinage with local nobles striking in their own names. Individual mints were, however, leased out to certain powerful bishops. The period of most base coinage occurred during the 1200s when one Danish king got the nickname Eric Plowpenny (1241-50) because he taxed plows in exchange for a promise not to further debase the coinage.

Coinage in Scandinavia became more common in the 1400s, but it was not until the following century that it can be considered common on the level of other European states. The difficulty collectors have today with obtaining medieval Scandinavian coins still calls witness to this.

Additional Specialized Books: Ahlström, Brekke and Hemmingsson *Norges Mynter - The Coinage of Norway. Bilingual.*
Bendixen, K. *Denmark's Money.*
Hauberg, P. *Danmarks Mønter indtil 1241.*
Lagerqvist, L. *Svenska Mynt*
Mansfeld-Bûllner, H.V. *Danske Mønter fra Tidsrummet 1241-1377.*
Skarre, K. *Coins and Coinage in Viking Age Norway.*

Sømod, J. *Danmarks Mønter.* Also covers Norway 1481-1813.
Known counterfeits: Counterfeits of medieval Scandinavian coins are not common.

DENMARK VF

Harold Bluetooth, 950-85. Penning. Degenerate Carolingian temple. semibracteate 500.00

Cnut, 1016-1035. Pennig. Porcupine-like head / Long cross, crescent in each angle. An imitation of a coin of Aethelred II of England 250.00

Sven Estridsen, 1047-1075. Penning. Crude bust l. with flowing hair, scepter before / Long cross, three pellets in each of three angles, circle with dot in last... 250.00

F

Eric Plougpenning, 1241-50. Billon Penning. RЄX ЄRIC, Fleur / DΛNORVM, Crown......... 150.00
Christopher II, 1319-32. Billon Penning. Large A / P and small crescent 60.00
Christian I, 1448-81. AR Hvid. Crowned K / Cross intersecting shield 50.00
Frederick I, 1523-33. Søsling. Crowned shield over cross / Shield.. 65.00
Frederick II, 1559-88. 8 Skilling. Crowned arms / Inscription 45.00
Christian IV, 1588-1648. 2 Skilling. similar.... 25.00

Frederick III, 1648-72. AV Ducat. Bust r. / Inscription 800.00
___. Crowned shield / Inscription...................... 20.00
Christian V, 1670-99. 2 Skilling. Similar. 20.00

NORWAY VF

Olaf Tryggvason, 995-1000. Penning. Bust l. with scepter / Short cross 800.00
Hans, 1481-1513. Hvid. Crowned O / Shield on cross 250.00
Frederick I, 1524-33. Skilling. Cross intersecting shield / Lion on shield 450.00

SWEDEN VF

Knut Eriksson, 1167-96. Penning. Dots intended to represent head facing, Λ l. bracteate........ 750.00
Eric of Pomerania, 1396-1439. Örtug. Shield with three crowns / Cross bisecting Є 175.00
Karl Knutson, 1448-70. Örtug. Ship on shield /Three crowns on shield........................... 200.00
Gustaf I, 1521-60. Billon Fyrk. Vasa shield / Crown 150.00

VF

Gustav II Adolf, 1611-32. AE Öre. Crowned shield / Crossed arrows, crown above. 85.00
Christina, 1632-54. AE Quarter Öre. Crowned Vasa shield / C R S, Three crowns 50.00

SPAIN

The history of Spain is dominated by two events: The Iberian peninsula being again taken from the Moslems, and the slow process of unifying the several Christian kingdoms into modern Spain. Both these events are easily seen in the coinage. The very first Spanish coins were actually imitations of Islamic ones. Of the several kingdoms it was not long before two, Castile and Leon, joined into one dominant power. When Queen Isabella of Castile and Leon married Ferdinand of Aragon, the next most powerful kingdom, Spain as it is know today, was nearly complete.

Queen Isabella did more than finance Columbus' voyage of discovery. She came to the throne to find a thoroughly debased coinage and mints out of control. She reestablished a sound currency and central authority, giving the nation a monetary system capable of dealing with the new wealth that the explorations she financed were to bring back.

Except for copper there is virtually no portraiture in the sixteenth and seventeenth centuries.

Additional Specialized Books:
Castán and Cayón, *Las Monedas Españolas desde Don Pelayo a Juan Carlos I.*

Known counterfeits: There are numerous counterfeits of Ferdinand and Isabella's coins, most of inferior quality.

LEON   VF

Ferdinand I, 1000-1065. Dinero. SPANIA, Bust facing / FERNAND REX, Short cross........Rare

CASTILE
                                                 VF
Alfonso VIII, 1158-1214. AV Dobla. Two lines of Arabic, cross above, ΛIF below / Five lines of Arabic, Arabic around both borders........Scarce

CASTILE & LEON
                                                 VF
Anonymous, 1100s-1200s. Millares in imitation of Almohad coin. Degenerate Arabic inscription. Square. 50.00

Alfonso VI, 1073-1109. Dinero. ANFNS REX, Cross / Cruciform monogram 100.00
Alfonso X the Wise, 1253-84. Billon Maravedi Preto. ALF: REX..., Castle / Lion r.......... 60.00
Sancho IV, 1284-95. Cornado. SAnCII REX, Crowned bust l. / Castle............................ 60.00
Ferdinand IV, 1295-1312. Billon Pepion. Castle / Lion l... 40.00
Alfonso XI, 1312-50. Billon Noven. Castle in square / Lion l. in square. 40.00

Peter the Cruel, 1350-69. Four Maravedis. Castle in arched border / Lion in arched border..... 150.00
                                                 VF
Henry II, 1369-79. Real. Crowned En within double inscription / Four-lobed arms. (25mm)... 200.00
Henry III, 1390-1406. Billon Blanca. Castle in six-arched border / Lion l. in six-arched border. (25mm) 50.00
Henry IV, 1454-75. Billon Dinero. Castle in diamond border / Lion l. in diamond border...................................... 38.00

UNITED SPAIN   VF

Ferdinand & Isabella, 1469-1504. AV Double Excellente. Crowned confronted busts / Eagle supporting shield................................... 800.00
__. Real. Crowned shield / Yoke and arrows. (27mm)...................................... 150.00
Philip II, 1556-98. Two Reales. Crowned shield / Arms in shape of a octafoil. (27mm) 125.00

                                                 VF
Philip IV, 1621-65. AE 16 Maravedis. Bust r. / Crowned shield 45.00

ARAGON   VF

James I, 1213-76. Dinero. Crowned bust l. / Patriarchal cross.. 90.00
Peter IV, 1335-87. Dinero. Similar 90.00

BARCELONA   VF

Alfonso II, 1291-1327. Croat. Crowned bust l. / Long cross, annulet and three pellets in alternate angles. (25mm) 225.00

SWITZERLAND

The coinage of medieval Switzerland is much like that of Germany and Austria. It began with silver denars in the 800s when only three or four cities were operating, mostly in the name of the Holy Roman Emperor. Over the next couple hundred years the right to strike coins was given by the emperor to various nobles, cities and clerics in order to win their support. Some inflation made the denar smaller. By the 1200s coinage ceased to be rare. Designs varied, some were derived from the original

Carolingian temple, cross and inscription types, others were local symbols. When the thin, one-sided bracteates evolved, they took on a distinct form in Switzerland. There they were often struck on square blanks, which would spread out to appear roundish except at the points because the dies were round. Bold pellet borders were also characteristic.

Like the Germans, many new denominations both larger and smaller developed in the 1400s and later, including gold and, in the 1500s, thalers. Copper was usually not favored and most coins of low value were struck in very base silver-copper alloy called billon.

Even though much of Switzerland was united over the 1200s through 1400s, each of the member cantons (provinces) maintained its own distinctive coinage.

Additional Specialized Books:
Craig, W.D., *Germanic Coinages.*
Metcalf, D.M., *Coinage of South Germany.*
Saurma, H. *Die Saurmasche Munzsammlung deutscher, schweitzerischer und polnischer.*

Known counterfeits: Counterfeits of medieval Swiss coins are not commonly encountered. Some are known from Chur of the 1600s.
                                                 VF
Basel. 1429-37. AV Goldgulden. Madonna stg. with Child / SIGISMVD, etc., royal orb.......... 300.00
Geneva. c.1200. Denier. S PETRVS, Head of St. Peter / GENEVAS, Cross........................ 100.00
__. 1590. 12 Sols. Shield within sun / PXII SOLS POVR LES SOLDATS DE GENEVE (AE, 30mm) 50.00
Lausanne. c.1300. Denier. S_D_S LAVSAN_, Temple / CIVITAS _QSTRI, Cross 75.00
Lindau. 1200s. Bracteate. Lime tree............... 65.00

                                                 VF
Schaffhausen. 1597. 3 Kreuzer. Ram leaping from tower / Double headed eagle with 3 on chest. 60.00
Schwyz. 1510-20. Scudo. Double headed eagle / Floral cross.. Rare
Solothurn. 1200s. Bracteate Denar. VRSVS, Head l. 40.00

                                                 VF
St. Gallen. c.1200. Bracteate. MONETA SANC GALLI, Facing bust, pellet border 300.00
Zug. 1609. Dicken. MON NO TVGI SAN OSW, Bust of St. Oswald / Eagle (30mm)......... 125.00

EUROPEAN COINS

Modern coinage as we know it began in Europe during the 1500s and spread throughout the world with the establishment of European colonies, or with the opening of European trade relations. Since this time the manufacture of coinage has progressed from hand hammering, to screw presses and roller dies, to steam powered presses. Today's high tech, electronic minting machines, capable of striking thousands of coins per minute, are basically an improved version of the steam-powered ones first used in the late 1700s.

Many people collect European and other world coins by "type." This means one of each design, or of each design in each different alloy in which it is struck. Others collect one of each date and mintmark much as United States coins are collected. There is no right or wrong way to collect coins. The most important thing to remember is to enjoy the experience, and perhaps to learn by the process. There is no series more extensively documented in catalogues than the coinage of modern Europe, so whatever path the collector chooses, he need not do it in the dark. With the introduction of the Euro, the new pan-European currency, people are becoming more and more aware of the changes in European coinage — past, present and future.

Because many colonial coins feature the name and symbolism of the colonizing power more prominently than any reference to the colony itself, such coins are included in this chapter. This should make it easier for the layman to find the type of coin he is trying to identify.

BOOKS ABOUT EUROPEAN COINS

While as in any field there are thousands of specialized books, a few very basic books will go a long way. Many collectors never feel the need to progress much further than the following volumes:

Bruce, Colin R., II. *Unusual World Coins.*
Krause, Chester, and Clifford Mishler. *Standard Catalog of World Coins, 1601-1700.*
Krause, Chester, and Clifford Mishler. *Standard Catalog of World Coins, 1701-1800.*
Krause, Chester, and Clifford Mishler. *Standard Catalog of World Coins, 1801-1900.*
Krause, Chester, and Clifford Mishler. *Standard Catalog of World Coins, 1901-date.*

The above books are virtually an entire library in compact form. Coverage is extensive from the 1600s through the mid-1700s, and is virtually complete with individual date and mint listings from that time to the present.

Yeoman, R.S. *Current Coins of the World.*
Yeoman, R.S. *Modern World Coins, 1850-1964.*

COUNTERFEIT EUROPEAN COINS

While many individual counterfeits will be listed under each specific country, it is always important to remember that new counterfeits of the more expensive European coins appear every year. This also applies to many more common gold bullion issues.

AUSTRIA

The modern coinage of Austria, until 1918, was used in a much larger area than is present day Austria. It circulated in the many lands of the Hapsburg dynasty, and of their dependent nobles. While modern coin production with the use of roller dies began before his reign, the later coinage of Leopold I the Hogmouth (1657-1705), took it to a new height of uniformity. Their excellent portraits are a perfect example of the Baroque style. Collectors should

remember that coins struck with roller dies usually appear slightly curved and that this is not a flaw.

The standard design formula is an obverse portrait, and a double headed eagle reverse. It continued through the 1890s, when a crown and values became the most common designs. A very few commemoratives were also struck during this time. Austria is one of three modern countries to have used the double headed eagle. They are easily distinguished. A Hapsburg shield is on its breast (see illustration). Russia's eagle has St. George slaying a dragon on its breast. Serbia's (later Yugoslavia's) eagle has a shield depicting a cross with C's in the angles. The later Yugoslav shield may be more complex but still contains this element.

After World War I, Austria became a republic and was reduced to its present size. Its circulating coins and commemoratives depict both aspects of local history and culture, such as a Royal Lipizzaner stallion or fauna such as the edelweiss. During World War II Austria was part of Germany, and Nazi coins with the mintmark B were struck in Vienna.

During most of Austria's history, powerful nobles and bishops were allowed to strike their own coins. The Counts of Tyrol were the most prolific issuers of coins. Their three kreuzers are particularly common. The Archbishops of Salzburg also struck vast numbers of coins at several mints from 996 through 1806.

Additional Specialized Books: Miller zu Aicholz, *Oesterreichische Munzpragungen, 1519-1938.*

Probszt, G. *Die Münzen Salzburgs.*

Known counterfeits: All 1780 Maria Theresa thalers with mintmarks SF are modern restrikes. The same is true for most 1915 gold 4 ducat, 1 ducat, 20 corona and 100 corona and 1892 8 florin and 4 florin.

VF

Leopold I the Hogmouth, 1657-1705. 2 pfennig (S).
  Three shields / blank 12.00
__. 3 Kreuzer. Bust r. / Double headed
  eagle. (S) 25.00
__. 15 Kreuzer. similar. (S) 35.00
__. Thaler. similar (S) 225.00

__. Double Thaler. similar (S) 350.00
Eighteenth Century   **F**
1800 Kreuzer Bust of Francis II r. / Eagle (C) 2.00
1714 3 Kreuzer. Bust of Charles VI r. /
  Eagle (S) 15.00
1765 3 Kreuzer. Bust of Maria Theresa
  (Billon) 15.00
1754 10 Kreuzer. Bust of Francis I in wreath /Eagle,
  10 on altar (S) 17.50
1795 12 Kreuzer. Eagle / Inscription (Billon) ... 5.00

1778 20 Kreuzer. Bust of Joseph II in Wreath /
  Eagle (S) 5.00
1800 24 Kreuzer. Eagle / Inscription
  (Billon) 20.00
1746 30 Kreuzer. Bust in diamond / Eagle in diamond (S) 40.00

Eighteenth Century   F

1751 1/2 Thaler. Bust of Francis I r. / Eagle
(S) 65.00
1780 SF Thaler restrike. Bust of Maria Theresa /
Eagle. Unc. 7.00
1798 Thaler. Bust of Francis II r. / Arms.
(S)..75.00
1773 Ducat. Bust of Maria Theresa r. / Eagle
(G) 200.00
1773 3 Ducat. Bust of Joseph II r. / Eagle
(G) 1,000.00

Nineteenth Century to 1920   VF

1816 Kreuzer. Crowned shield / Inscription
(C) 2.00
1860 4 Kreuzer. Eagle / Wreath (C)................. 6.00
1812 20 Kreuzer. Bust of Francis I in wreath / Eagle
(S)... 10.00
1870 20 Kreuzer. Bust of Franz Josef / Eagle
(Billon).. 2.00
1841 1/2 Thaler. Bust of Ferdinand I / Eagle
(S)..90.00

1857 2 Thaler. Bust of Franz Josef / Tower between
train and ship 800.00
1893 1 Heller. Eagle (C)..........................35
1901 2 Heller. Eagle (C)..........................50
1893 1 Corona. Head of Franz Josef / Crown
(S)... 3.00

Republic Coinage 1923 to 1938   XF

1924 100 Kronen. Eagle head / Oak sprig
(C) 1.50

1925 Schilling. Neo-classical building / Shield
(S)...3.50

Republic Coinage 1923 to 1938   XF

1928 2 Schilling. Schubert / Ten shields (S) ... 10.00
1935 5 Schilling. Madonna and Child / Eagle
(S) 28.00
1926 25 Schilling. Eagle (G) 125.00

Republic Coinage 1946 to date   BU

1972 2 Groschen. Eagle (AL)..............................20
1946 Schilling. Sower (AL)............................ 1.50
1957 10 Schilling. Shield / Girl's head (S)........ 6.00

1974 10 Schilling. Eagle / Girl's head (CN) 1.75
1996 20 Schilling. Anton Bruckner (ALB)....... 4.00
1956 25 Schilling. Mozart (S) 4.50
1982 500 Schilling. Printing press (S)............. 50.00

BALKANS

The Ottoman conquest of the Balkan Peninsula ended the use of European style coinage for most of the region, and it was not restored until the 1800s. The only surviving coinages were those of Transylvania, and the small Venetian and Ragusan settlements along the Adriatic coast. The former were all copper, the latter a variety of metals.

The first country to regain its independence from the Ottoman Turks was Greece. Its first coinage was very distinctive, and portrayed the mythological Phoenix bird reborn from its ashes, alluding to the rebirth of the Greek nation. After very few years, its coinage took on the less creative forms popular elsewhere in Europe: shields, royal portraits and a denomination within a wreath. The coinages of the two Greek republics, 1925-1935 and 1974 to date, are also distinctive in their harking back to ancient times for their inspiration.

Soon Serbia (1868), Romania (1867), Bulgaria (1881), and Montenegro (1906) struck their first modern coinages, on much the same European pattern as mentioned above. Albania lagged behind until 1926. After the first World War, Montenegro and the former Austrian territories of Slovenia, Croatia and Bosnia-Herzogovina were joined under the king of Serbia to form Yugoslavia. Following World War II these kingdoms were all overthrown by Communists. Most communist coins follow the typical pattern of a state seal on the obverse and a value or a symbol of agricultural or industrial labor on the reverse. As a result of the Yugoslav Civil War, Slovenia, Croatia, Macedonia, and Bosnia-Herzegovina were established as independent states. Moldova came into being as a result of the break-up of the Soviet Union.

Post-communist Balkan coinage varies from monotonous bank monograms and has exquisite depictions of flora and fauna. Some of these new governments have even chosen to use the same heraldic motifs which were found on their coinages during the 1930s. During the last few years all these countries have struck collectors' coins. Some, such as Bosnia's, have been actively marked in North America. Others, such as Romania's, have been very scantily distributed.

Because the alphabets and languages used may seem unusual to North American readers, it is useful here to give some Balkan country names in their native forms:

Albania .... SHQIPNI or SHQIPERI
Bulgaria ....БЪЛГАРИЯ
Croatia ....HRVATSKA
Greece .... ΕΛΛΑΣ
Macedonia......................... ΜΑΚΕΔΟΝИΙΑ
Montenegro............................. ЦРНА ГОРА
Serbia ....СРБИЈА or СРПИЈА
Yugoslavia..........................ЈУГОСЛАВИЈА

Additional Specialized Books: see general European listings.
Known counterfeits: Look for the Albanian gold and dollar-sized silver coins of the 1920s and 1930s, particularly the 1938 gold. Modern style counterfeits exist of the 1600s Venetian coppers for Dalmatia and Albania.

ALBANIA   XF

1935 Qindar Ar. Eagle (C) 10.00

1931 1/2 Lek. Arms / Man fighting lion (N) ... 10.00
1935 Frang Ar. Head of King Zog /
Arms (S).....................................25.00
1926 100 Franga Ar. Head of Amet Zogu / Chariot
(G) 800.00
1941 0.20 Lek. King of Italy in helmet / Eagle
between fasces (Steel).................... 4.00
1939 10 Lek. King of Italy / similar (S) 120.00
1947 1/2 Lek. Eagle (Z) 1.50
1964 1 Lek. Eagle (AL) 2.00

                                    BU

1988 5 Lek. Train / Train. (CN) 12.00
1996 50 Lek. Ancient horseman (CN) 2.00

BOSNIA-HERZEGOVINA   BU

1994 500 Dinara. Arms over bridge / Wolf
(CN) 8.50
1998 10 fennig. Triangle / Map
(C plated Steel) 1.00

BULGARIA   VF

1912 2 Stotinki. Arms / Wreath. (C)................. 1.00
1881 5 Stotinki. similar. (C)......................5.00
1925 1 Lev. similar (CN) 50
1882 2 Leva. similar (S) 7.00
1943 5 Leva. Medieval horseman r. / Wreath.... 1.00
1894 20 Leva. Head of Ferdinand I l. / Arms
(G) 100.00

Postwar Issues   BU

1951 1 Stotinka. Arms / Grain (ALB) 25
1977 50 Stotinki. Runner / Arms (CN)............. 2.00
1976 1 Lev. Gun and knife / Lion (C)............... 5.00

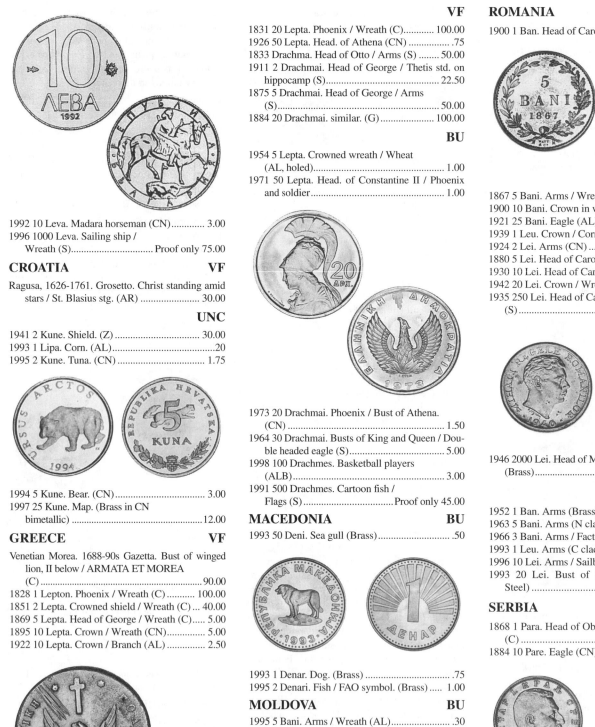

1992 10 Leva. Madara horseman (CN)............. 3.00
1996 1000 Leva. Sailing ship /
   Wreath (S)............................... Proof only 75.00

CROATIA   VF

Ragusa, 1626-1761. Grosetto. Christ standing amid
   stars / St. Blasius stg. (AR) 30.00

UNC

1941 2 Kune. Shield. (Z) 30.00
1993 1 Lipa. Corn. (AL).......................................20
1995 2 Kune. Tuna. (CN) 1.75

1994 5 Kune. Bear. (CN) 3.00
1997 25 Kune. Map. (Brass in CN
   bimetallic) 12.00

GREECE   VF

Venetian Morea. 1688-90s Gazetta. Bust of winged
   lion, II below / ARMATA ET MOREA
   (C) 90.00
1828 1 Lepton. Phoenix / Wreath (C) 100.00
1851 2 Lepta. Crowned shield / Wreath (C) ... 40.00
1869 5 Lepta. Head of George / Wreath (C)..... 5.00
1895 10 Lepta. Crown / Wreath (CN).............. 5.00
1922 10 Lepta. Crown / Branch (AL) 2.50

VF

1831 20 Lepta. Phoenix / Wreath (C)........... 100.00
1926 50 Lepta. Head. of Athena (CN) 75
1833 Drachma. Head of Otto / Arms (S) 50.00
1911 2 Drachmai. Head of George / Thetis std. on
   hippocamp (S)... 22.50
1875 5 Drachmai. Head of George / Arms
   (S)... 50.00
1884 20 Drachmai. similar. (G) 100.00

BU

1954 5 Lepta. Crowned wreath / Wheat
   (AL, holed).. 1.00
1971 50 Lepta. Head. of Constantine II / Phoenix
   and soldier.. 1.00

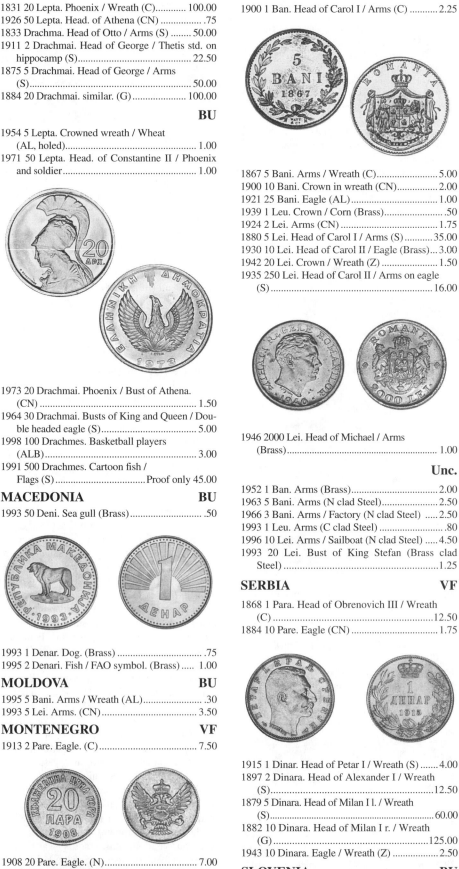

1973 20 Drachmai. Phoenix / Bust of Athena.
   (CN) 1.50
1964 30 Drachmai. Busts of King and Queen / Dou-
   ble headed eagle (S)................................... 5.00
1998 100 Drachmes. Basketball players
   (ALB)... 3.00
1991 500 Drachmes. Cartoon fish /
   Flags (S) ....Proof only 45.00

MACEDONIA   BU

1993 50 Deni. Sea gull (Brass)............................50

1993 1 Denar. Dog. (Brass) 75
1995 2 Denari. Fish / FAO symbol. (Brass) 1.00

MOLDOVA   BU

1995 5 Bani. Arms / Wreath (AL)........................30
1993 5 Lei. Arms. (CN) 3.50

MONTENEGRO   VF

1913 2 Pare. Eagle. (C) 7.50

1908 20 Pare. Eagle. (N)................................... 7.00
1912 1 Perper. Head of Nicholas / Arms (S)... 14.00
1910 2 Perpera. similar (S) 30.00
1910 10 Perpera. similar (G) 250.00

ROMANIA   VF

1900 1 Ban. Head of Carol I / Arms (C) 2.25

1867 5 Bani. Arms / Wreath (C)........................5.00
1900 10 Bani. Crown in wreath (CN)............... 2.00
1921 25 Bani. Eagle (AL) 1.00
1939 1 Leu. Crown / Corn (Brass)......................50
1924 2 Lei. Arms (CN) 1.75
1880 5 Lei. Head of Carol I / Arms (S) 35.00
1930 10 Lei. Head of Carol II / Eagle (Brass)... 3.00
1942 20 Lei. Crown / Wreath (Z) 1.50
1935 250 Lei. Head of Carol II / Arms on eagle
   (S) 16.00

1946 2000 Lei. Head of Michael / Arms
   (Brass)... 1.00

Unc.

1952 1 Ban. Arms (Brass)..................................2.00
1963 5 Bani. Arms (N clad Steel)...................... 2.50
1966 3 Bani. Arms / Factory (N clad Steel) 2.50
1993 1 Leu. Arms (C clad Steel) 80
1996 10 Lei. Arms / Sailboat (N clad Steel) 4.50
1993 20 Lei. Bust of King Stefan (Brass clad
   Steel) 1.25

SERBIA   VF

1868 1 Para. Head of Obrenovich III / Wreath
   (C) 12.50
1884 10 Pare. Eagle (CN) 1.75

1915 1 Dinar. Head of Petar I / Wreath (S) 4.00
1897 2 Dinara. Head of Alexander I / Wreath
   (S)..12.50
1879 5 Dinara. Head of Milan I l. / Wreath
   (S)... 60.00
1882 10 Dinara. Head of Milan I r. / Wreath
   (G) 125.00
1943 10 Dinara. Eagle / Wreath (Z) 2.50

SLOVENIA   BU

1992 10 Stotinov. Salamander (AL) 25
1996 50 Stotinov. Bee. (AL) 35

BU

1996 5 Tolarjev. Locomotive (Brass) 1.65
1994 500 Tolarjev. Quill pen.
   (S)............................Proof only 28.50
1993 5000 Tolarjev. Bees around hive.
   (G).........................Proof only 275.00

YUGOSLAVIA   VF

1925 50 Para. Head of Alexander I / Wreath
   (CN) 1.00
1938 2 Dinara. Crown (ALB)........................... 1.00
1932 50 Dinara. Head of Alexander I / Eagle.
   (S)..22.00
1945 Dinar. Arms. (Z) 1.00

BU

1953 50 Para. Arms (AL) 25
1990 1 Dinara. Arms. (CNZ) 25
1983 500 Dinara. Olympic symbols /
   Skier (S)..............................Proof only 17.50
1992 1 Dinar. Bank monogram (Brass) 60
1996 1 New Dinar. Eagle shield (Brass) 1.50

1996 20 New Dinar. Eagle shield / Bust of Nikola
   Tesla (CNZ) ....Proof only 16.00

BALTIC STATES

The regions that are today Estonia, Latvia, Lithuania and Finland were until 1918 submerged under the domination of Russia, Poland, Germany and Sweden in various combinations. Usually these greater powers would permit certain cities such as Riga, or certain nobles, to strike their own coins. These were somewhat common in the 1600s, but by the 1700s they ceased to be significant. During the 1800s, virtually none of these states were permitted their own coinage besides Finland, which was a semi-autonomous Grand Duchy under Russia.

The collapse of the great European Empires during World War I liberated these countries from Russia — the must recent power to dominate the area. The coats of arms of these newly independent states were used on one side or the other of virtually every coin struck between the wars. While in most cases the other side was a monotonous indication of value, certain other pieces were exceptionally attractive. Most notable are beautiful rendi-

tions of the personification of Latvia. Lithuania also struck interesting commemoratives.

With the exception of Finland, all these countries were conquered by the Soviet Union in 1940. They re-emerged with the breakup of the Soviet empire in 1989. It is almost shocking how closely some of the new post-Soviet Baltic coins resemble the coins struck by these countries in the 1930s. The exception of course is Finland, whose coinage had the opportunity to evolve naturally during its longer independence. Since 1951 its modernistic commemoratives have been released in quantity to the world collector market.

Additional Specialized Books: see general European listings.

Known counterfeits: Known Finnish counterfeits include the 1951 500 Markkaa and possibly the 1918 Red Government 5 pennia.

ESTONIA   F

Reval, 1663-67. 1 Rundstück. Crowned shield /
   MON NOV CIVITA REVAL (AR) 40.00

VF

1922 3 Marka. Three lions (CN) 4.50
1926 5 Marka. Shield in wreath (CN) 150.00
1929 1 Sent. Three lions / Oak leaves (C)......... 1.00
1935 20 Senti. Shield (CN)................................ 2.00
1934 1 Kroon. Shield in wreath / Viking ship
   (ALB)... 7.00
1930 2 Krooni. Shield in wreath / Castle (S) 7.00
1932 2 Krooni. Shield in wreath / University
   building (S) 20.00

BU

1991 5 Senti. Three lions (Brass) 25

1993 5 Krooni. Doe (Brass)............................... 3.00
1992 100 Krooni. Three lions / Three swallows
   (S).....................................Proof only 35.00

FINLAND   VF

1873 1 Penni. Crowned Aii (C).......................... 8.00
1889 5 Penniä. Crowned Aiii (C)....................... 5.00
1900 10 Penniä. Crowned Nii (C) 5.00
1917 25 Penniä. Russian eagle (S) 75
1890 1 Markka. similar (S)............................... 2.50
1882 10 Markkaa. similar. (G)........................ 80.00

XF

1918 5 Penniä. Trumpets. (C).......................... 55.00
1919 1 Penni. Lion. (C) 1.75

BU

1986 50 Penniä. Lion / Tree (ALB)....................50

BU

1993 10 Markkaa. Capercaille bird / Branches (Brass
   in CN, bimetallic)... 4.50
1956 100 Markkaa. Shield / Trees (S) 3.00
1990 100 Markkaa. Lyre / Owl (S).................. 40.00
1952 500 Markkaa. Olympic rings / Wreath
   (S)..40.00

LATVIA   F

Riga, 1660-65. Schilling. CR monogram / SOLIDVS
   CIVI RIG, crossed keys (Billon) 30.00

Republic   VF

1935 1 Santims. Shield. (C) 1.40
1939 2 Santimi. Shield (C)................................ 2.00
1922 5 Santimi. Shield (C)................................ 1.00
1922 10 Santimu. Shield (N) 1.00
1922 50 Santimu. Shield / Latvia gazing from
   rudder of ship (N)...................................... 3.00
1924 1 Lats. Shield / Wreath (S)....................... 3.00
1925 2 Lati. similar (S)..................................... 3.00
1931 5 Lati. Head of Latvia r. / Arms (S) 11.50

Restored Republic   BU

1992 2 Santimi. Shield (C plated Steel) 50

1992 1 Lats. Arms / Fish (CN) 3.75
1992 2 Lati. Arms / Cow (CN) 7.00
1995 10 Latu. Arms / Schooner
   (S)...Proof only 47.50

LITHUANIA   F

John III Sobieski, 1674-1696. 1679, 6 Groszy. Bust
   r. / Knight riding l. (S)............................... Rare
Augustus II, 1697-1704. 1706 6 Groszy. Crowned
   bust r. / Three shields (S) 150.00

Republic   VF

1936 1 Centas. Knight riding l. (C) 5.00
1936 2 Centai. similar. (C)................................ 8.00
1925 10 Centu. Knight riding l. / Ear of grain.
   (Brass) 3.00
1925 50 Centu. similar. (Brass) 7.00
1925 1 Litas. similar / Oak branch (S)............... 3.00
1925 2 Litu. similar / Wreath (S)...................... 5.50
1925 5 Litai. similar. (S) 8.00
1936 5 Litai. similar / Bust l. (S) 4.50
1938 10 Litai. Stylized castle / Bust l. (S) 20.00

Restored Republic   BU

1991 5 Centai. Knight riding l. (AL) 40
1997 50 Centai. similar. (Brass).........................85

1997 1 Litas. Bust / Knight riding l. (CN)......... 2.00
1995 10 Litu. Runner and globe / similar
   (CN) ....Proof only 15.00
1996 50 Litu. Basketball players /
   Shield (S)................................Proof only 40.00

LIVONIA & ESTONIA   F

1757 4 Kopeks. LIVO ESTHONICA, Two Shields /
   Double headed eagle (S)............................40.00

BRITISH ISLES

Despite successful experiments with milled (screw press) coinage during the reign of Elizabeth I (1558-1603), this method of striking uniform, well-made coins was not adopted in England until 1663, after the restoration of the monarchy. By this time there were a great many different denominations in silver, from the tiny silver penny, to the crown (60 pence) which had finally become common.

By the end of the century most of the silver denominations below six pence were being struck only for ceremonial distribution on Maundy Thursday, the Thursday before Easter. These silver coins were given to the poor but usually passed into circulation. After the mid-1700s their value as collectibles was so established that almost all were immediately sold by their recipients to collectors, and today survive in high grade.

Another change was the replacement of puny, privately made royal contract farthings with officially struck regal farthings and halfpennies of good weight. For awhile the government replaced these coppers with ones of tin, but this was soon abandoned due to their tendency to corrode.

The designs on British coins have usually been very conservative. The shield on a cross was used before and after the Civil War. New designs were often heraldic as well, sometimes showing one shield, other times showing arrangements of the shields of England, Scotland, Ireland and France. (England claimed France until the early 1800s.) The new copper coins show a seated female, Britannia, an allegory for Britain dating back to Roman days.

During the 1700s the government failed to provide enough coins to satisfy Britain's growing industrial economy. The industrial Revolution also provided the answer to this dilemma. Merchants and miners took matters into their own hands and contracted with modern factories to strike their own money. These tokens, common from the late 1780s and 1790s as well as from 1811-15 depict a delightful array of scenes from Gothic cathedrals to the very machines of the Industrial Revolution.

Gradually the government responded. New steam-power struck coppers were introduced in 1797-99, including the first penny to be struck in copper instead of silver. A massive issue of machine struck silver and gold was released in 1816. Notable is the powerful Baroque-style depiction of St. George slaying the dragon by Benedetto Pistrucci, used on the crown and gold pieces.

During the reign of Queen Victoria (1837-1901) old designs were sometimes given a beautiful neo-Gothic interpretation. Another innovation on the practical side was the replacement of the copper coins with slightly smaller ones of bronze. These wore much better than pure copper.

The two world wars took their toll on British coinage. The purity of the silver was lowered from 92-1/2 percent to 50 percent in 1920 after the First World War. It was replaced completely by cupro-nickel in 1947 after the Second World War. From the Great Depression onwards gold ceased to circulate. The gold sovereigns struck from then until today were solely for bullion or collector purposes.

After 1,100 years of using a coinage derived from the penny of Charlemagne, and based on multiples of 12, Britain finally replaced the pound of 240 pence with one divided into 100 decimal new pence. The new seven sided 50 pence introduced in 1969 proved so popular that since then, many countries have used this shape for their coinage.

During the second half of the twentieth century collectors' commemoratives were issued quite frequently. From the 1970s onward new creative designs were used for these coins. Many were sold at a premium and were never placed in circulation.

Scottish coins followed most of the same trends as on English coins quite closely. Where royal copper coins were needed, however, Britannia was not depicted. Instead a thistle, Scotland's national flower, or scepters were used. After 1707 Scotland and England were joined as the United Kingdom and separate Scottish coinage was ended. From 1937 to 1970, special Scottish shillings were struck, good throughout the United Kingdom. The current five pence and several brass pound coins also honor Scotland.

Irish coins continued longer but were usually limited to base metal. From the Restoration until 1823, Ireland was usually provided with distinctive halfpennies, farthings and ultimately pennies with a crowned harp as their reverse. The first machine made ones were struck in 1805. There were two important exceptions. After James II was forced to flee England in 1688, he managed to hold onto Ireland for several months. To help finance his war to keep the throne he struck high value coins in bras containing metal from melted cannon. These sixpences, shillings, half crowns and crowns were dated to the exact month and are called "gun money." Another exception came in 1804-13 when the Bank of Ireland struck silver five, ten and thirty pence and six shilling tokens to ease the coinage shortage.

Colonial coins struck during the 1700s and early 1800s, less so than the later ones, were very similar in style to British issues. Those for the American Colonies are discussed under the United States section. One big exception is the coinage of the East India Company. Many of these are hardly distinguishable from local Indian states and Moghal Empire coins. Usually they are identified by certain symbols or their machine-made fabric, but they were originally intended to circulate alongside local coins and their designs made this possible.

During the mid 1800s colonial coins became increasingly more practical in their designs, and many have no other motif than a large number indicating the value. Beginning in the 1920s in most territories, somewhat earlier in a few others, local color and creativity entered into colonial coin design. Native plants and animals were depicted. Some larger values bore the coat of arms of the individual colony. Many of the designs were so pleasing that they continued in use for decades, even after independence. Like in the homeland, silver was phased out after World War II.

Many independent former colonies still recognize the British monarch as Queen. These British Commonwealth members often voluntarily depict the monarch on the obverse of their coins, as they did before independence. Most are listed here for convenience, except Canada which is covered in depth in its own section.

Additional Specialized Books:

Dalton and Hamer, *The Provincial Token Coinage of the 18th Century*.

Pridmore, F., *The Coins of the British Commonwealth of Nations*. 4 vols.

Seaby, et al. *Coins of England and the United Kingdom*. The basic reference.

West, R. ed., *British Coins Market Values*. Current updated values but minimal numismatic information.

Known counterfeits: Vast numbers of contemporary counterfeits of 1700s copper were made, both by striking and casting. Those made in America and those in middle grade are worth more than the real ones. Many counterfeits of 1811-1820 silver were made at the time and have some small numismatic value. Collector counterfeits have been made of many coins with rare dates spanning the last 150 years. A partial list includes: 1905 half crown and 1847 Gothic crown. A great many sovereigns have been counterfeited, many originating in Lebanon. Some known examples include: 1887, 1910, 1911, 1918M, 1923SA (altered date), 1927SA. Other circulation counterfeits include shilling 1916, florin 1900, 1918, 1942, half crown 1818, 3 shillings 1815, guinea 1798.

ENGLAND   F

Charles II, 1660-85. 1672 Farthing. Bust l. / Britannia std. (C) 25.00

F

1675 Halfpenny. similar 35.00
1670 Threepence. Bust r. / Three interlocking C's (S)... 15.00
1680 Crown. Bust r. / Cross of shields, C's in angles (S).. 125.00
1676. Half Guinea. Bust r. / Cross of shields, scepters in angles (G) 225.00
James II, 1685-88. 1686 Halfpenny. Bust r. / Britannia std. (Tin)............................. 100.00

1685 Shilling. Bust l. / Cross of shields (S) 50.00
1686 Half Crown. Bust l. / Cross of shields (S). 80.00
1688 Guinea. Bust l. / Cross of shields, scepters in angles (G) 375.00
William and Mary, 1688-94. 1690 Farthing. Two busts r. / Britannia std. l. (Tin)................. 85.00
1694, similar but copper 35.00
1689 Twopence. Two busts r. / Crowned 2 (S)... 225.00

1693 Shilling. Two busts r. / Cross of shields, monograms in angles (S)......................... 40.00
1691 5 Guineas. Two busts r. / Crowned shield (G)...1,500.00
William III, 1694-1702. 1699 Halfpenny. Bust r. / Britannia std. l. 25.00
1696 Sixpence. Bust r. / Cross of shields (S) .. 20.00
1697 Shilling. similar (S) 30.00

1700 Half crown. Bust r. / Cross of shields (S)..50.00
1695 Crown. Bust r. / Cross of shields. (S) ... 100.00

GREAT BRITAIN   F

Anne, 1702-1714. 1714 Farthing. Bust l. / Britannia std. (C) 225.00

1708 Shilling. Bust l. / Cross of shields (S) 30.00
1708 Half Crown. similar (S) 45.00

F

1712 Guinea. Bust l. / Cross of shields, scepters in angles (G).. 225.00
George I, 1714-27. 1720 Halfpenny. Bust r. / Britannia std. (C) 10.00
1723 Shilling. Bust r. / Cross of shields, roses and plumes in angles (S) 18.00

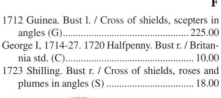

1716 Crown. similar. (S)................................. 210.00
1718 Quarter Guinea. Bust r. / Cross of shields, scepters in angles (G) 100.00
George II, 1727-60. 1754 Farthing. Bust l. / Britannia std. (C)...................................... 6.00

1749 Halfpenny. similar. (C) 6.00
1757 Sixpence. Bust l. / Cross of shields (S) 8.00
1759 Guinea. Bust l. / "Rose" shield (G) 175.00
George III, 1760-1820. 1773 Farthing. Bust r. / Britannia std. (C)................................... 6.00
1763 Three pence. Bust r. / Crowned 3 (S) 10.00
1787 Sixpence. Bust r. / Cross of shields, crowns in angles (S) 6.00

1798 Guinea. Bust r. / "Spade" shield (G) 150.00

Machine Made Coinage   VF

1799 Farthing. Bust r. / Britannia std. (C) 5.00
1797 Twopence. similar but broad border (C, 2 ounces!)... 35.00

VF

1817 Shilling. Bust r. / Arms within garter (S) ... 8.50
1817 Half Crown. similar................................. 35.00
George IV, 1820-30. 1826 Halfpenny. Bust l. / Britannia std. (C).................................. 7.00
1826 Sixpence. Bust l. / Lion on crown. (S).... 12.00
1826 Sovereign. Bust l. / Crowned shield (G)..200.00

1826 5 Pounds. Bust l. / Crowned arms. (G).... Rare
William IV, 1830-37. 1831 Farthing. Bust r. / Britannia std. (C).............................. 10.00

1837 Halfpenny. similar (C) 9.00
1836 Four Pence. similar (S) 5.25
1832 Sovereign. Bust r. / Crowned shield (G)..200.00
Victoria, 1837-1901. 1844 Half Farthing. Young head / Crown (C)...................................... 5.00
1858 Farthing. Young head l. / Britannia std. (C) 5.00
1886 Halfpenny. Bust / similar (C)................... 2.75

VF

1887 Sovereign. Crowned bust / St. George slaying dragon (G) 100.00
1893 2 Pounds. Veiled bust / similar (G) 325.00
1893 5 Pounds. similar (G) 750.00
Edward VII, 1901-10. 1903 Farthing. Head r. / Britannia std. (C) 1.75

1910 3 Pence. Head r. / Crowned 3 (S) 2.00
1902 Crown. Head r. / St. George slaying dragon (S) 45.00
1910 Sovereign. similar. (G) 100.00
George V, 1910-36. 1917 Farthing. Head l. / Britannia std. (C) .... .35
1928 Halfpenny. similar (C) .... .75
1935 Penny. similar (C) .... .50
1929 Sixpence. Head l. / Six acorns (S) 1.00

1916 Shilling. Head l. / Lion on crown (S) 2.50
1928 Florin. Head l. / Cross of shields, scepters in angles (S) 2.50
1935 Half Crown. Head l. / Shield (S) 3.00
1935 Crown. Head l. / St. George, armored, slaying dragon. (S) 8.00
1911 Half Sovereign. similar but saint nude (G) 60.00
1932 Maundy set. 1, 2, 3, 4 Pence. Head l. / Crown over value. (S) .... Unc. 75.00

XF

George VI, 1936-52. 1943 Farthing. Head l. / Wren (C) .... .30
1942 Halfpenny. Head l. / Ship (C) .... .60
1937 3 Pence. Head l. / Thrift plant (Brass) 1.00
1946 6 Pence. Head l. / Crowned GRI (S) 1.00
1950 Half Crown. Head l. / Shield (CN) 1.50

VF

1858 Penny. similar (C) 6.00
1900 Penny. Veiled bust / similar (C) 1.00
1881 3 Pence. Young head / Crowned 3 (S) 3.25
1838 4 Pence. Young head / Britannia std. (S) 5.25
1887 6 Pence. Crowned bust / Arms (S) 3.00
1893 Shilling. Veiled bust / Three crowned shields (S) 5.50

1852 Florin. Crowned "Gothic" bust / Cross of shields, flowers in angles (S) 32.00
1874 Half Crown. Young head / Crowned shield (S) 25.00
1887 Double Florin. Crowned bust / Cross of shields, scepters in angles (S) 17.50
1893 Crown. Veiled bust / St. George slaying dragon (S) 32.00
1880 Half Sovereign. Young head / Crowned shield (G) 75.00

XF

1951 Crown. Head l. / St. George slaying dragon (CN) 6.00
Elizabeth II, 1952—. 1954 Farthing. Young bust / Wren 30
1962 Penny. Young bust / Britannia std. (C) 10
1953 Shilling. Young Bust / Crowned shield (CN) 35
1964 Florin. Young bust / Rose within border. (CN) 30
1965 Crown. Young bust / Bust of Churchill (CN) 1.00
1958 Sovereign. Young Bust / St. George slaying dragon (G) 100.00

Decimal Coinage **BU**

1971 1 New Penny. Bust in tiara / Portcullis (C)..25

1990 20 Pence. Bust in tiara / Crowned rose (CN, heptagonal)...75
1981 25 Pence. Bust in tiara / Heads of Charles and Diana (CN) 1.75
1973 50 Pence. Bust in tiara / Wreath of hands (CN, heptagonal)... 2.00
1995 Pound. Bust in tiara / Welsh dragon (Brass)... 3.50
1988 50 Pounds. Bust in tiara / Britannia stg. (G, 1/2 ounce) 160.00

British Tokens **VF**

1667 Farthing. Shield with castle and lion / NORWICH FARTHING (C) 30.00

British Tokens   VF

1792 Halfpenny. Elephant with castle on back /
    Lady Godiva on horse (C) 12.00
1788 Penny. Hooded head of Druid / Monogram
    (C) 12.00
1813 Penny. Birmingham Work House / Shield
    (C) 10.00
c.1980s R&W London / I (Brass) 10

SCOTLAND   F

Charles II, 1649-1685. 1677 Bawbee. Bust l. /
    Crowned thistle (C) 30.00
1669 Merk. Bust r. / Cross of shields, C's in angles
    (S).. 70.00

James II, 1685-89. 1687 10 Shillings. Bust r., 10
    below / Shields in angle of X 120.00
1687 40 Shillings. Bust r., 40 below / Crowned
    shield (S) 140.00
William and Mary, 1689-94. 1691 Bawbee. Two
    busts l. / Crowned thistle (C) 40.00
1693 20 Shillings. Two busts l., 20 below / Crowned
    shield (S) 120.00

1692 40 Shillings. Two busts l., 40 below / Crowned
    shield (S) 125.00
William III, 1694-1702. 1695 Turner. Crowned
    sword and scepter / Thistle (C) 30.00
1696 5 Shillings. Bust l. / Three thistles (S) ... 40.00
1696 40 Shillings. Bust l. / Crowned shield
    (S).. 120.00
Anne, 1702-14. 1705 5 Shillings. Bust l., 5 below /
    Three thistles (S)..................................... 40.00
1705 10 Shillings. Bust l., 10 below / Crowned
    shield (S)... 100.00

IRELAND   F

Charles II, 1660-1685. 1682 Halfpenny. Bust r. /
    Crowned Harp (C) 25.00
James II, 1685-91. 1686 Halfpenny. Bust l. /
    Crowned Harp (C) 20.00

1689 Shilling. Bust l. / XII over crown (C) 20.00
William and Mary, 1688-94. 1693 Halfpenny. Two
    busts r. / Crowned Harp (C) 35.00
William III, 1694-1702. 1696 Halfpenny. Bust r. /
    Crowned Harp (C) 37.50
George I, 1714-27. 1723 Farthing. Bust r. / Hibernia
    std. with harp (C) 25.00
George II, 1727-60. 1760 Halfpenny. Bust l. /
    Crowned Harp (C) 20.00

George III, 1760-1820. 1806 Farthing. Bust r. /
    Crowned Harp (C) 4.00
1805 5 Pence Bank Token. Bust r. / Inscription
    (S).. 7.50

George IV, 1820-30. 1822 Halfpenny. Bust l. /
    Crowned Harp (C) 8.00

Irish Free State   VF

1928 Farthing. Harp / Woodcock (C) 1.50
1935 Penny. Harp / Hen and chicks (C) 1.00
1928 6 Pence. Harp / Wolfhound (N)................ 1.00
1928 Florin. Harp / Salmon (S) 7.00

Irish Republic   XF

1953 Halfpenny. Harp / Pig and piglets (C) .... .25
1964 3 Pence. Harp / Hare (CN)........................ .25
1939 Shilling. Harp / Bull (S) 4.50
1962 Shilling. similar (CN)............................ 1.00
1963 Half Crown. Harp / Horse (CN) 2.00
1966 10 Shillings. Bust of Pearse / Statue of Cuchu-
    lainn (S).................................... BU 9.00

Decimal Coinage   BU

1978 1/2 Penny Harp/Celtic Bird........................ .25
1971 1 Penny. Harp / Celtic bird (C) .... .20
1986 20 Pence. Harp / Horse (Brass)................ 1.50
1988 50 Pence. Harp / Arms of Dublin (CN)...... 2.50
1995 Pound. Harp / Stag (CN).......................... 4.50

BRITISH COLONIES & COMMONWEALTH

AUSTRALIA   VF

1813 5 Shillings. NEW SOUTH WALES counter-
    stamped on Spanish colonial 8 Reales with
    large central hole (S) 16,000.00
1927 Halfpenny. Bust of George V (C) .... .75
1949 Penny. Head of George VI / Kangaroo
    (C)... .25
1910 3 Pence. Bust of Edward VII / Arms (S).... 5.00

1936 6 Pence. Bust of George V / Arms (S) 4.50
1943 6 Pence. Head of George VI / Arms (S)...... .75
1942 Shilling. similar / Ram's head (S)............. 1.50
1910 Florin. Bust of Edward VII / Arms
    (S) 150.00
1927 Florin. Bust of George V / Parliament
    (S) 7.50
1937 Crown. Head of George VI / Crown
    (S) 10.00
1918 Sovereign. Head of George V / St. George
    slaying dragon (G) 100.00

Elizabeth II   XF

1961 Penny. Young bust / Kangaroo (C) .... .40
1964 3 Pence. Young head / Wheat (S) .... .50
1954 6 Pence. Young bust / Arms (S)................ 2.25

Decimal Coinage   BU

1961 Shilling. Young bust / Ram's head (S)........ .75
1960 Florin. Young bust / Arms (S).................. 3.50

1966 2 Cents. Bust in tiara / Frilled lizard (C)......50
1996 20 Cents. similar / Platypus (CN) 50
1966 50 Cents. similar / Arms (S).....................6.50
1996 5 Dollars. similar / Bust of Donald Bradman (ALB in Steel, bimetallic)..........................12.50

1995 40 Dollars. similar / Emu (Palladium) 225.00

BAHAMAS BU

1806 Penny. Bust of George III / Ship (C)... F 35.00
1971 1 Cent. Starfish (C)...25
1966 10 Cents. Two fish (CN, scalloped) 25

1972 25 Cents. Sloop. (N)..50
1966 1 Dollar. Conch shell (S) 5.00
1971 2 Dollars. Two flamingos (S) 8.00
1967 20 Dollars. Lighthouse (G)...................120.00

BARBADOS F

1788 Penny. Slave head wearing prince of Wales crown / Pineapple (C)..................................8.00

BELIZE BU

1973 1 Cent. Crowned bust (C)............................25
1979 50 Cents. similar (CN)...............................1.75

1990 1 Dollar. Bust in tiara / Columbus' ships (Brass, decagonal) 2.25
1990 2 Dollars. similar / EE monogram (CN) .. 6.00

BERMUDA F

c.1616 12 Pence. SOMMER ILANDS, Boar / Ship (C) 6,500.00
1793 Penny. Bust of George III / Ship (C) 25.00

BU

1964 Crown Crowned bust / Arms (S) 4.00
1970 1 Cent. Bust in tiara / Boar (C)..................20

1996 60 Dollars. Bust in tiara / Map above ship (G, curved triangle)..................Proof only 1,500.00

BRITISH CARIBBEAN TERRITORIES BU

1964 1 Cent. Crowned bust / Wreath (C).............35
1956 5 Cents. similar / Ship (Brass)..................1.00
1955 50 Cents. similar / Queen stg. over arms of islands (CN)..3.50

BRITISH GUIANA VF

1813 Half Stiver. Bust of George III / Crowned wreath (C) 12.50
1891 4 Pence. Bust of Victoria / similar (S)......4.50
1936 4 Pence. Bust of George V / similar (S)...2.50

BRITISH HONDURAS VF

1888 1 Cent. Head of Victoria (C)....................8.50
1907 5 Cents. Bust of Edward VII (CN).........50.00
1936 10 Cents. Bust of George V (S)..............12.00
1952 25 Cents. Head of George VI 3.50
1964 50 Cents. Bust of Elizabeth II (CN) 50
The above are usually found worn.

BRITISH VIRGIN ISLANDS BU

1983 10 Cents. Bust in tiara / Kingfisher (CN) 1.00
1973 25 Cents. similar/ Cuckoo (CN)...............1.50

BRITISH VIRGIN ISLANDS BU

1985 20 Dollars. similar / Spanish colonial cob coin (S) ....Proof only 16.50
1975 100 Dollars. similar / Tern (G).............110.00

BRITISH WEST AFRICA VF

1908 1/10 Penny. Titles of Edward VII / Six-pointed star (AL)..3.00
1908 similar (CN) 50
1920 1/2 Penny. Titles of George V / Six-pointed star (CN)..2.00
1936 Penny. Titles of Edward VIII / similar (CN) 75
1956 Penny. Titles of Elizabeth II / similar (C)..60
1940 3 Pence. Head of George VI / Wreath (Brass) 60
1913 6 Pence. Bust of George V / Wreath (S) 5.00

1938 Shilling. Head of George VI / Palm tree (Nickel-Brass) 1.00
1938 2 Shillings. similar (Brass)......................2.00

BRITISH WEST INDIES VF

1822 1/16th Dollar. Rose-shaped arms / Crowned anchor (S)...15.00
1822 1/8th Dollar. similar (S) 18.00
1822 1/2 Dollar. similar (S) 175.00

CAYMAN ISLANDS BU

1972 10 Cents. Elizabeth II / Green turtle (CN)...50

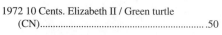

CAYMAN ISLANDS — BU

1992 1 Dollar Elizabeth II / Iguana
(S).. Proof only 55.00
1975 100 Dollars. Elizabeth II / Five queens
(G) 180.00

CEYLON — VF

1803 1/12th Rixdollar. Large 12 / Elephant l.
(C) 40.00
1821 Rix Dollar. Bust of George IV / Elephant l.
(S) 28.00
1891 1 Cent. Head of Victoria / Palm tree (C).....4.00

1910 5 Cents. Bust of Edward VII
(CN, square) 2.00
1929 50 Cents. Bust of George V / Palm tree
(S) 5.00
1951 50 Cents. Head of George VI (Brass) 35
1957 2 Cents. Elizabeth II (Brass, scalloped) 15

CYPRUS — VF

1881 1/4 Piastre. Head of Victoria (C) 16.00
1908 1/2 Piastre. Bust of Edward VII (C)..... 150.00

1931 1 Piastre. Bust of George V (C) 20.00
1934 1 Piastre. similar. (CN, scalloped)............ 2.50
1901 3 Piastre. Bust of Victoria / Crowned 3
(S)... 20.00
1921 9 Piastres. Bust of George V / Crowned shield
(S).. 10.00
1947 Shilling. Head of George VI / Two lions
(CN) 1.00

Unc.

1955 3 Mils. Bust of Elizabeth II / Fish (C)..........20
1955 50 Mils. similar / Ferns (CN) 1.00

EAST AFRICA — VF

1898 1 Pice. Head of Victoria (C) 10.00
1908 1/2 Cent. Titles of Edward VII / Tusks
(AL)..25.00
1923 1 Cent. Titles of George V / Tusks (C) 50
1936 5 Cents. Titles of Edward VIII / Tusks
(C) 50
1913 25 Cents. Bust of George V / Lion (S)..... 7.50
1963 50 Cents. Bust of Elizabeth II / Lion
(CN) 25

EAST AFRICA — VF

1946 Shilling. Head of George VI / Lion
(Billon)...2.00

EAST CARIBBEAN STATES — BU

1981 1 Cent. Bust in tiara / Wreath (AL) .... .20

1989 1 Dollar. similar / Ship (CN, 10-sided) 2.00
1994 10 Dollars. Mature bust / Soccer ball and Manhattan buildings (S) ....Proof only 45.00

FIJI — VF

1934 Halfpenny. Titles of George V
(CN, holed)....................................3.00
1936 Penny. Titles of Edward VIII (CN) 1.00
1950 3 Pence. Head of George VI / Hut
(Brass) 1.00
1965 6 Pence. Bust of Elizabeth II / Sea turtle
(CN) 30

1934 Shilling. Bust of George V / Outrigger
(S)..5.00
1943 Florin. Head of George VI / Shield (S) 2.50

BU

1976 1 Cent. Bust of Elizabeth II / Dish (C)....... .35
1987 50 Cents. similar / Sailing canoe
(CN, 12-sided)................................1.75
1995 1 Dollar. similar / Rattle (Brass)............... 3.50
1986 10 Dollars. similar / Fijian ground frog
(S)..............................Proof only 40.00
1978 250 Dollars. similar / Banded iguana
(G) 500.00

GIBRALTAR — VF

1813 1 Quarto. Lion holding key / Crowned wreath
(C) 30.00
1810 2 Quartos. similar / Castle (C)................ 17.50
1842 1/2 Quart. Head of Victoria / Castle
(C) 12.50

BU

1967 Crown. Bust of Elizabeth II / Castle
(CN) 1.50
1988 5 Pence. similar / Barbary Ape (CN) .... .75

BU

1996 50 Pence. similar / Five Dolphins
(CN, 7-sided)................................3.50
1996 Crown. similar / Audrey Hepburn
(CN)...7.50
1989 5 Sovereigns. similar / Una and lion
(G) ....Proof only 1,100.00

GOLD COAST — XF

1818 1/2 Ackey. George III / Arms (S) 225.00
1818 Ackey. similar (S)..................................450.00

GUERNSEY — VF

1903 Double. Shield (C) 30
1929 2 Doubles. Shield (C).............................. 1.25

1889 4 Doubles. Shield (C)................................ 1.25
1834 8 Doubles. Shield in wreath / Wreath
(C) 10.00

BU

1959 8 Doubles. Shield / Three lilies (C) 1.25
1966 10 Shillings. Elizabeth II / William the Conqueror (CN, square) 1.75
1971 2 New Pence. Shield / Windmill (C) 35

1983 Pound. Shield / Sailing ship (Brass) 3.50
1994 25 Pounds. Elizabeth II / Normandy invasion
(G) 245.00

HONG KONG — VF

1865 1 Mil. Crown / Chinese Inscription
(C, holed)......................................15.00
1905 1 Cent. Edward VII / Chinese Inscription
(C)...4.50
1932 5 Cents. George V / similar (S) 1.50
1948 10 Cents. George VI / similar (Brass) 50

HONG KONG   VF

1866 1/2 Dollar. Victoria / Ornament (S)...... 450.00
1891 50 Cents. Victoria / Value (S)................. 50.00

BU

1975 20 Cents. Elizabeth II / similar (Brass) 35

1960 1 Dollar. Elizabeth II / Lion (CN) 6.50
1993 2 Dollars. Bauhinia flower (CN,
    scalloped) 1.25
1994 10 Dollars. similar (Brass in CN,
    bimetallic) 4.50
1977 1000 Dollars. Elizabeth II / Snake (G) 325.00

INDIA - EAST INDIA CO.   F

1704-16 Pice. Crown / AUSPICIO REGIS ET
    SENATUS ANGLIA (C)........................... 45.00
1741 Pice. similar, BOMB below crown
    (Tin) 40.00
1179 AH (=1765) Rupee. Arabic inscriptions and
    ornament (S) 15.00
1835 1/12th Anna. Arms / Wreath (C).................75
1858 1/4 Anna. similar 85
1835 1/4 Rupee. William IV / Wreath. (S) 4.50
1840 Rupee. Victoria / Wreath (S) 3.00
1841 1 Mohur. Victoria / Lion and Palm tree
    (G) 150.00

INDIA - REGAL COINAGE   VF

1862 1/12th Anna. Victoria as queen / Wreath
    (C)..1.25
1916 1/12th Anna. George V / Wreath (C)...........50
1939 1/12th Anna. George VI / Wreath (C)..........50
1895 1/2 Piece. Victoria as empress / Wreath
    (C) 1.75

1862 1/4 Anna. Victoria as queen / Wreath
    (C) 1.50
1880 1/4 Anna. Victoria as empress / Wreath
    (C)..75
1906 1/4 Anna. Edward VII / Wreath (C)......... 1.25
1920 1/4 Anna. George V / Wreath (C) 40
1942 1/4 Anna. George VI / Wreath (C)..............35
1943 1 Pice. Crown / Wreath (C) 35
1862 1/2 Anna. Victoria as queen / Wreath
    (C)...20.00
1936 1 Anna. George V (CN) 35
1945 1 Anna. George VI (Brass) 25

INDIA - REGAL COINAGE   VF

1901 2 Annas. Victoria as empress / Wreath
    (S)..2.50

1918 2 Annas. George V (CN) 1.75
1940 2 Annas. George VI (CN)..........................30
1919 4 Annas. George V (CN) 5.00
1862 1/4 Rupee. Victoria as queen / Wreath
    (S) 5.00
1892 1/4 Rupee. Victoria as empress / Wreath
    (S) 3.00
1904 1/4 Rupee. Edward VII / Flowers (S)....... 3.00
19361/4 Rupee. George VI / Wreath (S)......... 82.25
1945 1/4 Rupee. George VI / Wreath (S) 85
1946 1/4 Rupee. George VI / Tiger (N)...............75
1919 8 Annas. George V (CN) 7.50
1899 1/2 Rupee. Victoria as empress / Wreath
    (S)..5.00

1885 Rupee. similar (S) 8.00
1903 Rupee. Edward VII / Flowers (S) 8.00
1914 Rupee. George V / Wreath (S) 8.00
1945 Rupee. George VI / Wreath (S) 3.00

INDIA - REGAL COINAGE   VF

1947 Rupee. George VI / Tiger (N)................... 2.50
1870 5 Rupees. Victoria as queen / Wreath
    (G)... 175.00
1870 10 Rupees. similar (G)......................... 275.00
1881 Mohur. Victoria as empress / Wreath
    (G)... 200.00
1918 15 Rupees. George V / Wreath (G) 165.00
1918 Sovereign. George V / St. George slaying
    dragon (G)....................................... 135.00

INDIA - PRINCELY STATES   VF

Alwar. 1891 Rupee. Victoria / Arabic inscription
    (S)... 10.00

INDIA - PRINCELY STATES   VF

Bharatpur. 1910 VS (=1858) Rupee. Victoria / Arabic
    inscription (S)................................... 85.00
Bikanir. 1895 1/4 Anna. Victoria / Inscription
    (C) 10.00
Bundi. 1989 VS (=1932) Rupee. EMPEROR
    GEORGE V, Dagger / Hindi inscription
    (S)... 13.50
Dewas, Junior Branch. 1888 1/12th Anna. Victoria /
    Wreath (C).. 20.00
Dewas, Senior Branch. 1888 1/12th Anna. Victoria /
    Wreath (C).. 12.00
Dhar. 1887 1/2 Pice. Victoria / Inscription (C)..5.00
Kutch. 1936 5 Kori. Titles of Edward VIII (S)..7.00
Sailana. 1912 1/4 Anna. George V / Inscription
    (C)... 7.50

*For princely states coins not struck in name of
British sovereign see India.*

IONIAN ISLANDS   F

1814 50 Paras. Bust of George III and 50 counter-
    stamped on Spanish 2 Reales (S)............300.00

1834 Lepton. Lion / Britannia std. (C) 3.00

ISLE OF MAN   VF

1733 Penny. Eagle on cap / Three legs (C)...... 25.00

1786 Penny. Bust George III / Three legs
    (C)...35.00
1786 1/2 Penny. George III / Three legs
    (C)...30.00
1839 Farthing. Victoria / Three legs (C)...........9.00

BU

1971 1 New Penny. Elizabeth II / Celtic cross
    (C) 35

1980 10 Pence. Elizabeth II / Falcon (CN)...........85
1990 1/5th Crown. Elizabeth II / Alley cat
    (G) 70.00

BU

1976 Crown. Elizabeth II / George Washington
(CN) 2.50
same (S) 8.00
1985 1 Angel. Elizabeth II / Archangel Michael
slaying demon (G, 1 ounce) 450.00

JAMAICA — VF

1882 Farthing. Victoria / Shield (CN) 1.75
1928 Farthing. George V / Shield (CN) 2.00
1950 Farthing. George VI / Shield (Brass) 25
1869 Halfpenny. Victoria / Shield (CN) 2.50
1907 Halfpenny. Edward VII / Shield (CN) 1.50
1940 Halfpenny. George VI / Shield (Brass) 75

1910 Penny. Edward VII / Shield (CN) 2.50
1920 Penny. George V / Shield (CN) 2.50
1937 Penny. George VI in high relief / Shield
(Brass) 1.75
1958 Penny. Elizabeth II / Arms (Brass)...............20

BU

1964 Halfpenny. Elizabeth II / Arms (Brass)........15
1966 5 Shillings. Crown in chain / Arms
(CN) 5.00

JERSEY — VF

1813 18 Pence. Shield / Wreath (S) 80.00
1841 1/52 Shilling. Victoria / Shield (C) 30.00
1909 1/24 Shilling. Edward VII / Shield (C) 2.50
1937 1/24 Shilling. George VI / Shield (C) 1.00
1877 1/12 Shilling. Victoria / Shield (C) 2.00
1931 1/12 Shilling. George V / Shield (C)........ 1.00

BU

1964 1/12 Shilling. Elizabeth II / Shield (C) 1.00
1981 Penny. Elizabeth II / Shield (C)....................15

BU

1983 10 Pence. Elizabeth II / Prehistoric stone
structure (CN).. 1.00
1972 2 Pounds 50 Pence. Elizabeth II / Lobster
(S)... 20.00

MAURITIUS — VF

(1822) 25 Sous. REÇU au TRESOR / pour 25 Sous
(S)... 50.00

MAURITIUS — VF

1969 1 Cent. Elizabeth II (C)..............................10
1949 2 Cents. George VI (C) 1.25
1917 5 Cents. George V (C) 4.50
1886 10 Cents. Victoria (S) 5.00
1975 1/4 Rupee. Elizabeth II / Crown and flowers
(CN) 30

1950 1/2 Rupee. George VI / Stag (CN) 1.00
1934 1 Rupee. George V / Shield (S) 8.00
1975 25 Rupees. Elizabeth II / Butterfly
(S)...BU 15.00

NEW GUINEA — XF

1929 1/2 Penny. Crown and scepters
(CN, holed) 350.00

1936 Penny. Crown and *ERI* (C) 2.00
1944 Penny. Crown and GRI (C)...................... 5.00
1944 3 Pence. similar (CN) 8.50
1935 Shilling. Titles of George V, crown and
scepters (S, holed).. 3.00
1938 Shilling. similar but George VI (S) 3.00

NEW ZEALAND — VF

1940 Halfpenny. George VI / Tiki idol (C) 65
1950 Penny. George VI / Tui bird (C) 50
1933 3 Pence. George V / Crossed clubs (S) 75
1952 3 Pence. George VI / similar (CN) 70
1943 6 Pence. George VI / Huia bird (S) 1.00
1952 Shilling. George VI / Maori warrior
(CN) 3.00

1935 Florin. George V / Kiwi bird (S) 3.00

NEW ZEALAND — VF

1940 Florin. George VI / Maori and two vies of
Aukland (S).. 4.00
1943 Half Crown. George VI / Arms (S) 3.50
1951 Half Crown. similar (CN) 1.00
1935 Crown. George V / Maori chief and British
naval officer shaking hands (S).............1,500.00

BU

1949 Crown. George VI / Fern leaf (S) 12.00
1965 Halfpenny. Elizabeth II wearing wreath /
Tiki idol (C) 1.00
1965 Penny. similar / Tui bird (C) 2.00
1956 6 Pence. similar / Huia bird (S) 5.00
1964 Shilling. similar / Maori warrior (CN)...... 1.50
1965 Florin. similar / Kiwi bird (S) 1.75
1953 Crown. similar / Crowned monogram
(CN)... 5.00
1967 5 Cents. Bust of Elizabeth II wearing tiara /
Tuatata lizard (CN) 25
1988 10 Cents. similar / Maori mask (CN) 25
1993 50 Cents. similar / H.M.S. Endeavor
(CN) 1.50

1994 50 Cents. similar (ALB in CN,
bimetallic).. 20.00
1967 Dollar. Bust of Elizabeth II wearing tiara /
Shield between branches (CN) 1.50

1990 Dollar. similar / Kiwi bird (ALB) 1.25
1996 5 Dollars. similar / Kaka Parrot (CN)..... 12.50
similar (S)................................Proof only 45.00

NIGERIA — BU

1959 1/2 Penny. Crown / Six-pointed star (C)......75
1962 Shilling. Elizabeth II / Palm branches
(CN) 3.50

NIGERIA — BU

1959 2 Shillings. Elizabeth II / Peanut-plant
(CN) 6.00

RHODESIA — BU

1964 6 Pence - 5 Cents. Elizabeth II wearing tiara /
Flame lily (CN) 1.25

1964 2 Shillings - 20 Cents. similar / Ancient bird
sculpture (CN) 3.00
1966 Pound. similar / Lion holding tusk
(G) .... Proof only 200.00

RHODESIA & NYASALAND — BU

1964 1/2 Penny. Giraffes (C, holed) 1.50

1957 2 Shillings. Elizabeth II / African fish eagle
holding fish (CN) 12.00

SEYCHELLES — VF

1948 2 Cents. George VI (C) 35
1944 25 Cents. similar (S) 3.50

BU

1959 2 Cents. Elizabeth II (C) 2.50

BU

1972 5 Cents. Elizabeth II / Cabbage (AL) 25
1974 1/2 Rupee. Elizabeth II (CN) 1.00
1972 5 Rupees. Elizabeth II / Beach scene with tree
and turtle (CN) 5.00
similar (S) 25.00

SOLOMON ISLANDS — BU

1977 2 Cents. Elizabeth II / Eagle spirit (C) 25

1988 10 Cents. Elizabeth II / Sea spirit (CN) 50
1996 50 Cents. Elizabeth II / Arms (CN,
12-sided) 2.50
1992 10 Dollars. Elizabeth II / Crocodile
(S) .... Proof only 42.50

SOUTH AFRICA, UNION OF — VF

1931 1/4 Penny. George V / Two sparrows
(C) 1.50
1942 1/4 Penny. George VI / Two sparrows
(C) 50
1953 1/2 Penny. Elizabeth II / Ship (C) 35
1929 1/2 Penny. George V / Ship (C) 5.00
1952 Penny. George VI / Ship (C) 50

1953 Penny. Elizabeth II / Ship (C) 35
1927 3 Pence. George V / Protea plant within three
bundles of sticks (S) 2.50
1943 3 Pence. George VI / similar (S) 1.00
1927 6 Pence. George V / similar but six bundles
(S) 4.00
1957 6 Pence. Elizabeth II / similar (S) 75
1943 Shilling. George VI / Allegory of Cape of
Good Hope (S) 2.50
1953 Shilling. Elizabeth II / similar (S) 1.25
1932 2 Shillings. George V / Shield (S) 6.00
1942 2 Shillings. George VI / Shield (S) 3.00

SOUTH AFRICA, UNION OF — VF

1932 2-1/2 Shillings. George V / Crowned shield
(S) 6.00
1955 2-1/2 Shillings. Elizabeth II / similar (S) . 3.00
1952 5 Shillings. George VI / Ship (S) 4.50
1958 5 Shillings. Elizabeth II / Springbok (S) .. 5.00

SOUTHERN RHODESIA — VF

1936 Penny. Crowned rose (CN) 1.25
1942 6 Pence. George VI / Two hatchets (S) 2.00

1951 2 Shillings. George VI / Antelope (CN) ... 3.00
1954 2 Shillings. Elizabeth II / Antelope
(CN) 75.00
1932 Half Crown. George V / Crowned shield
(S) 8.00
1953 Crown. Elizabeth II / Cecil Rhodes
(S) .... Unc. 15.00

STRAITS SETTLEMENTS — VF

1926 1 Cent. George V (C, square) 75
1901 5 Cents. Victoria (S) 2.50
1910 20 Cents. Edward VII (S) 3.50
1920 50 Cents. George V (S) 2.50

1920 Dollar. George V / Ornamental design containing Chinese and Malay inscription
(S) 20.00

CAUCASUS

The first modern, European style coins
struck in this region are the copper and silver
issues struck by Georgia (1804-1833) while
under Czarist Russian influence. It was not
until the break-up of the Soviet Union that
local coinage of the Caucasus region was
again placed in circulation. The first coins
were Azerbaijani and Armenian coins all
struck in aluminum. Both were of fairly plain
design. Well made coins with attractive
reverse designs were introduced by Georgia in
1993. A limited number of collector issues
have been struck by Georgia and Armenia.
Known counterfeits: None.

ARMENIA — BU

1994 10 Luma. Arms (AL) 25

1994 3 Drams. Arms (AL) 1.00
1996 100 Drachms. Stork with chess board / Arms
(CN) 7.50

AZERBAIJAN — BU

1992 10 Qapik. Eight-pointed star (AL) 50

AZERBAIJAN — BU
1993 20 Qapik. Crescent and star (AL) 75
1996 50 Manat. Romantic couple / Mohammed
Fuzuli (S) .... Proof only 60.00

GEORGIA — BU
1827 2 Abazi. Masonry crown / Inscription
(S)... F 30.00

1993 20 Thetri. Emblem / Stag (Steel)............... 1.50
1995 500 Lari. Profiles of Stalin, Roosevelt, Churchill
and DeGaulle (G)...................... Proof only 500.00

CZECHOSLOVAKIA

After four hundred years of Austrian rule, Czechoslovakia became and independent state in 1918, following the break up of the Hapsburg empire. While most of the coins circulating here were regular coins of the empire, special copper pieces were struck for Bohemia in the late 1700s. Also common were the coins struck by the local bishops of Olmuetz.

Additional Specialized Books: Miller zu Aicholz, Oesterreichische Münzpragungen, 1519-1938. Despite the title this is an excellent catalogue for later Bohemian coins.

Known counterfeits: Few.

BOHEMIA — F
1687 6 Kreuzer. Bust of Leopold I / Double headed
eagle, double tailed lion on chest (S) 40.00
1699 Ducat. Similar (G) 250.00
1782 Groeschl. Crowned shield (C)............... 12.00
1943 1 Koruna. Double-tailed lion / Ivy branches
(Z) .... VF .75

OLMÜTZ — F
1705 Kreuzer Bust / Arms (S)......................... 15.00

SCHLICK — F
1638 3 Kreuzer. Madonna and Child over arms /
Double headed eagle (S) 25.00

CZECHOSLOVAKIA — VF
1925 10 Haleru. Double-tailed lion /Bridge..........35
1938 20 Haleru. Double-tailed lion / Wheat and
scythe)CN)...35
1934 20 Korun. Shield / Three figures stg.
(S)...4.00

BU
1949 50 Korun. Stalin / Shield (S) 5.00
1965 10 Korun. Shield / Jan Hus (S)............... 15.00
1966 5 Haleru. Shield / Wreath (AL)....................25
1980 2 Koruny. Shield / Symbol (CN).................75
1991 1 Haler. CSFR over shield / Wreath (AL)....10
1993 500 Korun. Shield / Tennis player (S).... 40.00

CZECH REPUBLIC — BU
1993 1 Koruna. Double-tailed lion / Crown (N clad
Steel)..60

CZECH REPUBLIC — BU
1993 50 Korun. Double-tailed lion / City view
(Steel, Brass and Copper plated,
bimetallic) 7.50
1994 200 Korun. Shield / Cathedral (S) 16.50

SLOVAKIA — VF
1939 10 Halierov. Shield / Castle (C)............... 2.00
1941 1 Koruna. Shield / Wreath (CN).............. 1.00
1944 10 Korun. Shield / King, bishop and knight
(S)... 4.00

BU
1993 10 Haliers. Shield / Steeple (AL) 35
1993 10 Koruna. Shield / Medieval cross
(Brass)...2.50

BU
1993 100 Korun. Shield / Three doves (S) 9.00
1994 200 Korun. Logo / Hockey player (S).... 18.00

FRANCE

After centuries of deterioration, French royal coinage began to stabilize somewhat by the 1600s. This coincides with the introduction of milled coinage of neat manufacture during the same century. A silver dollar sized ecu and its fractions became common. Small values were struck in base silver and especially in copper. This included the old denier tournois, which had survived since the 1200s. The gold louis d'or became so recognized for its stability that it saw wide circulation internationally. Most coins bore the king's portrait, with fleurs or a shield of arms on the reverse. Sometimes an elaborate cross or monogram was still used, which had been used Renaissance. Despite the improved striking methods, imprecise means were used to manufacture blanks of exact weight so many had to be adjusted with a file before striking to remove excess metal. The resultant "adjustment marks" are not considered damage, but if they're severed they do reduce the coin's value.

Among the most important uses of coinage for the study of French history is the effect that the French Revolution had on the iconography. An entire new set of symbols replaced the traditional ones. Those reflecting new ideologies include one displaying a tablet inscribed "Men are equal before the law." An allegorical head, initially representing liberty was also quite popular. Even after Napoleon took the reigns as emperor he maintained the revolutionary name of the country as "French Republic" temporarily on the coinage. The Revolution's most lasting change on the coinage came with the decimal system. This system, used the world over today, divides the monetary unit, the franc or the dollar for example, into tenths or hundredths.

Most nineteenth century French coins were very conservative, depicting the monarch, and a coat of arms or a value. There was great artistic merit, however, in the beautiful coins of the 1898 to 1920 period.

In this dawn of the new European currency, the Euro, it is all the more important to mention that French coinage was the basis of an earlier international currency, that of the Latin Monetary Union, from 1865 to 1920. During this period the money of nations as diverse as Greece and Switzerland were struck on an international standard and held the same value.

The most common design to be used by the French republics is an allegorical female head or bust. This image, rooted in the 1790s allegory of liberty, is variously described today as the personification of the Republic of France, and as Marie Anne (the personification's nickname.)

Inflation hit France again after World War I and the currency did not finally stabilize until 1960. During this time most of the coins were of baser metals, including aluminum-bronze and aluminum. Some denominations were distinguished with holes in their centers. Many mintmarks were used on French coins before 1960 and some of the dates and mintmarks can be valuable. Only common ones for the type are listed here. Coins before 1960, and some outmoded ones struck later, don't have legal tender status.

In recent years a phenomenal amount of collector issues have been struck, sometimes in odd sizes and at a rate of one every few weeks!

During and immediately after World War I, many municipal chambers of commerce throughout France struck small denomination emergency tokens to facilitate commerce. Their designs run from utilitarian to breathtaking.

Colonial coins from India are the earliest common French colonials. Many of these are hardly distinguishable from local Indian states coins. Usually they are identified by certain symbols, such as a fleur or a cock. They were originally intended to circulate alongside crude local coins and their designs and crudeness made this possible.

178

Other colonial coins were struck occasionally from the 1890s through the 1930s, but were not abundant except in Indo-China. During World War and especially right after, they were struck in abundant quantities in base metals. Usually one side bore a female head representing an allegory of France. The reverse would allude to the individual colony. Since 1948 virtually all French colonial coins can be easily collected in mint state.

Additional Specialized Books: Duplessy, Jean, *Les Monnaies Francaises Royales, vol. II*.

Known counterfeits: Contemporary counterfeits of French coins have always been common. The gold 20 and 50 franc pieces should be examined with care. Counterfeits of smaller denominations are slightly less dangerous. A sampling of counterfeit French coins includes 1 Franc 1867BB and 1915, and 5 Francs 1875A, 1960 and 1975, but hundreds of others exist.

KINGDOM   F

Louis XIV, 1643-1715. 1696 Double denier. Bust r. / Crown and three fleurs (C) 20.00
1655 Liard. Crowned bust r. / LIARD DE FRANCE, fleurs (C) 18.00
1675 4 Sols. Bust r. / Four fleurs around mint mark (S) 25.00
1707 10 Sols = 1/8 Ecu. Old bust r. / Crown over crossed scepters (S) 28.00

1676 4 Sols, Bust Louis XIV R. Fleur-de-Lis Cross, Silver 25.00
1690 Ecu. Old bust r. / Cross of 8 L's (S) 125.00
1694 Louis d'or. Old bust r. / L's and crowned fleurs around mintmark (G) 300.00

Louis XV, 1715-74   F
1770 Sol. Bust r. / Crowned shield (C) 8.00
1750 2 Sols. Crowned L / Crowned crossed floral L's (Billon) 15.00
1744 6 Sols = 1/20 Ecu. Old bust l. / Crowned shield in wreath (S) 20.00
1729 24 Sols = 1/5 Ecu. Young bust l. / similar (S) 30.00
1741 Ecu. Bust l. / similar (S) 80.00

1745 2 Louis d'or. Head l. / Crowned shields of France and Navarre (G) 400.00

Louis XVI, 1774-93   F
1786 Liard. Head l. / Crowned shield (C) 8.00
1792 3 Deniers. Bust l. / Fasces (C) 20.00
1791 12 Deniers. similar (C) 8.00
1793 2 Sols. similar (C) 15.00
1783 6 Sols = 1/20 Ecu. Bust l. / Crowned shield in wreath (S) 30.00

Louis XVI, 1774-93   F
1791 30 Sols = 1/4 Ecu. Bust l. / Angel writing on tablet (S) 40.00
1783 1/2 Ecu. Bust l. / Crowned shield in wreath (S) 40.00
1792 Ecu. similar (S) 90.00
1786 Louis d'or. Bust l. / Crowned shields of France and Navarre (G) 200.00

Republic, 1793-1804   F
1793 24 Livres. Angel writing on tablet / Wreath (G) 1,000.00
1793 6 Livres. similar (S) 100.00
1793 1 Sol. Tablet below eye / Wreath on scales (C) 30.00

Republic, 1793-1804   F
L'An 2 (1793-94) 2 Sols. similar, no AD date 100.00
1792 5 Sols. Soldiers swearing oath (C). Common token of the time 10.00
L'An 6 (1797-98) 1 Centime. Bust of Liberty (C) 2.00
L'An 8 (1799-1800) 1 Decime. similar / Wreath (C) 10.00
L'An 7 (1798-99) 5 Francs. Liberty, Hercules and Equality (S) 40.00

Napoleon I, 1799-1815   F
1808 5 Centimes. N in wreath, raised border (C) 100.00
1810 10 Centimes Crowned N in wreath, raised border (Billon) 7.00
L'An 12 (1803-04) 1/4 Franc. Bust as Premier Consul / QUART in wreath (S) 32.50
1809 1/2 Franc. Bust as Emperor / DEMI FRANC in wreath (S) 10.00
1809 1 Franc. similar (S) 16.00

Napoleon I, 1799-1815   F
L'An 11 (1802-03) 5 Francs. Bust as Premier Consul / Wreath (S) 50.00
1811 5 Francs. Bust as Emperor / similar (S) 25.00
1812 20 Francs. similar (G) 100.00

Louis XVIII, 1814-1825   F
1815 Decime. Crowned L in wreath / Wreath (C) 7.50
1817 1/4 Franc. Bust l. / Crowned shield (S) .. 10.00
1822 1 Franc. Bust l. / Crowned shield in wreath (S) 12.00

1824 5 Francs. similar (S) 20.00
1816 20 Francs. similar (G) 100.00

Charles X, 1824-30
1827 1/4 Franc. Bust l. / Crowned shield (S) 6.00
1825 1 Franc. Bust l. / Crowned shield in wreath (S) 20.00

1830 40 Francs. Bust r. / similar (G) 200.00

Louis Philippe, 1830-48
1847 25 Centimes. Head r. / Wreath (S) 6.00
1840 1/2 Franc. similar (S) 5.00
1846 1 Franc. similar (S) 8.00

Louis Philippe, 1830-48

1848 5 Francs. Head r. / Wreath (S) 9.00
1831 20 Francs. Bust l. / Wreath (G) 100.00

Second Republic, 1848-52   VF

1849 1 Centime. Liberty head (C) 5.00
1849 1 Franc. Ceres head / Wreath (S) 45.00
1852 1 Franc. Head of Louis Napoleon / Wreath
(S) 80.00

1849 5 Francs. Liberty, Hercules and Equality
(S) 15.00
1851 10 Francs. Cered head / Wreath (G) 65.00

Napoleon III, 1852-70   VF

1862 1 Centime. Head l. / Eagle (C) 1.00
1854 2 Centimes. similar (C) 2.00
1855 5 Centimes. similar (C) 4.00
1862 10 Centimes. similar (C) 10.00
1867 20 Centimes. Head l. / Crown (S) 4.00
1867 50 Centimes. similar (S) 6.00
1858 1 Franc. Head l. / Wreath (S) 25.00

Napoleon III, 1852-70   VF

1867 1 Franc. Head l. / Arms (S)..................... 12.00
1866 2 Francs. similar (S)............................. 25.00
1868 5 Francs. similar (S)............................. 15.00
1862 10 Francs. Head r. / Wreath (G) 55.00
1868 20 Francs. Head r. / Wreath (G) 100.00
1869 100 Francs. similar (G) 500.00

Restored Republic, 1871-1958   VF

1895 1 Centime. Ceres head (C) 2.50
1908 2 Centimes. Republic head (C) 1.00
1916 5 Centimes. similar / Allegorical group
(C) 1.00
1897 10 Centimes. Ceres head (C) 3.00
1931 10 Centimes. Cap and RF (CN, holed) ...... .35
1945 20 Centimes. similar (Z) 5.00
1904 25 Centimes. Republic head / Fasces
(N) .... .75
1916 50 Centimes. Sower (S) 1.00
1939 50 Centimes. Head l. (ALB) .... .50
1872 1 Franc. Ceres head / Wreath (S) 4.00
1947 1 Franc. Head l. / Cornucopia (AL) .... .25
1915 2 Francs. Sower (S)................................. 2.00
1921 2 Francs. Mercury std. (ALB) 2.00
1873 5 Francs. Liberty, Hercules and Equality
(S) 9.00
1945 5 Francs. Head l. / Wreath (AL) .... .35
1901 10 Francs. Head l. / Cock l. (G).............. 55.00

1952 10 Francs. Head l. / Cock and branch
(ALB).. .35
1933 20 Francs. Head l. / Two ears of grain
(S).. 5.00
1953 50 Francs. Head l. / Cock and branch
(ALB).. 2.00

1909 100 Francs. Winged genius (G)............ 475.00
1955 100 Francs. Bust with torch / branches
(CN) 1.00

Vichy France   VF

1941 20 Centimes. VINGT over oak leaves
(Z).. 2.00
1941 20 Centimes. 20 over oak leaves (Z) .... .75
1943 1 Franc. Ax between wheat ears (AL) .... .25

Vichy France   VF

1941 5 Francs. Philippe Petain / Ax (CN) 100.00

Fifth Republic, 1959-date   BU

1968 1 Centime. Wheat ear (Steel).......................25
1987 5 Centimes. Bust l. (ALB) 10
1967 20 Centimes. Bust l. (ALB) 15
1976 1/2 Franc. Sower (N)................................30
1977 1 Franc. Sower (N)...................................40
1979 2 Francs. Modernistic sower (N) 65
1989 10 Francs. Winged genius (Steel in ALB,
bimetallic) 7.50
1989 10 Francs. Montesquieu (Steel in ALB,
bimetallic) 17.50

Fifth Republic, 1959-date   BU

1987 100 Francs. LaFayette (S) 20.00
1996 100 Francs. Clovis (S)............................35.00
1990 500 Francs = 70 Ecu. Charlemagne
(G) ....Proof only 450.00

ALGERIA   VF

1956 20 Francs. Head r. / Two wheat ears
(CN).. 1.00
1949 50 Francs. similar (CN) 3.00
1952 100 Francs. similar (CN) 4.00

CAMEROON   VF

1943 50 Centimes. Cock / Double cross (C) 3.50
1926 1 Franc. Head l. / Palm branches
(ALB).. 2.00
1948 1 Franc. Antelope head (AL) 25
1924 2 Francs. Head l. Palm branches
(ALB) 15.00

COMOROS   BU

1964 1 Franc. Head l. / Palm trees (AL)..............75
1964 5 Francs. similar (AL)............................. 1.25
1964 10 Francs. Shells and Coelacanth
(ALB).. 2.00

FRENCH AFARS & ISSAS   BU

1975 2 Francs. Antelope head (AL) 5.00
1975 5 Francs. similar (AL).............................4.00
1975 20 Francs. Ocean liner and small sailing ship
(ALB) 7.00

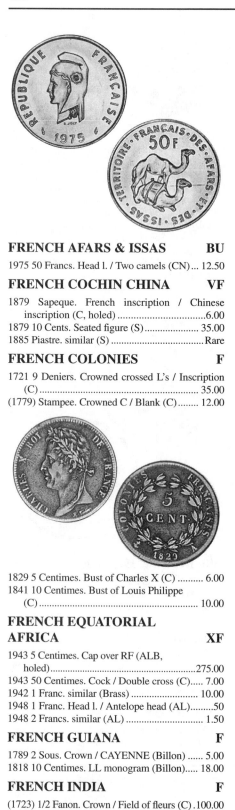

FRENCH AFARS & ISSAS   BU

1975 50 Francs. Head l. / Two camels (CN) ... 12.50

FRENCH COCHIN CHINA   VF

1879 Sapeque. French inscription / Chinese inscription (C, holed) 6.00
1879 10 Cents. Seated figure (S) 35.00
1885 Piastre. similar (S) .... Rare

FRENCH COLONIES   F

1721 9 Deniers. Crowned crossed L's / Inscription (C) 35.00
(1779) Stampee. Crowned C / Blank (C) 12.00

1829 5 Centimes. Bust of Charles X (C) 6.00
1841 10 Centimes. Bust of Louis Philippe (C) 10.00

FRENCH EQUATORIAL
AFRICA   XF

1943 5 Centimes. Cap over RF (ALB, holed) 275.00
1943 50 Centimes. Cock / Double cross (C) 7.00
1942 1 Franc. similar (Brass) 10.00
1948 1 Franc. Head l. / Antelope head (AL) 50
1948 2 Francs. similar (AL) 1.50

FRENCH GUIANA   F

1789 2 Sous. Crown / CAYENNE (Billon) 5.00
1818 10 Centimes. LL monogram (Billon) 18.00

FRENCH INDIA   F

(1723) 1/2 Fanon. Crown / Field of fleurs (C) .100.00
1720-1835 Doudou. Fleur / Inscription (C) 6.00

1753 Biche. Five fleurs / I753 (C) 20.00
1776 1/5 Rupee. Arabic inscription, P on rev. (S) 20.00

FRENCH INDO-CHINA   VF

1887 1 Sapeque. French inscription / Chinese inscription (C, holed) 4.00
1885 1 Cent. Std. figure / Chinese in rectangle (C) 4.00
1899 1 Cent. Allegories of France and French Indo-China std. (C) 2.00
1888 10 Cents. Figure std. (S) 10.00
1921 10 Cents. similar (S) 3.00
1899 20 Cents. similar (S) 20.00
1894 50 Cents. similar (S) 100.00
1886 Piastre. similar (S) 20.00
1926 Piastre. similar (S) 17.50

XF

1942 1/4 Cent. (Z) 40.00
1935 1/2 Cent. Cap over RF (C) 2.00
1943 1 Cent. Ears of grain (AL) 1.00

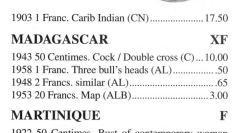

1939 5 Cents. Head above two cornucopiae (CN, holed) 1.00
1946 5 Cents. Bust with olive branch (AL) 1.00
1941 10 Cents. similar (CN) .... .75
1941 20 Cents. similar (CN) 1.00
1936 50 Cents. Figure std. (S) 6.00
1931 Piastre. Head l. (S) 15.00
1947 Piastre. Bust with olive branch (CN) 2.00

FRENCH OCEANIA   XF

1949 50 Centimes. Republic std. / Beach scene (AL) 1.50
1949 2 Francs. similar (AL) 1.50

FRENCH POLYNESIA   BU

1965 50 Centimes. Republic std. / Beach scene (AL) 1.50
1987 1 Franc. similar (AL) .... .45
1965 2 Francs. similar (AL) 1.00
1967 10 Francs. Carving (N) 1.75
1991 50 Francs. Beach huts below mountain (N) 2.00

1982 100 Francs. similar (N-Brass) 4.00

FRENCH SOMALIA   BU

1965 1 Franc. Antelope head (AL) 4.00

FRENCH SOMALIA   BU

1959 2 Francs. similar (AL) 5.00
1975 10 Francs. Ocean liner and small sailing ship (ALB) 5.00

FRENCH WEST AFRICA   XF

1944 1 Franc. Head l. / Two cornucopiae (ALB) 5.00
1948 2 Francs. Head l. / Antelope head (AL) .... .50
1956 10 Francs. similar (ALB) 1.50
1957 25 Francs. Antelope head / Root figure (ALB) 2.00

GUADELOUPE   F

1921 50 Centimes. Carib Indian (CN) 9.00

1903 1 Franc. Carib Indian (CN) 17.50

MADAGASCAR   XF

1943 50 Centimes. Cock / Double cross (C) ... 10.00
1958 1 Franc. Three bull's heads (AL) .... .50
1948 2 Francs. similar (AL) .... .65
1953 20 Francs. Map (ALB) 3.00

MARTINIQUE   F

1922 50 Centimes. Bust of contemporary woman (CN) 15.00
1897 1 Franc. similar (CN) 22.00

NEW CALEDONIA   BU

1949 50 Centimes. Republic std. / Kagu bird (AL) 3.50
1994 1 Franc. similar (AL) .... .50
1949 2 Francs. similar (AL) 4.50
1972 10 Francs. Small sailing ship (N) 2.00
1967 20 Francs. Busts of three bulls 5.00

1972 50 Francs. Hut and trees (N) 5.00
1976 100 Francs. similar (N-C) 6.00

NEW HEBRIDES   BU

1970 1 Franc. Bird (N-Brass) .... .75
1973 10 Franc. Carved head (N) 1.25
1966 100 Francs. Carving (S) 15.00

REUNION — VF

1816 10 Centimes. LL monogram / ISLE DE
BOURBON (Billon).................................. 85.00
1896 50 Centimes. Bust of Mercury (CN)...... 45.00

BU

1948 1 Franc. Palm trees (AL) 2.00
1955 10 Francs. Shield (ALB) 2.50
1964 100 Francs. Shield (N).............................. 3.50

SAINT PIERRE & MIQUELON — BU

1948 1 Franc. Sailing ship (AL)......................... 4.00
1948 2 Francs. similar (AL) 5.00

TOGO — VF

1924 50 Centimes. Palm branches (ALB) 6.00
1948 1 Franc. Antelope head (AL) 6.00
1925 2 Francs. Palm branches (ALB)............. 18.00
1956 5 Francs. Antelope head (ALB) 3.00

TONKIN — XF

1905 1/600th Piastre. French inscription / Chinese
inscription (Z)... 15.00

TUNISIA — VF

1938 5 Centimes. Arabic inscription / French
inscription (CN, holed)................................. 2.00
1945 50 Centimes. Wreath / Wreath (ALB)........25
1946 5 Francs. Arabic inscription / French inscription (ALB) 1.50
1939 20 Francs. Two branches / Wreath
(S).. 20.00

GERMANY

The coinage of Germany is by far the most complex of the modern era. As more and more nobles and bishops were given the right to strike coins as a favor to the Holy Roman Emperor, the number of issuing authorities in greater Germany became almost bewildering. Certainly at its greatest, it ran into several hundred. Most struck coins solely in their own names, others such as cities cited their own authority on one side, but paid homage to the Holy Roman Emperor on the other. The local side of a coin would usually depict the bust or arms of the local prince, or a city's patron saint. Some depicted symbolic animals or a wildman (a giant wearing nothing but a loin-encircling bush.) The Emperor was sometimes portrayed, but usually he was honored by inscribing his titles around a double headed eagle. Usually the Emperor was the head of the Austrian house of Hapsburg, but not always. Following the Napoleonic wars, many of the ecclesiastical territories were absorbed by the secular ones, the greater states began to take over the smaller ones, and the Holy Roman Empire ceased to exist. For the first time, the number of coin-issuing German states began to decline. This process continued until the German states were finally replaced by a republic in 1918.

While there were a great many local coinage standards, some basic ideas remained consistent. A thaler was a large, silver-dollar sized coin. A ducat was made of gold and uniformly contained 11/100 troy ounce of that metal. Good silver coins were often valued in terms of how many were needed to make a thaler. Thus the inscription 6 einen thaler meant that the coin was worth one sixth of a thaler. Guldens were not always used but when they were usually resembled an American half dollar. The albus and groschen were small silver coins. Other small coins such as the pfennig, heller, kreuzer, could be either copper or billon, but when they were created in the Middle Ages they were originally silver.

Almost fifty years before the German states passed into history, Germany became a unified nation. Each local prince retained his own territories and some aspect of local government, but after 1871 the national government fell to the hands of one German Emperor, who happened to be the hereditary King of Prussia — the most powerful of the German states. Throughout Germany, all copper and small silver coins (1 pfennig to 1 mark) were uniform. Larger silver and gold coins (2 through 20 marks) shared a common reverse design with the legend Deutsches Reich. The obverse bore the portrait of the local prince or the city arms.

During and immediately after World War I hundreds of municipal governments and companies throughout Germany struck small denomination emergency tokens or notgeld to facilitate commerce. Their designs run from traditionally heraldic to humorous to utilitarian.

The "Weimar" Republic of 1918 to 1933 struck minor coins of fairly bland agricultural designs, and a good number of exciting commemorative silver pieces. Its coins were replaced in the 1930s by ones bearing the notorious Nazi swastika held by an eagle. During World War II, like so many other countries, zinc replaced most coinage metals needed for the war effort.

From 1949 until 1990 there were two Germanies, the Federal Republic (West), and the smaller, Soviet dominated Democratic Republic (East). Each had its own coinage, the West with a traditional German eagle, the East with typical Communist industrial symbolism. Both states struck numerous commemoratives, often very similar in inspiration. With the fall of Communism, East Germany chose to join West Germany, which then attempted to bail the smaller state out of the economic morass of Communism.

The German Empire struck coins for two colonies, and both are very popularly collected. The issues for German East Africa were struck in gold, silver and bronze. The large silver pieces bear an exciting bust of Kaiser Wilhelm II wearing an elaborate griffin-topped helmet. The large silver pieces of German New Guinea display a detailed bird of paradise, considered by some to be among the most beautiful images of the entire European colonial series. All German New Guinea coins are scarce and in high demand.

Prices: In many specialized markets and in Europe many German coins can sell for prices in excess of those listed below. Also the prices shown here are for common dates. Rare date and mint combinations can be quite valuable.

Spelling: There are many spelling variations connected with German coins. Thaler is the earlier form of Taler. Kreuzer is the later form or kreutzer. Pfenning is a variant of pfennig. Also note that ü is a symbol for ue and both are quite common.

Additional Specialized Books: Money Trend magazine provides up to the month pricing updates for this volatile market.

Known Counterfeits: A great many contemporary counterfeits exist of Prussian 1/24 and 1/12 Thalers of the 1700s. Some also exist of 1/3 Thalers, 1773A, for example. Dangerous modern counterfeits exist of several 20 mark gold pieces. While rare patterns of Adolf Hitler portrait coins exist, virtually all those encountered are actually fantasy souvenirs made well after the war.

Some banks have restruck classic 17th and 18th century coins with new dies. These are easily distinguished from originals because of their brilliant proof finishes. Many also have a small date of restriking discreetly placed on the coin.

Beware of damaged coins. Solder marks and other mount marks severely reduce the value of a coin. So does smoothing out an unpleasant surface by heavy polishing or scraping. This practice is particularly common on German coins. Early coins struck with roller dies will be slightly curved. This is not damage and is to be expected.

GERMAN STATES TO 1871 — F

Aachen. 1759 12 heller. Eagle / Inscription
(C) 20.00
Anhalt. 1862 21/2 Silber Groschen. Shield / Inscrip-
tion (Billon)... 4.00
Augsburg. 1715 Heller. Pine cone / Cross with rose
at center and leaves in angles (C) 6.00
Baden. 1870 Kreuzer. Shield between griffins /
Wreath (C) 1.00
Bavaria. 1750 12 kreuzer. Bust r. / Crowned round
arms (S) 12.00
Brandenburg-Prussia. 1676 18 Groscher (1/4 Tha-
ler). Bust r. with sword / Eagle (S) 35.00

GERMAN STATES TO 1871   F

Bremen. 1781 Schwaren. Key / Inscription.
(C) 4.00
Brunswick-Luneburg. 1679 Thaler. Shield / Wildman standing (S)...................................... 165.00
Brunswick-Wolfenbuttel. 1823 1/24th Thaler. Horse leaping l. / Inscription (Billon) 3.00
Camenz. 1822 3 Pfennig. Wing / Inscription.
(C) 30.00
Frankfurt. 1786 Pfennig. Eagle / Inscription (C).2.00
Hamburg. 1727 4 Schilling. Double headed eagle / Castle (S) 18.00
1861 Ducat. Knight stg. / Inscription (G) 175.00

Hannover. 1834 Thaler. Head of William IV of England / Crowned shield (S) 115.00
Hesse-Cassel. 1843 3 Heller. Shield / Inscription
(C) 2.00
Lindau. 1689 Pfennig. Linden tree / blank
(C) 22.00
Lippe-Detmold. 1685 Thaler. Bust Simon Heinrich r. / Arms (S) 600.00
1860 Thaler. Bust of Paul F.E. Leopold r. / Arms
(S)... 40.00
Lübeck. 1732 8 Schilling. Double headed eagle / Shield (S) 25.00
Mainz. 1671 Ducat. Bust of Johann Philip r. / Shield
(G) 275.00
Munster. 1735 3 Pfennig. CA monogram / Inscription (C) 6.00

Nassau. 1861 Kreuzer. Crowned shield / Wreath
(Billon) 1.00
Nurnberg. (1700) 1/16 Ducat. Shield / Lamb holding banner (G) square 90.00
Oldenburg. 1858 Groschen. Crowned shield / Inscription (Billon) 3.50
Prussia. 1840 Pfennig. Crowned shield / Inscription (C) 1.50

GERMAN STATES TO 1871   F

1854 3 Pfenninge. similar (C)............................ 1.00
1821 Silber Groschen. Head of Friedrich Wilhelm III r. / Inscription (Billon) 3.00
1701 1/12 Thaler. Eagle surrounded by Fs and Rs / Crowned scepter (S) 25.00
Saxony. 1866 5 Pfennige. Crowned Baroque shield / Inscription 1.50

1668 1/24th Thaler. Arms / Royal orb (S)....... 15.00
1776 Thaler. Bust of Friedrich August r. / Shield
(S).. 35.00
Schwarzburg-Sondershausen. 1846 Pfennig. Crowned shield / Inscription (C)..................... 1.50
Stolberg-Werningerode. 1768 Ducat. Bust of Christian Ernst / Stag stg. l. (G) 400.00
Trier. 1695 3 Petermenger. Crowned shield / Bust of St. Peter (S) 14.00
Westphalia. 1812 2 Centimes. HN monogram / Inscription (C)... 2.50

1808 2 Franken. Bust of Jerome Napoleon / Wreath
(S) 400.00
Württemberg. 1798 1/2 Kreuzer. Crowned FII / 1/2
(Billon).. 7.00
1848 3 Kreuzer. Crowned shield / Wreath 2.00

GERMAN STATES 1873-1918   VF

(All reverses are the imperial eagle unless noted.)
Anhalt-Dessau. 1914 3 Mark. Heads of Duke and Duchess (S) 65.00
Baden. 1908 3 Mark. Head of Friedrich II l.
(S)... 22.00

Bavaria. 1876 2 Mark. Head of Ludwig II r.
(S)... 70.00
Bremen. 1904 2 Mark. Shield (S)................... 40.00
Brunswick-Wolfenbuttel. 1915 3 Mark. Heads of Duke and Duchess r. (S) 110.00

GERMAN STATES 1873-1918   VF

Hamburg. 1896 2 Mark. Shield between lions
(S) 20.00
Hesse-Darmstadt. 1904 2 Mark. Busts of Philipp and Ludwig l. (S) 40.00
Lippe-Detmold. 1906 2 Mark. Bust of Leopold IV l.
(S) 200.00
Lübeck. 1908 3 Mark. Double headed eagle
(S) 70.00
Mecklenburg-Schwerin. 1904 2 Mark. Busts of Grand Duke and Grand Duchess l. (S)...... 35.00
Mecklenburg-Strelitz. 1877 2 Mark. Bust of Friedrich Wilhelm l. (S) 250.00

Oldenburg. 1901 2 Mark. Bust of Friedrich August l. (S).. 200.00
Prussia. 1913 2 Mark. Bust of Wilhelm II (S)... 12.50
1913 3 Mark. King on horse, surrounded by followers / Eagle grasping snake (S)................... 14.00
1908 5 Mark. Head of Wilhelm II. (S) 22.50
1872 10 Mark. Head of Wilhelm I (G) 95.00
1888 20 Mark. Head of Friedrich (G)............ 120.00
Reuss-Greiz. 1899 2 Mark. Bust of Heinrich XXII
(S) 200.00
Reuss-Schleiz. 1884 2 Mark. Head of Heinrich XIV
(S) 300.00

Saxe-Altenburg. 1903 5 Mark. Bust of Ernst r.
(S) 200.00
Saxe-Coburg-Gotha. 1905 2 Mark. Head of Carl Eduard r. (S) 275.00
Saxe-Meiningen. 1915 2 Mark. Bust of Georg II l.
(S) 60.00
Saxe-Weimar-Eisenach. 1910 3 Mark. Heads of Grand Duke and Grand Duchess (S) 35.00
Saxony. 1913 3 Mark. Building (S) 20.00
Schaumburg-Lippe. 1911 3 Mark. Bust of Georg l.
(S) 75.00
Schwarzburg-Rudolstadt. 1898 2 Mark. Bust of Günther l. (S).. 250.00
Schwarzburg-Sondershausen. 1905 2 Mark. Head of Karl Günther r. (S) 40.00

GERMAN STATES 1873-1918   VF

Waldeck-Pyrmont. 1903 20 Mark. Head of Friedrich l. (G) 2,000.00
Württemberg. 1914 3 Mark. Bust of Wilhelm II r. (S)...................................... 17.50

GERMAN EMPIRE 1873-1918   VF

1915 1 Pfennig. Imperial eagle / Inscription (C) 50
1906 2 Pfennig. similar (C) 25
1874 5 Pfennig. similar (CN) 1.00
1919 5 Pfennig. similar (Iron) 20
1905 10 Pfennig. similar (CN) 25
1875 20 Pfennig. similar (S)............................ 8.00
1888 20 Pfennig. Eagle in wreath / Inscription (CN) 18.50
1909 25 Pfennig. Imperial eagle / Wreath (N) 7.00
1876 50 Pfennig. Imperial eagle / Inscription (S)...................................... 12.00
1918 1/2 Mark. Eagle in wreath / Wreath (S)...................................... 1.50

1874 1 Mark. Imperial eagle / Wreath (S) 6.00
1914 1 Mark. similar but larger eagle (S) 1.50

NOTGELD   VF

Aachen. 1920 10 Pfennig. Wolf. (Iron)............. 3.00

Coblenz. 1918 10 Pfennig. Arms (Iron)............ 2.00
Hamburg. 1923 5/100 Verrechnungsmarke. Arms (AL) 4.00
Leipzig. (1920) 20 Pfennig. Arms / Strassenbahn... (Iron) 3.00
similar but wooden 5.00

NOTGELD   VF

Westphalia. 1923 1/4 Million Mark. Von Stein / Horse rearing (AL) 6.00

REPUBLIC 1919-1933   VF

1923 1 Rentenpfennig. Sheaf of wheat (C)...........50
1925 2 Reichspfennig. similar (C) 30
1929 10 Reichspfennig. Stylized wheat (ALB) 50
1924 50 Rentenpfennig. similar. (ALB)........... 10.00
1931 50 Reichspfennig. Eagle (N) 4.00
1924 1 Mark. Eagle (S) 9.00
1922 3 Mark. Eagle within legend (AL) 1.00
1928 3 Mark. Eagle / Dinkelsbühl, Man over city walls (S)................................... 450.00

REPUBLIC 1919-1933   VF

1930 5 Mark. Eagle / Graf Zeppelin (S)........ 100.00
1931 5 Mark. Eagle / Oak tree (S)................... 75.00

NAZI STATE 1933-1945   VF

1937 1 Reichspfennig. Eagle holding swastika in wreath (C) 25
1940 5 Reichspfennig. similar (Z)......................20
1938 50 Reichspfennig. similar (N) 28.00

1941 50 Reichspfennig. / Eagle Holding Swastika in Wreath (AL) 5.00
1934 2 Reichsmark. Schiller. (S)..................... 55.00
1936 5 Reichsmark. Head of Hindenburg r. / Eagle holding swastika in wreath (S) 6.00

FEDERAL REPUBLIC   Unc

1950 1 Pfennig. Oak sapling. (C plated Steel) .. 1.00
1993 2 Pfennig. Oak sapling. (C plated Steel) .... .10
1949 5 Pfennig. Oak sapling. (Brass plated Steel) 30.00
1980 10 Pfennig. Oak sapling. (Brass plated Steel) 20
1950 50 pfennig. Woman planting sapling. (CN)..9.00
1977 1 Deutsche Mark. Eagle / Oak leaves (CN)..1.00
1951 2 Deutsche Mark. Eagle / Grapes and wheat (CN) 110.00

1971 2 Deutsche Mark. Max Planck / Eagle (CN) 3.00
1952 5 Deutsche Mark. Museum, Stylized eagle / Eagle (S)................................... 1,500.00
1968 5 Deutsche Mark. Bust of Gutenberg / Eagle (S).. 22.50

FEDERAL REPUBLIC   Unc

1970 5 Deutsche Mark. Eagle / Inscription (S)..8.50
1983 5 Deutsche Mark. Karl Marx / Eagle (CN clad N)..4.50
1972 10 Deutsche Mark. Olympic flame / Eagle (S)..8.50

1990 10 Deutsche Mark. Friedrich Barbarossa / Eagle (S)..8.00

DEMOCRATIC REPUBLIC (EAST GERMANY)   Unc

1952 1 Pfennig. Hammer, compass and wheat (AL)..6.00
1948 5 Pfennig. Wheat on gear. (AL)..............50.00
1989 10 Pfennig. Hammer and compass within wheat. (AL) 50
1950 50 Pfennig. Three smoke stacks. (ALB) ...32.50
1982 2 Mark. Hammer and compass within wheat. (AL)..2.00
1971. 5 Mark. Brandenburg Gate. (CN)............6.00

1979 5 Mark. Albert Einstein. (CN) 75.00
1972 10 Mark. Buchenwald Memorial (CN).. 7.50
1988 20 Mark. Microscope. (S) 220.00

GERMAN EAST AFRICA   VF

1890 Pesa. Eagle / Arabic inscription. (C) 3.00
1910 Heller. Crown / Wreath (C).................... 1.50
1909 5 Heller. similar (C) 30.00
1916 5 Heller. Crown over DOA / Wreath (C).. 12.00
1913 1/4 Rupie. Bust of Wilhelm II in griffin helmet / Wreath (S).. 12.00

GERMAN EAST AFRICA VF

1893 2 Rupien. similar bust / Arms (S)......... 285.00
1916 15 Rupien. Eagle / Elephant. (G) 800.00

GERMAN NEW GUINEA XF

1894 1 Pfennig. Inscription (C)...................... 90.00
1894 5 Mark. Bird of paradise (S)............. 1,250.00

1895 20 Mark. similar. (G) 4,250.00

KIAO CHAU VF

1909 10 Cent. Eagle on anchor / Chinese Inscription
(CN)..55.00

HUNGARY

The reign of Leopold I the Hogmouth (1657-1705) saw a far greater change for Hungarian coins than it did for the coinage of his Austrian dominions. Like the modern Austrian coin production under Leopold, which used roller dies, new heights of uniformity were reached. Their excellent portraits are a perfect example of Baroque style. Collectors should remember that coins struck with roller dies usually appear slightly curved and that this is not a flaw. But in Hungary before the mid 1600s, only three denominations — the small base silver denar, the big silver thaler, and the gold ducat were common in circulation. This period saw the increase in production of a whole range of middle denominations. For the most part the Madonna and Child still dominated the reverse, with portraits on the obverse. During the reign of Maria Theresa (1740-80) copper replaced base silver for the small denominations, and coats of arms became more common. The coppers in particular were ornamented with impressive, high relief portraits. Unfortunately the poor condition of most

surviving examples makes this difficult to appreciate today.

From 1892 until the Communist takeover, the Holy Crown of Saint Stephen, a relic of Hungary's patron saint, came to dominate the coinage, with the Madonna or a portrait to giving it diversity. The Communists replaced the old religious symbols with national heroes, architecture, and images idealizing industrial and agricultural labor. Interestingly, the new post-Communist republic combines both old and new imagery harmoniously, with a pleasant mixture of flora and fauna.

Additional Specialized Books: Huszar, L. *Münzkatalog Ungarn.*

Known counterfeits: Many gold coins have been restruck in quantity. These include 1892 10 and 20 Korona, 1907 and 1908 100 Korona, and some 1895 pieces. Also note that all coins marked UP are restrikes, regardless of type or metal.

Leopold I Hogmouth, 1657-1705 F

1662 Denar. Crowned shield / Madonna and Child
(Billon).. 18.00
1703 Duarius. Crowned shield / Small Madonna
and Child over denomination (Billon) 16.00
1680 3 Krajczar. Bust r. / Madonna and
Child (S) 17.00
1695 1/4 Thaler. Bust in diamond / Madonna and
Child stg. in diamond (S).......................... 30.00
1661 Thaler. Bust of Leopold, Hungarian shield and
Madonna and Child in margin / Double headed
eagle (S) 150.00
1694 Ducat. Leopold stg. / Madonna and Child
(G) 175.00

Other Rulers, 1705-1848 F

1711 Poltura. Joseph I / Small Madonna and Child
over denomination (S) 15.00
1705 10 Poltura. Crowned shield / PRO LIBER-
TATE X (C)... 18.00
1848 1 Krajczar. Crowned shield (C)............... 2.00
1849 6 Krajczar. Crowned shield (Billon)......... 5.00
1778 20 Krajczar. Maria Theresa in wreath /
Madonna and Child in wreath (S) 8.00
1839 20 Krajczar. Ferdinand I / Madonna and Child
(S) 3.50

Other Rulers, 1705-1848 F

1745 1/2 Thaler. Maria Theresa / similar
(S) 70.00
1785 1/2 Thaler. Angels over arms /
similar (S) 35.00
1833 Thaler. Francis I / similar (S) 80.00

Francis Joseph, 1848-1916 VF

1868 1 Krajczar. Angels over shield / Wreath
(C) 1.00
1870 10 Krajczar. Head r. / Crown of St. Stephen
(Billon) 7.50
1879 1 Forint. Head r. / Crowned shield (S)...... 8.00
1909 2 Filler. Crown of St. Stephen (C) 1.00
1915 Korona. Head r. / Crown of St. Stephen
(S) 3.00
1908 5 Korona. similar (S)............................. 18.00
1901 20 Korona Francis Joseph stg. / Arms
(G) 80.00

Regency, 1920-45 VF

1938 2 Filler. Crown of St. Stephen (C) 20
1927 1 Pengo. Crowned shield (S) 1.50
1942 2 Pengo. similar (AL) 30
1938 5 Pengo. Bust of St. Stephen / Arms (S) ..9.00

1943 5 Pengo. Bust of Nicholas Horthy / Arms
(AL) 1.00

Republics, 1946-date BU

1950 2 Filler. Wreath (AL) 50
1982 10 Filler. Dove (AL)................................ 1.50
1949 1 Forint. Arms (AL) 12.00
1971 5 Forint. Kossuth / Arms (CN) 1.50
1956 25 Forint. Parliament / Arms and gear
(S).. 22.50
1985 100 Forint. Turtle (S) 10.00
1961 500 Forint. Bela Bartok (G).................. 750.00
1997 5 Forint. Egret (Brass)...............................75
1996 100 Forint. Crowned shield (Steel, brass plated
center, bimetallic).. 5.00
1992 500 Forint. Tellstar satellite (S) 60.00
same but Proof......................................37.50

ITALY

Much like Germany, Italy, until 1861, was divided into a number of smaller independent countries. During most of the modern era the south was unified as one kingdom, the Kingdom of Naples and Sicily (more properly called the Two Sicilies). While artistically creative in the 1600s and 1700s, its more mundane later coinage is more commonly encountered. The island of Sicily itself usually had separate coinage.

Central Italy was ruled by the Pope. Despite being one unified Papal State, many of the larger cities under papal rule did have special designs and sometimes even different coinage standards. This local variation ended by 1800. Unlike the other Italian states incorporated into the new unified Kingdom of Italy in 1860-61, the Pope was able to maintain his independence until 1870. After decades of dispute with Italy, the Papal State was restored to independence in 1929 as the much smaller State of the Vatican City. Since then Papal coins have been routinely struck and can occasionally be found circulating not only at the Vatican but in and around Rome. Most Vatican coins today are collected in mint sets.

Throughout this period most papal and Vatican coins have depicted the pope or his coat of arms, along with some religious iconography or a Latin saying reflecting some moral precept. There are three kinds of "special" coins. Sede Vacante coins are struck between Popes and have the arms of the Papal Secretary of State. Holy Year coins are struck to celebrate the Jubilee when pilgrims are encouraged to come to Rome. Lastly, Lateran coins were given to the crowds when the pope took possession of the Cathedral of St. John Lateran in Rome. This is his church as Bishop of Rome, not St. Peter's Basilica.

Papal medals are quite common and are struck for commemorative purposes only. They should not be mistaken for coins. They are usually large and have very high relief. Most of those dated before 1775 are actually government restrikes struck from the original dies from the late 1700s and later. Those after 1550, which appear cast, are unofficial replicas, but aren't necessarily worthless.

Northern Italy was much more complex. It was a variable mix of small states. Some, like Venice, were international powers, while others were controlled by petty princes. Ultimately a good number of them fell into the hands of foreign powers such as Spain, France and Austria. The Duke of Savoy (who was also King of Sardinia) began to unify Italy by conquering these small states, and then moving south. One Italian state that has survived is San Marino. It has had coinage since 1864 but today most of its coins are sold to collectors. Like the Vatican's coins, they are struck to Italian standards and can be spent in Italy.

The first unified Italian coinage was struck to the standard of the international Latin Monetary Union (see France). Italian coins of the twentieth century are usually of high artistic merit. After World War I the Lira shrunk to one fifth of its value. Its value evaporated again after World War II and many coins of the 1940s to 1970s are aluminum or steel.

The colonial coins of Italy are very popularly collected, and are in high demand. Most silver is found cleaned and most copper is pitted. Despite this fact, collectors will often settle for these imperfect specimens.

Additional Specialized Books: Berman, Allen G. *Papal Coins.*

Gill, Dennis, *Coinage of Ethiopia, Eritrea and Italian Somalia.*

Muntoni, *Le monete dei Papi e degli Stati Pontifici.*

Known counterfeits: There are many contemporary counterfeits of Italian minors, including 1863M 1 lira, 1863N and 1911 2 lire, 1927 and 1930 5 lire, 1958- 500 lire. Vatican and papal pieces include 1736 1 grosso, 1796 2 carlini, 1797 5 Baiocchi and 1868 4 soldi, Naples include 1796 120 grana.

More dangerous counterfeits capable of fooling collectors are quite common. Mostly they are imitations of the old silver-dollar size 5 and 20 lire pieces. This is also true of similar Papal and San Marino 5 lire pieces. The overwhelming majority of Eritrea 5 Lire and Talero pieces are counterfeit. Many Italian, Papal and Vatican gold coins have also been counterfeited, but less commonly than the large silver. A partial list of counterfeits includes: Two lire 1895 and 1898, and 5 lire 1914. The 20 Lire depicting Mussolini is not a coin but a privately struck fantasy.

ITALIAN STATES   F

Bologna. 1680 Quattrino. Lion with banner / BONONIA DOCET (C) 18.00
1769 5 Bolognini. City arms / Cartouche (S).. 16.00
Genoa. 1814 10 Soldi. Arms / John the Baptist (S) 11.50
Gorizia. 1759 Soldo. Crowned arms / Cartouche (C) 6.50
Lombardy-Venetia. 1846 1 Centesimo. Two crowns (C) 3.00
Lucca. 1664 Quattrino. L / Holy Countenance (C)...10.00
Milan. 1665-1700 Quattrino. Charles II of Spain / Crowned MLNI DVX in wreath (C) 20.00
Naples. 1788 Grano. Ferdinand IV / Wreath (C)..8.00

ITALIAN STATES   F

1791 Piastra. King and Queen / Band of zodiac over Sun and Earth (S)...................................100.00
1857 2 Tornesi. Head r. / Crown (C)................2.50
Napoleonic Kingdom. 1813 5 Soldi. Head r. / Crown (S) 6.00
Papal State
Clement X, 1670-76. 1672 Piastra. Arms / Port of Civitavecchia (S).....................................500.00
Innocent XI, 1676-89 1/2 Grosso. Arms / NOCET MINVS (S).................................... 15.00

Alexander VIII, 1689-91. 1690 Testone. Bust r. / Two oxen plowing (S)............................. 145.00
Innocent XII, 1691-1700. Quattrino. Arms / St. Paul with sword (C) 10.00
Clement XI, 1700-21. Grosso. Arms / DEDIT PAV-PERIBVS (S) 20.00
Clement XII, 1730-40. 1738 Quattrino. Arms (C)..12.00
Benedict XIV 1740-58. 1750 Grosso. Arms / Holy door (S).................................... 20.00
Clement XIII, 1758-69. 1766 Zecchino. Arms / Church std. on cloud (G) 125.00
Pius VI, 1775-99. 1797 21/2 Baiocchi. Bust of St. Peter (C) 17.50
Pius VII, 1800-23. 1816 Quattrino. Arms (C)...7.50

Sede Vacante, 1830. 30 Baiocchi. Arms / Dove of Holy Spirit (S)..................................... 20.00
Gregory XVI, 1831-46. 1839 1/2 Baiocco. Arms / Wreath (C)..................................... 4.00
Pius IX, 1846-78. 1858 20 Baiocchi. Bust / Wreath (S) 4.00
1866 1 Soldo. Bust (C).....................................1.75
1868 10 Soldi. Bust / Wreath (S)..................... 2.50
1868 20 Lire. similar (G) 125.00
Savoy (as Kingdom of Sardinia). 1794 5 Soldi. Bust r. / St. Mauritius stg. (C) 7.00
1830 1 Lira. Bust r. / Arms (S)........................ 20.00

Sicily. 1737 Grano. Eagle / Cartouche (C) 20.00

ITALIAN STATES   F

1793 Oncia. Bust r. / Phoenix in flames
   (S)... 500.00
Tuscany. 1692 Tallero. Cosimo III / Port of Livorno
   (S)... 175.00
1859 2 Centesimi. Arms (C) 4.00
Venice. 1684-88 Soldo. S M V M A IVSTIN, Doge
   and lion / Christ (C)................................... 20.00
1676-84 Zecchino (Ducat). ALOYSIVS CONT,
   Doge and St. Mark / Christ (G)................. 80.00
1722-32 Scudo. ALOYSIVS MOCENICO...VQ,
   Cross / Bust of lion in shield (S)............. 85.00
1741-52 Soldo. S M V PET GRIM D, Doge and
   lion / Christ (C).. 15.00

ITALY   VF

Vittorio Emanuele II, 1861-78 . 1867 1 Centesimo.
   Head l. / Wreath (C) 1.50
1862 2 Centesimi. similar (C) 1.50
1861 5 Centesimi. similar (C) 1.50
1866 10 Centesimi. similar (C) 3.50
1863 1 Lira. Head r. / Wreath (S) 5.00
1874 5 Lire. Head r. / Arms (S)...................... 17.50
1863 20 Lire. Head l. / Arms (G) 100.00
Umberto II, 1878-1900. 1897 2 Centesimi. Head l. /
   Wreath (C) 1.50
1895 5 Centesimi. similar (C) 25.00
1893 10 Centesimi. similar (C) 3.50
1889 50 Centesimi. Head r. / Arms (S) 40.00
1886 1 Lira. similar (S)..................................... 6.00
1882 20 Lira. Head l. / Arms (G) 90.00
Vittorio Emanuele III, 1900-46. 1915 2 Centesimi.
   Bust l. / Italia on ship (C) 1.30
1921 10 Centesimi. Head l. / Bee (C) 1.25
1940 20 Centesimi. Head l. / Allegorical head r.
   with fasces (Steel)..40
1922 1 Lira. Italia std. (N) 1.00
1924 2 Lire. Bust r. / Fasces (N)...................... 2.00

1914 5 Lire. Bust r. / Italia in four horse chariot
   (S)... 850.00
1927 5 Lire. Head l. / Eagle (S)....................... 3.00
1927 10 Lire. Head l. / Italia in two horse chariot
   (S)... 15.00
1927 20 Lire. Head r. / Naked youth before std. Ita-
   lia (S) 90.00
1912 50 Lire. Bust l. / Italia and plow (G) 750.00

Republic, 1946-date   BU

1954 1 Lira. Scales / Cornucopia (AL) 1.85
1957 2 Lire. Bee (AL)...................................... 2.50
1969 5 Lire. Rudder / Porpoise (AL) 75
1950 10 Lire. Pegasus (AL)............................ 10.00
1975 50 Lire. Vulcan at forge (Steel) 75
1974 100 Lire. Minerva presenting olive tree
   (Steel) 85
1974 100 Lire. Marconi (Steel) 1.75

1959 500 Lire. Renaissance bust / Columbus' ships
   (S)... 8.00
1986 500 Lire. Donatello / Donatello's David
   (S)...65.00
1970 1000 Lire. Concord / Campidoglio pattern
   (S)...15.00

ITALIAN COLONIES   VF

Eritrea. 1890 50 Centesimi. Umberto II / Branches
   (S)... 50.00
1890 2 Lire. similar (S).................................. 70.00
1918 Tallero. Female bust r. / Eagle (S) 60.00
Italian Somalia. 1909 1 Besa. Bust l. (C) 22.00
1919 1/2 Rupia. Head r. / Crown and wreath
   (S)... 40.00
1925 5 Lire. Bust r. / Arms (S) 120.00

SAN MARINO   XF

1935 5 Centesimi. Arms (C)............................. 3.00
1893 10 Centesimi. Arms (C)......................... 25.00
1906 1 Lira. Arms / Wreath (S)...................... 40.00

                               BU

1972 1 Lira. Bust of St. Marino (AL)...................20
1974 20 Lire. Three towers / Lobster (ALB) 70
1992 100 Lire. similar / Columbus' ship
   (Steel).. 1.25
1982 500 Lire. similar / Garibaldi (S) 12.50

1996 10,000 Lire. Arms / Wolves
   (S)..Proof only 30.00
1979 9 Scudi. Three palm fronds / Three arms
   (G) 240.00

VATICAN CITY   BU

1930 5 Centesimi. Arms / Olive sprig (C).......... 6.00

VATICAN CITY   BU

1942 10 Centesimi. Pius XII / Dove (Brass) ...55.00
1934 20 Centesimi. Arms / St. Paul (N) 6.00
1941 50 Centesimi. Arms / Archangel Michael
   (Steel) 5.00
1931 1 Lira. Arms / Madonna stg. (N) 6.00
1942 2 Lire. Arms / Justice std. (Steel) 3.00
1962 5 Lire. John XXIII / Dove of Holy Spirit
   (AL) 1.50

1973 10 Lire. Arms / Fish (AL) 1.00
1985 20 Lire. John Paul II / Eagle (ALB) 1.00
1955 50 Lire. Pius XII / Hope (Steel)................ 3.00
1929 100 Lire. Pius XI / Christ stg. (G) 300.00
1978 200 Lire. Arms / Sermon on the mount
   (ALB) 2.50
1963 500 Lire. Sede Vacante, Arms / Dove of Holy
   Spirit (S) 10.00
1978 1000 Lire. John Paul I / Arms (S)........... 25.00

1990 1000 Lire. John Paul II treading over barbed
   wire / Arms (S).. 18.50
1995 100,000 Lire. John Paul II / Basilica of St.
   John Lateran (G) ....Proof only 875.00

LOW COUNTRIES

These countries are Belgium, the Netherlands and Luxembourg. They are called this
because most of their land is flat and barely
above sea level. They are sometimes also called
"BeNeLux" after their customs and trade union.
All three were controlled by the Spanish Hapsburgs until the late 1500s. At that time the Netherlands became Protestant and declared its
independence. The Spanish Hapsburgs continued to rule Belgium and Luxembourg until
1714 when they were transferred to the Austrian branch of the same dynasty. During the
Napoleonic Wars all three were part of the
French Empire. After that, a newly independent
Kingdom of the Netherlands was given all three
territories, only to lose Belgium in 1830 in a
revolt resulting from cultural and religious differences. In 1890 Luxembourg was lost when it
was decided that the Queen of the Netherlands,

could not legally succeed to the Grand Duchy of Luxembourg because she was a woman.

In addition to royal portraits and heraldry, the coins of Belgium (called Spanish Netherlands and later Austrian Netherlands) and Luxembourg had a few distinctive motifs. This included an X-cross and some purely inscriptional types. A few small territories such as Liege had the arms of the local bishop or the bust of a patron saint. The new Kingdom of the Belgians used the international standard of the Latin Monetary Union (see France) until World War I. Interestingly, most Belgian coins are struck in two different versions. Some have French and some have Flemish inscriptions, because both languages are commonly spoken.

The coins of the Netherlands have traditionally been struck by its constituent provinces. These almost always had a coat of arms on the copper. Some of the silver coins shared designs from province to province, such as arrows or a knight, but each individual province changed small details such as the shield and its name in the legend. Thus they could circulate interchangeably throughout the Netherlands. The Lion Dalders are particularly common in this series. These are usually poorly struck on irregular blanks. Sea-salvaged examples are worth less, unless accompanied by documentation. After the new kingdom was founded in 1815, the national arms, or the monarch's monogram or portrait were used on a more uniform national coinage. Since the 1500s Dutch gold ducats with a standing knight have been particularly common in international commerce. The word BELGII on their reverse does not refer to Belgium, which did not exist when they were first struck. Instead is derived from the ancient name for the region.

Belgian and Netherlands zinc coins struck during World War II were issued under the Nazi occupation. Fully brilliant specimens of these are virtually nonexistent.

Both Belgium and the Netherlands struck colonial coinages. The issues of the Belgian Congo (earlier called Congo Free State) are particularly attractive. Some are enormous copper coins, others depict a powerful elephant. Dutch colonials for the Netherlands Antilles are of homeland types, although some have a distinctive inscription. Coins for the Netherlands Indies (today Indonesia) are far more distinctive. They either appear European or East Asian depending on which side one examines. Dutch colonials from World War II were struck by United States Government mints, and bear their mintmarks.

Additional Specialized Books: De Mey, *Les Monnaies des Souverains Luxembourgeois.*

De Mey and Van Keymeulen, *Les Monnaies de Brabant 1598-1790.*

Mevius, J. *De Nederlandse Munten van 1795 tot Heden.*

Zonnenbloem, U., *Catalogus van de Zilvern Munten.*

Known counterfeits: Low Countries' coins have not been as extensively counterfeited as

many other countries' coins. A Holland 1791 2 stuiver exists and an occasional counterfeit gold ducat may be encountered.

BELGIUM under Austria   F

1789 Liard. Joseph II / AD USUM BELGII AUSTR (C) 6.00
1790 Liard. Lion holding hat on pole (C) Insurrection 7.50
1766 Kronenthaler. Cross, crowns in angles / Double headed eagle (S) 40.00
1750 1/2 Souverain d'or. Maria Theresa / Arms (G) 300.00

BELGIUM   VF

1862 1 Centime. Crowned L / Lion with tablets (C) 5.00
1876 2 Centimes. similar (C) .... .75
1919 2 Centimes. Crowned A / Lion with tablets (C) .... .35
1862 5 Centimes. Lion (CN) .... .25
1832 10 Centimes. Crowned L / Lion with tablets (C) 100.00

1944 25 Centimes. Monogram / Three shields (Z) .... .20
1844 1 Franc. Leopold I / Wreath (S) 140.00
1887 1 Franc. Leopold II / Arms (S) 15.00
1923 2 Francs. Belgium binding wound / Caduceus (N) 1.50
1869 5 Francs. similar (S) 8.00
1877 20 Francs. similar (G) 80.00
1932 20 France. Albert / Arms (N) 45.00
1934 20 Francs. similar (S) 2.50
1935 50 Francs. Train station / Michael the Archangel (S) 80.00

Post-War Coinage   BU

1971 25 Centimes. Crowned B (CN) .... .15

1986 5 Francs. Albert II (Aluminum) .... .50
1960 50 Francs. King and Queen / Crown over two shields (S) 9.00
1989 100 Ecu. Maria Theresa (G) 500.00

BELGIAN COLONIES   VF

Congo Free State. 1888 1 Centime. Star (C) 2.00
1887 2 Francs. Leopold II / Arms (S) 45.00
Belgian Congo. 1910 5 Centimes. Star (CN) ... 1.50
1955 50 Centimes. Crowned shield / Palm tree (AL) .... .15
1926 1 Franc. Albert I / Palm tree (CN) 2.75

BELGIAN COLONIES   VF

1943 2 Francs. Elephant (Brass, hexagonal) 4.50
1944 50 Francs. Elephant (S) 50.00
Rwanda-Burundi. 1961 1 Franc. Lion (Brass) .... .50

LUXEMBOURG   VF

1757 2 Liards. Maria Theresa / Wreath (C) 85.00
1789 1/2 Liard. Crowned shield (C) 16.00
1854 21/2 Centimes. Arms (C) 3.50
1908 5 Centimes. William (CN) 1.00
1901 10 Centimes. Adolphe (CN) .... .75
1924 2 Francs. Ch monogram / Iron worker (N) 2.25
1929 5 Francs. Charlotte / Arms at angle (S) 3.00
Post-War Coinage   **BU**

1970 25 Centimes. Arms (AL) .... .10
1957 1 Franc. Ch monogram / Iron worker (CN) .... .40
1946 100 Francs. Jean / Knight riding (S) 40.00
1964 100 Francs. Jean / Arms (S) 12.00

NETHERLANDS (PROVINCES)   F

Most coins below exist in several varieties with varying provincial shields and legends.

1794 Duit. Shield / D GEL RIE (C) 6.00
1681 1 Stuiver. Shield between I S / GRON ET OML (S) 17.50
1787 2 Stuivers. Shield between 2 S / TRA IEC TUM (S) 6.00
1764 1 Gulden. Crowned shield / Woman stg. (S) 22.00
1642 Lion Daalder. Bust of knight over shield / Lion (S) 50.00
1698 Ducat. Knight stg., shield at feet / Crowned shield (S) 100.00

1773 Ducat. Knight stg. / MON ORD PROVIN (G) 125.00

NETHERLANDS (KINGDOM)   VF

1823 1/2 Cent. Crowned W / Crowned shield (C) 28.00
1884 1/2 Cent. Lion / Wreath (C) 4.00
1876 1 Cent. Crowned W / Crowned shield (C) 5.50

NETHERLANDS (KINGDOM)   VF

1883 1 Cent. Lion / Wreath (C)......................... 4.00
1941 1 Cent. similar (C) 75
1942 1 Cent. Cross (Z) 50
1877 2-1/2 Cents. similar (C)............................ 5.00
1941 2-1/2 Cents. similar (C)............................ 2.00
1827 5 Cents. Crowned W / Crowned shield
   (S)... 50.00
1850 5 Cents. Willem III / Wreath (S) 5.00
1907 5 Cents. Crown (CN)................................ 10.00
1913 5 Cents. Orange plant (CN, square) 3.00
1827 10 Cents. Crowned W / Crowned shield
   (S)... 25.00
1849 10 Cents. Willem II / Wreath (S) 30.00
1897 10 Cents. Wilhelmina as child / Wreath
   (S)...12.00
1918 10 Cents. Wilhelmina as adult / Wreath
   (S).. 2.00
1826 25 Cents. Crowned W / Crowned shield
   (S)... 28.00
1890 25 Cents. Willem III / Wreath (S) 150.00
1943 25 Cents. Wilhelmina / Wreath (S) 1.25
1942 25 Cents. Viking ship (Z) 1.00
1818 1/2 Gulden. Willem I / Crowned shield
   (S)...280.00
1858 1/2 Gulden. Willem III / Crowned shield
   (S) 25.00
1922 1/2 Gulden. Wilhelmina / Crowned shield
   (S) 1.50

1848 1 Gulden. Willem I / Crowned shield
   (S)...110.00
1848 1 Gulden. Willem II / Crowned shield
   (S) 25.00
1892 1 Gulden. Wilhelmina as child / Crowned shield
   (S) 20.00
1929 1 Gulden. Wilhelmina as adult / Crowned shield
   (S) 3.00
1872 2 1/2 Gulden. Willem III / Crowned shield
   (S) 15.00
1930 2 1/2 Gulden. Wilemina as adult / Crowned
   shield (S)... 6.00
1831 3 Gulden. Willem I / Crowned shield
   (S)...450.00
1827 5 Gulden. similar (G)............................. 200.00
1823 10 Gulden. similar (G)........................... 275.00
1875 10 Gulden. Willem III / Crowned shield
   (S) 75.00
1927 Ducat. Knight stg. / MO AUR REG BELGII...
   (G).. XF 45.00

Post-War Coinage   Unc.

1948 1 Cent. Wilhelmina old (C) 1.50
1971 5 Cents. Juliana (C) 25
1948 10 Cents. Wilhelmina old (N) 1.00
1951 25 Cents. Juliana (N)................................ 1.75
1982 1 Gulden. Beatrix (N)............................... 1.00
1962 2 1/2 Gulden. Juliana (S)......................... 5.00
1988 5 Gulden. Beatrix (Brass) 3.50

Post-War Coinage   Unc.

1997 10 Gulden. Beatrix / George Marshall
   (S)...10.00
1982 50 Gulden. Beatrix / Lion and eagle
   (S) 35.00

NETHERLANDS COLONIES

Aruba   BU

1992 5 Cents. Arms (N clad Steel) 30
1995 5 Florin. Beatrix / Arms (N clad Steel,
   square)... 5.00
1995 25 Florin. Beatrix / Sea turtles (S).......... 35.00

Ceylon   F

1660-1720 2 Stuiver. IISt in wreath / same
   (C)..20.00
1791 1 Stuiver. T over Voc monogram / I over S T
   (C) 35.00

Curacao   VF

1821 1 Real. Caduceus and branch (S).......... 100.00
1944 1 Cent. Lion / Wreath (C)........................ 1.75

1900 1/4 Gulden. Wilemina as adolescent / Crowned
   shield (S)...20.00
1944 1 Gulden. Wilemina as adult / Crowned shield
   (S) 5.00

Netherlands Antilles   BU

1957 1 Cent. Lion / Wreath (C)........................ 1.00
1978 25 Cents. Shield (N) 75
1985 2 1/2 Gulden. Beatrix / Arms (N).............. 4.00
1977 25 Gulden. Juliana / Peter Stuyvesant
   (S)...200.00
1978 100 Gulden. Juliana / Willem I (G)........ 80.00

Netherlands East Indies   VF

1789 Duit. Shield / Voc monogram (C)............. 4.00
1807 Duit. 5 1/16 G, Shield / INDIA BATAV
   (C) 2.00
1802 1/4 Gulden. Crowned shield / Ship (S) .. 60.00
1859 1/2 Cent. Crowned shield / Indonesian inscrip-
   tion (C) 4.00
1945 1 Cent. Rice plant (C, holed) 25

Netherlands East Indies   VF

1899 2-1/2 Cents. Crowned shield / Indonesian
   inscription (C)...10.00

1913 5 Cents. Crown (CN, holed) 1.25
1857 1/10 Gulden. Crowned shield / Indonesian
   inscription (S)... 3.00
1945 1/4 Gulden. similar (S)................................50
1826 1/2 Gulden. Willem I / Wreath (S) 35.00
1840 1 Gulden. similar (S)................................ 40.00

Surinam   BU

1764 Duit. Plant / SOCIETEI VAN SURINAME
   (C).. F 30.00
1972 1 Cent. Arms (C)..................................... 1.00
1962 1 Gulden. Juliana / Arms (S) 8.00

POLAND

Early modern Poland was mostly ruled by the royal House of Saxony and its coins closely resembled the German States coins of the day. Mostly they were small coppers, small to medium size coins of base silver, and big, good silver Thalers, and gold. Most bore a bust, some had monograms on the obverse, and the royal arms dominated the reverse. Some of the most creative designs were memorial issues for the death of the king. Some of these depicted a butterfly.

Poland may have been dissolved in 1795 but there were still Polish coins struck after that. The remnant state, the Grand Duchy of Warsaw, struck some heraldic types, though briefly. Krakow even more briefly did the same as an independent republic. Also the part of Poland under Russian rule had its own distinctive coinage from 1816 to 1850. Some of these bore a portrait of the Czar even when Russian coins did not, others actually had the exchange rate on the reverse, giving values in both Polish and Russian currencies.

Polish independence was restored in 1918 and the crowned white eagle became a national symbol always depicted on the coins of the between-the-wars republic. Portraits of an idealized Polonia, and allegory of the nation, and the forceful bust of Marshall Pilsudski also were very common.

After World War II the Communist government removed the crown and changed most of the minor coins to aluminum. Initially monotonous, later Communist issues depict diverse national heroes and local animals. Post-Communist are very similar in style to late Communist issues, but with the crown replaced on the eagle's head.

Poland has produced collectors' issues in quantity since the mid-1960s. Virtually unique among world coinage of the era, Poland has since then actually distributed quantities of rejected designs. These patterns, or probas, are usually far from rare like most other countries' patterns, and can usually be bought for $10 to $20 each!

Additional Specialized Books: Gumowski, M. *Handbuch der Polnischen Numismatik.*

Kopicki, E. *Katalog podstawowych typow monet i banknotow Polski.*

Known counterfeits: Polish coins have not been the victims of significant counterfeiting in the past but may be slightly more so now because of Eastern European counterfeiting rings. A counterfeit exists of a klippe (square) 1933 Sobieski 10 Zlotych. An older circulation counterfeit of the 1932 5 Zlotych is known.

KINGDOM   F

1752 Solidus. August III / Arms (C) 8.00
1780 Grosz. SR monogram / Arms (C) 9.00
1755 Tympf. August III / Arms, 18 below (Billon)..................................... 27.50
(1733) 16 Groschen. AR monogram, 16 gr below / Butterfly (S) .... XF 1,250.00
1702 Thaler. August II / Arms (S)................ 550.00

KINGDOM   F

1775 Thaler. Stanislaus Augustus / Arms (S).. 95.00
1703 Ducat. August II / Crown over three shields (G).. 450.00

GRAND DUCHY OF WARSAW   F

1813 3 Grosze. Arms (C) 7.00
1814 1/3 Talara. Friedrich August / Arms (S) 35.00
1811 Ducat. similar (G)................................ 400.00

RUSSIAN RULE   F

1817 1 Grosz. Polish arms on Russian eagle (C)..4.00
1840 10 Groszy, Russian arms (Billon) 6.00
1838 2 Zlote = 30 Kopeks. similar (S) 12.00
1816 5 Zlotych. Alexander I / Polish arms on Russian eagle (S) 60.00

KRAKOW   F

1835 5 Groszy. Eagle in Crowned city gate (Billon)... 30.00

REPUBLIC   VF

1923 10 Groszy. Eagle (N) .... .45
same, Nazi restrike (Z)................................ .20

1925 5 Zlotych. Eagle / Polonia and youth (S).. 300.00
1934 5 Zlotych. Pilsudski / Eagle (S)................ 4.00
1925 20 Zlotych. King Boleslaus / Eagle (G) .... BU 150.00

POST-WAR COINAGE   BU

1949 5 Groszy. Eagle (C).................................. 1.00
1958 5 Groszy. Eagle (AL)................................. .20
1960 5 Zlotych. Eagle / Fisher (AL) 5.00
1967 10 Zlotych. Eagle / Marie Curie (CN) 2.25
1978 100 Zlotych. Moose / Eagle (S)...Proof only 25.00
1991 20,000 Zlotych. SAR monogram / Eagle (CN in Brass, bimetallic)................................ 20.00
1992 5 Groszy. Crowned eagle (Brass) .... .25

1997 2 Zlotye. Beetle / Crowned eagle (Brass) 4.00
1997 10 Zlotych. Pope with Eucharist / similar (S)...............................Proof only 28.00

PORTUGAL

Artistically the coins of Portugal before the twentieth century are distinctive in their consistent adherence to Baroque-style ornamentation generation after generation. They are also distinctive in their relative lack of portraiture, on silver and copper before the 1800s. The most common design is either a shield or a monogram. The reverse typically displays a cross or the denomination in Roman numerals.

During the 1600s much Portuguese silver was revalued by the application of a countermark with a new value.

Portugal maintained its colonial empire longer than most European powers, and had an extensive colonial coinage. During the 1600s and 1700s most of it was either of homeland types and bore a globe on the reverse. The coins of Portuguese India up to the 1800s is interesting in its very European designs combined with primitive methods of local manufacture. Early this century Portugal's colonial coinage was fairly uniform from colony to colony, by the 1930s a distinctive formula was developed: One side bore an emblem of Portugal, the other a heraldic symbol of the colony itself. One of these was sometimes replaced by the value on smaller denominations.

Additional Specialized Books: Gomes, *Moedas Portuguesas.*

Vaz, J. *Book of the Coins of Portugal.*

Known counterfeits: Contemporary counterfeits of Brazilian copper are not rare and are considered desirable. 1700s and 1800s gold should be inspected with care. The Azores crowned GP countermarked silver has been subject to cast counterfeits. Some lack the flat spot that would naturally occur on the back side corresponding to the countermark.

KINGDOM   F

Philip III, 1621-40. Tostao. PHILIPVS..., Crowned Shield, L B at sides / Cross (S) 275.00

John IV, 1640-56. 80 Reis. Crowned IoIII over LXXX / Cross (S) 65.00
Afonso VI, 1656-83. 40 Reis. Crowned XXX / Cross (S) 50.00
Peter II, 1683-1706. 1699 5 Reis. Crowned P II/ V in wreath (C) 7.00
John V, 1706-50. 1721 10 Reis. Crowned JV / X in wreath (C) 12.00
Joseph I, 1750-77. 1760 4 Escudos. Bust of Joseph r. / Arms (G) 300.00
Maria and Peter III, 1777-86. 1781 200 Reis. Crowned shield / Cross (S) 20.00

KINGDOM F

Maria alone, 1786-99. 1789 4 Escudos. Bust of Maria r. / Arms (G)....................................275.00
John, Regent 1799-1816. 1/2 Tostao. Crowned XXXX / Cross (S) 17.50
John VI, 1816-1826. 1820 400 Reis. Portuguese shield on crowned globe / Cross (S) 15.00
Peter IV, 1826-28. 1828 40 Reis. Bust r. / Crowned shield (C)..8.00
Michael, 1828-34. 120 Reis. Crowned shield / Cross (S)..10.00
Maria II, 1834-53. 1850 10 Reis. Crowned arms / X in wreath (C)..3.00

VF

Peter V, 1853-61. 1860 5000 Reis. Head r. / Arms (G)..175.00

Luiz I, 1861-89. 1883 20 Reis. Head l. / Wreath (C) 2.00
Carlos I, 1889-1908. 1900 100 Reis. Crowned shield / Value (CN) 75
1892 500 Reis. Head r. / Crowned arms (S)......4.50
Manuel II, 1908-10. 1909 20 Reis. Head l. / Crown in wreath (S) 3.00

REPUBLIC XF

1918 2 Centavos. Arms (C) 75
same but (Iron)..55.00
1910 Escudos. Bust with flag / Arms (S)........40.00
1933 5 Escudos. Ship / Arms (S) 1.50
1934 10 Escudos. similar (S)..............................7.50

BU

1968 20 Centavos. Cross of shields / XX (C) 50
1983 21/2 Escudos. Corn ear / Arms (CN) 50
1966 20 Escudos. Bridge / Arms (S)..................4.50

1986 50 Escudos. Ship / Arms (CN).................. 3.00
1997 200 Escudos. Francis Xavier / Ship (CN)... 5.50

PORTUGUESE COLONIES

Angola VF

1698 20 Reis. Crowned Shield / XX (C).........25.00
1762 2 Macutas. Crowned shield / Wreath (S)..25.00
1860 1/2 Macuta. Arms (C).................................20.00
1921 1 Centavo. Arms (C)...................................12.50
1927 10 Centavos. Bust l. / Arms (CN)..............4.00
1953 1 Escudo (C) 75
1952 10 Escudos. Portuguese arms / Angolan arms (S)..2.50
1972 20 Escudos. Portuguese arms / Angolan arms (N)...1.00

Azores VF

1750 5 Reis. Crowned II over V / Crown over five shields within wreath (C)..........................45.00
1830 5 Reis. MARIA II, etc., Arms (C)..........15.00
1901 5 Reis. Arms / Wreath (C)......................2.75
1980 25 Escudos. Arms (CN).....................BU 3.50

Brazil F

1695 320 Reis. Crowned shield / Globe over cross (S)..27.00
1768 5 Reis. Crowned V / Globe (C) 10.00

1819 20 Reis. Crowned XX / Arms on globe (C) 8.00
1821 960 Reis. Crown and Wreath / Arms on globe (S)..25.00
1810 4000 Reis. Crowned shield / Cross (G) 125.00

Cape Verde XF

1930 10 Centavos. Head l. (C)............................2.50
1949 50 Arms (CN)...1.50
1967 21/2 Escudos. Portuguese arms / Cape Verde arms (CN) 1.25
1953 10 Escudos. similar (S) 4.50

Portuguese Guinea XF

1933 10 Centavos. Head l. (C)..........................50.00
1946 50 Centavos. Arms (C) 4.00
1952 21/2 Escudos. Portuguese arms / Guinea arms (CN) 3.50
1973 5 Escudos. similar (CN)..............................5.50

1952 20 Escudos. similar (S) 25.00

Portuguese India Crude F

1706-50 5 Bazarucos. Shield between G A / Wheel (Tin, 5.3g.)...50.00
1769 10 Bazarucos. Shield between G A / IO in Wreath (Tin)...60.00
1854 41/2 Reis. Crowned shield / 41/2 R (C)...12.00
1750-77 12 Reis. Crowned shield / doze rei in wreath (C) 60.00
1746 Pardao. John V / Arms (S) 150.00
1650 2 Tangas. Shield between G A / St. John between S I (S)..65.00
1783 Rupia. Busts of Maria and Peter / Arms (S)...35.00
1857 Rupia. Peter V / Wreath (S) 55.00
1781 12 Xerafins. Arms / IIX, Cross (G) 950.00

Portuguese India, modern coinage VF

1871 3 Reis. Crowned shield / Wreath (C)......10.00
1881 1/8 Tanga. Luiz I / Crown (C)...................3.50
1881 1/8 Rupia. Luiz I / Arms (S) 6.00
1901 1/4 Tanga. Carlos I ./ Arms (C) 6.00

1934 2 Tangas. Indian shield / Portuguese shield (CN)..5.50
1935 Rupia. Portuguese shield / Indian shield (S)..8.00
1958 10 Centavos. Arms (C) 40
1958 1 Escudo. Portuguese arms / Indian arms (CN)..85
1959 6 Escudos. similar (CN)............................2.50

Macao BU

1952 5 Avos. Arms (C) 5.00
1972 50 Avos. Portuguese arms / Macao arms (CN)..75
1952 1 Pataca. similar (S) 4.00

1992 5 Patacas. Junk passing cathedral (CN, polygonal) 4.50
1989 100 Patacas. Arms / Snake (S)...............42.50

Madeira BU

1981 25 Escudos. Head of Zarco / Arms (CN)...4.00

Mozambique VF

1853 1 Real. Arms / Wreath (C)......................20.00
1820 80 Reis. Crown / Shield on globe (C).....35.00
1936 10 Centavos. Arms (C) 3.00
1945 50 Centavos. Arms (C) 2.50
1951 1 Escudo. Arms (CN)...................................1.50
1953 21/2 Escudos. Portuguese arms / Mozambique arms (CN)..75
1960 5 Escudos. similar (S) 2.00
1970 10 Escudos. similar (CN)............................60
1952 20 Escudos. similar (S) 3.00

St. Thomas and Prince — XF

1971 10 Centavos. Arms (AL)	35
1962 20 Centavos. Arms (C)	.85
1951 50 Centavos. Arms (CN)	12.50
1948 1 Escudo. Arms (N-C)	15.00
1939 2 1/2 Escudos. Portuguese arms / Colonial arms (S)	50.00
1951 5 Escudos. similar (S)	20.00
1951 10 Escudos. similar (S)	30.00

1971 20 Escudos. similar (N)	3.50
1970 50 Escudos. Two shields / Cross of shields (S)	BU 6.50

Timor — XF

1951 10 Avos. Cross of shields (C)	2.50
1945 20 Avos. Bust r. / Arms (CN)	35.00
1951 50 Avos. Arms (S)	10.00
1970 20 Centavos. Arms (C)	1.25

Timor — XF

1970 1 Escudo. Arms (C)	1.75
1970 2 1/2 Escudos. Portuguese arms / Timor arms (CN)	2.00
1958 3 Escudos. similar (S)	6.00
1970 5 Escudos. similar (CN)	2.50
1958 6 Escudos (S) similar (S)	12.00

RUSSIA

Russia has the dual distinction of being the last European country to abandon primitive medieval hammered coinage and the first country with a modern decimal-based coinage. The silver dollar sized ruble was introduced in 1704 it was valued at 100 of the old kopeks. Modern Russian coinage is attributable to the personal will of Peter the Great, who was determined to make Russia into modern country in a single lifetime. Before his reign portrait coins were virtually unheard of in Russia, and large silver or gold coins were generally imported foreign coins. He was also the first ruler since the 1400s to successfully circulate copper coinage.

The standards of copper coins changed several times in the 1700s and 1800s and often new coins were struck over old ones.

Specialized collectors consider these particularly desirable, but not every one cares.

During the early and mid-1800s portraiture was removed from silver coinage. It was replaced by a double headed eagle. Throughout the century the number of shields on its wings increased. Each shield represented an additional territory, such as Finland or Poland, that the Czar had incorporated into his empire.

One distinctive type of coin struck under Czarist Russia is the novodel. This is an official government "restrike" with new dies. Some novodels are actually new issues of old coins that were never actually struck. They can sometimes be identified by their unusually uniform quality, not representative of the earlier coins they resemble. They were generally struck for wealthy nineteenth century collectors, and today are considered rare and desirable.

From 1921-23 coins were struck in the name of the Russian Soviet Federated Socialist Republic. These pieces carried the communist slogan, "Workers of all countries unite!" and purely agricultural symbols. With the establishment of the Union of Soviet Socialist Republics and the addition of new territories, symbols of expansion began to appear. The new state symbol consisted of a hammer and sickle superimposed on a globe, with ribbons at its side. Each ribbon represented a republic added to the Soviet Union, much as the shields were added to the czarist eagle's wings. Among the most splendid depictions of Soviet iconography is the scene on the Soviet ruble of 1924. Nicknamed the "worker ruble" it shows an industrial worker pointing out the rising sun of Communism to a less enthusiastic agricultural worker. This relates clearly to the difficulties implicit in Russia, an agrarian nation, being the first one to implement Communism, a system intended for initial implementation in an industrial society.

During the 1970s and 1980s a wide range of commemoratives were released. Some base metal pieces were widely distributed within the Soviet Union. Others, mostly platinum or silver, were not even made available to the average Soviet citizen. Much of the commemorative coin program continued after the fall of Communism, but other changes occurred. Most of the low value circulating coins released over the last several years bear the double headed eagle, former symbol of Czarist Russia, for the first time since 1918! Another post-Communist phenomenon is rapid inflation. This has caused a revaluation of the currency, followed by more inflation.

After the fall of Communism the republics within the U.S.S.R. became independent nations. Among the most important — outside of Russia proper — is the Ukraine. Ukrainian coins were released after years of being distributed unofficially in small quantities. Because of

the initial difficulty in obtaining them, followed by abundant supplies, Ukrainian minor coinage has been the subject of one of the most precipitous drops in value in the recent world numismatic market. The trident symbol depicted on them goes back to the early coinage of Kievian Rus, virtually all of which are considered museum pieces.

Belarus, between Russia and Poland has yet to actively circulate coinage, but has made available some collectors' issues.

Additional Specialized Books: Spassky, I.G. *Russian Monetary System.*

Uzdenikov, V., *Russian Coins, 1700-1917.*

Known counterfeits: Many new counterfeits of czarist coins have appeared recently. Copper and gold has been counterfeited recently more than silver. (Most of the massive quantity of 1700s copper coming onto the market is authentic, however.) This includes Siberian coppers and many novodels. Know your dealer!

F

Peter I, 1689-1725. 1706 Denga. Two-headed eagle (C)	30.00
1705 Kopek. Peter riding horse r. (C)	25.00

F

1725 Ruble. Bust r. / Cross of four crowned P's (S)	175.00
Anna, 1730-40. 1734 Denga. Two-headed eagle / Cartouche (C)	7.00
Ivan IV, 1740-41. 1741 Grivennik (10 Kopeks). Bust r. as child / Crown (S)	300.00
Elizabeth, 1741-61. 1762 5 Kopeks. EE monogram in wreath / Two-headed eagle (C)	40.00
1752 Ruble. Bust r. / Two-headed eagle (S)	125.00
1756 2 Rubles. similar (G)	250.00
Peter III, 1759-62. 1762 4 Kopeks. St. George spearing dragon / Drum, cannon and flags (C)	45.00

F

Catherine II the Great, 1762-1796. 1791 5 Kopeks. *EI* monogram in wreath / Two-headed eagle (C) 10.00
1783 15 Kopeks. Bust r. / 15 on Two-headed eagle (S)..................................... 28.00
1769 Ruble. Bust r. / Two-headed eagle (S)... 90.00
Paul I, 1796-1801. 1798 2 Kopeks. Crowned P (C) 8.00
1800 Poltina (= 1/2 Ruble). Cross of four crowned TT's / Inscription in square (S) 75.00
1798 Ruble. similar (S)................................... 70.00

Alexander I, 1801-25. 1802 2 Kopeks. Two-headed eagle in thick border with two dots / Inscription in similar border (C) 27.00
1812 2 Kopeks. Two-headed eagle without border / Wreath (C) 2.50
1831 25 Kopeks. Two-headed eagle with wings down / Wreath (S) 10.00

F

1820 Ruble. Two-headed eagle / Wreath (S).. 25.00
Nicholas I, 1825-55. 1835 Kopek. Two-headed eagle with wings down (C)......................... 3.00
1844 Kopek. Crowned H (C)........................... 3.00
1850 20 Kopeks. Two-headed eagle / Wreath (S)...5.00

VF

Alexander II, 1855-81. 1875 1/4 Kopek. Crowned Aii monogram (C) 2.50
1869 20 Kopeks. Two-headed eagle / Wreath (S).. 2.00
1877 Ruble. similar (S)................................... 25.00
Alexander iii, 1881-94. 1889 1/2 Kopek. Crowned AIII monogram (C)............................... 2.00
1893 3 Kopeks. Two-headed eagle in ornate border / Wreath (C) 1.50

1894 50 Kopeks. Head r. / Two-headed eagle (S)...25.00
Nicholas ii, 1894-1917. 1909 1/2 Kopek. Crowned NII monogram (C)...................................... .50
1908 3 Kopeks. Two-headed eagle in ornate border / Wreath (C) 1.50
1905 5 Kopeks. Two-headed eagle / Wreath (S)..2.00
1896 50 Kopeks. Head l. / Two-headed eagle (S)..8.00
1899 Ruble. similar (S).................................. 17.50
1902 5 Rubles. similar (G).............................. 60.00

Communist Russia (РСФСР)   XF

1923 10 Kopeks. Hammer and Sickle / Wreath (S).. 2.00
1923 50 Kopeks. similar / Star (S).................... 7.00

Soviet Union (CCCP)   XF

1925 1/2 Kopek. CCCP (C) 14.50
1931 1 Kopek. Arms / Wreath (ALB)............... 1.50
1936 2 Kopeks. similar (ALB) 2.00
1943 3 Kopeks. similar (ALB) 1.00
1952 5 Kopeks. similar (ALB) 1.00
1957 10 Kopeks. Arms / Octagon (CN)............ 2.00

1965 15 Kopeks. Arms (CNZ) .... .40
1967 20 Kopeks. Arms / Ship (CNZ)................. .75
1991 50 Kopeks. Dome and tower (CN)............. .50
1924 Ruble. Industrial worker leading farmer towards sun / Arms (S) 25.00

BU

1981 Ruble. Cosmonaut / Arms (CNZ) 2.00
1991 5 Rubles. Cathedral / Arms (CN) 6.50
1979 150 Ruble. Wrestlers / Arms (Platinum)... 220.00

Russian Federation   BU

1992 1 Ruble. Two-headed eagle (Brass clad Steel)...1.00

1994 50 Rubles. Flamingos / Two-headed eagle (CN in ALB, bimetallic).............................. 2.50
1995 100 Rubles. Ballerina / similar (G) ....Proof only 695.00

SIBERIA   F

1768 Polushka (=1/4 Kopek). Crowned EII monogram in wreath / Cartouche (C) 75.00

1779 2 Kopeks. similar / Value on shield between sables (C)... 35.00

SCANDINAVIA

Scandinavian coins first become common in the 1500s. By the 1600s the small base-silver coins of Denmark were frequently found. During this period the coins of both Sweden and Denmark follow a typical European pattern of portraits, monograms, crowns and shields. Other features are distinctive. In both countries standing figures of the monarch become more common than elsewhere in Europe. Monograms in Denmark are more likely to use modern, rather than Roman, numerals. In Sweden the divine name, the Tetragramaton, in Hebrew is often depicted.

The single most distinguishing feature of Scandinavian coinage is the abundant use of copper. Large copper coins struck on crudely made blanks were common particularly in 1600s Sweden. There also large slabs of copper, called "plate money," that were used instead of silver coins. Each piece, weighing up to several pounds, was usually stamped five times with circular dies — once in each corner to prevent clipping, with an additional stamp in the center. Most of the plate money on the market in recent years is from one shipwreck, the

Nicobar, and is corroded. These are worth less than non sea-salvaged pieces. By the late 1700s plate money had ceased to be struck but large copper continued to be common throughout Scandinavia.

During the 1800s, Scandinavian coins were decimalized, and in 1872 a common monetary union was formed with all Scandinavian countries striking distinctive coins on a common standard. During this time most countries used portraits only on silver and gold, monograms on copper.

Norway has been part of either the Danish (1397-1814) or the Swedish (1814-1905) monarchy through most of the modern era. In 1905 it elected a king of its own, Haakon VII. Modern Norwegian coins usually resemble that of the kingdom with which it was united, sometimes with the distinctive Norwegian arms, a lion with a battle ax, other times differentiated only by small mintmarks.

Iceland had no separate coinage until 1922, Greenland until 1926. Before then Danish coins circulated on both islands. In 1941 Iceland became independent and royal symbols, such as the crown, were removed from above the arms. Many recent coins show the guardian spirits of Iceland, sometimes supporting the country's shield. After 1964 regular Danish coins were reintroduced to Greenland and today it is an integral part of Denmark.

All these countries have issued plentiful silver commemorative in the modern era, with some base metal ones more recently.

One convenient way to distinguish Swedish from other Scandinavian coins is that the word "ore" is spelled with ö in Swedish, and ø in the others.

It is convenient to mention the names of the Scandinavian countries in their native languages:

Denmark	DANMARK
Greenland	GRØNLAND
Iceland	ISLAND
Norway	NORGE or NOREG
Sweden	SVERIGE

Denmark struck colonial coins for its possessions in the West Indies. They are generally artistic and not particularly rare. In 1913 Denmark sold these islands to the United States and they became the United States Virgin Islands. Today these coins are popular with collectors not only of Danish coins, but with many U.S. collectors as well. The coins of Danish India are both scarcer and less popular.

Swedish issues for the West Indies are very rare. They consist only of countermarks on other countries' coins for local use.

Additional Specialized Books: Hobson, Burton, *Catalogue of Scandinavian Coins.*

Sømod, J. *Danmarks Mønter.* Also covers Norway 1481-1813.

Tonkin, Archie, *Myntboken.* Annual editions with up to date Swedish pricing.

Known counterfeits: Contemporary counter-

feits exist of some seventeenth and eighteenth century Danish minors. Swedish plate money has been the victim of dangerous counterfeits. The rare Danish 1776 2 skilling is known altered from 1778.

DENMARK   F

1719 1/2 Skilling. Crowned double *F4* monogram
   in wreath (C) 16.00
1771 1 Skilling. Crowned double C7 monogram
   (C) 8.00

1779 2 Skilling. Crowned C7 monogram / Crowned
   shield (Billon) 8.00
1764 4 Skilling. Crowned double F4 monogram
   (Billon) 10.00
1701 8 Skilling. Frederick IV / Crown (S) 25.00
1732 24 Skilling. Christian VI / Crowned shield
   (S) 100.00
1711 Krone. Frederick IV on horse r. / Arms
   (S) 125.00
1786 Daler. Large wildman with club supporting
   Danish arms / Norwegian arms (S) 550.00
1738 Ducat. Crowned double *C6* monogram / Fortress (G) 650.00

                                        VF

1869 1 Skilling. Crowned CIX in wreath (C) ... 4.50
1856 16 Skilling. Frederick VII / Wreath (S)..... 7.75
1855 1 Rigsdaler (S) similar (S) 40.00
1846 1 Species Daler. Christian VIII / Arms
   (S) 100.00
1899 1 Øre. Crowned CIX / Dolphin and wheat ear
   (C) 1.25
1907 2 Øre. Crowned F8 monogram (C) 1.50
1919 5 Øre. Crowned Cx monogram (C) 5.00
1897 10 Øre. Christian IX / Dolphin and wheat ear
   (Billon) 6.00
1924 25 Øre. Crowned CxR (CN, holed) 1.00
1942 similar (Z, holed) 1.50
1925 1/2 Krone. Crowned CxC monogram / Crown
   (ALB) 6.50
1875 1 Krone. Christian IX / Shield between Dolphin
   and wheat ear (S) 25.00
1923 2 Kroner. King and Queen / Arms (S) 8.00

1908 10 Kroner. Frederick VII / Arms (G) 80.00
1873 20 Kroner. Christian IX / Dania std. l.
   (G) 135.00

Post-war Coinage   BU

1962 1 Øre. Crowned *FRIX* monogram (Z)...... 1.25
1973 10 Øre. Crowned *M2R* monogram (CN).... .25
1957 1 Krone. Frederick XI / Shield (ALB) 3.00
1968 10 Kroner. Frederick XI / Princess Benedikte
   (S) 11.50
1992 200 Kroner. Queen and Prince / Stylized house
   (S) 50.00

GREENLAND   XF

1926 25 Øre. Crowned shield / Bear (CN) 6.50
1960 1 Krone. Crown over two shields / Wreath
   (CN) 5.50

ICELAND   XF

1931 1 Eyrir. Crowned Cx (C) 6.00
1942 2 Aurar. similar (C) 1.00
1963 5 Aurar. Shield in wreath (C) .... .75
1981 10 Aurar. Ox / Cuttle-fish (C) .... .20
1922 25 Aurar. Crowned shield (CN) 4.00
1940 1 Krona. similar (ALB) 2.00

                                        BU

1981 1 Krona. Giant / Cod (CN) .... .50
1970 10 Kronur. Arms (CN) .... .75
1974 500 Kronur. Four spirits / Woman leading cow
   (S) 8.00
1987 50 Kronur. Four spirits / Crab (CNZ) 3.00

NORWAY   F

1643 Skilling. Lion with battle ax / I SKILL ING
   DA (Billon) 45.00
1714 2 Skilling. Crowned double *F4* monogram /
   Lion with battle ax (Billon) 15.00
1778 4 Skilling. Crowned *C7* monogram / Crowned
   arms, crossed hammers below|
   (Billon) 20.00
1655 8 Skilling. Crowned F3 monogram / Lion with
   battle ax (S) 90.00
1763 24 Skilling. Crowned F5 monogram / similar
   (S) 15.00
1684 Mark. Crowned C5 / Lion with battle ax, in
   wreath (S) 250.00
1689 4 Mark. Crowned double *C6* monogram /
   Lion with battle ax, in wreath (S) 125.00
1673 1/2 Specie Daler. Christian V / Crowned shield
   (S) 2,200.00
1749 1 Riksdaler. Frederick V / Lion with battle ax,
   mountains behind (S) 275.00

                                        VF

1870 1 Skilling. Arms (C) 7.00
1825 8 Skilling. Carl XIV / Arms (S) 40.00

1847 24 Skilling. Oscar I / Arms (S)............... 30.00
1891 2 Øre. Arms, Ocr II at sides (C) 5.00
1917 10 Øre. Crowned H7 monogram
   (Billon).. 2.00
1939 50 Øre. Cross of monograms / Crown
   (CN, holed) .... .60
1906 2 Kroner. Arms / Tree within border of hands
   (S) 15.00

Post-war Coinage   BU
1957 1 Øre. Crowned H7 monogram (C) 2.50
1964 10 Øre. Crowned Ov monogram / Bee
   (CN) 1.25
1992 1 Krone. Harald V / Crown (CN)................ .75

Post-war Coinage   BU
1964 10 Kroner. Arms / Building (S)................ 7.00
1993 100 Kroner. Harald V / Figure skater
   (S)... 60.00

SWEDEN   F
1666 1/6 Öre. C R S, Three crowns / Crowned lion
   (C) 12.00
1720 1/2 Öre. F R S, Three crowns / Crowned arrow
   shield (C) 7.00
1690 1 Öre. Crowned CXI / Three crowns
   (Billon).. 12.00
1748 2 Öre. Crowned shield / Crown over crossed
   arrows (C) 8.00

SWEDEN   F
1669 4 Öre. Crowned C / Three crowns
   (S) 25.00
1719 1 Mark. Ulrica Eleonora r. / Crowned shield
   (S) 165.00
1676 2 Mark. Charles XI l. / Three crowns
   (S) 55.00
1753 4 Mark. Adolf Frederick r. / Arms
   (S) .... 150.00.
1697 8 Mark. Charles XII r. / Crowned shield
   (S) 550.00
1778 1/24th Riksdaler. Crowned GIII / Crowned
   shield (Billon) 15.00
1779 1/12th Riksdaler. similar (S).................. 27.50
1718 Daler. Jupiter and eagle (C) 10.00
1719 Daler. Hope (C) 10.00
1725 Riksdaler. Frederick I r. / Arms (S) 225.00
1781 Riksdaler. Gustav III r. / Arms (S).......... 75.00

(reduced)

1741 2-1/2 Daler "Plate money." Crowned FRS in
   each corner, 1/2 DALER SILF.MYNT in cen-
   ter (C).. 200.00
1709 Ducat. Carl XII r. / Crowned CC monogram
   (G) 850.00
1776 Ducat. Gustav III r. / Arms (G)............. 525.00

VF
1821 1/2 Skilling. Crowned CXIV / Crossed arrows
   (C) 5.00
1848 1/16th Riksdaler. Oscar I / Arms (S) 8.00
1721 Riksdaler, Anniv. of Liberation War, Busts of
   Gustaf Vasa, Gustaf II Adolf 400.00

VF
1806 Riksdaler. Gustav IV / Arms (S)........... 300.00
1866 1 Öre. Carl XV / Wreath (C) 3.00
1920 1 Öre. Crowned GvG monogram / Three
   crowns (C).. 50
1890 2 Öre. Crowned OII monogram (C) 2.00
1917 2 Öre. Crowned GvG monogram / Three
   crowns (Iron) 6.00
1907 5 Öre. Crowned OII monogram (C) 2.00
1941 5 Öre. Crowned GvG monogram / Three
   crowns (C).. 50
1898 10 Öre. Crowned OII monogram
   (Billon) 4.50
1934 10 Öre. Crowned shield (Billon) .... .60
1943 25 Öre. Crown (Billon) .... .75
1856 25 Öre. Oscar I / Wreath (S) 12.00
1907 50 Öre. Crowned OII monogram / Wreath
   (S) 10.00

1938 50 Öre. Crowned Gv monogram / Wreath
   (CN) 1.50
1898 1 Krona. Oscar II / Arms (S) 30.00
1936 1 Krona. Gustav V / Arms (S) 2.00
1897 2 Kronor. Oscar II crowned / Arms
   (S) 9.00
1944 2 Kronor. Gustav V old / Arms
   (Billon) 2.50
1874 10 Kronor. Oscar II / Arms (G) 85.00

BU
1953 1 Öre. Crown / Crown (C) 3.00
1967 2 Öre. similar (C) .... .50
1979 5 Öre. Crowned CXVIG monogram (C).....25
1988 10 Öre. similar (CN) .... .15
1956 25 Öre. Crown (Billon) 5.00
1968 50 Öre. Crowned GVIA monogram
   (CN)... 1.00

BU

1979 1 Krona. Carl XVI / Crowned shield
(CN) 60
1964 2 Kronor. Gustav VI / Crowned shield
(Billon) 5.00
1964 5 Kronor. Gustav VI / Crowned GVIA monogram (Billon) 28.00
1972 10 Kronor. Gustav VI / Signature (S) 8.50
1976 20 Kronor. King and Queen / Arms
(S) 15.00
1990 200 Kronor. Carl XVI / Ship Vasa (S) ... 55.00
1993 1000 Kronor. Queen / Arms (G) 275.00

SPAIN

During the 1500s through the early 1800s Spanish coins were among the most important international trade coins in the world, particularly those struck at Spain's colonial mints in the Americas. They were so respected that they were the standard of value on which the original United States dollar was based.

Spanish coinage, up until the mid-1800s, was based on the real, introduced by Ferdinand and Isabella. It was originally a silver coin larger than a quarter, although it had shrunk to the size of a nickel and thinner by the 1600s. From then until the Napoleonic Wars it remained quite stable. During most of this period it carried the coat of arms of Spain on the reverse, a portrait or variation on the arms on the obverse.

Gold coins were plentiful as well. They were denominated in escudos, worth 16 reales. They more often bore portraits than the silver did.

Copper coins were denominated in maravedi, 34 of which were worth one real. During most of this period the copper coinage was poor. There was often a shortage of new copper, causing old worn 0

out coins to continue in use long after they should have been replaced. Often these coins would be counterstamped to revalidate them. A number indicating a new value and sometimes a date would be impressed. When this was done repeatedly the coins took on a mutilated appearance, and sometimes ceased to remain flat. This practice of making resellados ended in the 1700s, but the practice of forcing worn out copper into continued use persisted.

Spanish coins from the mid-1800s until recently have carried two dates. The large date is the year of authorization but not when the coin was actually manufactured. The real date is usually indicated in tiny incuse numbers on the six-pointed star which is a Madrid mintmark.

After a few monetary experiments in the mid-1800s Spain joined many other European countries in 1869 in striking its coins according to the international standard of the Latin Monetary Union, and continued to do so until 1926. Most of the issues during this period uniformly bore the royal portrait and the coat of arms.

The final years of the monarchy and the period of the Civil War not only saw a deterioration of the value of the coinage but also an opening up of the designs to new ideas under all three governments. Despite the extremely modernistic eagle supporting the shield, Franco's later coinage, mostly of base metal, was fairly conservative in pattern.

The restoration of the monarchy not only promised a progressive government for Spain, but also changes in the coinage. Since the 1980s new shapes have been used to distinguish denominations, and a plethora of designs have been used to promote the recognition of various cultural sights and events throughout Spain. There have also been a vast number of collector issues sold at a premium. These too have had unusual and progressive designs.

COLONIAL COINAGE

The real, issued in the New World, was struck to the same standards as in European Spain but the designs often varied. The first issues of the early 1500s displayed the Pillars of Hercules and a coat of arms. In terms of style they seemed no different than European coins. The first copper coins struck in the New World, minted in Santo Domingo, featured monograms. They were far more carelessly made.

When the quantities of silver and gold being mined and shipped back to Spain became so great that they could not be struck into nicely finished coins, a rough, improvised coin was devised. Called "cobs" by modern collectors, these coins were struck to the same exacting weight standards but the designs were only hastily impressed, with no entire image being found on any one coin. The blanks on which they were struck were neither round nor flat. Originally it was intended that these be shipped back to Europe and remelted, but the pressing needs for money in the Spanish American colonies caused them to be pressed into service as regular coinage.

While dates are engraved on the dies of these cobs, they are usually not clear on the coins. Specialized references, however, sometimes permit the dating of these pieces by the correlation of mintmarks and assayers' initials, which are more often legible.

Many of the cobs on the market are recovered from shipwrecks or found on beaches near shipwrecks. Generally sea salvaged coins are either pitted or covered with black compounds called horn silver. This is bonded to the metal and cannot be removed without removing part of the coin. Such corroded coins are worth far less than other cobs and Spanish colonial coins. The exception is for those coins with pedigrees to known shipwrecks. If satisfactorily documented, the novelty value of their history can far exceed their value as low grade Spanish Colonial coins. Be careful of false documentation and made to order pedigrees. When possible, documentation from the original salvers is desirable.

From 1732 onward, more careful methods of manufacture were implemented. Initially the improved silver carried the crowned shield of Spain on one side, two globes between the Pillars of Hercules on the other. Later the designs were changed (1760) to bear the king's portrait and a Spanish shield. The face value of each silver coin was indicated in numbers of reales indicated as 8R through 1R, with the half real simply as "R" without a numeral. The improved gold had carried a similar design since the 1730s. Copper in the Spanish colonies was not common, and at most mints it wasn't struck at all.

Despite the vast expanse covered by the Spanish colonies in the Americas, most of the coins struck were of similar design from mint to mint. Some mints, however, are far scarcer than others, so it is important to recognize their marks. Usually the mintmark is incorporated into the reverse legend. The Colonial Listings below follow a large representation of the mintmark, which appears on the coins listed.

Later Spanish colonial coins of the Philippines and Puerto Rico resemble Spanish coins of the turn of the century. On these the name of the colony is clearly indicated.

Additional Specialized Books: Castan, C. and Cayon, J., *Las Monedas Españolas desde Don Pelayo a Juan Carlos I.*

Sedwick, D. and F., *The Practical Book of Cobs*, 3rd ed.

Known counterfeits: Gold coins of Isabella II have been counterfeited. So have many nineteenth century silver dollar sized coins. These include, among others: 20 reales 1852, 5 peseta 1870 (69), 1871 (73), 1897, 1899 The "star" dates are the ones in parentheses. Many are not silver but a nickel alloy. Other gold coins of Alfonso XII and XIII have been restruck by the Spanish mint but they bear the accurate "secret" dates of (19)61 and (19)62.

Counterfeits of Spanish colonial cobs are plentiful in both gold and silver. Examine any example for casting seams, raised pimples or a cloudy appearance. This is different from the graininess found on authentic sea salvaged coins. Also note that no two cobs are precisely identical, so if you have a pair of identical coins there is a good chance both are counterfeit. Many of the two globes and portrait pieces have also been counterfeited, both at the time of issue and recently. Most of the recent counterfeits are poor quality metal and will not ring correctly.

Be careful not to accidentally purchase Puerto Rican coins with solder marks on the edge.

EUROPEAN COINAGE

Carlos II, 1665-1700   F

1682 2 Reales. Arms in octolobe / Crowned CAR-
OLVSII monogram (C) 305.00

Carlos II, 1665-1700   F

1685 4 Reales. Crowned shield / Arms in octolobe
(S).. 275.00
1687 4 Reales. similar / Cross over MA monogram
(S).. 550.00

Carlos III Pretender, 1701-13   F

1711 2 Reales. similar / Crowned CAROLVSIII
monogram (S).. 30.00

Philip V, 1700-46   F

1719 4 Maravedi. Crowned shield / Lion holding
globes (C) 12.00
1726 1 Real. Crowned shield / Arms in octolobe
(S).. 20.00
1734 4 Reales. similar (S) 200.00
1743 1/2 Escudo. Bust r. / Crowned shield
(G)...80.00
Louis, 1724
1724 2 Reales. Crowned shield / Arms in octolobe
(S).. 45.00

Ferdinand VI, 1746-59   F

1757 2 Reales. Crowned shield / Arms in octolobe
(S).. 30.00
1747 1/2 Escudo. Bust r. / Crowned shield
(G)...75.00

Carlos III, 1759-88

1780 8 Maravedis. Bust r. / Castles and lions in
angles of cross (C) 15.00
1788 2 Reales. Bust r. / Crowned shield (S) ... 25.00
1786 4 Escudo. Bust r. / Crowned shield in collar
(G) 250.00

Carlos, IV, 1788-1808

1800 4 Maravedis. Bust r. / Castles and lions in
angles of cross (C) 12.00
1793 1 Real. Bust r. / Crowned shield (S)..... 152.00

Joseph Napoleon, 1808-13

1810. 4 Reales. Bust l. / Crowned shield (S) .. 12.50

Ferdinand VII, 1808-33 2

1824 2 Maravedis. Bust r. / Castles and lions in
angles of cross (C) 6.00
1809 4 Reales. Bust r. / Crowned shield
(S).. 125.00

Isabel II, 1833-68

1837 4 Reales. Bust r. / Crowned shield in collar
(S).. 25.00
1868 2-1/2 Centimos. Bust r. / Crowned shield
(C)... 4.50
1868 Escudo. Bust r. / Crowned shield between pillars
(S).. 10.00

Latin Monetary Union Standard   VF

1870 2 Centimos. Hispania std. / Lion holding
shield (C) 1.00
1879 5 Centimos. Alfonso XII / Arms (C) 3.50
1900 50 Centimos. Alfonso XIII as child / Arms
(S)... 3.00

Latin Monetary Union Standard   VF

1891 1 Peseta. Alfonso XIII as baby / Arms
(S)..15.00
1871 5 Pesetas. Amadeo I / Arms (S) 20.00
1883 5 Pesetas. Alfonso XII / Arms (S).......... 12.00
1878 25 Pesetas. Alfonso XII / Arms (G) 135.00

Republic & Civil War   VF

1938 10 Centimos. Arms (Iron).................... 650.00
1937 25 Centimos. Yoke and arrows / Crowned shield
(CN, holed).. .40
1937 1 Peseta. Head l. / Grapes (Brass) 1.00

Franco Regency   BU

1953 10 Centimos. Horseman / Arms (AL)...... 3.00
1959 10 Centimos. Franco (AL)...................... .10
1964 1 Peseta. Franco / Arms (ALB) .... .75
1949 5 Pesetas. similar (N) 2.00
1975 25 Pesetas. Franco / Eagle holding arms
(CN) .... .75
1966 100 Pesetas. Franco / Arms in octolobe
(S)... 6.00

Kingdom Restored   BU

1983 1 Peseta. Juan Carlos / Arms (AL)............. .20

1990 50 Pesetas. Juan Carlos / Globe (CN,
notched)... 2.50
1994 100 Pesetas. Juan Carlos / Prado Museum
(ALB)... 3.75
1989 5000 Pesetas. Arms / Ship Santa Maria
(S).. 100.00

COLONIAL COINAGE   F

Santo Domingo, Hispaniola

1506-1516 and later. 4 Maravedis. Crowned Y /
Crowned pillars (C) 40.00

C

Cartagena, Colombia

1634 8 Reales cob. Crowned shield / Pillars over
waves (S)... 2,500.00

C or C^A

Chihuahua, Mexico

1812 8 Reales. Ferdinand VII / Arms
(cast S) 60.00

D

Durango, Mexico

1814 1/8th Real. Crowned FoV monogram
(C)..27.00
1821 8 Reales. Ferdinand VII / Arms (S)........ 50.00

G^A

Guadalajara, Mexico

1821 8 Reales. Ferdinand VII / Arms (S)........45.00
1821 8 Escudos. similar (G)......................2,500.00

G

Guanajuato, Mexico

1822 8 Reales. Ferdinand VII / Arms (S)........45.00

ME

Lima, Peru

1689 1 Real cob. Pillars over waves / Castles and
lions in angles of cross (S)........................50.00
1740 2 Reales cob. similar (S) 45.00
1697 4 Reales cob. similar (S) 270.00
1746 8 Reales cob. similar (S) 100.00
1696 8 Escudos cob. similar (G)................2,250.00
1754 1/2 Real. Crowned shield / Two globes
between pillars (S) 15.00

COLONIAL COINAGE   F

1761 4 Reales. similar (S) 90.00
1769 8 Reales. similar (S) 150.00
1796 1/4 Real. Castle / Lion (S) 15.00
1812 1/2 Real. Ferdinand VII / Arms (S)..........7.00
1793 2 Reales. Charles IV / Arms (S) 20.00
1805 4 Reales. similar (S) 40.00
1782 8 Reales. Charles III / Arms (S).............35.00
1821 2 Escudos. Ferdinand VII / Arms
(G)...350.00
1775 8 Escudos. Carlos III / Arms (G)..........500.00

M

Mexico City, Mexico

1653 1/2 Real cob. CAROLVS monogram / Arms
in octolobe (S)..120.00
1714 1 Real cob. Crowned shield / Arms in
octolobe (S)..57.50

F

1613 2 Reales cob. similar (S)...................... 150.00
1733 4 Reales cob. similar (S)...................... 185.00
1664 8 Reales cob. similar (S)...................... 225.00
1688 4 Escudos cob. Cross, fleurs in angles (G)...................... 1,400.00
1755 1/2 Real. Crowned shield / Two globes between pillars (S)......................15.00
1736 2 Reales. similar (S) 30.00
1768 4 Reales. similar (S) 100.00
1769 8 Reales. similar (S) 100.00
1780 1/2 Real. Carlos III / Arms (S) 10.00
1817 1 Real. Ferdinand VII / Arms (S)............. 7.50
1788 2 Reales. Carlos III / Arms (S)............... 20.00
1805 4 Reales. Carlos IV / Arms (S)............... 40.00
1791 8 Reales. similar (S) 40.00
1808 1 Escudo. similar (G).......................... 165.00

1736 4 Escudos. Philip V / Arms (G) 1,000.00

NG or G

Nueva Guatemala, Guatemala

1743 1/2 Real cob. Crowned shield / Two globes between pillars (S)...................... 40.00
1752 8 Reales cob. similar (S)...................... 110.00
1758 2 Reales. similar (S) 60.00
1772 2 Reales. Carlos III / Arms (S)............... 30.00
1812 2 Reales. Ferdinand VII / Arms (S) 25.00

NR or SF

Nuevo Reino / Santa Fe de Bogotá
Colombia

1652 2 Reales cob. Crowned shield / Pillars over waves (S)...................... 525.00
1663 2 Escudos cob. Crowned shield / Cross, fleurs in angles (G) 1,000.00
1795 1 Real. Carlos IV / Arms (S)................. 25.00
1777 1 Escudo. Carlos III / Arms (G) 90.00

P

Popayan, Colombia

1772 1 Real. Carlos III / Arms (S) 150.00
1776 8 Escudos. similar (G) 475.00
1814 8 Escudos. Ferdinand VII / Arms (G).. 425.00

PTS or P

Potosi, Bolivia

1662 1/2 Real cob. PHILIPVS monogram / Castles and lions in angles of cross (S) 95.00
1749 2 Reales cob. Pillars over waves / Cross, castles and lions in angles (S)...................... 45.00
1648 8 Reales cob. Crowned shield / Arms in octolobe (S)...................... 150.00
1761 8 Reales cob. Pillars over waves / Cross, castles and lions in angles (S)...................... 135.00

F

1770 1 Real. Two globes between pillars / Arms (S)......................27.50
1770 8 Reales. similar (S)............................. 150.00

1799 1/4 Real. Lion / Castle (S) 15.00
1808 1 Real. Carlos IV / Arms (S) 9.00
1776 2 Reales. Charles III / Arms (S) 12.50
1823 4 Reales. Ferdinand VII / Arms (S)........ 30.00
1795 8 Reales. Charles IV / Arms (S) 35.00
1822 1 Escudo. Ferdinand VII / Arms (G).... 300.00
1784 2 Escudos. Charles III / Arms (G)........ 350.00

Ş

Santiago, Chile

1792 1/4 Real. Carlos IV / Castles and lions in angles of floral cross (S) 17.50

COLONIAL COINAGE F

1810 2 Reales. Imaginary bust of Ferdinand VII / Arms (S)...................... 35.00
1797 8 Reales. Carlos III / Arms (S) 100.00
1810 2 Escudos. Bust of Carlos III with titles of Ferdinand VII / Arms (G)....................... 400.00

Z or ZS

Zacatecas, Mexico

1820 1 Real. Ferdinand VII / Arms (S)........... 15.00
1821 8 Reales. 40.00

Philippines

1805 Octavo. Crowned shield / Lion with two globes (C)... 55.00

VF

1868 10 Centavos. Isabel II / Arms (S) 12.00
1864 20 Centavos. similar (S) 65.00
1868 50 Centavos. similar (S) 15.00
1868 2 Pesos. similar (G)............................... 65.00

VF

1880 10 Centavos. Alfonso XII / Arms (S) ...325.00
1885 20 Centavos. similar (S) 8.00
1885 50 Centavos. similar (S) 7.50
1882 4 Pesos. similar (G)..............................750.00

1897 Peso. Alfonso XIII / Arms (S) 30.00

Puerto Rico VF

(1884) 1/2 Dollar. Fleur-de-lis countermark on United States Liberty Seated half dollar (S) ....F 250.00

Puerto Rico VF

1896 5 Centavos. Arms (S) 25.00
1896 10 Centavos. Alfonso XIII / Arms (S)....35.00
1895 20 Centavos. similar (S)........................60.00
1896 40 Centavos. similar (S)......................275.00

1895 Peso. similar (S) 250.00

SWITZERLAND

While the Swiss cantons (provinces) gradually formed a union during the thirteenth through the fifteenth centuries, each one maintained its own coinage. During the early modern period most had a range of small silver denominations, with some striking silver-dollar sized talers and gold. Copper was not generally favored so very small denominations were usually struck in billon, a very base silver-copper alloy.

During the Napoleonic era a Swiss Republic was established (1798-1803) and even after its demise the various cantons maintained similar standards. After a new Swiss Confederation was founded a uniform national coinage was created, replacing the issues of the cantons in 1850. It was based on the French Franc, which became an international standard under the Latin Monetary Union.

Shooting competitions have for centuries been major events in Switzerland. Many of these festivities were commemorated, especially in the nineteenth century, by special silver talers and later 5 Franc pieces of very high artistic merit. These are much prized by collectors and should be examined carefully for signs of cleaning, which reduces their value.

The regular coinage of Switzerland is perhaps the most conservative in the world, reflecting its extreme stability and resistance to inflation. Bearing a female representation of Helvetia, the allegory of the nation, or the Swiss cross, the designs of many denominations have not changed in over 120 years. Like most countries, however, Switzerland moved from silver to base metal in the 1968. Interestingly, Swiss coins rarely bear any language spoken in Switzerland. Because of the awkwardness of inscribing the coins in the four different languages spoken there, most coins are inscribed only in Latin. Switzerland in Latin is Helvetia, Swiss is Helvetica.

Additional Specialized Books: Meier, Albert, *HMZ Katalog.*

Known counterfeits: Pre-1850 coins of Switzerland are not often counterfeited. Gold 20 Francs of the late nineteenth and twentieth centuries should be examined with reasonable care. A partial list of years counterfeited include 1897, 1900, 1902-04, 1911, 1912, 1915, 1919, 1922, 1927, 1930, 1931, 1933, 1935, all with the B mintmark. The 1935 with the LB mintmark is an official restrike form 1945-47.

CANTONAL ISSUES   F

Basel. 1749 1/4 Thaler. City view / Basilisk
(S)..100.00
Bern. 1809 1 Batzen. Shield / Wreath (Billon) . 9.00
Geneva. 3 Sols. Shield / Cross in quatrilobe
(Billon).. 80.00

1840 1 Centime. Arms (C) 2.50
St. Gall. 1790 6 Kreuzer. Bear l. / Wreath
(Billon) 17.50

CANTONAL ISSUES   F

Schwyz. 1655 Schilling. Two-headed eagle / Saint
(Billon).. 18.00
Zurich. 1848 1 Rappen. Arms / Wreath
(Billon).. 4.50
1810 Ducat. Lion with shield (G)................. 600.00

CONFEDERATION   VF

1895 1 Rappen. Arms / Wreath (C)................... 6.00
1942 5 Rappen. Head of Helvetia (CN) 1.00
1850 10 Rappen. Arms / Wreath (Billon) 15.00
1907 20 Rappen. Head of Helvetia (CN) 1.50
1906 1/2 Franc. Helvetia stg. / Wreath (S)........ 2.00
1894 1 Franc. similar (S) 10.00
1939 2 Francs. similar (S)................................ 2.25
1865 5 Francs. Woman and child / Shield in Cross
(S)... 125.00
1932 5 Francs. William Tell / Shield (S) 7.50
1883 20 Francs. Head of Helvetia / Wreath
(G) 70.00

Unc.

1963 2 Rappen. Cross / Wheat ear (C) .... .45
1993 5 Rappen. Head of Helvetia / Wreath
(CN)... .20
1967 1 Franc. Helvetia stg. / Wreath (S) 3.50

1984 5 Francs. High altitude balloon and deep
water submarine (CN)................................. 7.00
1922 10 Francs. Bust of Helvetia / Radiant cross
(G) 70.00

AFRICAN COINS

Coinage really did not come to sub-Saharan Africa until the colonial era, when Europeans introduced it for their territories, which at first lay along the coast, and later stretched inland. There were some earlier exceptions, however. The most important and distinctive coinage of early sub-Saharan Africa was that of the ancient kingdom of Axum, located in present-day Ethiopia. Beginning ca.270 and continuing as late as ca.640, the coins of this African monarchy were always of small size, but were struck in all three classic metals: gold, silver and bronze. Its most unusual and impressive feature was the use of a gold inlay on many of the bronze coins. Sometimes this was just a dot in the center, and other times a large area surrounding the king's bust. When intact, these inlays always make for a dramatic appearance. Another notable feature of Auxumite coinage is the first use of Christian symbolism as the primary motif of the design. The cross became quite common on these pieces. Also of interest was the use of Ge'ez, the distinctive Axumite alphabet, which today has the distinction of being the alphabet frequently used in Ethiopia for liturgical purposes.

Just because coins came late to Africa does not mean the region did without currency. Many distinctive forms of exchange existed, and they are today a collecting field unique to itself. Broadly speaking, three of the most common categories of this money were cowries, beads, and metal objects of various forms, Cowrie shells constitute a primitive form of currency common to most continents. They were traded in Asia, the Pacific, and the Americas as well. Later they were replaced or supplemented by manufactured beads. Trade beads were used as early as the 1400s in Niger, where they were made of terra cotta. Later more elaborate designs evolved in glass, simpler ones occasionally in stone. Many were made locally, and as trade with Europe expanded, more were imported.

By far the most famous currency of Africa is that of bronze and iron. The "kissie" or "Ghizzi" penny was popular among the Kissi, Bandi, Gbandia, Gola, Kpelle, Loma, Mandingo and Mendi tribes living in the areas of modern Guinea, Liberia, and Sierra Leone. Used from the 1880s to the 1930s, they consisted of twisted rods of iron about 9 inches to 15 inches in length. One end was formed into a "T" and the other a paddle. Its strange shape ultimately derives from a hoe. Another famous African metal trade currency were the various crosses of central Africa. Small H-shaped ingots and medium to large X-shaped ingots of copper were traded in Zambia and Katanga during the 1700s and 1800s. A third class of metal trade good was the bracelets. Originally of African manufacture, the Europeans quickly learned the utility of arriving with acceptable local currency and today most of the smaller, late form of these "manillas" are actually believed to have been cast in Birmingham.

The first sub-Saharan countries to strike their own modern coins were, logically, the only two to avoid European colonization: Ethiopia and Liberia. Ethiopia's first modern coins were struck by King Menelik II who unified the country in the 1880s. Though there had long been a royal dynasty in Ethiopia, traditionally descended from the biblical King Solomon, before Menelik's reign actual power had been divided between local feudal princes. The other country to strike early independent coinage, Liberia, was founded in 1822 as a refuge for freed American slaves. While the first Liberian cents of 1833 were distinctive in their design, later issues depicting a Liberty head looked more like United States patterns than African coins. It was, in fact, not until 1960 that Liberty took on African instead of European facial features. A third independent African country, although not native in culture, also began issuing coins in 1874. This was the Dutch Zuid Afrikaansche Republiek (the Transvaal). Its coinage was short-lived however, as the country was conquered by the British during the Boer War and incorporated into their empire in 1902.

Beginning in 1957 and finally completed in 1975, African countries began to gain their independence from the colonial powers. Most wasted little time in emphasizing their independence by exercising the sovereign prerogative of striking coins. Those new states not finding it useful to strike coins in quantity to circulate in commerce at the very least struck them in limited numbers for presentation and commemorative purposes. It is not unusual for central and west African countries not to strike their own coins for circulation. Many of these states have found benefit in belonging to one of two currency unions. A common currency throughout every country in such a union is used to facilitate both trade and economic stability. The most common obverse design to be used on these new African coinages was the portrait of a founding statesman. The coat of arms was also a common obverse, and when it was not used for that often found its way onto the reverse. One of the most common motifs, however, is the wonderful proliferation of exotic animals which have graced African coins since the 1960s. Such devices have made even the circulation strikes of Africa popular with collectors worldwide. Most of the precious metal coins of post-colonial Africa are struck solely for sale to collectors and many are struck only in proof quality.

Specialized Books: Gill, Dennis. *The Coinage of Ethiopia, Eritrea and Italian Somalia.*

Krause, Chester and Mishler, Clifford, *Standard Catalog of World Coins.* 19th and 20th century volumes updated frequently.

Munro-Hay, Stuart and Juel-Jensen, Bent. *Aksumite Coinage.* Up to date scholarship on this frequently redated series.

Known Counterfeits: The most commonly counterfeited African coins are the gold coins of Axum, and to an extent those in other metals. The most commonly counterfeited modern African coin is the gold Krugerrand of South Africa. Fraudulent pieces have been common since the 1970s, often cast, some with real gold shells around a tungsten core. Every example should be not only weighed, but also examined with a glass and given a "ring" test. Cast pieces will sound dull and have less resonance.

ANGOLA   Unc.

1978 1 Kwanza, Arms (CN).............................. 1.50
(1980s) 100 Kwanzas, Arms (C)..................... 14.00

BENIN (DAHOMEY)   Unc.

1971 1000 Francs, Somba woman / Arms
(S)...PF 90.00

BENIN (DAHOMEY)   Unc.

1994 200 Francs, Tyrannosaurous Rex / Arms
(C) 10.00
BOTSWANA...Unc.
1966 50 Cents, Seretse Khama / Arms (S)........ 5.00
1991 1 Thebe, Arms / Head of Turako bird
(AL).. .30

BURUNDI   Unc.

1965 1 Franc, Arms (B)................................... 3.00
1993 1 Franc, Arms (AL) 1.25
1965 10 Francs, King Mwanbutsa / Arms
(G)... 50.00
1968 10 Francs, Grain and Bannanas (CN) 3.00

CENTRAL AFRICAN STATES   Unc.

1971 1 Franc, Three giant eland (AL).............. 2.25

CENTRAL AFRICAN STATES   Unc.

1961 50 Francs, similar (CN) 10.00
1968 100 Francs, similar (N) 12.00

CHAD   Unc.

1970 100 Francs, Africa / Robert F. Kennedy
(S) .... PF 85.00
1985 100 Francs, Three giant eland (N) 30.00

CONGO, Peoples Republic   Unc.

1990 100 Francs, Three giant eland (N) 6.00
1993 100 Francs, Woman inscribing tablet / Sailing
ship (CN)... 10.00

CONGO, Democratic
Republic (ZAIRE)   Unc.

1965 10 Francs, Lion face (AL)........................ 7.00

CONGO, Democratic Republic (ZAIRE) Unc.

1987 1 Zaire, President Mobutu (B)................. 2.00
1971 100 Zaires, same / Hotel Intercontinental
(G)..PF 675.00

DJIBOUTI Unc.

1977 1 Franc, Arms / Antelope bust (AL) 2.50

1991 100 Francs, Arms / Camels (CN)............. 5.50

EQUATORIAL AFRICAN STATES Unc.

1990 1 Franc, Three giant eland (AL)............... 1.75
1982 25 Francs, similar (ALB) 2.25
1977 500 Francs, Woman r. / Stylized eland
(CN) 16.50

EQUATORIAL GUINEA Unc.

1969 1 Peseta, Tusks / Arms (ALB) 2.00
1970 100 Pesetas, Arms and tusks / Naked Maja
(S)...PF 35.00
1985 5 Francos, Three eland (ALB) 8.00

ERITREA Unc.

1997 1 Cent, Soldiers with flag / Antelope (N clad
Steel) 25

1997 25 Cents, same / Zebra (N clad Steel)...... 1.00
1994 1 Dollar, Arms / Cheetah (CN) 8.00

ETHIOPIA VF

1892-93 1 Mahaleki, Crown / Inscription
(S).. 150.00
1897 1 Matonya, Menelik II / Inscription
(C)... 8.00
1897 1/32nd Birr, Menelik II / Lion (C) 7.50
1903 1 Gersh, similar (S)................................. 3.50
1897 Birr similar (S)................................. 10.00
1903 1 Birr, similar (S)................................. 25.00
1925 1 Werk, Empress Zauditu / Lion (G).... 500.00
1931 50 Matonas, Haile Selassie crowned / Lion
(N).. 2.50

Unc.

1944 (1944-75) 1 Cent, Haile Selassie / Lion
(C) 50
1944 (1952-53) 25 Cents, similar (C, scallopped
and reeded) 3.00

Unc.

1972 5 Dollars, similar (S).........................PF 15.00
1966 100 Dollars, similar (G)...................PF 525.00
1977 10 Cents, Lion head / Antelope (B).......... 1.50
1982 2 Birr, Lion head / Two soccer players
(CN) 8.50

GABON Unc.

1960 10 Francs, Leon Mba / Arms (G) ......PF 75.00
1984 100 Francs, Three giant eland (N)............ 8.00

GAMBIA Unc.

1971 1 Butut, Bust / Peanuts (C) 20

1987 1 Dalasi, Bust / Crocodile (CN,
heptagonal)... 4.50
1977 40 Dalasi, Bust / Aardvark (S)............... 27.50

GHANA Unc.

1958 3 Pence, Kwame Nkrumah / Star (CN,
scallopped) 1.00
1958 5 Shillings, same (S) ....PF 12.50
1967 5 Pesewas, Cocoa beans / Arms (CN) .... .75

1991 20 Cedis, Cowrie / Arms (N clad Steel)... 1.00
1986 100 Cedis, Drums / Commonwealth games
(S) 17.50

GUINEA Unc.

1959 10 Francs, Ahmed Sekou Toure
(ALB)... 45.00
1962 1 Franc, similar (CN)............................. 7.00
1971 1 Syli, Bust l. (AL) 8.00
1985 5 Francs, Arms / Palm branch (B clad
Steel) 1.00
1988 100 Francs, Arms / Basketball players
(S)... 65.00

GUINEA-BISSAU Unc.

1977 50 Centavos, Arms / Palm tree (AL) 9.00

(1995) 2000 Pesos, Arms / Agricultural scenes
(N plated Steel) 17.50

IVORY COAST PF

1966 10 Francs, President Boigny / Elephant
(S) .... PF 50.00
1966 similar (G) 525.00

(reduced)

KATANGA Circ.

1700s-1800s. Katanga cross or Baluba cross. Large
X-shaped cast, copper cross, usually 9" across
and "thick. Authentic ones usually have a rasied
central ridge... 125.00
1961 1 Franc, Bananas / Katanga cross (C) 3.50

KENYA Unc.

1966 5 Cents, Jomo Kenyatta / Arms (B).......... 1.00
1969 10 Cents, similar but legend around bust
(B) 65
1975 50 Cents, similar (CN) 75
1980 1 Shilling, Daniel Arap Moi / Arms
(CN).. 1.00

1994 10 Shillings, similar (B around CN).........2.75
1991 1000 Shillings, similar (S) .... PF 275.00

LESOTHO Unc.

1979 1 Sente, King Moshoeshoe II / Hut (B).......40

LESOTHO   Unc.

1966 50 Licente, King Moshoeshoe I / Arms
(S) 10.00
1988 10 Maloti, Pope / Arms (S) ....PF 45.00

LIBERIA   VF

1833 1 Cent, Settler grasping tree, ship in distance
(C) 20.00

1847 2 Cents, Liberty head in cap / Palm tree
(C) 12.00
1896 10 Cents, Liberty head / Wreath (S) 10.00
1937 1/2 Cent, Elephant / Palm tree (B) 25

Unc.

1968 1 Cent, Elephant / Palm tree and ship (C) 35
1960 10 Cents, African Liberty / Wreath (S).... 3.00
1968 50 Cents, same (CN) 1.50
1995 1 Dollar, Captains James T. Kirk and Jean-Luc
Picard / Arms (CN)..................................... 8.50
1964 20 Dollars, William V.S. Tubman / Arms
(G)... 275.00

MALAWI   Unc.

1964 1 Shilling, President Banda / Corn
(CNZ)... 1.50
1971 1 Tambala, same / Rooster (C) 75
1995 5 Kwacha, President Muluzi / Child reading
(CN) 8.50

MALI   Unc.

1961 5 Francs, Hippopotamous head (AL)....... 1.25
1967 50 Francs, President Keita (G) ....PF 265.00

MOZAMBIQUE   Unc.

1975 5 Centimos, Head r. / Plant (CZ).......... 115.00
1986 20 Meticais, Arms / Armored tank (AL) 3.00

1994 10 Meticais, Arms / Cotton plant (B clad
Steel) 1.25

NAMIBIA   Unc.

1993 10 Cents, Arms / Tree (N plated Steel) 1.00
1996 10 Dollars, Arms / Runner and Cheetah
(S)...PF 45.00

NIGER   PF

1300s-1400s Djenné beads. Narrow, tubular
terracotta beads with tight ridges
strand Circ. 20.00
1960 500 Francs, President Hamani / Arms
(S) 35.00
1968 50 Francs, Lion / Arms (G) 450.00

NIGERIA   Unc.

1973 1/2 Kobo, Arms (C) 3.50

1991 1 Kobo, Arms / Oil wells (C plated Steel) 25
1993 1 Naira, Arms / Herbert Macaulay (N plated
Steel) 1.75

RWANDA   Unc.

1965 1 Franc, Head / Arms (CN) 1.75
1970 2 Francs, Person pouring grain / Arms
(AL, scallopped) 50
1987 5 Francs, Plant / Arms (C) 1.85
1990 2000 Francs, Nelson Mandela / Arms
(G) ....PF 200.00

SIERRA LEONE   Unc.

1964 1/2 Cent, Milton Margai / Two fish (C)...... .25
1978 10 Cents, Siaka Stevens / Arms (CN) 1.00
1987 1 Leone, Joseph Momoh / Arms (B,
octagonal)... 1.50

1998 10 Leones, Arms / Princess Diana
(S)...PF 47.50

SOMALIA   Unc.

1967 5 Centesimi, Arms (B)...............................60
1976 10 Senti, Arms / Lamb (AL, polygonal) .... .35
1984 25 Shillings, Arms / Turtle (CN)............ 15.00

SOUTH AFRICA, Z.A.R.   VF

1898 1 Penny, Paul Kruger / Arms (C).............. 2.00
1897 6 Pence, Paul Kruger / Wreath (S) 3.00

SOUTH AFRICA, Z.A.R.   VF

1874 1 Pond, Thomas Burgers / Arms
(G) 2,000.00
1900 1 Pond, Paul Kruger / Arms (G) 135.00

SOUTH AFRICA, Republic   Unc.

1963 1/2 Cent, Jan Van Riebeeck / Two sparrows
confronted (B)... 1.00
1969 1 Cent, similar / two sparrows (C)..............50
1971 2 Cents, Arms / Gnu (C) 35
1978 5 Cents, Arms / Crane (N) 50
1984 10 Cents, Arms / Aloe (N) 35
1988 20 Cents, Arms / Protea (N) 60
1992 50 Cents, Arms / Plant (B plated Steel).... 1.00
1971 1 Rand, Arms / Springbok (S) 6.00

1994 1 Rand, Arms / Building (S) .... PF 22.50
1994 5 Rand, similar (N plated C) 7.50
Above two for inauguration of Nelson Mandela.
1978 Krugerrand, Paul Kruger / Springbok (G,
1 ounce net)..................................bullion + 3%

SWAZILAND   Unc.

1974 1 Cent, King Sobhuza II / Pineapple (C).....20
1996 50 Cents, King Msawati III / Arms (CN)... 3.75

TANZANIA   Unc.

1966 10 Senti, Julius Nyerere / Ostrich (B)....... 1.50
1972 1 Shilingi, same / Arms with torch (CN) ... 1.50

1992 20 Shilingi, Ali Hassan Mwinyi / Mother and
Baby elephants (N clad Steel) 3.50
1974 1500 Shilingi, Julius Nyerere / Cheetah
(G) 420.00

UGANDA   Unc.

1966 10 Cents, Tusks (C) 35
1987 10 Shillings, Arms (Steel) 2.50
1993 10,000 Shillings, Arms / Pope (S).....PF 37.50

WEST AFRICA   Circ.

1700s-early 1900s Aggry beads. Millefiore type multicolored glass beads composed of cross-sections of component parts pressed against a central tube. Many are of Venetian manufacture. ....each 3.00

1700s-early 1900s Aggry beads. Similar but wholly extruded, not composite. ....strand 15.00

1500s-1948 Popo manilla. Cast bronze bracelet of varying size. They have an opening about 1/2" to 1-1/2" separating two enlarged flat ends. Mostly manufactured in Birmingham. At the time British colonial authorities forced their withdrawal they circulated at about 3 pence. 2" to 3-1/2" 12.00

Similar but 12" across.................................... 150.00

1880s-1930s Kissie penny. Twisted rod of iron 9" to 15" long. One end was formed into a "T" and the other a paddle... 8.00

WEST AFRICAN STATES   Unc.

1961 1 Franc, Ibex / Root (AL) .... .60

1980 25 Francs, Chemist / Root (ALB) 1.75
1972 5000 Francs, Root / Seven shields (S).... 37.50

ZAMBIA   Unc.

1964 6 Pence, Shield / Morning glory (CNZ)... 1.20
1968 1 Ngwee, Kenneth Kaunda / Aardvark (C) .... .80

1972 50 Ngwee, same / Arms (CN, polygonal) 4.00
1992 5 Kwacha, Arms / Oryx (B) 1.50

ZIMBABWE   Unc.

1600s-1700s. H-shaped cast, copper ingot of variable size, ranging from 1" to 12"....Circ. 125.00
1980 1 Cent, Ancient bird sculpture (C).............. .40

1980 50 Cents, same / Sunrise (CN).................2.25
1996 10 Dollars, Victoria Falls Bridge / Lions (S)... PF40.00

EARLY ISLAMIC COINS

For many Westerners the single most intimidating type of coinage to understand is Islamic coinage. There are two reasons for this, both of which can be partially overcome without having to become an expert. Whether it appears on coins or in newspapers, many find the appearance of written Arabic as intimidating as it is beautiful. This is because it is written exclusively in cursive. The letters in each word are connected. But just as one doesn't have to be able to read the Odyssey to identify Greek coins, one can often tell something about early Islamic coins without reading their inscriptions either. The second reason is that because it is often considered a violation of Islamic law to depict people or animals in art, most coins are lacking the symbols or iconography which would otherwise help to identify them. Nevertheless, there are often big differences in the size, shape, and style of many coins. One only has to be told what they are, and this chapter is the first lesson.

Prices listed are for the most common coins of the denomination. Illustrations may not the most common date or mint, but are chosen for their clarity. Valuations for gold are for XF preservation, silver for VF, billon and copper for Fine, all with average strikes and fully identified. Unidentified early Islamic coins are worth a fraction of the values indicated, even in decent grade.

Dates on Islamic Coins: The Moslem world uses a different calendar than the one used in the West (the A.D. calendar). It is based on Mohammed's flight from Mecca to Medina in 622 A.D., which in the Moslem (A.H.) calendar is the year 1. Also the year is lunar not solar, so it is 3 percent shorter. To convert an A.H. date into an A.D. date simply subtract 3 percent and add 622. All dates given in this section are A.D. unless A.H. is indicated. Dates on early coins are spelled out. From the 1400s onward, numerals begin to be used.

Arabic Numerals

0	½	1	2	3	4	5	6
٠	١/٢	١	٢	٣	٤	٥	٦

7	8	9	10	50	100	500	1000
٧	٨	٩	١٠	٥٠	١٠٠	٥٠٠	١٠٠٠

Denominations/Metals: Unless otherwise noted:

Dinar	18-19 mm, then broader and thinner	Gold
Dirham	21-29 mm	Silver
Akche	10-19 mm	Silver
Fals	15-22 mm	Copper

Specialized Books: Album, Stephen, *A Checklist of Islamic Coins*, Second Edition (Essential guide to arranging a collection. Lists most monarchs, what they struck and rarity. This chapter is roughly sequenced by the Checklist.)

Album, Stephen. *Marsden's Numismata Orientalia Illustrata.* (Outdated valuations but many clear line drawings, often better then photographs.)

Broome, Michael. *A Handbook of Islamic Coins.* (An excellent, nicely illustrated and readable history.)

Mitchiner, Michael. *Oriental Coins and their Values: World of Islam.* (Mammoth general work with extensive illustrations.)

Plant, Richard. *Arabic Coins and How to Read Them.* (Organized into simple lessons.)

Spengler and Sayles. *Turkoman Figural Bronze Coins and their Iconography,* 2 vols.

Known counterfeits: Because early Islamic coins are not as popularly collected as ancient or modern coins, they have less often fallen victim to high quality counterfeiting. Some very early gold coins are the exception. Lesser quality counterfeits exist, including Abbasid dirhams and Abbasid Yemen fractions, as well as many Ottoman silver and gold pieces. Some coins were also subject to counterfeiting in the era they were issued, particulary early silver dirhams.

PRE-REFORM HYBRID COINS (630s-c.698). When Mohammed's desert followers first emerged from their Arabian homeland to conquer most of the Middle East and Mediterranean basin in the 600s, they found complex monetary systems in use in two rival civilizations: the Byzantine Empire and Sassanian Persia. Not yet having developed a coinage suited to their new ideologies, they adopted what they found. From the Byzantines they adopted small bronzes imitating the follis, usually modeled after Constans II's or Heraclius' folles, which depicted standing emperors. Some bore both Arabic and Greek inscriptions. They dealt with the awkard situation of copying a coin with a Christian cross by replacing the horizontal crossbar with a circle. Before this hybrid coinage ended, it had even progressed to on that depicted a standing figure of the Calif. The Calif, after the death of Mohammed, was the somewhat universally acknowledged religious leader of all Moslems. During the first few hundred years he also ruled as an international emperor, much as the Holy Roman Emperor in the West. The first four (the Orthodox Caliphs, 632-661) were in-laws of Mohammed. The Umayyad and Abbasid dynasties followed.

The Moslems' first silver coins were imitations of drachms of the Sassanian Empire, and depicted the deceased Persian emperor. An Arabic inscription was added in the ample border area and before the bust to identify the real issuer. When this coinage was phased out for religious reasons, the last local issuers managed to circumvent the prohibition of portraiture by replacing the head with an abstract diamond shape.

Arab-Sassanian Drachm (4 gm.) 50.00
Tabaristan Drachm (2 gm.) 20.00
same but diamond replaces head on bust 50.00
Follis (Fals), Standing "Byzantine" emperor / Large M 30.00

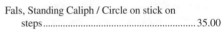

Fals, Standing Caliph / Circle on stick on steps.. 35.00

UMAYYAD (661-750). In 696-97 (77 AH) the first truly Islamic coins began to replace the old hybrid issues. In conformity with religious law all images were removed from gold and silver, and from most of the copper. The new gold dinars at 4.25 grams were physically similar to the Byzantine gold solidus. The silver dirham was a broad, thin coin like its predecessor, the Sassanian dirham, but it was slightly smaller, weighing about 3 grams. The copper fals varied somewhat in size but was usually a bit smaller than the old imitative folles. The central designs on most coins of all three metals was the same: the basic religious creed of Islam, called the kalima. It translates "There is no god but God, Mohammed is his prophet." Its presence is what defines the obverse of an Islamic coin, and it is recognizable by its tall Y-shaped characters. A legend around the border gives the value, date and, except on gold, the place of minting. More quotes from the Koran occupy the reverse. Arabic at this time was not written in the modern rounded script used today but in a more angular form called Kufic. This is easier to read and as a result many collectors who can't read modern Arabic can read coins of the Umayyads, the first dynasty of Caliphs. Three or four mints account for over 90 percent of all dirhams available, despite the existence of several dozen mints throughout the caliphate. The Wasit mint alone accounts for 80 percent of all Umayyad dirhams. Rare mints are very desirable to the specialist and can be worth many times the value given below for a common, representative coin. Most of the earlier coins do not bear the name of the ruler and can only be assigned to a particular caliph by the date.

Dinar 300.00
Dirham 25.00
Fals 3.00

ABBASID (750-1258). Most early Abbasid coins do not differ significantly from Umayyad ones, except for the choice of religious text on the reverse of the gold and silver. Like the Umayyads, the inscriptions are in the clear Kufic script, and is often fairly easy for a beginner to read. Three or four mints account for over 85 percent of all coins available, despite the existence of several dozen mints throughout the caliphate. The Madinat-al-Salam (Baghdad) mint alone accounts for 70 percent of all Abbasid silver. Rare mints are desirable to the specialist and can be worth many times the value given below.

The first step in divergence from the original Umayyad design was the use of additional lines of inscription to cite a local ruler or heir or governor. Still, the basic pattern was retained through to the end of the very long Abbasid dynasty. After its extinction, one or more rulers may have claimed the title, but there was no one Islamic empire.

Dinar 225.00
Dirham 20.00
Fals 6.00

IDENTIFYING OTHER DYNASTIES

Early break-away dynasties such as the Buwayhid in Iran retained this original format. As the caliphate's secular empire began to fragment into more regional states, local characteristics began to develop in the coinage. These traits today can be used by the non-Arabic reader to narrow down a coin's identity as to time or place. A brief summary of the characteristics of some early Islamic dynasties follows. It should be remembered that like ancient and medieval European coins, these were all hand struck. Hundreds of smaller dynasties have been omitted.

UMAYYADS OF SPAIN (756-1031). Very similar silver to regular Umayyad, except the style of the Khufic lettering which is characterized by distinct dots or circles at the intersections of the strokes. Many of the dirhams are found damaged by bumps or small bends.

Dinar .... VF 1,000.00

Dirham 35.00
Fals 20.00

BUWAYHID (932-1062, Iran and Iraq). Usually coins of standard Umayyad-Abbasid design but generally with two concentric obverse border legends around a four to six line central legend. The engraving is usually excellent but fully struck coins are unusual. Metal is good quality for most but not all reigns. No fals were struck.

Dinar 175.00
Dirham 25.00

ALMORAVID AND ALMOHAD (1053-1269, Morocco, expanding to Libya). These dynasties of Berbers struck very finely engraved gold coins, as well as average quality silver. Some gold bears the legend inside a square border. Almoravid dinars weigh four grams, Almohad dinars 4.6 grams. No fals were struck.

Dinar 250.00
Qirat (Almoravid) 25.00
Square Dirham (Almohad) 20.00

ALAWI SHARIFS (1664-present, Morocco). The inscription on the broad, thin gold dirham is often within a circle or an octagon of two superimposed squares. Later this was replaced by the thick benduqi often featuring central rosette on both sides. The most distinctive feature.

Dinar .... VF 200.00
Benduqi (AV) .... VF 135.00
Dirham 25.00

Four Fals (cast AE, 29 mm)) 3.00
Fals (cast AE) 4.00

FATIMID (A.D. 909-1171, Egypt, extending at times to Algeria and Syria). Most Fatimid coins encountered are struck in good quality silver and gold. Later in the dynasty the silver becomes debased. They usually bear concentric circles of inscription in a target pattern, still using the early Kufic script, but some other patterns also occur. Small glass tokens were used instead of copper. (Similar glass pieces for other dynasties are weights.)

Dinar 250.00
Dirham 25.00
Glass Token 15.00

AYYUBID (AD 1169-1284, additional branches 1149-1460s). The Ayyubids produced much silver that was anywhere from slightly to very poorly struck. Only 60 to 80 percent of the impression will be visible on a typical coin even if it has no wear. Inscriptions usually in and around a square or hexagram design. Copper fals are very similar to the silver drachms. Some large copper dirhams were also struck with the image of a kneeling prince, similar to the common Artuqid ones (see below).

Dinar 200.00
Dirham (AR) 18.00
Dirham (AE) 30.00
Fals 6.00

MAMLUK (1250-1517, Egypt and Syria). Mamluk gold is common and silver is small and quickly becomes base until after 1412. They small copper fals of this dynasty is interesting because of its variety of designs. Most coins are only partially struck and not well engraved.

Dinar (1250-1421), variable weight 300.00
Ashrafi (1421-1517), gold, 3.5gm. 150.00

RASULID (1229-1439, Yemen). Distinctive silver dirhams with animal images in a border have recently been available in the Western market. Before this Rasulid coins rarely appeared outside specialized circles.

Dirham. Two fishes or Lion in circle 60.00
Dirham, non-pictorial 40.00
Fals ....VG 10.00

MOGADISHU (1322-1600s, Somalia). Small, thin coppers, very poorly struck with Arabic inscriptions.

Fals ....VG 35.00

SELJUQS OF RUM (1116-1308, Turkey). Gold and silver of good metal and nice engraving are common. Strike is not always full. Many coins have a recognizable calligraphy with U-shaped well carved out of the end of the strokes.

Dinar ....Rare
Dirham 25.00

same with lion.. 50.00
Fals 10.00

OTTOMAN EMPIRE (1324-1922, Balkans, Turkey, Middle East, Iraq, and most of North Africa). The only significant Islamic empire after the Rennissance besides the Moghul, its coins are extremely common. Much of the coinage was base silver, struck concurrently with rather pure gold. The standards of both changed frequently. The easiest way to identify that a coin is Ottoman is by the tougra design, a stylized rendition of the Sultan's signature vaguely resembling a hand. Other countries have used this symbol, but 99 percent of the coins a collector is likely to encounter with it are Ottoman. Ottoman coins are easily dated by reign because the year of accession of the Sultan is usually indicated in Arabic numerals plainly on each coin. The AH dates below are those dates, not dates of issue. Representative coins below have inscriptions without a tougra if not described.

Mustafa Celebi, 1419-20. Akche (AR,
    10mm)...Rare
Murad II, 1421-51. Akche (AR, 10mm) 12.00
Mohammed II, 1451-81. 855 AH Akche (AR,
    10mm).. 12.00

Bayzit II, 1481-1512. 886 AH Akche (AR,
    10mm).. 12.00
Selim I, 1512-20. 918 AH Akche (AR,
    10mm).. 12.00
Suleyman I the Magnificent, 1520-66. 926 AH
    Akche (AV, Sultani, 20mm)..................... 200.00
Selim II 1566-74. 974 AH Dirham (AR,
    19mm).. 45.00
Murad III, 1574-95. 982 AH Mangir (AE, Four pet-
    als in square) 9.00
Mohammed III, 1595-1603. 1003 AH Akche (AR,
    10mm).. 12.00
Ahmed I, 1603-17. 1012 AH Akche (AR,
    10mm).. 12.00
Osman II, 1618-22. 1027 AH Akche (AR,
    10mm).. 12.00
Mustafa I, 1617-18, 1622-23. 1031 AH Onluk (AR,
    17mm).. 60.00
Murad IV, 1623-40. 1032 AH Akche (AR,
    10mm).. 12.00
Ibrahim 1640-48. 1049 AH Akche (AR,
    10mm).. 12.00
Mohammed IV, 1648-87. 1058 AH Dirhem (AR,
    18mm) Tougra 40.00
Suleyman II, 1687-91. 1099 AH Mangir (AE,
    18mm) Tougra 6.00
Ahmed II, 1691-95. 1102 AH Mangir (AE, 18mm)
    Tougra... 50.00
Mustafa II, 1695-1703. 1106 AH Kurus (AR,
    37mm)... 30.00
Ahmed III, 1703-30. 1115 AH Para (AR, 15mm)
    Tougra... 15.00
Mahmud I, 1730-54. 1143 AH Para (AR, 15mm)
    Tougra... 10.00
Osman III, 1754-57. 1168 AH Para (AR, 15mm)
    Tougra... 35.00

Mustafa III, 1757-74. 1171 AH Kurus = Piastre
    (AR, 38mm) Tougra 30.00
Abdul Hamid I, 1774-89. 1187 AH 1/2 Zeri Mah-
    bub (AV, 18) Tougra................................. 100.00
Selim III, 1789-1807. 1203 AH Para (Billon,
    15mm) Tougra 1.25
Mustafa IV, 1807-08. 1222 AH Para (Billon,
    15mm) Tougra.. 35.00
Mahmud II, 1808-39. 1223 AH 100 Para (Billon,
    35mm) Tougra.. 5.00
Abdul Mejid, 1839-61. 1255 AH 5 Para (AE,
    22mm) Tougra 1.00

Abdul Aziz, 1861-76. 1277 AH 10 Para (AE,
    27mm) Tougra..3.00
Murad V, 1876. 1293 AH 20 Kurush (AR, 37mm)
    Tougra This coin has been counterfeited. Tougra
    should be different than Abdul
    Hamid II's...60.00
Abdul Hamid II, 1876-1909. 1293 AH Kurus =
    Piastre (AR, 15mm) Tougra........................3.00
Mohammed V, 1909-18. 1327 AH 20 Kurus (AR,
    37mm) Tougra..15.00

__. 1327 AH 10 Para (N, 19mm) Tougra 1.00
Mohammed VI, 1918-23. 1336 AH 40 Para (CN,
    24mm) Tougra.....................................VF 4.00

OTTOMAN EGYPT (1517-1914). Egypt under the Ottoman Empire was ruled by hereditary governors with almost independent power. Their coins were usually distinct from regular Ottoman coins but generally similar, including the tougra (see above). The main distinguishing feature is the use of the Arabic word Misr (مصر) instead of the mint name.

Mohammed III, 1595-1603. 1003 AH Medin (AR,
    15mm)..75.00

Ahmed I, 1603-17. 1012 AH Mangir (AE, 16mm)
    Grid pattern 30.00
Mahmud I, 1730-54. 1143 AH Zeri Mahbub (AV,
    20mm) Tougra..175.00
Selim III, 1789-1807. 1203 AH Para (Billon,
    15mm) Tougra...6.50

Abdul Mejid, 1839-1861. 1255 AH 5 Para (AE,
    21.9mm) Tougra...5.00
Abdul Mejid, 1839-61. 1255 AH 5 Para (AE,
    21mm) Tougra...1.00
Abdul Aziz, 1861-76. 1277 AH 10 Para (AE,
    31mm) Tougra...1.00
Murad V, 1876. 1293 AH Qirsh (AR, 18mm)
    Tougra...150.00
Abdul Hamid II, 1876-1909. 1293 AH 2 Qirsh (AR,
    18mm) Tougra and quivers 3.00
Mohammed V, 1909-14. 1327 AH 5/10 Qirsh (CN,
    21mm) Tougra...1.00

SAMANID (819-1004, Afghanistan and Central Asia). Most coins were struck on the traditional Umayyad-Abbasid pattern. Single dirhams may even be confused for Abbasid ones until they are read. Enormous, (35+mm) multiple dirhams were often evenly but weakly struck. Reasonably well made copper fals often resemble silver dirhams.

Dinar (AV) 175.00
Multiple Dirham (AR).................................... 65.00

Dirham 30.00
Fals 12.00

SIND (800s-1000s, Southern Pakistan). Only inscriptions appear on these coins that are found frequently. The fraction described may have been called a damma or a sixth dirham.

Fractional Dirham (AR, 9mm) 12.00
Fals 50.00

GHAZNAVID (949-1186, Iran, Afghanistan, India). These are similar to Saminid but multiple dirhams often bear a sword below legend. Carelessly struck gold on the traditional pattern is common. Copper is less so. Because their territories stretched into India, some of the Ghnaznavids dirhams are inscribed in both Arabic and Sanskrit, stouter.

Dinar 175.00
Multiple Dirham (AR)................................... 65.00
Dirham 25.00

Dirham, bi-lingual 65.00
Fals 12.00

GREAT SELJUQS (1038-1157, Iran). A Turkish dynasty in Iran, they are mostly gold. Some of these dinars are so base they appear silvery, and vary in weight from 1 to 6 grams. The average is 4 grams. Typical coins have two border legends on the obverse, one on the reverse, around central legends. Engraving is decent but striking is often uneven.

Dinar (Sometimes base gold) 150.00
Dirham (Base silver).. 20.00
Fals 10.00

KHWARIZMSHAHS (1127-1231, Central Asia). Calligraphy is bold but thick and unrefined. Gold is similar to that of the Great Seljuqs. Jitals are small and thick.

Dinar 125.00

Dirham.. 25.00
Jital (Billon or copper), sometime with
    horseman 5.00

ARTUQID (1118-1408, Syria and Iraq). Most common are the unusual large copper dirhams depicting a variety of images, some inspired by ancient coins. Reversed are inscriptions, often in ornamental borders.

Dirham (AR) hexagram pattern....................... 25.00

Dirham (AE) Facing head / Two heads 35.00
Dirham (AE) Four figures mourning............... 40.00

ZANGID (1127-1251, Syria and Iraq). See comments under Artuqid.

Dirham (AE) Man holding crescent 40.00
Dirham (AE) Double headed eagle 40.00
Fals, standing "Byzantine" figures 35.00

GREAT MONGOLS (1206-1270s, Central Asia) The Mongols often continued coinage in the local style of the lands they conquered. Thus while not Moslems themselves they struck extensive Islamic-style coinage.

Dinar with name of Genghis Khan............. 1,500.00

Dirham / Jital of Genghis Khan with titles only
    (Billon)... 65.00
Dirham of later Mongols 35.00

ILKHANS (1256-1357, Iran). The Ilkhans were the Mongol governors of Persia. They struck much silver, gold, and copper. Some coins have both Mongol and Arabic inscriptions. Later ones have very mostly fine Arabic script, framed with ornate borders of various design including an architectural arch and a curved pentagon. Strikes are usually weak at the edge but not the center.

Dinar (AV) 175.00
Dinar of 6 Dirhams (AR) 50.00
Double Dirham..20.00
Dirham 20.00
Fals..15.00

TIMURID (1370-1579, Iran, Iraq, Afghanistan and Central Asia). This dynasty was descended from the conqueror Tamerlane. Silver tankas often have either an inscription in the ancient Khufic script constructed into a square, or of regular Arabic bounded by a square with border-ornaments in the form of brackets { } on each side. They are thicker.

Tanka (AR) 20.00

SAFAVID (1501-1756, Iran). These are often large silver coins with and without marginal legends. Horizontal lines of legend often are divided by underlines. Often thick calligraphy with occasional floral ornaments or pellets around edge or throughout. Some feature poetic couplets.

Shahi (AR)...20.00

Abbasi (AR) 15.00

AFSHARID (1729-1803, Iran). Distinctive for the use of large empty border confining a small round central inscription.

Ashrafi (AV, 3.5gm) 200.00

Six Shahi (AR, 6.9gm) 10.00

CIVIC COPPER (1600s-1800s, Iran, Afghanistan, Central Asia). During this period most rulers did not strike copper coins, but left that task to local governments. Unlike most Islamic coins they often bore animals in addition to a variety of other designs. Most are nickel to quarter size and thick.

Fals, Peacock 25.00
Fals, Lion 12.00
Fals, Camel 25.00

QAJAR (1750-1925, Iran). This was the last dynasty to strike hand hammered coins. The coins usually have no marginal legends, and smaller sizes are more common than the earlier Safavid ones. Some early ones still feature poetic couplets. Listings here are for hammered coins.

Toman (AV) c.1230s AH 130.00
Kran (AR, 18mm) 15.00

Kran (AR, 18mm) Lion 45.00
50 Dinars (AE, Sun-face) 15.00

DELHI (1206-1500s, North India and Pakistan). Mostly small billon coins called jitals, sometimes depicting a bull and/or a horseman. Occasional fals were very small, and large silver tanka were almost half-dollar size. Copper tankas of the same value as the silver ones were forced on the people in the 1300s. These are slightly thick and nickel-sized, with fine script.
Tanka (AV) 350.00
Tanka (AR) 30.00

Tanka (AE) 8.00
Jital (Billon) 4.00
Fals (AE) 4.00

MUGHALS (1526-1857, India, Pakistan, Bangladesh). This powerful empire shrunk to triviality by the end of the 1700s. It stuck fine silver rupees with inscriptions punctuated by various ornaments. They were thick coins of quarter size. Copper fals or paisas were cent to quarter size and very thick. Regnal dates often appear.
Mohur (AV) 250.00

Rupee (AR) 20.00
Paisa (AE).. 10.00

HYDERABAD (1700s-1949, Central India). This was the most powerful of the princely states during the colonial era. Its machine struck coins often depict a building with a tower at each corner or a tougra, similar to Ottoman coins. Its hand-struck copper paisas are very common and very crude, being almost as thick as they are wide.
Rupee with inscription 12.00
Rupee with building 9.00
2 Pai (AE, holed, machine struck) 25
Paisa (AE, hand struck)..75

ASIAN & PACIFIC COINS

Most early Asian coins fit neatly into the category of either Islamic or Oriental. Some pieces, particularly those of Southern India and Southeast Asia had a distinctive appearance reflecting neither of these influences. However, over the course of the 1800s, nearly all coinage based on these traditions, be they Islamic, Oriental or local were replaced by machine made European style coinage. The images on these new, modern coins varied from an attempt to preserve traditional designs with modern forms, to overt imitation of European motifs.

Trends in Islamic coinage changed following the fall of the Ottoman Empire after World War I. Today very few countries follow the strict Muslim prohibition of depicting persons or animals on coins. The traditional tougra symbol rarely appears these days and Turkey even abandoned the Arabic alphabet for the Roman one. Also, a great number of Islamic countries produce bilingual coins. Generally, English or French appears on the coins in a secondary position to Arabic. This is almost always the case with commemorative coins, which are, to a large extent, produced for the international collector market. Also Western A.D. calendar dates often supplement the Islamic A.H. date as the former is used in some Islamic countries for business purposes.

In the center of the Middle East is its one non-Moslem country, Israel. Founded in 1948 as a safe haven for Jews persecuted throughout the world, and who sought to return to their Biblical homeland, it is the only nation whose coins are inscribed in Hebrew. Israeli minor coins frequently have motifs from ancient Judaean coinage. The extensive series of commemoratives features an extremely diverse array of motifs, often rendered in modern styles of art. During the 1960s and 1970s Israeli commemorative coins were so widely purchased by the collecting public that now the number of coins and mint sets available from that point in time greatly exceeds demand, resulting in very low prices. This was further complicated by the use of government issued holders composed of a plastic that corroded the coins' surfaces. Lower mintages and distribution, especially during the 1990s have resulted in collector issues of a somewhat more stable value.

Those looking for coinage struck by India before the colonial era will find listings for a sampling of numerous small states with unfamiliar names. This is because until 1947 India was not one unified country, but a group of hundreds of princely states. Even during the period of British rule, only about half the country was directly controlled by the crown. Princely states, from the size of a city to those larger than most modern countries, often struck their own coins.

The first ancient Indian coins were not struck with a pair of dies like Western coins were, and not cast in molds like Chinese coins. Instead they were impressed by several different punches on each side, each being some indication of sequence or authority. After the invasion of Alexander the Great, Western methods gradually took over. For a few hundred years after, most Indian coins were stylistic descendants of either Greek or Sassanian (Persian) coins. After the advent of Islam in the eighth century most of central and northern India, regardless of the religion of the population, used the Islamic style coins discussed above. The largest states during this period were the Sultanate of Delhi, and later the Moghul Empire. While all this occurred, southern India followed a different course. Most of the coins of this region freely bore images, generally of deities or their symbols. Gold, silver and copper were common in both the north and the south during most periods. Interestingly, however, Indian gold included very tiny pieces called fanams. Struck in great quantities by both princes and merchants, they were common from the 1600s to the 1800s, but some are much earlier.

By the 1700s most Indian coins were very thick and were struck with dies larger than their blanks, thus only part of the design was impressed. The nickname for this style coin is "dump" coinage. Sometimes broad, ceremonial versions were struck of the very same coins. These are nazarana coins and are scarce for all but a few states. As time progressed, thinner European style coins began to replace dump coinage. Also from the 1700s to the present century, designs consisting solely of inscriptions gradually gave way to images. It is interesting to note that Indian states' coins are presently so poorly published and sparsely collected that completely uncatalogued dates and varieties of many coins are occasionally only a few dollars more than the price a common one would fetch. Many of the silver and gold from this period bears small digs called shroff marks, applied by bankers. If minor, they only moderately reduce the value of coins in average condition.

After independence from Britain was achieved, the Indian subcontinent was divided into Bangladesh, the Republic of India, and Pakistan, with Ceylon, now Sri Lanka, off the coast. India's coinage is among the most common in the world with massive mintages. Its designs almost always features the Asoka Pillar, a third century B.C. sculpture featuring lions facing in four directions. Recent Pakistani coins have omitted English legends but are characterized by the star and crescent motif. Both Bangladesh and India have used their coins extensively to promote increased agricultural production.

Until recently Himalayan countries rarely placed portraits on their coins, but like non-Islamic India, they used religious symbols. Tibetan coins show some Chinese influence in the 1800s. Other Central Asian countries, during the medieval through early modern ages, are properly discussed under Islamic coins. They then fell under Russian domination, first Czarist then Communist. Only Mongolia and Tuva maintained modern coinage during this period, that of the latter being quite scarce. After the fall of the Soviet Union, many of these areas resumed coinage, combining European style coinage with traditional artistic motifs.

Late in the 1800s, domestically made silver coins became common in China. These pieces struck with European style machinery by the Imperial Government generally depicted a dragon, a motif picked up by Japan and Korea as well. As the Western style silver became common, so Western style copper coins, generally without a central hole, began to replace the old cast cash coins described in the Early Oriental chapter above. All three monarchies frequently dated their coins by the regnal year of their emperors. China also used the traditional Oriental cyclical calendar. When the Republic replaced the Empire, portraits of politicians replaced the imperial dragon on silver, flags on copper. Architecture also became common beginning in the 1940s, both in China and Japan. Today portraiture is not overwhelmingly favored in the Far East, but plants and animals have become popular, especially when they're symbolically significant.

In addition to China, discussed above, many other areas of Asia progressed through a stage of primitive implement money. What is unusual about some of this is that it occasionally followed the initial introduction of coinage proper and continued in use concurrently with it. This is particularly true of Southeast Asia. Most of the coinage of Vietnam over the last several hundred years has been cast, as discussed in the Early Oriental chapter, although silver was more common. As European style coinage was adopted in Southeast Asia, portraiture became common. Usually kings were depicted in Thailand and Cambodia, politicians in Vietnam. This trend continued in the postwar era in many countries, although buildings, flora and fauna became common too, particularly with the independence of Indonesia, Malaysia and Singapore. None of these countries have issued precious metal coinage for circulation since 1942.

Independent Pacific coinage is a relatively recent phenomenon. many nations did not even begin coinage until the 1970s. All the circulating coins are base metal, and a large percentage of the coins in both base and precious metals are struck for international collector distribution, rather than circulation. Some countries, such as the Marshall Islands, have bolstered sales by making false claims of legal tender status. As a result many are traded today at a fraction of their nominal face values or issue prices.

Specialized Books: Bruce, Colin R., et al., *The Standard Guide to South Asian Coins and Paper Money.*

Haffner, Sylvia, *The History of Modern Israel's Money.*

Japanese Numismatic Dealers Association, *The Catalog of Japanese Coins and Banknotes* (Contains annually updated prices,. in Japanese but usable).

Krause, Chester and Mishler, Clifford, *Standard Catalog of World Coins* (17th, 18th, 19th and 20th century editions, frequently updated.)

Mitchiner, Michael, *Oriental Coins and their Values: The Ancient and Classical World.*

Mitchiner, Michael, *Oriental Coins and their Values: Non-Islamic and Colonial Series.*

Opitz, Charles, *Odd & Curious Money - Descriptions and Valuations.*

Known Counterfeits: Most portrait silver dollars of China have been extensively counterfeited. Those depicting Sun Yat Sen are often less deceptive than the others. Dragon dollars have also been counterfeited. Both types often have a grey cast and are of incorrect weight. Counterfeits of dragon coppers made originally to circulate are often worth more than the real thing.

The Japanese 1000 Yen for the 1964 Olympics has been counterfeited. The details of the mountain differ. A number of experts have challenged the Japanese government's claims that counterfeits exist of the gold 100,000 Yen. Counterfeits exist of both the Japanese silver Yen and the Korean silver Whan of the late 1800s.

There have been a number of circulating counterfeits made of Thailand's coins, particularly in the mid 1800s and 1970s. More dangerous counterfeits of rarer coins may also have been made to fool collectors.

AFGHANISTAN   VF

1289 AH 1 Rupee, Inscription (S) 7.50
1306 SH 2-1/2 Afghani, Tougra / Mosque
    (S) 20.00

                                        Unc.
1316 SH 2 Pul, Mosque (C) 1.00
1332 SH 50 Pul, Mosque (C) 1.00
1340 SH 5 Afghani, Bust of shah (N clad
    Steel) 1.50
1352 SH 50 Pul, State seal (C clad Steel) 3.50
1978 AD 500 Afghani, State seal / Siberian
    Crane (S) 30.00
1357 SH 50 Pul, Inscribed wreath (ALB) 2.50

ALGERIA   Unc.

1964 1 Centime, Arms (AL) 45

ALGERIA   Unc.

1964 50 Centimes, Arms (ALB) 1.00
1974 5 Centimes, 1974-1977 inside gear (AL) ... .50
1992 2 Dinars, Camel head (Steel) 5.00
1993 100 Dinars, Horse head (Steel around
    ALB) 25.00

BAHRAIN   Unc.

1965 1 Fils, Palm tree (C) .... .30
1992 100 Fils, Arms (B around CN) 3.50
1968 500 Fils, Bust of Amir / Arms (S) 10.00

BANGLADESH   Unc.

1973 5 poisha, State seal / Hoe (AL, square) .... .20

1975 Taka, State seal / Family (CN) 1.00
1992 Taka, State seal / Runners (S) .... PF 47.50

BHUTAN   VF

1835-1910 Deb Rupee, Crude inscriptions in
    three registers (C) 3.50
(1928) 1/2 Rupee, King / Symbols in nine compartments (S) 15.00

(1928-68) same but (N) 1.00

                                        Unc.
1974 20 Chetrums, Farmer / Four-fold ornament
    (ALB) .... .50
1995 300 Ngultrum, Dragons / Dag Hammarskjold
    (S) .... PF 50.00

BURMA   VF

1781 1/4 Pe, Two fish (C) 145.00
1852 Rupee, Peacock (S) 12.50

                                        Unc.
1952 1 Pya, Lion (C) .... .35
1966 25 Pya, Gen. Aung San (AL) 1.00

                                        Unc.
1953 1 Kyat, Lion (CN) 2.00
1975 1 Kyat, Rice plant (B) 2.00

CAMBODIA   VF

802-1450AD Unit, Dot and crescent pattern (Lead,
    hole) 5.00
1700s-1800s 2 Pe, Bird (Billon) 10.00
1860 5 Cent, Norodom I / Arms (C) 12.00

                                        Unc.
1959 10 Sen, Bird (AL) .... .75
1974 10,000 Riels, Bust of Lon Nol (S) 95.00
1979 5 Sen, Arms (AL) 3.00
1993 4 Riels, Flag / Dinosaur (CN) 15.00
1994 100 Riels, Angkor Wat (Steel) 1.00

CHINA, Empire   VF

1 struck cash Fukien 1896-1903 20 Cents, Dragon
    (S) 6.00

Kiangsi 1890s 10 Cash , Dragon (C) 3.50
Kwangtung 1890-1908 10 Cent, Dragon (S) 4.00
Pei Yang (Chihli) 1908 Dollar, Dragon, 34th year
    (S) 15.00
Taiwan, (1894) 10 Cents, Dragon (S) 175.00
Szechuan (1901-08) Dollar, Dragon (S) 25.00

CHINA, Republic
(General Issues)   VF

1916 1/2 Cent, Diamond with border of buds (C,
    holed) 10.00
1936 1/2 Cent, Sun / Ancient spade money
    (C) 1.50
(1912-27) 10 Cash, Crossed flags (C) .... .75
1936 1 Cent, Sun / Ancient spade money (C) ...... .75

1940 1 Cent, Ancient spade money (AL) .... .25
(1912-27) 20 Cash, Crossed flags (C) 2.50
1933 2 Cents, Diamond with border of buds
    (C, holed) 60.00
1936 5 Cents, Sun Yat-sen / Ancient spade money
    (N) 1.00
1940 5 Cents, Ancient spade money (AL) .... .60
1914 1 Chiao, Bust of Gen. Yuan Shi-kai
    (S) 10.00
1941 10 Cents, Sun Yat-sen / Ancient spade money
    (CN) 1.50
1926 20 Cents, Phoenix and dragon (S) 15.00
1927 20 Cents, Sun Yat-sen facing / Crossed flags
    (S) 25.00
1914 1/2 Dollar, Yuan Shi-kai / Wreath (S) 30.00
1942 1/2 Dollar, Sun Yat-sen / Ancient spade
    money (CN) 3.00

CHINA, Republic
(General Issues) VF
1914 Dollar, Yuan Shi-kai / Wreath (S) 12.50
1917 Dollar, Yuan Shi-kai in high hat / Dragon (S) 250.00
(1912-27) Dollar, Sun Yat-sen / MEMENTO over wreath (S) 10.00
1932 Dollar, Sun Yat-sen / Junk sailing into sunrise, birds over head (S) 200.00
1934 Dollar, similar but no birds or sun (S).... 12.50
1916 10 Dollars, Yuan Shi-kai / Dragon (G) 3,000.00

CHINA, Republic
(Province Issues) VF
Chekiang 1924 10 Cents, Crossed flags (S) 7.00
Fengtien 1929 1 Cent, Sun over wreath (C)...... 3.00
Fukien 1923 20 Cents, Three flags (S).............. 7.00
Honan (1912-27) 10 Cash, Crossed flags (C) ... 1.50
Hunan (1912-27) 10 Cash, Star (C) 4.00
Kansu 1928 Dollar, Sun Yat-sen / Star (S).... 300.00
Kiangsi 1912 10 Cash, Star (C) 5.00
Kwangsi 1926 20 Cents, "20" (S) 6.50
Kwangtung 1919 20 Cents, "20" (S)................. 1.25

Kweichow 1928 Dollar, Automobile (S) 550.00
Shensi (1928) 2 Cents, Crossed flags and IMTYPEF (C)..................................... 25.00
Singkiang 1949 Dollar, Value (S)................... 20.00
Szechuan 1912 Dollar, Seal script (S)............ 20.00
Yunnan 1949 20 Cents, Building (S)................ 7.50

CHINA, Republic on Taiwan Unc.
1949 1 Chiao, Sun Yat-sen / Map of Taiwan (C) 4.00
1954 5 Chiao, similar (B) 1.00
1960 1 Dollar, Flowers (CNZ) 50
1970 5 Dollars, Chaing Kai-shek left (CN) 80

Unc.
1989 10 Dollars, Chaing Kai-shek facing (CN).. .65
1965 100 Dollars, Sun Yat-sen / Deer (S) 25.00

CHINA, Peoples Republic Unc.
1976 1 Fen, Arms (AL) 50
1956 2 Fen, Arms (AL) 1.50
1986 5 Fen, Arms (AL) 45

1992 1 Jiao, Arms / Flower (AL) 50
1980 1 Yuan, Great wall (CN) 2.00
1995 5 Yuan, Monkey (C) 8.00

CHINA, Peoples Republic Unc.
1995 10 Yuan, Building / Two pigs (S, scalloped) ....PF 65.00
1996 20 Yuan, City gate / Yangtze river (S, rectangular)......................................PF 60.00
1989 100 Yuan, Arms / Snake (Platinum) ....PF 575.00
1991 10,000 Yuan, Temple of Heaven / Panda encircled by coins (G), Proof only 180,000.00

EGYPT, Kingdom VF
1917 1 Millieme, Inscription (CN) 1.00
1917 2 Piastres, Inscription (S)...................... 2.50
1916 100 Piastres, Inscription (G)................ 100.00
1935 1 Millieme, King Fuad (C) 50
1935 5 Milliemes, King Fuad (CN)................... 1.00
1923 10 Piastres, King Fuad (S) 12.50
1930 50 Piastres, King Faud (G) 70.00
1938 5 Milliemes, King Farouk (C, scalloped) 1.00
1941 10 Milliemes, King Farouk (CN) 1.00
1944 2 Piastres, King Farouk (S, hexagonal).... 1.00

1938 100 Piastres, King Farouk (G).............. 150.00

EGYPT, Republic Unc.
1956 1 Millieme, Sphinx (ALB)....................... 4.00
1962 2 Milliemes, Falcon (ALB)........................60
1975 5 Milliemes, Nefertiti (B) 30
1984 1 Piastre, Tougra / Pyramids (ALB) 20
1958 20 Milliemes, Gear (ALB)....................... 5.00
1964 5 Piastres, Dam (S) 4.00

1955 10 Piastres, Sphinx (S) 18.00
1967 10 Piastres, Falcon (CN) 2.00
1977 10 Piastres, Clasped hands (CN) 2.25
1980 10 Piastres, Sadat (CN) 3.50
1992 10 Piastres, Mosque (CN)....................... 1.25
1956 20 Piastres, Sphinx (S) 5.00
1970 25 Piastres, Nasser (S) 6.50
1958 1/2 Pound, Ancient chariot (G)............. 175.00

1980 1 Pound, Fist (S)..................................... 8.00

EGYPT, Republic Unc.
1960 5 Pounds, Dam (G) 600.00
1994 10 Pounds, Ancient Hippopotamus figure (S) .... PF 47.50
1983 100 Pounds, Nefertiti (G).............. PF 725.00

INDIAN STATES VF
Assam 1818 Rupee, Four lines Sanskrit inscription each side (S, octagonal) 50.00
Baroda 1885 Paisa, Horse hoof over sword (C)... 1.25
Bijapur 1600s, Leaf containing dot pattern both sides (C) 5.00
Bikanir 1937 Rupee, Facing bust (S)............. 16.50
Dungarpur 1944 Paisa, Arms (C, square)........ 25.00
Gwalior 1942 1/4 Anna, Bust left (C) 60
Indore 1935 1/4 Anna, Facing bust (C) 2.00
Jaipur 1944 1 Anna, Bust / Branch (B) 40
Jaora 1893 Paisa, Flag (C) 6.50
Kachar 1601-11 1/4 Rupee, Three lines Sanskrit inscription each side (S)............................50.00

INDIAN STATES   VF

Kutch 1936 5 Kori, Inscriptions (S) 7.00
Mewar 1928 Rupee, City walls (S) 10.00
Mysore 1700s Kasu, Elephant / Grid pattern
    (C) 5.00
Mysore 1800s Fanam, Stylized Narasimha
    (G) 13.50
Nawanagar 1570-1850 Dokdo, Barbarized inscrip-
    tion (C) 1.50
Pudokkatai 1889-1906 1 Cash, Goddess Brihad-
    amba (C) 50

Tonk 1932 Pice, Arms / Leaf (C) 1.00
Travancore (1790-1895) Fanam, Design rendered in
    series of dots and lines (G) 8.50
Travancore (1938-49) 1 Cash, Conch shell (C) 25
Tripura 1934 Rupee, Lion (S) 37.50

INDIA   Unc.

1950 1 Pice, Asoka pillar / Horse (C) 1.50
1954 1 Anna, similar / Bull (CN, scalloped)..... 1.25
1950 1 Rupee, similar / two ears of grain (N)... 4.50

INDIA   Unc.

1972 1 Paisa, Asoka pillar (AL, square) 50
1961 2 Paise, similar (CN, scalloped) 80
1970 3 Paise, similar (AL, hexagonal) 50
1957 5 Paise, similar (CN, square) 1.00
1993 10 Paise, similar (Steel) 35
1968 20 Paise, similar / Lotus (ALB) 1.50
1996 25 Paisa, Rhinoceros / Asoka Pillar
    (Steel) 35
1972 50 Paise, Couple with flag / similar (CN) 85
1964 1 Rupee, Nehru / similar (N) 2.00
1991 1 Rupee, Rajiv Gandhi / similar (CN) 60
1997 1 Rupee, Asoka pillar / Two ears of grain
    (Steel) 30
1994 2 Rupees, Water drop / Asoka pillar
    (CN) 2.00

INDIA   Unc.

1997 2 Rupees, Map / similar (CN) 40
(1985) "1984" 5 Rupees, Indira Gandhi / similar
    (CN) 3.00
1974 10 Rupees, Family in triangle / similar
    (CN) 3.50
(1969-70) 20 Rupees, Mahatma Gandhi / similar
    (S) 6.00
1986 20 Rupees, Fishermen / similar (S) 10.00
1975 50 Rupees, Woman and ear of grain / similar
    (S) 10.00
1982 100 Rupees, Games logo / similar (S).... 17.50

INDONESIA   Unc.

1952 1 Sen, Rice (AL, hole) 1.00
1970 1 Rupiah, Bird (AL).................................25
1971 10 Rupiah, Wreath (CN).........................45
1991 100 Rupiah, Eagle / Cow racing (ALB)......75
1993 1000 Rupiah, Eagle / Tree (CN around
    B).. 3.75

1974 100,000 Rupiah, Eagle / Komodo dragon
    (G) 450.00

IRAN, Qajar dynasty   VF

1167AH Fals, Peacock, Mazandaran (C) .....F 25.00
1194AH 2 Abbasi, Inscriptions (S) 45.00
1235AH Fals, Lion and sun, Tabriz (C) ....F 10.00
1318AH 50 Dinars, Wreath / Lion and sun
    (CN) 1.50
1323AH 1000 Dinars, Shah with large moustache /
    Lion and sun (S).. 30.00
1342AH 5000 Dinars, Shah with fat cheeks / Lion
    and sun (S) 15.00

Pahlavi dynasty   XF

1310SH 1 Dinar, Lion and sun (C)................. 30.00
1320SH 10 Dinars, similar (ALB) 2.00
1311SH 1 Rial, similar (S)................................ 5.00

Pahlavi dynasty   XF

1346SH 10 Rials, Shah / Lion and sun in wreath
    (CN).. 1.00
1338SH 10 Rials, similar but FAO under lion
    (CN).. 1.00
1971AD 100 Rials, Ruins of Persepolis
    (S) .... PF 25.00
1352 1 Pahlavi, Shah / Lion in wreath (G) 100.00

Islamic Republic   Unc.

1358SH 50 Dinars, Lion and sun without crown
    (B).. 12.00
1371 5 Rials, Tomb of Hafez (B)...................... 2.75
1370 50 Rials, Oil refinery / Map (CN)............. 8.00
1375 1 Azadi, Mosque / Ayatollah Khomeini
    (G) 140.00

IRAQ, Kingdom   VF

1933 1 Fils, Faisal I (C)................................... 3.00
1938 20 Fils, Ghazi I (S)................................. 3.00
1953 100 Fils, Faisal II (S).............................. 7.50

Republic   Unc.

1959 1 Fils, Grain in star (C, polygonal).............75

1971 5 Fils, Palm trees (Steel, scalloped).............75
1970 100 Fils, similar (CN) 1.50
1981 1 Dinar, Saddam Hussein and airplanes
    (N) 12.00

ISRAEL   Unc.

1949 25 Mils, Grapes (AL).............................. 25.00
1949 1 Pruta, Anchor (AL) 2.00

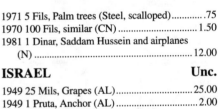

1957 10 Prutot, Ancient jug (AL)...................... 2.50
1954 100 Prutah, Date palm (N clad Steel)....... 3.00
1949 500 Prutah, Three pomegranates (S) 25.00
1965 1 Agorah, Three ears of grain (AL,
    scalloped) 25
1979 1/2 Lirah, Menorah (CN).........................50
1967 10 Lirot, Sword and olive branch / Western
    Wall (S) 8.00
1969 10 Lirot, Helmet and inscription (S)....... 10.00

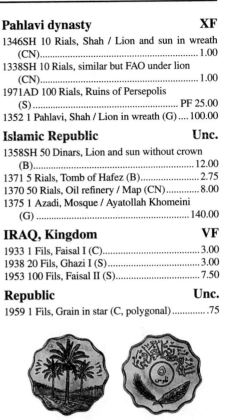

ISRAEL   Unc.

1974 25 Lirot, David Ben Gurion / Menorah
(S).. 10.00
1980 1 New Agorah, Date palm (AL).................10
1982 1/2 Sheqel, Lion (CN) 50
1984 1 Sheqel, Theresianstadt Lamp (S) 15.00
1984 100 Sheqelim, Ancient coin with menorah
(CN) 2.00
1986 1 New Sheqel, Lily (CN).................... 1.50
1988 1 New Sheqel, Maimonides (N)............... 1.75
1996 1 New Sheqel, Yitzak Rabin (S) 30.00

JAPAN, Meiji 治明,

1867 = year 1   VF

1883 1 Rin, Chrysanthemum (C) 6.00
1875 1 Sen, Dragon (C)............................. 2.00
1889 5 Sen, Sunburst (CN)......................... 5.00
1907 20 Sen, Sunburst (S)......................... 5.50
1903 1 Yen, Dragon (S)........................... 27.50

1872 5 Yen, Dragon / Sunburst, wreath and banners
(G) 1,000.00
1876 Trade Dollar, Dragon (S)................... 650.00

Taisho 正大, 1912 = year 1   VF

1918 5 Rin, Paulowina crest (C)................... 1.00
1913 1 Sen, Sunburst (C)........................... 3.00
1917 10 Sen, Sunburst (S)......................... 2.00
1925 50 Sen, Sunburst / Two phoenixes (S) 1.50

Showa 和昭, 1926 = year 1   Unc.

1941 1 Sen, Mt. Fuji (AL)..........................50
1938 10 Sen, Cherry blossom / Waves (ALB,
hole) 4.75
1946 50 Sen, Phoenix (B)........................... 2.50
1968 5 Yen, Rice plant (B) 15
1978 50 Yen, Chrysanthemums (CN, hole) 1.00
1958 100 Yen, Phoenix (S)........................... 6.00
1964 1000 Yen, Mt. Fuji (S)........................ 45.00
1986 100,000 Yen, Chrysanthemum / Two Phoe-
nixes (G) 1,250.00

Heisei 平成, 1989 = year 1   Unc.

1989 500 Yen, Paulowina (CN)...................... 10.00

| | Unc. |

1993 5000 Yen, Chrysanthemum / Two cranes
(S) 70.00
1990 Yen, Sapling (AL) 10
1997 10 Yen, Temple (C)...............................45
1994 50 Yen, Chrysanthemums (CN, hole) 1.00

JORDAN   Unc.

1949 1 Fils, Crown (C) 2.25
1975 50 Fils, King Hussein (CN) 1.25
1977 21/2 Dinars, King Hussein / Gazelle
(S) 25.00
1995 1 Dinar, similar / FAO logo (B) 10.00

KAZAKHSTAN   Unc.

1993 2 Tyin, Arms (B) 45
1995 20 Tenge, Arms / U.N. logo (CN) 4.00
1995 100 Tenge, Arms / Old man and hut
(S)...PF 55.00

KOREA   VF

1898 5 Fun, Two dragons (C) 5.00
1910 10 Chon, Dragon (S) 18.00
1893 1 Whan, Two dragons (S) 5,925.00

KOREA, NORTH   Unc.

1959 1 Chon, Arms (AL) 1.00
1987 1 Won, Building / Arms (AL).................. 3.50
1995 10 Won, Arms / Cartoon tiger (CN) 8.00

KOREA, SOUTH   Unc.

1959 100 Hwan, Syngman Rhee / Two Phoenixes
(CN) 6.00
1978 1 Won, Rose of Sharon (AL) 15

1972 50 Won, Rice plant (CN) 7.50
1982 50 Won, similar..................................35
1983 500 Won, Manchurian crane (CN) 2.50
1984 10,000 Won, Cross / Saints (S).............. 25.00

LAOS   Unc.

1952 20 Cents, Elephants (AL) 1.50
1971 2500 Kip, King / Arms (S) 35.00
1980 20 Att, Arms / Plower (AL)......................85

LEBANON   Unc.

1955 1 Piastre, Wreath (ALB, hole) 25
1975 10 Piastres, Cedar (B) 20
1952 50 Piastres, Cedar (S) 3.50

LEBANON   Unc.

1968 1 Livre, Cedar / Fruit (N)....................... 3.00
1980 400 Livre, Monogram / Olympic logo
(G) ....PF 450.00

LIBYA   Unc.

1952 1 Millieme, King Idris (C) 50

| | Unc. |

1979 5 Dirhams, Horseman (B clad Steel)........ 9.00
1981 70 Dinars, Hands embracing handicapped
symbol / Logo (G)............................... 400.00

MALAYSIA   Unc.

Malacca 1247AH 1 Keping, Rooster (C) ...... VF 4.00
1967 1 Sen, Building (C) 15
1989 5 Sen, Top (CN) 15
1993 1 Ringgit, Dagger and scabbard (B) 2.00
1976 500 Ringgit, Malayan Tapir (G) 500.00

MARSHALL IS.   Unc.

1986 1 Dollar, Arms / Triton shell (S)............. 27.50

1988 5 Dollars, Arms / Space shuttle Discovery
(CN).. 6.00
1993 10 Dollars, Arms / Elvis Presley (B) 14.00
1995 50 Dollars, Arms / Marilyn Monroe
(S) .... PF 56.00

MONGOLIA   XF

1925 1 Tugrik, National emblem (S) 22.50
1937 20 Mongo, similar (CN) 10.00

1937 5 Mongo, similar (ALB) 6.00
1945 5 Mongo, Arms (ALB) 5.00
1959 2 Mongo, Wreath (AL, hole) 1.50
1981 1 Mongo, Arms (AL) 85
1992 250,000 Tugrik, Chengis Khan / National
emblem (G) .... PF 30,600.00

MOROCCO   VF

1314AH 1 Dirham, Six pointed star each side
(S) 7.00

MOROCCO — VF

1340AH 10 Mazunas, Star / Ornamental pattern
  (C) 1.50
1951 1 Franc, Star (AL)..................................... .10
1953 100 Francs, Star within star (S) 2.50

Unc.

1975 5 Santimat, Arms / Wheel and fish (B) 30
1965 1 Dirham, Hasan II / Arms (N) 1.00
1987 5 Dirham, similar (Steel around ALB) 8.50

NEPAL — VF

Patan 1654 1/4 Mohar, Sword / Lion (S) 100.00

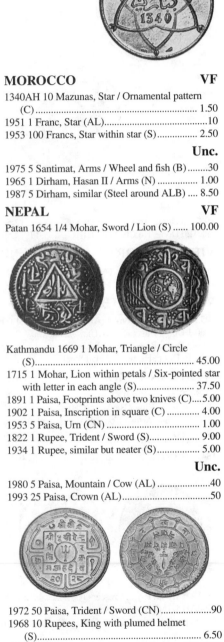

Kathmandu 1669 1 Mohar, Triangle / Circle
  (S)... 45.00
1715 1 Mohar, Lion within petals / Six-pointed star
  with letter in each angle (S)...................... 37.50
1891 1 Paisa, Footprints above two knives (C)....5.00
1902 1 Paisa, Inscription in square (C) 4.00
1953 5 Paisa, Urn (CN) 1.00
1822 1 Rupee, Trident / Sword (S)................... 9.00
1934 1 Rupee, similar but neater (S)................ 5.00

Unc.

1980 5 Paisa, Mountain / Cow (AL) 40
1993 25 Paisa, Crown (AL)...................................50

1972 50 Paisa, Trident / Sword (CN) 90
1968 10 Rupees, King with plumed helmet
  (S)... 6.50
1993 500 Rupees, Bear (S).........................PF 45.00

NIUE — Unc.

1997 1 Dollar, Arms / Princess Diana (CN) ... 10.00
same (S) ....PF 47.50
1992 5 Dollars, Arms / HMS Bounty (S) 22.00

PAKISTAN — Unc.

1951 1 Pie, Tougra (C) 2.50
1948 2 Annas, Tougra / Star and crescent
  (CN) 1.00

PAKISTAN — Unc.

1974 1 Pice, Tower, star and crescent (AL)......... .30
1962 5 Paisa, Tougra, star and crescent / Ship
  (B) 70
1976 50 Paisa, Mohammad Ali Jinnah (CN) 1.00
1976 150 Rupees, Tower, star and crescent / Croco-
  dile (S) 35.00

PHILIPPINES — Unc.

1958 1 Centavo, Arms / Man seated with hammer
  (C) .... .25
1964 25 Centavos, Arms / Woman with hammer
  (CNZ).. .35
1947 50 Centavos, MacArthur / Arms (S) 4.00
1967 1 Peso, Flaming sword / Arms (S) 7.50
1974 1 Sentimo, Bust of Lapulapu (AL)............. .10

1983 50 Sentimos, Bust of Pilar / Eagle (CN) .... .50
1970 1 Piso, Marcos / Pope (N).......................... 4.00
1990 2 Pisos, Bonafacio / Tree (CN)................. 1.00
1974 25 Pisos, Arms / National bank (S) 10.00
1992 10,000 Pisos, Corazon Aqino / Map
  (G) ....PF 900.00

QATAR — Unc.

1973 1 Dirhem, Ship and trees (C) .... .50
1993 50 Dirhems, similar 2.00

SAUDI ARABIA — VF

1346AH 1/4 Ghirsh, Inscription (CN).............. 8.00
1378AH 1 Ghirsh, Palm and swords (CN).......... .25
1354AH 1/4 Riyal, Inscription (S) 2.50
1374AH 1 Riyal, similar (S)............................. 2.50

1397AH 10 Halala, Palm and swords (CN) .... .25
1414AH 100 Halala, similar (CN) 1.00

SOUTH EAST ASIA — VF

Funan 190-627AD Unit, Sun / Temple with symbol
  inside (S) 75.00
Mekong River valley 1600s-1800s Long ingot with
  rounded ends and rough bumps on one side,
  called "Tiger tongue" money (Billon)....... 20.00
___. 1700s to late 1800s, similar but no bumps,
  called "Canoe" money (base billon).......... 10.00

SHARJAH — Unc.

1964 5 Rupees, John F. Kennedy / Crossed flags
  (S) 12.50

SINGAPORE — Unc.

1986 1 Cent, Arms (C)... .10
1971 5 Cents, Fish (AL) .... .35

SINGAPORE — Unc.

1967 20 Cents, Swordfish (CN).......................... .60

1967 50 Cents, Zebra fish (CN)........................... .80
1978 10 Dollars, Satellite dish (S) 7.50
1981 5 Dollars, Airport (CN).............................. 6.50
1990 100 Dollars, Arms / Lion head (G).......485.00

SRI LANKA (CEYLON) — Unc.

1963 1 Cent, Arms (AL) .... .10
1975 25 Cents, Arms (CN) .... .25
1981 2 Rupees, Dam (CN)................................ 1.25
1995 5 Rupees, U.N. logo (ALB) 2.50

SUDAN — Unc.

1956 1 Millim, Postman on camel (C) .... .30

1970 10 Millim, similar (C, scalloped)................ .90
1989 25 Ghirsh, Building (Steel) 2.25
1976 5 Pounds, Hippopotami (S)..................... 30.00

SYRIA — Unc.

1935 1 Piastre, Lion heads (B, hole)................ 22.50
ND (World War II emergency issue) 1 Piastre,
  Inscription (B) 6.00

1971 5 Piastres, Arms / Grain (ALB) .... .35
1950 1 Lira, Arms (S) 25.00
1978 1 Pound, President Assad / Arms (N)....... 3.00

TANNU TUVA — VF

1934 1 Kopejek, (ALB) 45.00
1934 20 Kopejek (CN)....................................55.00

THAILAND — VF

1782-1809 1 Baht "bullet money" with Conch
  countermark (S) 25.00
1800s 100 Cowries, circulating gambling token
  (Porcelain)... 4.00
(1862) 1/16th Fuang, Three crowns / Elephant in
  border (Tin) 6.00
1890 1 Att, Rama V / Siam seated (C) 12.00
1908 1 Baht, Rama V l. / Elephants (S)......3,200.00

THAILAND VF

1918 1 Baht, Rama VI r. / Elephants (S)......... 10.00
1929 50 Satang, Rama VII l., / Elephant l. (S) 6.00
1946 25 Satang, Rama VIII as child / Garuda
(Tin) 2.50

Rama IX Unc.

1957 5 Satang, Bust / Arms (B) 25
1961 1 Baht, King and Queen / Arms (CN)...... 2.00
1972 5 Baht, Bust / Garuda (CN, polygonal).... 1.20
1980 10 Baht, Bust / Wheel (N)........................ 2.25
1996 20 Baht, King with camera / King and people
(CN) 3.25
1971 50 Baht, Bust / Wheel (S)....................... 16.50

TIBET VF

1795 1 Sho, Chinese inscription around square /
Tibetan inscription around square (S)....... 60.00
1875-1930 Ga-den Tanka, Lotus / Symbols
(S)... 6.00
1919 1 Sho, Lion (C) 5.00

1936 3 Srang, Lion before mountains (S)....... 10.00
1952 10 Srang, similar (S).............................. 12.00
1918 20 Srang, Lion (G)................................. 400.00
1902-42 Rupee, Chinese bust / Floral wreath (S)
Struck by Chinese. 14.00

TONGA Unc.

1967 1 Seniti, Queen Salote (C)........................ 1.00
1981 20 Seneti, King Taufa'ahau / Roots
(CN) 1.50
1985 1 Pa'anga, King / Dove
(CN, heptagonal) 4.00
1981 5 Hau, King / Charles and Diana (G)... 275.00

TUNISIA Unc.

1954 5 Francs, Monogram / Crescent (CN)...... 3.50

TUNISIA Unc.

1960 2 Millim, Tree (AL) 25
1976 1/2 Dinar, Bourguiba / Hands (CN) 7.50
1982 75 Dinars, same / Children (G) ....PF 225.00

TURKEY VF

1341 100 Para, Wheat / Oak branch (ALB) Arabic
alphabet... 2.50
1928 25 Kurus, similar. Arabic alphabet (N) 3.00
1936 1 Kurus, Star in crescent (CN) 1.00
1948 1 Lira, Star and crescent (S) 3.00

Unc.

1959 5 Kurus, similar / Oak branch (C) 30
1967 1 Lira, Ataturk (Steel)................................50

1979 5 Lira, Ataturk on horse (Steel)................ 1.00
1960 10 Lira, Ataturk / Symbols of revolution
(S)... 9.00
1988 50 Lira, Ataturk (ALB)..............................15
1997 5000 Lira, Ataturk (B) .... .75
1992 500,000 Lira, Ship (Turkish Jews)
(G) ....PF 320.00

TURKMENISTAN Unc.

1993 1 Tennesi, President Nyyazow (C plated
Steel) 25

TURKMENISTAN Unc.

1993 50 Tennesi, Same / Rhyton (N plated
steel).. 3.00

UNITED ARAB EMIRATES Unc.

1973 1 Fils, Palm trees (C) 20
1988 50 Fils, Oil wells (CN) 1.65

1995 1 Dirham, Pitcher (CN) 1.85
1981 5 Dirhams, Falcon (CN) 6.50
1996 50 Dirhams, Bust of Sheikh (S)............. 60.00

UZBEKISTAN Unc.

1994 1 Tiyin, Arms (B clad Steel)......................30
1997 10 Som, Arms (N clad Steel)................... 1.50

VIETNAM VF

1832 7 Tien, Sun / Dragon (S) 300.00
1848-83 1 Tien, Scepter and swastika (S) 120.00

Unc.

1976 1 Hao, Arms (AL).................................... 2.50

Unc.

1987 10 Dong, Arms / Orangutan (CN) 12.50
1989 20 Dong, Ho Chi Minh (B).............. PF 14.50

VIETNAM, NORTH XF

1946 5 Hao, Stove / Star (AL) 18.00
1958 1 Xu, Wreath (AL, hole)........................... 2.00

VIETNAM, SOUTH Unc.

1953 10 Su, Three women (AL) 1.00
1960 1 Dong, Bust / Rice (AL)........................ 2.50
1966 5 Dong, Rice (CN, scalloped)................. 1.00
1974 10 Dong, Farmers (B clad Steel) 60

WESTERN SAMOA Unc.

1967 1 Sene, King (C)..20
1974 50 Sene, King / Bananas (CN)................. 1.75
1988 100 Tala, Arms / Kon-Tiki (G) .... PF 120.00

YEMEN, Kingdom VF

1343AH 1 Zalat, Inscription (C).................... 40.00

1381AH 1/80th Riyal, Crescent (C) 75
1368AH 1/16th Riyal, Crescent
(S, pentagonal) 5.00

Arab Republic Unc.

1963 1 Buqsha, Leaves (ALB) 50
1985 50 Fils, Eagle (CN) 2.50
1975 100 Riyals, Eagle / Arab Jerusalem
(G) 325.00

EARLY ORIENTAL COINS

Coins were invented three times, each independently. The sole surviving strand of evolution is the Western method of striking a coin with an impression from a single die on each side. But until early this century another tradition prevailed in the Far East. Beginning in roughly the 8th century B.C., round coins were produced there by casting in moulds. These were the result of centuries of evolution. One of the earliest currencies in China, like in many other countries, was cowrie shell. But in China it did not disappear with the first stage of monetary development. Instead, it evolved with its replacement of carved bone and jade cowries. Trade in actual tools and farm implements such as knives and hoes also occurred. Eventually cowries, knives and hoes were replaced in circulation by small bronze replicas of these items. These trade items were made by casting and were usually very thin and fragile. It followed naturally that as more convenient round coins evolved they would also be made by casting. From the first millennium B.C. until the 19th century most coins in the far east were copper or copper alloys such as brass and bronze. Occasionally low value pieces were cast of iron or zinc. In the 19th century, European manufactured equipment for striking rather than casting coins began to be imported and within few generations the speed and uniformity these machines allowed caused the old method casting to be abandoned.

All Far Eastern coins ultimately were derived from Chinese coins. China was, for thousands of years, the most powerful state in the region and long before Japan, Korea and Vietnam produced their own coins, they were importing millions of coins from China. The typical Chinese coins used from roughly the eighth B.C. century onward were cast with holes in the center for stringing. The common English name for these coins is "cash." Most were between the size of a nickel and a mini-dollar. Larger coins were worth multiple of the smaller ones. All the values below are for average size unless noted otherwise. From the first millennium B.C. until the 19th century most Far Eastern coins were copper or copper alloys such as brass and bronze. All coins below are made of these metals unless noted. In China and Japan low value pieces were occasionally cast of iron. In Annam (Vietnam) zinc was used for low values. Both iron and zinc cash corroded quite quickly and most examples found will show corrosion. Tin coins influenced by Chinese cash were also cast in the East Indies.

Chinese cast coins almost never have any images, just inscriptions. The most common types of inscription for the first few hundred years of Chinese coinage consisted of two characters indicating the theoretical weight, although the actual weights rarely coincided. Sometimes before, and almost always after the 600s Chinese coins bore a very standard formula of obverse consisting of four characters. Two of the characters indicated that the coin was money. They generally were T'ung Pao (current money).

Current Money	Yuan Pao (first money)	Chung Pao (heavy money)

The other two characters were the reign title of the emperor. This was not the actual name of the emperor (which was forbidden to be uttered) but the name by which he chose to be called. On great occasions an emperor may have even changed his reign title. Most early Chinese coins had no dates, but because the reign titles changed so frequently the coins can be dated fairly narrowly. During the last two dynasties, most emperors kept the same reign title throughout their reigns.

There were often different ways of writing characters, similar to different type fonts in the West. Most resembled modern Chinese writing. One, however, was very different and was called Seal Script. The following list indicates the reign title in regular script and, when it appears on the coins, seal script. All a collector has to do is ignore the two characters that mean money (see above) and match up the other two to the list below. Most of the time this is all one needs to date the coin.

Reverse legends were not common on Chinese coins. On occasion a regal year appeared. Only during the Ch'ing dynasty did mintmaks come into fashion for the reverse. Most of these were written in Manchu rather than Chinese. Manchu uses a cursive script and is written vertically.

Japanese, Korean and Vietnamese coinage begin later and are greatly influenced by and take the basic form of Chinese coins. Different reverses help distinguish non-Chinese cash. Japanese cash, for example, often has a pattern of arcs on the reverse. Korean coins developed with three (or sometimes two) characters. Annamese (Vietnamese) coins often have two characters on the reverse clearly indicating the value in numerals. All four countries used Chinese characters during this period. Similar coins with Chinese and Arabic or only Arabic were cast in the East Indies.

Specialized Books: Japanese Numismatic Dealers Association, *The Catalog of Japanese Coins and Banknotes*. In Japanese.

Mandel, Edgar, *Cast Coinage of Korea*.

Schjoth, F., *Chinese Currency*.

Known counterfeits: Counterfeits of cast Chinese coins are quite common and some collector counterfeits many be hundreds of years old themselves. Most pre-round coins have been counterfeited. Poorer fakes are very roughly cast and have a painted-on patina, but many more dangerous counterfeits exist. Any Chinese coin over $200 in value and much cheaper implement money should be examined by an expert.

The most counterfeited cheap cast cash are those of Annam. These were made by the tens of thousands to sell as souvenirs to U.S. soldiers and other foreigners during the Vietnam War.

CHINA

Pre-Coin Currencies	Avg.
First Millenium B.C. Stone Cowrie Imitation	90.00
First Millenium B.C. Stone Cowrie Imitation	90.00
First Millenium B.C. Jade Cowrie Imitation	150.00
First Millennium B.C. Copper Cowrie Imitation	125.00

500s B.C. "Ant-Nose" Money 15.00
ca.770-375 B.C. Hollow Handle Spade (often 31-40gm.) 400.00

ca.770 B.C. and later Ch'i Knife Money (ca.45-50 gm.) 250.00

(reduced)

ca.500-250 B.C. Pu Spade Money (usually 5-6 gm.) 30.00

(reduced)

ca.400-250 B.C. Ming Knife Money (thin, usually 14-16 gm.) 20.00

Early Round Coinage   **F**

200s B.C. Ming Tao 100.00

200s B.C. Yi Tao 20.00

100s B.C. Pan-liang 5.00

1st Century B.C. - 6th Century A.D. Wu-shu 4.00

Usurper Wang Mang 7-22 A.D.

Ta-ch'üan wu-shih, 50 Cash 12.00

Hsiao-chüan chih-yi [oS-139] 7.00

Huo Ch'üan [o149] 5.00

Spade Money (thick, 14-17 gm.) 25.00

Knife Money resembling a key .... Rare

529 A.D. Yung-an wu-shu 20.00

553 A.D. Ch'ang-p'ing wu-shu [o242o] 22.00

T'ang Dynasty 618-907

600s - 700s A.D. K'ai-yüan 3.00

756-62 Ch'ien Yüan 5.00
similar but larger 16.00

Five Dynasties Period 907-60

917-42 Ch'ien-heng [S-436v] (Lead) 16.00

960-61 T'ang-kuo 8.00

Northern Sung Dynasty 960-1127

968-75 Sung-yüan 3.00

976-84 T'ai-p'ing 3.00

990-994 Shun-hua 3.00

995-98 Chih-tao or 3.00

998-1004 Hsien-p'ing 3.00

1004-07 Ching-te 3.00

1008-16 Hsiang-fu 3.00

1017-21 T'ien-hsi 3.00

1023-31 T'ien-sheng 3.00

1032-33 Ming-tao 5.00

1034-37 Ching-yu 3.00

1038-39 Huang-sung 3.00

1040 K'ang-ting 5.00

1041-48 Ch'ing-li 22.00

1049-53 Huang-yu 3.50

1054-55 Chih-ho 3.00

1056-63 Chia-yu 5.00

1064-67 Chih-p'ing 3.00

1068-77 Hsi-ning 3.00

1078-85 Yüan-feng 3.00

1086-93 Yüan-yu 3.00

1094-97 Shao-sheng 3.00

1098-1100 Yüan-fu 3.00

坚宋

1101 Sheng-sung 3.00

崇寧

1102-06 Ch'ung-ning 8.00

大觀

1107-10 Ta-kuan Large .... VF 38.00
similar, normal size 3.00

政咪

1111-17 Cheng-ho 3.00

重和

1118 Chung-ho 6.50

宣咪

1119-25 Hsüan-ho 6.50

靖爾

1126 Ching-k'ang 6.50

Southern Sung Dynasty 1127-1280

建炎

1127-30 Chien-yen 38.00

紹興

1131-62 Shao-hsing 12.00

隆興

1163-64 Lung-hsing 55.00

乾道

1165-73 Ch'ien-tao 35.00

燿熙

1174-89 Shun-hsi 3.00

紹熙

1190-94 Shao-hsi 3.00

1195-1200 Ch'ing-yüan, (Large size, Iron)..... 38.00
same, copper, normal size 3.00

嘉泰

1201-04 Chia-t'ai 12.00

開禧

1205-07 K'ai-hsi 12.00

嘉定

1208-24 Chia-ting 5.00

大宋

1225-27 Ta-sung 7.00

紹定

1228-33 Shao-ting 4.00

2145

1234-36 Tuan-p'ing 27.00

嘉熙

1237-40 Chia-hsi 15.00

淳祐

1241-52 Shun-yu.. 3.00

皇宋

1253-58 Huang-sung 6.00

開慶

1259 K'ai-ch'ing 22.00

景定

1260-64 Ching-ting.. 5.00

咸淳

1265-74 Hsien-shun... 12.00

Ki-tan Tartar (Liao) Dynasty 907-1125

天贊

922-924 T'ien-tsan ....Scarce

重熙

1032-54 Ch'ung-hsi ....Scarce

清寧

1055-65 Ch'ing-ning 90.00

咸雍

1066-73 Hsien-yung... 95.00

大康

1074-82 Ta-k'ang 90.00

大安

1083-91 Ta-an 90.00

壽昌

1092-1100 Shou-ch'ang 95.00

乾統

1101-09 Ch'ien-t'ung.. 90.00

天慶

1110-20 T'ien-ch'ing.. 90.00

Western Hsia Dynasty 982-1227

天盛

1149-68 T'ien-sheng 22.00

乾祐

1169-93 Ch'ien-yu .... Scarce

皇建

1210-12 Huang-chien.. 100.00

光定

1212-22 Kuang-ting 80.00

Nü-chen Tartars 1115-1260

正隆

1156-61 Cheng-lung 5.00

大定

1161-89 Ta-ting 5.00

泰咪

1201-08 T'ai-ho, Large 55.00

Mongol (Yüan) Dynasty 1280-1368

大德

1297-1307 Ta-te ....Scarce

至大

1308-11 Chih-ta 7.00

1308-11 Ta-yüan Large size, Mongol script 40.00

皇慶

1312-13 Huang-ch'ing...................Scarce

至正

1335-67 Chih-cheng ....Scarce

Ming Dynasty 1368-1644

洪武

1368-98 Hung-wu.......................... 3.00

建文

1399-1402 Chien-wen ....Scarce

永樂

1403-24 Yung-lo 3.00

洪熙

1425 Hung-hsi ....Scarce

宣德

1426-35 Hsüan-te 10.00

正統

1436-49 Cheng-t'ung [S-1171] .....Scarce

景泰

1450-56 Ching-t'ai ....Scarce

天順

1457-64 T'ien-shun ....Scarce

成化

1465-87 Ch'eng-hua......................Scarce

弘治

1488-1505 Hung-chih 5.00

正德

1506-21 Cheng-te ....Scarce

嘉靖

1522-66 Chia-ching 5.00

隆慶

1567-72 Lung-ch'ing 25.00

萬歷

1573-1619 Wan-li 5.00

泰昌

1620 T'ai-ch'ang........................... 20.00

天啓

1621-27 T'ien-ch'i 6.00

崇禎

1628-44 Ch'ung-chen 6.00

Ch'ing (Manchu) Dynasty 1644-1911

1616-27 T'ien-ming, Manchu script 40.00

順治

1644-61 Shun-chih....................... 3.50

康熙

1662-1722 K'ang-hsi 1.50

雍正

1723-35 Yung-cheng..................... 3.50

乾隆

1736-95 Ch'ien-lung...................... .35

嘉慶

1796-1820 Chia-ch'ing 50

道光

1821-1850 Tao-kuang 40

咸豐

1851-61 Hsien-feng........................ 1.00

咸豐

1851-61 similar but large, 50 Cash, ... 25.00

祺祥

1861 Ch'i-hsiang................................. Rare

Virtually all known examples of the Ch'i-hsiang are counterfeit.

同治

1862-74 T'ung-chih 4.00

光緒

1875-1908 Kuang-hsu...................... 2.75
similar but machine struck .... .25

宣統

1908-11 Hsüan-t'ung 10.00

Republic 1911—
1912 2 Cash, Flags on rev. 15.00

For non-cast coinage see modern Asia.

JAPAN   F
708-14 Mon 1,750.00
759-65 Mon 925.00
765-70 Mon 825.00
1606 Mon 150.00
1626-1769 Mon 50
1739-1867 Mon (Iron) 4.00

	VF
ND (1768) 4 Mon rev. Curves	3.00
1707-09 10 Mon	20.00

(reduced)

1835-70 100 Mon, Oval	9.00
1853-65 Isshu Gin (Silver, small rectangle)	12.00
1832-58 Nishu Kin (Electrum, small rectangle)	25.00
1736-58 Koban (Gold, oval)	1,250.00

KOREA   F

1700s-1800s Mun	2.00
1679-1752 2 Mun	3.00

1883 5 Mun	5.00
1866 100 Mun	14.00
1882-83 2 Chon (Silver, enameled center	VF 300.00

ANNAM (Vietnam)   F

1342-69 1 Phan, Yü-tsung Wang	7.00
1655-61 1 Phan, Vinh-tho	6.00

ANNAM (Vietnam)   F

1739-66 1 Phan, Thien Minh	30.00
1740-87 1 Phan, Canh Hung	3.50
1788-92 1 Phan, Quang Trung	3.00
1792-1801 1 Phan, Canh Thinh	3.00
1802-20 1 Phan, Gia Long	2.75
1820-41 1 Phan, Minh Mang	2.00
1841-47 1 Phan, Thieu Tri	1.75
1848-83 6 Phan, Tu Duc	3.50
1883-84 1 Phan, Kien Phuc	50.00
1884-85 1 Phan, Ham Nghi	100.00
1885-88 1 Phan, Dong Khanh	7.50
1888-1907 10 Phan, Than Thai	1.25
1907-1916 10 Phan, Duy Tan	1.25
1916-25 1 Phan, Khai Dinh	15.00

same, machine struck	4.50
1926-45 10 Phan, Bao Dai	7.50

MALAYSIA   VF

Kelantan 1321 A.H. Pitis (Tin) Arabic inscription	5.00
Pahang, 1884-96 A.D. Cent (Tin) Chinese inscription / 1 C and Arabic inscription	75.00
Trengganu 1222 A.H. Pitis (Tin) Arabic inscription	40.00

THE AMERICAS

The images and symbolism that adorned the newly independent Latin American countries' coins in the early 1800s found their origins in the coinages of the early United States and the French Revolution. This was only natural. After all, most of these states had rejected monarchy in favor of a representative republican form of government, quite unusual on earth at the time. There were few examples of republican coinages on which to base theirs. The Unites States' was the closest, and its struggle showed that a colony can throw off its master's yoke. The French Republic had been the most important in terms of the development of political thought. Hence the first generations of Latin American coins were mostly dominated by female personifications of liberty, as well as symbols of liberty and prosperity such as the liberty cap and the cornucopia. This was not to the exclusion of real human portraiture. Haïti, the hemisphere's second oldest independent nation, Mexico and Brazil all established monarchies. These and many other countries depicted their heads of state, be it king or president, or the liberator Simon Bolivar. Almost all the new countries proudly displayed their new, distinctly American coats of arms.

If the primary inspiration for images was the United States and France, the primary source for the physical form and standard of the coinage was clearly Spain, the former colonizing power for most of the New World. Most countries retained a silver coin the size of the old Spanish milled dollar or eight real piece. Some even kept its division into pieces of eight. Many gold pieces were also struck on the old escudo standard as well. Many of the big bullion-exporting areas during colonial days continued to do so after independence, and the Mexican eight real peso was a favorite coin in the Orient until the early 1900s.

Latin American coinage proved to be far less stable than the old Spanish colonial coinage. Within a generation or two many of these new eight reales or pesos began to decline in weight or purity. Some were even replaced by copper emergency coins. By 1967 all Latin American and Caribbean counties had abandoned precious metal for all but bullion and commemorative coins.

Iconography remained fairly consistent throughout the 1800s. Some of the biggest changes in the imagery reflected the overthrow of the Haitian (1806, 1821, 1858), Mexican (1823, 1867), and Brazilian (1889) monarchies. The extremely diverse and creative allegories of Bolivian proclamation coins often incorporated books, buildings, crowds and dragons, as well as images of the presidents, who seemed to take power and be forced out with the vagaries of fate. Another change was the replacement of the screw press with steam powered machinery for the

manufacture of coinage, generally within the first 50 years of independence. As a transition to modern minting technology, many Latin American countries toward the end of the century contracted to have their coins struck in Paris, Brussels, Birmingham (England), or Waterbury (Connecticut). Improvements in local die engraving were spotty, however, and images usually varied from quaint to cartoonlike. European mints offered not only high-capacity machines capable of producing uniform coins, but expert die engraving as well.

New images began to appear toward the beginning of the twentieth century, along with new metals. Commemoratives were introduced, first in Colombia in 1892 to honor the 400th anniversary of Columbus' discovery of America. During the period before the 1950s, Brazil and Mexico were the only other countries to release commemorative coins. Late in the twentieth century most New World countries struck commemoratives, both for circulation and for sale to collectors at a premium. The flora and fauna depicted on many Caribbean and Central American coins have given them particular appeal to collectors. Many New World collectors' issues have been distributed in Europe and North America by marketing firms. Overdistribution, particularly in the case of Caribbean collector issues, caused a sharp drop in their market prices, and many can today be purchased at well below their original issue prices. Unknowingly, some collectors have further reduced the value of their holdings by discarding the original mint holders, which collector coins must remain in to maintain their maximum value.

One of the most fascinating aspects of Latin American numismatics is plantation or hacienda tokens. Some plantations were so large they allowed for company-run towns with exclusively company-run stores. Often the workers were paid with tokens issued by the plantation and good at these stores. They were usually simple, devoid of all but inscriptions and numbers, but form a valuable record of local history.

Specialized Books: Bruce, Colin R., *Standard Catalog of Mexican Coins,* Paper Money, Stocks, Bonds and Medals.

Burnett, Davis, *Bolivian Proclamation Coinage.*

Rulau, Russell, *Latin American Tokens.*

Known Counterfeits: Contemporary counterfeits of the early coppers of Brazil are quite common and actively collected. Cast counterfeits exist of Cuban 1915 10, 20 and 40 centavos and 1 Peso. A counterfeit of the 1928 Ecuador 1 Condor was struck with cast dies. Early Haitian silver coins were counterfeited at the time, but the counterfeits are collected along with the official issues. Contemporary counterfeits of Mexican cap-and-

rays 8 reales abound. Most are struck either nickel-silver (an alloy of copper, nickel and zinc, but no silver), or of a baser silver alloy. A partial list includes 1835PiJS, 1836ZsOM, 1840GJ, 1843MoML, 1894MoAm and 1904ZsFM (peso). Counterfeits of two and four reales of this type also exist. There are collector counterfeits of several of the Mexican revolutionary issues, and very dangerous counterfeits of some of the Mexican twentieth century bullion gold coins, the 1947 50 Peso in particular. Examine the latter carefully. A 1982 counterfeit Mexico silver onza is not dangerous due to its significant difference in style. It has been suggested that there are dangerous counterfeits of the 1889 Paraguay 1 Peso, but this is not certain. Another bullion piece, the Peru 1962 100 Soles have been the victim of a dangerous counterfeit of about 75 percent pure gold.

ARGENTINA   VF

Buenos Aires 1823 1 Decimo, Arms (C)......... 12.00
Buenos Aires 1844 2 Reales, Wreath /
    Wreath (C).. 11.50
Cordoba 1849 2 Reales, Castle / Sun (S)........ 30.00
Entre Rios 1867 1/2 Real, Arms (S).............. 150.00

La Plata 1826 2 Soles, Sun face / Arms (S)..... 25.00
1854 1 Centavo, Sun face (C) 15.00
1884 1 Centavo, Arms / Liberty head (C) 1.00
1897 10 Centavos, Head of Argentina /
    Wreath (S) 1.50
1903 5 Centavos, similar (CN) .... .50
1915 10 Centavos, similar (CN) 1.00
1926 20 Centavos, similar (CN) .... .50
1941 50 Centavos, similar (N) 1.00

Unc.

1957 1 Peso, similar (N clad Steel)...................... .85
1968 5 Pesos, Sailing ship (N clad Steel)............ .60
1973 1 Centavo, Head of Argentina / Olive
    branch (AL) .... .30
1985 5 Centavos, Wildcat (B) .... .60
1991 1000 Australes, 14 coats of arms / Globes
    and pillars (S) .... PF 40.00

Unc.

1997 1 Peso, Eva Peron (CN around B)............ 3.75
1994 50 Pesos, Three coats of arms /
    Book (G)...............................PF 255.00

BAHAMAS   Unc.

1974 1 Cent, Arms / Starfish (B)..........................40
1974 50 Cent, Arms / Swordfish (CN).............. 2.00
1994 5 Dollars, Arms / Gold course (S).....PF 45.00
1974 10 Dollars, Arms / Milo Butler (CN)..... 12.00

BARBADOS   Unc.

1973 5 Cents, Arms / Lighthouse (B) 35
1970 4 Dollars, Arms / Plant (CN)................... 4.50

1981 10 Dollars, Arms / Neptune (CN) 12.50
1994 50 Dollars, Arms / SIDS conference
    logo (G)................................PF 550.00

BELIZE   Unc.

1974 10 Cents, Arms / Hermit bird (CN).......... 2.00
1977 25 Cents, Arms / Motmot bird (CN)........ 2.00
1981 5 Dollars, Arms / Toucan (CN) 6.50
1982 100 Dollars, Arms / Kinkajou (G) 450.00

BOLIVIA   VF

1828 2 Soles, Bolivar / Tree between
    llamas (S)................................... 20.00
1831 8 Soles, similar (S) 45.00
1844 8 Scudos, Bolivar / Mountain (G) 650.00
1852 1 Sol, Victory or Fame blowing
    trumpet / Small temple (S) .... holed 18.00
1868 1/8th Melgarejo, Bust of Melgarejo /
    Dragon about to be beat by hand with
    club (S).................................... 25.00
1873 1 Boliviano, Arms / Wreath (S) 25.00
1883 5 Centavos, similar (CN, hole)................ 8.00

VF

1897 20 Centavos, similar (S) 5.00
1900 50 Centavos, similar (S) 9.50
1909 5 Centavos, Mountain scene / Caduceus
    (CN) 1.00
1935 10 Centavos, similar (CN) 1.00
1942 20 Centavos, similar (Zinc) 2.50

Unc.

1951 10 Bolivianos, Bolivar / Wreath (C)......... 3.50

1965 50 Centavos, Mountain scene (N clad
    Steel) 1.50
1979 200 Pesos Bolivianos, Arms / Children
    (S)....................................PF 17.50
1987 20 Centavos, Arms (Steel)........................ .75
1998 1 Boliviano, Arms / Bank emblem
    (S)....................................PF 65.00

(1876) 5 Centavos token of Daniel Quiroga, Cocha-
    bamba. Eagle-topped fountain (CN) 8.50

BRAZIL   VF

1823 20 Reis, Wreath / Arms (C)................... 12.50
1831 80 Reis, similar (C)................................ 10.00
1847 1200 Reis, similar (S) 175.00
1857 20,000 Reis, Pedro II / Arms (G) 260.00
1868 10 Reis, similar (C)................................ 2.00
1871 200 Reis, Arms / Value (CN)................... 1.50
1888 1000 Reis, Pedro II / Arms (S).............. 12.50
1896 100 Reis, Constellation (CN) 3.00
1900 400 Reis, Cross / Wreath (S) 25.00
1900 4000 Reis, Cabral with flag / Arms of
    Portugal and Brazil (S) 300.00

*Above two commemorate the 400th anniversary of
the discovery of Brazil.*

1918 50 Reis, Female bust r. (CN) .... .35

VF

1935 100 Reis, similar (CN) 1.00
1938 200 Reis, Maua / Locomotive (CN) 75
1937 300 Reis, Oswaldo Cruz / Lamp (CN) 1.00
1925 400 Reis, similar (CN) 1.75
1936 1000 Reis, Jose de Anchieta / Open
    book (ALB)................................. 1.00
1936 5,000 Reis, Dumont / Wing (S) 2.00
1922 10,000 Reis, Bust of Brazil / Arms
    (G) 400.00
1947 20 Centavos, Getulio Vargas (ALB)............15

Unc.

1953 1 Cruzeiro, Map of Brazil (ALB) 1.00

1961 2 Cruzeiros, Arms (AL) 1.00
1972 1 Cruzeiro, Two portraits / Map of Brazil
    (N) 1.65
1972 300 Cruzeiros, similar (G) 300.00
1980 5 Cruzeiros, Coffee (Steel) 75
1988 100 Cruzados, Child's portrait (Steel) 3.00
1992 500 Cruzeiros, Sea Turtle (Steel)................75

1993 5 Cruzeiros Reals, Two parrots (Steel)........60
1998 5 Centavos, Bust of Tiradentes
    (C plated Steel)................................25
(1995) 3 Reais, BC30 / Jerusalem Cross
    (S) .... PF 40.00

CENTRAL AMERICAN
REPUBLIC   VF

1842 1/4 Real, Mountains / Tree, no legends
    (S)... 9.00
1825 8 Reales, similar with legends (S) 50.00
1850 2 Escudos, similar (G)........................... 200.00

CHILE VF

1817 1 Peso, Volcano / Column (S) 650.00
1822 1 Peso, similar (S) 175.00
1834 1/2 Real, similar (S) 40.00
1848 2 Reales, Condor / Arms (S) 8.00
1851 1 Centavo, Star / Wreath (C) 12.50
1861 1/2 Decimo, Condor flying / Wreath
  (S) 10.00
1879 1 Decimo, Condor with shield / Wreath
  (S) 2.00
1883 1 Peso, Condor with shield / Arms (S) .. 12.00
1892 10 Pesos, Arms / Chile stg. (G) 235.00
1904 1 Centavo, Bust / Wreath (C) 2.00
1915 5 Centavos, Condor / Wreath (S) 3.00
1922 20 Centavos, similar (CN) 75
1933 1 Peso, similar (CN) 50
ND 1 Peso token. Oficina Aguado (Red
  vulcanite) 10.00

Unc.

1946 100 Pesos, Female bust l. / Arms (G) 300.00

1967 10 Centavos, Condor (ALB) 1.00
1975 1 Peso, O'Higgins (CN) 25
1980 5 Pesos, Liberty breaking chains (CN) 2.00
1995 100 Pesos, Arms (ALB) 2.50

COLOMBIA VF

1820 1/4 Real, Liberty cap / Pomegranate
  (S) 60.00
1831 1 Real, Fasces between two cornucopias /
  Wreath (S) 17.50
1842 2 Reales, "Nueva Granada" and bird over cor-
  nucopia / Wreath (S) 55.00
1855 1 Decimo, Pomegranate between two cornu-
  copias / Wreath (S) 8.00
1864 1/2 Decimo, Pomegranate / BOGOTA and
  stars (S) 9.50
1874 2 Decimos, Liberty head / Arms (S) 11.50
1881 2-1/2 Centavos, Liberty cap (CN) 25
1897 10 Centavos, Liberty head / Arms (S) 1.50
1918 1 Centavo, Liberty bust (CN) 12.00
1921 2 Centavos, similar (CN) 75
1935 5 Centavos, similar (CN) 1.50
1942 10 Centavos, Bolivar / Arms (S) 1.25
(1839-40) 1 Mitad token of Manuel Angulo,
  Cannon / Logo (C) 100.00

Unc.

1970 20 Centavos, Santander (N clad Steel) 20
1965 50 Centavos, Gaitan / Arms (CN) 60
1956 1 Peso, Old mint doors / Arms (S) 22.50
1918 5 Pesos, Stone cutter / Arms (G) 125.00
1981 10 Pesos, Equestrian statue / Map
  (CNZ) 1.25
1993 500 Pesos, Tree (CN around ALB) 3.25

COSTA RICA VF

1847 1 Real, Tree / Bust (S) 15.00
1855 1/8th Peso, Arms / Tree (S) 22.50
1875 25 Centavos, similar (S) 18.00

1899 20 Colones, Arms / Columbus (G) 225.00
1903 2 Centimos (CN) 1.00
1936 5 Centimos, Arms / Wreath (B) 75
1948 25 Centimos, similar (CN) 20
1954 1 Colon, similar (Steel) 35

Unc.

1970 5 Colones, Arms / Renaissance portrait
  (S) ....PF 12.50
1974 50 Colones, Arms / Sea Turtle (S) 16.50
1997 50 Colones, Arms (B) 2.50

CUBA VF

1916 2 Centavos, Arms / Star (CN) 1.25
1943 5 Centavos, similar (B) 1.00
1915 10 Centavos, similar (S) 4.00
1920 20 Centavos, similar (S) 3.00
1952 40 Centavos, Lighthouse and flag / Tree
  growing through wheel (S) 2.50
1953 50 Centavos, Jose Marti / Scroll (S) 2.50
1932 1 Peso, Arms / Star (S) 9.00
1916 2 Pesos, Jose Marti / Arms (G) 70.00
1916 10 Pesos, similar (G) 200.00

Unc.

1963 1 Centavo, Arms / Star (AL) 60
1972 20 Centavos, similar (AL) 3.00
1982 1 Peso, Don Quixote and Sancho Panza /
  Arms (CN) 8.00
1990 3 Pesos, Che Guevara / Arms (CN) 6.00
1993 20 Pesos, Fidel Castro / Arms (S) ..... PF 90.00

DOMINICAN REPUBLIC VF

1844 1/4 Real, Value (B) 8.50

1877 5 Centavos, Book (CN) 20.00
1888 21/2 Centavos, Arms (CN) 2.00
1897 20 Centavos, Arms / Indian head
  (Billon) 7.50
1937 1 Centavo, Arms / Palm tree (C) 1.50
1942 10 Centavos, Arms / Indian head (S) 2.00
1956 25 Centavos, similar (S) 2.50

Unc.

1955 1 Peso, Arms / Trujillo (S) 25.00
1984 1 Centavo, Arms / Caonabo (C plated
  Zinc) 25
1967 1/2 Peso, similar (CN) 1.50
1976 1 Peso, Arms / Duarte (CN) 2.00
1983 1 Peso, Arms / Three portraits (CN,
  polygonal) 2.50
1979 100 Pesos, Arms / Pope (G) 160.00

ECUADOR VF

1834 1 Real, Fasces between two cornucopias /
  Sun over two mountains (S) 60.00

1849 2 Reales, Liberty as on 1830s United
  States coin / Arms (S) 65.00
1855 8 Escudos, Bolivar / Arms (G) 1,750.00
1886 1/2 Decimo, Arms (CN) 16.50
1893 1 Decimo, Sucre / Arms (S) 1.75
1909 1 Centavo, Arms / Wreath (CN) 7.50
1912 1/2 Decimo, Sucre / Arms (S) 1.25
1928 10 Centavos, Arms / Bust (N) 1.00
1937 20 Centavos, Arms / Wreath (N) 50
1928 50 Centavos, Sucre / Arms (S) 2.00

Unc.

1928 1 Condor, Bust / Arms (G) 350.00
1943 5 Sucres, Sucre / Arms (S) 10.00
1964 10 Centavos, Arms / Wreath (N clad
  Steel) 50
1979 50 Centavos, similar (N clad Steel) 50
1988 1 Sucre, Arms / Sucre (N clad Steel) 40
1991 10 Sucres, Arms / Ancient sculpture
  (N clad Steel) 1.00

EL SALVADOR   VF

1828 2 Reales, Pillar / Mountain (S) 165.00
1835 1 Real, similar (S) 275.00
1889 1 Centavo, Morazán (CN) 3.00
1892 50 Centavos, Arms / Flags with hands
  (S) 50.00
1908 1 Peso, Arms / Columbus (S) 10.00
1914 5 Centavos, Arms / Wreath (S) 3.00
1942 1 Centavo, Morazán (C) 50
1951 10 Centavos, similar (CN) 1.50
1953 20 Centavos, Priest l. / Wreath (S) 1.00

1800s Token of Finca (Plantation) San Luis (N
  plated Z) 10.00

Unc.

1976 1 Centavo, Morazán (B) 20
1970 50 Centavos, similar (N) 60
1988 1 Colon, Columbus (Steel) 2.25
1992 2500 Colones, Four interlocking hands
  (G) 375.00

GUATEMALA   VF

1829 1 Real, Sun over five mountains / Tree
  (S) 225.00
1859 1/2 Real, Carrera / Arms (S) 30.00
1861 4 Reales, Carrera / Wreath (G) 30.00
1874 1 Real, Shield / Wreath (S) 16.50
1880 1/2 Real, Guatemala std. / Scroll, wreath
  and rifles (S) 4.50
1895 2 Reales, similar (S) 4.50

VF

(1893-97) 1 Dia token of Las Camelias (AL,
  triangular) 17.50
1900 1/4 Real, Mountains / Wreath (CN) .... .35
1915 12-1/2 Centavos (C) 1.25
1923 5 Pesos, Barrios (B) 2.75
1932 1 Centavo, Arms (B) 1.00
1949 5 Centavos, Arms / Tree (S) 1.50
1958 10 Centavos, Arms / Monolith (S) 1.25

Unc.

1963 25 Centavos, Arms / Female portrait (S).. 5.55
1978 25 Centavos, similar (CN) 85
1992 1 Quetzal, Arms / Carlos Merida (S) ... PF 50.00

HAÏTI   VF

1807 15 Sols, Liberty / Arms (S) 125.00

1814 (year 11) 12 Centimes, Snake grasping tail /
  Arms (S) 30.00
1827 (year 24) 25 Centimes, President Boyer /
  Arms (S) 15.00
1831 (year 28) 50 Centimes, similar (S) 18.00
1846 1 Centime, Wreath / Fasces (C) 3.00
1850 61/4 Centimes, Emperor Faustin / Arms
  (C) 7.50
1863 10 Centimes, President Geffrard / Arms
  (C) 4.50

1905 5 Centime, Pedro Nord-Axesis/Arms
  (CN) 1.00
1881 1 Centime, Head of Haïti / Arms (C) 3.50
1906 10 Centimes, Pedro Nord-Alexis / Arms
  (CN) 1.50
1949 10 Centimes, Dumarsais Estime / Arms
  (CN) 25

Unc.

1953 10 Centimes, Paul Magliore / Arms
  (CNZ) 1.25
1970 20 Centimes, Francois Duvalier / Arms
  (CN) 80
1981 50 Centimes, Jean-Claude Duvalier / Plant
  (CN) 1.50
1986 50 Centimes, Peralte / Arms (CN) 1.00
1995 1 Gourde, Fortress / Arms (ALB) 1.75
1970 40 Gourdes, Emperor Dessalines / Arms
  (G) ....PF 220.00

HONDURAS   F

1832 1 Real, Sun over five mountains / Tree
  (33% silver) 22.50
1845 2 Reales, similar (20% silver) 15.00
1854 4 Reales, similar (4% silver) 10.00
1862 1 Peso, Pyramid / Tree (C) 7.50
1871 25 Centavos, Arms / Tree (S) 5.50
ca.1880 Ceiba municipal token, Star (B) 500.00

VF

1884 50 Centavos, Femal stg. with book / Arms
  (S) 15.00
1892 1 Peso, similar (S) 45.00
1907 1 Centavo, Pyramid (C) 1.50
1912 2 Centavos, Pyramid (C) 2.50
1922 1 Peso, Liberty head / Arms (G) 250.00
1939 1 Centavo, Arms (C) 50
1949 2 Centavos, Arms (C) 25
1934 1 Lempira, Arms / Indian (S) 3.50

Unc.

1956 5 Centavos, Arms (CN) 60

1967 50 Centavos, Arms / Indian (CN) 1.25
1978 50 Centavos, Arms / Indian (CN) 1.00
1992 100 Lempiras, Arms / Sailing ship
  (S) .... PF 60.00
1992 500 Lempiras, Arms / Morazan
  (G) .... PF 240.00

JAMAICA   Unc.

1969 1 Cent, Arms / Ackee fruit (C) 25
1977 10 Cents, Arms / Butterfly on plant (CN) ..40
1982 25 Cents, Arms / Hummingbird (CN) 1.00

1976 50 Cents, Marcus Garvey / Arms (CN,
  polygonal) 1.50
1972 10 Dollars, Bustamante and Manley / Arms
  (S) 10.00
1995 25 Dollars, Parrots / Arms (S) .... PF 50.00
1995 50 Dollars, Bob Marley / Arms (S) .. PF 45.00

(reduced)

MEXICO, Pre-Columbian — Circ.

1500s Mushroom-shaped or T-shaped, thin copper sheet with upturned edge. Usually 4-5" high by 6" wide... 85.00

1500s Chisel-shaped, thin copper sheet with unfinished edge. Usually 7" high by 2" wide.... 25.00

MEXICO, Local Copper — F

Chiapas 1911 Token of Guatimoc Plantation, Coffee plant (B) 7.00

Chihuahua 1835 1/4 Real, Indian / Wreath (C) 12.00

Colima 1830 1 Octavo, Inscription (C)........... 25.00

Durango 1852 1/8th Real, Eagle / Large 8o (C) 8.00

Guanajuato 1856 1 Quartilla, Eagle / Hands about to strike coin (C) 11.00

Jalisco 1860 1/2 Octavo, Flag, bow and quiver / Liberty std. (C) 10.00

San Luiz Potosi 1828 1/4 Real, Book / Std. figure (C) 6.75

Sinaloa 1866 1/4 Real, Liberty head in wreath / Wreath (C) 4.00

Sonora 1835 Cuartillo, Two quivers / Cap and rays (C) 11.00

Tacambaro ND 1/8th Real, Caduceus (C)....... 25.00

Zacatecas 1853 1 Quartilla, Monument / Cherub (B) 8.00

MEXICO — VF

1822 1/2 Real, Emperor Augustin I / Eagle (S)... 25.00

	VF
1823 2 Reales, similar (S)..............................	45.00
1824 2 Reales, Hook neck eagle / Cap and rays (S)...	50.00
1830 1/8th Real, Eagle / Wreath (C)	5.00
1842 1/8th Real, Liberty std. / Wreath (C)......	10.00
1847 1/4 Real, Liberty head (S).......................	4.00
1852 1/2 Real, Eagle / Cap and rays (S)...........	5.00
1858 1 Real, similar (S)...................................	6.00
1862 2 Reales, similar (S)................................	10.00
1869 4 Reales, similar (S)................................	30.00

1893 8 Reales, similar (S)................................	12.00
1840 1/2 Escudo, Eagle / Hand holding liberty cap and pointing to book (G)	60.00
1856 1 Escudo, similar (G).............................	100.00
1868 2 Escudos, similar (G)	200.00
1829 4 Escudos, similar (G)	450.00
1839 8 Escudos, similar (G)	500.00

Empire of Maximilian — VF

1864 1 Centavo, Eagle / Wreath (C)................	60.00
1864 5 Centavos, similar (S)............................	20.00
1864 10 Centavos, similar (S)	25.00
1866 50 Centavos, Head r. / Arms (S).............	95.00

	VF
1866 1 Peso, Head r. / Arms with supporters (S)...	45.00
1866 20 Pesos, similar (G)............................	800.00

Republic Decimal Coinage — VF

1863 1 Centavo, Liberty std. / Wreath (C)	18.00
1886 1 Centavo, Eagle / Wreath (C)................	2.00
1883 1 Centavo, Bow and quiver / Wreath (CN)..	.75
1900 1 Centavo, Eagle / 1 over ¢ (C)................	4.00
1883 2 Centavos, Bow and quiver / Wreath (CN)..	.75
1867 5 Centavos, Eagle / Cap and rays (S)	40.00
1888 5 Centavos, Eagle / Wreath (S)................	2.50
1882 5 Centavos, Bow and quiver / Wreath (CN)..	1.00
1868 10 Centavos, Eagle / Cap and rays (S) ...	40.00
1891 10 Centavos, Eagle / Wreath (S).............	3.00
1898 20 Centavos, similar (S).........................	8.00

1884 25 Centavos, Eagle / Scroll, cap and balance scale (S)..	20.00
1878 50 Centavos, similar (S).........................	25.00
1872 1 Peso, similar (S)	20.00
1898 1 Peso, Eagle / Cap and rays (S).............	10.00
1870 1 Peso, Eagle / Wreath (G)	60.00
1889 2 1/2 Pesos, similar (G)..........................	300.00
1900 5 Pesos, Eagle / Scroll, cap and balance scale (G)	300.00
1889 10 Pesos, similar (G)............................	500.00
1891 20 Pesos, similar (G)............................	600.00

Estados Unidos — XF

1906 1 Centavo, Eagle / 1 over ¢ (C)..................	.75
1915 2 Centavos, Eagle / 2 over ¢ (C).............	13.50
1927 5 Centavos, Eagle / 5 over ¢ (C)...............	6.75
1936 10 Centavos, Eagle / Value in Aztec border (CN)..	.65
1942 20 Centavos, Eagle / Cap and rays (S)	2.00

1950 50 Centavos, Eagle / Realistic portrait of Cuauhtemoc (Billon) 1.80

1956 50 Centavos, Eagle / Stylized portrait of Cuauhtemoc (C)... 1.00

Unc.

1961 1 Peso, Morelos / Eagle (Billon) 2.25

Unc.

1921 2 Pesos, Eagle / Independence winged
(S)...................................... XF 55.00
1948 5 Pesos, Eagle / Stylized portrait of
Cuauhtemoc (S).......................... 8.00
1959 (1959-72) 10 Pesos, Eagle / Hidalgo
(G,.24 oz. net)................... bullion + 7%
1960 10 Pesos, Eagle / Hidalgo and Madero
(S).. 9.00
1980 20 Pesos, Eagle / Mayan figure (CN)....... 2.50
1968 25 Pesos, Eagle / Aztec playing ball (S).. 4.75

1947 (1947-72) 50 Pesos, Eagle / Winged Independence (G, 1.2 oz. net.) .... bullion + 3%
1977 100 Pesos, Eagle / Morelos (S) 6.00
1985 200 Pesos, Eagle / Four revolutionaries
(CN) 3.25
1985 250 Pesos, Eagle / Soccer ball (G)....... 100.00
1987 500 Pesos, Eagle / Madero (CN)............. 2.00
1992 1000 Pesos, Eagle / Juana de Asbaje
(ALB).. 2.25
1986 2000 Pesos, Eagle / Soccer (G)........... 900.00
1988 5000 Pesos, Eagle / Monument (CN) 7.75
New Pesos
1992 5 Centavos, Eagle (Steel) 25
1993 10 Centavos, Eagle (Steel) 25
1994 20 Centavos, Eagle / Wreath (ALB) 35
1995 50 Centavos, Eagle (ALB) 75
1996 1 New Peso, Eagle (Steel around ALB)... 1.25
1997 2 Pesos, Eagle / Symbols around border
(Steel around ALB) 2.35
1992 5 New Pesos, Eagle (steel around
ALB)... 4.00

Unc.

1993 10 New Pesos, Eagle / Aztec Image
(ALB around S) 8.50
1994 20 New Pesos, Eagle / Hidalgo (ALB around
S).. 13.50
1995 50 New Pesos, Eagle / "Niños Heroes"
(ALB around S) 26.50
Bullion Issues
1991- 1/20 oz., Eagle / Winged Independence
(S).. 2.45
1991- 1/10 oz., similar (S) 2.55
1991- 1/4 oz., similar (S) 4.50
1991- 1/2 oz., similar (S) 6.00
1949 1 oz., Coining press / Balance scale
(S).. 17.50
1978-80 1 oz., similar (S) 6.76

1982- 1 oz., Eagle / Winged Independence
(S).. 8.00
1996- 2 oz., similar (S) 22.00
1996- 5 oz., similar (S) 45.00
1987- 1/20 oz., Eagle / Winged Independence
(G) .... bullion + 30%
1987 1/15 oz., similar (G)................. bullion + 25%
1991-93 1/10 oz., similar (G) .... bullion + 20%
1981-93 1/4 oz., similar (G) .... bullion + 11%
1981-93 1/2 oz., similar (G) .... bullion + 8%
1981-93 1 oz., similar (G)................... bullion + 3%
1943 1.2057 oz., similar (G)........................ 525.00
1989 1/4 oz., similar (Platinum) ....PF 240.00

Revolutionary Issues   VF

Aguascalientes 1915 20 Centavos, Eagle / Cap and
rays (C)... 9.00
Atlixtac 1915 10 Centavos, Eagle / Wreath
(C) 6.50
Chihuahua 1915 5 Centavos, Cap and rays / 5 over
¢ (C) 3.50

Durango 1914 1 Centavo, Date / Wreath
(C) 35.00
Jalisco 1915 2 Centavos, Cap and rays / 2 over ¢
(C) 17.50

VF

Oaxaca 1915 1 Centavo, Inscription
(C, rectangular) 125.00
Oaxaca 1915 5 Centavos, Juarez (C) 4.50
Puebla 1915 10 Centavos, Eagle / X over C
(C)... 17.50
Sinaloa 1915 20 Centavos, Eagle / Value
(S, cast)... Rare

NICARAGUA   VF

1800s Token of Hacienda Elvira, Tree (CN) ... 30.00
1878 1 Centavo, Arms / Wreath (CN) 6.00
1887 10 Centavos, similar (S).......................... 2.50
1899 5 Centavos, similar (CN) 1.50
1912 1/2 Centavo, Triangular arms / Wreath
(C).. 2.50
1928 1 Centavos, similar (C) 4.00
1936 5 Centavos, similar (CN) 1.00

1936 10 Centavos, Francisco Hernandez de
Cordoba / Sun over five mountains (S) 2.00
1946 25 Centavos, similar (CN) 50

Unc.

1954 50 Centavos, similar (CN) 5.00
1972 1 Cordoba, similar (CN) 4.00
1967 50 Cordobas, Triangular arms / Ruben Dario
(G) 450.00

1975 50 Cordobas, similar / USA's Liberty bell
(S).. 21.50
1974 5 Centavos, Triangular arms (AL).............50
1981 50 Centavos, Sandino (CN) 1.75
1987 5 Cordobas, Sandino's hat (ALB) 4.00
1994 10 Centavos, Triangular arms / Dove flying
over Nicaragua (Steel) 75
1997 1 Cordoba, Triangular arms (N clad
Steel)... 2.50

PANAMA   VF

1907 1/2 Centesimo, Balboa (CN) 1.00

1904 21/2 Centesimos, Balboa / Arms (S) Popularly
called the "Panama Pill" 3.50
1904 5 Centesimos, Balboa / Arms (S) 5.00
1929 21/2 Centesimos, Balboa (CN)................. 3.50
1930 1/10th Balboa, Arms / Balboa (S) 3.00
1947 1/4 Balboa, similar (S) 2.00

Unc.

1953 1 Centesimo, Uracca (C) 3.00
1966 1/10th Balboa, Arms / Balboa
    (CN clad C)....................................1.00

Unc.

1971 1/2 Balboa, similar (CN clad C).......... PF 3.00
1970 5 Balboas, Discus thrower / Arms (S)...... 7.50
1982 20 Balboas, Balboa up to knees in water /
    Arms (S) ....PF 110.00
1983 500 Balboas, Butterfly / Arms
    (G, scalloped) 800.00

PARAGUAY   VF

1903 5 Centavos, Lion (CN) 2.00
1925 50 Centavos, Star (CN)........................... 1.50
1938 2 Pesos, Star (AL)................................... 1.50

Unc.

1947 5 Centimos, Passion flower (ALB) 1.00

1953 25 Centimos, Liou/Wreath (ALB,
    Scalloped) 75
1953 50 Centimos, Lion / Wreath
    (ALB, scalloped) 75
1975 5 Guaranies, Woman with Jar (Steel)...........50
1988 50 Guaranies, Estigarribia / Dam (Steel) . 1.00
1974 150 Guaranies, Einstein / Arms (S) .... PF 85.00
1968 300 Guaranies, Stroessner / Lion (S) 8.50
1997 500 Guaranies, Caballero / Bank building
    (B) 2.50

PERU   VF

1826 1/4 Real, Llama (S)................................. 14.00
1833 1/2 Real, Arms / Liberty stg. (S) 6.00
(ca.1860s) 1/2 Real token of Hotel of Commerce,
    Trujillo. Chicken on plate / Wreath
    (C) ....Scarce
1849 2 Reales, similar (S) 15.00

PERU   VF

1854 4 Reales, similar (S)................................ 25.00
1863 1 Centavo, Sun / Two cornucopias (CN) 2.50
1876 2 Centavos, similar (C) 3.00
1888 1/5th Sol, Arms / Peru std. (S).................. 3.50
1891 1 Sol, similar (S) 7.00
1901 1 Centavo, Sun / Two cornucopias (C)..... 2.50
1919 2 Centavos, similar (C) 75
1921 10 Centavos, Head of Peru / Fern branch
    (CN) 75
1945 10 Centavos, similar (B) 50
1935 1/2 Sol, Arms / Peru std. (S) 2.50
1951 1 Sol, Arms (B)..50

Unc.

1966 1 Sol, Arms / Llama (B) 60
1972 10 Soles, Arms / Tupac Amaru (CN) 1.25
1962 100 Soles, Arms / Peru std. (G)............ 650.00
1984 100 Soles, Adm. Grau (B) 1.00
1987 1 Inti, Arms / Adm. Grau (CN) 75
1991 5 Centavos, Arms (B) 45
1996 1 Nuevo Sol, Miner and oil derrick / Arms
    (S) 30.00
1994 5 Nuevos Soles, Arms / Bird (Steel
    around B) 6.50
1926 1 Libra, Arms Indian (G)...................... 160.00

TRINIDAD & TOBAGO   Unc.

1966 1 Cent, Arms (C)..15
1971 10 Cents, Arms (CN) 30

Unc.

1976 5 Dollars, Arms / Ibis (S)........................ 25.00
1982 10 Dollars, Arms / Flag (CN) 15.00
1994 10 Dollars, Arms / Bird (S).............. PF 47.50
1984 200 Dollars, Arms / Bank building
    (G) .... PF 115.00

URUGUAY   VF

1844 1 Peso, Arms (S) 350.00
1857 5 Centesimos, Sunface / Wreath (C0)...... 12.00
1869 1 Centesimo, similar (C)........................... 2.00

URUGUAY   VF

1877 10 Centesimos, Arms / Wreath (S)........... 6.00
1895 1 Peso, similar (S) 25.00
1901 1 Centesimo, Sun (CN)..............................75
1924 2 Centesimos, Sun (CN) 1.00
1936 5 Centavos, Sun (CN) 1.00
1930 10 Centesimos, Head of Uruguay / Couger
    (ALB) 2.50
1917 50 Centesimos, Arms / Artigas (S)........... 7.00
1942 1 Peso, Artigas / Couger (S) 2.25
early 1900s 10 Centesimos token of Villegas Bros.
    Vinyard, Carmelo (B) 10.00

Unc.

1953 10 Centesimos, Artigas (CN)......................75
1965 1 Peso, Artigas / Arms (ALB) 60
1961 10 Pesos, Gaucho / Wreath (S)................ 7.00

1977 5 Centesimos, Bull (AL)..............................45

Unc.

1981 2 Nuevos Pesos, Five ears of grain
(CNZ).. 1.00
1989 100 Nuevos Pesos, Gaucho (Steel) 75
1994 2 Pesos Urugayos, Artigas (B) 1.50

VENEZUELA　　　　　　　　　　F

Guaiana 1814 1/2 Real, Castle / Lion (C) 25.00
1822 1/4 Real, Star around "19" (S) 275.00
1830 1/4 Real, Cornucopia / Wreath (S)......... 38.50
1843 1/4 Centavo, Liberty head / Wreath (C)... 7.50
1858 1 Centavo, similar (C) 6.00
1863 10 Reales, Esclarecido / Wreath (S).........Rare
1876 1 Centavo, Arms / Wreath (CN) 6.00
1886 1/2 Bolivar, Bolivar / Arms (S) 20.00
1893 1 Bolivar, similar (S) 12.00

VF

1858 1 Real token of J.B. Hellyer, Allegator
(C) 45.00
1887 1 Real token of F.B. Leon (CN) 70.00

1921 5 Centimos, Arms (CN)............................ 2.00
1938 12 1/2 Centimos, Arms (CN) .... .30
1929 1/4 Bolivar, Bolivar / Arms (S)..................75
1935 1/2 Bolivar, similar (S)...............................75
1911 1 Bolivar, similar (S)................................ 5.00
1954 1 Bolivar, similar (S)................................ 1.25

1945 2 Bolivares, similar (S) 2.00
1902 5 Bolivares, similar (S) 16.00
1936 5 Bolivares, similar (S) 11.50
1912 20 Bolivares, similar (G) 70.00

Unc.

1983 5 Centimos, Arms (N clad Steel)................10
1977 25 Centimos, Bolivar / Arms (N) 20
1977 1 Bolivar, similar (N) 75
1973 10 Bolivares, Bolivar in rounded rectangle /
Arms in rounded rectangle (S) ....PF 11.50
1975 50 Bolivares, Arms / Armadillo (S) 25.00
1980 75 Bolivares, Sucre / Donkey running
(S).. 12.50

1983 100 Bolivares, Bolivar standing/ Building
(S) .... PF 13.50
1975 500 Bolivares, Bolivar in rounded rectangle /
Oil wells in rounded rectangle (G) 10,000.00
1990 500 Bolivares, Jose Paez / Arms
(S) .... PF 25.00

WORLD PAPER MONEY

Paper money was created to make several things possible. The original reason for the invention of paper money in China in the 1200s was to permit the government to spend an increased amount of money without having to incur the expense of that value. Such deficit financing has, over the last few centuries, been the cause for hundreds of countries printing billions of pieces of paper money. Most governments have had the ability to force their citizens to accept their paper money through coercion, but they have not always had to. Historically, most governments' notes have been backed up by full or partial reserves of precious metal, and such notes have been able to be redeemed for that bullion under specified conditions. This has been less and less the case over the past thirty or so years. There are also advantages to the general public in the use of paper money. It permits the convenient transportation of a fixed amount of value. Because it is physically small, it is also easier to hide, therefore making such transportation and storage not only more convenient, but also more secure. Unfortunately, when a government that has issued paper money is overthrown, its paper, unlike its precious metal coins, often becomes worthless. Many countries even declare their own paper money obsolete every ten or twenty years as a matter of course.

There are no surviving examples of the first paper, issued in China 700 years ago, but specimens are known of notes printed on Mulberry bark paper in the 1300s during the Ming dynasty. The first European notes were printed in France in the 1600s when the King of France wished to raise funds without having to part with gold or silver bullion. It was at that time a failure, and it wasn't until over a century later that paper money became accepted in any serious way by any European population. This was during the French Revolution, when the government printed assignats backed up by confiscated Church property.

Because of the potential for counterfeiting, most paper money is made with a number of deterrents incorporated, all of which are intended to make reproduction difficult. Many of these devices have recently been incorporated into United States paper money and are explained in that section. Several countries have even considered replacing paper (actually combinations of paper and cloth) with plastic notes. Australia has circulated these plastic notes for years with great success. Multicolored inks and intricately engraved designs might be used to thwart counterfeiters, but they have had the secondary result of encouraging collecting.

Over the last decade the market for collectible paper money has been very strong. Many prices have increased and at shows, over-the-counter sales are far more brisk than they were a decade ago. Like coins, the value of a piece of paper money varies based on its state of preservation. The proper handling and grading of world paper is similar to that for United States paper, and the reader should refer to the discussion in that section. The nature of paper money design admits of extremely minute differences in details between varieties. The dates of the notes listed below are the series or law dates appearing on the notes themselves. However, dates appearing on paper money are not necessarily the actual dates of printing, which often can only be identified by an analysis of the signatures printed on the notes. A book such as this can do no more than simply introduce the collector to this aesthetically pleasurable hobby. Thus it is particularly important for anyone interested in collecting world paper money to acquire one or more of the excellent specialized books listed below.

Illustrations: Illustrations shown here are not to actual size. A typical piece of world paper money will usually range from 4" to 6" on its side. Notes that are longer or shorter than this length will be noted in the text as either "Large" or "Small."

Specialized Books:

Bruce, Colin R. II, ed., *Standard Catalog of World Paper Money, Specialized Issues*.

Bruce, Colin R. II, and Shafer, Neil, eds., *Standard Catalog of World Paper Money, Modern Issues*.

Monetary Research Institute, *MRI Bankers' Guide to Foreign Currency*.
Pick, Albert, *Standard Catalog of World Paper Money*, General Issues.

Known Counterfeits: Good counterfeits of British notes were made during World War II by the Germans. Many counterfeits are not made with the same process as the real notes they imitate. Often, counterfeits lack the precise detail of the originals. Notes of significant value should be authenticated by an expert.

ALBANIA	F
(1926) 5 Franka Ari, Boy in fez	20.00
(1939) 20 Franga, Roma std.	7.00

	Unc.
1957 10 Leke, Arms	2.00
1964 1 Lek, Peasant couple / Mountain fortress	1.50
1976 5 Leke, Bridge / Freighter ship	1.50
1992 1000 Leke, Skanderbeg / Arms and tower	22.50

ANGOLA	VF
1861 1000 Reis, Portuguese Arms	Rare
1921 1 Escudo, Francisco de Oliveira Chamico and steamship / Woman looking out at ships	20.00
1956 20 Escudos, Porto r. / Gazelle running	4.00

	Unc
1962 20 Escudos, Dock / Gazelles running	17.50
1976 100 Kwanzas, Antonio Neto / Agricultural workers	7.50
1995 1000 Kwanzas Reajustados, Jose Dos Santos and Antonio Neto / Antelope	4.00

ARGENTINA	F
1884 5 Centavos, Avellanda	15.00
(1900-02) 1 Peso, Argentina std.	110.00

	Unc.
(1935) 1 Peso, Argentina std.	4.00
(1960) 5 Pesos, Young Jose de San Martin / People in plaza	5.00
(1983-84) 1 Peso Argentino, Old Jose de San Martin / Mountain lake	.20

(1990) 500,000 Australes, M. Quintana / Progress std. with torch	75.00

AUSTRALIA	VF
(1923) 1 Pound, George V	700.00
(1938-52) 1 Pound, George VI / Shepards and sheep	10.00

	Unc.
(1961-65) 10 Shillings, M. Flinders / Parliament building	40.00

	Unc.
(1974-83) 1 Dollar, Elizabeth II / Aboriginal art	2.00
(1994-) 20 Dollars, Biplane and Rev. J. Flynn / Sailing ship and M. Reiby	24.00

AUSTRIA F

1759 10 Gulden, Inscriptions	Rare
1847 100 Gulden, Austria, Atlas and Minerva	600.00
1858 100 Gulden, Austria l., Danube r.	450.00
1880 100 Gulden, Boys with sheaf and book	160.00

	VF
(1919) 1000 Kronen, Imperial eagle, female bust r.	.75
1927 10 Schilling, Mercury / Harvest	10.00
1936 100 Schilling, Woman with Edelweiss	350.00
1945 10 Schilling, Woman / Mountain	1.00

	Unc.
1956 20 Schilling, A. von Welsbach / Mountain village	15.00
1967 20 Schilling, C. Ritter von Ghega / Railway bridge over Semmering Pass	4.50
1986 20 Schilling, M. Daffinger / Albertina Museum, Vienna	3.25
1988 5000 Schilling, Wolfgang A. Mozart / Opera House, Vienna	475.00

BAHAMAS VF

1870s Bank of Nassau 5 Shillings, Victoria I	Scarce
1919 1 Pound, George V and ship	500.00
1936 4 Shillings, George VI and ship	40.00
(1953) 4 Shillings, Elizabeth II and ship	7.50

	Unc.
1965 1/2 Dollar, Elizabeth II / Underwater scene of fish	7.00
1974 1/2 Dollar, Elizabeth II / Smiling woman at market	1.50
1996 100 Dollars, Elizabeth II / Swordfish	170.00

BELGIUM VF

1851-52 100 Francs, Two cherubs	Rare
1910-20 20 Francs, Minerva and lion	12.00

1919 1000 Francs, Allegorical figures	300.00

BELGIUM VF

1927-32 100 Francs, Albert and Elizabeth	2.50
1952-59 100 Francs, Leopold I	5.50

	Unc.
1964 20 Francs, King Baudouin / Molecule	2.00
(1978-81) 100 Francs, H. Beyaert / Geometric design	10.00
(1995-) 100 Francs, J. Ensor and theatrical masks / Beach scene	4.50

BERMUDA F

1914 1 Pound, Arms	1,750.00
1920-35 5 Shillings, George V / Ship	800.00

	VF
1937 5 Shillings, George VI and Hamilton harbor	40.00
1952-57 5 Shillings, Elizabeth II and Hamilton harbor	7.50

	Unc.
1970 1 Dollar, Elizabeth II / Two sailboats	18.00

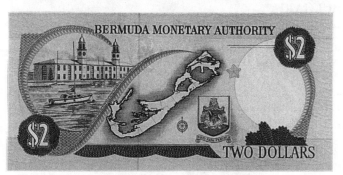

1988 2 Dollars, Elizabeth II / Two towered building and map	5.00
1996 100 Dollars, Elizabeth II / House of Assembly	160.00

BOLIVIA VF

1902 1 Boliviano, Arms and Vegitation	5.00
1928 1 Boliviano, Bolivar and mountain	1.00
1942 500 Bolivianos, Miner	85.00
1945 500 Bolivianos, Busch / Miners	1.50

	Unc.
1962 5 Pesos Bolivianos, G. Villarroel / Oil refinery	10.00
1981 500 Pesos Bolivianos, Avaroa / Puerto de Antofagasta in 1879	1.00
1986 50 Bolivianos, M. Perez de Holguin / Early church	18.50

BOSNIA-HERZEGOVINA Unc.

1992 100 Dinara, Dove of Peace	6.00
1992 100 Dinara, Shield containing arm with sword	.50
1994 500 Dinara, Shield containing six fleurs-de-lis	6.00

BRAZIL F

1833 1 Mil Reis, Arms l., Commerce std. center / blank	45.00

F

(1860-68) 5 Mil Reis, Arms between Justice and Commerce...................... 50.00

(1870) 1 Mil Reis, Pedro II and arms.. 15.00

Unc.

(1885) 2 Mil Reis, Pedro II and Church / Rio de Janeiro Post Office........... 20.00
Estampa 3A (1893) 500 Reis, Woman with sheep 12.00
Estampa 11A (1907) 5 Mil Reis, Woman std. with flowers and fruit 30.00
Estampa 17A (1925) Pres. Manuel Ferraz de Campos Salles........................ 6.00
Estampa 17A (1936) A. Santos Dumont.. 20.00

VF

(1943) 10 Cruzeiros, Getullio Vargas / Allegory of Industry 5.00
1955-59 50 Cruzeiros, Princess Isabel / Allegory of Law 4.00

Unc.

(1961-62) 5 Cruzeiros, Bust of male Indian / Flower floating 1.25
(1972-80) 1 Cruzeiro, Liberty head in circle / Bank building in circle .... .50
(1988) 5000 Cruzados, Bust of C. Portinari / C. Portinari painting 4.00
(1991-93) Vital Brazil and snake being milked for venom / One snake swallow-
    ing another 1.00

BULGARIA   F

1885 20 Leva, Arms 450.00
(1904) 5 Leva, Value / Arms 25.00
1922 5 Leva, Arms / Bee hives 4.00
1947 500 Leva, Tsar Boris III / Allegorical woman 7.00
1943 20 Leva, Tsar Simeon II and Arms / View of Tirnovo 5.00

Unc.

1947 20 Leva, Bank building 10.00

1951 100 Leva, G. Dimitrov and arms / Woman with grapes .... .25
1962 1 Lev, Arms / War monument 2.00
1974 2 Leva, Arms / Woman picking grapes.. 2.50

Unc.

(1992) 20 Leva, Portrait of medieval duchess / Boyana church .... .65

CAMBODIA   VF

(1955) 10 Riels, Temple of Banteay Srei / Phnom-Penh central market....... 10.00

Unc.

(1963-72) 100 Riels, Preah Vihear Temple / Areal view of Preah Vihear Temple .60
(1973) 1000 Riels, Children at desks / Ancient stone face .... .75
(1995) 5000 Riels, King Sihanouk / Phnom-Penh central market................... 6.50

CANADA

A much fuller treatment of Canadian paper money is provided here than for any other country but the United States. This is due to the wide popularity of collecting in North America.

As in the United States, many of Canada's earlier notes were actually issued by banks and not by the government. They were gradually eliminated by the 1940s. Fractional notes, with face values under one dollar were common well into the twentieth century. They are frequently found in very worn condition.

Note that the prices here are for the most common date appearing on the note and most common variety for each design described. There are sometimes many varieties, and a specialized reference should be consulted.

Additional Specialized Reference:

Charlton, J.E. *Standard Catalogue of Canadian Charter Bank Notes.*

Charlton, J.E. *Standard Catalogue of Canadian Government Paper Money.*

Known Counterfeits: The series of 1954 is known to have been counterfeited in the $20, $50, $100, and $1,000 dollar denominations. Counterfeits are also know of some of the earlier private bank notes.

Twenty Five Cents   VF

1870 Bust of Britannia...37.50
1900 Britannia std. 9.00

1923 Bust of Britannia...10.00

One Dollar   F

1866 Champlain and Cartier...700.00
1870 Cartier, and Woman with child and globe...............................200.00
1878 Countess of Dufferin 90.00

VF

1897 Countess and Earl of Aberdeen, Lumberjacks between / Parliament build-
     ing 75.00
1911 Earl and Countess of Grey / Parliament building 50.00
1917 Princess of Connaught..38.00
1923 George V..28.00
1935 George V...22.50
1937 George VI 6.00

Unc.

1954 Elizabeth II with "Devil's face" in hair / Prarie scene 25.00

Devil's Face hair   ReDesigned Hair

1954 similar, no "Devil's face" 5.00
1967 Elizabeth II / Parliament...3.50
1973 Elizabeth II / Floating logs in river near Parliament..............4.00

Two Dollars   F

1866 Indian woman, Britannia scene, sailor...........................1,000.00
1870 Gen. Montcalm, Indian chief, Gen. Wolfe...................2,000.00
1878 Earl of Dufferin...785.00
1887 Marchioness and Marquis of Lansdowne 300.00

VF

1897 Prince of Wales and fishermen in boat / Wheat threshing scene........125.00
1914 Duke and Duchess of Connaught / Arms.............................90.00
1923 Prince of Wales..70.00
1935 Queen Mary...35.00
1937 George VI...15.00

Unc.

1954 Elizabeth II with "Devil's face" in hair / Quebec scene 55.00
1954 similar, no "Devil's face" 9.50
1974 Elizabeth II / Inuit scene...7.50
1986 Elizabeth II / Two robins 3.00

Four Dollars   F

1882 Duke of Argyll..300.00

VF

1900 Countess and Earl of Minto, ship in lock between / Parliament building 350.00
1902 similar but ship on Canadian side of lock 350.00

Five Dollars   F

1866 Victoria, arms, sailing ship 3,000

VF

1912 Locomotive 300.00

One Dollar (right column)

VF

1924 Queen Mary...1,250.00
1935 Prince of Wales...85.00
1937 George VI..12.50

Unc.

1954 Elizabeth II with "Devil's face" in hair / Otter Falls 65.00
1954 similar, no "Devil's face"..27.50
1972-79 Sir Wilfred Laurier / Fishing boat....................................25.00
1986 Sir Wilfred Laurier / Kingfisher...6.50

Ten Dollars   F

1866 Sailors, lion and beaver...6,000.00

VF

1935 Princess Mary...50.00
1937 George VI...21.00

Unc.

1954 Elizabeth II with "Devil's face" in hair / Mt. Burgess 80.00
1954 similar, no "Devil's face"..40.00
1971 Sir John MacDonald / Oil refinery 25.00

1989 Sir John MacDonald / Osprey 12.00

Twenty Dollars   F

1866 Princess of Wales, Beaver, Prince Albert .... Rare

VF

1935 Princess Elizabeth 200.00
1937 George VI..27.50

Unc.

1954 Elizabeth II with "Devil's face" in hair / Laurentian Hills.................135.00
1954 similar, no "Devil's face"..75.00
1969-79 Elizabeth II / Lake Moraine and Rocky Mountains 40.00
1991 Elizabeth II / Loon..22.50

Twenty Five Dollars   VF

1935 George V and Queen Mary..625.00

Fifty Dollars   Unc.

1975 W.L. MacKenzie King / Mounted Police in formation.......130.00
1988 W.L. MacKenzie King / Snowy owl.......................................47.50

VF

1935 Duke of York..400.00
1937 George VI...75.00

Unc.

1954 Elizabeth II with "Devil's face" in hair / Nova Scotia coastline 200.00
1954 similar, no "Devil's face" 150.00

One Hundred Dollars   VF

1935 Duke of Gloucester 350.00
1935 Sir John MacDonald 150.00

Unc.

1954 Elizabeth II with "Devil's face" in hair / Okanagan Lake 285.00
1954 similar, no "Devil's face" 235.00
1975 Sir Robert Borden / Nova Scotia harbor scene 150.00
1988 Sir Robert Borden / Canada Goose 95.00

Five Hundred Dollars   VF

1896 Genius, Marquis of Lorne and Parliament building .... Canceled 5,000.00
1911 Queen Mary .... VG 3,500.00

1925 George V 3,850.00
1935 Sir John MacDonald 3,500.00

One Thousand Dollars   VF

1896 Queen Victoria .... Canceled 6,500.00
1901 Lord Roberts .... Canceled 6,500.00
1911 George V .... VG 3,500.00
1924 Lord Roberts .... Canceled 6,500.00
1925 Queen Mary 3,850.00
1935 Sir Wilfred Laurier 900.00
1937 similar 1,200.00

Unc.

1954 Elizabeth II with "Devil's face" in hair / Landscape 1,750.00
1954 similar, no "Devil's face" 1,350.00
1988 Elizabeth II / Two pine grosbeaks 875.00

Five Thousand Dollars   VF

1896 J.A. MacDonald .... Canceled 6,500.00
1901 Queen Victoria .... Canceled 7,000.00
1918-24 similar .... Canceled 6,500.00

Fifty Thousand Dollars   VF

1918-24 George V and Queen Mary .... Canceled 9,000.00

CHILE   F

1881 5 Pesos, Village and Gen. Freire 60.00
1918-22 5 Pesos, Chile std. with shield 10.00
1929 1000 Pesos, Condor 200.00

VF

1939-47 20 Pesos, Capt. Valdivia / Park scene 3.50
1958-59 5 Pesos, O'Higgins .... .25

Unc.

(1962-70) 1/2 Escudo, Bernardo O'Higgins / Early explorer 2.50
1975-81 50 Pesos, Capt. A. Prat / Sailing ship 1.00
1989-95 10,000 Pesos, Capt. A. Prat / Hacienda 37.50

CHINA, EMPIRE   F

1368-99 300 Cash, Three strings of coins .... Rare
1856-59 5000 Cash, Inscription with dragons 60.00

VF

1904 5 Dollars, "Imperial Bank of China," Confucius stg. / same in Chinese,
   Confucius stg. 125.00
(1910) 10 Dollars, Prince Chun l., Dragon above Great Wall 900.00

CHINA, REPUBLIC   VF

1931 5 Yuan, Temple of Heaven 5.00
1937 5 Yuan, Sun Yat-sen / Skyscraper .... .25
(1940) 10 Cents, Temple of Heaven 75
1947 1000 Customs Gold Units, Sun Yat-sen / Building 2.00

Republic, on Taiwan   Unc.

1946 1 Yuan, Bank building and Sun Yat-sen / Naval battle 6.00
1954 1 Yuan, Sun Yat-sen / Bank building 5.00
1961 1 Yuan, Sun Yat-sen / Presidential Office Building 2.50
1972 50 Yuan, Sun Yat-sen / Chungshan building 5.50
1987 100 Yuan, similar 8.00

CHINA, PEOPLES REPUBLIC   Unc.

1948 5 Yuan, Sheep .... XF 18.00

	Unc.
1953 2 Fen, Airplane	.25
1953 5 Fen, Freighter	.30
1962 1 Jiao, Farm workers	.40
1972 5 Jiao, Textile workers	1.00
1980 1 Jiao, Two Taiwanese	.15
1990 50 Yuan, Three portraits / Waterfalls	11.50
1979 10 Fen Foreign Exchange Certificate, Waterfall	1.25

COLOMBIA

	F
(1819) 2 Reales / 25 Centavos Donkey with pack	100.00
1860s 1 Peso = 10 Reales, Steamship	150.00
1888 1 Peso, Arms and Bolivar	18.00

	VF
1929-54 1 Peso, Santander and Bolivar / Liberty	.75
1941-63 10 Pesos, Gen. Nariño / Bank emblem	1.50

	Unc.
1959-77 1 Peso Oro, Bolivar and Santander / Condor	2.25

1974-75 200 Pesos Oro, Bolivar / Coffee picker	7.50
1997 5,000 Pesos, J. Asuncion Silva / Woman amid trees	11.00

COSTA RICA

	F
1871 2 Pesos, Arms l., woman r.	400.00
1910-14 1 Colon, Columbus and Arms	40.00

	F
1914-32 10 Colones, Coffee pickers	60.00

	VF
1942-48 10 Colones, Carazo / Sailing ship	15.00
1951-62 10 Colones, Echeverria / Oxcart	6.00

	Unc.
1963-67 5 Colones, B. Carrillo / Coffee worker	20.00
1977-88 100 Colones, R. Jimenez / Supreme Court building	5.00
1996 5000 Colones, Ancient sculpture / Ancient stone sphere and animals	37.50

CROATIA

	Unc.
1942 10 Kuna	10.00
1991 1 Dinar, R. Boskovic and geometry / Zagreb Cathedral	.10
1995 10 Kuna, J. Dobrila / Pula Arena	5.00

CUBA

	F
1857-59 100 Pesos, Allegorical scene	Rare
1872--83 5 Centavos, Arms / Allegory	5.50
(1905) 10 Pesos, T. Palma	Rare

1934-48 10 Pesos, Cespedes	80.00

	Unc.
1949-60 1 Peso, Jose Marti	22.50
1961-65 1 Peso, Jose Marti / Castro entering Havana	7.00
1971-90 20 Pesos, C. Cienfuegos / Soldiers on beach	15.00
1995 3 Pesos, Ernesto Che Guevara / Guevara cutting sugar cane	1.50
(1985-) 1 Peso Foreign Exchange Certificate, San Salvador de la Punta castle	3.50

CZECHOSLOVAKIA

	VF
1919 1 Koruna, Arms	1.50

	VF
1920 100 Korun, Bohemian lion and Pagan priestess / Femal portraits at each side	60.00
1932 1000 Korun, Figure scanning globe	40.00
(1945) 1000 Korun, King George Podebrad / Castle	3.00
1953 25 Korun, Equestrian statue / View of Tabor	7.50

	Unc.
1961 3 Korun, Arms	2.00
1973 500 Korun, Soldiers in rain gear / Medieval fortress	30.00
1986 10 Korun, P. Orszagh Hviezdoslav / Orava mountains	2.00

DENMARK

	F
1713 5 Rigsdaler, Crowned F4 monogram	Rare

1819 1 Rigsbankdaler, Inscriptions and ornaments	90.00
1819 100 Rigsbankdaler, Inscriptions	600.00
1875-90 10 Kroner, Arms	300.00

	VF
1916-21 1 Krone, Value / Arms	3.00
1910-42 50 Kroner, Fishermen pulling net into boat / Arms within vine	25.00

	Unc.
1950-60 5 Kroner, B. Thorvaldsen and three graces / Kalundborg city view	25.00
1972-78 10 Kroner, S. Kirchhoff / Eider bird (duck)	5.00

	Unc.
1997 500 Kroner, N. Bohr / Medieval relief of knight fighting dragon	110.00

DOMINICAN REPUBLIC

	VF
(1810) 4 Escalins, Arms	Rare
1848 2 Pesos = 80 Centa with 40 Pesos overprint, Boy l., Arms center	225.00
1867 10 Pesos, Arms	175.00
1947-59 100 Pesos, Woman with coffee pot	90.00

	Unc.
(1961) 10 Centavos Oro, Reserve Bank building	12.00
1977-88 5 Pesos Oro, Sanchez / Hydroelectric dam	4.50
1992 1000 Pesos Oro, National Palace / Columbus's fortress	125.00

ECUADOR

	VF
1928-38 5 Sucres, woman std. with fruit and sickle	F 17.50
1939-49 100 Sucres, Woman scanning globe	75.00

	Unc.
1957-74 10 Sucres, Conquistador	4.00
1961-65 100 Sucres, Bolivar / Arms	30.00
1976-82 1000 Sucres, Ruminahui / Arms	12.00
1995 50,000 Sucres, E. Alfaro / Arms	28.50

EGYPT

	VF
1899 50 Piastres, Sphinx	1,500.00
1917-51 25 Pistres, Nile scene	8.50
(1940) 5 Piastres, King Farouk	3.00
(1952-58) 5 Piastres, Queen Nefertiti	2.00

	Unc.
1961-66 25 Piastres, Arms	7.50
1967-78 50 Piastres, Al Azhar Mosque / Ramses II	6.00

Unc.

1978 25 Piastres, statue and sphynx/arms with 3.25
1994 100 Pounds, Mosque / Sphinx.. 70.00

EL SALVADOR   VF

1934 5 Colones, Woman reclining with branch / Columbus 40.00
1955-58 2 Colones, Coffee bush / Columbus 10.00

Unc.

1963-66 1 Colon, Columbus / Central Bank building 20.00
1974-76 25 Colones, Columbus / Port 25.00
1997 200 Colones, Columbus / Monument 38.50

ETHIOPIA   F

1915-29 10 Thalers, "Bank of Abyssinia," Leopard.......................................Rare
1932-33 5 Thalers, Head of gazelle 100.00
1932-33 100 Thalers, Elephant 175.00

VF

1945 1 Dollar, Haile Selassie and Farmer plowing..................................... 15.00
1945 100 Dollars, Haile Selassie and Palace 225.00

Unc.

(1961) 1 Dollar, Haile Selassie and coffee bushes...................................... 45.00

(1966) 100 Dollars, Haile Selassie and Church cut from rock 225.00
1969EE (1976) 50 Birr, Science students / Castle at Gondar...................... 45.00
1969EE (1991) 100 Birr, Menelik II / Man with microscope 45.00
1989EE (1997) 1 Birr, Portrait of boy / Tisisat Waterfalls on Blue Nile......... 1.00

FINLAND   F

1790 8 Skilling Specie, Arms.. 1,200.00
1862 20 Mark, Arms with supporters 300.00
1897 5 Markkaa, Allegorical bust / Arms 20.00

VF

1918 25 Penniä, Group of four flowers.. 1.50
1939 50 Markkaa, Allegorical group of six people, ship in background 15.00

1945 1000 Markkaa, Allegorical group of 13 people with heavy rope 30.00

Unc.

1963 1 Markka, Wheat / Lion rampant with sword 1.25
1975 500 Markkaa, President Kekkonen / Arms 150.00
1993 20 Markkaa, V. Linna / Tampere Street....................................... 6.50

FRANCE   F

1701-07, 200 Livres, Crowned monogram..3,500.00
1789-90, 1000 Livres, Louis XVI..2,200.00

VF

1792 10 Sous, Value in triangle between allegorical figures 3.00

1792 50 Livres, Republic std. 15.00
1864-66 50 Francs, Two cherubs.. Rare
1889-1927 50 Francs, Two cherubs, two portraits and ornate oval border.... 55.00
1939 20 Francs, Science and Labor / Scientist.. 15.00
1941-49 10 Francs, Miner / Farm woman...75
1944 5 Francs, Flag...40
1946-51 50 Francs, Leverrier / Neptune...3.50

Unc.

1966-70 5 Francs, Louis Pasteur / Louis Pasteur 20.00
1981-94 200 Francs, Baron de Montesquieu / Baron de Montesquieu 45.00
1996 200 Francs, G. Eiffel / Base of Eifel tower 48.50

GERMANY   F

1874 20 Mark, Herald wearing tabbard 3,500.00

1908 100 Mark, Reichskassenscheine Medallic women's head supported by two
women standing 6.00

VF

1910 1000 Mark, Inscription / Arms with supporters .... .50
1923 1,000,000 Mark, Inscription 1.50
1939 20 Reichsmark, Woman with edelweiss 5.00
1944 1 Mark, Large M .... .75
1948 5 Deutsche Mark, Europa on Bull 7.50

Unc.

1960 5 Deutsche Mark, Young Venetian Woman by Albecht Dürer / Oak
leaves 16.50

1970-80 10 Deutsche Mark, Young Man by Albecht Dürer / Sailing
Ship 11.00
1991-93 1000 Deutsche Mark, Brothers Grimm / Open book 665.00

GHANA   Unc.

(1965) 1 Cedi, Kwame Nkrumah / Bank building 7.00
1979-82 5 Cedis, Old man with hat / Men cutting tree 2.50
1994-96 5000 Cedis, Arms / Freighter in harbor 22.00

GREAT BRITAIN   F

1694 5 Pounds, Inscription (handwritten) .... Rare
1751 10 Pounds, Inscription (handwritten details) .... Rare
1797 1 Pound, Inscription and Small arms .... Rare

                                                                        F

1855 5 Pounds, similar but "payable to the bearer" .... Rare
1902 10 Pounds, similar 500.00
1917 1 Pound, St. George and George V / Parliament 100.00

1944-47 5 Pounds, Inscription and small arms 60.00
(1957-61) Head of Britannia and St. George / Lion .... VF 30.00

Unc.

1960-70 10 Shillings, Elizabeth II / Britannia std. 7.00
(1978-82) 1 Pound, Elizabeth II / Sir Isaac Newton 5.00
1990 5 Pounds, Elizabeth II / G. Stephenson 13.50

GREECE   F

1822 100 Grossi, Inscription and seals 300.00
1852 10 Drachmai, Arms .... Rare
1897 5 Drachmai, Arms and Stavros / Athena 175.00
1922 100 Drachmai, Stavros, reclining women, arms / Acropolis see between
columns 65.00

VF

(1946) 10,000 Drachmai, Aristotle 50.00
1955 50 Drachmai, Pericles / Pericles speaking 5.00

Unc.

1964 50 Drachmai, Arethusa / Shipyard 2.00
1978 50 Drachmai, Poseidon / Sailing ship 1.00
1983 500 Drachmes, Capodistrias / Fortress at Corfu 4.50
1996 200 Drachmes, R. Velestinlis Ferios / Secret school for Greek priests .. 3.25

GUATEMALA   F

(1882) 5 Pesos, Locomotive 125.00
1934-45 5 Quetzales, Freighter between two quetzales 30.00

	VF
1948-54 1/2 Quetzal, Building l., Quetzal flying at center / Two figures	6.00

	Unc.
1966-70 100 Quetzales, Indio de Nahuala / Mountain	300.00
1971-83 10 Quetzales, Gen. Granados / National Assembly of 1872	15.00
1994-95 100 Quetzales, F. Marroquin / Univ. of San Carlos de Borromeo	30.00

HAITI

	F
1790s 4 Escalins, Arms	Rare
1851 2 Gourdes, Arms	60.00
1875 1 Piastre, Pres. Domingue l., Agriculture r.	25.00
1914 2 Gourdes, J.J. Dessalines and arms / Mining scene	50.00

	Unc
1919 (1964) Castle / Arms	8.50
1973 1 Gourde, Francois Duvalier / Arms	2.00
1979 5 Gourdes, Jean-Claude Duvalier / Arms	4.00
1989 1 Gourde, Toussaint L'Ouverture	.60
1992 5 Gourdes, Statue of several figures / Arms	1.50

HAWAII

	VF
(1880) 10 Dollars, Sailing ship, cowboy, locomotive	10,000.00
1895 5 Dollars, Woman, building, bull's head	15,000.00

HONG KONG

	VF
1931-56 10 Dollars, Chartered Bank of India, Australia and China	F 75.00
(1935) 1 Dollar, George V	300.00
(1949-52) 1 Dollar, George VI	20.00
1952-59 1 Dollar, Elizabeth II	2.00

	Unc.
1961-95 1 Cent, Elizabeth II	.25
1973-76 500 Dollars, Hongkong and Shanghai Banking Corp.	450.00
1985-91 10 Dollars, Standard Chartered Bank	5.00
1994-97 20 Dollars, Bank of China issue	4.50

HUNGARY

	VF
1920 20 Korona, Matyas Church	.50
1929 10 Pengo, Deak / Parliament	10.00

	VF
1939 5 Pengo, Girl / Man playing balalaika	4.00

	Unc.
1965-89 50 Forint, Rakoczi / Battle scene	2.00
1990 500 Forint, Endre Ady / Aerial view of Budapest	4.00
1997 10,000 Forint, St. Stephen / View of Esztergom	65.00

ICELAND

	VF
1792-1801 1 Rigsdaler, Inscription, triangle above	Rare
1928 10 Kronur, Sigurdsson	10.00
1957 5 Kronur, Viking / Farm	1.50

	Unc.
1961 10 Kronur, J. Eiriksson / Ships at port	4.00

1961 1000 Kronur, Bishop Sveinsson / Church	25.00
1986 2000 Kronur, J.S. Kajarval / Leda and the Swan	45.00

INDIA

	VF
1861-65 10 Rupees, Queen Victoria	Rare
1910-20 10 Rupees, Inscription	F 40.00
1917 1 Rupee, George V	3.00
(1937-43) 5 Rupees, George VI	1.50

	Unc.
1957 1 Rupee, Coin	5.00
1966 1 Rupee, Coin	3.00
(1962-67) 5 Rupees, Asoka pillar	10.00

238

	Unc.
(1996) 10 Rupees, Mahatma Gandhi / Tiger	1.25

INDONESIA
	Unc.
1945 1 Rupiah, President Sukarno / Smoking volcano	6.00
1961 21/2 Rupiah, President Sukarno	7.50
1964 50 Sen, Soldier	.25
1980 5000 Rupiah, Diamond Cutter / Three Torajan houses	20.00
1994 50,000 Rupiah, President Soeharto / Airplane over airport	50.00

IRAN
	F
1890-1923 1 Toman, Lion and Nasr-ed-Din Shah	200.00
1924-32 50 Tomans, Nasr-ed-Din / Lion	1,250.00

	VF
1315AH (1936) Reza Shah / Mountains	15.00
(1948) 50 Rials, Shah Mohammad Reza / Five ancient figures	12.50

	Unc.
1340SH (1961) 10 Rials, Shah Mohammad Reza / Amir Kabir Dam	2.75
(1971-72) 5000 Rials, Shah Mohammad Reza / Trees before Golestan Palace	250.00
(1981) 200 Rials, Imam Reza Shrine / Tomb of Ibn-E-Sina	5.50

	Unc.
(1993) 5000 Rials, Ayatollah Khomeini / Flowers and Birds	15.00

IRAQ
	Unc.
(1971) 1/4 Dinar, Ship at port / Palm trees	9.00
1986 25 Dinars, Saddam Hussein / Monument	7.50

1994 100 Dinars, Saddam Hussein / Building with tower	4.50

IRELAND
	F
1808 1 Pound, Hibernia std.	Rare
1890-1917 10 Pounds, Hibernia stg. l. and r.	275.00
1929-39 5 pounds, Man plowing with horses	120.00

	Unc.
1962-68 10 Shillings, Lady Hazel Lavery / Face of river god	18.00
1977-89 1 Pound, Queen Medb / Medieval writing	6.50
1995-96 50 Pounds, D. Hyde / Statue of Parnell	110.00

ISRAEL
	VF
(1948-51) 500 Mils, Anglo-Palestine Bank	75.00
(1952) 1 Pound, Bank Leumi Le-Israel	15.00

	Unc.
1958 1/2 Lira, Woman with oranges	5.00
1968 5 Lirot, Albert Einstein / Atomic Reactor	6.00
1975 500 Lirot, David Ben Gurion / Golden Gate	27.50
1985-92 10 New Sheqelim, Golda Meir / Jews in Moscow	12.50

ITALY

	VF
1874 2 Lire, Bust of Italia	F 8.00
1888-1925 10 Lire, Umberto I	10.00

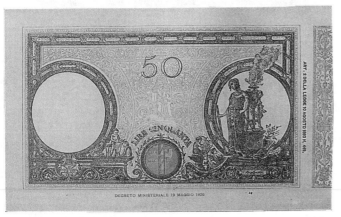

1926-36 50 Lire, Woman with three children / Woman standing	50.00
1935-44 10 Lire, Victor Emmanuel III / Italia	2.00

	Unc.
1966-75 500 Lire Eagle and Arethusa	10.00
1990 1,000 Lire, Montessori / Teacher and student	1.00
1975 20,000 Lire, Titian / Painting	90.00
1984-90 50,000 Lire, Bernini / Equestrian statue	50.00
1997 500,000 Lire, Raphael / Painting "School of Athens"	325.00

JAMAICA

	F
1904-18 2 Shillings 6 Pence, George V / Woman with hat	1,250.00
1939-48 10 Shillings, George VI / Value	40.00

	Unc.
1960 5 Shillings, Elizabeth II / River rapids	75.00
1978-81 10 Dollars, G.W. Gordon / Bauxite mining	7.50
1991-93 100 Dollars, D. Sangster / Dunn's River Falls	6.50

JAPAN

	VF
(1872) 1 Yen, Two phoenixes and two dragons	F 120.00
(1930) 100 Yen, Pavilion and Shotoku-taishi / Temple complex	50.00
1938 50 Sen, Mt. Fuji	1.25
(1947) 10 Sen, Dove / Diet building	.50

(1950) 1000 Yen, Shotoku-Yaishi / Yumedono Pavilion	15.00

	Unc.
(1969) 500 Yen, Iwakura Tomomi / Mt. Fuji	7.50
(1984-93) 1000 Yen, Soseki Natsume / Two cranes	12.50
(1993-) 5000 Yen, Inazo Nitobe / Mt. Fuji	55.00

JORDAN

	Unc.
1959 1/2 Dinar, Young King Hussein / Collonade	15.00
(1975-92) 1/2 Dinar, King Hussein / Jerash	3.00

1992 20 Dinars, King Hussein / Dome of the Rock in Jerusalem	50.00

KENYA

	Unc.
1966-68 5 Shillings, Jomo Kenyatta / Woman picking coffee	45.00

	Unc.
1978 10 Shillings, Jomo Kenyatta / Cows	6.00
1980-88 50 Shillings, Daniel Arap Moi / Airplane over airport	10.00
1995 20 Shillings, Daniel Arap Moi / Runner and stadium	1.75

LATVIA

	VF
(1919) 5 Rubli, Head l. / Flame	10.00
1937-40 10 Latu, Fishermen / Man sowing	5.00

	Unc.
1992 1 Rublis	.30
1992 5 Lati, Tree	13.50
1992 50 Latu, Sailing ship / Crossed keys	115.00

MEXICO

A much fuller treatment of Mexican paper money is provided here than for any other country but the United States and Canada.

As in the United States, many of Mexico's earlier notes were actually issued by banks and not by the government. They were eliminated by the issues of the Bank of Mexico about 1920. This introductory reference only deals with federally issued notes.

Note that the prices here are for the most common date appearing on the note and most common variety for each design described. There are sometimes a wide number of varieties, and a specialized reference should be consulted.

Additional Specialized Reference: Bruce, Colin, *Standard Catalog of Mexican Coins, Paper Money Stocks, Bonds and Medals.*

Empire of Augustin Iturbide

	F
1823 1 Peso, Arms	25.00
1823 2 Pesos, Arms	40.00
1823 10 Pesos, Arms	75.00

Fifty Centavos

	F
1920 Minerva	15.00

One Peso

	F
1920 Plenty with Cherubs	25.00
(1936)-43 Aztec calendar / Statue of Victory	3.00

	Unc.
1943-48	6.00
1948-50 similar	12.00
1954 similar	12.00
1957-70	.75

Five Pesos

	F
1925-34 G. Faure / Victory statue	8.00
1936	50.00

	Unc.
1937-50 similar	5.00
1953-54 similar	4.00
1957-70 similar	2.00
1969-72 Josefa / Aquaduct	.75

Ten Pesos

	F
1925-34 Two winged Victories / Statue of Victory	8.00
1936 similar	15.00

	Unc.

1937-42 Woman with large headdress / Road to Guanajuato	15.00
1943-45 similar	10.00
1946-50 similar	6.50
1951-53 similar	6.50
1954-67 similar	3.00
1969-77 Hidalgo / Dolores Cathedral	.75

Twenty Pesos

	F
1925-34 Freighter at dock by locomotive	25.00
1937 Josefa / Federal Palace courtyard	VF 25.00

	Unc.
1940-45, similar	15.00
1948 similar	10.00
1950-70 similar	5.00
1972-77 Morelos / Pyramid	1.00

Fifty Pesos

	F
1925-34 Navagation std. / Statue of Victory	60.00
1937-40, Zaragoza / City view	125.00

	Unc.
1941-45 de Allende / Statue of Victory	12.00
1948-72 similar	4.00
1973-81, Juarez / Aztec deity	.75

One Hundred Pesos

	F
1925-34 Maritime Commerce and Youth / Statue of Victory	100.00
1936 Madero / Bank building	225.00

	VF
1940-42	20.00
1945 Hidalgo / Coin	20.00

	Unc.
1950-61 similar	12.00
1974-82, Carranza / Stone altar	.75

Five Hundred Pesos — F

	F
1931-34 Electricity std. / Statue of Victory	400.00
1936 Morelos / Miners' Palace	400.00
1940-43 Morelos	VF 40.00

	Unc.
1948-78 similar	7.50
1979-84, Madero / Aztec calendar	2.50

One Thousand Pesos — F

	F
1931-34 Wisdom with globe / Statue of Victory	1,350.00
1936 Cuauhtemoc / Pyramid	450.00
1941-45 Cuauhtemoc / Pyramid	VF 40.00

	Unc.
1948-77 similar	10.00
1978-85, de Asbaje / Santo Domingo plaza	2.00

Two Thousand Pesos

1983-89, J. Sierra / 1800s courtyard	1.50

Five Thousand Pesos

1980-89 Cadets / Chapultepec castle	3.00

Ten Thousand Pesos

1943-53 Romero / Government Palace	VF 300.00
1978 Romero / National palace	75.00
1981-91 Cardenas / Coyolxauhqui	7.00

Twenty Thousand Pesos

1985-89 A. Quintana Roo / Pre-Columbian art	12.50

Fifty Thousand Pesos

1986-90 Cuauhtemoc / Spaniard and Aztec fighting	50.00

One Hundred Thousand Pesos

1988-91 Calles / Stag	90.00

Reform, 1000 Pesos = 1 New Peso

Ten Nuevos Pesos

1992 Cardenas / Coyolxauhqui	6.00
1992 Zapata / Statue of Zapata	4.50
1994, same without Nuevos	3.50

Twenty Nuevos Pesos

1992 A. Quintana Roo / Pre-Columbian art	12.00
1992 Juarez / Statue	8.00
1994, same without Nuevos	6.50

Fifty Nuevos Pesos

1992 Cuauhtemoc / Spaniand and Aztec fighting	26.50
1992 Morelos / Fisherman	20.00
1994, same without Nuevos	15.00

One Hundred Nuevos Pesos

1992 Calles / Stag	50.00
1992 Nezahualcoyotl / Xochipilli statue	40.00
1994, same without Nuevos	28.50

Two Hundred Nuevos Pesos

1995, de Asbaje / Temple of San Jeronimo	50.00

Five Hundred Nuevos Pesos

1992, Zaragoza / Puebla Cathedral	145.00
1994, same without Nuevos	120.00

MOROCCO — Unc.

	Unc.
1965-69 5 Dirhams, King Muhammad V / Man with sheaf	27.50
1970-85 10 Dirhams, King Hassan II / Woman sorting oranges	5.50
1987 200 Dirhams, similar / Sailboat	40.00

NETHERLANDS — F

	F
1846 10 Gulden, Inscriptions	Rare
1904-21 25 Gulden, Arms and ornate border	450.00

1939-41 20 Gulden, Queen Emma and sailing ship / Church	12.00
1943 2-1/2 Gulden, Queen Wilhelmina	VF 7.00
1966 5 Gulden, Vondell / Mondernistic depiction of building	10.00
1985 250 Gulden, Lighthouse	185.00
1992 100 Gulden, Abstract pattern	77.50
1997 10 Gulden, different abstract pattern	9.00

NEW ZEALAND — VF

	VF
1934 1 Pound, Kiwi, Arms and Maori chief	55.00

	Unc.
(1967-81) 1 Dollar, Elizabeth II / Bird	7.00
(1981-92) 1 Dollar, similar but older portrait	2.50
(1992-) 5 Dollars, Sir Edmond Hillary / Penguin	6.50

NICARAGUA — F

	F
1984 10 Centavos, Arms	55.00
1938 50 Centavos, Liberty / Arms	45.00

	Unc.
1962 1 Cordoba, Building / Cordoba	4.00
1972 20 Cordobas, Woman lighting cannon / Treaty signing ceremony	3.50
1985 1000 Cordobas, Sandino	1.25
(1991) 50 Cordobas, Chamorro / Polling place	12.50

NIGERIA — **Unc.**

(1967) 1 Pound, Bank building / Man beating plant	7.00
(1973-78) 1 Naira, Bank building / Workers stacking bags of grain	11.00

(1984-) 10 Naira, A. Ikoku / Women carrying bowls on heads	2.00

NORWAY — **F**

1695 10 Rixdaler Croner, Inscription with wax seals	2,000.00
1877-99 5 Kroner, Oscar II	400.00
1940-50 1 Krone	8.00

	Unc.
1972-84 10 Kroner, F. Nansen / Fisherman	4.00
1984-95 50 Kroner, A.O. Vinje / Medieval stone carving	12.50
1996 50 Kroner, P.C. Asbjornsen / Water lilies	11.50

PAKISTAN — **Unc.**

(1953) 5 Rupees, Small boat / Mountain scene	12.50
(1969) 1 Rupee, Archway	3.50

(1982-) 1 Rupee, Tomb of Allama Iqbal	.25
(1986) 50 Rupees, Mohammad Ali Jinnah / Gate of Lahore fort	5.00

PALESTINE — **F**

1927-45 500 Mils, Rachel's Tomb l. / Tower of David	100.00
1927-44 1 Pound, Dome of the Rock l. / Tower of David	100.00

PANAMA — **VF**

1941 1 Balboa, Balboa	650.00
1941 5 Balboas, Uracca	1,500.00

PARAGUAY — **F**

1856 1/2 Real, Flowers and seal	80.00

1903 1 Peso, Woman in straw hat	7.50

	Unc.
1943 5 Guaranies, Gen. Diaz	15.00
1952 1 Guarani, Soldier / Building	4.00
1952 500 Guaranies, Gen. B. Caballero / Freighter	1.85
1995 5000 Guaranies, D.C.A. Lopez / Lopez Palace	5.00

PERU — **F**

1879 5 Soles, Women with children	10.00
1922 10 Libras, Tapping tree for rubber	90.00

	Unc.
1958 5 Soles, Liberty (or Peru)	6.00
1962-68 5 Soles de Oro, Liberty (or Peru) std. / Arms	3.00

1977 50 Soles de Oro, Tupac Amaru / Town of Tinta 1.00
1995 10 Nuevos Soles, J. Abelardo Quiñones / Biplane flying upside-down. 7.00

PHILIPPINES F

1852-65 25 Pesos, Isabel II ....Rare
1908 50 Pesos, Woman with flower, "Banco Español Filipino" 500.00
1928 50 Pesos, similar, "Bank of the Philippine Islands" 40.00

Unc.

(1943) 5 Pesos, Monument, "Japanese Government" 2.00
(1949) 2 Pesos, Rizal 1.50
(1969) 1 Piso, Rizal / 1898 Independence declaration 1.50
(1970s) 10 Piso, Mabini / Barasoain church 2.00
(1987-94) 500 Piso, B. Aquino / Scenes of Aquino's life 25.00

POLAND F

1794 5 Groszy, Eagle and mounted knight 15.00
similar, F. Malinowski on back ....Copy
1917 20 Marek, White eagle 20.00

VF

1931 20 Zlotych, E. Plater / Woman with children... 2.00
1948 50 Zlotych, Bust of fisherman 1.25

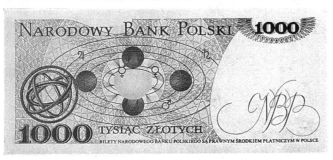

Unc.

1962-65 1000 Zlotych, Copernicus / Diagram of Copernican view of solar
    system.. 16.50

Unc.

1977-82 2000 Zlotych, Mieszko I 7.00
1994 20 Zlotych, Boleslaw I / Medieval coin 12.00

PORTUGAL F

1798-99 2400 Reis, Walled cities and cherubs.. Rare
1891 500 Reis, Arms / Arms 80.00
1918-20 50 Centavos, Woman holding ship / Justice 5.00
1920-25 5 Escudos, J. das Regras / Church and convent 60.00
1944-52 500 Escudos, Joao IV / King with crown .... VF 40.00

Unc.

1960 50 Escudos, Pereira / "The Thinker" statue 15.00
1971 20 Escudos, G. de Orta / Market in Goa 2.00
1996 1000 Escudos, Cabral / 1500s Sailing ship 11.00

PUERTO RICO F

1813 8 Reales, Paschal lamb..G 1,500.00
1895 1 Peso, Bearded Bust l. / Crowned arms of Spain 35.00
1909 10 Dollars, Ponce de Leon / Liberty.. 1,750.00

ROMANIA F

1877 5 Lei, Two women std.. 250.00

1877 50 Lei, Ancient Romans 800.00
1914-28 5 Lei, Woman with distaff / Woman picking apples, child at s
    ide... VF 3.00

Unc.

1966 1 Leu, Arms .... .50
1991 500 Lei, Bust of Brancusi / Brancusi std.. 2.75
1993 5000 Lei, A. Iancu / Elaborate gateway 1.75

RUSSIA F

1787-1818 5 Rubles, Inscriptions.. 500.00
1866-80 5 Rubles, Monogram / D. Ivanovich Donskoi 350.00

Unc.

1909 5 Rubles, Arms.. 1.50

	Unc.
1918 500 Rubles, Two-headed eagle	2.50
1938 5 Rubles, Pilot	4.50
1961 3 Rubles, Kremlin tower	.50
1991 50 Rubles, Lenin / Dome at Kremlin	3.00
1997 100 Rubles, Chariot monument / Bolshoi Theater	37.50

RWANDA

	Unc.
1964-76 50 Francs, Map / Miners	2.00
1978 100 Francs, Zebras / Woman and child	6.00
1988-89 1000 France. Two Watusi warriors / Two gorillas	15.00

SAUDI ARABIA

	Unc.
1379AH (1961), 1 Riyal, Hill of Light / Arms	35.00
1379AH (1976) 50 Riyals, King Faisal / Arches in mosque	40.00
1379AH (1984) 1 Riyal, King Fahd / Landscape	1.25

SOUTH AFRICA

	VF
1867-68 1 Pond, Arms, "Zuid-Afrikaansche Republiek"	Rare
1920 1 Pound, Arms	F 150.00
1928-47 10 Shillings	22.00

1928-47 1 Pound, Sailing ship	18.00

	Unc.
(1961-62) 1 Rand, Jan van Riebeeck / Lion crest	25.00
(1978-93) 10 Rand, Jan van Riebeeck / Bull and ram	9.00
1994 100 Rand, Water buffalo / Zebra herd	32.50

SPAIN

	VF
1874 50 Pesetas, D. Martinez	F 2,000.00
1925 (1925-36) Philip II / Philip II in scene	2.00
1935 500 Pesetas, H. Cortez / Cortez burning his ships	75.00
1949 1000 Pesetas, de Santillan / Goya painting	55.00
1951 5 Pesetas, Balmes / Building	3.00

	Unc.
1965 1000 Pesetas, St. Isidoro / Medieval sculpture	35.00
1976 5000 Pesetas, Charles III / Prado Museum	75.00
1985 10,000 Pesetas, Juan Carlos I / Prince of Asturias	110.00
1992 1000 Pesetas, Cortes / Pizarro	13.50

SWEDEN

	F
1666 10 Daler Silvermynt, Inscription	7,000.00
1802-34 8 Schillingar Specie, Inscription	65.00
1907-17 5 Kronor, Svea std. / Gustav Vasa	45.00
1918-52 5 Kronor, similar	1.00

	Unc.
1954-61 5 Kronor, Gustav VI Adolf / Svea stg.	6.00
1965-81 5 Kronor, Gustav Vasa / Stylized rooster	2.25
1986-92 100 Kronor, Carl XI / C. Polhem	140.00
1996 50 Kronor, Jenny Lind / Violin	13.50

SWITZERLAND

	F
1907 50 Franken, Helvetia and child	1,000.00
1924-49 100 Franken, Female portrait / Man chopping tree	VF 55.00

	Unc.
1961-74 50 Francs, Little girl r. / Apple harvesting	55.00
1979-90 10 Francs, L. Euler / Water turbine	12.00
1994 50 Francs, S. Taeuber-Arp / Her abstract art	50.00

TANZANIA

	Unc.
(1966) 5 Shillings, Young Julius Nyerere / Mountain	9.00
(1978) 20 Shilingi, Julius Nyerere / Cotton knitting machine	4.50
(1985) 20 Shilingi, Old Julius Nyerere / Tire factory workers	2.00

	Unc.
(1996) 200 Shilingi, Pres. Mwinyi / Two fishermen	5.00

TURKEY — **XF**

1259AH (1843) 250 Kurush, Inscription	Rare
1334AH (1918) 10 Livres, Inscription in ornamental border	300.00
same, WWI British military counterfeit	5.00

Note: The counterfeits far outnumber authentic notes.

1930 50 Kurush, Ismet Inonu / Building	8.00

	Unc.
1930 (1961) 5 Lira, Ataturk / Three women with baskets	45.00
1970 (1971-82) 10 Lira, Ataturk / Lighthouse view	4.00
1970 (1984-97) 10 Lira, Ataturk / Children giving flowers to Ataturk	.50
1970 (1997) 100,000 Lira, Ataturk / similar	2.00

VENEZUELA — **F**

1811 1 Peso, Seal	800.00
1861 8 Reales, Inscription	Rare

	Unc.
1945-60 10 Bolivares, Bolivar and Sucre / Arms	25.00
1961 10 Bolivares, Bolivar and Sucre / Carabobo Monument	25.00
1974-79 20 Bolivares, j. Antonio Paez / similar	7.50
1990-95 50 Bolivares, A. Bello / Bank building	.50

VIETNAM — **F**

(1946) 100 Dong, Farmers with buffalo	20.00

	Unc
1976 5 Hao, Arms / River scene	2.50
1980 100 Dong, Ho Chi Minh / Junks sailing amid rocks	4.00

	Unc
1994 50,000 Dong, Ho Chi Minh / View of docks	12.50

YUGOSLAVIA — **VF**

1920 10 Dinara, Progress moving wheel / Mountain scene	40.00
1931 50 Dinara, King Alexander / Equestrian statue	3.00
1939 10 Dinara, King Peter II / Woman in local costume	8.00

	Unc.
1944 1 Dinara, Soldier	1.00
1963 100 Dinara, Woman in folk dress / View of Dubrovnik	1.75
1985 5000 Dinara, Tito / View of Jajce	2.50
1993 10,000,000,000 Dinara, Nikola Tesla / High frequency transformer	9.00

ZAMBIA — **Unc.**

(1963) Elizabeth II & Fisher with net / Bird	Rare
(1968-69) Pres. Kenneth Kaunda / Mining facility	45.00

(1980-88) Older Pres. Kenneth Kaunda / Bank building	5.00
1992 500 Kwacha, Bird / Elephant head and cotton pickers	3.50

ILLUSTRATION CREDITS

The illustrations in this book are used with the permission of and are copyright 1999 by the firms and individuals listed below. Numbers indicate the page on which the illustration is located and letters: **A**, **B**, **C** indicate the column. All photos not credited below are from the Krause Publications photo archive and are copyright 1999 Krause Publications.

Stephen Album ....204 B & C, 205 A, 206 A & C

Allen G. Berman............................Cover, 85 A, 85 C, 86 A, 86 B, 87 A, 87 B, 87 C, 88 B, 88 C, 89 C, 90 A, 94 A, 95 A, 95 B, 113 B, 149 B & C, 150 B, 151 B, 152 A, 153 A, 154 C, 155 A, 157 A, 158 A, 160 B, 163 B, 206 C, 216 A, 244 A

Paul Bosco ....79 C, 80 A, 136 C, 156 A, 159 A, 162 B

Civil War Token Society.................83 A, 84 A

Frederick Fleischer ....Cover

M & M Numismatics, Ltd ....135 C, 136 A, 136 C, 137 C, 139 A, 139 B, 139 C, 140 C, 143 C, 144 B, 145 B, 145 C, 146 C, 158 C, 159 C, 203 C, 204 A, 204 B, 206 A

Dmitry Markov ....161 C, 162 A, 162 B, 204 C, 206 A

Pegasi Numismatics........................136 A, 149 A, 149 B, 149 C, 150 A, 150 B, 150 C, 151 A, 151 B, 151 C, 152 A,   152 C, 153 A, 153 B, 153 C, 154 A, 154 C, 155 A, 155 C, 156 A, 156 B, 156 C, 157 C, 158 A, 158 C, 160 A, 160 C, 161 A, 162 C, 163 C, 204 A, 205 A, 206 B

RaBenco ....110 B

William Rosemblum.......................200 C

Sam Sloat Coins, Ltd......................88 B, Cover

R.M. Smythe...................................140 A, 153 A

Spink America ....136 A, 137 A, 140 A, 153 B, 156 B, 156 C, 157 B, 163 B

Stack's...13 C, 21 A, 90 A, 137 B, 138 B, 144 C, 156 A, 159 A, 161 B, 169 B

Italo Vecchi, Ltd ....136 B, 136 C, 137 A, 137 B, 137 C, 138 A, 138 C, 139 A, 138 C, 139 A, 140 C, 141 A, 141 B, 142 B, 142 C, 143 A, 143 B, 143 C, 144 A, 144 B, 144 C, 145 A, 145 B, 145 C, 146 B, 146 C, 147 A, 147 B, 147 C, 159 A, 159 B

Silver Bullion Chart

Price $	3.00	3.50	4.00	4.50	5.00	5.50	6.50	7.00	7.50	8.00	8.50	9.00	9.50	10.00
0.020	0.060	0.070	0.080	0.090	0.100	0.110	0.130	0.140	0.150	0.160	0.170	0.180	0.190	0.200
0.030	0.090	0.105	0.120	0.135	0.150	0.165	0.195	0.210	0.225	0.240	0.255	0.270	0.285	0.300
0.040	0.120	0.140	0.160	0.180	0.200	0.220	0.260	0.280	0.300	0.320	0.340	0.360	0.380	0.400
0.050	0.150	0.175	0.200	0.225	0.250	0.275	0.325	0.350	0.375	0.400	0.425	0.450	0.475	0.500
0.060	0.180	0.210	0.240	0.270	0.300	0.330	0.390	0.420	0.450	0.480	0.510	0.540	0.570	0.600
0.070	0.210	0.245	0.280	0.315	0.350	0.385	0.455	0.490	0.525	0.560	0.595	0.630	0.665	0.700
0.080	0.240	0.280	0.320	0.360	0.400	0.440	0.520	0.560	0.600	0.640	0.680	0.720	0.760	0.800
0.090	0.270	0.315	0.360	0.405	0.450	0.495	0.585	0.630	0.675	0.720	0.765	0.810	0.855	0.900
0.100	0.300	0.350	0.400	0.450	0.500	0.550	0.650	0.700	0.750	0.800	0.850	0.900	0.950	1.000
0.110	0.330	0.385	0.440	0.495	0.550	0.605	0.715	0.770	0.825	0.880	0.935	0.990	1.045	1.100
0.120	0.360	0.420	0.480	0.540	0.600	0.660	0.780	0.840	0.900	0.960	1.020	1.080	1.140	1.200
0.130	0.390	0.455	0.520	0.585	0.650	0.715	0.845	0.910	0.975	1.040	1.105	1.170	1.235	1.300
0.140	0.420	0.490	0.560	0.630	0.700	0.770	0.910	0.980	1.050	1.120	1.190	1.260	1.330	1.400
0.150	0.450	0.525	0.600	0.675	0.750	0.825	0.975	1.050	1.125	1.200	1.275	1.350	1.425	1.500
0.160	0.480	0.560	0.640	0.720	0.800	0.880	1.040	1.120	1.200	1.280	1.360	1.440	1.520	1.600
0.170	0.510	0.595	0.680	0.765	0.850	0.935	1.105	1.190	1.275	1.360	1.445	1.530	1.615	1.700
0.180	0.540	0.630	0.720	0.810	0.900	0.990	1.170	1.260	1.350	1.440	1.530	1.620	1.710	1.800
0.190	0.570	0.665	0.760	0.855	0.950	1.045	1.235	1.330	1.425	1.520	1.615	1.710	1.805	1.900
0.200	0.600	0.700	0.800	0.900	1.000	1.100	1.300	1.400	1.500	1.600	1.700	1.800	1.900	2.000
0.210	0.630	0.735	0.840	0.945	1.050	1.155	1.365	1.470	1.575	1.680	1.785	1.890	1.995	2.100
0.220	0.660	0.770	0.880	0.990	1.100	1.210	1.430	1.540	1.650	1.760	1.870	1.980	2.090	2.200
0.230	0.690	0.805	0.920	1.035	1.150	1.265	1.495	1.610	1.725	1.840	1.955	2.070	2.185	2.300
0.240	0.720	0.840	0.960	1.080	1.200	1.320	1.560	1.680	1.800	1.920	2.040	2.160	2.280	2.400
0.250	0.750	0.875	1.000	1.125	1.250	1.375	1.625	1.750	1.875	2.000	2.125	2.250	2.375	2.500
0.260	0.780	0.910	1.040	1.170	1.300	1.430	1.690	1.820	1.950	2.080	2.210	2.340	2.470	2.600
0.270	0.810	0.945	1.080	1.215	1.350	1.485	1.755	1.890	2.025	2.160	2.295	2.430	2.565	2.700
0.280	0.840	0.980	1.120	1.260	1.400	1.540	1.820	1.960	2.100	2.240	2.380	2.520	2.660	2.800
0.290	0.870	1.015	1.160	1.305	1.450	1.595	1.885	2.030	2.175	2.320	2.465	2.610	2.755	2.900
0.300	0.900	1.050	1.200	1.350	1.500	1.650	1.950	2.100	2.250	2.400	2.550	2.700	2.850	3.000
0.310	0.930	1.085	1.240	1.395	1.550	1.705	2.015	2.170	2.325	2.480	2.635	2.790	2.945	3.100
0.320	0.960	1.120	1.280	1.440	1.600	1.760	2.080	2.240	2.400	2.560	2.720	2.880	3.040	3.200
0.330	0.990	1.155	1.320	1.485	1.650	1.815	2.145	2.310	2.475	2.640	2.805	2.970	3.135	3.300
0.340	1.020	1.190	1.360	1.530	1.700	1.870	2.210	2.380	2.550	2.720	2.890	3.060	3.230	3.400
0.350	1.050	1.225	1.400	1.575	1.750	1.925	2.275	2.450	2.625	2.800	2.975	3.150	3.325	3.500
0.360	1.080	1.260	1.440	1.620	1.800	1.980	2.340	2.520	2.700	2.880	3.060	3.240	3.420	3.600
0.370	1.110	1.295	1.480	1.665	1.850	2.035	2.405	2.590	2.775	2.960	3.145	3.330	3.515	3.700
0.380	1.140	1.330	1.520	1.710	1.900	2.090	2.470	2.660	2.850	3.040	3.230	3.420	3.610	3.800
0.390	1.170	1.365	1.560	1.755	1.950	2.145	2.535	2.730	2.925	3.120	3.315	3.510	3.705	3.900
0.400	1.200	1.400	1.600	1.800	2.000	2.200	2.600	2.800	3.000	3.200	3.400	3.600	3.800	4.000
0.410	1.230	1.435	1.640	1.845	2.050	2.255	2.665	2.870	3.075	3.280	3.485	3.690	3.895	4.100
0.420	1.260	1.470	1.680	1.890	2.100	2.310	2.730	2.940	3.150	3.360	3.570	3.780	3.990	4.200
0.430	1.290	1.505	1.720	1.935	2.150	2.365	2.795	3.010	3.225	3.440	3.655	3.870	4.085	4.300
0.440	1.320	1.540	1.760	1.980	2.200	2.420	2.860	3.080	3.300	3.520	3.740	3.960	4.180	4.400
0.450	1.350	1.575	1.800	2.025	2.250	2.475	2.925	3.150	3.375	3.600	3.825	4.050	4.275	4.500
0.460	1.380	1.610	1.840	2.070	2.300	2.530	2.990	3.220	3.450	3.680	3.910	4.140	4.370	4.600
0.470	1.410	1.645	1.880	2.115	2.350	2.585	3.055	3.290	3.525	3.760	3.995	4.230	4.465	4.700
0.480	1.440	1.680	1.920	2.160	2.400	2.640	3.120	3.360	3.600	3.840	4.080	4.320	4.560	4.800
0.490	1.470	1.715	1.960	2.205	2.450	2.695	3.185	3.430	3.675	3.920	4.165	4.410	4.655	4.900
0.500	1.500	1.750	2.000	2.250	2.500	2.750	3.250	3.500	3.750	4.000	4.250	4.500	4.750	5.000
0.510	1.530	1.785	2.040	2.295	2.550	2.805	3.315	3.570	3.825	4.080	4.335	4.590	4.845	5.100
0.520	1.560	1.820	2.080	2.340	2.600	2.860	3.380	3.640	3.900	4.160	4.420	4.680	4.940	5.200
0.530	1.590	1.855	2.120	2.385	2.650	2.915	3.445	3.710	3.975	4.240	4.505	4.770	5.035	5.300
0.540	1.620	1.890	2.160	2.430	2.700	2.970	3.510	3.780	4.050	4.320	4.590	4.860	5.130	5.400
0.550	1.650	1.925	2.200	2.475	2.750	3.025	3.575	3.850	4.125	4.400	4.675	4.950	5.225	5.500
0.560	1.680	1.960	2.240	2.520	2.800	3.080	3.640	3.920	4.200	4.480	4.760	5.040	5.320	5.600
0.570	1.710	1.995	2.280	2.565	2.850	3.135	3.705	3.990	4.275	4.560	4.845	5.130	5.415	5.700
0.580	1.740	2.030	2.320	2.610	2.900	3.190	3.770	4.060	4.350	4.640	4.930	5.220	5.510	5.800
0.590	1.770	2.065	2.360	2.655	2.950	3.245	3.835	4.130	4.425	4.720	5.015	5.310	5.605	5.900
0.600	1.800	2.100	2.400	2.700	3.000	3.300	3.900	4.200	4.500	4.800	5.100	5.400	5.700	6.000
0.610	1.830	2.135	2.440	2.745	3.050	3.355	3.965	4.270	4.575	4.880	5.185	5.490	5.795	6.100
0.620	1.860	2.170	2.480	2.790	3.100	3.410	4.030	4.340	4.650	4.960	5.270	5.580	5.890	6.200
0.630	1.890	2.205	2.520	2.835	3.150	3.465	4.095	4.410	4.725	5.040	5.355	5.670	5.985	6.300
0.640	1.920	2.240	2.560	2.880	3.200	3.520	4.160	4.480	4.800	5.120	5.440	5.760	6.080	6.400
0.650	1.950	2.275	2.600	2.925	3.250	3.575	4.225	4.550	4.875	5.200	5.525	5.850	6.175	6.500
0.660	1.980	2.310	2.640	2.970	3.300	3.630	4.290	4.620	4.950	5.280	5.610	5.940	6.270	6.600
0.670	2.010	2.345	2.680	3.015	3.350	3.685	4.355	4.690	5.025	5.360	5.695	6.030	6.365	6.700
0.680	2.040	2.380	2.720	3.060	3.400	3.740	4.420	4.760	5.100	5.440	5.780	6.120	6.460	6.800
0.690	2.070	2.415	2.760	3.105	3.450	3.795	4.485	4.830	5.175	5.520	5.865	6.210	6.555	6.900
0.700	2.100	2.450	2.800	3.150	3.500	3.850	4.550	4.900	5.250	5.600	5.950	6.300	6.650	7.000
0.710	2.130	2.485	2.840	3.195	3.550	3.905	4.615	4.970	5.325	5.680	6.035	6.390	6.745	7.100
0.720	2.160	2.520	2.880	3.240	3.600	3.960	4.680	5.040	5.400	5.760	6.120	6.480	6.840	7.200
0.730	2.190	2.555	2.920	3.285	3.650	4.015	4.745	5.110	5.475	5.840	6.205	6.570	6.935	7.300
0.740	2.220	2.590	2.960	3.330	3.700	4.070	4.810	5.180	5.550	5.920	6.290	6.660	7.030	7.400
0.750	2.250	2.625	3.000	3.375	3.750	4.125	4.875	5.250	5.625	6.000	6.375	6.750	7.125	7.500
0.760	2.280	2.660	3.040	3.420	3.800	4.180	4.940	5.320	5.700	6.080	6.460	6.840	7.220	7.600
0.770	2.310	2.695	3.080	3.465	3.850	4.235	5.005	5.390	5.775	6.160	6.545	6.930	7.315	7.700
0.780	2.340	2.730	3.120	3.510	3.900	4.290	5.070	5.460	5.850	6.240	6.630	7.020	7.410	7.800
0.790	2.370	2.765	3.160	3.555	3.950	4.345	5.135	5.530	5.925	6.320	6.715	7.110	7.505	7.900
0.800	2.400	2.800	3.200	3.600	4.000	4.400	5.200	5.600	6.000	6.400	6.800	7.200	7.600	8.000
0.810	2.430	2.835	3.240	3.645	4.050	4.455	5.265	5.670	6.075	6.480	6.885	7.290	7.695	8.100
0.820	2.460	2.870	3.280	3.690	4.100	4.510	5.330	5.740	6.150	6.560	6.970	7.380	7.790	8.200
0.830	2.490	2.905	3.320	3.735	4.150	4.565	5.395	5.810	6.225	6.640	7.055	7.470	7.885	8.300
0.840	2.520	2.940	3.360	3.780	4.200	4.620	5.460	5.880	6.300	6.720	7.140	7.560	7.980	8.400
0.850	2.550	2.975	3.400	3.825	4.250	4.675	5.525	5.950	6.375	6.800	7.225	7.650	8.075	8.500
0.860	2.580	3.010	3.440	3.870	4.300	4.730	5.590	6.020	6.450	6.880	7.310	7.740	8.170	8.600
0.870	2.610	3.045	3.480	3.915	4.350	4.785	5.655	6.090	6.525	6.960	7.395	7.830	8.265	8.700
0.880	2.640	3.080	3.520	3.960	4.400	4.840	5.720	6.160	6.600	7.040	7.480	7.920	8.360	8.800
0.890	2.670	3.115	3.560	4.005	4.450	4.895	5.785	6.230	6.675	7.120	7.565	8.010	8.455	8.900
0.900	2.700	3.150	3.600	4.050	4.500	4.950	5.850	6.300	6.750	7.200	7.650	8.100	8.550	9.000
0.910	2.730	3.185	3.640	4.095	4.550	5.005	5.915	6.370	6.825	7.280	7.735	8.190	8.645	9.100
0.920	2.760	3.220	3.680	4.140	4.600	5.060	5.980	6.440	6.900	7.360	7.820	8.280	8.740	9.200
0.930	2.790	3.255	3.720	4.185	4.650	5.115	6.045	6.510	6.975	7.440	7.905	8.370	8.835	9.300
0.940	2.820	3.290	3.760	4.230	4.700	5.170	6.110	6.580	7.050	7.520	7.990	8.460	8.930	9.400
0.950	2.850	3.325	3.800	4.275	4.750	5.225	6.175	6.650	7.125	7.600	8.075	8.550	9.025	9.500
0.960	2.880	3.360	3.840	4.320	4.800	5.280	6.240	6.720	7.200	7.680	8.160	8.640	9.120	9.600
0.970	2.910	3.395	3.880	4.365	4.850	5.335	6.305	6.790	7.275	7.760	8.245	8.730	9.215	9.700
0.980	2.940	3.430	3.920	4.410	4.900	5.390	6.370	6.860	7.350	7.840	8.330	8.820	9.310	9.800
0.990	2.970	3.465	3.960	4.455	4.950	5.445	6.435	6.930	7.425	7.920	8.415	8.910	9.405	9.900
1.000	3.000	3.500	4.000	4.500	5.000	5.500	6.500	7.000	7.500	8.000	8.500	9.000	9.500	10.000

Gold & Platinum Bullion Chart

Price $	270.00	280.00	290.00	300.00	310.00	320.00	330.00	340.00	350.00	360.00	370.00	380.00	390.00	400.00	410.00
0.020	5.40	5.60	5.80	6.00	6.20	6.40	6.60	6.80	7.00	7.20	7.40	7.60	7.80	8.00	8.20
0.030	8.10	8.40	8.70	9.00	9.30	9.60	9.90	10.20	10.50	10.80	11.10	11.40	11.70	12.00	12.30
0.040	10.80	11.20	11.60	12.00	12.40	12.80	13.20	13.60	14.00	14.40	14.80	15.20	15.60	16.00	16.40
0.050	13.50	14.00	14.50	15.00	15.50	16.00	16.50	17.00	17.50	18.00	18.50	19.00	19.50	20.00	20.50
0.060	16.20	16.80	17.40	18.00	18.60	19.20	19.80	20.40	21.00	21.60	22.20	22.80	23.40	24.00	24.60
0.070	18.90	19.60	20.30	21.00	21.70	22.40	23.10	23.80	24.50	25.20	25.90	26.60	27.30	28.00	28.70
0.080	21.60	22.40	23.20	24.00	24.80	25.60	26.40	27.20	28.00	28.80	29.60	30.40	31.20	32.00	32.80
0.090	24.30	25.20	26.10	27.00	27.90	28.80	29.70	30.60	31.50	32.40	33.30	34.20	35.10	36.00	36.90
0.100	27.00	28.00	29.00	30.00	31.00	32.00	33.00	34.00	35.00	36.00	37.00	38.00	39.00	40.00	41.00
0.110	29.70	30.80	31.90	33.00	34.10	35.20	36.30	37.40	38.50	39.60	40.70	41.80	42.90	44.00	45.10
0.120	32.40	33.60	34.80	36.00	37.20	38.40	39.60	40.80	42.00	43.20	44.40	45.60	46.80	48.00	49.20
0.130	35.10	36.40	37.70	39.00	40.30	41.60	42.90	44.20	45.50	46.80	48.10	49.40	50.70	52.00	53.30
0.140	37.80	39.20	40.60	42.00	43.40	44.80	46.20	47.60	49.00	50.40	51.80	53.20	54.60	56.00	57.40
0.150	40.50	42.00	43.50	45.00	46.50	48.00	49.50	51.00	52.50	54.00	55.50	57.00	58.50	60.00	61.50
0.160	43.20	44.80	46.40	48.00	49.60	51.20	52.80	54.40	56.00	57.60	59.20	60.80	62.40	64.00	65.60
0.170	45.90	47.60	49.30	51.00	52.70	54.40	56.10	57.80	59.50	61.20	62.90	64.60	66.30	68.00	69.70
0.180	48.60	50.40	52.20	54.00	55.80	57.60	59.40	61.20	63.00	64.80	66.60	68.40	70.20	72.00	73.80
0.190	51.30	53.20	55.10	57.00	58.90	60.80	62.70	64.60	66.50	68.40	70.30	72.20	74.10	76.00	77.90
0.200	54.00	56.00	58.00	60.00	62.00	64.00	66.00	68.00	70.00	72.00	74.00	76.00	78.00	80.00	82.00
0.210	56.70	58.80	60.90	63.00	65.10	67.20	69.30	71.40	73.50	75.60	77.70	79.80	81.90	84.00	86.10
0.220	59.40	61.60	63.80	66.00	68.20	70.40	72.60	74.80	77.00	79.20	81.40	83.60	85.80	88.00	90.20
0.230	62.10	64.40	66.70	69.00	71.30	73.60	75.90	78.20	80.50	82.80	85.10	87.40	89.70	92.00	94.30
0.240	64.80	67.20	69.60	72.00	74.40	76.80	79.20	81.60	84.00	86.40	88.80	91.20	93.60	96.00	98.40
0.250	67.50	70.00	72.50	75.00	77.50	80.00	82.50	85.00	87.50	90.00	92.50	95.00	97.50	100.00	102.50
0.260	70.20	72.80	75.40	78.00	80.60	83.20	85.80	88.40	91.00	93.60	96.20	98.80	101.40	104.00	106.60
0.270	72.90	75.60	78.30	81.00	83.70	86.40	89.10	91.80	94.50	97.20	99.90	102.60	105.30	108.00	110.70
0.280	75.60	78.40	81.20	84.00	86.80	89.60	92.40	95.20	98.00	100.80	103.60	106.40	109.20	112.00	114.80
0.290	78.30	81.20	84.10	87.00	89.90	92.80	95.70	98.60	101.50	104.40	107.30	110.20	113.10	116.00	118.90
0.300	81.00	84.00	87.00	90.00	93.00	96.00	99.00	102.00	105.00	108.00	111.00	114.00	117.00	120.00	123.00
0.310	83.70	86.80	89.90	93.00	96.10	99.20	102.30	105.40	108.50	111.60	114.70	117.80	120.90	124.00	127.10
0.320	86.40	89.60	92.80	96.00	99.20	102.40	105.60	108.80	112.00	115.20	118.40	121.60	124.80	128.00	131.20
0.330	89.10	92.40	95.70	99.00	102.30	105.60	108.90	112.20	115.50	118.80	122.10	125.40	128.70	132.00	135.30
0.340	91.80	95.20	98.60	102.00	105.40	108.80	112.20	115.60	119.00	122.40	125.80	129.20	132.60	136.00	139.40
0.350	94.50	98.00	101.50	105.00	108.50	112.00	115.50	119.00	122.50	126.00	129.50	133.00	136.50	140.00	143.50
0.360	97.20	100.80	104.40	108.00	111.60	115.20	118.80	122.40	126.00	129.60	133.20	136.80	140.40	144.00	147.60
0.370	99.90	103.60	107.30	111.00	114.70	118.40	122.10	125.80	129.50	133.20	136.90	140.60	144.30	148.00	151.70
0.380	102.60	106.40	110.20	114.00	117.80	121.60	125.40	129.20	133.00	136.80	140.60	144.40	148.20	152.00	155.80
0.390	105.30	109.20	113.10	117.00	120.90	124.80	128.70	132.60	136.50	140.40	144.30	148.20	152.10	156.00	159.90
0.400	108.00	112.00	116.00	120.00	124.00	128.00	132.00	136.00	140.00	144.00	148.00	152.00	156.00	160.00	164.00
0.410	110.70	114.80	118.90	123.00	127.10	131.20	135.30	139.40	143.50	147.60	151.70	155.80	159.90	164.00	168.10
0.420	113.40	117.60	121.80	126.00	130.20	134.40	138.60	142.80	147.00	151.20	155.40	159.60	163.80	168.00	172.20
0.430	116.10	120.40	124.70	129.00	133.30	137.60	141.90	146.20	150.50	154.80	159.10	163.40	167.70	172.00	176.30
0.440	118.80	123.20	127.60	132.00	136.40	140.80	145.20	149.60	154.00	158.40	162.80	167.20	171.60	176.00	180.40
0.450	121.50	126.00	130.50	135.00	139.50	144.00	148.50	153.00	157.50	162.00	166.50	171.00	175.50	180.00	184.50
0.460	124.20	128.80	133.40	138.00	142.60	147.20	151.80	156.40	161.00	165.60	170.20	174.80	179.40	184.00	188.60
0.470	126.90	131.60	136.30	141.00	145.70	150.40	155.10	159.80	164.50	169.20	173.90	178.60	183.30	188.00	192.70
0.480	129.60	134.40	139.20	144.00	148.80	153.60	158.40	163.20	168.00	172.80	177.60	182.40	187.20	192.00	196.80
0.490	132.30	137.20	142.10	147.00	151.90	156.80	161.70	166.60	171.50	176.40	181.30	186.20	191.10	196.00	200.90
0.500	135.00	140.00	145.00	150.00	155.00	160.00	165.00	170.00	175.00	180.00	185.00	190.00	195.00	200.00	205.00
0.510	137.70	142.80	147.90	153.00	158.10	163.20	168.30	173.40	178.50	183.60	188.70	193.80	198.90	204.00	209.10
0.520	140.40	145.60	150.80	156.00	161.20	166.40	171.60	176.80	182.00	187.20	192.40	197.60	202.80	208.00	213.20
0.530	143.10	148.40	153.70	159.00	164.30	169.60	174.90	180.20	185.50	190.80	196.10	201.40	206.70	212.00	217.30
0.540	145.80	151.20	156.60	162.00	167.40	172.80	178.20	183.60	189.00	194.40	199.80	205.20	210.60	216.00	221.40
0.550	148.50	154.00	159.50	165.00	170.50	176.00	181.50	187.00	192.50	198.00	203.50	209.00	214.50	220.00	225.50
0.560	151.20	156.80	162.40	168.00	173.60	179.20	184.80	190.40	196.00	201.60	207.20	212.80	218.40	224.00	229.60
0.570	153.90	159.60	165.30	171.00	176.70	182.40	188.10	193.80	199.50	205.20	210.90	216.60	222.30	228.00	233.70
0.580	156.60	162.40	168.20	174.00	179.80	185.60	191.40	197.20	203.00	208.80	214.60	220.40	226.20	232.00	237.80
0.590	159.30	165.20	171.10	177.00	182.90	188.80	194.70	200.60	206.50	212.40	218.30	224.20	230.10	236.00	241.90
0.600	162.00	168.00	174.00	180.00	186.00	192.00	198.00	204.00	210.00	216.00	222.00	228.00	234.00	240.00	246.00
0.610	164.70	170.80	176.90	183.00	189.10	195.20	201.30	207.40	213.50	219.60	225.70	231.80	237.90	244.00	250.10
0.620	167.40	173.60	179.80	186.00	192.20	198.40	204.60	210.80	217.00	223.20	229.40	235.60	241.80	248.00	254.20
0.630	170.10	176.40	182.70	189.00	195.30	201.60	207.90	214.20	220.50	226.80	233.10	239.40	245.70	252.00	258.30
0.640	172.80	179.20	185.60	192.00	198.40	204.80	211.20	217.60	224.00	230.40	236.80	243.20	249.60	256.00	262.40
0.650	175.50	182.00	188.50	195.00	201.50	208.00	214.50	221.00	227.50	234.00	240.50	247.00	253.50	260.00	266.50
0.660	178.20	184.80	191.40	198.00	204.60	211.20	217.80	224.40	231.00	237.60	244.20	250.80	257.40	264.00	270.60
0.670	180.90	187.60	194.30	201.00	207.70	214.40	221.10	227.80	234.50	241.20	247.90	254.60	261.30	268.00	274.70
0.680	183.60	190.40	197.20	204.00	210.80	217.60	224.40	231.20	238.00	244.80	251.60	258.40	265.20	272.00	278.80
0.690	186.30	193.20	200.10	207.00	213.90	220.80	227.70	234.60	241.50	248.40	255.30	262.20	269.10	276.00	282.90
0.700	189.00	196.00	203.00	210.00	217.00	224.00	231.00	238.00	245.00	252.00	259.00	266.00	273.00	280.00	287.00
0.710	191.70	198.80	205.90	213.00	220.10	227.20	234.30	241.40	248.50	255.60	262.70	269.80	276.90	284.00	291.10
0.720	194.40	201.60	208.80	216.00	223.20	230.40	237.60	244.80	252.00	259.20	266.40	273.60	280.80	288.00	295.20
0.730	197.10	204.40	211.70	219.00	226.30	233.60	240.90	248.20	255.50	262.80	270.10	277.40	284.70	292.00	299.30
0.740	199.80	207.20	214.60	222.00	229.40	236.80	244.20	251.60	259.00	266.40	273.80	281.20	288.60	296.00	303.40
0.750	202.50	210.00	217.50	225.00	232.50	240.00	247.50	255.00	262.50	270.00	277.50	285.00	292.50	300.00	307.50
0.760	205.20	212.80	220.40	228.00	235.60	243.20	250.80	258.40	266.00	273.60	281.20	288.80	296.40	304.00	311.60
0.770	207.90	215.60	223.30	231.00	238.70	246.40	254.10	261.80	269.50	277.20	284.90	292.60	300.30	308.00	315.70
0.780	210.60	218.40	226.20	234.00	241.80	249.60	257.40	265.20	273.00	280.80	288.60	296.40	304.20	312.00	319.80
0.790	213.30	221.20	229.10	237.00	244.90	252.80	260.70	268.60	276.50	284.40	292.30	300.20	308.10	316.00	323.90
0.800	216.00	224.00	232.00	240.00	248.00	256.00	264.00	272.00	280.00	288.00	296.00	304.00	312.00	320.00	328.00
0.810	218.70	226.80	234.90	243.00	251.10	259.20	267.30	275.40	283.50	291.60	299.70	307.80	315.90	324.00	332.10
0.820	221.40	229.60	237.80	246.00	254.20	262.40	270.60	278.80	287.00	295.20	303.40	311.60	319.80	328.00	336.20
0.830	224.10	232.40	240.70	249.00	257.30	265.60	273.90	282.20	290.50	298.80	307.10	315.40	323.70	332.00	340.30
0.840	226.80	235.20	243.60	252.00	260.40	268.80	277.20	285.60	294.00	302.40	310.80	319.20	327.60	336.00	344.40
0.850	229.50	238.00	246.50	255.00	263.50	272.00	280.50	289.00	297.50	306.00	314.50	323.00	331.50	340.00	348.50
0.860	232.20	240.80	249.40	258.00	266.60	275.20	283.80	292.40	301.00	309.60	318.20	326.80	335.40	344.00	352.60
0.870	234.90	243.60	252.30	261.00	269.70	278.40	287.10	295.80	304.50	313.20	321.90	330.60	339.30	348.00	356.70
0.880	237.60	246.40	255.20	264.00	272.80	281.60	290.40	299.20	308.00	316.80	325.60	334.40	343.20	352.00	360.80
0.890	240.30	249.20	258.10	267.00	275.90	284.80	293.70	302.60	311.50	320.40	329.30	338.20	347.10	356.00	364.90
0.900	243.00	252.00	261.00	270.00	279.00	288.00	297.00	306.00	315.00	324.00	333.00	342.00	351.00	360.00	369.00
0.910	245.70	254.80	263.90	273.00	282.10	291.20	300.30	309.40	318.50	327.60	336.70	345.80	354.90	364.00	373.10
0.920	248.40	257.60	266.80	276.00	285.20	294.40	303.60	312.80	322.00	331.20	340.40	349.60	358.80	368.00	377.20
0.930	251.10	260.40	269.70	279.00	288.30	297.60	306.90	316.20	325.50	334.80	344.10	353.40	362.70	372.00	381.30
0.940	253.80	263.20	272.60	282.00	291.40	300.80	310.20	319.60	329.00	338.40	347.80	357.20	366.60	376.00	385.40
0.950	256.50	266.00	275.50	285.00	294.50	304.00	313.50	323.00	332.50	342.00	351.50	361.00	370.50	380.00	389.50
0.960	259.20	268.80	278.40	288.00	297.60	307.20	316.80	326.40	336.00	345.60	355.20	364.80	374.40	384.00	393.60
0.970	261.90	271.60	281.30	291.00	300.70	310.40	320.10	329.80	339.50	349.20	358.90	368.60	378.30	388.00	397.70
0.980	264.60	274.40	284.20	294.00	303.80	313.60	323.40	333.20	343.00	352.80	362.60	372.40	382.20	392.00	401.80
0.990	267.30	277.20	287.10	297.00	306.90	316.80	326.70	336.60	346.50	356.40	366.30	376.20	386.10	396.00	405.90
1.000	270.00	280.00	290.00	300.00	310.00	320.00	330.00	340.00	350.00	360.00	370.00	380.00	390.00	400.00	410.00

Foreign Exchange Table

The latest foreign exchange fixed rates below apply to trade with banks in the country of origin. The left column shows the number of units per U.S. dollar at the official rate. The right column shows the number of units per dollar at the free market rate.

Country	Official #/$	Market #/$
Afghanistan (Afghan)	4,750	20,200
Albania (Lek)	140.45	–
Algeria (Dinar)	64.463	75.00
Andorra uses French Franc and Spanish Peseta		
Angola (Readjust Kwanza)	257,128	–
Anguilla uses E.C. Dollar	2.70	
Antigua uses E.C. Dollar	2.70	
Argentina (New Peso)	.9999	–
Armenia (Dram)	420.0	–
Aruba (Florin)	1.79	–
Australia (Dollar)	1.6123	–
Austria (Schilling)	12.4821	–
Azerbaijan (Manat)	3,950	–
Bahamas (Dollar)	1.00	–
Bahrain Is. (Dinar)	.38	–
Bangladesh (Taka)	48.40	–
Barbados (Dollar)	2.00	–
Belarus (Ruble)	11,500	–
Belgium (Franc)	36.593	–
Belize (Dollar)	2.00	–
Benin uses CFA Franc West	595.03	–
Bermuda (Dollar)	1.00	–
Bhutan (Ngultrum)	42.72	–
Bolivia (Boliviano)	5.70	–
Bosnia-Herzegovina (New Dinar)	141.00	195.0
Botswana (Pula)	4.6544	–
British Virgin Islands uses U.S. Dollar	1.00	–
Brazil (Real)	2.045	–
Brunei (Ringgit)	1.722	–
Bulgaria (Lev)	1,765	–
Burkina Faso uses CFA Fr. West	595.03	–
Burma (Kyat)	6.3411	–
Burundi (Franc)	511.69	–
Cambodia (Riel)	3,770	–
Cameron uses CFA Franc	595.03	–
Canada (Dollar)	1.5136	–
Cape Verde (Escudo)	94.71	–
Cayman Is. (Dollar)	0.8333	–
Central African Rep.	595.03	–
CFA Franc Central	595.03	–
CFA Franc West	595.03	–
CFP Franc	102.23	–
Chad uses CFA Franc Central	595.03	–
Chile (Peso)	498.74	–
China, P.R. (Renminbi Yuan)	8.279	–
Colombia (Peso)	1,577	–
Comoros (Franc)	446.23	–
Congo uses CFA Franc Central	595.03	–
Cook Islands (Dollar)	1.47	–
Costa Rica (Colon)	275.92	–
Croatia (Kuna)	6.8677	–
Cuba (Peso)	23.00	35.00
Cyprus (Pound)	.5262	–
Czech Republic (Koruna)	34.403	–
Denmark (Danish Krone)	6.7412	–
Djibouti (Franc)	177.72	–
Dominica uses E.C. Dollar	2.70	–
Dominican Republic (Peso)	15.75	–
East Caribbean (Dollar)	2.70	–
Ecuador (Sucre)	7,610	–
Egypt (Pound)	3.4188	–
El Salvador (Colon)	8.755	–
England (Sterling Pound)	.6249	–
Equatorial Guinea uses CFA Franc Central	595.03	–
Eritrea, see Ethiopia		
Estonia (Kroon)	14.19	–
Ethiopia (Birr)	6.9875	7.25
Euro	9070	
Faroe Islands (Krona)	6.7412	–
Fiji Islands (Dollar)	1.9912	–
Finland (Markka)	5.3934	–
France (Franc)	5.9503	–
French Polynesia uses CFP Franc	102.23	–
Gabon (CFA Franc)	595.03	–
Gambia (Dalasi)	11.05	–
Georgia (Lari)	1.30	–
Germany (D. Mark)	1.7742	–
Ghana (Cedi)	2,403	–
Gibraltar (Pound)	.6249	–
Greece (Drachma)	291.94	–
Greenland uses Denmark Krone	6.7412	–
Grenada uses E.C. Dollar	2.70	–
Guatemala (Quetzal)	6.8348	–
Guernsey uses Sterling Pound	.6249	–
Guinea Bissau (CFA Franc)	595.03	–
Guinea Conakry (Franc)	1,300	–
Guyana (Dollar)	162.80	–
Haiti (Gourde)	16.797	–
Honduras (Lempira)	14.01	–
Hong Kong (Dollar)	7.7477	–
Hungary (Forint)	229.82	–
Iceland (Krona)	72.18	–
India (Rupee)	42.72	–
Indonesia (Rupiah)	8,840	–
Iran (Rial)	3,000	4,800
Iraq (Dinar)	1,200	1,690
Ireland (Punt)	.7144	–
Isle of Man uses Sterling Pound	.6249	–
Israel (New Sheqalim)	4.0473	–
Italy (Lira)	1,756	–
Ivory Coast uses CFA Franc West	595.03	–
Jamaica (Dollar)	36.65	–
Japan (Yen)	119.95	–
Jersey uses Sterling Pound	.6249	–
Jordan (Dinar)	.709	–
Kazakhstan (Tenge)	65.00	–
Kenya (Shilling)	63.80	–
Kiribati uses Australian Dollar	1.6123	–
Korea-PDR (Won)	2.20	170.0
Korea-Rep. (Won)	1,224	–
Kuwait (Dinar)	.3047	–
Kyrgyzstan (Som)	11.05	–
Laos (Kip)	4,203	–
Latvia (Lat)	.5842	–
Lebanon (Pound)	1,508	–
Lesotho (Maloti)	6.185	–
Liberia (Dollar)	1.00	30.00
Libya (Dinar)	.45	2.00
Liechtenstein uses Swiss Franc	1.4411	–
Lithuania (Litas)	4.0018	–
Luxembourg (Franc)	36.593	–
Macao (Pataca)	8.0034	–
Macedonia (New Denar)	54.94	–
Madagascar (Franc)	5,220	–
Malawi (Kwacha)	43.88	–
Malaysia (Ringgit)	3.80	–
Maldives (Rufiya)	11.77	–
Mali uses CFA Franc West	595.03	–
Malta (Lira)	.3794	–
Marshall Islands uses U.S. Dollar	1.00	–
Mauritania (Ouguiya)	204.4	–
Mauritius (Rupee)	24.95	–
Mexico (Peso)	9.975	–
Moldova (Leu)	4.55	–
Monaco uses French Franc	5.9503	–
Mongolia (Tugrik)	817.61	–
Montenegro uses Yugoslavia	10.6349	–
Montserrat uses E.C. Dollar	2.70	–
Morocco (Dirham)	9.6504	10.50
Mozambique (Metical)	11,495	12,100
Myanmar (Burma) (Kyat)	6.2481	202.0
Namibia (Rand)	6.185	–
Nauru uses Australian Dollar	1.6123	–
Nepal (Rupee)	67.68	
Netherlands Antilles (Gulden)	1.79	–
New Caledonia uses CFP Franc	102.23	–
New Zealand (Dollar)	1.9102	–
Nicaragua (Cordoba Oro)	11.3443	–
Niger uses CFA Franc West	595.03	–
Nigeria (Naira)	87.0	–
Northern Ireland uses Sterling Pound	.6249	–
Norway (Krone)	7.8955	–
Oman (Rial)	.385	–
Pakistan (Rupee)	51.25	–
Palau uses U.S. Dollar	1.00	–
Panama (Balboa) uses U.S. Dollar	1.00	–
Papua New Guinea (Kina)	2.2371	–
Paraguay (Guarani)	2,900	–
Peru (Nuevo Sol)	3.4725	–
Philippines (Peso)	39.07	–
Poland (Zloty)	3.9035	–
Portugal (Escudo)	181.86	–
Qatar (Riyal)	3.641	–
Romania (Leu)	12,816	–
Russia (Ruble)	22.86	–
Rwanda (Franc)	320.3	370.0
St. Helena (Pound)	.6249	–
St. Kitts uses E.C. Dollar	2.70	–
St. Lucia uses E.C. Dollar	2.70	–
St. Vincent uses E.C. Dollar	2.70	–
San Marino uses Italian Lira	1,756	–
Sao Tome e Principe (Dobra)	2,390	–
Saudi Arabia (Riyal)	3.7523	–
Scotland uses Sterling Pound	.6249	–
Senegal uses CFA Franc West	595.03	–
Seychelles (Rupee)	5.301	–
Sierra Leone (Leone)	1,475	–
Singapore (Dollar)	1.722	–
Slovakia (Sk. Koruna)	39.865	–
Slovenia (Tolar)	155.64	–
Solomon Is. (Dollar)	4.7915	–
Somalia (Shilling)	2,620	–
Somaliland (Somali Shilling)	1,800	3,000
South Africa (Rand)	6.185	–
Spain (Peseta)	150.9	–
Sri Lanka (Rupee)	69.53	–
Sudan (Dinar)	196.0	–
Surinam (Guilder)	401	–
Swaziland (Lilangeni)	6.185	–
Sweden (Krona)	8.166	–
Switzerland (Franc)	1.4411	–
Syria (Pound)	46.25	–
Taiwan (NT Dollar)	33.08	–
Tajikistan uses Russian Ruble	22.86	–
Tanzania (Shilling)	692.25	–
Thailand (Baht)	37.365	–
Togo uses CFA Franc West	595.03	–
Tonga (Pa'anga)	1.6054	–
Transdniestra (New Ruble)	630,000	675,000
Trinidad & Tobago (Dollar)	6.2525	–
Tunisia (Dinar)	1.1542	–
Turkey (Lira)	354,830	–
Turkmenistan (Manat)	195	6,500
Turks & Caicos uses U.S. Dollar	1.00	–
Tuvalu uses Australian Dollar	1.6123	–
Uganda (Shilling)	1,233	–
Ukraine (Hryvnia)	3.85	–
United Arab Emirates (Dirham)	3.673	–
Uruguay (Peso Uruguayo)	10.995	–
Uzbekistan (Som)	24.00	–
Vanuatu (Vatu)	129.25	–
Vatican City uses Italian Lira	1,756	–
Venezuela (Bolivar)	5861.0	–
Vietnam (Dong)	13,892	–
Western Samoa (Tala)	3.0157	–
Yemen (Riyal)	141.34	–
Yugoslavia (Novikh Dinar)	10.6349	–
Zaire (Noveaux Zaire)	245,000	–
Zambia (Kwacha)		

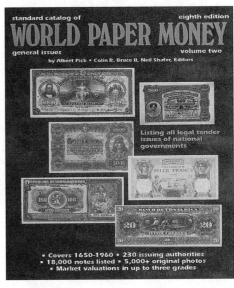
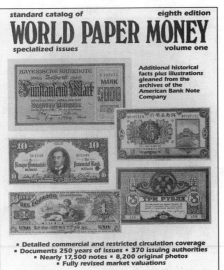

STANDARD CATALOG OF WORLD COINS SERIES

For thousands of prices on coins from around the world, experienced and beginner collectors turn to the Standard Catalog of World Coin series from Krause Publications. Each volume, authored by Chester Krause and Clifford Mishler and edited by Colin Bruce, contains crisp clear photographs and prices in up to four grades of condition listed by country and denomination for easy reference.

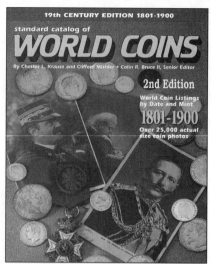

1801-1900, 2nd Edition
Softcover • 8-1/2 x 11
1,032 pages • 24,000+ b&w photos
SCN02 • $45.00

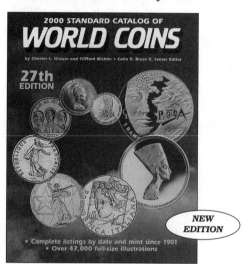

1901-Present, 27th Edition
Softcover • 8-1/2 x 11
1,936 pages • 47,000 b&w photos
SC27 • $47.95

1601-1700, 2nd Edition
Softcover • 8-1/2 x 11
1,200 pages • 18,500 b&w photos
C402 • $65.00   Avail. 11/99

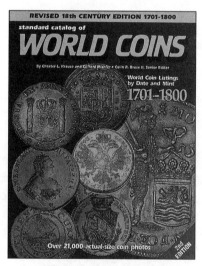

1701-1800, 2nd Edition
Softcover • 8-1/2 x 11
1,248 pages • 20,000 b&w photos
SE02 • $65.00